An Introduction
to
Philosophical Analysis

Lively and readable, this third edition of *An Introduction to Philosophical Analysis* offers clear and detailed presentations of the issues and conflicts present in philosophy. Professor Hospers engages readers with a narrative style and informal method of presentation, using hundreds of examples and engrossing dialogues by real and imaginary disputants to dramatize the issues and convey a sense of ongoing discussion and argument.

Among the book's many distinguishing features is a new chapter on the problems of ethics, including the philosophy of law and of society, the nature of moral judgment, and theories of normative ethics. This extensive revision includes new emphases on the philosophy of science and problems of personal identity, as well as different approaches to a variety of issues.

"I think this book will provide a guide which should help to prevent people getting lost in the labyrinth without pretending that there isn't a labyrinth. I congratulate Dr Hospers. I think he has done wonders with a very difficult job." *Professor John Wisdom, Fellow of Trinity College, Cambridge*

"Anyone who wishes to familiarize himself with the methods and approaches to philosophy current in universities in England and the United States will find this book a useful guide."
Philosophical Studies

John Hospers is Professor at the School of Philosophy at the University of Southern California, Los Angeles. He has written many books and articles on philosophical questions, including *Readings in Introductory Philosophical Analysis* (1969), *Understanding the Arts* (1982) and *Human Conduct* (1982).

THIRD EDITION

An Introduction to Philosophical Analysis

John Hospers

London

First published in Great Britain in 1956
by Routledge & Kegan Paul

Second edition published in 1967

Third edition published in 1990
by Routledge
11 New Fetter Lane, London EC4P 4EE

Reprinted in 1992, 1995, 1996

© 1953, 1967, 1988 Prentice-Hall
A Division of Simon & Schuster

Printed in England by Clays Ltd, St Ives plc

British Library Cataloguing in Publication Data
A catalogue record for this book is available
from the British Library

ISBN 0–415–05575-X (hbk)
ISBN 0–415–05576–8 (pbk)

CONTENTS

7
THE PHILOSOPHY OF RELIGION, *287*

8
PROBLEMS IN ETHICS, *338*

GLOSSARY, *407*

INDEX, *411*

PREFACE

One reason for preparing a new edition of *An Introduction to Philosophical Analysis* is the obvious one of updating the material and the bibliography. This reason is less important than it might seem, for neither the main problems of philosophy nor their proposed solutions are likely to go out of date in a few years' time. Introductory students are not in a position to appreciate the last ten years of philosophy before they know anything about the previous two thousand years, and the latest developments can be understood only against the background of the earlier. Though there is some change in the materials and arguments presented in the present edition—it has been about 75 percent rewritten—a bigger change has been in the method of presentation, which is more informal and (it is hoped) easier for students to grasp. Most of the distinctively new developments of the last twenty years are highly technical and presuppose a considerable previous acquaintance with philosophy. If one were expected to present the latest developments in the field and at the same time "keep it simple," the two demands would be quite incompatible.

The main structural change in the present edition is the omission of the 100-page introductory chapter on language. Many have apparently found it helpful, yet few instructors seem to have used it in their classes. The strategy in the present edition is to begin with certain traditional problems of philosophy (beginning with epistemology) and to bring in considerations of language as these are needed along the way. This alteration may make the book more usable; and it may attract the introductory reader's interest much more quickly than the previous format of laying an elaborate foundation before proceeding to the problems themselves.

Other changes have been made as well. In line with the current emphasis on applied ethics, the entire ethics chapter is new and contains sections on topics of increasing interest such as philosophy of law and of society, which did not appear in previous editions. New emphases in philosophy of science and problems of personal identity have been included, as well as different approaches to a variety of other issues. An attempt has been made not to oversimplify the problems, while yet rendering them as easy to comprehend as possible, largely through the constant use of examples designed to "rock the reader's mind to its foundations"; such examples, it is hoped, will lead readers to think the problems through for themselves rather than repeat sentences they have learned but barely understand. In many philosophy courses, especially those based on anthologies, the material is so difficult for undergraduates of the 1980s to read that they soon give up trying; anything they get out of the course comes from what they hear in the classroom. My strongest hope with regard to the present edition is that it will stimulate students (as well as nonstudent readers) to read the material on their own and think through the problems beyond the point that the text carries them. Philosophy, as Moritz Schlick said, is less a subject matter than an activity; and it is this sense of ongoing activity that I wish more than anything else to convey.

For comments and counsel in the preparation of this edition, I would like to express my appreciation to Professor Edward Johnson of the University of New Orleans, Professor Joseph Croic of the University of Florida, and Professor John Dupre of Stanford University. For permission to quote from books and articles published by them, I would like to express my thanks to Unwin Hyman Ltd. for quotations from G. E. Moore's *Some Main Problems of Philosophy;"* to Routledge & Kegan Paul for quotations from C. D. Broad's *The Mind and Its Place in Nature;* to Oxford University Press for excerpts by Norman Malcolm and Frederick Will in *Mind;* and to Princeton University Press for passages from W.T. Stace's *Time and Eternity.* And for many hours of overtime in the typing of the manuscript I would like to express my special thanks to Lucine Andonian.

J. H.

PREFACE
TO THE SECOND EDITION

Those who approach philosophy for the first time do so from a variety of motives. Some are drawn into philosophy from their interest in the sciences, some from the arts, some from religion; others come to philosophy without any academic background, motivated by an uneasiness about "the meaning of things" or "what the world is all about"; still others have no motivation more specific than that of wanting to know what kind of thing people are talking about when they use the word "philosophy." Accordingly, the demands which different people make of philosophy, the questions they expect it to answer, are as diverse as the motives leading them to it; and as a result, the books which are written to satisfy these demands are similarly diverse. Often two books professing to introduce readers to philosophy contain little or none of the same material. For these reasons it is impossible to write a book that will satisfy all, or even (perhaps) a majority of readers.

One might try to overcome this difficulty by writing a book so comprehensive that all the problems which anyone considered philo-sophical would be treated in it, and the reader would have only to select portions in which he was most interested. This, however, is hardly possible in practice: A book of a thousand pages would not begin to suffice. Nor would it be feasible to devote just a few pages to each problem: This would leave only outline summaries of the various issues, which would mean little to the reader; he might learn the meanings of some terms and absorb a few "general trends" from such a presentation, but he would not have been given enough material to make the problems come alive for him. The capsule method is even less successful in philosophy than it is elsewhere. The only apparent solution, then, would be to include not all, but only some, of the problems in the field. This method has its drawbacks, for no matter which problems are included and which are excluded, many readers are bound to object both to some of the inclusions and some of the exclusions. Yet this is the policy that has been followed in this book, as the one with the fewest all-round disadvantages.

INTRODUCTION

What is philosophy? The question sounds easy, yet to answer it at the outset is far from easy. This is not merely because different persons who write and teach what they call philosophy have different ideas of what philosophy should be—though this is true enough. But even if that were not so, it would be virtually impossible to give any impression of what goes on in philosophy without going into philosophical controversies themselves in the process. We can fairly easily tell others what is the subject matter of biology, or astronomy, or art history, or chemical engineering. But if we try to answer the question, What is philosophy?, in the same easy way we seem doomed to failure.

What is philosophy?, people ask, unaware of the traps concealed in "what is . . . " questions. What is water? It is H_2O, says the chemist; it is the liquid that I see in rivers and lakes, says someone else. Are they giving the same answer? They are talking about the same thing, but they have different means of identifying the thing: The chemist will call nothing water unless it is two parts hydrogen and one part oxygen; but human beings for many thousands of years have correctly identified many examples of water without knowing anything about chemistry. What they drank was indeed H_2O, although they didn't know this. If they had a definition of "water" at all, was it incorrect or mistaken because it wasn't the chemist's definition? Or did the word "water" mean the same to both because the word served to identify the same kind of liquid for both of them? This itself is a philosophical question ("If two descriptions always denote the same objects, have they the same meaning?"); one must look into this issue in order to understand "what is . . . " questions—including the question, What is philosophy?

Philosophy studies reality, one might say. But so do the sciences; so in one way or another does every subject we study. And when we ask, What is meant by the word "reality"?, the kind of answer philosophers give us is likely to strike most people as too complicated, difficult, confusing, even evasive. But philosophers have the thankless task of pointing out to those who want "capsule culture in three easy lessons" that such questions are not so simple. Consider the word "real": "That's not a real duck—it's a decoy"; "it's not a giraffe out there—it's a configuration of shapes that looks like a giraffe against the sunset sky." "That's not a real pink rat—you're having the DTs, you're hallucinating." "That didn't really happen—it was a dream; or you were misinformed; or you read it wrong; or somebody lied." "That's not a real problem—it's a phony one, you think there's a problem but there isn't." and so on.[1] Each of these uses of the word "real" has an opposite; we can identify what *this* occurrence of the word means only when we know what it is being *contrasted* with, and what it is contrasted with is an enormous variety of different things. Besides all that, the word "real" is often used merely as an "intensive": "That really happened" is an emphatic way of saying "That happened." Thus we can't give a simple answer to the question, What is real? We have to go through the cumbersome and tiring business of pointing out the various things that the word "real" can mean by contrasting it with what, in that specific context, is not called real (it could change again in a different context). Is a dream real? Well, it's not like the tree out there, but it's a real experience, isn't it? To a beginner this may be bewildering, frustrating, even anger-provoking. People want simple answers to simple questions. But what they don't see is

that the question isn't simple. To get them to see this is already to have taken a brief excursion into philosophy.

Not all answers are sharp and clear—this is another source of frustration. Do you see objects or images of objects? If I look at a tree, I see the tree. When I look at it through yellow glasses, what I see is yellow—is that the tree? If I look at it through a mirror, do I see the tree or the mirror-image of a tree? If I look at it through a telescope, do I see the tree or a telescopic image of it? If that's an image, why not also when I look at it through a pane of glass? Do I see any of it at all when a bit of it is viewed through an electron microscope and seems grayish although the tree is not? When I detect its presence on a radar screen, am I seeing the tree or simply a blob on the screen? And what about a photograph of it? or an x-ray? We are fairly familiar in each of these cases with the scientific facts, but quite confused as to how to *describe* them, what to call them and why. But in philosophy, every question we encounter is filtered through *language,* and language can be inadequate to express what we want to say; language can distort what we mean, clarify what we mean, even create what we mean but thought we hadn't. The way we put things in language can determine how we will understand an issue, how we will "come at" a question. It can also lead us to create phony questions that ask nothing, though we think they are asking something: More frequently we are asking a variety of different questions at once, all clothed in the same words, and we haven't bothered to distinguish the various questions that are concealed "under the words."

For example, What is the meaning of life? This is often believed to be *the* question which philosophy must answer. But when we ask it at first, we don't see the traps in the question. "What's the meaning of that phone call?" we ask when a voice utters a few hostile words and the line clicks dead. We can be asking,

[1]See J. L. Austin, *Sense and Sensibilia* (Oxford: Oxford University Press, 1962).

who made it? what does the caller want? what does it portend for the future? and many other things. "What does 'perihelion' mean"? It means the point on the orbit of a planet where it's nearest to the sun (or of a satellite, when it's nearest to the planet around which it revolves). That's an example of the dictionary sense of the word "meaning"; it tells us how a word is used in a language. "What's the meaning of that remark?"—that is, what did you intend by it? Are you trying to communicate what I think you are? "What's the meaning of a falling barometer?" It means that a storm is on the way, it's an indicator of future events. "If everyone on board the plane was killed, what does that mean?" It means that if your friend was on board, she too was killed; that is, it logically *implies* it; the conclusion is inescapable if you grant the premise.

In these cases we have *multiplicity* of meanings (in this case of the word "meaning" itself): meaning as definition; meaning as intention; meaning as implication; meaning as purpose; meaning as import for the future; and so on. But there usually isn't much confusion in figuring out the kind of answer that is appropriate—we can tell that from the context of the discussion. But suppose someone asks, "What is the meaning of her death?" Unless the questioner fills us in on what information is wanted, we are rather at a loss to give an answer—because the question is unclear. Is the questioner asking, "What effects will her death have?" or "What will it do to my life from here on?" or "Was some purpose served by her death?" or "Is it an indicator that future deaths of the same kind (such as, by terrorists) will probably follow?" or "Did God cause her death and if so for what reason, for what purpose?" Until we know how to take the question, we cannot hope to provide an answer.

So it is with the question, "What is the meaning of life?" What information is the questioner requesting? Does she want to know whether her life serves some overall purpose? why she should continue living? whether there is a pattern of events in her life that she hasn't discovered, but discovering it may be important for her future? or what she ought to do with her life? or perhaps, whether God has created her for a reason, and she is trying to find out what that reason is? "Tell me in other words what you want to know," we may say. But to do this, especially for one who hasn't made distinctions like these and isn't very good at articulating incoherent thoughts and impressions, may be extremely difficult—even impossible—at the start. She feels that she is being made to go through an uncomfortable effort and concentration that isn't necessary: All she wants to know is, "What is the meaning of life?", and here we are throwing dust in her face, forcing her to choose between alternative formulations before we'll so much as entertain her question. Understandably, this is extremely frustrating.

But until we have cut through the fog we can't get far in philosophy. She doesn't even realize that she has asked a foggy question, and wonders why we don't answer her with simple directness. Most people at this point stick with their foggy question, obtain somebody's equally foggy answer in some obscure but impressive-sounding bit of pontification ("The meaning of life is to fulfill your destiny"), and then walk away satisfied. But these people have evaded the issues of philosophy.

How then are we to define the word "philosophy"? Many definitions have been offered, but they cast very little light on the subject. If someone says, "Philosophy is the interpretation of all experience," we have an impressive-sounding formula; but what is an "interpretation," and what is meant by "experience"? We know what it is to interpret a sentence in a foreign language, or to interpret the notations on a musical score; but what is it to interpret *experience?* Aren't we shifting words about from a context in which they have a clear meaning to one in which they don't? If someone said, "Your theory is mistaken," and someone else later said, "Your theory is blue," would you think you understood the second question just because you understood the first plus all the individual *words* in the second? Wouldn't you want to ask, not "Is it blue?" but "What do you mean by your question?"

Besides, most people seem to have the impression that giving a definition will answer their questions. But the word in a definition may be as obscure or ill-understood as the word or phrase one is trying to define; then the definition is no help. "A flubjub is a blue dingbat" is no help unless you already know the meaning of "dingbat." For a definition of the term "philosophy" to succeed, you would have to know the meanings of the words in the definition, and these are likely to be as confusing as the word "philosophy" itself. And some words entirely defy definition by means of other words. "A pungent smell," "a bitter taste," "a creepy sensation," "a feeling of terror"—try to communicate what these words mean to anyone who has not already smelt a pungent smell, tasted a bitter taste, and so on. Throwing more words at him won't do the trick; you have to confront the person with the *experience* for which the words are labels: "Here's a bottle of chlorine; smell it—that's what you call a pungent smell." Now you know from experience what at least one kind of pungent smell is like. No amount of words expended on an attempted *verbal* definition will succeed. And even when verbal definitions are given, the words in the definition can cause as much trouble as the words being defined.

Philosophical *argument* is also full of pitfalls for the *unwary*. Let's consider, for example, a comparatively simple view, "psychological egoism," that is often put forward. Notice some of the confused arguments that are often

used to support it. We shall follow only a few steps of an imaginary dialogue that could go on and on:

A: Everybody is really selfish. People are only out to help themselves.

B: Not so. I know lots of people who do things for others.

A: They do things for others, but they still do it for a selfish reason—because they *want* to.

B: Wrong again. We all do things we don't want to do. I don't want to wash the dishes, but I do it anyway. I want a drink, but if my doctor has told me to lay off alcohol I follow his advice and don't do what I want to do.

A: But you're still doing what you want to do. You don't want to wash the dishes, but you'd rather do that than have them pile up dirty in the sink. You want a drink, but you want your health even more.

B: But there's nothing in *wanting* something that's selfish, or even self-interested. There's a difference. Selfish people *use* others for their own purposes. But if I'm ill and go to a physician, this is a self-interested act—I do it to get better—but you'd hardly call it selfish. I may want to do lots of things that aren't selfish or even self-interested: I may want to help a friend out of a jam, or I may want to help the needy or feed the hungry, even though I get nothing out of this myself. Don't confuse "I want to do X" with "I want X for self-interested reasons."

A: But you do get something out of it—if not money or fame or reputation, at least an inner satisfaction, perhaps even pride.

B: Sometimes, but that's not why I do it. I'd do it even if I didn't get the satisfaction. Many times I've performed unpleasant duties with no satisfaction either gained or anticipated beforehand. I do it because I think I ought to, not because I *want* to.

A: Even then you do it because you want to. You'd have guilt feelings if you didn't, and to escape these guilt feelings you do it.

B: Sometimes, but sometimes not. If it's something not expected of me, which neither I nor others would blame me for not doing—something "over and above the call of duty"—I'd have no guilt feelings at not doing it. But sometimes I do it anyway. Don't confuse "I did it, and I got satisfaction from doing it" with "I did it *in order* to get the satisfaction."

A: I still say that if you did it, you got some kind of personal reward from it—pleasure, pride, gratification, feeling of self-worth.

B: And how do you know that I get this? What if I tell you that sometimes I don't? Do you know more about my motives and inner feelings than I do myself? What if I say I neither get nor expect to get satisfaction or any other kind of personal reward from doing it?

A: I'd say you're kidding yourself. You wouldn't have done it otherwise.

B: And you're saying that not just I, but everyone, does a deed for personal satisfaction or whatever? You say that *all* people are motivated only by self-interest. How do you know this? Have you met every person who's ever lived and will live on this planet? Do you know enough about the motives of each and every one of them to be able to say this? After all, you don't even *know* most of them. Maybe you can say it for yourself; then I say "Speak for yourself." Don't tell me how *I* am motivated; I know that better than you do. At least, you have no way of knowing what my motives are or that of the rest of the human race—certainly not people long since dead and people who haven't yet been born. You have no evidence for such a huge generalization about *all* human beings, past, present, and future.

A: Evidence? Isn't it a plain fact about hu-man nature that people don't do something if they don't get *something* out of it for themselves?

B: And what entitles you to be so sure? Whether it's true or not there's an obvious fallacy in the way you reason about it. If someone does something, you take this very fact as evidence that the person did it from self-interested motives. If she helped someone, she did it to gain personal satisfaction or reward; if she didn't, but did something else instead, then she did that from the same motive—that's your argument. But this is a clear case of begging the question—assuming the point that's at issue. You can't take the point you're trying to prove—"Everyone is motivated exclusively by self-interest"—and *assume* it in the argument leading to that very conclusion. You're assuming the truth of psychological egoism in the very process of trying to establish it.

The point here is not that psychological egoism is false, but that the arguments that are used by A in this dialogue to prove that it's true are all defective.

As philosophical arguments go, this one is very simple; the fallacies are fairly easy to detect. But in many philosophical arguments this is far from being so. Philosophical arguments often become extremely complicated and hard to follow; sometimes after you have finally succeeded in following the complexities of the issue, you feel the arguments are equally balanced on both sides of a question. Then comes a feeling of frustration: "I went through all this because I expected to get a definite answer at the end of it, and I haven't." You then feel disappointed, even resentful and perhaps more confused at the end than at the beginning.

Still, if you work carefully through the various arguments, you do become clearer about them in time—enough to feel that you have at least mastered the reasons for and against holding a certain view. If no definite conclusion has been reached, isn't it better to know that there is something to be said on both sides than to take one position dogmatically and not be able to defend it against opponents? In philosophy, the *reasons* we can adduce for or against a conclusion are as important as the conclusion that is reached. There is a satisfaction in reaching a position that has been well established, but there is also a satisfaction in having gone thoroughly through the reasons for or against it. "If you gave me the choice," it has been said, "between the truth and the search for truth, I would take the search." Not everyone would echo this sentiment; it seems that the more people want definite conclusions, the more they tend to be impatient with complex arguments. But in the issues to be discussed in this book there are very few conclusions that everyone, including those who have thought about the subject for years, would accept. In the following pages we shall examine the pros and cons of numerous philosophical positions. Sometimes the author's bias may be showing, but the purpose of the discussion is not to get agreement (agreement is easy, if you're in the right frame of mind) but to let the discussion of the issues spur you on to thinking about them for yourself. It is for you, the reader, to absorb the arguments and assess them as carefully as you can.

But we still haven't come to grips with the question, "What is philosophy?" Many people who have been studying and teaching the subject for years wouldn't agree on a definition. And a definition wouldn't tell you much anyway—it would give you some *words* which you could memorize and copy down in notes and spew forth on tests, but they would still not succeed in giving you an experience of philosophical thinking. Just as you can learn to swim only by getting into the water, you can only find out what goes on in philosophy by engaging in it.

Nevertheless, to describe philosophy, let's try at least one plausible suggestion which covers most if not all of what people who are engaged in thinking and writing about the subject are constantly doing. The suggestion is that philosophy is the *study of justification*. People have many beliefs, but many of them are not justified—that is, they have no good reason for holding them. Philosophy asks, of even the most ordinary, everyday statements, "What are your reasons for believing this?" and "How will you prove to me that what you said was true?" and "If someone denied what you claim, what could you say in defense of your claim against your opponent?" Philosophy is a study of "How do you know?" questions, applied to lots of different kinds of issues, but especially to very *general* questions about the physical world, the mind, and scientific, religious, and ethical theories.

In the last few lines several words have already been used to explain "what philosophy is," and these words in turn require clarification: "true," "know," "reason," "evidence." We have to ask, When is a statement true? When can you be said to *know* it? What is a good reason for believing something and why? In Chapter 1 we shall be concerned with "true" and "know," as well as reasons for believing we can have knowledge (or that we can't). In Chapter 2 we shall ask how we know (if we do) that statements about the world such as "There's a desk in front of me" are true. In Chapter 3 we shall ask how we know whether another group of statements, called "necessary" statements, such as "Dogs are dogs" and "2 + 2 = 4", are true. In Chapter 4 we shall ask how we know that the statements of science, especially atoms and other things we can't perceive with our senses, are true. In Chapter 5 we shall investigate the meaning of "cause" and try to discover whether, if all our actions are caused, we are yet free. In Chapter 6 we shall consider a group of related questions concerning the mind: What is it? How is it related to the body? What is a person? and What makes someone the same person? In Chapter 7 we shall discuss various claims of religion, whether they are justified, and how or whether we are in a position to know whether they are. In Chapter 8 we shall examine another kind of claim—moral ones involving the use of such terms as "good" and "right" and "just," and how such claims can be established, if they can, and how they are connected with one another and with others outside of ethics.

The first three chapters are devoted to what is often called *epistemology,* the theory of knowledge—the study of whether we are justified in claiming to know anything, and if so what. The fourth chapter considers epistemological questions in the area of the sciences. Chapters 5 through 7 are devoted to what is often called metaphysics, "the investigation of the nature of reality"—Chapter 5, problems of determinism and freedom; Chapter 6, problems of mind and self; Chapter 7, problems of religion. However, the grandiloquent phrase "the nature of reality" is not a very precise one. Science surely attempts to discover the nature of reality, and all disciplines claim to investigate some aspect or other of reality, or "what is." In fact these chapters are as epistemological as the others. The question, "How do you know?," is as appropriate

to religious claims discussed in Chapter 7 as to scientific claims discussed in Chapter 4. The same could be said for the brief introduction to ethics in Chapter 8: What do ethical claims mean and how are we to know whether they are true? Thus the problem of justification will be with us from start to finish.

Why should we ask such questions? They may not make you any richer, possibly not even any happier, but they will enable you better to *understand* when we are justified in asserting what we do and why. They will give an indication of what reasons can be given for or against numerous beliefs you have—and many more you haven't encountered. And thus, it is hoped, they will increase your understanding and enlightenment, even though many distinctions will have to be drawn which are confusing at the outset. "A little philosophy (like a little learning) is a dangerous thing," because we think too soon that we know all the answers; we want to impress our friends with our newfound "knowledge." But if we persevere, we can gradually cut through the confusions and the popular oversimplifications; and then the feeling of mastery we experience will make it seem more than worth all the effort we put into it and all the frustrations we encountered along the way.

CHAPTER
1
KNOWLEDGE

1. TRUTH

In the popular mind, philosophy is concerned with profound questions such as, What is truth? What is goodness? What is beauty? What is the meaning of life? Philosophy does indeed deal with these questions—along with many others that the newcomer to philosophy frequently has never heard of and doesn't even suspect. But a discussion of these questions often leads into very intricate pathways of argument, with many traps for the unwary.

"What is truth?" asked Pontius Pilate, who did not stay for an answer. Well, what *is* the answer to this seemingly simple question?

To give a thoughtful answer to such a question requires us to separate the different senses of the word; "true" is used in different ways. We say "She was true to her word," which means simply that she kept her word, that she did what she said she was going to do. "She is a true friend" means that she really

was a friend, not someone who merely pretended to be. "This characterization in a novel is true to human nature" means approximately that the character is depicted as behaving in the way that people of that kind do generally behave under the circumstances described. "It's a true diamond" means that it's a real diamond and not imitation. And so on.

We also call *statements* true: "What you just said is true"; "Truer words were never spoken"; and so on. So what does "true" mean when we talk about true statements, or people uttering true statements?

In practice we have no trouble with this so-called problem. "What you just said is true"; "It's true that the earth is round"; "It's true that I returned home before midnight." Doesn't every child know what it means to say these things? What problem is there about truth, that we should even bother to consider it? "I returned home before midnight," a woman says; someone questions this and the woman says, "But it's *true* that I returned home by midnight." Isn't she merely saying the same thing over again, with emphasis?

And indeed, there is a very simple answer to the question "What is truth?" when it's true statements we're asking about. If a certain state-of-affairs exists or occurs in the world, and we assert that it does, then our statement is true. The statement "Snow is white" is true if and only if snow *is* white. And if you did return home before midnight last night, the statement "I returned home before midnight" is a true statement.

Or we could put it a different way. A true statement is one that states a *fact*. But the word "fact" is ambiguous. Sometimes the word "fact" is used to mean the same as "true statement"—for example, "It's a fact that I returned home by midnight." But sometimes we speak of a fact as the state-of-affairs in the world, which the statement expresses. The fact that snow is white (a condition of the world, not something in language) is what makes the statement that snow is white true. A fact in this sense is some state-of-affairs in the world, so the answer "A true statement is one that expresses a fact" comes to the same thing as the answer "A true statement is one that asserts the existence of some actual state-of-affairs (or any fact about the world)." "Snow is black" does not describe any state-of-affairs in the world, and so the statement is false.

All this may seem very disappointing. It is quite a comedown after what seemed like a very profound question, "What is truth?" But it *does* answer the question "What is a true statement?" even though some people may have the feeling that there is something wanting in the answer—they had expected something very profound and enlightening, and all they got was "A true statement expresses a fact." Slim pickings, one might say, as an answer to a deep philosophical question.

It is possible, though, that we may have confused the question "What is a true state-

ment?" with a very different question, namely "How do we *discover* whether a statement is true?" And the answer to this last question is much more complicated, because we discover the truth of different statements in different ways. We don't discover the truth of "87 + 85 = 172" in the same way that we discover the truth of "There is a book on this table" or "Marjorie is happier today than she was last year" or "All lions are carnivorous." How we discover the truth of various kinds of statements is something we cannot fruitfully discuss until we have first examined these kinds of statements—and that is what we shall be doing in the coming chapters.

It is also easy to confuse our original question, What is a true statement?, with the question, What *criteria* do we use for calling a statement true? We constantly use the word "cause" in daily life, without asking ourselves what exactly is involved in calling something a cause; we may give synonyms like "produce" and "bring about," but then the same question arises as to what is the criterion for the use of *these* terms. Perhaps we can give some account of truth (true statements) by giving a criterion for its application.

Thus, *correspondence* has often been suggested as a criterion for the truth of a statement: "A statement is true if it corresponds with the facts" or ". . . if it corresponds with some actual state-of-affairs in the world." Which of the solutions to the mystery is true—that Jones attacked her because they had a domestic quarrel, or that Smith attacked her because she wouldn't consent to sexual relations with him, or that Brown attacked her because she wouldn't hand over the money he said she owed him? "The true answer is whichever one corresponds with the facts." A criterion of truth is *"correspondence with reality."*

This account gives us a mental picture of a series of states-of-affairs on one side and a series of statements on the other side; truth then consists of matching up the statements with the right states-of-affairs. But have we really gained anything by this process? Why do we have to talk about correspondence at all? Why isn't it enough just to say that a true statement is one that states the facts (or reports an actual state-of-affairs)? You might ask, "Talk about correspondence if you wish, but what does it add?" This way of explicating the concept of truth seems to be only a blind alley—as so many in philosophy will turn out to be.

Besides, the notion of a fact or state-of-affairs seems clear enough when we are talking about ordinary situations such as a book being on the table. But what is the fact that is supposed to be expressed by sentences like "The hydrogen atom has one electron" and "Honesty is a virtue?" We may *say* "It's a fact that honesty is a virtue," but what kind of fact is that? To which fact or situation is the statement "Honesty is a virtue" supposed to "correspond"? By talking about correspondence, have we said anything to clarify or enlighten the answer to such a question, or have we merely obfuscated it with a word?

There are other suggested criteria of truth, the most usual being the one that is called *coherence*. But coherence requires not just a single statement (thus far we've been discussing only single statements) but entire bodies or systems of statements. When we have discussed an entire interconnected system of statements such as we find in the sciences, we shall return to the topic of truth in Chapter 4.

Meanwhile, a few distinctions are needed before we proceed.

Sentences and Propositions

We have said that statements are true or false; but the word "statement," though it will do for ordinary purpose, is ambiguous. It can mean a *sentence*—a string of words with a subject and a predicate—or it can mean a *proposition*. It is propositions that philosophers ordinarily talk about as being true or false, and they symbolize a proposition with the letter *p* (a second proposition is symbolized as *q,* a third as *r,* and so on). But what exactly is a proposition? A sentence, like a word, has a meaning; a sentence is not merely a string of marks on paper or a series of noises but is either or both of these things *with* a meaning. But when we talk about a proposition, we are talking not about the sentence itself but about what the sentence means.

Two or more sentences can be used to express the same proposition—that is, the same meaning. "New York is larger that San Francisco" and "San Francisco is smaller than New York" are two different sentences, and they are quite different from one another: For example, the first sentence contains the word "larger" but the second one does not; the first sentence begins with the letter *N,* but the second does not, and so on. Yet they state, or express, the same proposition. They both give the same information; they both assert the existence of the same state-of-affairs. If you believe that the first sentence expresses a truth, you are committed to believing that the second one does also; and if someone said, "I'll give you two bits of information: New York is larger than San Francisco, and San Francisco is smaller than New York," we would say that this person was giving us not two pieces of information but one. The reverse also occurs; the same sentence can be used to express different propositions, when the sentence is ambiguous. "He rents the house" could mean that he rents it *to* someone or that he rents it *from* someone—two different meanings, but one sentence.

It is the proposition that is true or false, but the sentence that has meaning or fails to have it. A sentence is only a vehicle of meaning, and only when we know what that meaning is can we know whether the proposition it expresses is true or false. A proposition has, indeed, often been defined as *"anything that is true or false."*

The word "proposition" is used in philosophy in a special sense—not the popular sense in which we say "I have a proposition to put to you." Many pages could be spent—and largely wasted—in discussing propositions. We could ask questions such as "Are propositions temporal or nontemporal entities?" "Do propositions exist before anyone states them in a sentence?" "What are propositions, apart from their expression in sentences?" So many questions arise here that many students of the subject have been led to abandon the use of the term "proposition" entirely and speak only of sentences and classes of sentences. Yet the distinction is useful, for it marks an important difference: between the sentence itself (as it would be studied by grammarians) and the meaning that it conveys. Philosophers are concerned with sentences only insofar as they are carriers of meaning; the analysis of sentences (and the words they contain), together with their history, origin, and relations, is the concern of linguists, philologists, etymologists. Our concern with sentences in philosophy is simply that in order to state propositions we must use sentences. There are nonlinguistic substitutes for sentences—for instance, when I tell a friend that I am going to pull a handkerchief out of my coat pocket during a party to indicate that I'm going to leave within the next 10 minutes. But such a signal has to be arranged in advance, and I have to use language in order to explain what proposition the signal is to express.

We shall have occasion to use the technical term "proposition" quite often in our inquiry. Sometimes we shall employ the more usual word, "statement," which can mean either the proposition expressed or the sentence expressing it. In many cases it is clear from the context which of these is meant. But in many cases the distinction is important to avoid confusion, and then we shall employ the more precise language of "sentences" and "propositions."

Sometimes the meaning is quite clear to most readers even though the sentences designed to express them are ungrammatical, garbled, and hardly sentences at all. A letter published in the *Los Angeles Times* reads:

Mr. Baggage Man
American Airlines
U.S. of Los Angeles

Gentlemen Dear sir

I damn seldom where my suitcases are. She no fly. You no more fit to baggage master than for crysake that's all I hope. What's the matter you?

Itu Hisuki

Though the sentences are (to say the least) defective, aren't the propositions they are intended to express clear enough?

Truth and belief. The sentences "*p* is true" and "I believe that *p* is true" clearly have different meanings. A person may believe that a proposition is true even though it isn't: Everyone once believed that the earth is flat, although this proposition is false. And of course a person may believe that a proposition is false even when it is true. One might put it this way: "A true proposition correctly reports reality, but what people *think* correctly reports reality may not do so." The point may appear too obvious to be worth mentioning, but people sometimes mislead others, and themselves as well, through being confused about these seemingly simple matters.

Here are a few examples:

1. "A proposition is false until it's proven true" and "A proposition is true until it's proven false" reveal equally obvious mistakes. It may be that some people will not *believe* a proposition until it has been proven true — or sometimes not even then; and others will not disbelieve a proposition until it has been proven false (if then). But the degree of one's belief concerning a proposition has nothing to do with its truth. A person who says, "It's false till it's proven true," may mean (even though saying it in a very mislead-

ing way), "I'll *believe* it's false until it's proven true."

Assuming that this is what is meant, what are we to say of such belief? Believing a proposition is false until it is proven true would seem to be as unjustified as believing it's true till it is proven false. If it has been shown to be false, then one should disbelieve it; if it has been shown to be true, one should believe it; and if it has not been shown to be either, one should not believe it or disbelieve it. One's belief should be proportioned to the evidence; if it is very likely true but not proved, the proper attitude is "I believe that it's very *probably* true." (When can we be *sure* that it's true? This question will occupy us later in this chapter.)

2. During an argument, when a proposition has been attacked, one sometimes hears, "Well, at least *as far as I'm concerned,* it's true." But what on earth does this mean? When you say it, are you saying that it *is* true, or that you *believe* that it is true? More likely it is the latter; but when you say you believe it is true, remember that you believing that it is true is quite compatible with its not *being* true—that is, your belief may be false. To say "As far as I'm concerned, it's true" is extremely misleading: It sounds as if you are saying *more* than that you believe it (rightly or wrongly) to be true—that not only do you believe it to be true, but that it *is* true. But if you are saying that it *is* true, then what does the "as far as I'm concerned" add? Is it said in order to let you off the hook in case the statement turns out not to be true? But you can't have your cake and eat it. You can't declare that it *is* true and, when it is shown to be false, claim as a defense that you said it was true only as far as you're concerned.

3. The most misleading of all the formulations of this kind is "*To me* it's true, *to you* it may not be." What does it mean to say "To me it's true?" Perhaps it just means "It's true *according to me*"—that is, "I *believe* it's true." But this, as we have seen, is quite com-

patible with the statement's actually being false. If all you mean is that you believe it's true, then why not say just that, instead of generating confusion by saying "*To me* it's true"? Perhaps the answer is that this last formulation makes it sound as if it *is* true and that your believing it guarantees it.

Discussions often end with one person saying "Well, to me it's true" while another one says "And to me it isn't." But what do these statements mean? If they mean simply that the first person believes it and the second person doesn't, then the statements only repeat what is already known to both disputants. And if they mean something more, what is it? This kind of conclusion to a discussion leaves entirely unanswered the question "*Is* it true or *isn't* it?" What is "To you it's true, to me it isn't" except a confusing and somewhat dishonest way of saying "According to you there is, according to me there isn't"—that is, "You believe there is, I believe there isn't?"—thus leaving it an open question which of the beliefs is true.

If White says "*p* is true" and Black says "*p* is not true," they are contradicting one another, and one of them must be mistaken. But if White says "I believe *p* is true" and Black says " I believe *p* is not true," their statements do not contradict one another, and both of them may be true (both *are* true if the speakers are not lying).

What may mislead people into saying such things as "It's true for me" is that some characteristics of things are *relative*—that is, they are to-me and to-you characteristics. "Calculus is fascinating," says one person. "I find it utterly boring," says another. Both statements are true: It *is* interesting to one person and uninteresting to the other. The same applies to many statements, such as "The music was moving," "The information was surprising," "The news was heartening," and in general to statements about what effects something has on a person: Clearly something can have one effect on one person and a very different effect on another, and their reports do not contradict each other. But truth is not relative in this way: If it is true that there are four trees in a certain enclosure at certain time, then it is true, period—not true-to-you and false-to-me, and anyone who says there are not four trees is mistaken.

Truths are not relative to the individual, even when they are truths *about* an individual. The statements "The information was surprising to White" and "It was not surprising to Black" may both be true. Suppose Smith has a toothache and Jones does not; is the statement "I have a toothache" true for Smith but false for Jones? Not at all: The pronoun "I" refers to different persons in the two sentences. Two propositions are true, that Smith has a toothache, and that Jones does not. It is not true merely for Smith that Smith has a toothache; it is simply true, period (not *to* anyone). The sentence "I have a toothache" merely expresses a different proposition when Smith utters it than it does when Jones utters it, since each person is referring to himself.

4. Can a proposition be true at one place or time but not at another place or time? Is "Chicago has more than 3 million people" true when someone says it in 1990, but false if someone said it in 1890? One could indeed *say* this, and probably it would not be misleading to say it, yet wouldn't it be more accurate to say there are two propositions and not one: "Chicago had more than 3 million people in 1890" (false) and "Chicago has more than 3 million people in 1990 (true)? The sentence "Chicago has more than 3 million people" doesn't tell you *when* the statement is uttered, so its meaning is *incompletely specified*. Once the meaning of the sentence is completely specified as to time, the alleged relativity disappears. The same happens with regard to place: "There is a book on this desk" may be said to be true when it's your desk we're talking about, but not when it is my desk (in a different room); but again this is not a case of the same proposition being both true and false. One must make clear to what desk the phrase "this desk" refers: It can refer to one desk when you're in one room, to a different one when you're in another room. Demonstrative pronouns like "this" and "that," as well as "here" and "there" and "now" and "then," are a kind of substitute for acts of *pointing*. The sentence by itself doesn't tell you where the thing is; it is the utterance of the sentence *in* a certain spatial and temporal context that does so: "Now" is the time when the speaker is speaking (whenever that is) and "here" is the place or vicinity in which the speaker is speaking. To know when or where that is, you have to go beyond the sentence itself and examine the *conditions of its utterance*. If you came into a classroom and found on the blackboard the words "You are a liar," would this be true or false? You can't tell until you know to whom the words are addressed (if anyone), and when: The sentence itself will not tell you. However, if you provide a specification of the time and place (January 21, 1990 at 4 P.M., at such-and-such an address in a certain city) and who the "you" is, then the sentence *will* provide sufficient information, and will, once again, be true or false, period.

5. One might ask: "But how can a proposition about the future be true *now?* Is it already true today that tomorrow there will be an earthquake in Japan?" Questions of this kind have induced mental cramps in many of those who have raised them; they feel that the question is somehow strange, yet they want to ask it. How are we to deal with such questions? Well, if someone had said in 1780 that in 1880 New York City would have the largest population of any city in the United States, the statement would have been true, wouldn't it? In 1780 the speaker would be in no position to *know* that in another century New York would be the largest city—it would at best be an "educated guess." Still, if anyone had said it, it would have been true, even without the speaker's *knowing* that it was true. Similarly, you may not be in a position to know that to-

morrow there will be a storm in the city where you live, but if you say there will be, and there is a storm the next day, then the statement was true. Was it true at the time that you made it (before you knew whether it was true)? Of course, we may reply, because the truth of a statement is *tenseless:* It was, is, and always will be true that Abraham Lincoln died in 1865. The proposition is not "true at a certain time" but true, period. What changes when the future becomes the present and the present becomes the past is not the truth of the statement but our knowledge of it.

What if someone nevertheless says "It doesn't become true till tomorrow, when it happens. Today, the statement about tomorrow's weather is neither true nor false"? We *could* simply say that the person is mistaken—that it's *discovered* to be true tomorrow, but it is true regardless of when the statement is made. "Truth is tenseless." Don't ask, "Is it true today?"; ask rather, "Is it true?" Is it true today that Lincoln died in 1865? Of course it's true, but it isn't true merely today. "Is it then true at all times?" Yes, if you want to put it that way—but why not just simply say, It's true, period? Or you might prefer to say, "Say if you like that it won't be true until next Tuesday that there will be a tornado here next Tuesday." But if someone predicted the event today, and this person later turned out to be right, how could you deny that the statement was true—not known, but true—even at the time it was made?

6. Can a proposition be partly true and partly false? In a true-false test, if any part of the statement is false, the whole statement is counted as false. The statement "Snow is white and dogs are green" is false although half of it is true. But that sentence is a compound sentence, which is a conjunction of two different sentences, one about snow and one about dogs. In a conjunctive sentence, both parts have to be true for the statement to be true. But "Either I am a human being or Napoleon is still alive" is true because the "or"

indicates that only one of the two parts needs to be true.

But what about simple sentences like "Doris is a scheming, selfish brat"? One might say, "It's partly true—she is that sometimes, but not all the time," or "It has some truth in it, but as it stands it's an exaggeration." Both objectors are taking exception to the statement as it stands and suggesting that it would be true if it were revised a bit so as to be less extreme. As it now stands, it is false; but you would only have to revise it a little to make it true. This seems to be what such objectors are saying.

7. Must every proposition be either true or false? Suppose someone said: "It could be true, or it could be false, or it could be unknown." This statement confuses truth with our knowledge of it. For example, it is either true or false that there is an intruder in the house next door at this moment, but since the family is gone for the weekend nobody knows; still, it is either true or false that there is an intruder there. We should not confuse the truth of a proposition with our (or anyone's) knowledge of its truth. There are doubtless many truths which no one yet knows; more truths are being discovered all the time. For example, it is either true or false that tomorrow it will rain in your neighborhood, but at the moment we don't yet know which.

Meaningless Sentences. "A sentence is either true or false or *meaningless*. If it's meaningless, it is neither true nor false." A meaningless sentence expresses no proposition at all, so we can't say that the proposition is meaningless, only that the sentence is. Propositions themselves remain either true or false. Consider these examples: (1) "Pirots carulize elatically" is meaningless because it contains noises or ink-marks, but no words; (2) "Walking say eat very" is meaningless because, though it contains words, the words don't add up to a sentence; (3) "He stood between the post" is meaningless because the word "between" requires a relation between two things—he would have to stand between the post *and* something else, and the something else is not specified.

Consider the word "motion." Motion, we say, is change of position. But change of position is always *with respect* to something. The train is moving—that is, it is changing its position with respect to the point on the surface of the earth from which it started (or for that matter any point on the earth's surface). But the table in this room is not moving: That is, it is not changing its position with respect to the floor on which it rests; nor is the floor, with respect to the house of which it is a part, unless we're in the midst of an earthquake; nor is the house, with respect to the earth on which it stands. In this context, it is not only meaningful but true to say that the table is not moving; and this is the context that is usually implicit in our daily discourse. But at the same time, the table, the floor, the house, and the portion of the earth on which it rests are all moving with respect to the sun, for the earth and everything on it revolve around the sun at approximately 18 miles per second. "But how can it be moving and standing still at the same time?" It is standing still with respect to the earth below it, but moving with respect to the sun. Motion is change of position with respect to something, and to know whether something is moving you have to know the reference point implicit in the assertion. The sun itself is moving with respect to other things, carrying the solar system with it—it is revolving around the center of our galaxy (many thousands of light-years distant from the sun) at a speed of over 200 miles per second; and the same may be true of our galaxy itself, with respect to a system of galaxies or something else of which we are so far ignorant. Once a reference point (to provide a "with respect to") is supplied, talk about motion has meaning, though of course many statements about it may be false; but without such a reference,

any talk about motion is meaningless, even though the sentence in question may have a subject and a verb and be in impeccable grammatical form.

But why does a word have no meaning outside a certain context? Why does "above" have no meaning apart from reference to space, or "between" apart from reference to two other places? Is it because we haven't bothered to give it one? If this were so, we could easily remedy the deficiency by simply extending the meaning of the word to cover the new cases. But this is not the source of the trouble in the examples we have considered. Of course we could always *stipulate* some new and entirely different meaning for the old word: We could use the word "between" so as (in its new meaning) to mean the same as "against," and then "He stood between the post" would be meaningful because it would mean the same as "He stood against the post." All this is true, but trivial. What we cannot do, however, is mean the same thing we always have by the words "above" and "between"—or even anything similar to it that merely extends the usage somewhat—and yet meaningfully say, "She stood above the universe" or "He stood between the post."

Category mistakes. There are many possible reasons for a sentence to be meaningless (hence express no proposition), but among the chief reasons are *category mistakes.* Suppose someone said to you, "Saturday is in bed." Puzzled, you ask, "Who is Saturday?" "I don't mean any person by that name, I mean the seventh day of the week, Saturday." "But how can a day of a week be in bed? What does it mean to say it?" The speaker is, as we say, mixing categories. The word "Saturday" describes a 24-hour span of time; a span of time is not like a thing, which is in a certain *place.* How can a span of time be in a place?

Everything we can talk about, it is said, falls into certain broad classes, or categories. Thus we can say that books are used for reading, that they contain pages and print, that they have certain sizes and weights, but not that they are numbers (for numbers are non-temporal entities, while books exist in time), or that they themselves read books (for books are inanimate objects, and reading is something applicable only to conscious beings), or that they are days of the week. It is meaningful (it is suggested) to ascribe a characteristic to something in a given category only if the characteristic also belongs in that category. Let us take a few examples of category mistakes to see how they operate.

If someone claimed that he had tasted a smell or smelled a taste, he would be guilty of a category mistake. Whatever you smell, whether it is acrid or pungent or stale, it is always a smell and not a taste. Smell-words apply to smells and taste-words to taste. True, we smell things—such as roses and ammonia—but it is the smell of it we are aware of through our sense of smell and not the taste or sight or touch. Each of our senses, according to this account, constitutes a special category, and the rule for every category in relation to every other is "no trespassing." One may think there are exceptions to this: For example, people say they see sounds when they look through an oscilloscope and see waves of various kinds when certain sounds are heard and simultaneously fed into the machine. But of course we don't see sounds in this case or in any other: We can ask about any sound, "What did it sound like?" but we cannot meaningfully ask this of the waves that we *see*. What happens is that *when* we hear a certain sound we simultaneously see a set of visual curves on the machine. But this goes no distance whatever toward saying that we see the sound itself; the sound is something we hear, and we see the sight that accompanies the sound.

"The number 7 is blue." Numbers are not physical objects and do not have the characteristics of physical objects. Numbers are

timeless entities; they have no history, no before and after; it would be meaningless to say that the number 7 came into existence yesterday or had a heart attack today. Temporal characteristics—those that characterize things existing in time—cannot be attributed to timeless entities, or vice versa. Here are two very general and very important categories that should not be intermixed. Mixing them accounts for many cases of meaninglessness. Thus "Quadruplicity drinks procrastination" would be neither true nor false but meaningless. Quadruplicity is a characteristic, or, as philosophers often say, a property, and a property of something cannot *do* anything, such as drink. For that matter, neither can procrastination, which is a property of individuals, do anything or have anything (such as drinking) done to it; that would be another category mistake.

"Quadratic equations go to horse races." Is this true, false, or meaningless? Equations are not the kind of thing that can do things in time, such as go to horse races; quadratic equations are mathematical entities, which have no histories. You might think: "I can write a quadratic equation on a piece of paper, put the paper into my pocket, and go to the horse race; thus the equation has had the trip along with me." But it is not the equation that you put into your pocket but a piece of paper with certain marks on it, marks that stand for the equation. Other persons may have written on other pieces of paper certain marks that also stand for the same equation. By destroying the piece of paper you would not destroy the equation but only one representation of it. Even if all such representations were destroyed, a certain portion of mathematics would not thereby be destroyed—to the great disappointment of some students. You would destroy certain marks (numerals, equals signs, etc.) but not what they stand for.

But perhaps "Quadratic equations go to horse races" is simply *false*. In that case,

"Quadratic equations do not go to horse races" is true. Well, isn't it true? They don't go, do they? Still, what would it be like for a quadratic equation (not marks on a piece of paper) to go to a horse race? Quadratic equations just aren't the kind of things that *can* go to horse races—*or fail to go,* for that matter. If "Quadratic equations go to horse races" is meaningless, then its negative, "Quadratic equations do not go to horse races," is meaningless also. And isn't it? If a category mistake is meaningless in the affirmative form of the statement, it would seem to be equally so in the negative form.

Self-contradictoriness. Suppose we said, "He drew a square circle," "She was naked but wore a red dress," "She lay in her bed, striding indignantly out of the room," "The room was empty but full of books." If we were speaking literally and not using the words in some new and different sense, we would be guilty of contradicting ourselves, for we would be saying of something, X, that it had one characteristic, A, and in the same breath that it had another characteristic, not-A, which was inconsistent with it. To be a cube is *not* to be a sphere; to be naked is *not* to be clothed, in a red dress or anything else; and so on. A thing could not have both of these characteristics at the same time. It is not merely that we could not *imagine* anything having these incompatible properties. This is true enough: You cannot imagine a circle that is also square. But, your failure to imagine such a thing would not by itself prove that it was meaningless. If it is meaningless, it is so for a different reason: that the sentence describing this alleged state-of-affairs is self-contradictory.

Are self-contradictory statements meaningless? Some might say that they are not: "I do know," one might suggest, "what is meant by 'That's a square circle,' and it's *because* I know what it means to say this that I know

it's self-contradictory. I grant you that there are no square circles—the statement is false; and it *has* to be false, for there couldn't be any square circles; but it isn't meaningless. Don't you know what it means? I do, and it's just because I know what it means that I can assert with confidence that it is self-contradictory."

One might reply, however, "You know what the *word* 'square' means, and also what the word 'circle' means; but I submit that you do not know what the phrase 'square circle' means. What could its meaning possibly be? It's true that the words taken *individually* have a meaning, but it doesn't follow that the words *taken in conjunction* (together) have a meaning." We know what "fall" means (it means at least going downward, though doubtless another characteristic should be added about the manner of going downward, since you can jump or plunge or dive, and these cases of going downward are not falling); you also know what "upward" means. But do you know what "falling upward" means? "Falling upward" is a contradiction in terms; one can fall, and one can go upward, but one can't *fall* upward. "Certainly it's self-contradictory, but it does have a meaning, else I wouldn't even be able to say that it's self-contradictory."

But has it? Have the two words in conjunction a meaning? What possible state-of-affairs could be described by "I fell upward"? None, for there is no such possible state-of-affairs. "But," one might still contend, "this doesn't prevent the sentence from having a meaning; a sentence can have meaning without describing any possible situation, just as the word 'unicorn' means without describing any creature. 'Falling upwards' doesn't describe anything, for it has no instances; let's even add that it could have no possible instances—and yet it has defining characteristics, doesn't it? The defining characteristics are that (1) one goes downward (2) in a certain way (not jumping or diving), and (3) one goes upwards.'' ''But these defining characteristics are incompatible with one another.'' ''True, but that's just the point: the sentence is self-contradictory, but it has meaning just the same.''

Admittedly, self-contradictory expressions are peculiar; they are not like the cases of meaninglessness we find in ''Walking very eat aha'' or ''The watch was above the universe.'' Still, one could make a case for saying that the sentences ''There is a square circle'' and ''I fell upwards'' are meaningless: Their individual words have meaning, but the sentence as a whole does not. But why should one say this? Why insist that such a sentence is meaningless? Isn't it quite enough to say that it is self-contradictory—isn't that condemnation enough?

These are only some of the kinds of sentences that can plausibly be described as ''meaningless.'' No complete list can be attempted here; some would call certain sentences meaningless and others would say they are only ''very difficult to figure out.'' Many sentences in students' term papers, and others by philosophers in their writings, would be examples. ''She was only a shadow'' in a figurative way of saying that she was very thin or emaciated, but ''The world is a mere shadow'' would be labeled as nonsense (meaningless) by some and as a far-out metaphor by others. Our aim here has been only to distinguish problems of meaning from problems of truth.

2. KNOWLEDGE

One of the fundamental problems of philosophy is the nature and extent of human knowledge. We all have many *beliefs;* but how can we be sure that the beliefs are true? What we want is not merely belief, but *knowledge.*

We want to be able to be *certain.* But about what things can we be certain? Can we be certain about anything? Can we know anything about the fundamental nature of the universe?

about God? about electrons? We can't see or touch God or electrons, so how can we know? Even about things we *can* perceive with the senses (sight, touch, hearing, smell, taste), we often seem to make false claims: We think we hear someone knocking at the door, but it's only the wind; we seem to see a man in the forest at twilight, but it's only a tree stump. And so on. What *can* we be certain about?

When we speak of being certain, we don't mean that we merely *feel* certain about it. People feel certain about all kinds of things that turn out not to be true. A woman is certain, absolutely certain, that her husband is still alive, although he may have been dead for years. Many people used to be (feel) certain that other people were inhabited by devils; but how could they be sure? And how can we be sure, as most of us are today, that they are not? There probably isn't anything that some people, at some time, haven't *felt* certain about; people can feel certain of the craziest things. You yourself probably feel certain of many things, but what *entitles* you to feel certain? You have *beliefs*—but do you have *knowledge?*

When we desire knowledge, what exactly is it that we desire? What exactly *is* knowledge? People are in the habit of asking ''Is there X, yes or no?'' without first asking ''What *is* the X that I am seeking?'' But before we ask ''How can we get X?'' we have to know what X is. In other words, before we ask what we can know or what we can't know, let's first ask *what it is* to know.

This is a characteristic philosophical question. In fact, most of the questions of philosophy will come under the headings of ''What do you mean?'' and ''How do you know?'' Questions about meaning, such as ''What do you mean by 'know'?,'' tend to irritate most people; finding the answer is often laborious, time-consuming, and boring. People think they already know what they mean by such common words as ''know''—after all, haven't they used such common words all their lives?—and that the only question is what things the word applies to. But before you are in a position to find out what things, if any, the word "X" applies to, don't you first have to know what you mean by the word "X"? If I asked you, "Are there any flubjubs in the world—yes or no?", wouldn't you first ask me, "What *are* flubjubs?" Don't you have to know that before you can answer my question?

Like so many words, the word "know" is not always used in the same way. There are overlapping senses of the word which are apt to be confused with one another until someone points them out. A person who has never studied philosophy is especially likely to be confused by such words, slipping from one sense of the word to another one without knowing it. The ordinary person is aware that some words are *ambiguous* (have more than one meaning): People know the difference between the bark of a tree and the bark of a dog, or between the bank of the river and the Bank of Manhattan. If someone said to you that she went to the bank, you might ask which kind of bank she meant. But in most cases people seem quite unaware of the ambiguity of many of the words they use. And it seems as if the word "know" is one of them. Let's distinguish several ways we use the word "know".

1. Knowing how. Do you know how to ride a horse? to swim? to use a welding torch? to build a house? This means, at least approximately, "Do you (now) have the *ability* to do it?" If you don't, then you don't know how. If you throw me into the water, you will find out soon enough whether or not I know how to swim.

This sense of *know* is not restricted to human beings. Animals know how to do all kinds of things; sometimes they know how without ever having to learn. When they are able to do something they've never had to learn to do, we say that they "know by instinct" or that their behavior is "genetically programmed." Almost every kind of creature except human beings knows how to swim: People have to be taught, and only then do they know how. Chickens know how to avoid predators: They can hide and play dead from the day they hatch. Most animals know how to distinguish foods that will nourish them from things that won't: Dogs will eat meat but (usually) not leaves, and rabbits will eat leaves but not meat. They don't have to be taught, they just "naturally" are able to do this. Non-human animals have many more of these abilities—to do things without having learned them—than people have; in this sense they have far more "natural-know-how" than we do.

2. Acquaintance. When you are asked "Do you know Susie Smith?" you normally take this to mean "Have you met her?" not "Do you know any facts *about* her?" Whether you know her is decided by whether you have run into her at least once (not necessarily that you'd recognize her now, years later). Similarly, if someone asks "Do you know that old country lane near the red barn?" the person normally is asking if we've seen it or been on it, whether we've confronted it through our senses at some time in some way. You know (are acquainted with) Yosemite Falls if you have been there and have seen it; you may know nothing at all *about* it except that you saw it. A person who has never been there but read all about it in a book or encyclopedia may know many more facts about it than the person who has seen it.

"Seeing it for yourself" is sometimes called knowledge by acquaintance. Many philosophers, however, say that this isn't knowledge at all: It is only acquaintance. Having a headache isn't knowledge, though you certainly experience (are acquainted with) the headache; but knowing *that* you have a headache is. Seeing some colors in your visual field isn't knowledge; but forming concepts from your sensations and recognizing that it's an animal stalking in the underbrush, is. You couldn't have knowledge of the world without acquaintance, but acquaintance alone is not yet knowledge.

3. *Knowing that.* The sense of the word "know" that interests philosophers the most, and over which there is the most controversy and confusion, is what is called "knowing that": Do you know that there's a God, that you are now reading a book, that Caesar crossed the Rubicon, that there aren't any unicorns in the world?

If *knowing that* involves understanding statements or sentences, then this sense of knowing is pretty much limited to human beings, since animals (for the most part, at least) don't understand statements, questions, suggestions, and other things expressed in the sentences that human beings utter. Tell your dog that there are seven trees in the yard, and he won't understand you. Still, one might say, can't animals as well as humans know *that* some statements are true? Doesn't your dog know you when he sees you? Doesn't he know that that's a bone and not a twig? Doesn't he know that you usually feed him at dusk, or that you come back from work at 3 o'clock?

Your dog knows you: That is, he recognizes you, and acts in accordance with that recognition; and he knows *how* to distinguish you from other people. Your dog knows that a particular object is a bone in the sense that he knows *how* to distinguish a bone from a twig; he can even tell the difference between a real bone and a phony bone from the pet store—that is, he *knows how* to tell the difference (they don't smell the same). And surely he knows nothing about 3 o'clock; but he does seem to have an "inner time-clock" so that he knows *how* to tell at about what time of day you usually come home, and acts anxious if you don't show up. It is plausible to conclude that the dog's knowledge is limited to acquaintance and knowing how. Even if a dog can be made to understand some brief sentences,

such as commands (Heel! Stop! Come! Stay! Get off the couch!), that only shows that he can respond to certain cues, not that he knows *that* any statements are true or false. Still, one could argue this matter both ways.

Restricting ourselves to human beings, and thus omitting speculations about creatures that don't have a language, what is the meaning of "know" in the sense of "knowing that"? What are the requirements for knowing something—as opposed to just believing it, or wondering about it, or dreaming about it, or having a favorable attitude toward it? Philosophers have examined a set of three standard, or *classical* requirements in this area; we refer to this as *the classical analysis of the concept of knowing.* We'll examine the requirements first, and then turn to some objections.

First requirement: The statement must be true. (This is sometimes called the *objective component of knowledge.*) Nevermind at this point how we discover that it's true; the point is that what isn't true can't be knowledge. If a person claims to know that someone is dead, and then the person turns up alive, she will have to admit that she didn't really know it: She only *thought* she knew. If I say I know that tomorrow it will rain in Chicago, and tomorrow comes and no rain falls in Chicago, I'll have to admit that I didn't know, for my claim turned out to be mistaken. When the statement is false, the claim to know that it's true *has to be withdrawn.* You can't know what isn't so.

In this respect knowing is different from believing, wondering, speculating, hoping, and so on. These words all describe a person's state of mind. When you believe something you have a certain state of mind toward it (confidence in its truth), as well as a disposition or tendency to act on the basis of the belief (to bet in its favor, or to take a raincoat in case it's a prediction of rain). You can perfectly well believe a statement is true although it is not. But unlike the others, "know" is a *success-word*. It does not merely describe your state of mind, it also puts the stamp of truth upon your statement. If you read in a novel that the character believed, was sure, was convinced, etc., that her husband was going to leave her, you can conclude that it still might not turn out that way; but if the author says she *knew* it (not just that she felt sure), then you as a reader can conclude that her belief is true. That's the way the word "know" functions, in contrast to the others.

But the requirement of truth is not enough. It was true that the earth was round long before most people believed it; and although it was true, you couldn't say that they *knew* it. Knowing involves not only its truth, but the speaker's awareness of its truth. Thus we get the second requirement:

*Second requirement: **You must believe that the statement is true.*** (This is sometimes called the *subjective component of knowledge*.) "She knew *p*" (*p* stands for any proposition or statement) "but *p* was not true," is a contradiction in terms; but "She believed *p*, but *p* was not true," is all right—people have false beliefs all the time. Can I say I know *p* without believing it? Yes, I can say it—I can utter the words -- I may be trying to deceive you, or be a perennial liar; but I can't *sincerely* say I know it unless I also believe it. Wouldn't it be odd to go around saying "I know the earth is round, but I don't believe it"? Couldn't you be accused of being ignorant of how the word "know" is used in our language?

Still, people do sometimes say things like "I know it's true, but I still can't believe it." She realizes her husband is dead, but still can't believe it; you have just won a million dollars, but still can't believe it. Here it's a matter of your mental attitude not having yet caught up with your intellectual realization; you do know it's true, and you do believe it, too (if asked "Is it true? Yes or no?" you'd say

"Yes"), but winning the lottery was such a surprise to you that you haven't yet digested the realization even though the check is in your hand; or, the woman knows her husband is dead, his body lies in state at the funeral home and she has seen it, but she hasn't yet adapted herself emotionally to what she realizes is true. It's not a matter of belief, but of adaptation to that belief.

But even these two requirements for knowing aren't enough. You can believe something and it may be true, but you don't yet *know* that it's true. Suppose that for some crazy reason, or no reason at all, a person believes strongly that there's going to be a hail storm tomorrow in the city she lives in. The sky is clear, the weather clam, and the weather forecasts predict nothing of the kind. She just "got it in her head" that this was going to happen, and to everyone's surprise (because there hasn't been a hail storm here for years) it does happen. Her statement was true (here we are, surrounded by hailstones) and she believed it; but did she *know* it? Or suppose there's a person who has inordinate confidence in his predictions. He strongly believes that the next throw of the dice will be double-sixes. The throw is made, and it's double-sixes. "I knew it!" he exclaims. But did he? Wasn't it just a lucky guess? After a person's guess has turned out correctly, people often say "I knew it all the time" though if it doesn't turn out the way they predicted, they are silent about it. This tends to irritate us, because we believe the person's claim is mistaken: The statement was indeed true, and he believed it, but he still didn't *know* it. A lucky guess isn't knowledge. So we need to add another condition:

*Third requirement: **There must be good evidence for believing the statement.*** In other words, there must be good reason to believe it. For example, suppose a person had no reason to believe something—and no more reason to believe the opposite. He made a guess, and his guess turned out to be right, but he lacked any *evidence* for his claim. The person must not only believe *p,* he must have good *reason* to believe *p,* otherwise his belief is just a lucky "shot in the dark." There must be some good reason to make the claim to know, or else the claim to know is unfounded. Consider this example: "How did you know the right answer? You never studied the course." "I peeked in the textbook during the exam." This explains to the inquirer how the student knew an answer on a test, for we now know the route by which he got it right: The fact that the textbook said that Nepal has an area of 54,000 square miles is good reason to believe that it does—not a conclusive reason perhaps (one might resurvey it and find an error?) but good reason nevertheless.

But goodness of evidence or reasons is a matter of *degree.* "Good" is a comparative term; you can have good evidence, better evidence, best evidence. To know *p,* how good must the evidence for it be? Surely the evidence must be considerable, the reasons very good. But how good is that? If the weather is fair today, no clouds in the sky, no predictions of rain or cold winds, you may say "I know the weather tomorrow will be fair." And suppose you turn out to be right. What about your statement "I *know* that tomorrow it will be fair"? Do you know just because you believe it and you have *some* reason to believe it is true? It isn't exactly a lucky guess, but it doesn't seem quite to be knowledge either—more like what we call "an educated guess."

This third requirement of knowing is not always formulated in the same way. Sometimes it is said that one must have good evidence, or adequate evidence, or excellent evidence, for *p.* Sometimes it is said that one must have good reason, or excellent reason, or sufficient reason, for believing *p.* Sometimes it is said that we must be *justified* in believing *p.* One must "have a right to be sure" of the truth of *p.* In all of these formulations, however, the requirement is somewhat vague:

How much evidence is adequate? *How much* reason is good enough reason? We would ordinarily say, for example, that we have excellent reason, and a right to be sure, that a particular chair exists. After all you've been sitting on it for years (or thought you have). But how good must the evidence, or reason to believe, or justification for believing, be in order for us to *know* something exists? Don't I know that I have lived on this earth for some years, and that the earth was here long before I was born? Do I have adequate or sufficient evidence for this to be said to know it? (Bertrand Russell once suggested that the earth might have been created, complete with memories, five minutes ago.) Do I know that this book is not going to suddenly turn into an elephant? Do I know that I shall never be mother or father to an orange?

We shall try to shed some light on questions like these in the next chapter, but meanwhile we should remember that evidence is a matter of degree, and that "reason to believe" too becomes stronger by degrees, increasing as evidence accumulates. One may be more justified, less justified, or entirely justified in believing *p.* As result, there are likely to be many borderline cases in which we won't be quite sure whether to say that we know *p* or not—just as there are clear cases of yellow and orange, but also borderline cases in which we wouldn't be sure whether to say that a certain color-sample is yellow or whether it is orange.

This third requirement of knowing is by far the most troublesome of them all, hinging as it does on the question of how much evidence is required. Do I *know* that there are chairs in the classroom next door? I passed by there 10 minutes ago, and there were lots of chairs there then. Of course, someone could have removed them in 10 minutes—but the doors were open and surely I would have heard some sounds, of treading feet or scraping chairs. But what if someone made a thousand-dollar bet with some movers that they couldn't remove the chairs silently in 10 minutes? Can I really be sure that this can't be done? Would I stake my life on it? Is this genuine knowledge, or must I say that although I have excellent reason to believe it, I don't really know it? If I go there later and see for myself that the chairs are still there, I know the statement was true—thus satisfying the first condition; but *before* I saw it myself, did I know?

Do you know that the earth is round? It looks flat, but then people do go around it all the time, don't they? Aerial photographs show the curvature; and astronauts on the moon saw the earth as a round ball, the way we see the moon from the earth. Still, do you know? Photographs can be faked or doctored up; and when people say what they saw they may be lying or mistaken. And I haven't been up there myself. So do I *know* that the earth is round? Don't I just believe it, with excellent reason to do so, without having the decisive evidence that would entitle me to say "I know it"?

At this point an unreflective person may say, "Come now, you've got to be kidding. I know (1) those true statements which (2) I believe (3) with good reason. I have excellent reason for believing that the earth is round, and that there are still chairs in the next room. Anyone who says I don't know these things is a fool." Still, the suspicion persists that although I might have excellent evidence, I don't have enough evidence, and surely not *all* the evidence, and therefore I don't really *know*. The person who is careful—more careful at any rate that the average layperson—about the use of the word "know" will be inclined to say that you had reason to believe, but that the reason still fell short of being knowledge. On the basis of the evidence you had at hand, you still *could* have been mistaken. So even the statement about the chairs in the next room was not knowledge but still an educated guess.

In that case, when do I know? Only (one might suggest) when the evidence is *complete,* so that *nothing* could any longer be discovered

that could place the statement in doubt. I didn't really know the chairs were next door at the time I made the statement. If I had looked and to my surprise found no chairs there, the statement "There are chairs in the next room" would have been false. Consider these two possible cases. Case 1: You say the chairs are there, you go next door to see, and sure enough, there they are as expected. Case 2: You say the chairs are there, you go next door to see, and to your great surprise the room is empty. The only difference between the two cases is that in the first case the chairs turned out to be there and in the second case they didn't. At the time you made the statement, *the evidence in the two cases was exactly the same.* Now, you surely didn't know the chairs were there in case 2, when they weren't there; so you didn't know in the first case either, when they were. Your educated guess isn't knowledge.

At this point it is customary to make a further distinction in the meaning of the word "know". We distinguish between knowing in the *weak* sense and knowing in the *strong* sense. In the weak sense, you did know, because you believed a proposition that turned out to be true, and you believed it for very good reasons. But in the *strong* sense, you didn't know, because your evidence—though very good—was still *incomplete*. There was still more evidence you *could* have had, therefore you don't *know* until you have this *additional* evidence. You don't *know* until *nothing more could go wrong* to cast doubt on your statement.

In the strong sense, then, you can't know anything that you're not perceiving now (such as the room next door), not even that there *is* a room next door. What then *can* you know? We have assumed thus far that if you go next door and take a look, that will provide the needed decisive evidence, because it is the direct evidence of your senses. You didn't hear about it, you didn't infer it from something else, you *saw it for yourself*. But one could now raise the question, Is even that enough? People do sometimes have hallucinations; sometimes they see what they want to see instead of what's there; sometimes they think that what they see is one kind of thing and actually it's another kind of thing (they think it's a fox in the distance, but it's a coyote). So even direct inspection isn't always decisive. And thus we are led to consider the possibility that if at least *sometimes* the direct evidence of your senses isn't decisive, then perhaps it *never* is. Certainly, you don't always know it at the time; and so possibly you *never* really know, even under circumstances we consider ideal.

The view just described is called *skepticism,* or at any rate, one kind of skepticism—skepticism concerning sensory knowledge. (There are other kinds, as we shall see.) As seekers after knowledge in the strong sense, we may convince ourselves that what we are seeking is never to be found—and in that case *nothing* is ever certain, and we never *really know* anything—at best we have well-based opinions or beliefs, but not knowledge.

The advocate of knowledge in the weak sense will probably call us "certainty-chasers" and claim we have turned our back on common sense completely. But what is wrong with chasing certainty? Isn't that what we (or at least some of us) want? And as for common sense, it's not very clear what the phrase "common sense" means (doesn't common sense tell people that the earth is flat?); at any rate, there is no reason to believe that common sense, whatever it is, is always right. When we study philosophy we should (it is said) graduate from such naive ideas.

At any rate, "ordinary language" advocates (those using a weak sense of "know") may raise a few points in reply. "We admit," they may say, "that the only difference between the first case and the second case is that in the first case the chairs were in the room and in the second case they weren't. The evidence was the same in both cases. But this still doesn't show that we didn't know in both cases. What it shows is that *although we might have been mistaken, we weren't mistaken.* If the chairs hadn't been there, we couldn't have claimed to know that they were; but since they were, we *did* know, although (on the basis of the evidence we had) we *might* have been mistaken. But we *weren't* mistaken, so we did know."

"Not so. You had good reason to believe that they were there, but not *sufficient* reason. You weren't observing the chairs, you *inferred* from past experience that they were; and that isn't enough."

How much *is* enough? Seeing something for yourself, or taking pictures of it, some would say; then you do know in the strong sense. But, since even our own senses can sometimes lead us to mistaken conclusions, how can we be sure they aren't doing so in this case? Can we be sure when they do and when they don't? Thus, every statement—even a seemingly obvious one such as "I am looking at some chairs"—is always *perpetually* on trial. I can have well-grounded belief, but not knowledge.

Nevertheless, we do use the word "know"; the word does have a use in our language. We use it for something—and not only laypersons, but some philosophers have suggested that it is not only foolish but mistaken to say that we an never have knowledge about the world. A contemporary philosopher, Norman Malcolm, contrasts two cases:

Suppose after a routine medical examination the excited doctor reports to me that the x-ray photographs show that I have no heart. I should tell him to get a new machine. I should be inclined to say that the fact that I have a heart is one of the few things that I can count on as absolutely certain. I can feel it beat. I know it's there. Furthermore, how could my blood circulate if I didn't have one? Suppose that later on I suffer a chest injury and undergo a surgical operation. Afterwards the astonished surgeons solemnly declare that they searched my chest cavity and found no heart, and that they made incisions and looked about in other likely places but found it not. They are convinced that I am without a heart. They are unable to understand how circulation can occur or what accounts for the thumping in my chest. But they are in agreement and obviously sincere, and they have clear photographs of my interior spaces. What would be my attitude? Would it be to insist that they were all mistaken? I think not. I believe that I should eventually accept their testimony and the evidence of the photographs. I should consider to be false what I now regard as an absolute certainty. [When I say I know I have a heart, I know it in the weak sense.]

Suppose that as I write this paper someone in the next room were to call out to me, "I can't find an ink-bottle; is there one in the house?" I should reply, "Here is an ink bottle." If he said in a doubtful tone, "Are you sure? I looked there before," I should reply, "Yes, I know there is; come and get it."

Now could it turn out to be false that there is an ink-bottle directly in front of me on this desk? Many philosophers have thought so. They would say that many things could happen of such a nature that if they did happen it would be proved that I am deceived. I agree that many extraordinary things could happen, in the sense that there is no logical absurdity in the supposition. It could happen that when I next reach for this ink-bottle my hand should seem to pass through it and I should not feel the contact of any object. It could happen that in the next moment the ink-bottle will suddenly vanish from sight; or that I should find myself under a tree in the garden with no ink-bottle about; or that one or more persons should enter this room and declare with apparent sincerity that they see no ink-bottle on this desk; or that a photograph taken now of the top of the desk should clearly show all of the objects on it except the ink-bottle. Having admitted that these things *could happen,* am I compelled to admit that if they did happen, then it would be proved that there is no ink-bottle here *now?* Not at all. I could say that when my hand seemed to pass through the ink-bottle I should *then* be suffering from hallucination; that if the ink-bottle suddenly vanished, it would have miraculously ceased to exist; that the other persons were conspiring to drive me mad, or were themselves victims of remarkable concurrent hallucinations: that the camera possessed some strange flaw or that there was trickery in developing the negative: . . . Not only do I not *have* to admit that those extraordinary occurrences would be evidence that there is no ink-bottle here; the fact is that I *do not* admit it. There is nothing whatever that could happen in the

next moment or the next year that would by me be called *evidence* that there is not an ink-bottle here now. No future experience or investigation could prove to me that I am mistaken. Therefore, if I were to say, "I know that there is an ink-bottle here," I would be using "know" in the strong sense.[1]

In Chapter 2 we shall be concerned with such questions as the trustworthiness of our senses, as well as problems of language in making statements we claim to know. *What,* if anything, we can know will concern us soon enough. At the moment we are concerned with the *meaning* (or meanings) of "know," and the examples have been introduced only by way of illustration, to make the distinctions clear.

Perhaps we can make the present distinctions clearer by introducing two terms important in studying philosophy: the difference between *confirmation* and *verification.* I am said to *confirm* a statement when I adduce evidence in its favor; the more confirmation of it I have, the greater the probability that it is true. I am said to *verify* a statement when I have *completely* confirmed it—when the process of confirmation is complete. Thus, I have confirmed that all of the marbles in this bag are black when I have examined half of them and found them all to be black; but I have not verified it until I have examined all of them and found them all to be black. The proponent of knowledge in the strong sense might still say I don't *know* they're all black, even in the second case, because how do I know they're really black? or perhaps I have miscounted? and so on. But the difference between the senses of "know" comes out if we say that for the weak sense, a high degree of confirmation is sufficient for knowing, whereas for the strong sense, nothing short of verification is

---

[1]Norman Malcolm, "Knowledge and Belief," in *Knowledge and Certainty* (Englewood Cliffs: Prentice-Hall, 1963), pp. 66–68.

required for knowing (whether or not that verification can ever be achieved).

Can we ever really verify—confirm "all the way"? No matter how much we confirm, isn't there always more that remains to be confirmed? Isn't the process infinite, and thus never completable? Many philosophers have said yes to this—that we have only a high degree of confirmation, or "warranted assertability," but not total certainty. But others have rejected this view.

Suppose, for example, that I open a page of a book at random, and the first word on the page is "in". Or so it looks to me; I look again and it still appears to be "in". I ask other people and they also say the first word on the page is "in". I take a picture of it with a Polaroid and it also shows the word as "in". How long am I supposed to keep on with this? What more confirmation do I need to provide, before I can say I *know* that the word is "in"? I can continue to *stare* at the page, but if someone then asked what I was doing and I said "I am confirming the statement that the first word on this page is 'in'," wouldn't she properly consider this a bad joke? I can continue to stare at the page indefinitely, but that doesn't show that I am continuing to confirm the statement. *The confirmation comes to an end.* (Besides, if I'm still staring at it 5 minutes later, wouldn't I be confirming that the word is "in" at *that* moment, not the original moment 5 minutes earlier when I started looking?) Even if as I looked I found to my surprise that the environment suddenly changed, and instead of looking at a book I was looking at swans in a garden, that wouldn't disconfirm the statement that I *was* looking at the page of a book, whose first word was "in".

What if, in spite of all this, a person still doubts that the page begins with this word? Some would say, "He's just a pathological doubter, like the person who has locked his front door, then on getting into his car he says he isn't certain, and so he goes back to make sure, and a moment later still isn't certain,

and goes back again and again to make sure. What such a person needs is a psychiatrist." But this is a psychological observation, hardly a philosophical argument against perpetual doubt. A philosophical argument would be: "I can well understand how you could question some statements, even most statements. But if you carry on this merry game until you have covered *all* statements, you are simply mistaken. You may see someone in a fog or in a bad light and not know (not be certain) whether he has a right hand. But don't you know that *you* have a right hand? There it is! Suppose I now raise my hand and say, 'Here is a hand.' Now you say to me, 'I doubt that there's a hand.' But what evidence do you want? What does your doubt consist of? You don't believe your eyes, perhaps? Very well, then come up and touch the hand. You still aren't satisfied? Then keep on looking at it steadily and touching it, photograph it, call in other people for testimony if you like. If after all this you still say it isn't certain, *what more do you want?* Under what conditions *would* you admit that it *is* certain, that you *do* know it? I can understand your doubt when there is some condition left *unfulfilled,* some test left uncompleted. At the beginning, perhaps you doubted that *if* you tried to touch my hand you would find anything there to touch; but then you did touch and so you resolved *that* doubt. You resolved further doubts by calling in other people and so on. You performed all the relevant tests, and they turned out favorably. So now, at the end of the process, what is it that you doubt? Oh, I know what you *say:* 'I still doubt that that's a hand.' But isn't this saying 'I doubt' now an empty formula? I can no longer attach any content to that so-called doubt, for there is nothing left to doubt; you yourself *cannot specify any further test that, if performed, would resolve your doubt.* 'Doubt' now becomes an empty word. You're not doubting now that *if* you raised your hand to touch mine, you would touch it, or that *if* Smith and others were brought in, they would also testify that this is a hand—we've already gone through all that. So what is it specifically that you doubt? What possible test is there *the negative result of which you fear?* I submit that there isn't any."

"You see, there is nothing left to doubt—when the tests have been carried out and their results are all favorable. Suppose a physician examines a patient and says, 'It's probable that you have an inflamed appendix.' Here one can still doubt, for the signs may be misleading. So the physician operates on the patient, finds an inflamed appendix and removes it, and the patient recovers. *Now* what would be the sense of the physician's saying 'It's *probable* that he had an inflamed appendix'? If seeing it and removing it made it only *probable*, what would make it certain? Or you are driving along and you hear a rapid regular thumping sound and you say, 'It's probable that I have a flat tire.' So far you're right; it's only probable—the thumping might be caused by something else. So you go out and have a look, and there is the tire, flat. You find a nail embedded in it, change the tire, and then resume your ride with no more thumping. Are you *now* going to say 'It's merely *probable* that the car had a flat tire'? But if given all those conditions it would be merely probable, what in the would *would* make it certain? Can you describe to me the circumstances in which you would say it's certain? If you can't, then the phrase 'being certain' has no meaning as you are using it. You are simply using it in such a special way that it has no application at all, and there is no reason at all why anyone else should follow your usage. In daily life we have a very convenient and useful distinction between the application of the words 'probable' and 'certain.' We say appendicitis is probable *before* the operation, but when the physician has the patient's appendix visible before him on the operating table, now it's certain—that's just the kind of situation in which we apply the word 'certain,' as opposed to 'probable.' Now you, for some reason, are so fond of the word 'probable' that you want to use it for everything—you use it to describe *both* the preoperative and postoperative situations, and the word 'certain' is left without any application at all. But this is nothing but a verbal manipulation on your part. You have changed nothing; you have only taken, as it were, two bottles with different contents, and instead of labeling them differently ('probable' and 'certain'), as the rest of us do, you put the same label ('probable') on both of them! What possible advantage is there in this? It's just verbal contrariness. And since you have preempted the word 'probable' to cover *both* the situations, we now have to devise a *different* pair of words to mark the perfectly obvious distinction between the situation *before* the surgery and the situation *during* the surgery—the same difference we previously marked by the words 'probable' and 'certain' until you used the word 'probable' to apply to both of them. What gain is there in this verbal manipulation of yours?"

"It is not just verbal manipulation," the skeptic replies. "The issue between us is not one of words but of fact. I do not call a proposition certain, or claim that I know it to be true, until *all the evidence for it is in.* Now the reason I decline to say that it's certain that the patient had appendicitis, or that the tire was flat, is that the evidence for these propositions is not all in; there always could be more, and that more could turn out negatively. Your examples sounded plausible because in describing them you assumed without proof that certain *other* statements were certain—that there really was a car, that you weren't dreaming it all, that the physician really was looking at the patient's appendix, that there really was an operating table, and so on. Now all *these* statements, I contend, are subject to the same uncertainty as the original statements about the patient having appendicitis and the tire being flat. You had no right to smuggle them in as if *they* were certain. I would want to question each of these in turn, and for the very same reasons. They are not certain because the evidence for them is never complete; there always could be more, and that more could have a negative result. That's why I have to object even to your example of the hand. If I admit that I'm really seeing and touching the hand, I can't very well turn around and doubt that it exists, for the statement 'I am *really* seeing it' already entails 'It exists.' But how do I know that I am really seeing and touching a hand; or, to put it differently, that I am seeing and touching a real hand? If I admit that I am, then of course you have me. But this initial admission, which you take for granted in your example, is precisely what I will not grant.''

And thus the opponents remain deadlocked. But what are they deadlocked about? Is it simply a disagreement about *words*—a verbal dispute? Is it merely that one person uses the word "know" in the ordinary, looser or more flexible sense, and the other refuses to use the word "know" until every bit of possible evidence is in? Many philosophical disputes turn out to be verbal in this way, and it may be that the present one is too. But on the other hand, there may be more to it than that. May there not be an underlying disagreement about our human abilities? Aren't the skeptic and the "certainty-chaser" saying something about what they believe are the limitations of our capacities as would-be knowers? If so, underlying the verbal disagreement is a disagreement about human potential, and that disagreement is only reflected in the refusal to use the word "know" in situations where those who are innocent of philosophical investigations, or uncorrupted by philosophical arguments, do not hesitate to do so.

Objections to the Standard Account of Knowing

The standard account of knowing has been attacked for various reasons. Some of them can be understood only after a course in

logic[2]; others are so complex and involuted that it would take many pages just to set them forth clearly.[3] But some idea can be gained of the thrust of these objections by considering a few quite simple examples.

1. Suppose that holography has been so perfected that when a hologram of a vase is placed at a distance of, say, ten feet from a person, it looks to him exactly as if there were a vase, say, 15 feet in front of him. Now suppose that there actually is a vase 15 feet in front of S, but that S's view of the vase is blocked by a holographic photograph of another vase. Since the hologram makes it *appear* as if there is a vase in front of him, however, S forms the belief that there is one in front of him, S is clearly justified in believing that there is a vase in front of him—at any rate, he is *as* justified in believing this as he is on many other occasions when we could credit him with knowledge. Moreover, his belief is true. In this case, however, we would not be willing to say the S *knows* that there is a vase in front of him. The reason for this concerns the casual process by which S's belief is formed. There simply is no causal connection between the fact that there is a vase in front of him and S's belief that there is a vase.[4]

In other words, his belief is not brought about by perception of the actual vase. His true belief that there is a vase out there is justified, but not by what he sees, which is only a hologram. So we hesitate to grant that S *knows* there's a vase there. The reason we hesitate to say that S knows is that what he actually saw a hologram provides no justification for what he believes. According to this view, there must be some causal connection

---

[2]Edmund Gettier, "Is Justified True Belief Knowledge?" in *Analysis,* 23, 6 (1963), pp. 121–123.

[3]For example, in Robert Nozick, *Philosophical Explanations* (Cambridge:Harvard University Press, 1981), Chapter 3, and Paul Moser and Arnold Vander Nat, eds., *Human Knowledge* (New York: Oxford University Press, 1987).

[4]Alvin Goldman, "A Causal Theory of Knowing," *The Journal of Philosophy* 64, 12 (1967): 357–372.

(cause-and-effect relation) between what he sees and his justification for making his knowledge-claim; usually there is, but in this case there isn't.

Examples like this one would lead us to revise the third condition for knowledge: In order to know that there's a vase there, my belief must have been *caused* (at least in part) by the actual presence of a vase there; if what caused my belief was a hallucination or a bit of visual trickery, then the belief was not caused by the actual object, and therefore my claim to knowledge is unjustified.

2. You see some solidified lava in a region of the country-side, and you quite reasonably conclude that a nearby mountain erupted many centuries ago. And it's true, let's say, that a mountain did erupt nearby many centuries ago, spewing forth lava. But a century after the eruption some people came along and removed all the lava; a century after that others came along and decided to make it look as if there had been a volcanic eruption, and put lava in the right places. Then you do not *know* that the mountain erupted. Your true belief is based on evidence, but what you think is evidence (the lava you see) isn't: What you see is the hauled lava, not the natural lava from the volcano. What you see is not the result of the volcano erupting. Your statement that there was lava was "true by accident," so to speak. Your belief was justified, but not on the basis of what you saw.

We have here a case of justified true belief—thus fulfilling all the three conditions of the standard analysis. But is it knowledge? One could adduce many more examples to "crack" the standard analysis; some of them seem just clever or cute, but they all try to show how the standard analysis can be criticized.

Another kind of objection comes from a different quarter: that one can know even in the *absence* of evidence.

3. You hear a few strains of music on the radio and immediately you exclaim, "That's Beethoven!" or "That's Shostakovich!" And

let's say you were right. If you knew, *how* did you know? What was your evidence? It would be virtually impossible to state exactly what your evidence was. Even if you were a musicologist and knew all the relevant terminology, that wouldn't be enough to enable you to describe the passage in a way that would distinguish Beethoven's work from that of all other composers. If you made a stab at it by saying "It is full of pride and passion . . ." etc., such description would also fit some works of other composers. Anyway it probably wasn't just these features that enables you to identify the composer so unerringly after a few bars (time after time); it was some indescribable combination of stylistic features which sets Beethoven's works apart from those of other composers.

Did you know? In the weak sense, the answer is probably yes; you had excellent reason to believe it, it was far from being guesswork. You had reason enough to place a large bet on it, a bet which you would have won. Perhaps in this case it was not *lack* of evidence, but ability to *articulate* what the evidence was; the evidence was in the passage you heard, but you could not isolate in words the features of the passage that entitled you to be so sure.

4. Suppose that you are in telephone communication every day with a friend who is taking a 2-year trip to numerous obscure places in the world. I have no knowledge of your friend and have not seen her itinerary. But every day, when you ask me where she is today, I come up with the right answer: I may not know how, but I say what comes to my mind—"Today she is in Timbuktu," "Today she is in the Seychelle Islands," and so on—and it turns out that I am always right. How I am able to come up with the right answer every time may be a mystery to you and to everyone else who investigates the matter, and even to me. But wouldn't it be correct in these circumstances to say that I know from day to day where she is? "But you have no evidence—no reason to give the answers you do!" That may be so; but still, don't I know?

We could say knowledge is *the ability to be always right*—being right is what counts; even my believing it isn't required. In that case we come up with a different conception of knowledge than we had before. Let us develop this view:

5. Suppose that for four hours every evening for a year you sit in a room some hundreds of feet away from me—I can't see or hear you, there are no telephones, etc. Each minute a bell rings, and when it does I pull a card from a deck in my hand, and you write down on a pad what card you think it is. And suppose that in thousands of tries, you always get it right: You correctly identify the 9 of spades, the ace of hearts, and so on. At first we suspect trickery: A battery of scientists is on hand to make sure that there is no secret way we could communicate with each other. But there is no trickery, no faking: Without any secret communication with me, every time you write down the right answer. I am amazed and mystified as to how you are able to do this: With 52 different cards in a deck, the chances against being right even ten times in a row are staggeringly small, and even more so with a hundred thousand times in a row. It's just extending the long arm of coincidence too far to say it is mere guesswork. Surely you *know?*

As for you, you just write down the first number and suit that pops into your head—you have no special *belief* that you are right, no particular confidence in your abilities. I may not tell you about the results till after it's all over, and you may not even be aware that you are getting it right every time: You may be bored by the whole procedure and only keep on with it because you're being paid to do it. But you do have this peculiar ability to get it always right. You have no *evidence* that your answers are the right ones, and equally surprising, you don't even have the *belief* that they are. Still, don't you *know* the right answers? When we ask in amazement, "How do you know?" we can't come up with an an-

swer: But can't we say "We don't know *how* you know, but you know"? The fact that we ask "How do you know?" assumes that you do know.[5]

"But," one may say, "the person lacks evidence." "On the contrary," someone could reply, "the fact that you're always right *itself constitutes the evidence.* Your response after a thousand tries in which you're always right *is* good reason to say that you know. The difference in these ESP cases is that we don't know *why* it's evidence—we have no explanation for what happens—but nevertheless we can say *that* it is; the evidence criterion is fulfilled, even if the belief requirement isn't." Yet can we speak of knowing something if the person had no idea whether the statement was true?

There is yet another kind of objection to the third condition of the standard definition of knowing. Knowing p requires having evidence for $p;$ let us say that this evidence is another proposition, q. But don't we then have to know that q is true? If I don't know that q is true, how can q be good evidence for $p?$ And how do we know q? Perhaps by another proposition that is evidence for q, namely r. And so on—it seems that we are caught in an infinite regress. The requirement of evidence always takes us beyond the original proposition, p, to another one, and then we have to know the truth of that one in order to know the truth of the original one.

One way out of this that has been suggested is that we don't really know *any* of them in isolation, but that p, q, r, and others simply lend support to one another, and each one of them makes the other more probable. (This is a rather complicated business, and we shall not discuss it until we have discussed the idea

---

[5] Cases somewhat like this have actually occurred and are described, for example, in S. G. Soal and F. Bateman, *Modern Experiments in Telepathy* (London: Faber & Faber, 1954) except that the subjects didn't *always* get it right.

of coherence after dealing with scientific theories in Chapter 4, where the idea is most prominently displayed.)

Another way is simpler to explain: There is no infinite regress because in this process we soon come to propositions which are known to be true *without* having to adduce evidence for them. Many such propositions will be discussed in the next two chapters. An example would be "I see in my visual field what appears to be a tree" and "I feel drowsy." If you were asked, "How do you know that you feel drowsy? What *evidence* do you have for this?", what could we say except simply "I just do feel drowsy, that's all. I have the experience, and that's all the evidence I could ever have or need." In certain circumstances, one might say, we have a *right to be sure* that a proposition is true:

In certain cases one acquires the right to be sure of a proposition not through holding any other beliefs, but simply because one is having or has had certain experiences. What, for example, gives me the right to be sure that this is a sheet of paper? Well, partly my seeing what I now do, partly the fact that my past experiences have been such that I can identify sheets of paper when I see them . . . It is enough that I am having the experience that I am and that I have acquired the necessary skill in identifying what I see.[6]

Some philosophers have held that certain propositions don't require evidence because they are *self-evident*. It's not very clear what "self-evident" means, however. Can a statement be *evidence for itself?* Or does it merely mean that it is *obvious,* too obvious to require evidence? But obviousness is a rather subjective matter; what seems obvious to you may not seem obvious to me. It may seem obvious that the earth is flat, but that's no guarantee that it is.

Still, there are statements that are alleged to be known, not because there is evidence for them, but because they *don't require* evidence. We shall see in coming chapters what such statements are and evaluate their claims. Don't I know that A is A (that everything is itself and not something else)? Don't we know that if no dogs are cats, then no cats are dogs either? Don't I know that everything that's colored must have some specific color and not just color in general (must be perfectly determinate)? Don't I know that something can't have two colors all over at the same time, that an object can't be both round and square? Most of us would say that such statements are self-evident, or obvious, or too "basic" to require evidence. Perhaps the very notion of "evidence" doesn't even apply to such statements. But that story will be unfolded in the coming chapters.

Some philosophers have held that knowledge is limited to a fairly small class of these seemingly self-evident statements, such as "I feel pain now" and "I am hearing what sounds like a train whistle." But others have held that such a conception of knowledge is on the wrong track, and that these examples are at best limiting cases. Knowledge, they would say, is an *achievement,* and to be able to report that you have a headache is an achievement. To be able to say "I know that all the drawers of this desk are empty" after examining them all thoroughly is an achievement; the statement, far from being self-evident, rests on solid (conclusive?) evidence. And to know, through various lines of evidence that take considerable skill and patience, that the moon is approximately 240,000 miles from the earth, is a considerable achievement—as opposed to just repeating what others have told you, in which case the only evidence you have for it is other people's word. On this conception, knowledge is the conclusion of a process of inquiry, in which you didn't know something at the beginning of the inquiry but did know it at the end.

---

[6]Alfred J. Ayer, "Knowledge, Belief, and Evidence," in *Metaphysics and Common Sense* (San Francisco: Freeman, Cooper & Co., 1967), p. 121.

Conclusions. What shall we conclude from all this—that the standard theory of knowing has to be patched up, now at one place and now at another? Or that it should be scrapped entirely? If we patch it up to fit one example, doesn't the revised definition then fail to fit other examples? Do any of the suggested definitions give *the* meaning of the word "know"?

Before we go further, it is important to become aware of an important philosophical point, which will be relevant to many issues that will be discussed in the coming pages. *Words* don't just "mean"; *people* mean by the words they use. And people don't always use the same word to mean the same thing. What one person might grant to be knowledge, another might not, because they don't attach quite the same meaning to the same word. There is no such entity as knowing "out there somewhere," waiting to be discovered, the way we discover the characteristics of a mineral-rich rock. A word means what we *make* it mean; but when we use it we are usually not conscious of exactly what shades of meaning we are putting into it,—in what circumstances exactly we would use the word and in what circumstances we would decline to use it. We may have thought only of typical cases, not of cases at the outer limits; that's why so many far-out examples can be dredged up to test our intellects, as well as our patience: "If such and such happened . . . would you still call it knowledge?"

Is there perhaps some central *core* of meaning that is indispensable, and around which the others (so to speak) revolve, becoming more expendable as they approach the periphery? Sometimes there is and sometimes there isn't—in the coming pages we shall encounter numerous examples of both. We have seen that in the case of "know" we may be able to do without the evidence requirement, and also the belief requirement. Yet the first requirement by itself (truth) is not enough, for a statement can be true without you or I or any-

one knowing that it is. So something more is required, but what the "more" is doesn't seem to be always the same.

According to one writer, the "central core" of the meaning of "know" can be described as follows:

"Know" is used to assure others in a special way. It indicates that the evidence is not merely good but is as good as can be, that further investigation has lost its point. "Know" closes questions, stops debates. Allowing that someone knows or knew something is incompatible with continued inquiry and caution. This is what constitutes the gravity of the claim: in authorizing others to consider matters closed, I assume a special responsibility for the consequences of error . . . If "know" merely signaled evidence of a certain weight, we could allow that people knew even if they have proved wrong. But "know" signals conclusive evidence . . .[7]

The account is insightful; yet not everyone would agree with it. For one thing, it seems to be concerned primarily with the strong sense of "know"; and for another, it speaks of knowledge's connection with evidence, thus eliminating what some philosophers would insist on, that there can be knowledge without any need for evidence. Still, with these qualifications, the passage does seem to convey the general thrust of what we mean to signify when we use the word "know." And perhaps—in this as in so many other cases—that's about as much precision as we can get.

3. CONCEPTS

From whence comes our knowledge? Before we can answer that question, a few remarks must be made about concepts. Before we can have knowledge of even a simple statement such as "Ice melts," we must understand the meanings of the words "ice" and "melts." And to do that we need to have a *concept*

---

[7]Douglas C. Arner, "On Knowing," *Philosophical Review 68,* 1 (Jan. 1959): Sec. 5.

of ice and of melting. How do we acquire these concepts?

It was once thought that at least some of our concepts are *innate*—that they are, so to speak, "wired into us." Suppose that the concept of redness (or being red) were innate: Then we would have it without having to experience any instances of it—that is, without ever having to see anything red. A person born blind could have the concept just as well as a person who could see. It seems so obvious that a person born blind does not possess the concept of redness, or of any other color, that no one has held that this concept, or the concept of any other sensory property, is innate.

Some concepts, however, have been believed to be innate: for example, the concept of cause and the concept of God. If the concept of cause is innate, then we could know what the word means, and be in full possession of the concept, without ever having seen causes operating. This was the view of René Descartes (1596–1650).

This may seem quite implausible to us today—how could we have the concept of cause without having opened our eyes on the world and seen causes operating in nature? It is also difficult to believe that the concept of God is innate. But at a time when it was believed that God had imposed a certain structure on the mind at birth, such beliefs were more easily accommodated. Today we are more inclined to believe that what is innate are not concepts but *dispositions to behave* in a certain way: For example, we have an innate tendency to be frightened of loud noises. Concepts, however, come only with learning. Animals have much more in the way of innate dispositions than human beings do: As we mentioned earlier, much of their behavior is not learned but genetically "programmed." The chicken plays dead to avoid the hawk when it is only a few days old—but that doesn't show that it has innate concepts; rather, it shows only that it has built-in dispositions to behave in certain ways in response to certain stimuli.

The obvious next step, then, is to say that all concepts are acquired through *experience*. (This view is sometimes called "empiricism," and the view that some concepts are innate is called "rationalism," but these names are liable to be misleading because they become confused with other senses of these terms, yet to be discussed.) This view was defended by three British philosophers: John Locke (1632–1704), George Berkeley (1685–1753), and David Hume (1711–1776).

Instead of the word "concepts," these philosophers all used the word "ideas," and the problem they undertook to answer was: "How do we come by the ideas we have?" All the ideas we have or ever shall have, they said, come from *experience:* (1) some through the "outer" senses, such as sight, hearing, and touch, and from these all our concepts involving the physical world are drawn; and (2) some from the "inner" senses, such as experiences of pain and pleasure, feelings of love and hate, pride and remorse, experiences of thinking and willing—from these we get all the ideas about our inner life. All our concepts are derived from these two kinds of experience. (Locke called the first "ideas of sensation" and the second "ideas of reflection.")

The use of the word "idea" was so general in the seventeenth and eighteenth centuries as to include all experiences, of whatever kind; but Hume made a clear distinction among experiences, between "impressions" and "ideas." Neither word was used in the twentieth century sense, in which we say "I have the impression that someone is watching me" and "The idea of human progress is a delusion." Hume's use of these words can be illustrated as follows: If I see a green tree, I have an *impression* of green (sense-impression), and then if I close my eyes and imagine something green, I have an *idea* of green—an idea being a kind of weak copy of an impression. You have the impression when your eyes are open, but you can have the idea of something whenever you care to imagine it. Hume's main thesis in connection with these terms was *"No ideas without impressions."* If you have never seen anything green—that is, if you have never had a green sense-impression—it is impossible for you ever to have any *idea* of green. You must first have the impression in order to have the idea, and a person born blind could never have any idea of green or any other color, because the person has never had any sense-impressions of colors. Similarly, a person born deaf could have no idea of tones, nor would a person born without a sense of smell have any idea of odors, and so on. For every idea X', there is a corresponding sense-impression X; and without first having the sense-impression X, we cannot have the corresponding idea X'. The same considerations apply to the ideas gleaned from the "inner" senses: a person who has never experienced pain can have no idea of pain; a person who has never experienced fear can have no idea of fear; and so on. And a child who has not yet experienced sexual love can have no idea of love: The child can observe how people having this experience *behave,* but the child does not yet have any idea of what the feeling is like that impels them to behave in this way.

So much for the outlines of the theory. But as it stands it will not do, as Locke and Hume were well aware. Can't we have ideas of lots of things of which we have never had any impressions? We can imagine a golden mountain even though we have never seen one; and we can imagine a creature that is half man and half horse. True, we have seen pictures of centaurs, mythical creatures that are half man and half horse, but we could imagine these without ever having seen the pictures, and the persons who first drew such pictures must have been able to imagine them before they drew the pictures. And we can imagine (have an idea of) black roses even though the only roses we have ever seen are red, yellow, pink, and white. We can have ideas of all these things before we have ever had sense-experi-

ences of them, and even if we never experience them at all.

Thus Locke was led to distinguish between *simple* ideas and *complex* ideas. We can imagine golden mountains and black roses without ever seeing them because, after all, we have seen the colors gold and black in other things. The idea of golden mountains and black roses are complex ideas: We simply take ideas we have *already* acquired through other experiences and put them together in our imagination in new combinations. The human mind can create all sorts of complex ideas from simple ideas already gleaned from experience; but the human mind cannot create a single simple idea. If we have never seen red, we cannot imagine red; and if we have never felt a pain, we cannot imagine pain. Red and pain are simple ideas. It is true that we might well be able to imagine a mountain or a rose without ever having seen one, but that is only because the ideas of mountain and rose are themselves complex ideas. If we have seen a hill and also have the idea of height from having seen some things higher than others, we can then form the idea of something higher and steeper than a hill, namely a mountain, even if we have never seen one. Similarly, we can have an idea of God, because we can combine certain ideas we derive from our experience of human beings, such as power, intelligence, kindness, and so on, and imagine these as being present to a greater degree than in any person we have ever encountered. (There are problems here that we shall consider in detail in Chapter 7.)

The relation of simple to complex ideas is somewhat like the relation of atoms to molecules. Without atoms, you cannot have molecules; and atoms can be combined in different ways to form different molecules. Without simple ideas, you cannot form complex ideas; but once you have a number of simple ideas, you can combine them in your imagination in all sorts of different ways to form the ideas of countless things that never existed on land or sea.

Nothing, at first view, may seem more unbounded that the thought of man, which not only escapes all human power and authority but is not even restrained within the limits of nature and reality. To form monsters, and join incongruous shapes and appearances, costs the imagination no more trouble than to conceive the most natural and familiar objects. And while the body is confined to one planet, along which it creeps with pain and difficulty, the thought can in an instant transport us into the most distant regions of the universe . . .

But though our thought seems to possess this unbounded liberty, we shall find, upon a nearer examination, that it is really confined within very narrow limits, and that all this creative power of the mind amounts to no more than the faculty of compounding, transposing, augmenting, or diminishing the materials afforded us by the senses and experience. When we think of a golden mountain, we only join two consistent ideas, gold and mountain, with which we were formerly acquainted. . . . In short, all the materials of thinking are derived either from our outward or inward sentiment; the mixture and composition of these belongs alone to the mind and will.[8]

It has never been made quite clear *which* of the ideas we have are simple ideas and which are complex; no complete list of them has ever been offered, but only scattered examples. In general, the ideas of sensory qualities have been the stock examples of simple ideas: red, sweet, hard, pungent; pain, pleasure, fear, anger; thinking, wondering, doubting, believing. It may not be of great importance to decide in every case which ideas are simple ideas, but there is a problem about them nevertheless. "Simple ideas are those that cannot be broken down, or analyzed, into other ideas"—so runs the suggested criterion. But this provides no help to us in trying to determine which ideas can, and which cannot, be further analyzed.

There is even a problem in the case of color-ideas, such as red, which are usually taken as the standard case of simple ideas: It is doubtless true that if you have never seen

[8]David Hume, *An Enquiry Concerning Human Understanding,* Section II, paragraphs 4 and 5.

any shade of red, you cannot imagine any; but what if you have seen two or three shades of red? Can you then imagine only those shades but not the others? Or can you imagine (have an idea of) *any* shade of red after you have experienced (had an impression of) a few samples? Hume discussed such a case: Suppose that you have seen all the shades of blue there are except one, but you are told where that missing shade of blue lies in relation to the other shades on a scale ranging from the lightest to the darkest. Is it really impossible for you to imagine that shade without ever having seen it? Many persons would say that you *can* imagine it; or at least—what is not the same thing—that whether you can imagine it prior to seeing it or not, that you can *recognize* it as the missing shade after you *have* seen it. But if you *can* have an idea of it before you have had an impression of it, what happens to the view that "for every (simple) idea there must be a corresponding impression?" Is the idea of it then not a simple idea? Or if it is a simple idea, must there be perhaps a million simple ideas of blue corresponding to each of the million or more specific shades of blue? If the idea of each of these million shades is a simple idea, then it should be impossible to imagine the missing shade without having first seen it. On the other hand, if the simple idea is only blue-in-general (not any specific shade of blue), then presumably you *could* imagine the missing shade; but then you would have to say that the idea of this missing shade is a complex idea, composed of (1) the idea of blue-in-general and (2) the idea of being darker than, or lighter than, some other shade.

Here problems multiply: If you have seen only primary red, can you imagine scarlet, crimson, magenta? Are the ideas of these simple or complex ideas? If you have seen many shades of yellow and many shades of red, but no orange, can you imagine orange without ever having seen it? (Might some people be able to, but not others? Could an idea then be simple for some people but complex for others?) And if you answer "Yes" to the previous question, try this one: If you have seen blue and yellow, but no green, can you imagine green? (It is important not to confuse the physical and the psychological here. Orange, we say, is a mixture of red and yellow, and green is a mixture of yellow and blue. But green doesn't *look* like a mixture of yellow and blue the way orange looks like a mixture of red and yellow. What color you get when you mix different paints, or combine different lights, has nothing to do with the question of what colors you can imagine without having seen them.)

Whatever the outcome of these speculations, it seems to be quite clear that without some impressions we cannot have certain ideas. A person born blind can have no idea of colors. And if we had never experienced shapes of *any* kind, we could have no idea of shape—not of triangular, rectangular, circular, or any other—though it may well be that if we had experiences (impressions) of *some* shapes, say a triangle and a pentagon, we could form the idea of other shapes, such as a rectangle and a hexagon, without having seen them. Clearly *some* impressions are indispensable before we can form *some* ideas, though it may be a matter of dispute just which ones these are.

Concept vs. image. But the word "idea" is ambiguous. One can mean by it either a *concept* or an *image.* Most of the time, Locke and his followers seem to have been talking about images, but sometimes the discussion of "ideas" shifted in such a way that it would be more appropriate to a discussion of concepts. Without having seen red we cannot form in our minds red *images;* but from this we cannot conclude that we can have no *concept* of red. Let us consider the example of ultraviolet. No human being can have ultraviolet images, since the human eye is not sensitive to that part of the spectrum; bees and certain other creatures can see it, but we cannot. Since we

have no ultraviolet impressions, we can have no ultraviolet images. But we do appear to have a *concept* of ultraviolet. Physicists speak of ultraviolet light, and can identify it and relate it to other parts of the spectrum; indeed, they can talk about ultraviolet just as easily as they talk about red. Similarly, human beings do not have any sense that acquaints them with the presence of radioactivity the way they have senses like sight and hearing and touch that acquaint them with the sensible properties of physical objects. ("Sensible" in philosophy means "capable of being sensed.") We can't see, hear, smell, or touch radioactivity; we have to rely on instruments like Geiger counters to detect its presence. If any creature did have a sense acquainting itself directly with the presence of radioactivity, we would have not the faintest conception of what it would be like; we simply have no "image" of radioactivity. (Remember that images need not be visual: There are auditory images, tactile images, olfactory images, and so on. When you imagine the smell of ammonia or the taste of scalloped potatoes, you are having olfactory images and gustatory images respectively.) Yet we do, it seems, have the concepts—at any rate physicists do—and physicists work as easily and familiarly with concepts like radioactivity as they do with concepts of which they *do* have sense-impressions (and consequently images). Hume's dictum "If no impressions, then no ideas" applies to images; it does not seem to apply to concepts.

A person born blind might become a physicist and specialize in the physics of color; this would be a somewhat peculiar choice, no doubt, but it would be a possible one. Such a person would never have seen any colors, and therefore the blind physicist would have no color-images. But she might well know more *facts* about colors than you or I: She could tell us more about the light waves and other physical properties of colored objects, and more about the physical conditions under which colors are seen, than most people can. She would in fact be able to tell us what the color of every object is; not by looking at it as we do, but by reading in Braille the pointer readings on instruments that record the wavelengths of light emanating from the objects. She would be able to impart to us a great deal of knowledge about color and colored objects; and how could she do this if she did not have the concept of color? If she did not possess this, how could she know what she was talking about? Of course, she could correctly identify colors only as long as the correlation held between the seen color and the wavelengths of light; if this correlation were no longer to hold, she would start making mistakes in color identification because she could not see the colors but had only the indirect evidence of the instruments recording lightwaves. Still, must we not admit that she has the concept of color, even though she is unable to experience any color-images? How could she use the word, and even impart to us new knowledge that presupposes knowledge of what the word means, unless she had the concept?

What is a concept? There is something other than images, something that we have called concepts. But what is a concept? How do we tell when we have one? Let's examine a few suggested answers to this question.

1. We have a concept of X when we know the definition of the word "X". But this is far too narrow: We do know the meanings of countless words—"cat," "run," "above"— and use them constantly without being able to give a definition of them in words. Whatever having a concept involves, it does not require being able to state a definition—something that even the compilers of dictionaries often have a hard time doing. And words like "red" and "sweet" don't seem to be verbally definable at all; we can exhibit instances of red, but we cannot communicate to others what that shade of color looks like by words alone. We

learn the meaning of "red" *ostensively,* that is, by being shown instances of it: "Yes, that's red," "No, that isn't, it's pink," and so on. If verbal definitions were required, we would have to conclude, according to this view, we can never have a concept of redness.

2. Let's try again: We have a concept of X when we can apply the word "X" correctly; we have a concept of redness and orangeness when we can correctly apply the words "red" and "orange" to every example we are shown. This criterion doesn't require us to give a definition but only to use the word with uniform correctness. It is also much more in line with our actual use of the term "concept": for example, "He must have some concept of what a cat is, for he always uses the word 'cat' in the right situations; he never applies it to dogs or weasels or anything else."

People born blind can *use* the word "red" correctly (blind persons can test for redness using Braille instruments in an optics lab) and can have *a* concept of redness, but not the same one that sighted people have: Sighted people can have it by seeing instances of redness; blind persons cannot. They can only talk about wavelengths, a physical phenomenon that is highly *correlated* with our experiences of red.

This second criterion, however, is still too restrictive: It assumes that in order to have a concept we must first be acquainted with a *word.* Doubtless this is often the case, but not always. A person may have something in mind for which no word yet exists, and may then invent a word for it; or a person may use an old word in a new sense, giving it a meaning it didn't have before. Didn't the person have the concept *prior* to devising a new word (or new sense of an old word)? When physicists first adopted the common word "energy" for their own special purposes, they had in mind a highly abstract concept, and presumably they had it in mind before devising a word for it. Doubtless there are many concepts that one can't have without much prior knowledge of language, but this cannot be the case for all concepts, else how would language have gotten started? Using a word correctly seems to be a *consequence* of having the concept, but not a prerequisite for having it; that is, if you have a concept, *and* know the word for it, you will then be able to use the word correctly; but having the concept is not the same thing as being able to use the word.

3. Let us, then, try once more, so as not to involve the acquaintance with a word in the having of a concept. We have a concept of X (of X-ness) when we are able to distinguish Xs from Ys and Zs and indeed from everything that is not an X. We might well do this whether we had a word for X or not, though of course it would be most convenient if we did have a word, and normally we do have. Thus if a child can distinguish cats from dogs and pigs and all other things, she has a concept of what is a cat, even though she cannot state a definition and she has never heard the word "cat" and connected the word with the thing by way of ostensive definition.

We have now specified what a concept is in such a way as to make it possible to have a concept without knowing any words. A dog that can distinguish cats from birds can be said to have these concepts, although it knows no words. Even this definition might be objected to, however, for the reason that being able to distinguish Xs from Ys is, once again, a *consequence* of having the concept of X, but not what having the concept consists of. One is tempted to say that if you have a concept of X, you can, *as a result,* distinguish Xs from other things; but you have to have the concept first. But what then would having the concept be? Moreover, we can devise machines that can effectively differentiate some things from others; do we wish to say that these machines have concepts?

4. In reply to such objections, we might say that to have a concept of X is simply to have some *criterion-in-mind*. It would consist in some kind of "mental content" quite independent of words and quite independent of distinguishing Xs from Ys and Zs. But it is not easy to state what such a criterion-in-mind would be like, or how one would know, through introspection alone, whether one possessed such a criterion. Surely the way one would know whether one had a criterion for X would be whether it would enable one to distinguish Xs from Ys and Zs. A criterion for identifying Xs would (it would seem) automatically be a criterion for distinguishing Xs from non-Xs. And so we would be back with our third criterion after all.

I can, of course, have a concept of X even though there are no Xs in the world at all. I may have a concept of a sort of thing that is a reptile, larger than an elephant, and flies through the air. I could easily identify such a creature if it existed, and the fact that it does not exist does not prevent me from having the concept of such a creature. I have such a concept, then, although no such creature exists and there is no word to designate this peculiar combination of characteristics. In many cases I can have the concept even if I cannot state any characteristics at all; I cannot state in words what distinguishes red from orange, though I know how to make the distinction in practice, and so I have a concept of these colors.

If scientists can have a concept of ultraviolet without being able to visualize it, surely we may say, a blind person can have a concept of red without being able to visualize red; after all, scientists and blind persons both have a criterion for distinguishing X (ultraviolet, red) from non-X. But it would seem that blind persons, though they have *a* criterion for distinguishing X from non-X, do not have *the same* concept as sighted persons do, for they do not have the same criteria for distinguishing red from non-red. Blind persons must use wavelengths as their criteria, whereas sighted persons use (as they have from time immemorial) the easily distinguishable difference in the way red *looks*. There is a high degree of correlation between the two concepts; but they are not the same concept, for there is not the same means of distinguishing red from non-red. (Sighted people, of course, *can* use both ways of distinguishing red from non-red, whereas the blind can use only one.) Similarly, a person who could see ultraviolet would have a concept of it over and above the one we have, for such a person would be able to distinguish that color from others by means of direct inspection, without having to resort (as we do) to instruments for distinguishing it. For most scientific concepts—which will be discussed in Chapter 4—there are no images.

Does your dog have the concept of a bone? of a cat? In any sense involving language, it clearly does not. The dog doesn't know the definition of these words, nor can it use them. But it is clearly able to identify something as a bone when it sees it, and it chases cats but not sticks and stones; it can distinguish many different kinds of things and creatures from one another, and in that sense it has the concept. Does it do so by having a criterion-in-mind? We can't say much about what goes on in a dog's mind—whatever it is, it is surely very different from ours; but the fact that it consistently is able to distinguish cats from stones, and male from female dogs, can hardly be put down to coincidence. It has an ability to *recognize* different kinds of things and to act on that recognition. The dog wags his tail when his owner comes home but not when an intruder enters the yard. Presumably there is some criterion which the dog has for distinguishing the one from the other.

Are all concepts based on experience? What are we to say of the view that all concepts are based on experience—which means that in the case of simple "ideas" a concept of X is impossible without a prior experience of X, and in the case of "complex ideas" that the concept of X is impossible without a prior experience of the simple ideas of which it is constituted? The view seems not only plausible but inevitable, for what is the alternative? We are not born with concepts, nor do we (as Plato thought) remember them from a state of existence prior to our birth; so how else could we acquire them except through experience?

The difficulty lies in showing in each case how the concept was actually derived from experience. With sensory concepts such as redness, the case is relatively easy. As small children we had various red things pointed out to us, and by acts of successive abstraction we came to recognize the characteristic, redness, that all the cases pointed to had in common. But how did we derive through experience the concept of liberty, of honesty, of marginal utility, of four, of logical implication? We do have these concepts, and we have them *without* any corresponding images. When we think of liberty, we may imagine the Statue of Liberty, and when we think of slavery, we may imagine African slaves on a plantation; but neither of these images constitutes the meaning of the words "liberty" and "slavery"—others may imagine something very different when they think of liberty or slavery, and still others may have no images at all. There is no image *of* liberty or slavery the way there is an image of red or sweet. These are abstract concepts, to which there are no corresponding images. If we have images, they are not *of* liberty but of particular things or situations that may or may not exemplify liberty. We can all understand the same concept, liberty, even though we all have different images (or none at all) when we think about it. What we *think* of when we think of liberty is very different from what we *imagine* when we think of it; what we imagine, if anything, is only an incidental accompaniment.

This is not to say that we could have the concept of liberty if we had never had any sense-experiences at all. Our having the concept is in some way or other dependent on experience; but it is far from easy to say how. Perhaps if we had always lived under a tyranny and never seen or heard of people who could express their opinions without fear of punishment, we would not be able to form the concept of liberty—though even this is doubtful, for as long as we were aware of restraints upon our behavior, we could conceive of a state-of-affairs in which these restraints were absent. It is, indeed, very difficult to know upon *what* experiences our concept of liberty is dependent. The relation between the concept and sense-experience is indirect: There is no particular sense-experience, or even any single kind of sense-experience, that we must have had before we can have this concept. Whatever the connection is between the concept and experience, it is sufficiently indirect that no one has given a clear account of exactly what this connection is in every case.

Let us consider another type of concept, those of arithmetic. Since we can distinguish between two things and three things, where did we get our concepts of two and three? "From experience," Hume would say. But exactly how? Arithmetic, we might say, studies the *quantitative* aspects of things; when we consider the sum of two and three, we don't care whether it's three apples, three boats, or three bales of hay. The concept of three (or three-ness) is formed through abstraction from many cases. What three apples, three boats, and three bales of hay have in common is their numerical *quantity;* that there are three *of* them is relevant to mathematics, not what it is that there are three *of.* The concepts of arithmetic are all quantitative—that is what defines them as arithmetical; and they are abstracted from experience, from our experience of things in the world. Without any experience of quantities of things, we would have no arithmetical concepts. So far so good. But don't we have a concept of 12,038,468 just as much as we have of 3? Yet we have probably never

observed exactly that number of things, and did not know it even if we did. What, we can then ask, is the relation between that number and our sense-experiences?

Or consider the meanings of such terms as "equality," "infinity," "implication," "deduction." We have concepts of all of these, for we can distinguish cases of the application of these words from cases of their non-application. Yet they do not seem to correspond to anything that confronts us in experience. If they are derived from experience in some remote way, it is not clear how, or what exactly the steps are.

Perhaps the experience we must have gone through in order to derive our concepts of numerical equality and of 12,038,468 is simply our experience of learning mathematics, or the experience of learning to use these words. But if so, this is a broader sense of the word "experience" than we have thus far been using, namely sense-experience (or sense-impressions).

Indeed, there are words that we can use with systematic accuracy that do not seem to be connected with experience, even by way of abstraction: consider connective words like "and" and "about," which have a function in a sentence but do not correspond to any distinguishable items in the world:

One must not only know the meanings of nouns, verbs, and adjectives, one must also understand the significance of the syntactical form of the sentence; and for many sentences, one must understand various kinds of words that serve to connect nouns, adjectives, and verbs into sentences so as to affect the meaning of the sentence as a whole. One must be able to distinguish semantically between "John hit Jim," "Jim hit John," "Did John hit Jim?," "John, hit Jim!," and "John, please don't hit Jim." This means that before one can engage in conversation one must be able to handle and understand such factors as word order; "auxiliaries" like, "do," "shall," and "is"; and connectives like "is," "that," and "and." These elements can neither get their meaning by association with distinguishable items in experience nor be defined in terms of items that can. Where could we look in our sense-perception for the object of work-order patterns, pauses, or words like "is" and "that"? And as for defining these elements in terms of words like "blue" and "table," the prospect has seemed so remote that no one has so much as attempted it.[9]

The acquiring of such concepts as these seems to require experiences of a different kind: learning a language, understanding sentences and sets of sentences, and the operations or performances with such symbols that are governed by linguistic rules.

According to empiricism, every word or phrase that we use must be traceable back to sense-experience in some way, whether the route be short (as with "red") or long (as with "liberty"). Or to put it in a different way, every word, to have meaning, must be either capable of ostensive definition itself or defined by means of other words, and these perhaps by still others, which are ultimately definable by ostensive definition. If this cannot be done, then the word or phrase is meaningless. If anyone claims, says Hume, that he has some idea (concept), we need only ask him,

From what impression is that supposed idea derived? And if it be impossible to assign any, this will serve to confirm our suspicion . . . Commit it then to the flames; for it can contain nothing but sophistry and illusion.[10]

But is this criterion satisfactory? In the light of the last few pages, it seems that the answer must be no. There is nothing in reality corresponding to the square root of minus 1. Yet mathematicians have this concept and use it constantly. It is only with regard to ideas that come from what Hume called *impressions* that his theory of concepts has any plausibility.

---

[9]William Alston, *Philosophy of Language* (Englewood Cliffs, NJ: Prentice-Hall, 1963), p. 68.

[10]David Hume, *An Enquiry Concerning Human Understanding,* concluding sentences of Chapters 2 and 11.

4. THE SOURCES OF KNOWLEDGE

We are now in a position to consider the question, How do we know what we claim to know (if we do)? What are the sources of human knowledge? What are the avenues by which we acquire it? We shall first consider the principle candidates for this position and briefly consider their merits or demerits.

1. Perception. The most obvious way we claim to have knowledge is by means of our *senses*. "How do you know there's a table there?" "I see it; and I touch it; and if that isn't enough I can take pictures of it; you can also take a look yourself and call in others if you like." Most of Chapter 2 will be devoted to examining the claim to knowledge via sense-perception. We have already encountered some of the problems involved in assessing these claims.

2. Introspection. Often we simply state how we feel or what we are thinking or wondering about. The psychiatrist asks, "Tell me how you feel at this moment," and you may say, "I feel sort of down in the dumps—depressed, I don't know why, I'm just not with it today. I feel as if something awful is about to happen to me." Or, "I don't feel energetic—sort of like a vegetable. I just want to curl up on the beach and sleep all afternoon." Don't we know the truth of such statements in a way we don't know anything else? Don't you *know* how you feel, in a way that no one else can know it? Others can only *infer* how you feel from how you look and behave, but you know because you have the feelings yourself.

Yet psychologists are often skeptical about introspective reports. Some don't accept the data of introspection at all, but only people's behavior. Why should this be? You may not know what the world is really like, but don't you know how you yourself feel?

There is the possibility that the person may be lying. Much more frequently, however, we *misdescribe* how we feel. We may say we feel resentful when we only feel angry (resentment is more like the "demand that other people feel guilty"). We may say that we are in love when we are only infatuated for a short time. A woman may say sincerely that she hates her husband, but she doesn't really, especially if she is all hearts and flowers when he returns an hour later. We can often tell more about how people feel by how they behave than by what they say. Most people aren't very good at articulating their feelings in words.

We also tend to "read into the script." We put much more into the report than we are actually feeling. Our report may be permeated by importations from psychological theories which are no part of the feeling itself: "I feel as if I have an Oedipus complex"; "I feel that I am a paranoid schizophrenic, and that I am being persecuted by everyone . . . "; "I feel that I have an unconscious wish to be hurt, and even though I really don't want to be hurt, somehow I do . . . " And the therapist may say, "Forget about what you've read in books; forget about psychological theories. Just tell me what you *feel* at this moment." Simply to give an introspective report, without adding to it bits of knowledge or theory which are *not* a part of what you introspect (what you "find within you when you search your soul"), is an extraordinarily difficult achievement for most people. They feel what they feel, but exactly *what* they feel, with the interpretative material pared away, is often difficult to describe.

Most of the words we use to describe our feelings aren't merely descriptions of inner states occurring at that moment. "I feel bored" and "I feel a stab of pain" probably come quite close to stating what we feel at a given time. These are *occurrent* states. But "I am in love" is not. If you're in love, you want to do things for the person you love, you are willing to give up things for the beloved; and if you say you're in love but show no tendency to do these things, can we still say you're in love? Someone else in your family may be quite convinced from your behavior that you are not in love, even while you insist that you are. And you yourself may later admit, "I thought it was love but it was only temporary infatuation."

Can you tell by introspection that you're happy? You can tell whether you are feeling pleasure, an occurrent state that comes and goes. But when you say you are happy, you are saying much more than this. Happiness is more of an enduring thing; you can feel pleasure at noon and displeasure half a minute later, but it would be strange to say "I felt happy at 12, unhappy at 12:01, and happy again at 12:02." Happiness involves a relatively permanent *disposition* to feel a certain way about things and respond to them in certain ways. No report of what you experience at the present moment will entitle you to say you are happy: Such dispositional states involve your state of mind *and* your behavior over a period of time.

In the simplest cases, it is doubtful whether the word "introspect" even fits. Do you have to stop and introspect ("examine your mind") in order to know that you have a headache? Ordinarily we speak of introspection only when our state of mind is quite complicated, and it isn't easy to say just how it is that we feel. You don't *find out* that you have a sudden feeling of relief when you learn that your loved one is safe after all—you don't ask yourself and then give yourself the answer. Don't you just know? This issue, too, will be discussed in subsequent chapters.

3. Memory. "How do I know what I had for breakfast this morning? I remember it, that's how I know." Isn't remembering it just as good as perceiving it right in front of you? Wouldn't it be strange to say that you *don't* remember it? Isn't memory a perfectly good way of knowing something?

But memory can play tricks on us too. You may say quite sincerely, "I remember that I had eggs for breakfast this morning." And then it occurs to you that it was yesterday morning, not this morning, that you had them—this morning you were in a hurry and ran to class without eating breakfast. People sometimes have the experiences of *deja vu*— "I remember when I was a child how I used to play with the neighbor boy Charlie in the back yard." But it is possible that you have been told this so often that you have come to believe that it's true—that what you are remembering is your parents' repeated stories about you and Charlie, and that you have confused their reports (together with what you imagined while they were telling them) with what actually happened. Remembering something is no more a guarantee of knowing it that perceiving it is—even less, it would seem: Aren't you more likely to be right if you see something at the present moment than if you remember seeing it at some time in the past?

You might say, "Then I don't *really* remember it, I only *seem* to remember it." True enough; but then how do you tell the difference between those things you only *seem* to remember because they never happened, and those that you *really* remember, because they did happen?

Yet we shouldn't jump from saying "Some perceptions are fallible" to saying "All perceptions are fallible"; and neither should we jump from "Some memories are fallible" to "All memories are fallible." How would we know that all memories are fallible? Doesn't that statement rely on memory too?

Besides, how can I know that a past memory was mistaken, unless I know that this act of remembering really did occur in the past, and that there was a previous state-of-affairs of which it was a memory? And how do I know *this?* If I know that my memory has deceived me in the past, I have to know some facts about the past—and how do I know these, except through memory?

Suppose I remember that I spent last week in Chicago, and suppose some argument convinces me that this memory-judgment was mistaken. How might I become convinced of this? Suppose I run into someone today who describes a conversation he had with me (or says he had) last week in Los Angeles; and then still another person, unknown to the first one, also tells me that she had lunch with me last week in Los Angeles. I have never known either of these people to lie; perhaps they were just mistaken—but on the other hand, perhaps it was I who was mistaken. They are as convinced that they remember seeing me in Los Angeles as I am that I was in Chicago. Suppose that I keep a daily diary and look up what appears in it for last Wednesday's date, and the record indicates that I was in Chicago that day. Doesn't that prove my case? Not quite. Sometimes people write only what they *think* has happened, not really happened.

But could I have deceived myself on so important a point? I may say to myself, "What I write in my diary, since it's written the same day, is usually true" — but in concluding this, am I not again relying on memory? Not only that, I am assuming other things which are in turn based on memory—for example, that the ink-marks on the page of my diary have not changed their shape, and that the words written in it have not somehow turned into very different words, which I now read. If the shape of the words changed overnight, what I read in the diary now wouldn't be evidence for what really happened last Wednesday. And what makes me so sure that ink-marks don't change their shape in this way? Again, the fact that thus far they never have. But how do I know *this?* This belief too is based on memory. I *remember* that in all my experience ink-marks never change their shape in this way. And so I am propping up my memory-judgment by reference to the diary, but that judgment in turn has to be propped up by all manner of assumptions, such as "Ink-marks don't change their shape," which are also based on memory of how ink-marks have behaved in the past.

We are thus led to the conclusion that we have no good reason to say that some memory-judgments are false, unless the truth of *some* memory-judgments is assumed. Unless we grant that some memory-judgments are true, our judgment that some memory-judgments are false can even get off the ground, for there could be no evidence to support them. All such evidence comes from the past and is itself derived from memory.

4. Reason. Another alleged source of knowledge is *reason.* But this elusive word doesn't always have the same meaning. Sometimes it means *reasoning.* And we do sometimes attain knowledge—or believe we do—by means of reasoning: That is, we don't look and touch, we "figure it out." If A is larger than B, then B is smaller than A. If A is larger than B and B is larger than C, then A is larger than C. If all human beings are mortal and Jones is a human being, then Jones is mortal. If all dogs are mammals and you own a dog, then you own a mammal. And so on for countless other cases. These are simple cases of reasoning with which we are all familiar.

We aren't saying that A *is* larger than B (we would have to discover that by the use of our senses), but that *if* A is larger than B, B is smaller than A. We don't have to observe that A is larger than B, and then make a second observation to discover that B is smaller than A; we know it without making any second observation.

There are many things that we discover solely by reasoning: Mathematics is a prime example. We figure out that $8 \times 8 = 64$, that the square root of 9 is 3, that $100 - 53 = 47$, and so on. We don't *look*, we *reason* to the conclusion.

But again, we don't always reason correctly. A child may be quite certain that 6 times 8 is 68. Anyone can make a mistake in addition or subtraction. Anyone can also make a mistake in logic—in reasoning from premises (A is larger than B, and B is larger than C) to conclusion (A is larger than C). For example, some people reason that if something isn't hot it must be cold; but this is incorrect—it might be lukewarm. As a source of knowledge, reasoning isn't foolproof.

There are also statements we don't arrive at through reason*ing* at all—statements so basic, so fundamental, as to be what we reason *from* rather than reason *to.* How do you know that A is A, that dogs are dogs, and teeth are teeth? How do you know that if no cats are dogs, then no dogs are cats? or that if either *p* or *q* is true, then either *q* or *p* is true? Of such statements we are inclined to say "They are necessarily true" and "They can't be false"—but how do we know this? Such statements are sometimes called "truths of reason." But they invite many questions. If we can't prove them, how do we know that they are true? If someone denied them, how would you prove the person wrong? We shall examine statements of this kind at some length in Chapter 3.

The word "reason," however, is not limited to reason*ing*—that is only one aspect of reason. Reason is a power or capacity that human beings have, and which no other animal has, at least not to the same extent. Reason involves the power to form concepts, the power to understand, the power to think. In this very general sense, the use of reason is presupposed in every subject we study, including philosophy. Reason is even involved in ordinary perception; we not only see the lion, we *recognize* it as a lion, *understand* what may happen if we just stand there, and *respond* (perhaps by running away).

Even in this general sense of "reason," however, reason is fallible like our other faculties. We may take what we see to be something different from what it is, or we may recognize it correctly but misconceive the situation because of misinformation ("Lions are harmless"), or react inappropriately (try to tempt it with carrots). An imbecile, a generally stupid person, an insane person, or just someone who "doesn't have all his oars in the water" or "is missing some of his marbles"—is said to suffer from "a defect of reason."

Meanwhile, there are other alleged sources of knowledge.

5. Faith. "How do you know that God exists?" "I know by faith." If faith is *all* that is appealed to, not accompanied by evidence or reasoning, there is one thing about this claim to knowledge that stands out at the beginning: "Two can play at that game." If you say you know by faith that a certain statement is true, someone else can say with equal sincerity that she knows by faith that it isn't. And where do we go from there? How do we tell who is right? It would seem that the appeal to faith, by itself, can't give an answer to this question. "Then ends the argument and begins the fight."

Many people who appeal to faith to justify their own beliefs are unwilling to grant the truth of their opponents' beliefs when *they* appeal to faith. Yet the same criteria that would justify the one would justify the other. And when the two claims contradict each other, both of them can't be true.

We may sometimes have a *reason* for "having faith." " I have faith in you," you say to a friend you have known for years, and who has always proven to be truthful and reliable; you wouldn't have the same faith in a complete stranger or someone who had deceived you many times. But this is somewhat different sense of the word "faith"; here "having faith" in someone means having confidence or trust in that person. There can often be good reasons from past experience with someone for *having* faith in her; your confidence is then based on those reasons, not merely on faith. If you merely say "I have faith that I'll hit it lucky at the gambling table tonight," unsupported by evidence, you may well turn out

to be lucky, but you had no basis (reason) for making the statement, and you could hardly claim to know it.

6. Intuition. Much the same kind of criticism can be made of people who claim to have knowledge by intuition. "How did you know that that was the way out of the forest?" you may ask someone after having been lost for hours. "I knew it by intuition," the person may say, or "It's just a woman's intuition." Such a response often sounds impressive to her hearers, but the question remains, If she knew, *how* did she know? Not through seeing, hearing, or any of the usual sensory channels, it would seem. She just had a sudden conviction, and it turned out to be right—but how? "She knew by intuition" doesn't really tell us anything; it gives us a *word* -- but what does the word refer to? What kind of process is it, that enables people to be right all the time? (And it raises another question: If the person claimed intuition only that one time, and was right that one time, did she *know?* There is no *pattern* of being right that might enable us to say that she knew.) The mere claim "I knew it by intuition" provides no evidence at all that she knew.

Often, however, what's called "knowledge by intuition" is actually something different. Sometimes the person has been a more careful observer than most people are, or has noticed "minimal cues" in the environment that have escaped the notice of others; it is on this that she bases her "woman's intuition." In such a case it's not just intuition, it's the careful use of her senses and memory in noticing things that justifies her belief. Perhaps she remembered having passed an odd-shaped stump on the way, or that the foothills in the distance were definitely to the west because the sun was setting above them. If she noticed such things and others didn't, this would account for her success. Some people are very good at the childhood game "hide the thimble"; they observe carefully the direction in which the person who hid the thimble consistently does *not* look, and that's where it is.

Through careful observation of minimal cues in the behavior of others, some people quickly develop a keen sense of what other persons are like—"If they do A, they'll probably do B and C and D" based on past observation—and thus they become unusually good predictors of others' behavior. "He won't come back as he promised," she will say confidently; "he gave us the slip; he's secretly been looking for an opportunity for some time." The others hadn't noticed his eye-movements and gestures and subtle cues in his past behavior, but she has; so it's no wonder that she is more often right than they. But again, this isn't intuition, though that's what the person calls it—it is careful use of the senses, combined with a memory for relevant details.

However, if the claim to intuition is not based on any such things, but is *merely* a "shot in the dark," then there is a powerful objection to intuition as a claim to knowledge. "I know by intuition that *p* is true" invites the counterclaim "I know by intuition that it isn't." By itself intuition provides no method for weeding out true intuitions from false ones.

What then can be said about claims to extra-sensory perception (ESP)? These are not claims to know something by intuition; they are claims to have knowledge without the use of eyes, ears, or other sense-organs. "In telepathy," for example, "one mind affects another without any discoverable physical intermediary, and regardless of the spatial distance between their respective bodies."[11] If one person can report minute by minute exactly what the thoughts are of another person who is many miles away, and always reports them correctly to the last detail, we would

have excellent reason (depending on our definition of "know") to say that the first person knows what the second person is thinking. But if this happens it isn't knowledge by intuition, but knowledge by a process that is not presently understood.

7. Testimony. Most of what we claim to know is not anything we perceive with our own senses. We would probably claim to know (at least in the weak sense) that the earth is many millions of years old, that we were born on a certain year and day at a certain place, that George Washington was the first president of the United States, that Brutus killed Caesar, and countless other things that we were told or that we read in books of history and science. But we haven't ourselves *observed* these things—not even our own birth. We were there, but not in a position to discover anything for ourselves; usually we just take our parents' word for the time and place.

As to the oral testimony of others, we normally assume it's true unless there is some reason to believe that it isn't. "Where's the post office?" we ask in a strange town, and a stranger tells us; we follow the directions and find the post office. Of course, often we do have reason to believe that the testimony is false—for example, assertions made by perennial liars, or people who don't observe very carefully (they aren't lying, they're just mistaken in saying what they observed), or people who habitually exaggerate claims, or who "read into the script" by saying they saw a dinosaur behind the trees when actually it was an elephant or a peculiar configuration of leaves and branches. Accepting the claims of others unless there is some reason not to is a very timesaving device. Trying to find everything out for yourself would be impossible in a lifetime, besides being a colossal waste of time.

As to written testimony—for example, from encyclopedias and history books—again we tend to take such claims as true unless we

---

[11]H. H. Price, "Psychical Research and Human Personality," in J. R. Smythies, ed., *Science and ESP* (London: Routledge & Kegan Paul, 1967), p. 36.

find some reason not to. A doubtful historical claim by one professor is very likely to be questioned by another professor who wants to advance to eminence in his field. But the historical researcher herself depends on the testimony of books that *she* reads—she can't perceive George Washington for herself any more than you can. When we claim to know facts about George Washington, we believe the chain of written testimony—and this may be a very long chain, of one person depending on what another wrote, and he or she in turn depending on what a predecessor wrote—will end up with what people at the time and place observed by means of their senses. Presumably there were people who saw Washington inaugurated, and some left records of the event. In the case of more remote claims, such as that there were dinosaurs on the earth 70 million years ago, when nobody was around to observe them, the claim is a complex *inference* of a kind we shall examine in Chapter 4. In either case, however, we believe that the chain of testimony will lead back either to what some people *did* perceive, or what people *would have* perceived *if* they had been there (even if they weren't). If we want to expand our knowledge beyond what we can perceive for ourselves, the testimony of others is vital. I want Tacitus to tell me what happened in the reign of Claudius because I wasn't there.

Of course, as the saying goes, there's many a slip between cup and lip. The longer the chain of testimony, the more chances there are of a mistake. We tend to accept the claim unless it conflicts with something else we know. Most of what Herodotus tells us in his famous history can be checked in other sources, but we don't believe him when he writes that in Egypt cats jump into the fire (this conflicts with everything *we* have observed about cats). In matters of testimony, the motto "Nothing ventured, nothing gained" pays off better than "Safety first" (I won't believe it unless I can see it for myself). Most of the time, when we

accept testimony, we can learn countless truths we either wouldn't have the time or leisure to observe or couldn't possibly observe ourselves because the event is long ago or far away.

But do we *know,* just because Herodotus wrote it? or because the passerby said the post office was two blocks to the right? We would probably admit many well confirmed examples of testimony as genuine knowledge, at least in the weak sense. If someone walks in the door and says the house next door is still there, we believe it—that is the norm, even though it involves accepting both the person's testimony and memory. But knowledge in the strong sense is more than we can expect from the testimony of others. If you can't even know in the strong sense that the chairs are still next door—because they may have been removed, or because you misremember—how can you know something if there is an added hitch, that the other person may be giving unreliable testimony? Testimony is by its nature derivative: The testimony to an event is worthless unless *someone* observed the event; and if that person's observation is faulty, so is the testimony.

EXERCISES

1. Can you think of a statement that is true (or false) although there is no possible way in which anyone could ever discover which, or even obtain any evidence one way or the other?

2. In D. H. Lawrence's story "The Rocking Horse Winner," a little boy, every time he rocks frantically on his rocking horse in the evening, is able to predict which horse will win a race the following afternoon. His uncle is skeptical about this until it turns out time after time that the little boy's predictions are always right. Would you say that the little boy *knew* which horse would win the next day's race?

3. "A man who knows a sheep when he sees one, says 'There is a sheep.' But it is not a sheep but a dog. So he does not know that he sees a

sheep. But an object further away which he also sees but doesn't think is a sheep *is* a sheep. So it is true that he sees a sheep, and also he believes he does and is completely justified in believing it . . . He still doesn't know that he sees a sheep because what he takes to be a sheep isn't, and the sheep he sees he doesn't take to be one."[12] Would you say that in this example the man knows he sees a sheep? *If* not, would you further revise the definition of knowing to read that "If S knows that *p, S* is justified in believing that *p* in some way *does not depend on any false proposition*"?

4. A skeptic says he doesn't know he has a hand in front of him. Does he know, in spite of what he says?

5. A person who has recently studied geometry is asked "What is the expansion of *pi* four decimal places?" He says "I don't know." A minute later he remembers, and says "Yes, I do know; its 3.1416." (This example is used in Keith Lehrer, *Knowledge,* p. 60.) Did he know the first time, even when he said he didn't? Comment on the following responses.

   a. "If he knows *p,* he believes that he knows *p*. And he didn't believe the latter. So he didn't know *p* at the time of his initial report."

   b. "He knew the correct answer, though he didn't know that the answer was correct."

   c. "He knew it because he had memorized it."

6. A woman is asked on a television quiz program, "In what year did George Washington die?" She says "1799," the correct answer, and wins a new car. "She new the answer," we say.

   a. Did she know it if she just happened to guess it right?

   b. Did she know it because she remembered reading it in a history book?

   c. Suppose she read it in a history book, but wasn't sure she remembered it correctly at the time she gave the answer; did she know it?

7. Can you ever say truly (a) "I am dreaming"? (b) "I am asleep"? (c) "I am not breathing"? (d) "I am dead"?

8. Do you require anything other than your present experience, plus knowledge of what the words mean, to know that the following propositions are true?

   a. I have a toothache.
   b. I ate breakfast this morning.
   c. I exist.
   d. I hope it rains tomorrow.
   e. I think it will rain tomorrow.
   f. It will rain tomorrow.

9. Do you consider the following to be occurrent states, or dispositional, or both?

   a. He is angry.
   b. She is quick-tempered.
   c. He is religious.
   d. She is boiling over with rage.
   e. He is fat.
   f. She is restless.
   g. The fruit is rotten.
   h. Her face is ashen.
   i. The coffers are empty.
   j. His tastes are expensive.

10. Which of the following pairs of sentences express the same proposition?

    a. Johnny is taller than Billy.
       Billy is shorter than Johnny.
    b. Mary is prettier than Jane.
       Jane is uglier than Mary.
    c. I like custard pudding.
       I do not dislike custard pudding.
    d. They got married and had children.
       They had children and got married.

11. Do you consider the following suggestions (or apparent suggestions) meaningful? Why?

    a. "How do you know there isn't a big hole in space?" "In space? Don't you mean in some *bodies* in space? Planets might have holes." "No, I mean not a hole in any body of matter, but a hole in space itself."

    b. "I might be able to jump in one second from the earth to a star a million light-years away, by traveling through the fourth dimension."

    c. "Perhaps the chair on which you're sitting and the floor on which your feet rest have thoughts and feelings and pains just as you do."

    d. "Perhaps there was nothing at all for 20 billion years, and then all of a sudden there was something—matter."

12. Analyze the meaning of the word "true" or "truth" in each of the following:

    a. She is a true friend.
    b. He is true to his wife.

---

[12]From Keith Lehrer, *Knowledge* (Oxford: Claredon Press, 1974), p. 20.

c. This character (in a novel) is true to the way people of that kind behave in actual life.

d. The equator is not a true physical place.

e. The true way of solving this problem is . . .

f. This line is not a true plumb.

g. The true meaning of "democracy" is . . .

h. It's the truth that hurts.

i. This is certainly a true portrait of her.

j. You can't draw a true circle.

13. In which of the following cases does the "feeling" guarantee the truth of the statement about what is felt? Give your reasons.

a. I feel anxious.

b. I feel sick.

c. I feel as if I'm about to be sick.

d. I feel that I am about to be sick.

e. I feel able to do anything.

f. I feel as if I have a frog in my throat.

g. I feel that she has been unjustly treated.

h. I feel that God exists.

14. Is it true now that the sun will rise tomorrow?

15. In which of these cases is the "knowing" in question propositional? Explain in each case, stating the propositions where there are any involved.

a. Do you know what the solution is to this problem?

b. Do you know her intimately?

c. Can the human mind know reality?

d. Do you know how to perform an appendectomy?

e. Do you know why he walked out on his family like that?

f. Do you know which of the suitors she accepted?

g. A person doesn't know war until he's seen war.

h. Do you know what the feeling of *deja vu* is like?

i. I wouldn't know what to do in such a situation.

j. Do you know the meaning of that word?

16. Can you know (as opposed to having good reason to believe) any proposition about the future? Give your reasons.

17. In each of the following examples, do you *know* (not merely believe, or even have some rea-

son to believe) that the proposition is true? Defend you answer.

a. The road continues on the other side of the hill.

b. If I let go of this piece of chalk it will fall.

c. The first floor of this building is not now submerged in water.

d. The table has a back side and an inside even though I'm not now perceiving them.

e. This crow before me is black.

f. All crows are black.

g. You have an optic nerve.

h. You are not now a multimillionaire.

i. Julius Caesar once lived.

j. You had breakfast this morning.

k. The sun will rise tomorrow.

l. I have blood and bones and vital organs and am not made of straw.

m. This table won't turn into an elevator and carry us all downstairs.

n. A dog will never give birth to kittens.

o. You will not some day be father (or mother) to an orange.

p. You are not now asleep (or dead).

q. You did not eat mothballs for dinner yesterday.

r. This table is the same one that was in this room yesterday.

s. You were born (not hatched or spontaneously generated).

t. All human beings are mortal.

u. The earth is (approximately) spherical.

v. The earth did not come into existence five minutes ago.

w. You are not dreaming at this moment.

x. You are now seeing several colors.

y. You are younger than your parents.

z. You are not a nightengale.

18. Which of the above propositions would you claim to know in the strong sense, and why?

19. Evaluate this assertion: "Some propositions must be certain, for if none were certain, none could be probable. Probability is a concept derived from that of certainty. If we didn't know what it was for something to be certain, we would have no standard of reference for estimating probability. We wouldn't even be able to know what the word 'probable' would mean."

20. Evaluate the following definition of "knowing": Knowing is the ability to be regularly right. If I

can always tell you what your thoughts are, I know what they are—even though I don't know how I know (I can't state any evidence), and I may not even believe what I say (I may just say whatever pops into my mind, without giving it any particular credence). So belief and evidence both should be deleted from any definition of knowledge: All that knowing requires is the ability to be regularly right.

21. Could you imagine what a sweet taste was like if you had experienced only sour and bitter tastes? Could you imagine the taste of a tangerine if you had tasted only lemons and oranges? or the the taste of a nectarine if you had tasted only plums and peaches? Could you tell in advance what the experience of sadness at the death of a loved one would be like, if you had experienced only sadness in other contexts, such as sadness at the cessation of enjoyment and sadness at the theft of a prized possession? Could you tell in advance what the sadness of a Mahler andante would be like if you had experienced (in music) only andantes by Mozart? Can you know what it is to be greedy if you have never yourself experienced greed? If Mr. X was described to you as greedy, would you have no idea what his feeling-states were like? what to expect from him?

22. Can you have any idea of the following without having experienced them firsthand? Would you consider the ideas of them simple or complex in Locke's sense? State whether you are using "idea" in the sense of image or of concept. (a) space; (b) bookends; (c) nothing; (d) motion; (e) swimming; (f) life; (g) novelty; (h) regret.

23. Can you state in what way(s) if any the following concepts are based on experience? What experiences or kind of experiences must a person have in order to have each of these concepts? (a) doorknob; (b) racial integration; (c) morally deserving; (d) welcome; (e) probability; (f) economic opportunity; (g) infinity.

24. Aren't we assuming, when we trust the evidence of sight and hearing and so on, that our senses *do not distort* reality, the way mirrors at a "Fun House" distort images? That our senses are reliable at all—is this an assumption, or is there evidence for it?

25. If your physician tells you that taking some Vitamin C tablets would be good for you, and you follow his advice, are you accepting his advice on faith? What about a person who accepts the same advice from a friend who knows nothing about medicine or nutrition? or a person who hears a stranger saying it, and acts on it?

26. Can you imagine looking out your window in the morning and seeing *nothing*—no white, no black, no red, no green, no shapes, just nothing at all?

SELECTED READINGS

ALSTON, WILLIAM P. *Philosophy of Language.* Englewood Cliffs, NJ: Prentice-Hall, 1964.

ARMSTRONG, D. M. *Belief, Truth, and Knowledge.* Cambridge: Cambridge University Press, 1973.

AUSTIN, J. L. *Philosophical Papers.* Oxford; Oxford University Press, 1961.

AYER, ALFRED J. *The Problem of Knowledge.* London: Macmillan, 1956.

AYER, ALFRED J. "Truth," in *The Concept of a Person and Other Essays.* London: Macmillan, 1963. Also included in Olshewsky.

AYER, ALFRED J. *Philosophical Papers.* London: Macmillan, 1963.

AYER, ALFRED J. *The Central Questions of Philosophy.* London: Weidenfeld and Nicolson, 1973.

DRANGE, THEODORE. *Type Crossings.* The Hague: Mouton, 1966.

DRETSKE, FRED. *Seeing and Knowing.* London: Routledge & Kegan Paul, 1969.

FLEW, ANTONY, ed. *Logic and Language,* 1st & 2nd series. Oxford: Blackwell, 1953.

FLEW, ANTONY, ed. *Essays in Conceptual Analysis.* London: Macmillan, 1956.

FOGELIN, ROBERT. *Evidence and Meaning.* London: Routledge & Kegan Paul, 1967.

GRICE, PAUL. "Meaning." *Philosophical Review, 1966* (1957): 377–388. In numerous anthologies.

HARTLAND-SWANN, JOHN. *An Analysis of Knowing.* London: Allen & Unwin, 1958.

HILL, THOMAS E. *The Concept of Meaning.* New York: Humanities Press, 1967.

HUME, DAVID. *An Enquiry Concerning Human Understanding.* 1751. Many editions.

LEHRER, KEITH. *Knowledge.* Oxford: Clarendon Press, 1974.

LOCKE, JOHN. *Essays Concerning Human Understanding,* books 2 and 4. 1689. Many editions.

MALCOLM, NORMAN. "Knowledge and Belief" and "The Verification Argument" in *Knowledge and Certainty*. Englewood Cliffs, NJ: Prentice-Hall, 1963.

MOORE, G. E. *Some Main Problems of Philosophy*. London: Allen & Unwin, 1952.

MOORE, G. E. *Philosophical Papers*. London: Allen & Unwin, 1959.

NOZICK, ROBERT. *Philosophical Explanations*. Cambridge: Harvard University Press, 1981.

OLSHEWSKY, THOMAS, ed. *Problems in the Philosophy of Language*. New York: Holt, 1969.

PITCHER, GEORGE, ed. *Truth*. Englewood Cliffs, NJ: Prentice-Hall, 1964.

PRICE, H. H. *Thinking and Experience*. London: Hutchinson University Library, 1953.

RUSSELL, BERTRAND. *The Problems of Philosophy*. London: Oxford University Press, 1912.

RUSSELL, BERTRAND. *Human Knowledge: Its Scope and Limits*. New York: Simon & Schuster, 1946.

UNGER, PETER. *Ignorance*. Oxford: Clarendon Press, 1975.

WITTGENSTEIN, LUDWIG. *The Blue and Brown Books*. Oxford: Blackwell, 1935.

YOLTON, JOHN. *John Locke and the Way of Ideas*. London: Oxford University Press, 1956.

Note: Most of the important articles in philosophical periodicals are included in anthologies of readings. As a rule these anthologies are listed in the reading lists rather than the periodicals in which the essays first appeared.

2

PERCEPTUAL KNOWLEDGE

One of the main questions of philosophy, some would say *the* main question, is: How do you know? This doesn't mean How do you come to be sure? but What *entitles* you to be sure? (We may have come to be sure by having the statement repeated to us countless times since early childhood, but that doesn't entitle us to be sure of it.)

One of the most basic beliefs we all have is that there is a world out there, a world of soil and mountains and trees and oceans and buildings and stars. How could one possibly doubt this? After all, we see these things constantly, don't we? Can there be any doubt that they exist? Not only do we believe they exist, but we believe they have certain characteristics, or properties. We believe that here before us is a real book: It is made of paper; it has print on it; it contains covers; the pages are white and the print is black—and so on. No matter how often we check, our senses seem to tell us the same thing. There it is—we can see and touch it and photograph it as well. We also believe it has a certain shape (approximately rectangular) and is blue in color, and

that it retains this shape and color until something happens to change it. The truth of all this seems so plain, wouldn't it be silly to doubt it? Isn't the truth of these beliefs so obvious that it's a waste of time to doubt them or even discuss the possibility of their being mistaken? What is there in all this that could possibly create a problem?

1. APPEARANCE AND REALITY

We have already had some indications that the perceptual process is not perfect. We all know, or think we know, that there are times when our senses lead us to make incorrect judgments; things aren't always the way they appear.

First of all, there are *illusions*. For example, (1) The trees on the distant hillside look grayish-blue, yet we believe they are green. (2) The stick looks bent when it is half immersed in water; when we pull the stick out it looks straight, but when we put it back in the water it looks bent again. Yet we are quite sure that it remains straight all the time, and that the bent appearance is an illusion. (3) The whistle of the train sounds higher in pitch as the train approaches and lower in pitch as the train recedes, yet we believe that the pitch is the same throughout. (4) The two parallel lines in the Müller illusion (one with arrows pointing inwards, the other with arrows pointing outwards) look different in length—the one with the arrows pointing outwards looks longer; yet when you measure the lines with a ruler they turn out to be the same length. (5) You place one hand in hot water, the other hand in cold water, then you place both hands in a vessel of lukewarm water. The lukewarm water feels cold to the one hand, warm to the other. Yet we believe the water *is* lukewarm all the time, it just *seems* hot or cold. (6) The stars look very small as we look up at the night sky; in fact they seem to be little points of light; yet, we are told, they are enormous spheres of gas like the sun, often much larger than the sun—but they certainly don't *look* that way.

When we believe that something *appears* (looks, sounds, smells, tastes, feels) to have one quality but actually *has* a different quality, we are misled by *perceptual illusions*. We encounter many of these every day. We become so accustomed to them that we learn to correct for them: The distant tower looks smaller than the nearby tower, but we learn not to believe that it really is smaller, for when we get within a hundred feet of it, it looks the same size as the other one does from the same distance.

Illusions can be of varying origin. Sometimes they are caused by some external condition: For example, forgetting that we have red glasses on, we say that the sky is red. (Anybody wearing red glasses would see the sky as red.) Sometimes illusions are caused by some internal condition, as when we take a drug like santonin and everything looks yellow for some time. In either case, we perceive something as having a quality that it doesn't have.

Secondly, there are *hallucinations*. We sometimes perceive, or seem to perceive, something when there's nothing there at all. The alcoholic, in a state of delirium tremens, sees pink rats going up and down the wall, but of course there are no pink rats at all. If you expect someone to come to the house, you may hear a knock at the door numerous times during the evening, when there is no one there. You may see water in the desert, but it is only a mirage.

What if we incorrectly take one thing, say a treestump seen in the forest at twilight, to be something else—a man? Is this a hallucination, because there is no man there, or an illusion, because we do see a treestump (although we don't take it as being that)? Or, for example, you are walking down a strange hallway and think you see a person resembling yourself in a floor-to-ceiling mirror. This is ordinarily called an optical illusion; yet if you really believe that there is someone there other than yourself, and there isn't, this would seem to make it count as a hallucination. Or: A Vietnam veteran on LSD sees every mailbox as an enemy gun-emplacement. Is this a hallucination because there's no enemy pillbox there, or is it an illusion because he is mistaking an object that's there for another that isn't?

As long as we know the nature of the error, it doesn't particularly matter what we call it. What does matter is that the error does not lie in our senses, but in the *judgments* we make. Perceptual errors are errors of judgment. If you merely looked and listened and drew no conclusions, you would not make any errors. The error comes when you mistakenly judge that this is an X when it isn't, or that X has quality Y when it doesn't: when we judge that the stick really is bent in water (because it looks bent when submerged), or that there really is an animal in the underbrush when it's only an unusual configuration of leaves and branches. When we make such claims we stick our necks out, so the speak—the claim goes beyond what our senses reveal to us at that moment. If we made no claims, there couldn't be any erroneous claims.

People often make mistaken perceptual claims because they "read too much into the script": Their judgments go far beyond the evidence on which they make the judgment. A person says he sees a star falling to the earth, but it's only a small rock or particle of dust entering the earth's atmosphere (a meteor). A person sees a moving light in the sky and says she sees a spaceship from another galaxy. It's true that she sees a light in the sky—others see it too—but the others don't jump at once to the conclusion that it's a spaceship. Maybe it is, but it would require a lot more evidence than seeing a light in the sky to prove it.

We are said to perceive *veridically* (truly, correctly) when we perceive something the way it is: We say there is a tree there, and there is; we say it has green leaves, and it does. When we make judgments based on illusion or hallucination, we are said to perceive nonveridically (falsely, incorrectly).

But how do we tell the difference? In our daily life we don't seem to have much trouble with this. If we make a mistaken claim on the basis of sight, touch, and so forth, how do we later discover that we were mistaken? It is *further sense-experience* that shows us that our original judgment was mistaken. We beat the underbrush and find no animal, but simply twigs and branches; we change our angle of vision and see that the steps don't lead to that doorway after all. The woman we thought we saw is really a statue; we think we see a light in the next room, but we look more carefully and see that it was only a reflection. If a momentary experience leads us to make a mistaken perceptual judgment, further experience is what leads us to discover that the original judgment was mistaken. The same senses that may lead us to make a mistake also enable us to correct that mistake.

Still, one might ask, if we distinguish—as we do—between the way something *is* and the way it *appears,* how do we get from the "appears" to the "is"? Isn't "appears" all we can get? How then do we make the transition from the one to the other?

If the question is put in this way, we seem to have encountered an insoluble problem: "We only see appearances, never reality; we never can get past appearances, so we can never know what things are *really* like." And yet in daily life we have no problem with this at all. We say confidently that the coin is round and only looks elliptical from certain angles, that the dress is dark blue but looks black under yellowish light; that the trees really are green though they look purplish-gray in the distance, and so on. How can we say such things if "we see only appearances"?— don't we have good reason to say that the trees are really green, that the coin is really round?

In daily life, we say that a thing *has* the quality it *appears* to have *under certain conditions.* We say the curtains in the room are blue; they look blue now, with the sunshine coming in through the windows. In artificial light they may look black. And in the dark they surely look black, as everything else does in the dark. Yet we don't say that at night everything—the curtains, the chairs and tables, and so on—have all *become* black. We say the curtains are blue all the time even though they look black in the dark. We take the way they look in sunlight to be the color they "really have." Is this because sunlight is the condition in which we see them most of the time? No, sometimes it isn't: People who sleep during the day and are awake at night seldom see the "true color" of the curtains. It's not because it's the most usual condition, but because sunlight is the condition in which the *maximum color discrimination* is possible. A black dress and a dark blue dress may both look black in artificial light, but in sunlight we can tell the difference. We want to be able to describe that difference, which we all perceive, and so we take that as the *standard condition.* Thus we say "It's really dark blue, but it looks black under artificial light," and we do not say "It's really black, but only looks dark blue in sunlight."

We might say that something is blue because it emanates light waves of a certain length, and each color has its associated wavelength. And though this is doubtless a fact discovered by modern physics, it's not the way we distinguish black from blue. People could do that long before they knew anything about light waves. Do we really want to say that people in ancient times couldn't distinguish one color from another because they didn't know anything about light waves? What physics has told us is that when we say something *is* blue (because it looks blue in sunlight) it *also* has a characteristic wavelength of light emanating from it; but we could distinguish blue from other colors as children long before we knew anything about physics.

We say that blood is red, because it looks red under standard conditions. But when we look at a drop of blood with a microscope, we see something that is largely transparent with a few flecks of red in it. Shall we say then that blood isn't really red, that it only looks red to the normal human eye? We might indeed say that; on the other hand, we might say that the color that something has is the color it appears to have under standard conditions *to the unaided eye.* Or we could say: "To the ordinary vision, it *is* red, but under a microscope it *is* . . .", thus employing a different criterion in each context.

Color is something that can be discerned only by sight. Shape can be discerned by sight *and* touch. We say that the coin is round, though as I look at it now it appears elliptical in shape. But it does always appear round when I see it from a perpendicular angle. The round appearance is the center of a *distortion series,* from which all the other appearances "radiate": The further we get from the perpendicular, the more elongated the shape appears to be. But in the case of shape we also have the sense of touch to go by: The coin

feels round. We can also trace a line around it with a pencil and the resulting shape on the paper will be (roughly) circular. And the stick *feels* straight even when it *looks* bent in water.

We could carry this further. Sir Arthur Eddington alleged that a table isn't really solid at all, though it feels solid enough—but this, he said, is an error. If we had "atomic vision," we would see that the molecules in a table are quite far apart from one another, at least in relation to their diameters—the table, in fact, is mostly empty space. It is, in fact, a "whirligig of atoms and electrons," and the rectangular solid thing we see is appearance only—the way the table appears to human senses.

Once again, we could say that, and doubtless again it is true that the table is composed of molecules that are comparatively far apart. But if we said "The table isn't really solid," this would be misleading. What we mean by saying "It is solid" isn't that its molecules are closely packed together: What we mean is that we can sit on it without its giving way beneath us; that we can't put our hands through it as we could with melting butter; that it doesn't have holes in it; and so on. If we said to someone "Careful, that table isn't solid" we would be warning the person that it isn't safe to sit or stand on it or to put your books on it. But such advice would be misleading: We would be telling our hearers that the table is like a rotten staircase that will give way beneath their feet. And it isn't like that; it does withstand our weight, it *is* safe to stand on, and so on. That's *what we mean when we say it is solid.* It's an interesting fact about the table that it's composed of billions of tiny molecules, but that bit of knowledge—again from modern physics—has nothing to do with our ordinary judgments about what is solid and what isn't. In the ordinary sense, which we are accustomed to using every day of our lives, the table *is* solid; just try it and see.

We have here an example of something we shall encounter over and over. It's not what we see that generates a problem, or causes a mental cramp. It is what we *say* about what we see. We could agree about the table and the molecules, yet when we try to express or formulate them, our words and Eddington's come out very differently. The facts themselves are interesting, but there is nothing contradictory about them; it is only people's *claims* about them that seem to contradict each other. We say the table is really solid; Eddington denies it; but what he means by "solid" is simply something different from what we mean. As one early American philosopher put it:

Light passes through a solid crystal. This many persons deem a standing miracle. What we see excites no surprise. The passage through solid crystal is the marvel. We know the difficulty which would attend the passage of our hand through the crystal, and we deem the passage of the light identical with the passage of the hand. Nothing is more fallacious than thus to construe the word "passage" in these different uses of it. The two operations possess the requisite analogy to make the word "passage" applicable to both, but its meaning in each application is what our senses reveal, and not what the identity of the word implies.[1]

When we want to discover not the qualities, but the very *existence,* of something, we tend to consider the verdict of our sense of touch as decisive. If you see what you think is a tree in the yard, and on going to it you find to your surprise that you can *walk through* the place where you thought it was without bumping into anything, then you would surely be inclined to say that it was an optical illusion of some sort, that "there really was no tree there." (You would also consult other people or discover whether a tree appeared on a photograph.) If you thought you saw two iron bars side by side, but when you tried to feel them with your fingers you found only one continuous surface, you would conclude that in spite of visual appearances it was one bar,

not two. But if you thought you saw one bar and on touching it found two (you could trace the shape of each one with your fingers), you would surely conclude that there were two bars that looked like one.

This would work for iron bars and trees and other physical things. Still, you can't touch shadows, and yet they are there; and you can't touch rainbows and yet they exist. But for that very reason we don't call a rainbow a physical *object;* it is a physical phenomenon—something that can be seen by all and photographed. A shadow or a rainbow isn't the *sort of thing* we can touch; so the standard conditions for determining whether there's really a shadow there are not the same as the standard conditions for the tree that casts the shadow. The criteria we use for determining which conditions are the standard ones varies from one context to another; yet in every case, it would seem, there are conditions of perception that are decisive for determining whether an object exists, and what its qualities are.

2. PERCEPTUAL SKEPTICISM

A *skeptic* is a person who doubts the truth of every judgment, at least within a certain field of inquiry. A person who is a skeptic about religion may not be a skeptic about anything else. A person who is a skeptic about moral judgments may not be at all skeptical about the truth of mathematics. But let us consider the *perceptual* skeptic, a person who says that we are *never* entitled to be sure about our perceptual judgments—or, in other words, that we never are in a position to *know* that our perceptual judgments are true.

"It's all a dream." The perceptual skeptic might make the following suggestion: Can't we be *dreaming* all the time? How do we know that your whole life isn't one vast dream? Maybe there isn't a world out there at all, and you're just dreaming the whole thing. True, you are now reading a book; but perhaps that

---

[1]Alexander B. Johnson, *A Treatise on Language* (Berkeley: University of California Press, 1948), p. 85. Originally published 1836.

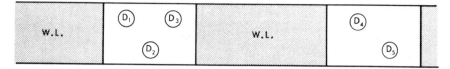

too is part of your dream. In your dreams you dream of things that never existed anywhere; and if your whole life is a dream, then it's *all* a series of dream-experiences, and perhaps there is no real physical world "out there" at all.

Common sense rebels at this conclusion. Don't we all know the difference between dreams and waking life? Like the difference between hallucinations and veridical perceptions, the difference may be hard to describe, but we have no particular trouble with it in practical life. We may not know for a moment on awakening whether we are still dreaming, but don't we discover this soon enough? You dream that your sister is dead, but you wake up and there she is, walking about. You find yourself in bed, the same bed you went to sleep in earlier, the same furniture and windows you have seen a thousand times, and you remember going to bed, getting drowsy, turning off the light. So you conclude that the experience you had of the South Seas must have been a dream.

But how do you know that it was the South Seas experience that was the dream? Maybe *that* was the reality, and your present experience is the dream; perhaps you were dreaming that you werc in your bedroom just waking up. How can you tell which is which?

It isn't that dreams are a weak copy of waking-life experiences; dreams can be as vivid as, or even more vivid than, waking-life experiences. Nightmares can be more vivid than anything you experience in waking hours. Rather, the dream-experiences are those that *don't fit in* with the rest. You eat lunch, you go to class, you return home, you read and watch television, you go to bed and sleep. Then you have all kinds of strange experiences (which we ordinarily call dreams) in

which you are far away or living long ago, or in which the law of gravity doesn't operate; perhaps you have several of these far-out experiences during the night and then you wake up to the old familiar surroundings. Not only do dream-experiences not fit in with waking-life experiences, they usually don't even fit in with each other: Your situation and nature in one dream is utterly different from what it is in another. Dreams are experiences all right, but they are anchorless; they do not *cohere* with the mass of experiences we call waking-life experiences.

When we are suddenly roused from a vivid dream, we may be momentarily dazed, not knowing the dream from the actuality. How do we establish which is which? Mere vividness does not decide the matter; the dream may be of nightmare intensity while the perception of our familiar surroundings may be comparatively dim. The deciding factor in the battle is what may be called the mass and the integration of the household troops. The bureau and windows of our familiar bedroom and the sound of a familiar voice throw out innumerable lines of connection that bring our everyday world around us again in irresistible volume. Against the great bulk of this world, and without any lodgment in it, the figures of our dream appear unsubstantial and fugitive, quickly dissolving for want of support; and it is just the recognition that what we have been experiencing will not fit into our common-sense world that we mean when we say wake from a dream.[2]

This is how we distinguish dreams from waking experiences; indeed, the ones that don't fit in are the ones we *call* dreams. But now the skeptic asks, "How do you know that *the whole thing*—what we call dreams and what you call waking-life experiences—isn't a dream? The experiences that fit in and those

[2]Brand Blanshard, *The Nature of Thought* (New York: Macmillan, 1939, Vol. 2), pp. 278-279.

that don't — maybe they're all a part of the *one big dream* which is your life. How do you know that this isn't so?"

The suggestion sounds profound, but one might object that it doesn't turn out to be anything more than a verbal maneuver. Suppose someone said to you, "All colors are blue," and you said "Ridiculous—there's red, there's green, etc.," and he said, "No, there's red-blue, there's green-blue, there's yellow-blue, and there's also blue-blue." What now does his contention come to? He uses different labels for colors than we do: When we call the leaves green, he says they are green-blue; when we call snow white, he says it white-blue. But what has this labeling gained us, except confusion? The colors haven't changed; they are exactly what they were before; all that has changed is what he *calls* them. His statement at first was surprising—"There's only one color, blue"—until we realize that the colors are the same as before, all that has changed is the labeling.

The same can be said of the skeptic's latest suggestion concerning dreams: "All experiences are dream-experiences." We all make the commonsense distinction between dream-experiences and waking-life experiences, and we have no difficulty in telling them apart. That there are those two main kinds of experiences remains a fact just as before. All that has changed is what the skeptic *calls* them. He has slapped the label "dreams" on *all* experiences, just as in the other example he slapped the label "blue" on all colors. But this did not extinguish one iota of the variety of colors (in the one case) and of experiences (in the other case) that can occur. You could apply the label "aspirin" to every bottle in your medicine cabinet, but that act of labeling doesn't turn every pill into an aspirin tablet.

The new labeler has only caused confusion. If he has his way, we can't even use the term "dream" to label the experiences that don't fit in with the rest of experience, because he has preempted the word "dream" to refer to *all* experiences, of whatever kind. What possible gain is there in this? We would not be changing any of the features of our experience; we would only be extending the use of a word—using it to describe all experience instead of the part that it has always been used to distinguish, and which everyone already understands.

One might say, "If the word means that much to you, *say* if you like that it's all a dream. But even if you do, within that one big dream we are all in all the time, you still have to distinguish between those 'islands' of experience that don't fit in with the others (the ones we have always called dreams) and the vast remainder that occur in a uniform and predictable way."

There is another consideration that favors waking life. On the basis of waking-life experiences we can *explain* dreams: The content of dreams can be explained by means of waking-life experiences we've had, often going back into childhood; but dreams do not in turn explain why we have the waking-life experiences we do—that we are now seeing a bed, tables, chairs, wallpaper, and so on. Science, as we shall see in Chapter 4, tries to provide explanations of why events occur as they do—and that which has explanatory power is accordingly favored over what does not.

One may try to undermine all these considerations, however, in this way: "None of this provides the real difference between dreams and waking life. The difference is that waking life experiences are experiences of a world out there—there really are chairs and tables in the room, quite apart from our perceiving them. But the same is not true of dreams: Dreams exist in the mind alone, and have no 'objective' existence—if the dreamer died he or she would have no more dreams, but the physical world would still be there. *That* is the difference between dreams and waking-life experiences: The dream-experiences don't report reality, and the waking-life experiences do."

This claim, however, brings up a very large

question, how our sense experiences are related to an independently existing world. We shall begin our consideration of this question in the next section. Meanwhile, skeptics have another arrow in their quiver, which we must consider first.

The evil demon. Rene Descartes (1596–1650), who is often called the founder of modern philosophy, attempted to doubt all that he was capable of doubting, to try to find something that he could not possibly doubt. And he found that he could easily doubt that there was a physical world; for, he said, he could easily imagine a powerful demon "feeding" him all the sense-experiences of sight, touch, smell, and so forth that he now has without there being a real world at all. The demon might write in his diary every night, "Made Descartes think there was a chair, table, etc."

How do you know that there isn't a powerful demon causing you to have the experiences that you do, planting the experiences in you to make you think there is a physical world, when in fact the whole physical world you believe in is nothing but a delusion? Skeptics can hardly claim to *know* there *is* such a demon; but they will turn the tables on us, asking how we know that there isn't. (And here the reply given in the case of dreams, that we distinguish between dream-experiences and waking-life experiences, won't suffice; for the demon causes *both* kinds of experience in us—though, of course, the demon cannot be perceived to cause either of them.)

Descartes wrote in his *Meditations:*

I will suppose, then, not that there is a supremely good God, the source of truth; but that there is an evil spirit, who is supremely powerful and intelligent, and does his utmost to deceive me. I will suppose that sky, air, earth, colours, shapes, sounds and all external objects are mere delusive dreams, by means of which he lays snares for my credulity. I will consider myself as having no hands, no eyes, no flesh, no blood, no senses, but just having a false belief that I have all these things . . . I suppose, therefore, that whatever things I see are illusions; I believe that none of the things my lying

memory represents to have happened really did so; I have no senses; body, shape, extension, motion, place are chimeras. What then is true? Perhaps only this one thing, that nothing is certain.[3]

"I have convinced myself" wrote Decartes, "that nothing in the world exists—no sky, no earth, no minds, no bodies; so am I not likewise nonexistent?" But if I did convince myself of anything then, *I* must have existed. If there is some deceiver, supremely powerful, supremely intelligent, who always deceives me, I exist; "Let him deceive me as much as he may, he will bring it about that, at the time of thinking that I am something, I am in fact nothing." If I think, then I the thinker must exist; if I doubt, then I the doubter must exist.

What is this "I" that thinks, doubts, wonders, believes? A body? No, a body is a physical thing like a chair or a tree, and the demon could delude me into thinking falsely that these exist. The demon could be feeding me hallucinations of body as well as of tables and trees. Or I could be dreaming all these things. But at least I am conscious of having all these experiences.

At this point I come to the fact that there is consciousness; of this and this only I cannot be deprived. *I* am, *I* exist; that is certain. For how long? For as long as I am experiencing . . . I know for certain that I am, and that at the same time it is possible that all these images, and in general everything of the nature of body, are mere dreams . . . What then am I? A conscious being. What is that? A being that doubts, understands, asserts, denies, is willing, is unwilling; further, that has sense and imagination . . . Even if I am all the while asleep; even if my creator does all he can to deceive me; how can any of these things be less of a fact than my existence?[4]

The deceiver must have someone to deceive, else there is no deception. I, who am

[3]René Descartes, *Meditations,* from (Meditation I and II.) *Descartes Selections,* Modern Students' Library. First published 1641 (New York: Scribners 1927), pp. 94–5, 96.

[4]Ibid., p. 99.

deceived, must exist. But not the "I" one ordinarily thinks of, a body of certain height and weight, but a mind that thinks, wonders, doubts, and so on, and also has sense-experiences even if those sense-experiences are not of a real world. The deceiver may deceive me into thinking there's a world including my body, but not that I, who am deceived, do not exist. I, the thinker, must exist.

I am, then, a thinking mind. But what is involved in saying that one is a mind, or has a mind, or is a person? This is a tangled issue that will be treated in detail in Chapter 6. At the moment we are concerned with the issue of knowledge and certainty. Of what, then, do I have knowledge? I know that I, a mind, exist; that I think, wonder, doubt, and so on; that I have certain feelings, moods, and emotions; and that I have sense-experiences.

Doesn't this last item require that there be a physical world from which the sense-experiences come? Not at all, says Descartes; the demon gives me the sense-experiences I have: *He,* not a physical world, causes the sense-experiences. The physical world is the main thing that he deceives us into believing exists. Is there any way that we can disprove the existence of such a demon?

Descartes tried to disprove the existence of the demon by attempting to prove the existence of a benevolent God who would not systematically deceive him. (Apparently God could deceive him sometimes, for such things as hallucinations and so on do occur.) We shall examine the arguments for God in due course. At the moment, it may be enough to say that virtually every commentator on Descartes has remarked that the introduction of God as a source of sensations was a mistake in Descartes' argument. Descartes eliminated the evil demon by postulating a nondeceiving God; but how did he substantiate the belief in such a God? How could he know that God was the source of sensations? Isn't the view that God causes one's sensations subject to

the same criticisms as the view that the evil demon causes them? Hasn't Descartes jumped from a demon-who-causes-experiences to a God-who-causes-experiences? And how can he have knowledge of the one any more than of the other?

Let us consider a hypothetical dialogue between an advocate of Descartes' demon-hypothesis (A) and a proponent of the idea that our experiences are caused by objects in the physical world (B).

A: Well, maybe we can't *know* that there is a demon causing our experiences; after all we can never see the demon. So the demon-hypothesis has not been proved. But on the other hand, how do you know that there isn't one? The demon-hypothesis hasn't been proved, but neither has it been disproved. So how can you be sure that the demon-hypothesis is false? Maybe we just have no way of knowing, one way or the other. Maybe there is such a demon as Descartes suggested, who is causing us to believe there is a world of trees and rocks and hills out there, whereas all the time we are being fed the experiences *as if* there were trees and rocks and so on, but there really aren't any—there is only the demon who is causing us to have the experiences that lead us to *believe* that there are trees and rocks. How can you know that this demon-hypothesis is not true?

B: But we haven't the slightest reason to believe the demon-hypothesis; there is not a shred of evidence in its favor.

A: That may be so. But even though we have (and perhaps can have) no evidence in its favor, neither have we any evidence *against* it. For all we know, the demon-hypothesis may be true, and we are being deceived all the time.

B: But what possible difference does it make to our experiences? Either way, we can perceive trees and rocks and hills—not only see and touch them but climb them. And we can distinguish these experiences from dream-experiences which don't fit into the main body of our experiences.

A: Doubtless it makes no practical difference; our experiences are the same either way. Still, it would be interesting to know whether there really are trees and rocks out there or whether the demon is feeding us experiences that cause us to believe falsely that there are trees and rocks. As philosophers we should be interested in that question, even though as practical human beings we may not care.

B: But even if the demon-hypothesis is true, there are some things the demon cannot deceive us about. Suppose that each night the demon writes in his diary, "Today again I deceived Jones into believing that there were really trees and rocks out there." But if he wrote, "Today I deceived Jones into believing that he exists," such a statement would be false, wouldn't it? He couldn't deceive Jones into believing that he exists, because Jones *would have to exist in order to be deceived:* "If I am deceived, I must exist." Even a powerful demon couldn't deceive if there's no one around to *be* deceived.

A: That was Descartes' argument: If I think, I must exist; if I doubt, I must exist; if I perceive, I must exist; if I am deceived, I must exist. Jones couldn't be deceived into believing that *he* exists, for he must exist before he can be deceived. But he *can* be deceived by the demon into thinking that trees, rocks, and so on exist. That hypothesis still hasn't been disproved.

B: But if Jones exists, then at least one physical organism exists. And Jones, or Jones' body, is a physical thing just as trees and rocks are physical things. So for the argument to get off the ground there has to be at least one physical thing. And if you admit that there has to be one real physical

thing, Jones, then there would seem to be no reason why there can't be lots of other physical things, such as rocks and trees.

A: That argument assumes that Jones is a physical body, or at least *has* a physical body. But Descartes argued that Jones could be deceived into thinking he is a physical body just as much as he could be deceived into thinking there are rocks and trees. Descartes believed that all that the demon-hypothesis entitled him to be sure of was that he, not a body but a *thinking mind,* exists—a mind that thinks, believes, doubts, is capable of being deceived, and so on. That he has a physical body is no more assured than that there are trees and rocks.

B: But that's a totally incorrect theory of what a person is. A person is a physical organism just as much as a person is a mind. In fact, isn't a person a physical organism who *has* a mind? So at least one physical organism must be assumed to exist after all.

At this point, however, we get into very deep waters; the nature of the self is now at issue. And on this issue there are conflicting opinions. We shall discuss this problem at length in Chapter 6.

The mad scientist. A currently fashionable version of the demon-hypothesis does assume that there is at least one physical organism, that of a scientist whose principal aim in life is to deceive us into believing that there are trees, rocks, and so on.

This scientist uses electrodes to induce experiences and thus carries out his deceptions, concerning the existence of rocks or anything else. He first drills holes painlessly in the variously colored skulls, or shells, of his subjects and then implants his electrodes into the appropriate parts of their brains, or protoplasm, or systems. He sends patterns of electrical impulses into them through the electrodes, which are themselves connected by wires to a laboratory console on which he plays, punching various keys and buttons in accordance with his ideas of how the whole thing works and with his deceptive designs . . . [5]

The scientist's purpose is to deceive. The ordinary person would probably assent to the statement "I know that there are rocks" (and so on). However, if there are no rocks, but only a scientist manipulating our brains so that we *think* there are rocks, then the statement "I know that there are rocks" cannot be true: We cannot know it if the belief is false. If we do know that there are rocks, then we can know that there is no scientist doing this to us. But no one can ever *know* that there is no scientist doing this. Therefore, no one can ever *know* that there are rocks, and so on.

This argument seems to be immune to the "ordinary language" arguments we considered earlier: I believe that there's a flat tire when I hear the thumping sound, but I know it when I get out and take a look; the doctor believes you have appendicitis when she taps your abdomen, but she knows it when she sees the inflamed appendix. As a way of distinguishing direct evidence from indirect evidence this suffices well enough; but if either the demon-hypothesis or the scientist-hypothesis is correct, then we are deceived into thinking that we see a flat tire or that we see an inflamed appendix—these are all parts of the Grand Deception. So even though this distinction between knowing and not knowing is sufficient for practical purposes, advocates of the demon-hypothesis and the scientist-hypothesis will argue that it doesn't go deep enough: In both cases persons are being deceived into thinking that physical objects are really there. What then remains? Only the deceiver (demon or scientist) and the person who is deceived. And again the question arises (which we must here postpone), What is the nature of the de-

ceived entity—a mind, a body, or both? As we shall see in Chapter 6, a great deal hangs on how this issue is resolved.

3. REPRESENTATIVE REALISM

We need not resort to far-out hypotheses like evil demons and mad scientists in order to arrive at skeptical conclusions. We turn now to a much more "commonsense" view. It is called *realism* because it holds that there are really rocks and trees and so on out there, existing independently of ourselves—that is, existing whether or not any perceivers exist. It is called *representative* because it holds that we are never directly aware of these physical objects; rather we are aware of the sense-impressions that somehow represent them.

The mind "hath acquaintance only with its own ideas," said John Locke; but he used the word "idea" more broadly than we do today. We speak of having ideas "in our minds," but when we see a red rose we do not call the red we see an idea. Rather, in the terminologoy of David Hume, it is an *impression,* or sense-impression. When we see a red object we are having an impression of red, but when we close our eyes and imagine it, we are having an idea of red. Our knowledge of the world is obtained through our sense-impressions of sight, touch, hearing, smell, and taste. In vision, for example, light waves (they were "corpuscles" in Locke's day, prior to the wave theory of light) emanate from the tree, some of which strike the eye, whereupon an impulse or message is conveyed along the optic nerve to the brain, and we have a sense-impression of the tree. Sometimes, as in the theory of the ancient Greek philosopher Democritus (ca. 460 B.C.), the tree is thought of as giving off tiny replicas of itself, some of which strike the eye and constitute our sense-impressions. Locke's own view waffles somewhat between the representative view we are now discussing and the causal theory to be dis-

---

[5] Peter Unger, "A Classical Form of Skeptical Argument," in *Ignorance* (Oxford: Oxford University Press, 1975), p. 13.

cussed below. At any rate, our knowledge of the physical world comes via sense-impressions, and it is these sense-impressions of which we have direct knowledge.

What could be more obvious than this view? one might ask; isn't it just plain physiology, which we all accept? If so, the seeds of skepticism are quickly sown in this account. For if we can know only that we have certain sense-impressions, how can we know that there is a physical order beyond them, which continues to exist whether we have sense-impressions or not? Isn't the physical world merely an unknowable source-of-sensations, much like the evil demon of Descartes' hypothesis?

Imagine an old-fashioned telephone exchange, before the advent of direct dialing. The operator receives an incoming call, hears a voice at the other end of the wire, records the number, and connects the customer with that number. All he knows of the people placing or receiving the calls are the voices he hears through the wires. He never sees the customers themselves; he only hears the voices as they are transmitted via the telephone to his end of the wires. In the same way, all we know of an external world is what comes in via the optic nerve, the auditory nerve, and so forth—the impressions of sight and sound and so on which we get after the nerves and brain have received the appropriate stimulus from the outside world. Each perceiver is like the operator of the telephone exchange whose knowledge of the customers is limited to the sound of their voices as conveyed along the wire. The situation is dramatically described by the late-nineteenth-century philosopher Karl Pearson:

How close then can we actually get to this supposed world outside ourselves? Just as near but no nearer than the brain terminals of the sensory nerves. We are like the clerk in the central telephone exchange who cannot get nearer to his customers than his end of the telephone wires. We are indeed worse off than the clerk, for to carry out the analogy properly we must suppose him *never to have been outside the telephone exchange, never to have seen a customer or any one like a customer—in short, never, except through the telephone wire, to have come in contact with the outside universe.* Of that "real" universe outside himself he would be able to form no direct impression; the real universe for him would be the aggregate of his constructs from the messages which were caused by the telephone wires in his office. About those messages and the ideas raised in his mind by them he might reason and draw his inferences; and his conclusions would be correct—for what? For the world of telephonic messages, for the type of messages that go through the telephone. Something definite and valuable he might know with regard to the spheres of action and of thought of his telephonic subscribers, but outside those spheres he could have no experience. Pent up in his office he could never have seen or touched even a telephonic subscriber *in himself.* Very much in the position of such a telephone clerk is the conscious ego of each one of us seated at the brain terminals of the sensory nerves. Not a step nearer than those terminals can the ego get to the "outer world," and what in and for themselves are the subscribers to its nerve exchange it has no means of ascertaining. Messages in the form of sense-impressions come flowing in from that "outside world," and these we analyze, classify, store up, and reason about. But of the nature of "things-in-themselves," of what may exist at the other end of out system of telephone wires, we know nothing at all.[6]

In this theory, the sense organs, nerves, and brain are the connecting links between the physical objects outside and the sense-experiences that occur after the brain has been stimulated by way of the sense organs. But brain, sense organs, and nerves are just as much physical objects as are table, trees, and rocks. If we are acquainted with them, then *they* must be sense-experiences also. But a sense-experience can hardly be the connecting link between physical objects and sense-experiences. On the other hand, if we are *not* acquainted with them, how can we know that

_____
[6] Karl Pearson, *The Grammar of Science* (Oxford: Everyman Library, 1892), pp. 57–58.

the sense-organs, nerves, and brains exist? At this point the analogy of the telephone exchange breaks down. The telephone operator can be acquainted with nothing except the sounds that come in along the wires of the exchange; but how can he then know that there are wires, or that he is in an exchange at all? It would appear that the entire telephone exchange has now collapsed into the operator.

What has happened? The telephone exchange theory proceeds on the assumption that it itself is not true. In the very process of trying to show that we have no knowledge of an outside world but only of our own sense-experiences (messages at the end of a wire), it has assumed that there is an outside world and that we have knowledge of it—at least enough to be able to say that there are things in the outside world that stimulate sense organs, which in turn stimulate nerves and send messages to the brain. Only if we know these things can our analogy get into operation; but if the telephone exchange theory is true, we can never know these things. The sounds we hear at the end of the wire are causally related to the exchange; later the very possibility of knowing that there is such a thing as an exchange has to be denied, but meanwhile it has played an indispensable part in the analogy. Once we are clear about this, we shall have to reject the analogy; we cannot both know that there is an exchange (as the theory requires us to) and also not know (as the theory also requires, since we know only the sounds at the end of the wire). Doesn't it seem as if the representative theory of perception, starting with commonsense beliefs shared by almost everyone, leads us into an utter skepticism about the existence of nature of a physical world?

Not necessarily: At this point Locke's successor in British philosophy, Bishop George Berkeley (1685–1753), steps in to rescue us from the skepticism in which the representative theory seems to land us. But at a cost, as we shall see.

4. BERKELEY'S IDEALISM

Berkeley attempted to solve the problem by getting rid of the world-out-there. No such world exists, he said, and we could have no knowledge of it if it did; all we have knowledge of is our sense-impressions. (Berkeley, like Locke, called these "ideas"; hence the term for his theory is *"idealism"*—taken not from the word "ideal" but from the word "idea.") And so we are easily led to Berkeley's main conclusion: *All that exists is minds and their ideas* (not merely all we can know, but all that exists). That's all we need, and "that's all there is, there ain't no more." There are not trees *and also* representations of them called experiences-of-trees, with veridical perception consisting of a correspondence between our tree-impressions and the trees, and hallucination consisting of having tree-impressions when no trees exist. If there were both these things—trees and tree-experiences—how could we ever compare the two to determine whether there is a correspondence? Have you ever compared a tree with your experience of a tree to determine whether there was a correspondence, perhaps some kind of resemblance, between them? Of course not, Berkeley would say; you couldn't; the suggested experiment doesn't even make sense. All we experience are our experiences, not something outside them to "correspond" to them.

The first response Berkeley's view creates is simply that of indignant disbelief: "What! No trees and mountains out there? He must be mad!" Samuel Johnson, when asked how he would refute Berkeley's view, kicked his foot against a stone and said, "I refute it thus!"

But Johnson's refutation was no refutation at all. Berkeley didn't believe all our experiences were hallucinations. He didn't deny that a certain visual experience is followed by a certain touch-experience (which is all that Johnson experienced when he kicked the stone). He didn't deny that there was a stone, or a tree, or a chair. He only denied the existence of anything outside the realm of our sense-impressions. Berkeley did indeed believe that there are chairs, but *not* that our chair-experiences "represent" anything existing outside us and independently of us. He believed, rather, that "chair" and all other physical-object words are names for *recurring patterns,* or complexes, *of sense-experiences,* and nothing else. Berkeley would say, "If by 'physical objects' you mean anything other than our sense-experiences, I insist that they do not exist, nor could we know that they existed even if they did. But if by 'physical objects' you mean groups or complexes of sense-experiences, then they undoubtedly *do* exist— indeed, we are aware of them every waking moment of our lives, since we are constantly having sense-experiences that fall into ordered patterns or groups."

What exactly is meant by saying that a chair, or any other physical object, is a pattern, or complex, of sense-experiences? This is somewhat difficult to convey in a few words; let us first take an example. Consider a table, which we believe to have a rectangular top. Now as I look at this tabletop (ordinarily speaking), I find that my experience has the following characteristics:

1. The appearance of the tabletop varies in systematic ways. If I move away from it, it appears to get smaller, and when I approach it it appears to become larger again. When I view it from above, it looks rectangular, but if I look at it from any other angle, it looks more like a trapezoid with the acute angles on the nearer side. The apparent shape and size vary systematically with the angle of vision.

2. As I stand still, it continues to look the same; but when I move, the apparent shape changes, and when I get back to my former position, it looks as it did before. After I have had a little experience of the way the apparent shape changes, I can predict how it will look after my next change of position: The whole series of sense-experiences is systematic and predictable.

3. As I move, the visual sense-experiences from moment to moment resemble one another: Shape A shades into shape B, B into C, C into D, etc., though A may not greatly resemble D. Apparent shape 1 may not resemble apparent shape 50, but the two are connected by a series of apparent shapes, each of which closely resembles the one on each side of it. Again, the change is gradual and regular.

4. There is no discontinuity in the series. As I look, or walk while looking, there is no moment at which I do not have the sense-experience (unless I turn my head or blink). The shape does not jump out of my field of vision and then pop back into it again somewhere else.

5. The series of apparent shapes has a center from which the others deviate in a progressive *distortion series.* (Referring back to our earlier example: The round apparent shape of the penny is the center around which all the elliptical ones congregate.)

6. My visual experiences act as *signs* of my tactual ones: If I go up to what I believe (on the basis of my visual sense-experiences) to be the table, I have tactual sense-experiences. My visual experiences are lightly correlated with tactual ones. Occasionally they are not, to be sure: If I don't know I am looking in a mirror I may approach what I believe to be the table, only to bump into the mirror—there will be no tactual sense-experience corresponding to the visual one. The tactual experience will be of the mirror, not of the table; there is no table beyond the mirror.

In short, the tabletop sense-experiences form an *orderly series.* The entire series of shapes constitutes, as it were, a *family:* They all "belong together" in a different way from the way the series of shapes we see looking at a coin do—these constitute another, and very different, family. A physical object is nothing more or less that a *family of sense-experiences*. When we have hallucinations, on the other hand, we have sense-experiences which don't belong to a family: They are *"wild"* (unattached). The pink rats the man sees in a state of intoxication are "wild," for they belong to no family.

It is a fortunate fact about the universe that the vast majority of our sense-experiences belong to families, thus making them, on Berkeley's analysis, real things—what we would call "physical objects." We could easily imagine a state-of-affairs in which this would not be so. Imagine for a moment that all our sense-experiences occurred hit-or-miss, with visual sense-data hopping all about our visual field, changing shapes and sizes in chaotic and unpredictable ways, each visual sense-experience discontinuous with the next one, coming and going and changing character every moment, visual sense-experiences not being followed by tactual ones, and tactual ones occurring unpredictably without visual ones having occurred to warn us. You could easily imagine most or even all of your sense-data being "wild," and in this case there would be no such things as physical objects, since there would be no such things as families of sense-experiences. One might say that there would be at least one family present, your own body. But that could also be otherwise: You might have the chaotic series of sense-experiences without even having any of the sense-experiences you now attribute to your own body. But fortunately, our experiences are not like this: Most of our sense-experiences belong to families.

The criterion we actually use in determining whether something is a hallucination, says Berkeley, is to observe whether the sense-experience in question belongs to a family. In doing this, we relate our sense-experiences *to one another*. We do not do what representative realism would seem to require: relate our sense-experiences to a reality outside our sense-experience to see whether they correspond. According to Locke, if we have a table-experience and there's no table, it's a hallucination; and if there is a table, it's not a hallucination (it is then *veridical*—a "true" perception). But we could never apply such a correspondence test, for we could never get outside our sense-experiences to discover whether or not there is something outside them to correspond to them. We never in fact even attempt to apply such a test: We compare our sense-experiences with one another, not with something else that isn't sense-experience. It is true, of course, that in hallucination "there is no table there"; but this means, according to Berkeley, only that in hallucination there is no family of table-experiences. It takes only a little time to discover whether or not the experience we are having is wild. The distinction between veridical perception and hallucination is always to be found in the relation of sense-experiences *to one another*—specifically, in whether or not they belong to a family. Those that don't belong to a family we call hallucinations.

Much misinterpretation of Berkeley has occurred on this point. Some have alleged that according to Berkeley everything is imaginary. But there is plenty of difference between a real table and an imaginary table. I can't sit on an imaginary table, or place books on it, nor will it hold my weight if I try to step on it: The sense-experiences don't cohere as a family. Samuel Johnson refuted nothing when he kicked a stone and exclaimed, "I refute it thus!" because Berkeley, of course, did not deny the existence of the stone. He would have said merely that a stone is a family of sense-experiences (not at all a hallucination), and that kicking the stone only confirmed his point: Visual stone-experiences are followed by tactual stone-experiences, just as they could be expected to do in any well-ordered family of sense-experiences.

And as for dream-experiences, they are also "wild" in relation to the well-ordered series of sense-experiences that constitute what we call waking life. These are also "outside the family." All these perceptual distinctions that we make—illusions, hallucinations, dreams— are made by relating and comparing sense-experiences *to one another,* not by comparing sense-experiences with some unknown something to which our sense-experiences "correspond." The test for veridicality is *coherence* among sense-experiences, not correspondence with something that is *not* sense-experience.

Esse est percipi. We must now consider another aspect of idealism. According to idealism, physical objects are families of sense-experiences. But obviously experiences do not exist unexperienced. Physical objects, then, do not exist unexperienced either.

This last assertion certainly conflicts sharply with our commonsense beliefs. We believe that physical objects continue to exist whether they are experienced or not. Idealism is committed to denying this. According to idealism, *esse est percipi* ("to be is to be perceived") as far as physical objects are concerned. Idealism says about physical objects the same thing that common sense says about experiences of all kinds: That they do not and cannot exist unexperienced; and if they cannot do so singly, combinations of them (by which idealism defines physical objects) cannot do so either. Pains and pleasures do not exist unexperienced: for them to exist *is* for them to be experienced. The same applies to trees and tables. There can be no reality apart from experience, says idealism. Tables, trees, and other physical objects are families of experiences.

But, you might say, surely the table doesn't cease to exist when I go out of the room! No, not if someone else stays in the room and continues to perceive it. But suppose everyone leaves the room; does the table then cease to exist? Yes, if no one is having table-experiences. If we think no one is in the room, and we leave for 15 minutes and then go back, we

may find our friend Jones saying, "It existed all the time; I was looking through a peephole in the wall, and I can assure you that I had table-experiences while you were gone exactly as I did when you were here." No idealist would deny this. But suppose that *no* one is in the room—no person, no organism of any kind that could have table-experiences. Does the table exist during that period? No; *esse est percipi,* and there is no *esse* because there is no *percipi.*

"Well, what difference does it make?" one might ask. "As long as the table is always there when we get back, what do we care? The question whether it exists during intervals between perceptions can make no difference whatever to our actual experiences." The idealist, of course, would not deny this. Still, whether it is a practical question or not, it would be interesting to know what the answer is, and how it can be known to be true.

"Physical objects do exist during interperceptual intervals, and I can easily prove it," one might suggest. "Bring a motion-picture camera into the room, set it going, and then have everyone leave. Come back a few minutes later, develop the film, and project it on the screen. We will then all witness the exciting drama of table-continuing-to-exist-during-our-absence." But the idealist would not be convinced by any such experiment. The motion-picture camera is itself a physical object, and is also, according to idealism, a family of sense-experiences that also ceases to exist when not experienced. The camera, the table, and indeed the room itself and the building it is a part of are all in the same boat; *esse est percipi* applies equally to all of them. Moreover, our account of the entire series of events is all given in terms of experiences: we have table-experiences, then table-and-camera experiences, then other-room experiences, then table-and-camera experiences again, and later table-projected-on-a-screen experiences. No one, certainly not the idealist, doubts that we have this sequence of experiences. And that is all there is—just this sequence of experiences. Nothing apart from the series of experiences exists, and we wouldn't know it even if it did.

Our frustration at this point may be similar to that of the boy who was told by his brother that the street light went out whenever his eyes were shut. He watched the street light intently, studiously shut his eyes, then furtively opened them again for a moment; the street lamp was shining as usual. The little boy said: "But you told me it went out!" "Yes," said his brother, "when your eyes are shut; but when you peeked, they were open." How could the boy ever prove otherwise? Is idealism, as one eighteenth-century critic remarked, "utterly absurd, and utterly irrefutable"?

Here is another argument: "We have to believe that physical objects exist unperceived in order to account for what we see when we perceive them again." You light a fire in the fireplace, watch it burn for a time, then leave the room for half an hour. When you return, nothing is left in the fireplace but a pile of glowing embers. Surely the fire must have burned down even though no one was perceiving it; how else can you explain the fact that there were burning logs on the fire when you left and only embers when you returned? The wood must have burned while you were gone, and in order to burn, it must have existed while you were gone. Or: Many times you have seen a house and also its shadow; this time you see the shadow but are not yet in a position to see the house. But surely the house must be existing at this moment even though neither you nor anyone else is perceiving it, else what would be casting the shadow?

In these examples we are appealing to well-established laws of nature about the behavior of fire and shadows. But, the idealist reminds us, we have known these laws to hold true only for cases we could observe; we have no justification for extending them to unobserved cases. For example, one might say: "Every time I have observed X I have observed Y; therefore it is probable that this time

when I observe X I shall observe Y." But this says nothing whatever about what happens when I do *not* observe X. No observation can possibly tell me what exists when nobody observes it. Even if physical objects continue to exist when no one perceives them, how can we have any reason to believe that they do, since no one can observe them existing unobserved?

Weak vs. strong idealism. It is misleading, however, to say that "even if physical objects do continue to exist unobserved . . ." for this assumes something that Berkeley would never grant, namely that it is possible, or even conceivable, for physical objects to exist unobserved. According to Berkeley, it's not that physical objects *might* exist unobserved but that we can't know even if they did (weak idealism). Rather, to speak of physical objects existing unobserved is a *contradiction in terms* (strong idealism)—or as Berkeley called it, a "manifest repugnancy," such as a square circle. Remember that physical objects are *nothing but* families of sense-experience. We don't believe that sense-experiences can exist unexperienced—we all admit that that's a contradiction in terms—and since physical objects are only complexes of sense-experiences, the physical objects too can't exist unobserved. The reasoning goes like this:

1. We do have knowledge of physical objects (trees, mountains, buildings, etc.).
2. Our knowledge is limited to our experiences. Therefore,
3. Physical objects are experiences (families of experiences).
4. But experiences can't exist unexperienced, so physical objects can't exist unexperienced either.

The idealist says that if we find this conclusion surprising it's because we have really never digested the initial premise, that physical objects *are* families of sense-experiences. We are surprised by the conclusion only because we still have lurking in the back of our minds the idea of tables and trees as inhabiting a world of things that are independent of minds—that is, of tables and trees as *not* being families of sense-experiences. Once we really grasp this, we shall no longer bring up any question of their existing unperceived, any more than we do now in the case of pains or pleasures, thoughts or ideas.

Causation of sense-experiences. But don't our sense-experiences have a *cause?* Ordinarily we say that our experience of the tree is caused by the tree itself, existing independently of our perception. This avenue is not open to Berkeley, who said that the tree simply *is* the complex of sense-experiences. But what then causes us to have the sense-experiences that we do?

Berkeley *might* have said, "Since physical objects are families of sense-experiences, when we say that A causes B, we are saying that A is regularly followed by B *in our experience*. We cannot use the idea of cause, so useful *in* our experience, to go *beyond* experience, where in any case we would have no knowledge of it." (We shall discuss the nature of cause in Chapter 5.)

But, good bishop that he was, Berkeley did not say this. He said that all our sense-experiences are caused directly by God. The reason the sense-experiences occur in an orderly way—barring hallucinations and so on—is that God gives us our sense-experiences, and he does so in an orderly way so that we can make predictions on the basis of them and thus guide our actions accordingly. God *could* have made our experiences so chaotic that there were no families-of-sense-experiences at all, and hence no regularities of experience that we could call physical objects. But God, being good, has chosen instead to give us orderly sets of sense-experiences. He plants these in our minds directly: He does not need the intermediary of the realist's physical objects. (Since we could not know the existence of these physical objects anyway, they wouldn't do us any good even if they did ex-

ist.) Reality thus consists of *minds* and *their experiences*. God is an infinite mind, and you and I finite minds. Thus, there are minds (God's and ours) and their experiences (God's and ours). Experiences are events in the history of minds. That is all there is—there is no more. God causes us to have our experiences in the order that we have them. There is no need for anything else.

Why is it that when we both look in the same direction we have similar sense-experiences? Because God feeds us similar sense-experiences in similar contexts, so that we may communicate with one another. If you saw a tree where I saw an elephant, and the next moment you saw in that place a sofa and I a bushel of apples, we would not be able to communicate. But by correlating the series of your experiences with mine, God makes prediction and communication possible. God works in an orderly manner—so orderly, indeed, that God not only enables different minds to communicate but also regulates the course of various persons' sense-experiences, so that we can notice regularities within the total series. Thus is science made possible. The laws of nature are the will of God manifested in the orderly series of sense-experiences that we have.

Berkeley's theory has been aptly commented on in the following limerick:

There was a young man who said "God
Must think it exceedingly odd
If he finds that this tree
Continues to be
When there's no one about in the Quad."

Reply

Dear Sir: Your astonishment's odd.
I am always about in the Quad.
And that's why the tree
Will continue to be
Since observed by

Yours faithfully,

God.[7]

---

[7]By an Oxford scholar, Ronald Knox, a critic of Berkeley.

Criticisms. (1) Many readers who have followed Berkeley up to this point may throw up their hands at his introduction of God into the scene. First, Berkeley began by saying "The mind hath knowledge only of its own ideas [experiences]." If this is true, how can we know that there is a God who causes the experiences, since God is not himself one of the experiences? If knowledge is only of sense-experiences and God is not a sense-experience, how can we know there is a God who causes the sense-experience? If we do know this, then we know something other than sense-experiences after all. And if we *can* know something other than sense-experiences, namely God, why can't we just as well bring in a world of independently existing physical objects as the causes of our experiences? Hasn't Berkeley, in bringing in God as cause-of-experience, betrayed his own basic premise, that we can have knowledge only of our own experiences?

(2) Berkeley said that we can have knowledge only of our minds and their ideas; but what of *other people's minds?* I can have knowledge of my own experiences; one family of experiences is the desk, another the tree out there, still another your body and clothing. I cannot have your experiences; I can only observe your body, its movements, facial expressions, and so on. My knowledge of you is limited to these sense-experiences of mine. Similarly, your knowledge of me is limited to those sense-experiences of yours which constitute my body. This is surely a very strange situation. To you, I can be nothing more than certain sense-experiences of yours; and to me, you can be nothing more that certain sense-experiences of mine. But *I* know that I am more than certain sense-experiences of yours, and presumably you know that you are more than certain sense-experiences of mine. Aren't we *both* minds who have sense-experiences? But how can either of us know this? If all I can know is that I (a mind) exist, together with the experiences of that mind, then, since my knowledge is limited to my experiences,

shouldn't I believe that my mind and its experiences are *all that exist?* In other words, shouldn't I be a *solipsist?* Solipsism (myself-alone-ism) is the belief that all that exists is my mind and its experiences. I have no knowledge of, and therefore no reason for believing in, the existence of minds other than my own. So I assert that mine is the only one.

Almost no one in the history of thought has been a solipsist. We all believe there are other persons, with minds like ours, who think and feel and have sense-experiences as we do. A person would be in a curious position who said "I am so convinced of solipsism that I believe everyone ought to be a solipsist!" If a solipsist writes books to advance his views, to whom is he addressing them, since he believes there are no minds other than his own to read and understand them? Besides all this, solipsism breaks down into as many views as there are persons: If Jones is a solipsist, he believes that only Jones exists; but if Smith is a solipsist, she believes that only Smith exists — which is a very different view, and in fact conflicts with the first one. It can't be true both that Jones is the only person existing *and* that Smith is the only person existing.

Berkeley was not a solipsist; but how did he avoid being one? Isn't solipsism the view that his own premises would drive him to? Berkeley, it should be noted, said that "Esse est percipi" applies only to physical objects, not to minds: For minds the motto is "Esse est percipere" (to be is to perceive, rather than to *be* perceived). But how could Berkeley know this? If human minds have no windows to observe anything but the course of their own sense-experiences, it would appear that Berkeley's mind must have had at least a door, else how could he know, on his own premises, that other minds than his exist?

(3) According to Berkeley, the statement that physical objects exist unexperienced is self-contradictory, because physical objects are families of sense-experiences and sense-experiences can't exist unexperienced. One's

first reaction to this definition—"Physical objects just *are* (families of) sense-experiences"—is that such a definition is absurd. "You can define terms as you wish," we may say; "I can define 'circle' as an eighteen-sided polygon," and thus the statement "Circles have no corners" will be self-contradictory by that definition. But why in the world should one accept such a definition?"

Berkeley, of course, argues that there *is* a good reason for accepting that definition: that if you do not, you are left with complete skepticism about the existence of physical objects. Try, he says, to imagine something as existing apart from a mind:

But, say you, surely there is nothing easier than to imagine trees, for instance, in a park, or books existing in a closet, and nobody by to perceive them. I answer you may so, there is no difficulty in it; but what is all this, I beseech you, more than framing in your mind certain ideas which you call books and trees, and at the same time omitting to frame the idea of anyone that may perceive them? But do not you yourself perceive or think of them all the while? This therefore is nothing to the purpose; it only shows you have the power of imagining or forming ideas in your mind; but it does not show that you can conceive it possible the objects of your thought may exist without the mind. To make out this, it is necessary that you conceive them existing unconceived or unthought of, which is a manifest repugnancy.[8]

The statement "Physical objects cannot be thought of as existing apart from a thinking mind" is ambiguous, however. If you mean that

Physical objects cannot be thought-of-as-existing apart from a thinking mind,

this is doubtless true. You cannot think of them or anything else as existing without first having a mind to think with. But this should

---

[8]George Berkeley, *Principles of Human Knowledge* (paragraph 23).

not be confused with a very different statement containing the same words,

Physical objects cannot be thought of as existing-apart-from-a-thinking-mind,

which is not trivial at all, and in fact is false: We do think of them in this way all the time. I cannot think without a mind, but I can think of something as *existing* without a mind. Thought cannot exist without minds, but this doesn't prove that tables and trees cannot exist without minds. Whether they do exist or not—and perhaps we can't know whether they do or not—at least we *think* of them as existing without minds. Doesn't the realist think of them thus—even if, as Berkeley said, the realist is wrong? And the same with perception as with thought: you can't perceive without a mind any more than think without a mind, but it doesn't follow that *what* you perceive can't exist without a mind. Maybe it doesn't, of course, but at least we can't prove that it doesn't by Berkeley's argument. *Perceiving* can't occur without a mind, but *that which you perceive* can—at least it is logically possible. Whether there is some positive way of defining "physical object" other than as a family of sense-experiences remains to be seen. But if the logical barrier is removed, we may go further.

(4) If we think—correctly or incorrectly—of physical objects existing apart from a mind, then perhaps we should take another look at weak idealism, which says that perhaps objects may exist apart from minds, but that we have no reason to believe that they do because we can't observe them existing unobserved. But now let us ask whether even this is true. In daily life we do not hesitate to believe that physical objects exist unobserved. If I leave the tub running in the bathroom and come back later and find that it is full of water, I assume that water flowed into the tub during my absence—how else, I believe, could

I explain how the water got there? And so on. The idealist (weaker version) argued, however, that there is no way of proving this: I cannot perceive it unperceived, and no argument will enable me to conclude anything about the unobserved when all the data we have to go on are about the observed. Thus the view that physical objects exist unobserved, even if not self-contradictory, is one for which there is absolutely no evidence.

But is this true? *Is* there no evidence? If I am alone in the room, and I shut my eyes for a moment, must I say that there was no table during the moment I shut my eyes? If the table is covered completely by a cloth, so that I see the cloth but not the table, must I say that the cloth exists but not the table?

According to Berkeley, the series of my sense-experiences are just what they would be *if* the tub and the water had existed during my absence, but of course they didn't, because there were no table-experiences during that time (except for God's—God held the fort and kept the table existing by perceiving it even if no other perceiver was there). But why go this circuitous route if we can say the tub and water and table *did* actually exist during my absence? Well, we can *say* it, but what *evidence* can we adduce? We can't perceive it existing unperceived, and we can't deduce its existence when it is unperceived from its existence when it is perceived.

In ordinary life we claim knowledge, not only from *observation* but from *inference*. We see bear-tracks in the mud, and we infer that a bear was there even though we didn't see one. We wake up and find the yard is wet, and we infer that it rained during the night while we were asleep. Why can't we say, similarly, that the existence of physical objects unobserved is an inference? We didn't *see* the bathtub fill up during those few minutes we were gone, but we *infer* that it did, and isn't our inference justified? Saying that the tub did exist during those minutes, and that water continued to enter it during that time, is the *best*

explanation we have of why the tub was full when we returned. How else would we account for it?

The same with the existence of other minds: I ask you "What would it take for me to persuade you to go to Mazatlan for four days during the next fortnight?" and you think for a moment (or furrow your brows and at least give the appearance of thinking) and then answer "Since I have other important plans for next week, I wouldn't do it for less than ten thousand dollars." Surely the best explanation of the fact that you respond thus to my question is that you are (or have) a mind and that you think, deliberate, choose, and give reasons for your choices, just as I do. How else would I explain the occurrence of the sentences I hear in the English language coming from your lips?

It seems that Berkeley will accept only *direct* evidence: Seeing or touching a tree is direct evidence, the evidence of our senses. But what's wrong with *indirect* evidence, one may ask, such as seeing only a tree's shadow? We don't observe the table under the cloth (though we could if we lifted the cloth), but we infer that it is still there; how else would the cloth stay up there? If we see the cat sleeping under the table, but our view of the cat is partially obscured by the table-leg, aren't we entitled to say that the whole cat is there, not just the part we are seeing? We *infer* from the part that we see that the whole cat is there, and isn't that a justified inference too? We use indirect evidence every day, almost every moment, of our waking lives. What is so bad about it, that we can't accept it?

Berkeley said that what's wrong with indirect evidence is that our knowledge is limited to our own sense-experiences, and we have no sense-experiences of part of the cat. And that is after all Berkeley's fundamental premise: We know only what we experience. That fundamental premise is something we have yet to come to grips with. The views we have yet to consider have different ways of handling such a premise. We shall now consider the first of these views, the theory call *phenomenalism*.

5. PHENOMENALISM

Of all the features of idealism, the one that is most likely to elicit scorn and disbelief is "Esse est percipi"—to be is to be perceived. That the physical world exists unperceived is not only one of our most deeply held beliefs, it is one that we feel completely justified in believing—not because we perceive it existing unperceived, which would be a contradiction in terms, but because it shows absolutely no signs of depending for its existence on anyone's perceiving it. The bathtub fills with water whether we are there or not; the house is still there even if we have left it for years; people die and the stars and the earth continue as before, and we have every reason to believe that they will continue when you and I are no longer here.

At the same time, it seems plausible to say—as Locke and Berkeley both held—that "the mind hath knowledge only of its own ideas." Whatever exists out there, we can know only though our experiences; and isn't the content of these experiences all we can really know?

The theory called *phenomenalism* attempts to incorporate both of these elements. It doesn't say "to be is to be perceived," but only "to be is to be perceiv*able*," at least as far as the physical world is concerned. The table exists when I see it; but it also exists when I don't see it—it's in the next room—because when I do go to the next room, there it is. The sense-experiences of the table are *available* to me any time I want to place myself in the right perceptual circumstances (looking around the corner, or going to the next room). If the tree has been cut down and burned, then it no longer exists and I can no longer perceive it; but if it is still out there, and I'm just at the other side of the building, if I doubt that the tree still exists I can walk to the other side of the building and see it for myself. Matter, said John Stuart Mill, is the "permanent possibility of sensation."

But if I say that a physical object exists, I must be able to *put this assertion to the test:* If it is not being perceived, I must be able to specify the conditions under which it *would* be perceived. If I say there's a watch in my desk drawer, and I open the desk drawer and it's empty, then I have to admit that my statement was false. Not all perceptual claims, of course, are as easy to check as this one, in which I only have to open the desk drawer. If I say there are certain flora and fauna at the bottom of the sea, I must be able to produce evidence, such as from underwater photographs. One can also talk about what went on during the long geologic ages before there were any human or other perceivers; here it is *not* possible for us to go back to that time and perceive it, but we must rely on *indirect* evidence, for example, the fossil record; we must have reason to say "If I had been there at the time (which I wasn't), I *would* have perceived . . ." and back it up with reasons. Isn't this what geologists do all the time? They look in the present for traces of the past, which they were not here to see; but they provide reasons for believing that the past was as they describe—that is, what they *would* have perceived *if* they had been there at the time. The statement "Dinosaurs lived on the earth 70 million years ago" doesn't mean that perceivers saw them, but that they *would* have perceived them if they had been there at the right place and time. It is the *possibility* of sensation, not the actual occurrence of it, which phenomenalists assert when they say that such-and-such really happened at a remote time in the past.

Sense-data. Much of the controversy surrounding phenomenalism has to do with exactly *what* it is that we see, hear, and so on, in perception. You might say, "We see trees, tables, and so on." True enough; but what exactly is it that we are aware of in perception—what is it that we are *immediately* aware of, without any element of inference? Locke and Berkeley said "ideas," used in a very broad sense of the word; Hume said "impressions"; Mill said "sensations." But all these terms are confusing. Even the word "sensation" does not tell us whether it is *what we sense* or *our sensing of it* that is meant. You might say that you have a sensation but not that you *see* a sensation. What then is it that you see? You *have* certain visual sensations, but *what* you see is not these sensations but a certain pattern of colors and shapes (which you may then *take* to be a tree). Even if you are having a hallucination you are still experiencing a pattern of colors and shapes. What you see, regardless of whether you are hallucinating or sensing veridically, has been called *sense-data* by many twentieth-century philosophers.

Consider this discussion by the contemporary philosopher G. E. Moore:

I hold up this envelope: I look at it, and I hope you all will look at it. And now I put it down again. Now what has happened? We should certainly say (if you have looked at it) that we all *saw* that envelope, that we all saw *it, the same* envelope: I saw it, and you all saw it. We all saw *the same* object. And by the *it,* which we all saw, we mean an object, which, at any one of the moments when we were looking at it, occupied just *one* of the many places that constitute the whole of space . . .

But now, what happened to each of us, when we saw that envelope? I will begin by describing *part* of what happened to me. I saw a patch of a particular whitish color, having a certain size, and a certain shape, a shape with rather sharp angles or corners and bounded by fairly straight lines. These things: this patch of a whitish color, and its size and shape I did actually see. And I propose to call these things, the color and size and shape, *sense-data,* things *given* or presented by the senses—given, in this case, by my sense of sight. Many philosophers have called these things which I call sense-data, *sensations.* They would say, for instance, that that particular patch of color was a sensation. But it seems to me that the term "sensation" is liable to be misleading. We should certainly say that I *had* a sensation, when I saw that color. But when we say that I *had* a sensation, what we mean is, I think, that I had the experience which consisted in my *seeing* the color. That is to say, what we mean by a "sensation" in this phrase, is my *seeing* of the color, not the color which I say: this color does not seem to be what I mean to say that I *had,* when I say I *had* a sensation of color. It is very unnatural to say that I *had* the color, that I *had* that particular whitish grey or that I *had* the patch which was of that color. What I certainly did *have* is the experience which consisted in my seeing the color and the patch. And when, therefore, we talk of *having* sensations, I think what we mean by "sensations" is the experiences which consist in apprehending certain sense-data, *not* these sense-data themselves. I think, then, that the term "sensation" is liable to be misleading, because it may be used in two different senses, which it is very important to distinguish from one another. It may be used either for the color which I saw or for the experience which consisted in my seeing it . . .

Part, at least, of what happened to me, I can now express by saying that I saw certain sense-data: I saw a whitish patch of color, of a particular size and shape. And I have no doubt whatever that this is part, at least, of what happened to all of you. You also saw certain sense-data; and I expect also that the sense-data which you saw were more or less similar to those which I saw. You also saw a patch of color which might be described as whitish, of a size not very different from the size of the patch which I saw, and of a shape similar at least in this, that it had rather sharp corners and was bounded by fairly straight lines. But now, what I want to emphasize is this. Though we all did (as we should say) see *the same* envelope, no two of us, in all probability, saw exactly the *same sense-data.* Each of us, in all probability, saw, to begin with, a slightly different shade of color. All these colors may have been whitish; but each was probably at least slightly different from the rest, according to the way in which the light fell upon the paper, relatively to the different positions you are sitting in; and again according to differences in the strength of your eye-sight, or your distance from the paper. And so too, with regard to the size of the patch of color which you saw: differences in the strength of your eyes and in your distance from the envelope probably made slight differences in the size of the patch of color, which you saw. And so again with regard to the shape. Those of you on that side of the room will have seen a rhomboidal figure, while those in front of me will have seen a figure more nearly rectangular . . .

Now all this seems to me to show very clearly, that, if we *did* all see the same envelope, the envelope which we saw was not *identical with* the sense-data which we saw: the envelope cannot be exactly the same thing as each of the sets of sense-data, which we each of us saw; for these were in all probability each of them slightly different from all the rest, and they cannot, therefore, *all* be exactly the same thing as the envelope.[9]

You and I are both seeing an envelope; but what appears in our vision is somewhat different. You are looking at the envelope from a slightly different angle, or I am further away from it than you so what I see is somewhat smaller; so although we are both seeing the same envelope, we are experiencing somewhat different sense-data. If I change my position, or angle, or the light changes, I myself see sense-data somewhat different sense-data from those I sensed a moment ago. I can't *describe* them in words other than saying that I see the envelope rather differently than I did before; nevertheless, *what* I see—the sense-data, not the envelope—is somewhat different from what it was a moment ago.

That I am sensing certain sense-data, phenomenalists would say, I cannot doubt; these are indubitable. But that I am perceiving a real physical object, that I *can* doubt. For example, I can sense reddish, roundish sense-data without there being a tomato in front of me:

When I see a tomato there is much that I can doubt. I can doubt whether it is a tomato that I am seeing, and not a cleverly painted piece of wax. I can doubt whether there is any material thing there at all. Perhaps what I took for a tomato was really a reflection; perhaps I am even the victim of some hallucination. One thing however I cannot doubt: that there exists a red patch of a round and somewhat bulgy shape, standing out from a background of other color-patches, and having a certain visual depth, and that this whole field of color is directly present to my consciousness. What the red patch

is, whether a substance, or a state of a substance, or an event, whether it is physical or psychical or neither, are questions that we may doubt about. Whether the something persists even for a moment before and after it is present to my consciousness, whether other minds can be conscious of it as well as I, may be doubted. But that it now *exists,* and that *I* am conscious of it—by me at least who am conscious of it this cannot possibly be doubted. And when I say that it is "directly" present to my consciousness, I mean that my consciousness of it is not reached by inference, nor by any other intellectual process.[10]

Whether I am perceiving a real tomato or having a hallucination, what I am (immediately, that is, noninferentially) aware of are sense-data. In a hallucination there is no physical thing that does the appearing, yet there are sense-data. The hallucinatory sense-data look the same as the veridical sense-data do; if they looked different, you wouldn't be taken in by the hallucination. The sense-data are just what *appear* to you, and the appearance (at least at the moment) is the same whether or not you are having a hallucination. If you are sensing sense-data in the hallucination case—where there is nothing *but* the sense-data—then you are also sensing sense-data in the veridical case; the appearance is the same. Physical objects can be other than they appear, but sense-data cannot, for the language of sense-data *is* the language of appearance: Sense-data cannot appear to be other than they are.

It would be logically possible for there to be sense-data but no physical objects at all. If none of the sense-data you experienced had stable characteristics—for example, if one moment you seemed to see someone's head and the next moment you saw a flash there and the next moment what appeared like a tree and the next moment just a black expanse, all in less than a second, and if *all* your sensory experience was like this, like a rapidly

[9]G.E. Moore, *Some Main Problems of Philosophy* (London: Allen & Unwin, Ltd.,) pp. 30–33.

[10]H. H. Price, *Perception,* (London: Methuen & Co., 1933), p. 3.

shifting kaleidoscope of colors and shapes—you would not have the concept of an enduring physical world at all. It is only because sense-data occur in regular and recurring patterns that we are entitled to speak of an enduring physical order.

Physical objects, according to phenomenalism, are *inferences* from sense-data. This assertion goes contrary to the way we ordinarily speak: When we see bear tracks we infer that a bear has been there, but when we see the bear for ourselves we don't call that an inference, but a direct observation. What, then, is the point of saying that even when we see the bear this too is an inference? It certainly isn't a *conscious* inference: We don't say to ourselves, "I have such-and-such sense-data, therefore I conclude that that's a bear standing out there." But although it isn't *psychologically* an inference—we don't go through a process of inferring as we do in the case of the bear tracks—it is, phenomenalists say, *logically* an inference: That is, whatever we conclude about the bear, even when it's standing before us in plain sight, is *totally based upon* the sense-data we experience, and indeed *goes beyond* the sense-data we experience at any moment. If we didn't experience sense-data, we would have no reason for saying that we perceive something real (a physical reality).

One might say, "But hallucinations at least, aren't real." This statement trades on the ambiguity of the word "real." When we have a hallucination we are not seeing a real bear; nevertheless we are having a *real experience*. An inventory of the creatures in the world would not include your hallucinatory bear, but a history of *all your experiences* would have to include that experience along with all the others, for the experience really occurred.

Usually this leap from sense-data to physical object is justified, for in most cases, when we see, for example, the "red bulgy something," our statement ("That's a real tomato") is true; hallucinations are the exception, not the rule, in our experience. But if we have any reason to suspect that our initial sense-data are misleading, we can make a more guarded claim: "I see what looks like a tomato," "That appears to be a tomato," "I seem to see a tomato," and so on. We do not say "I sense round, reddish sense-data," since the term "sense-data" is a technical one devised by epistemologists; we *can* do without this technical term, but we cannot do without an appearance-language of some sort ("This looks like a tomato," "There appears to be a tomato there," etc.), which enables us to distinguish the full physical-object claim from the milder claim about the momentary sensory presentation, or sense-data. If you said "There's a tomato" and there was none, you would have to withdraw your statement; but if you merely said "I seem to see a tomato" or something of that sort, then the fact that there is no tomato would not require you to withdraw your statement—even if there is no tomato there, it would still be true that you seemed to see one, or saw something that looked like one. When you make only a sense-data claim, your statement cannot be proved false by subsequent sense-experience, as it can when you make a physical-object claim.

When we assert that there is a tomato out there (or make any other physical-object statement) we are making an *implicit prediction*. We are predicting that the sense-data will succeed each other in regular and predictable ways. If it's a real tomato it won't suddenly disappear from our vision (unless we turn our heads or close our eyes) and it won't suddenly turn into an elephant or a cabbage. If the sense-data don't continue in the expected ways, then we will have to reconsider or rescind our assertion that it really was a tomato. What we will *not* have to reconsider or rescind is the judgment that we experienced certain reddish, roundish sense-data, for *that* statement is true even if the tomato turns out to be a hallucination.

For the phenomenalist, sense-data constitute the very *foundation of empirical knowledge*. From sense-data we get to physical objects; without sense-data this would be impossible. The structure of our knowledge of the world has sense-data as its ground floor, or foundation.

Certainty. Not only are sense-data the foundation of empirical knowledge, but statements describing our sense-data are *certain* in a way that physical-object statements are not. We may have to withdraw our statement that we saw a tomato in the light of later evidence, but we will not have to withdraw our statement that we saw what *looked* to us like a tomato. It would seem, then, that sense-data statements are *certain*.

Can sense-data statements never be mistaken? Of course they can: We may be lying to others about what we experience; or we may mean one thing and say another—we "get the wrong words out." But most important, we may unintentionally *misdrescribe* what we see. This is as true of statements about sense-data as of statements about physical objects. If you look steadily at a green square, and then close your eyes, you may see a reddish after-image in the shape of a square (many people do); and if someone says to you later, "Are you sure it was red? Couldn't it possibly have been magenta?" and then shows you a color-chart showing the difference between primary red and magenta, you may well say, "You're right, I think it was magenta that I saw." Here there is no question of being mistaken about the color of a physical object, for there was no physical object; there was only your after-image. But an after-image can be misdescribed as well as anything else. It would seem that *that* source of possible error can never be entirely eradicated.

Or suppose that you are having your eyes tested by an optometrist. You are asked to read the letters on a chart, and some of them look somewhat blurred to you. You are asked whether a certain letter is and E or an F. The optometrist knows well enough what the letters *are;* he is not interested in that—he is interested in what they *look like* to you so that he can prescribe the right glasses for you. And you aren't sure whether this letter looks more like an E or more like an F. It looks rather like both. You don't know which description fits best: you see what you see, but you don't know how to *describe* what you see—whether to call it a blurry-looking E or a blurry-looking F. (It is the sense-data that are blurred, not the letters themselves; looking blurred is a matter of how it *appears* to you, not how it *is*.)

When you are dizzy and see red spots before your eyes, you do not believe that there really are red spots on the wall. But there is no doubt that you *do* see spots before your eyes; that is part of your immediate experience at that moment. (They're sense-data spots, not physical spots on the wall.) But can't you misdescribe them in calling them red? As we have just seen, it is always possible that you may be using the wrong word to describe them.

But what if instead of saying "They *are* red spots" you say "They *look* red to me"? Isn't *that* statement certain? Not even this innocuous statement is free of the possibility of error; for there is another point here which we have not yet considered. When you call the spot "red," even when you merely say that it *looks* red to you at the moment, you are *going beyond the experience of the moment* in using the descriptive words that you use. The word "red", after all, is used not merely to describe *this* experience of yours, but many others as well; using it *connects* what you are experiencing now with what you have experienced many times in the past and will probably experience again in the future. Calling it "red" serves to lump your present experience (of the spots) together with lots of *other* experiences, implying that the experiences *all belong in the same color-category,* that the experiences are similar enough to all be describable by the same word. And in saying or implying this, might you not be mistaken? In calling the experience "red," aren't you relying on *memory?* And isn't memory fallible, as we have seen? Even in calling the spots "red" you are in effect saying that they are *like* other experiences you have had before—enough like them to make it appropriate for you to use the same word to describe them.

In calling it "red" you are not *naming* this sense-datum; if you were, you could never use the word again, for this sense-datum disappears forever; rather, you are *describing* it, saying what it is like. And that is just the point; you are saying what it is *like,* that it is like other data for which you have used the same descriptive word. If you could give every sense-datum a different proper name—in the way that you might call your cat "Rumplestiltskin," the name applying to just this one individual cat—you could get around this difficulty, though it would require an infinite number of proper names, none of them repeatable. But, as language is, it remains a fact that when you use language for any purpose other than to assign proper names, you inevitably go beyond the sense-datum of the moment and *relate* your present sense-data to past ones. In the very act of trying to report this momentary sense-datum only, you use words that connect it (through a relation of similarity) to *other* sense-data and commit you to saying that *this is like those.* And in doing this, of course, you go beyond the sense-data of the moment, with all the possibilities of error pertaining thereto. It is certain, of course, that you sense what you sense, and that you experience what you experience—but this is trivial; the moment you try to *describe* the experience in words, even using a simple sense-datum word like "red," you are going beyond the momentary sensory experience whose occurrence you are attempting to report. A possibility of error thus arises in the very act of using language. Sense-data reports are certain, but no pure sense-data report can

be made. Every report uses words, and words connect the experience reported with other experiences that at that moment are not present.

Still, it remains true that physical-object statements are capable of *more* sources of error that sense-data statements are; for a physical-object statement is an implicit prediction, and it is always possible for predictions to go awry. Sense-data statements make no such predictions. In making a physical-object claim, you are "sticking your neck out" further that if you make only a sense-data claim, so there is more chance that your claim may be in error.

The given. Suppose that an aborigine from a remote part of Australia were suddenly to be brought into your study; and suppose that he is not nearsighted, color-blind, etc. Would he be seeing chairs, desk, and books? We unhesitatingly say that he would, if he had his eyes open. He would see them, but he might not *know that* they were chairs and books. Never having seen any of those things, he would not have the *concept* of chairs and books, and of course he wouldn't call them that (even in his own language, which probably would have no names for these things). It's not that what you and he would see would be different; it's that he has a different system of *concepts* than you do. He might look at the chair and say it was a good weapon to throw at somebody, or that the red book would be something he could use to extract color from to put on his poisoned arrow. His sense-data would be similar to ours, but his classification of them would not, because he has a different system of concepts with which to *interpret* and *classify* his experience.

When a newborn baby first looks upon the world, it is for him what William James called "a blooming buzzing confusion." Only gradually would certain features stand out, to which he would attach names as his parents taught them to him. A fountain pen to a baby would not be an instrument used for writing, but (though she wouldn't be able to verbalize this) would be something like "shiny smooth biteable." It's not the sense-experiences themselves that would be different from yours or mine, but the *interpretation*—the *conceptual scheme* which the baby imposes on these sense-experiences.

What is presented to our senses, prior to interpretation or conceptualization, has often been called *the given,* since we play no active part in it: We are passive recipients of the sense-data. They are, as it were, *given* to us, without our having anything to say about it. (We can change what we see by turning our head or closing our eyes, but once our eyes are open we can't help what we see.) On the other hand, the concepts by means of which we interpret our experience (as a pen, or a smooth biteable) reflect the activity of the human mind working on the data presented by experience.

The combination of the two elements provides knowledge and belief. If we just stare at the given, thinking nothing and drawing no conclusions, we do not yet have knowledge. We have knowledge in the sense of *acquaintance* (see pp. 19–20)—which philosophers would not call knowledge at all—but we do not yet have knowledge *that*—knowledge in the fundamental sense we have been examining. If you go further and say, "That's a chair," this is indeed knowledge, but then you are doing more than passively "drinking in" sense-data: you are employing a concept you have, that of a chair, and saying that what you now see falls under that general concept. You can't be mistaken about the sense-data you have, but you can be mistaken in interpreting them in the way you do. Perhaps what you saw is not a chair but a footstool. You can even be mistaken in attributing to your sense-data the characteristics you do, even in calling them red or round; redness and roundness are also concepts. If you merely "drink in" the experience passively, you make no claims— hence there can be no false claims. But the

moment you say "This is red," or even "This *looks* red", you are making a claim. To have knowledge *that,* you must first make an assertion that could be true or false. Staring at the wall won't give you that—you can't be mistaken if you don't stick your neck out to assert something.

According to phenomenalism, there are two components in knowledge: the given, and the mind's interpretation of the given. Without the second, there are no concepts; without the first, there is nothing for the concepts to be about. Says the American philosopher C. I. Lewis:

"There are in our cognitive experience, two elements, the immediate data such as those of sense, which are presented or given to the mind, and a form, construction, or interpretation, which represents the activity of thought . . . If there be no datum given to the mind, then knowledge must be altogether contentless and arbitrary; there would be nothing which it must be true to. And if there be no interpretation which the mind imposes, then thought is rendered superfluous, and the possibility of error becomes inexplicable, and the distinction of true and false is in danger of becoming meaningless.[11]

He adds:

The distinction between this element of interpretation and the given is emphasized by the fact that the latter is what remains unaltered, no matter what our interests, no matter how we think or conceive. I can apprehend this thing as pen or rubber or cylinder, but I can not, by taking thought, discover it as paper or soft or cubical.[12]

Thus, Bertrand Russell, who introduced the term "sense-data" in his book *The Problems of Philosophy,* (1912), wrote:

We shall say that we have *acquaintance* with anything of which we are directly aware without the

[11]C. I. Lewis, *Mind and the World Order* (New York: Scribners, 1929) p. 38.

[12]Ibid., p. 52.

intermediary of any process of inference or any knowledge of truths. Thus in the presence of my table I am acquainted with the sense-data that make up the appearance of the table—its color, shape, hardness, smoothness, etc.; all these are things of which I am immediately conscious when I am seeing and touching my table. The particular shade of color that I am seeing may have many things said about it—I may say that it is brown, that it is rather dark, and so on. But such statements, though they may make known truths *about* the color, do not make me know the color any better than I did before: so far as concerns knowledge of the color itself, as opposed to knowledge of truths about it, I know [am acquainted with] the color perfectly and completely when I see it and no further knowledge of it itself is even theoretically possible.[13]

On sense-data in relation to knowledge, Russell says:

The actual sense-data are neither true nor false. A particular patch of color, which I see, for example, simply exists: it is not the sort of thing which is true or false. It is true that there is such a patch, true that it has a certain shape and a certain degree of brightness, true that it is surrounded by certain other colors. But the patch itself is of a radically different kind from the things that are true or false, and therefore cannot properly be said to be *true*.[14]

But now a problem arises. According to phenomenalists, sense-data are the basis of all perceptual knowledge. But simply *experiencing* sense-data is not knowledge, for in experiencing sense-data *no claim is made*. To have knowledge, there must be an assertion which is true or false. If the assertion is true and justified, we have knowledge, but first there must be an assertion. Sense-data themselves do not constitute an assertion. To get an assertion, even an assertion *about* sense-data, you must have *concepts*—that is, you must not have only the given data but the conceptualizing activity of the mind upon the given data. If

sense-data, then, are to be the basis of knowledge, it can't be just the sense-data themselves, but *statements* concerning sense-data—statements which, as we have seen, involve more than sense-data because they involve concepts as well. Without concepts there can be no assertions.

Knowledge *that* is always propositional knowledge. Sensing sense-data is not knowledge; it is simply acquaintance. Knowledge comes in when we utter true and justified *propositions*. Sense-data may be the basis for knowledge, but it is not the sense-data but the *propositions* about them that come to be knowledge. And as we have seen, it is difficult—some say impossible—to utter even one single proposition that is wholly about sense-data. Whenever we try, we always go *beyond* the given content of our experience. We apply to the given a concept, which already takes us beyond the given and connects it with other givens previously experienced—as we already saw in the example of red (see p. 79). The result is that no such propositions—not even "It looks red to me now"—are beyond the possibility of error.

The given itself cannot be described without going beyond it in the attempt to describe it, for to describe it ("It looks red and round") is already to go beyond the given content presented to sense. First, we may be making an error of labeling (Did it really look red? Didn't it look more like pink, mauve, or saffron?). And second, to say it looks red is to say that it looks like other colors we have seen before, and thus we connect the present sense-experience with past ones, of which our memory may be faulty.

Moreover, we don't often *notice* our sense-data very much. We drive past someone's house and see our friend working in the front yard. We are sure we saw her in the front yard; but if we were asked, "What color dress was she wearing?", we can't answer because we didn't notice. We couldn't even say what color her shirt *appeared* to be, because we

[13]Bertrand Russell, *The Problems of Philosophy* (London: Oxford University Press, 1912), pp. 46–47.

[14]Ibid., p. 113.

didn't notice that either. What we noticed was where she was and what she was doing. It seems that we are much more often certain of statements like this, about the physical world, than we are about the details of the way it appears to us.

Many philosophers have concluded that propositions about sense-data do not really constitute a *foundation* for empirical knowledge. There is no one class of propositions that regularly is the basis for inferring others. Sometimes we say, "It looked red to me, and since I saw it in normal conditions of light, I conclude (unless further evidence develops to the contrary) that it *was* red." But sometimes we say, "I noticed that my cat was sitting on the porch. And since I remember that my cat is black, I conclude that this cat was black, though I didn't notice it at the time. It probably must have *looked* black to me too, for if if had looked any other color I would probably have noticed it." In that case the sense-data statement is the one that is inferred.

Following this line of thought, *all* propositions are amendable in the light of other propositions; there is no class of specially privileged propositions on which others are always based. If the content of my vision looks blurred or distorted, I may infer that this is because the glass through which I am looking is cracked; but if I see first that the glass is cracked, I infer that what I see through it will look blurred. The inference can go either way. Each proposition can be questioned if other ones related to it in a system of propositions is questioned. If I already know that the letter on the chart is a P, I will be more likely to say that it looks like a P (and it *will* be more likely to look like a P, when the optometrist asks me). If you remember that you were driving along a freeway but don't remember what color the vegetation was, I may say "It must have looked greyish, because they always plant ice-plant along the freeway and ice-plant is greyish."

It seems, then, that all propositions—whether about sense-data or not—are constantly subject to doubt or amendment if other propositions related to them are subject to question; there is no one class of specially privileged propositions on which other propositions are always based. The general conclusion from this is: There is no class of propositions which are the *foundation of empirical knowledge.* Much of the attractiveness of phenomenalism arose from the presumed fact that sense-data propositions constitute the indubitable foundation of knowledge, and that other tiers of knowledge—first, ordinary physical-object propositions, and second, propositions of scientific theory (about unobservable entities such as electrons, which we shall discuss in Chapter 4)—were erected on this indubitable base. If the alleged base now turns out to be no base at all, much of the appeal of phenomenalism as an account of the foundation of human knowledge disappears.

Are sense-data themselves—not propositions about them—indubitable? The question makes no sense, for it is only propositions that can be known, doubted, wondered about, theorized about. Sense-data just *are:* they are neither dubitable nor indubitable, because only propositions can be that and sense-data aren't propositions (just as theories can be neither green nor any other color).

Criticisms of the phenomenalistic program. One aim of phenomenalism it to provide a basis for human knowledge: to provide a set of propositions, the foundation of the tabernacle of knowledge, which would support propositions on a "higher" level, such as propositions about the physical world (and at a still "higher" level, scientific constructs). But in the opinion of many philosophers, sense-data provide no such basis of certainty. If this is true, one aim of the phenomenalist program is doomed to failure. But other criticisms abound as well.

"Physical objects," said Mill, "are permanent possibilities of sensation." For the word "sensation" (used today in other ways) we can substitute the term "sense-data." But physical objects *aren't* sense-data, not even combinations of them as Berkeley thought, not even *possible* sense-data as phenomenalists have held. Physical objects have mass; sense-data don't. Physical objects bump into other objects and cause them to move, and so on; sense-data don't do these things. Physical objects are not *possible* sense-data, the way an acorn is a possible oak tree; the acorn is a potential oak tree, in that it may grow into one, but sense-data have no such relation to physical objects. Besides, in what way do possibilities exist? If you see a tablecloth but not the table under it, how can the *possibility* of table-sense-data hold up a tablecloth? Can a possibility *do* anything?

But twentieth-century epistemologists have greatly amended Mill's formula about possibilities. Instead of talking about possible things or possible experiences, they talk about *propositions*. It's not that there are two kinds of things or entities, but rather, there are two kinds of propositions. It is *propositions* about physical objects that are translatable into propositions about sense-data. Most of these propositions will be *hypothetical* (If . . . then . . .) propositions—propositions about what we *would* perceive *if* we fulfilled certain conditions. For example, I see a tree outside the window now (I sense a series of sense-data that constitutes a family). But if I change my position I no longer see it, yet the tree is still there. What do I mean by saying it is still there? That *if* I were in the position I was a moment ago (when it was in full view), then I *would* perceive it (but don't because I am not now in that position). This hypothetical (If . . . then . . .) proposition is still true, even though its if-clause remains unfulfilled, because I am not now in a position to see the tree. Indeed, it is a *contrary-to-fact* hypothetical statement. It is contrary to fact that I am in that position now, yet it is true that *if* I were

in that position I would see the tree (sense the appropriate sense-data). If I lifted the tablecloth I *would* see the table. Nobody is now seeing the book in my desk drawer, so no one is experiencing any sense-data of it; yet it is true that *if* someone were to open the drawer, he or she *would* sense the book-sense-data. Statements about what I'm perceiving now can be translated into statements about sense-data I'm experiencing now; and statements about what I'm not perceiving now can be translated into *hypothetical* statements about what I *would* be experiencing *if* I did certain things (like opening the drawer). The proof of the pudding is in the eating, and the proof of statements about physical objects existing unobserved lies in getting oneself into the appropriate conditions of observation.

But this still doesn't give us a *translation* of physical-object statements into sense-datum statements. Consider these points: (1) Physical objects aren't sense-data, so how can a statement about the one be translated (without change of meaning) into a statement about the other? Statements about sense-data are about the content of our experiences; statements about physical objects are about a stable and continuing physical order that exists independently of our experience. Besides, (2) hypothetical statements often contain *other* untranslated physical-object references: For example, in the case of the tree outside, there is the reference to "I," and I am at least a physical body, not a collection of sense-data. And (3) hypothetical statements may refer to a change of position (if I opened the drawer, if I moved in relation to the window), and these are *physical* changes, any description of which involves a reference to physical objects. So physical objects have in no way been eliminated; indeed, we cannot translate a physical object statement into a sense-data statement—they are not even about the same thing.

In view of all this, we might water down

phenomenalism into a much weaker version: We could merely say that any physical-object statement must be *verified* (or confirmed) by sensing sense-data. Physical-object statements don't *mean* the same as sense-datum statements do, and the one can't be translated into the other. But the way we *find out* whether a physical-object statement is true is by sensing sense-data. You find out if there's a tree out there by seeing and touching, that is, by having sense-experiences; and if they are of the right sort and occur in the regular and predictable order associated with real trees (they look smaller if you move away, they change their appearance depending on the light and the angle of vision, and so on), then you have verified—or at least highly confirmed—that there's a tree out there.

Such a version of phenomenalism seems innocent enough—even obvious. *How else could we possibly know there's a tree out there other than by having sense-experiences?* Yet even this seemingly bland contention has been called into question. There are matters yet to be considered about the status of physical objects themselves; and there are also considerations we have not yet broached about sense-data, the very foundation of phenomenalism, whose very existence has been called into question. Indeed, the phenomenalistic theory has been subjected to an all-out attack from so many quarters that, in the opinion of many contemporary epistemologists, little if anything of it remains.

The Attack on Sense-Data

You can say of a physical object, "It looks like a dog, but it really is a fox," or "It looks grayish in the distance , but I believe it's really blue." Physical objects aren't always as they appear to be. But the same cannot be said of sense-data; the sense-data language is the language of appearance, and sense-data can't appear to be other than they are. Whatever qualities they appear to have, those are the qualities they have. If the blue tower looks gray in the distance, then the sense-data you sense *are* gray.

But can't there be just as much of a problem describing sense-data as in describing physical objects? We have already noticed that it's difficult to say whether the letter on the chart looks to you more like an E or like an F. What are the sense-data then—E-like, F-like, both, or neither? One might reply, "Well, they *are* just blurry and indeterminate; that's the way they look, so that's the way they are."

But there is a problem. Suppose you pass hastily through a rose garden and you don't notice the color of most of the roses; a few look red to you, but the rest of them you don't particularly notice, except that they are all dark in color—there are no white or yellow roses. All you can say about the way they looked to you is that they looked dark in color. You might say, "Well then, the sense-data *were* dark, but not dark red, dark purple, etc." But isn't this peculiar, to say the least? How can something be dark in color but not dark of any particular color? Clearly, the roses themselves have a perfectly definite (determinate) color: dark red, dark purple, and so on. But don't sense-data also have to be perfectly determinate in color? You can go back and look again, and then the sense-data will be, let's say, dark red; but what about the sense-data-colors *before* you took time to notice? Will we have to say of these that they *were* dark but not any particular shade, because all that appeared to us was dark but not any particular shade? But this seems very peculiar. Can anything, even sense-data, possess the quality of darkness without having any particular shade of darkness?

One might reply that the problem arises because we are applying to sense-data the same considerations we apply to physical objects.

All physical objects have perfectly determinate colors, but (it is said) the same need not hold true of sense-data. Sense-data can be dark without being dark red or dark anything else. Nevertheless, many people have found this conclusion strange. "Anything with color has a determinate color" seems to them axiomatic, and if this principle doesn't apply to sense-data there must be something wrong with the concept.

A similar difficulty arises with number. When I *glance* at a speckled hen I notice that it has many speckles on it, but I don't notice how many (I didn't stay to count them). The real physical hen, of course, has a definite number of speckles. But I am talking not about the number of speckles it *has,* but the number it *appears* to have; and how many speckles did it appear to have? No definite number at all. It just appeared to have "lots of speckles," and that is as definite as I can get if I am talking only about appearances. The real hen either has 1247 speckles or it hasn't; it must be one or the other; but must it *appear* to have either 1247 speckles or not have 1247 speckles? It only appeared to have—well, a rather large number, an indeterminate number of speckles, not a definite number. But how is this possible? Can there be "numerosity without definite number"?

Again, objectors will say that we are creating a problem for ourselves by applying the same considerations to sense-data as we do to physical objects. The real hen has a definite number of speckles; the appearance of the hen need not. Still, numerosity without number seems strange. How can anything at all, including sense-data, have numerous apparent speckles without having a definite number of apparent speckles? Some say that the idea of "numerosity without a definite number" is nonsense.

This is only a small sample of questions that have been asked about sense-data. Consider: (1) The real hen occurs in physical space; it is three feet from that bush. What of the appearance of the hen? Is it also three feet from (the appearance of) that bush? Can you measure distances among sense-data as we we do among physical objects? (2) If a red spot in your visual field grows larger as you look, is it one sense-datum that is growing larger, or is it a succession of sense-data, each larger than the one that preceded? (3) Can the same red sense-datum move across a screen, or is it a different sense-datum at every moment of its journey because the spatial position is different? Does it remain the same sense-datum only as long as it doesn't move or vary its size? (4) If I blink my eyes while looking at the spot, are there two sense-data separated in time, or is there only one, which however ceases to exist during my blink? (5) If a change occurs in my visual field, have the sense-data changed or been replaced by others? If no change is observed, shall I say that the same sense-data continue to exist? Or if you get in the same spatial position I was in when I saw the tree, and neither of us is nearsighted, is it possible that you sense the same sense-data that I was sensing a moment ago when I looked at the tree? And so on.

One may say that none of this matters—we can say that what we see on the screen is one continuous moving sense-datum or a series of successive sense-data, just as we can say that the cup is half empty or that it is half full. If sense-data are just what they appear to be—if the sense-data language *is* the language of appearance—then for sense-data what appears *is,* even though this may involve numerosity without number and color without a determinate color; these things seem strange only because we are accustomed to physical-object talk and don't ordinarily engage in sense-data talk. In practical life we note how things appear only in order to discover how they are. But in this section, we are concentrating only on the appearances themselves, hence the seeming strangeness.

The Theory of Appearing

But a greater challenge lies in wait for sense-data theorists. The very existence of sense-data has been contested. According to the theory of appearing, I see things—physical objects—directly, not through the intermediary of sense-data. The entire idea of sense-data can be dispensed with. Physical objects exist; sense-data do not. Physical objects, to be sure, *appear* to me in different ways, but that is not to say that each mode of appearance is some kind of *existent* entity. Suppose I am looking at a sheet of white paper. It appears yellow to me because I'm wearing yellow lenses, or because I have jaundice, or because I have taken a drug. This apparently yellow sheet of paper has on it the same words as the really white sheet of paper does:

Now, if the yellow sheet of paper which I see *exists* —a yellow sheet of paper with the relevant words upon it—it must be somewhere in this room. Indeed, the yellow sheet which is seen by me (with my yellow lenses on) is, as I also see, in a certain spatial relation to this podium. It is roughly in the *same* relation to this podium as the white sheet which you see. But when we look about the podium, there are not two sheets of paper with those words on them, but only one. So either you are seeing something which does not exist, or I am. In either case, it follows that some things which are perceived do not exist.[15]

Can one sheet of paper have two surfaces on each side (one white, one yellow)? When you write on or tear up the one, have you written on or torn up both? Willard comments:

There must not only be two surfaces on each side of one sheet; there must also be as many surfaces there as can be seen by varying the circumstances of the perception. This seems to me to be far too high a price to pay to save the premise we are dis-

cussing—that whatever is perceived must exist . . . To say that the side of a sheet of paper has more than one surface is to say what is false.[16]

But is that what the sense-data theorist is saying? Not that there are two pieces of paper, one white and one yellow. If there are ten people in the room each looking at the paper with different-colored glasses, there will be ten *apparently* different-colored pieces of paper. There is only one real color, white, but ten apparent colors—and what is this but to say that the sense-data of each person are different in color?

Still, the point being insisted on is that only one piece of paper *exists* (on that podium), and that it is white. That is all that exists there. The different colors seen are just *manners of appearing* (through the glasses) of the one sheet of paper. But to say that X has a certain peculiar manner of appearing does not imply that there is something else besides X existing, namely Y. There need be no existent Y at all. Sense-data theorists have been led down the garden path with their arguments going from (1) "It seems to me that I perceive X," to (2) "I perceive a seeming-X," and thus to (3) "There is a seeming-X which I perceive."

The claim that now emerges is that the whole idea of sense-data is a mistake. Consider this coin on the table before me. We all agree that the coin is round, that from a 45° angle (for example) it *looks* elliptical. The conclusion that sense-data theorists then draw is that what I see is an elliptical sense-datum. But, critics argue, we need not draw this conclusion. I am not seeing anything elliptical at all. What I am seeing is a *round coin* that *looks* elliptical from an angle. There is nothing whatever in the situation that *is* elliptical. There is nothing elliptical to be sensed; there is only the round coin that exhibits to us an

---

[15] Dallas Willard, "Perceptual Realism," *Southwestern Journal of Philosophy 1,* 3 (1970): 81.

[16] Ibid, p. 81.

elliptical appearance from our angle of vision. All there is in the situation is (1) a round coin that (2) looks elliptical. But there is no *existent*—nothing that exists—that *is* elliptical. The only existent in the situation is the round coin.

"But no!" we may object. "The coin *is* round, granted; the coin from this angle *appears* elliptical, also granted. But there *is* something elliptical—here it is in my visual field, I see it now, an elliptical appearance. And this isthe sort of thing I call sense-data. How could I see something ellptical if there were nothing elliptical (there in my visual field) to be seen? And that elliptical something is a sense-datum!"

Not at all, says the critic. There is no elliptical existent, only a round existent that appears elliptical. Physical objects have different *ways of appearing:* The green trees on the distant mountainside look purplish-gray; the round coin looks elliptical. Physical objects often appear in different ways to different people; the green necktie appears gray to the color-blind person. Ways of appearing often give a clue to the nature of what exists; but they *are not existents themselves*. A mode of appearing does not *exist*. You can ask whether the coin exists, and whether it is round, and in doing so you consider how it appears under different perceptual conditions. But modes of appearing are not themselves existents (part of the "furniture of the universe"); they are only ways we have of discovering the nature of existents.

Physical objects appear—in different ways, under different conditions, to different people. (Would one *expect* them to always appear the same? Would you expect the tower to look as large far away as close up?) But there is no such thing as the sense-datum that *is* the appearance. No such entity exists.

Objects themselves appear to us in sense-perception . . . When I see a circular penny as elliptical I am seeing the circular surface of the penny, not some elliptical substitute. This circular surface, it is true, appears elliptical to me, but that fact has no tendency to show that I am not directly aware of the circular surface.[17]

Still, isn't there *something elliptical* there that I am (directly) aware of? And isn't that what we call a sense-datum?

Let us try a more difficult case. Here is a penny before me; I press my eyes and see double—two pennies. One of them at least must be only an apparent penny, since there aren't two pennies out there. There appear to be two pennies, yet only one penny exists to do any appearing. If I were to describe what exists in the world, I would say there is one penny on the table; if I were to describe what appears in my visual field, I would say two pennies. Which of them is real, and which is only a sense-datum penny? It's not as if there were one penny which looks one way from one angle and another way from another angle; it is one penny that looks like *two*. Can two-ness be a property of one penny?

The reply would probably be the same as before. Being double can't be a property of one penny, but *looking* double can be. One penny can't be two, but one penny can (under certain circumstances) *appear* a number of ways, including looking like two pennies.

This reply may cause a certain discomfort. When we see double, there are two apparent extended expanses. Don't I, in the most direct sense of "see", see *two* things before me? or at least two appearances? There *is* something double in my field of vision, and isn't that what we call sense-data?

Finally, what of hallucination? What of the dagger that Macbeth saw ("Is this a dagger that I see before me?" he says, while he is hallucinating)? Or what of after-images? After concentrating on a black square on the

---

[17] Winston H. F. Barnes, "The Myth of Sense-data," *Proceedings of the Aristotelian Society, 45* (1944–1945): 112.

white wall, you close your eyes and see a white square. There isn't, of course, any white square there to *do* any appearing. Nevertheless you see something, don't you? You see the white square (even with your eyes closed) as clearly as you ever see anything. This case is not like the round coin that appears elliptical; in this case there is no black square on the wall to present any appearances whatever. There is only the white square in your field of vision. There is no question of a physical white square existing out there in the physical world. But it *does* exist, doesn't it? It must, since you are seeing it! It has a sense-datum existence, but no physical-object existence. What now?

As a refutation of sense-data theory, the arguments above seem hardly conclusive. In hallucinations aren't you aware of *something?* If you were to give a complete inventory of the physical world (chairs, trees, mountains), your white after-image would not be part of that inventory; but if you were to give a complete inventory of what you experienced, the white square *would* be a part of it; a history of your life would be incomplete without it. There it is; you are looking at it right now; surely in some sense it *exists.* Maybe it doesn't exist "out there," maybe it exists as a projection from the brain—but whatever its cause it *exists.* There it is—you see it, don't you?

In the case of the white square, it seems plausible to say that what we are aware of is a sense-datum; it is an object of awareness, yet not a physical object. This doesn't prove, of course, that in the case of the coin we are also seeing an elliptical sense-datum, rather than the round coin. But the fact is that they *seem* to be in the same category—the one looks as real as the other, and there is no warning tag on one of them saying "Beware, I'm only a sense-datum." According to phenomenalists, at any rate, what we are immediately aware of in both cases is sense-data, but in the coin example the sense-data present a coherent pattern of both touch and sight that entitles us to believe that the sense-datum

points (as it were) to something beyond itself, a real physical thing. Physical objects, according to phenomenalists, are *logical constructs* out of sense-data: It is because the sense-data are as they are, and occur in the regular patterns that they do, that we are entitled to say that a real physical object exists.

6. DIRECT REALISM

Consider the following dialogue:

A: When I look at the coin, I am directly aware of an elliptical sense-datum.

B: No. You are directly aware of a round coin, which *looks* elliptical from your angle of vision.

A: But there is *something* that is elliptical, which I am now directly aware of—and that is what we call a sense-datum.

B: No, sense-data are a myth. I am aware of a round coin. But of course a round coin may look elliptical from an angle, may look dark in inadequate light, and so on. But it's a coin you're directly aware of all the time.

A: When I look at the North Star tonight, the point of light I see in the sky started on its way 450 years ago (at the speed of light, which is 186,000 miles per second). What I am aware of is this whitish sense-datum in the surrounding darkness. That's what I see *now;* for all we know the North Star may by now have ceased to exist—we won't know that for 450 years. Surely you don't want to say that I am seeing what may not even exist any longer.

B: But I do. I see tonight the star as it was 450 years ago; but I still see the star. There is still no need for sense-data.

A: I may see the star, but I see it by means of the sense-data I am experiencing now.

B: What you are experiencing now is the star as it was. But you are still experiencing the star, not sense-data. I grant that when you see a star you *have sensations,* but they are not *what* you see, as sense-data are supposed to be.

What is being defended in this dialogue is a theory of *direct realism,* to which "the theory of appearing" easily leads. In perception we are directly aware of physical objects; there are no such entities as sense-data standing, as it were, between us and physical objects.

A statement such as "We are directly aware of physical objects" is bound to elicit widespread assent. *Of course* we are directly aware of physical objects, even when we see them through a glass, even when we see them in a mirror or through a microscope or telescope. What could be more direct that seeing a tree? We don't infer their existence, we directly observe it. We are not aware of any act of inferring on our part, as we are when we infer from seeing the wet street that it has rained during the night. But it may (as we saw on p. 76) be an inference just the same: Aren't the sense-data we experience evidence for the existence of physical objects? But this is just what must be denied by anyone who dismisses sense-data as a myth.

Are we *always* aware in perception of some property of physical objects? When I look at the star, I see a point of light; is *that* a property of the star? If we see the paper through yellow glasses, it looks yellow; yet the paper is not yellow but white. Isn't there something in the situation that's yellow, our sense-data? No, says the direct realist, what we see is the white paper, which looks yellow through the glasses. Very well then, consider a hallucination: It looks as if there's a light under the archway, but there isn't, it's only a reflection. There is no light there to do any appearing; yet in hallucination I am directly aware of something, am I not? Since there's no light there, what is it that I am directly aware of? Certain sense-data (which I may incorrectly take to indicate the presence of a light), one

is inclined to say; but according to the direct realist, there are no sense-data; so what is it that I am directly aware of in this case? The direct realist may not call it sense-data, because that term is often taken to refer to *what* I see, which is what the direct realist finds objectionable. The direct realist might say, then, that we're having certain sensations, as Mill did, or sense-impressions, as Hume did, or even ideas, as Locke did. Still, isn't there something, which is not a physical object, which I experience? If I see red spots before my eyes, am I not seeing the red spots—though there are no such red spots in the physical world? And aren't they what I experience? Surely there is *something* that I am aware of that is not the state of a physical object.

However, it is not primarily the occurrence of hallucinations that have led epistemologists to question direct realism. Even if we never made mistaken claims about the physical world, such as when we take a hallucination to be a physical object, there is the fact that the nature of our sense-experiences depends on the *conditions of observation;* and what we are aware of in sense-experience may not be any state of the physical object at all. The world may be utterly different from the way it is "reported" to us in sense-experience. Consider:

What we perceive depends to a large extent on the nature of our sense organs. Our visual experiences would be quite different if we had one eye on each side of our heads, like horses, so that we could see on almost a 180° arc but without spatial depth (three-dimensionality). (In general, animals that hunt have binocular vision, being able to concentrate on one object, the better to catch it, whereas animals that are hunted have vision that lacks spatial depth but is much more extensive, the better to escape their predators.) Or suppose we had a thousand eyes, like some insects; what would the world look like then? Even within the human species there is enormous variability of perception: In a bright light an object looks one color, in the twilight another, and in the dark it looks black. Its apparent color depends not only on the light but on the condition of the observer. A color-blind person will not perceive certain colors at all; some people lack peripheral vision; some people have more depth-vision than others; to people who are astigmatic or nearsighted, everything (without glasses) looks blurred; to a person under the influence of LSD, things are luminous at the edges and move constantly like the patterns in a kaleidoscope. The same variability affects other senses as well: A piece of cake will taste sweeter to someone who has just eaten something sour than it will after eating ice cream. The rose garden will smell fragrant at first, then soon the smell will no longer be noticeable. And your dog or cat experiences thousands of smells which we human beings can't experience at all—and can't even imagine.

Even the average person who has never thought about these matters—let us call him Typical Tom—is not consistently a direct realist. He does not deny that the world would look very different to creatures with eyes very different from ours. And he is aware as any philosopher is of the existence of hallucinations. He is not even surprised at the suggestion that perhaps the ball is not red at all, but only looks red because of the nature of the rods and cones of the human retina, and that most creatures don't see colors at all, but see the world much as we do in viewing a black-and-white movie. The ball doesn't look red to them, but (perhaps) dark gray. What things look like depends on the nature of the perceiver's sense organs and on the conditions of observation—whether there is enough light to see by, whether the perceiver is wearing spectacles, whether the object is near or far away, and so on. Typical Tom is not likely to deny these things.

Of course we say that grass is green and roses are red. But does this mean more than that if we look at them under suitable conditions green and red are the color of what we see?[18]

But Typical Tom also believes that physical objects have certain properties that belong to the object regardless of the presence of observers.

When I conclude that this brick must have made that hole in the window, though nobody saw it do so, I credit the brick with having a size and weight at a time when it was not being perceived. But size and weight are not sensory properties. Blueness is a way things look; but heaviness is not a way things look or feel. A thing can, of course, look or feel heavy; but its *being* heavy is something different— it is heavy if it will hold down or make dents in other objects, if you can't lift it with one hand, and so on; and these causal characteristics are not ways of looking or feeling.[19]

It would seem, then, that much of what we see, hear, and so on, are not properties of physical objects at all. But if this is so, how do we tell which properties they only appear to have and which ones they really have? The problem for realism would seem to be not *that* physical objects are (for they do exist) but rather *what* they are (what properties they have, as opposed to what properties they appear to us to have). If some of the *apparent* properties of objects are not their *real* properties, then of course the data of our senses don't always show us what the object is really like.

Centuries before anything was known about the physics of light and sound, Democritus (an early Greek philosopher) set forth a primitive, but remarkably prescient, version of atomic theory: The universe, he said, consists of tiny particles moving in a void; these tiny particles he called "atoms" (ironically, in Greek this means "unsplittable"). These

[18] C. H. Whiteley, "Physical Objects," in *Philosophy*, Vol. 34 (1959), p. 149.
[19] Ibid.

atoms have definite size and shape and weight, but they do not have any color or smell or taste—color, smell, and so on are not really properties of the object, though in sense-experience they appear to be; our senses simply mislead us on this point.

Following the development of modern physics in the seventeenth century, Democritus' theories were set forth again, more systematically, by John Locke (1632–1704). According to Locke, physical objects have what he called *primary qualities* and *secondary qualities.*

Primary qualities, he said, are those qualities an object has even in the absence of perceivers. Objects have a certain size, shape, mass, density; they have these whether or not anyone is there to perceive them. These are intrinsic to the object. But there are also secondary qualities, which are not intrinsic to the object at all, but only depend on the presence of perceivers with sense organs; these qualities include color, smell, taste. Vinegar has a certain chemical composition regardless of perceivers, but its pungent smell exists only for perceivers.

Isn't the secondary quality "in the object" at all? Yes, said Locke, it exists as a *power* or *capacity* in the object—the capacity to produce certain sense-experiences under certain conditions (conditions of the organism, and of the perceptual environment). The power that the object has depends on what he called the "insensible parts" of the object, that is, on its molecular structure and (in the case of color) on the nature of the light waves emanating from it. These qualities, hidden from ordinary perception, give the object the power to affect our senses in certain ways, so that we experience certain colors, tastes, smells, and "feels" (touch-experiences). Objects we call red are not red in themselves; they have only the power to produce in us the sense-experience we call red; and the objects we call blue, having somewhat different "insensible parts" as Locke called them, have the power to produce in us the sense-experiences we call blue.

The power is in the object, but the red and the blue exist only as sense-impressions. Not until the sense-organ is affected do those so-called qualities come into existence.

According to Locke, the primary qualities are

. . . such as are utterly inseparable from the body, in what state soever it be; and such as in all the alterations and changes it suffers, all the force can be used upon it, it constantly keeps; and such as sense constantly finds in every particle of matter which has bulk enough to be perceived; and the mind finds inseparable from every particle of matter, though less than to make itself singly be perceived by our senses: e.g. Take a grain of wheat, divide it into two parts; each part has still solidity, extension, figure, and mobility; divide it again, and it retains still the same qualities; and so divide it on, till the parts become insensible [incapable of being sensed]; they must retain still each of them all those qualities. For division (which is all that a mill, or pestle, or any other body, does upon another, in reducing it to insensible parts) can never take away either solidity, extension, figure, or mobility from any body, but only makes two or more distinct separate masses of matter, of what which was but one before; all which distinct masses, reckoned as so many distinct bodies, after division, make a certain number. These I call *original* or *primary qualities* of body, which I think we may observe to produce simple ideas in us, viz. solidity, extension, figure, motion or rest, and number.

Secondly, such qualities which in truth are nothing in the objects themselves but powers to produce various sensations in us by their primary qualities, i.e. by the bulk, figure, texture, and motion of their insensible parts, as colors, sounds, tastes, etc. These I call *secondary qualities.*[20]

Does this mean that according to Locke size and shape are in the object, but that colors and sounds are only "in the mind"—or that only sense-data and not objects are colored? No, this is far from being Locke's view. The words we use for sensory qualities are ambiguous; they have more than one meaning, and we often skip from one to the

---

[20] John Locke, *An Essay concerning Human Understanding,* from Sections 9 and 10.

other without being aware of the ambiguity. High school students often argue for hours about the question "If a tree falls in the forest and nobody hears it, is there a sound?" But the answer to this one is easy: The word "sound" is ambiguous. If you mean the physical *sound waves,* they continue to exist whether there are perceivers or not and can be recorded on instruments regardless of the presence of anyone there to hear them. But if you mean the *sound-experiences,* the auditory sense-data, of course, don't come into existence until there is someone with ears to hear them: There is no sound-experience without a sound-experiencer. The sense-data—whether of size, shape, or color—only come into existence when there are perceivers; that is as true of the sense-data of so-called primary qualities like shape, as of so-called secondary qualities like color.

What Locke insisted on can now be described as follows: that in the physical sense of these words, there *is* a difference between shape and color. The object has a certain shape, but it has a color only in that it has a *power* to produce visual sense-data in perceivers. The power is there whether there are perceivers or not, but the power is actualized only when perceivers have experiences of color. In both cases there is something in the object, independent of perceivers; but the difference according to Locke is that the object itself has the quality in the case of the primary qualities, but in the case of the secondary qualities the object itself does not possess the quality but only the *power* to produce certain sense-data. The sulfuric acid has a certain chemical combination, H_2SO_4, but it has a strong acrid smell only in the sense that the acid has the power to produce that smell-experience in perceivers who have the right kind of noses.

Locke does not deny that the balloon is red, any more than that it is round. Indeed the balloon *is* red—it is not blue, not green, not any other color; and when we say commonsensically that the balloon is red, we are quite

right, and a person who says it is blue is mistaken. But what is meant by saying that it is red? Not, said Locke, that it has color as something intrinsic to it, but rather that it gives off light rays which cause us to experience red sense-data when they strike the retina of our eyes. The light waves (Locke still thought of them as corpuscles) are of such a nature as to cause us to experience red, not blue—the balloon has *that specific power.* It's not that redness comes into existence only when we see it—that's only true of the red sense-data (the other sense of "red")—but rather that the redness of the object is only a *power* or *capacity* to produce red sense-data, under the appropriate perceptual conditions.

Color is in the object in the sense that the object has the power (through the action of light waves reflected from it to our eyes) to produce color-experiences in us. Is heat in the object? Only in the sense that the molecules constituting the object are moving rapidly; this is heat in the physical sense (the only sense relevant to physics)—but the sense-impression of heat is not in the object but in us. Locke wrote:

. . . What is sweet, blue, or warm in idea, is but the certain bulk, figure, and motion of the insensible parts, in the bodies themselves, which we call so.

Flame is denominated hot and light; snow, white and cold; and manna, white and sweet, from the ideas they produce in us. Which qualities are commonly thought to be the same in those bodies that those ideas are in us, the one the perfect resemblance of the other, as they are in a mirror, and it would by most men be judged very extravagant if one should say otherwise. And yet he that will consider that the same fire that, at one distance, produces in us the sensation of warmth, does, at a nearer approach, produce in us the far different sensation of pain, ought to bethink himself what reason he has to say—that this idea of warmth, which was produced in him by the fire, is *actually in the fire;* and his idea of pain, which the same fire produced in him the same way, is *not* in the fire. Why are whiteness and coldness in snow, and pain not, when it produces the one and the other idea in us; and can do neither, but by the bulk, figure, number, and motion of its solid parts?

The particular bulk, number, figure, and motion of the parts of fire or snow are really in them—whether anyone's senses perceive them or not: and therefore they may be called *real* qualities, because they really exist in those bodies. But light, heat, whiteness, or coldness, are no more real in them than sickness or pain is in manna. Take away the sensation of them; let not the eyes see light or colours, nor the ears hear sounds; let the palate not taste, nor the nose smell, and all colours, tastes, odours, and sounds, as they are such particular ideas, vanish and cease, and are reduced to their causes, i.e., bulk, figure, and motion of parts.[21]

Berkeley, eager to attack Locke's view, believed that the reason Locke made the distinction between primary and secondary qualities was that the experience of the secondary qualities is extremely *variable:* The object looks red in one light, black in another, iridescent when you've taken a drug. Smells quickly go unnoticed, and a dish that tastes good when you're hungry is unbearable after you've had dessert. But, said Berkeley, the argument from variability won't work, because our experience of the so-called primary qualities involves just as much variation. Indeed, he contended, if variability of quality is supposed to show that the qualities do not really inhere in the object, then the so-called primary and secondary qualities are in the same boat, because both of them are variable. A thing looks smaller when it is further away. A round coin looks elliptical from most angles. A weight is heavier to lift when you are tired. Or to take Berkeley's classic example, if you have just had one hand in hot water and another in cold water and plunge both hands into lukewarm water, the water will feel hot to the one hand and cold to the other.

One might say that these changes occur in regular and predictable ways; you would *expect* an object to look smaller when it's fur-

ther away. Yes, but so do the changes in secondary qualities occur in regular and predictable ways; you would expect a red object to look black in the dark, and to look green through green glasses. The first illustrates laws of optics, the second illustrates laws of transmission of light.

Yes, but only the *apparent* shape and size change; the real size and shape do not. The box *is* five-by-six and rectangular no matter how it may appear to us from various angles and distances. Very well, but so is the book red even though it looks dark gray in the twilight and black in the dark. In both cases, the object has a certain quality even though it doesn't appear under all circumstances to have it.

Locke, however, would not have been at all disturbed at Berkeley's argument. Our experiences (sense-data) of both kinds of qualities depend on the conditions of perception, both external (your distance from the object, the conditions of illumination) and internal (whether you have normal vision, whether you've just ingested a drug). Locke's aim was rather to give a scientific account of the world and the relation of our perceptions to it. You can *explain* the occurrence of the secondary qualities in terms of the primary, but not the other way round. Color-experiences are the effect of light waves reflected from the surfaces of objects; smell-experiences are the effect of an object's interaction with parts of the nose. As long as sulfuric acid regularly smells a certain way, it doesn't much matter *how* it smells; the secondary qualities aren't needed in attempting to give scientific explanations. But primary qualities matter a great deal. If a barrel is heavy and is rolling downhill, you can predict that it will strike the boulder at the bottom, and can explain the series of events by laws of mass and momentum. Virtually all laws of physics and chemistry depend on the primary qualities, not on the secondary. Thomas Nagel wrote:

---

[21] Ibid., Sections 15–17.

To be red simply *is* to be the sort of thing that looks or would look red to normal human observers in the perceptual circumstances that normally obtain in the actual world. To be square, on the other hand, is an independent property which can be used to explain many things about an object, including how it looks and feels.[22]

Physical scientists today on the whole accept the distinction between primary and secondary qualities as obvious. They need size, shape, and weight (more precisely, mass—the mass of an object remains the same when transported to the moon, but its weight is much less). They need light waves to explain color; but the color of something doesn't do anything to explain the occurrence of the primary qualities; rather, the color is explained by the presence of certain primary qualities.

Another objection Berkeley gave to Locke's view is relevant at this point. Shape and color, said Berkeley, are inseparable; how can you imagine a color without a shape or a shape without a color? The shape of something, said Berkeley, is "the limit" (boundary of its color. Try to imagine a box that has a certain shape but no color, not even black; unless the box is transparent (in which case you see the color of whatever is behind it), you can't do it. Try to imagine a box that has a certain color but no shape; you can't do that either. The two are inseparable. Yet we are told that shape is a primary quality and color a secondary quality—the shape is a property of the box but the color is not (it's only a power). According to Berkeley, this is simply unintelligible.

Can Locke's theory deal with this objection? He might say, "You can't imagine apparent shape without apparent color" or "Visual sense-data that have shape also have color, and vice versa, but that isn't true of the objects." But then what are real objects like?

How are we to conceive them? Let us try to see what matter is like *at the the molecular level*—which Locke constantly referred to in talking about the "insensible parts" of physical objects. A table is composed of billions of molecules; the table has a certain mass, which is the sum of the mass of each molecule constituting it. So molecules do have mass. The table has a certain size; do molecules have size? Yes, we are told there are so many billions of them per cubic inch. The table has a certain shape, but the shape is that of a collection of molecules; rearrange the molecules and you'd have a table of a different shape, though the individual molecules could retain the same shape. But do individual molecules have shape at all? Are molecules round, or is this only the way we picture them, as we do when we think of the nucleus of the atom as being like the center of the solar system (the sun) and the electrons circling around it like planets? You might say, "They are only positive and negative charges"; in that case, do they have shape? If they have no shape, and we can't conceive them without shape, what then? Shall we say they are not imaginable?

It would appear that even some of Locke's primary qualities, such as shape, don't apply to individual molecules. Nor do other qualities: The table is smooth, because along its surface are countless molecules at about the same elevation; but are the individual molecules smooth? Or is smoothness only a feature of a huge collection of molecules like the table? As our example from Eddington (p. 55) illustrates, the submicroscopic qualities of the table ("a whirligig of atoms and electrons") are very different from its macroscopic qualities (smoothness, shininess, heaviness). The table is hard, but are its constituent molecules hard, like marbles? But hardness is something we can detect by the sense of touch, and an individual molecule is far too small to be touched; should we say that if we *could* touch it, it would feel hard?

---

[22] Thomas Nagel, *The View from Nowhere* (Oxford: Oxford University Press, 1986), p. 75.

Physicists speak of the mass of molecules and of their diameters—so many billions of them per cubic centimeter at such-an-such a temperature. But they do not speak of the color of electrons; color, they say, is a characteristic exhibited only when photons of lights impinge on *many* molecules. Well then, what color *has* a single molecule? No color at all, we are told. It's transparent then? No, it's not that either; color is simply not a property that is applicable to individual molecules. If we could see them, what would they look like? Would they be round in shape but "having no color at all" (and what would they have to look like for *this* description to apply?). If a drop of water could be expanded to the size of the earth, we are told, the molecules in it would be about the size of tennis balls; but what would the tennis balls look like? Wasn't Berkeley right—isn't color what "fills up" the shape? If they had size, wouldn't their perimeters have to be "filled up" by some color or other?

We could answer, *"In themselves,* apart from perception, they do not possess color." But how are we to imagine something "as it is in itself, apart from perception"? The fact seems to be that we can't. We can only imagine the way an object looks (or sounds, or smells, or feels, etc.) *to* someone.

We can *try* to imagine it as it would look to a fly with a thousand eyes; but we can't imagine how it would look *to no perceiver at all.* If someone said "What would it look like if no one was looking at it?" We would have to reply, "It wouldn't look at all." Period. With no one to do the looking, there would be no looks. If we do see it, we have to see it (or imagine it) as looking some way or other.

We can, of course, ask what things would look like if we had different kinds of optical equipment. If we could see ultraviolet, as bees can, it would look different from any color we now see, and we have no way of imagining (never having seen it) what that would be. If

we had eyes so sensitive and penetrating that could detect the molecular structure of the table before us, it would doubtless look very different from what it does now: Presumably we could see the individual molecules, each separated by empty space from one another—quite different from the way the table looks now, solid and continuous and impenetrable. Still, the answer raises further questions. "If we could see the individual molecules . . ." we say; but individual molecules, physicists tell us, have size and mass, but no color.

The subatomic world apparently defies the powers of human imagination. We can imagine only the kind of thing we have perceived, and we have never perceived subatomic particles. Even to call them "particles"—as if they were tiny marbles—is misleading. The properties of the subatomic world are peculiar, to say the least: An electron is described as a particle, but it is also described as a wave; but "how could an electron be a particle that bounced and ricocheted like a tiny bullet yet be described by an equation for a wave?"[23] Or again, it isn't merely that we can't determine both the momentum and the position of an electron at the same time, it seems that it can't simultaneously *have* both properties—is this imaginable? "Perhaps momentum and position were large-scale concepts, qualities that required a little breadth of scale before they took on meaning."[24] But what "takes on meaning"—the qualities? or the sentences describing them? Countless questions like this assail us when we try to imagine what are called "the ultimate constituents of the world." Physicists seem torn between saying that the subatomic world is unimaginable and trying to present us models or analogies by means of which we can imagine it just the same.

---

[23]Robert Crease and Charles Mann, *The Second Creation* (New York: Macmillan, 1986), p. 58.

[24]Ibid., p. 62.

Sometimes it is said that "we can have no idea what the content of the real world is, science only reveals to us its *structure*.[25]

But it is far from clear—and in any case would take a long time to sort out—what the distinction between structure and content comes to. Perhaps a few analogous cases will help. When we detect an object by means of radar, we cannot discern most of its qualities; we can only see, through the blips on the radar screen, that "there is something out there" (radar can't tell us whether it's iron, gold, or wood). Again, if we examine an x-ray of a part of someone's body, the x-ray reveals only certain things. It can show you whether a bone is broken, but not whether a muscle is twisted. Perception through instruments tells us very little about what properties an object has. It does give us genuine knowledge, but it doesn't tell us very much. The suggestion is, then, that shapes or colors we see, and which we attribute to the physical world of tables and trees, tell us no more about the real nature of tables and trees, than radar and x-rays tell us about the properties of the objects they reveal. As to "what objects are really like," concludes H. H. Price, at the end of the most careful and sustained book on perception in our century, "we have no knowledge, and no prospect of getting any."[26]

Yet all this is enormously puzzling. Physicists try to give us a "picture" (is that what it is?) of submicroscopic reality, nature "as it *really is.*" It is the use of the phrase "really is" that is puzzling. We can understand "The balloon really is red, although it looks black in the dark"; we can understand "The tower really is very tall though it looks very small from 5 miles away"; we can understand "The table really is composed of billions of tiny molecules." But how can we describe anything other than how it would appear to someone? Can you describe the view from the mountaintop, not as it looks to you with the naked eye, or the way it looks to you through a telescope, not as it would look to a dog or a gnat, but as it looks to *nobody*—just "the way it really is"? Remember our earlier problems with the word "really": It is tempting to assume that just because it has a meaning in this context and in that one, therefore it has a meaning in no matter *what* context we set this phrase. And perhaps that is the source of the trouble. Is it meaningful to speak of how something looks when there is no one to do the looking? Is it meaningful to speak of appearance, but appearance to no creature? Is it meaningful to ask of "how it is" when there is nothing that would constitute an answer? When we ask a question, we don't know the answer to it, else we shouldn't ask the question; but when we ask a question, mustn't we know what *would* constitute an answer to it if we found it? And if we haven't the faintest idea what an answer *would* be, do we really understand the question?

7. THE CAUSAL THEORY

"In perception we are directly aware of objects and their properties, not of sense-data." We have already considered what might be meant by the word "directly." But if there is one thing we have learned from our discussion of primary and secondary qualities, and our subsequent discussion of the qualities of individual molecules, it is that we are far from always aware of the real properties of objects—indeed, if we are always visually aware of colors and yet color is not a real property of objects, then we are *constantly* aware of qual-

[25]See, for example, Grover Maxwell, "Scientific Methodology and the Causal Theory of Perception," in H. Feigl, W. Sellans, and K. Lehrer (eds.), *New Readings in Philosophical Analysis* (New York: Appleton-Century-Crofts, 1972), pp. 298–314.

[26]H. H. Price, *Perception* (London: Methuen & Co., 1933), p. 333.

ities that are *not* real qualities of the objects around us. The American philosopher Alfred Whitehead wrote:

Bodies are perceived as having qualities which in reality do not belong to them, qualities which in fact are purely the offspring of the mind. Thus nature gets credit which should in truth be reserved for ourselves: the rose for its scent; the nightingale for its song; and the sun for its radiance. . . . Nature is a dull affair, soundless, scentless, colorless, merely the hurry of material, endless, meaningless.[27]

What, then, shall we say of physical objects themselves? According to the causal theory of perception, about all we can say is that the physical object is whatever causes us to have certain kinds of experiences. If you perceive a tree, your sense-impressions (or sense-data, for those who accept that term) can be described as green, roundish in appearance, "leafy" in structure, and so on; that's what we would say if we were asked to describe the sense-impression—as in the case of the optometrist who asks us what letter of the alphabet it *looks* like on the chart, as opposed to what letter it is. We also say that we *perceive* a tree, since the tree is the cause of our sense-impressions, not a lion or a lily pad. But we need not conclude that the sense-impression we have in any way *resembles* a tree. We are only committed to saying that it is *caused* by the tree. The tree may be very different from the sense-impression it causes in us. A cause is often very different from the effect it produces—a telegram is very different in nature from the emotional effect it produces, and the act of lighting a fuse is very different from the ensuing explosion. The casual theory leaves open the possibility that the tree itself

is quite different from the effect it produces on our senses.

Locke speculated on such effects and concluded that they don't matter so long as our sense-impressions enable us to identify objects. It is of practical importance that we recognize a physical object as a tree, so that we won't stumble against it or mistake it for something else. This much knowledge, says Locke, "God hath given us". If he has not seen fit to reveal to us what the tree is really like, this should be no cause for complaint; we have enough knowledge, said Locke, for our practical purposes of getting about in the world. *That* there is a physical world has been revealed to us, but *what* its intrinsic features are has not.

What then is the relation between our sense-impressions and the tree? According to many causal theorists at any rate, the tree is something whose existence we *infer* from our sense-impressions. It is not a conscious inference like "The ground is wet, so it must have rained." When something becomes habitual, inference is no longer conscious. When we see another car approaching we don't say to ourselves "If I don't step on the brakes, I'll hit the other car; therefore I should step on the brakes." The process has become unconscious. So it is with inferring objects from sense-experiences.

The existence of the tree, says the causal theorist, is not "directly given" to your consciousness as are your sense-experiences themselves. There is something "given" about your sense-impression that is just "present to your consciousness" in a way that the tree is not. Suppose you see red spots before your eyes and someone asks "How do you *know* that you're seeing red spots?"—what could you reply? "I just see them, that's all; I am directly (immediately, that is, without mediation) aware of them." And if you feel drowsy and someone asks "How do you know you feel drowsy?", again what could you say but

---

[27]Alfred North Whitehead, *Science and the Modern World* (Cambridge: Cambridge University Press, 1932), pp. 68–69.

"I just know that I feel drowsy, that's all." But if someone asks you "How do you know that that's a tree out there?" you could *justify* the belief: You could say, "Look in that direction yourself. Go out and walk around it. Touch it. Photograph it. Ask other people." In other words, there are things you could do that would *substantiate*—give further *evidence* for—the existence of a tree. There is such a thing as *justifying* the assertion that there's a tree out there in a way that you couldn't justify the assertion that you're now feeling drowsy.

You could also say that "There's a tree out there" is a *hypothesis* that *explains* the fact that you have certain sense-impressions. What better way to explain my sense-impressions— particularly their orderliness and occurrence in "families"—than to believe there really is a tree out there causing them? "That there are physical objects is not something we observe or perceive, but something we suppose or assume (to call it a 'hypothesis' or 'postulate' is to suggest something rather too deliberate and self-conscious). In old-fashioned language, it is a transcendent belief; it goes beyond the evidence."[28]

If someone declined to make the inference from sense-impressions to physical objects— "sense-impressions, yes; physical objects, no"—he would not be contradicting himself. He would, however, be at a great practical disadvantage. He would be unable to make reliable forecasts of his future experience. Regularities occur in nature, but there is very little regularity among sense-impressions. "Whenever there is lightning, there is thunder" is (we believe) true in nature, but "Whenever I have a sense-impression of lightning, I have a sense-impression of thunder" is not true: If I close my eyes I do not see the lightning, and

if I am asleep I may not hear the thunder. In nature, when someone travels from A to B she has to traverse all the points in between; but if I watch you travel from A to B, even the blink of my eye will interrupt the succession of my sense-experiences. "There is no type of sense-datum A of which it is true that whenever it occurs another type of sense-datum B accompanies or follows or precedes it."[29]

Practically no scientific or even merely commonsense predictions about our future perceptions can be made without introducing as an intermediate link between the prediction and the direct observations on which it is based the notion of a physical object existing unperceived, and practically no causal laws can be stated in terms only of actually perceived states of objects. We have thus in order to make predictions to assume at least that our experience will go on *as if* there were physical objects existing independently of us in the realist sense. This at least we must admit, even if we say that independent physical objects are only methodological fictions. But this itself is a very strong argument for their really existing. That experience should persistently go on as if something were true is the strongest empirical argument we can have for its really being true.[30]

We have to introduce these independently existing things and events in order to obtain any true statement of regularities.

Moreover, a generalization about sense-impressions always has to include a reference to the *conditions of observation,* whereas physical generalizations are quite independent of these. The sense-impressions are occasional, intermittent, variable. But the physical order is a steady, continuous, reliable, ongoing "ocean of reality" in which from time to time, under proper conditions, droplets of sense-impressions emerge.

[28]C. H. Whitely, "Physical Objects," *Philosophy 34* (1959): p. 143.

[29]Ibid., p. 145.

[30]Alfred C. Ewing, "The Causal Argument for Physical Objects." *Proceedings of the Aristotelian Society 19,* suppl. (1945): 37.

Whether I have a visual sense-impression depends on whether my eyes are open; whether the tree of which I have an impression exists does not depend on this physiological condition at all. If I am to hear something, the sound must be loud enough for me to hear it, and there must be air or some other physical medium to transmit the sound; but the sounds occur regardless of whether anyone hears them (they can be recorded on tape, and so on). Laws of nature hold true regardless of the conditions of anyone's observation. But the sense-impressions we have do depend on such conditions, and do not occur when those observation-conditions are absent. And thus the inference from sense-impressions to physical objects is an extremely useful one; one we could hardly do without in daily life if we were to continue to "make do" in this world. Without the concept of a physical order existing independently of its observers, science and many other human activities would never have arisen.

EXERCISES

1. Consider hallucination and illusion:

a. We look at a motion picture. What's on the screen appears to be moving, but in fact it's a series of still pictures, succeeding each other so rapidly that we have the illusion of motion when we look at them. Shall we call this an illusion, because there are still pictures that we misperceive, or a hallucination, because we see motion when there isn't any?

b. How would you classify the following experiences (under LSD)? "The wall began to be covered with an incredibly beautiful series of patterns—embossed, drawn, painted, but *continuously changing.* More color. Indescribable color. And all the colors, all the patterns, *were in the wall* in any case — only we don't usually see them, for we haven't eyes to . . . Looking at my bright blue pyjamas on the bed eight feet away, I saw that the blue was *edged with flame:* a narrow flickering,

shifting nimbus, incredibly beautiful, which filled me with delight to watch. Clear flame: golden scarlet. Then I understood that this flame was *music,* that I was *seeing sound* . . . [31] "The faces of people around me were slightly distorted as if drawn by a cartoonist, often with the emphasis on some small, humorous, but nevertheless rather characteristic feature."[32]

2. "Light proceeds at a finite speed (186,000 miles per second). Over short distances, such as on the earth, the explosion and my seeing the explosion are only a very small fraction of a second apart—but they still are separated in time. When I look at the North Star tonight, what I see is what was happening there 450 years ago. Doesn't this prove that what I see is not what is happening at time t_1 when it occurred, but something *else,* that is occurring at time t_2, the time when I become aware of it?" Discuss.

3. Would you be more inclined to say that (a) There may well be an evil demon such as Descartes hypothesized (making me believe falsely that there's a physical world) —I can neither prove nor disprove it; or that (b) there is no such evil demon, and I know this; or that (c) it is possible that there may be such an evil demon, but I have no reason for believing it? or what?

4. Assess Berkeley's view that "the real object is the touch-object." Can you think of any exceptions to this? (Note: Humans have not yet touched any of the planets besides the earth. Why nevertheless do we consider them to be real physical objects? What about flashes of lightning? rainbows?)

5. It is sometimes said that we take our touch-experiences as decisive because "experience has shown that we have more visual illusions and hallucinations than tactual ones." Is anything wrong with this reasoning?

6. If we had no visual or tactual sense-experiences but only experiences of hearing and

---

[31]R. H. Ward, "A Drug-taker's Notes," quoted in Sir Russell Brain, *The Nature of Experience* (Oxford: Oxford University Press, 1959) pp. 12–13.

[32]W. Mayer-Gross, "Experimental Psychoses and Other Mental Abnormalities Produced by Drugs," *British Medical Journal 2* (1951): 317.

smell, would we have been able to form the concept of a physical object? If you had never seen or touched a bell but only heard the ringing, would you be able to say "The sound comes from a bell" or even "The sound comes from a physical object"?

7. What are the criteria in making the following distinctions?

a. We say that the trees on the distant mountaintop are really green, although they look purplish-gray in the distance.

b. We say that a certain area in a pointillist painting looks green but really is dots of blue and yellow side by side.

c. We say that the curtains are blue, although they don't look blue when seen through red spectacles.[33]

d. We say that the whistle of the railway engine has a constant pitch, although if you are moving away from the engine the pitch appears to be falling and if you are approaching it the pitch appears to be rising.[34]

e. We say the orange really has a certain taste-quality, although we have one kind of taste experience if we eat it without anything preceding, another if we eat it after eating a lemon, and still another if we eat it after eating a lump of sugar.[35]

f. Could the after-image I had have really been red, though it appeared yellow to me at the time?

8. We approach an object that appeared to have one uniform color, say green, and on closer approach find that it consists of small blue and yellow squares. This closer view is more differentiated—has more specific detail—and so we consider it the preferable view. But what if I see double? I see two things and you see only one. Is that not more differentiated? Or when I "look through uneven glass, is not my view more differentiated than usual? . . . I see a kinked object of complex shape when you see only a homogeneous straight-sided one. Then ought not my view to be called

the better one of the two? But of course everyone holds that it is the worse." Explain why this is.[36]

9. State as precisely as you can (a) how we know whether a certain sense-experience is hallucinatory; (b) how we know when a certain sense-experience is illusory; (c) how we know when we are dreaming (or have been dreaming); (d) how we know that all of our experience isn't one big long dream.

10. I am the only perceiver about, and I see only the top half of a building. But the bottom half must be there even if I don't see it: How could it continue to stand there without the bottom half existing to support it? Would Berkeley have a reply?

11. What would you say to someone who declared that he or she was a solipsist? Do you think that solipsism can be disproved?

12. Set forth arguments either defending or attacking each of the following views:

a. ("Weak" idealism:) Even if physical objects do exist when no one is observing them, we can have no reason to believe that they do, for no one can observe them existing unobserved.

b. ("Strong" idealism:) The proposition that physical objects exist unobserved is not only without supporting evidence: there *could* be no evidence for (or for that matter against) it, for it is *self-contradictory*.

13. Would the following help in determining which is dream and which is waking life?

a. Just before experiencing the series T_2 I remember going to bed, becoming drowsy, and trying to sleep; so T_2 must have been a dream.

b. As Freud has shown, a person's dream-experiences are a good basis for inferring what his waking-life experiences (especially conflicts) are; but his waking-life experiences provide no basis for inference about his dreams. So we can tell which is which by discovering from which group inference is the more successful.

c. All the people in a given locality have very similar waking-life experiences (seeing the same buildings, etc), but the dreams of each per-

---

[33]H. H. Price, *Perception*, pp. 210–213.

[34]Ibid., p. 214.

[35]Ibid., pp. 214–215.

[36]Ibid., p. 224. Price suggests an answer on pp. 224–225.

son will be wildly discrepant with those of every other person. I can distinguish the waking-life experiences from the dream-experiences by checking with other people to see if they had experiences similar to mine.

14. Explain why phenomenalists consider the term "sense-data" preferable to (a) "ideas" (b) "sense-experiences" (c) "sensations."

15. If there were no hallucinations, no illusions, and no dreams, would the introduction of sense-data be required? Would the distinction between sense-data and physical objects become unnecessary, pointless, or meaningless? Explain.

16. "Nobody knows what physical objects are like really; we only know how they *appear* to us, not how they really *are*, what qualities they really have." What would phenomenalists say about this view, and why?

17. "Provided one is not making a verbal error or lying, sense-data statements are certain." "But no pure sense-data statements can be made." Evaluate both of these assertions. Do they have any bearing on the acceptability of phenomenalism?

18. Since, according to phenomenalism, all physical-object sentences are translatable into sense-data sentences, why has no such translation been achieved? Cite as many reasons as you can. Does this failure show that phenomenalism is false?

19. Defend one of the following views: Some physical-object propositions are (a) absolutely certain; (b) practically certain but never theoretically certain; (c) relatively certain (near enough to certain to be a basis for action) but never absolutely certain.

20. Explain the meaning of the assertion that every physical-object proposition is an implicit prediction. Prediction of what? Is the series of predictions involved in "That's a table over there" infinite or finite? Justify your answer.

21. Attack or defend the view that laws of nature can be expressed entirely as regularity-relations among sense-data. (Actual or possible sense-data? And if possible sense-data, what kind of proposition would this involve, and why?)

22. Sometimes, when you have three shades of color, you can't detect any difference between A and B or between B and C, but you *can* detect a difference between A and C. Since for sense-data

what appears is, you will say accordingly that (speaking of appearance only) A was identical with B and B was identical with C, but that A was not identical with C. But isn't it a necessary proposition that things identical to the same thing are identical to each other?[37]

23. Is belief in Berkeley's God just as satisfactory an explanation of the order of our sense-experience as is the belief in enduring physical objects? Defend your opinion.

24. According to phenomenalism, "There is ice at the South Pole now" becomes, "If I were there, I could perceive . . . " etc. But no one is there now, so how do I know? Of course I could fly there and see; but then I would have verified the statement for a *later* time, t_2, when I arrive there—not for the original time, t_1, at which the statement was made. But at t_1 when I say the ice is there, I mean that it is there *now*, not later when I verify it.

Do you think this objection is fatal to phenomenalism? What do you think, and why, of the following reply? "It's true that I can't verify it until later but nevertheless when I say the ice is there I mean that if someone were there *now* he would experience ice-data. And I *now* have reason to believe that this is true. I won't have direct evidence (seeing it) until later when I go there, but I have indirect evidence now—indirect, but evidence just the same."

25. Assess Berkeley's argument from inseparability (against Locke's primary vs. secondary qualities). Do you consider it valid, and why? Then assess his argument from variability.

26. Here are six suggested ways of distinguishing primary from secondary qualities. Try each of them in turn. Is there a distinction in each case, and when there is, does shape become primary and color secondary (that is, does the distinction into "primary" and "secondary" yield the Lockean position)?

a. Primary qualities are present in the world even when they are not being perceived; secondary qualities are not.

b. Primary qualities are perceived by more than one sense; secondary are not.

[37]See A. J. Ayer, *Foundations of Empirical Knowledge*, (London: Macmillan, 1955) pp. 131–134.

c. Primary qualities have not the variability of secondary qualities: for example, color may change, while shape remains constant.

d. Primary qualities are those left in the object after we break it down physically. (Descartes said that if we melt wax it loses its solidity and shape—both of which Locke called primary qualities—but never loses its extension, and accordingly Descartes considered extension the only "primary" quality of matter. Note: Does the wax lose shape, or only a particular shape?)

e. Primary qualities are those left after we remove as many properties from things by abstraction as we can and still have objects. (Something without color or smell would still be an object, but not without shape or size.)

f. Primary qualities are qualities of the "insensible parts" of objects. They are the qualities the individual molecules have.

27. Can you ever have experiences you don't think you're having?[38]

a. Someone is blindfolded and told that he will be branded with a red-hot poker. A piece of ice is pushed into his bare stomach and he screams. Does he mistake the sensation of cold for one of warmth?

b. I have been suffering from a severe toothache. I get a tingling in my check and for a moment I think it is the toothache again. Can I think I have it when I don't?

c. Is it possible to think that you feel a pain when you feel nothing at all, but only see blood on your knee?

28. State, in the light of your knowledge of physical science, (a) whether a molecule should be called a physical thing; (b) whether it is solid; (c) whether it is impenetrable, (d) whether it can be called hard or smooth; (e) whether atoms or electrons have any of these properties.

29. If you can say "I was aware of a greenish blob in my visual field, so I infer that I was seeing a tree," can you also say "I saw all the roses on that bush, and since they were all red, I infer that I must have been aware of red sense-data"?

30. "Our knowledge of the physical world is based upon, and could not occur without, our experiencing sense-data (or, if you prefer, having sensations). Sense-data statements thus constitute the *foundation* of empirical knowledge." (Foundationalism.) "Not at all: statements about sense-data are just as corrigible (subject to correction) as are physical-object statements. No one class of statements is in a preferred position over the others. What we take to be true are those statements that are maximally coherent with one another." Discuss.

SELECTED READINGS

AUNE, BRUCE. *Knowledge, Mind, and Nature.* New York: Random House, 1970.

AUSTIN, JOHN L. *Sense and Sensibilia.* Oxford: Oxford University Press, 1962.

AYER, ALFRED J. *Foundations of Empirical Knowledge.* London: Macmillan, 1955.

BERKELEY, GEORGE. *A Treatise Concerning the Principles of Human Knowledge.* Many editions. 1710.

BERKELEY, GEORGE. *Three Dialogues between Hylas and Philonous.* 1713. Many editions.

BOUWSMA, O. K. "Descartes' Evil Genius" and "Descartes' Skepticism of the Senses," in *Philosophical Papers.* Lincoln: University of Nebraska Press, 1965.

BOUWSMA, O. K. "Moore's Theory of Sense-data," in *The Philosophy of G. E. Moore.* La Salle, IL: Open Court Publishing Co., 1944.

DESCARTES, RENE. *Meditations on First Philosophy.* 1641. Many editions.

BENNETT, JONATHAN. *Locke, Berkeley, and Hume.* London: Oxford University Press, 1971.

EDDINGTON, ARTHUR S. *The Nature of the Physical World.* Cambridge: Cambridge University Press, 1928.

EWING, ALFRED C. *Idealism: A Critical Survey.* London: Methuen, 1936.

HIRST, R. J. *Problems of Perception.* London: Macmillan, 1959.

HUME, DAVID. *Treatise of Human Nature*, book 1. 1739.

KELLEY, DAVID. *The Evidence of the Senses.* Baton Rouge: Louisiana State Univ.Press, 1986.

LEWIS, CLARENCE I. *Mind and the World Order.* New York: Scribners, 1929.

LEWIS, CLARENCE I. *Analysis of Knowledge and*

---

[38] Examples a–c are taken from Don Locke, *Perception and the External World* (London: Allen & Unwin, 1967), pp. 86–87.

Valuation. LaSalle, IL: Open Court Publishing Co., 1946.

LOCKE, DON. *Perception and Our Knowledge of the External World.* London: Allen & Unwin, 1967.

LOCKE, JOHN. *Essay concerning Human Understanding,* book 2. 1689. Many editions.

MALCOLM, NORMAN. *Dreaming.* London: Routledge & Kegan Paul, 1959.

MALCOLM, NORMAN. *Thought and Knowledge.* Ithaca: Cornell University Press, 1977.

MARHENKE, PAUL. "Phenomenalism," In *Philosophical Analysis,* ed. Max Black. Ithaca: Cornell University Press, 1950.

McGINN, COLIN. *The Subjective View.* Oxford: Clarendon Press, 1983.

MILL, JOHN STUART. *An Examination of Sir William Hamilton's Philosophy.* London: Longmans Green, 1865.

MOORE, G. E. "A Defense of Common Sense," in *Philosophical Papers.* London: Allen & Unwin, 1959.

MOORE, G. E. *Philosophical Studies.* London: Routledge & Kegan Paul, 1922.

NAGEL, THOMAS. *The View from Nowhere.* New York: Oxford University Press, 1986.

PRICE, H. H. *Perception.* London: Methuen, 1933.

PRICE, H. H. *Hume's Theory of the External World.* London: Oxford University Press, 1940.

PRICHARD, H. A. *Knowledge and Perception.* London: Oxford University Press, 1950.

ROSS, J. J. *The Appeal to the Given.* London: Allen & Unwin, 1970.

RUSSELL, BERTRAND. *Our Knowledge of the External World.* London: Allen & Unwin, 1914.

SLOTE, MICHAEL. *Reason and Skepticism.* London: Allen & Unwin, 1970.

STACE, WALTER T. *Theory of Knowledge and Existence.* Oxford: Clarendon Press, 1932.

STRAWSON, P. F. *The Bounds of Sense.* London: Methuen, 1966.

SWARTZ, R. J., ed. *Perceiving and Knowing.* New York: Anchor Books, 1965.

WILLIAMS, MICHAEL. *Groundless Belief.* New Haven: Yale University Press, 1977.

YOLTON, JOHN, ed. *Theory of Knowledge.* New York: Macmillan, 1965.

CHAPTER

3

THE REALM OF NECESSITY

Thus far we have been considering statements about the world—whether about physical reality, such as "There are five trees in the yard," or about our sense-experiences, such as "I seem to see a dagger before me." Much more remains to be said about such statements, particularly when we consider the nature of scientific laws and theories, and again when we consider mind and its contribution to knowledge. These types of statements are *contingent* statements; they are contingent on what exists or occurs in the world. There are three chairs in this room now; but there might have been two, or five, or none. That there are three at this moment is a truth about the world, but it could easily be imagined as being different—and *would* be different if someone brought more chairs in. To know that there are three chairs in the room I have to perceive it, or at least someone does—one can't just "figure it out" as one would a problem in mathematics.

But, as we saw in Chapter 1, there are other truths, which are sometimes called "truths of reason." These are different in ways that are variously expressed: that they could not be otherwise than they are; that they could not possibly be false; that they are true in this world and in all possible worlds. They are sometimes called *necessary truths*.

Among the statements that many philosophers would be inclined to call necessary truths are:

A chair is a chair.
Red is a color.
Colors have spatial extension.
Dogs are mammals.
Fathers are male parents.
2 + 2 = 4.
The past cannot be changed.
You can't be in two places at the same time.
If A is larger than B and B is larger than C, then
   A is larger than C.

These statements are quite different from one another, and their necessity has been defended by very different kinds of arguments. What they all have in common is that they are all—or at least have been argued to be—necessarily true; it is impossible for them to be false. But what makes these statements necessarily true, if they are?

1. PROOF AND NECESSITY

If someone where to say,

(1) All dogs are mammals.
(2) All mammals are animals.

Therefore,

(3) All dogs are animals,

we might respond without hesitation, "That's true!" We might mean that each of the three statements is true. But we might also mean something else. What we have here is not merely a series of three statements but an *argument*. The first two statements are called *premises*; the third statement is the *conclusion* which is drawn from the premises and separated from them by the word "therefore," which indicates that it's an argument and not merely a series of assertions. Should we describe the argument as *true*? No, we say that the argument is a *valid* one. To say that the argument is valid means that *if* the premises are true, then the conclusion *must* be true; the conclusion *follows logically* from the premises: You cannot consistently assert the premises and yet deny the conclusion.

For an argument to be valid, it is not necessary that the premises be true. For example,

(1) All dogs are insects.
(2) All insects are green.

Therefore,

(3) All dogs are green.

In this case, each of the three statements is false, and yet the argument is valid: That is, *if* the two premises are true (which they are not), then the conclusion also must be true. It matters not at all to the validity of an argument whether or not the premises are true; the conclusion follows necessarily from the premises in both cases.

On the other hand, if one were to argue

(1) All dogs are mammals.
(2) All cats are mammals.

Therefore,

(3) All dogs are cats,

this argument would be *invalid*; the conclusion would not follow necessarily from the premises. In fact, both premises are true, yet the conclusion drawn from it is false. Even if all three statements are true,

(1) All dogs are mammals.
(2) Albany is the capital of New York.

Therefore,

(3) Many houses are lighted by electricity,

the result would not be a valid argument; as an argument, it is invalid—indeed, it could hardly be described as an argument at all—it's just three statements set next to one another, all of which happen to be true.

Consider another argument, as stated in the following *syllogism*:

All As are Bs;
All Bs are Cs;

Therefore,

All As are Cs,

or in a different formulation,

If p implies q, and q implies r, then p implies r;
That is: If (if p is true then q is true)

and (if *q* is true then *r* is true),
then (if *p* is true then *r* is true).

Such arguments are valid *no matter what* A, B, and C, or *p*, *q*, and, *r* may be. These are called *tautologies* (from the Greek word "tautos," the same). The argument is valid no matter what propositions *p*, *q*, and *r* are. *If being red implies being round, and if being round implies being smooth, then being red implies being smooth.*

"If *p* implies *q* and *p* is true, then *q* is true" is called a *propositional form*—not a proposition; you can substitute whatever propositions you like for *p* and *q*, and the argument holds. *Any* argument of that form is valid. On the other hand, the propositional form "If *p* implies *q*, then *q* implies *p*" is *not* valid; no matter what propositions you put in place of *p* and *q*, the argument is still invalid. "If being a dog implies being a mammal, then being a mammal implies being a dog" is an argument of this form; and, of course, the argument is invalid. Being a dog does imply being a mammal, but being a mammal doesn't imply being a dog. (There are many mammals besides dogs.)

Examples of valid propositional forms include:

1. If no As are Bs, then no Bs are As. (If no dogs are cats, then no cats are dogs.)
2. If A is larger than B, and B is larger than C, then A is larger than C.
3. If some As are Bs, then some Bs are As. (If some dogs are white creatures, then some white creatures are dogs.)

On the other hand, here are a few examples of invalid forms:

1. If all As are Bs, then all Bs are As. (If all dogs are mammals, than all mammals are dogs.)
2. If some As are not Bs, then some Bs are not As. (If some clocks are not things that give correct time, then some things that give correct time are not clocks.)

3. If *p* implies *q* and *q* implies *r*, then *r* implies *q*. (If being a square implies being a rectangle, and being a rectangle implies being a quadrilateral, then being a quadrilateral implies being a square.)

Logic is the study of valid reasoning. In logic we consider which propositional forms are valid, which are not, and why. Logic is a separate branch of study, and we shall not consider it here. Our purpose here is to introduce the topic of *necessary truth*. The statement "Billy is taller than Johnny" is not necessarily true; it is a *contingent* truth (contingent on what the world is like); you can't just "figure out" whether it is true, you have to measure the heights of both Billy and Johnny to discover whether it is true. But the statement "If Billy is taller than Johnny, then Johnny is shorter than Billy" is necessarily true; *any* statement of the form "If A is taller than B, then B is shorter than A" is necessarily true. You don't have to measure Billy's and Johnny's heights to discover *that*; you can know it without even having seen either one of them. The entire if-then statement is necessarily true, even though the component statements about Billy's and Johnny's heights are not.

"If that cat is black, and all black cats will bring bad luck, then that cat will bring bad luck"—the argument is valid enough, and the statement as a whole is necessarily true. But this will not suffice to convince the listener that her cat will bring bad luck. She sees that the argument is valid, but she wants to know whether the premises from which the conclusion is deduced are *true*. The arguer will not be said to have "proved his point" to her if he presents a valid argument containing false premises. She wants not only a valid argument but a *sound* one—one from which she can draw a true conclusion—and for this she needs not only logic (to test validity) but observation of the world (to test truth).

If you get your monthly bill from a department store and only check whether the addition is correct, you will not have completed your examination of the bill; the arithmetic may be correct, but the items added may not—you may have been billed for items you never purchased. To know that the bill is correct, you have to know (1) that the addition is correct and (2) that the items listed are indeed items you purchased (at the price listed). An argument is said to be *sound* if (1) the reasoning is valid *and* (2) the premises are true. But logic won't tell you whether the premises are true. Logic will only take whatever premises you please and tell you whether you can validly infer your conclusion from them.

"But how then can logic provide us with new information? Whatever appears in the conclusion (of a valid argument) is already contained in the premises of the argument." In a way this is true, but it depends on what we mean by the word "contained." The conclusion is not literally contained within the premises as a marble is contained in a bag. Nor is it contained in the sense that it *occurs* in the premises, for in the argument "All persons have heads, John Stewart is a person, therefore John Stewart has a head" the statement "John Stewart has a head" does not occur in the premises. The conclusion is, however, contained in the premises in the sense that is is *deducible from* the premises. But to say this is only to repeat what has already been said. The question, then, still faces us (and we shall phrase it now without using the word "contain"): When the conclusion is deducible from the premises, are we learning anything from the conclusion that we did not already know in stating the premises?

We can answer this quite simply: Sometimes we do and sometimes we don't. It all depends on the complexity of the argument and the intelligence of the individual. The question "Do we learn through deductive reasoning what we did not know before?" is a psychological question, the answer to which varies from person to person. In the case of

the syllogism about John Stewart, the conclusion probably does not give us any new information; before we get to the conclusion we already know what it is. Sometimes, however, the conclusion does give us new knowledge—we had not put the premises together before to draw the conclusion.

Mr. X, a man of high reputation and great social standing, had been asked to preside at a big social function. He was late in coming, and so a Roman Catholic priest was asked to make a speech to pass the time till his arrival. The priest told various anecdotes, including one which recorded his embarrassment when as confessor he had to deal with his first penitent and the latter confessed to a particularly atrocious murder. Shortly afterwards, Mr. X arrived, and in his speech he said: "I see Father——is here. Now, though he may not recognize me, he is an old friend of mine, in fact I was his first penitent."[1]

The audience of course remembered the premises—the first penitent was a murderer, Mr. X was the first penitent—and validly drew the conclusion, which probably came to most of them as a considerable surprise.

In a deductive argument of any complexity, the conclusion probably *will* come as a surprise to most people. Consider this argument:

If the guard was not paying attention at the time, the car was not noticed when it came in.
If the witness's account is correct, the guard was not paying attention at the time.
Either the car was noticed or Jones is hiding something.
Jones is not hiding anything.

Therefore,

The witness's account is not correct.

To a person with perfect reasoning powers, who could instantly see the implications of every statement or combination of statements;

---

[1] Alfred C. Ewing, *The Fundamental Questions of Philosophy* (London: Macmillan, 1951), p. 29.

doubtless no conclusion would come as new information; but since human beings are not thus gifted, there are many conclusions of valid deductive arguments that do come as new information, in spite of the fact that "the conclusion is contained in (deducible from) the premises."

Whenever we discuss an issue with others, we are constantly confronted by the demand, "*Prove* it." To prove something is presumably to establish it beyond a doubt (or, sometimes, beyond a reasonable doubt). But how you prove something depends on what kind of situation you are talking about. (1) In the most commonly used sense of "prove," you can prove something by giving very strong evidence for it; "I'll prove my case in court," a defendant says. "Prove to me," says the prosecuting attorney, "that you were in Atlanta the night of the murder." (Since the murder was committed in Chicago, that would let the defendant off.) He may then provide evidence: His parents testify that he was indeed in Atlanta that night; friends claim that they saw him in Atlanta; someone saw him board a plane from Chicago earlier in the day. Of course that doesn't *prove* that he didn't commit the murder, for all these people might have been lying to protect him, or mistaken in their identification (the person they saw might have been his identical twin). In court cases the evidence is almost always circumstantial, but a large body of evidence nevertheless is well on the way to proof—particularly if police find someone else's fingerprints on the gun and in the house where the murder took place. Indeed, the prosecution is not required to prove its case beyond all possible doubt, but only "beyond a reasonable doubt."

(2) In the sense in which the term "proof" is used in mathematics and logic, to prove something is to deduce it validly from true premises. Merely to perform a valid deduction isn't enough, as long as the premises from which the deduction is made can still be questioned.

Sometimes in a deductive argument, we must use premises that are not known to be true. Sometimes we use as premises certain propositions which are called *axioms*. Axioms are "assumed to be true" for purposes of the argument; they are *posited*—accepted in the context of the argument—and that which is posited may not be known to be true. One can carry out elaborate and valid deductions, while yet not questioning the axioms which constitute the premises of the argument; these will perhaps be questioned later. Thus, much of the Euclidean geometry can be deduced if you assume Euclid's axiom of parallels: "Taking a straight line and a point outside the line, only one straight line can be drawn through that point which is parallel to the first line." The premise seems plausible enough—many would consider it to be obviously true—but a problem for geometers has been that the axiom of parallels has never been proved. But if you assume this axiom, then (together with other premises) many propositions can be deduced which are of relevance to geometry, to surveying, to engineering.

Systems of geometry begin with certain axioms and definitions and proceed from there to deduce theorems, which (using more axioms and definitions along the way), yield more theorems, and so on. Assuming there are no errors in deduction, the conclusions are valid. But are they true? That depends on whether the premises (in this case the axioms) are true. The Axiom of Parallels is part of the Euclidean geometry we all learned in high school. But in the newer geometrical systems of Riemann and Lobatchevsky, the Axiom of Parallels is not included, and different conclusions are validly drawn. The premises of the Euclidean system seem to most people to be obviously true; but geometers tell us that while they suffice for ordinary finite distances, they will not do for the millions of light years of outer space, because of "the curvature of space."

At any rate, whether premises are *true* is

something that must be discovered empirically, by observation and measurement. Whether deductions are *valid* is discovered by following the rules of deductive logic. *Pure* geometry is concerned only with the validity of deductive systems; *applied* geometry (as in surveying and engineering) is concerned also with whether the premises from which the deductions are made are true. Pure geometry consists of arguments (premises and conclusions) which yield tautologies; applied geometry is an empirical science, the truth of whose premises must be discovered through experience.

2. THE "LAWS OF THOUGHT"

"Mt. Everest is higher than Annapurna" is not an example of a necessary truth; it might not have been true, and only observation of the world can tell us whether it is. What *is* necessarily true is that if Everest is higher than Annapurna, Annapurna isn't as high as Everest.

But there are many other propositions that have laid claim to the title of being necessarily true. Prominent among these, and historically the first, were the three "Laws of Thought" laid down by Aristotle (384–322 B.C.) which he not only considered to be necessary truths but believed that all other necessary truths presupposed them. They are:

1. The Law of Identity: A is A: Everything is itself.
2. The Law of Noncontradiction: Nothing can be both A and not-A.
3. The Law of Excluded Middle: Everything is either A or not-A.

Our first impression of these is likely to be that they're not very informative, even that they are so obvious as to be not worth mentioning. They were certainly not intended to convey any specific information, only the most general kind of truth. It is also mislead-

ing to call them "laws of thought," as if they were laws of psychology that describe the way people think. Some people don't think in accordance with them—when people contradict themselves, as they often do in arguments, they are violating the Law of Noncontradiction.

Consider the Law of Identity, A is A (everything is itself). Let us take one instance of the law, that water is water. This gives us no specific information about water that could be used by a chemist. It doesn't tell us that it is a liquid at ordinary temperatures, that it is wet, that it is transparent, that it is drinkable. It just says that water is water.

Why should such a statement be worth mentioning at all? It's not that we would doubt that it's true, even that it is necessarily true, but only that it seems trivial and pointless. Yet Aristotle considered it a fundamental law of reality. What happens if we deny it?

A: I deny that A is A.
B: I see. And is your denial a denial?
A: Of course.
B. Then A is A—you presupposed that A is A in what you just said. You can't even *think* about anything without presupposing this principle. Take anything at all, call it A; then it is A that you are talking about or thinking about and not something else. How could the A you are thinking about also be non-A? If it's a chair you are thinking about, then it's a chair, not a tomato.

Or suppose someone were to deny the Law of Noncontradiction:

A: This is a table and also not a table.
B: Well, what is it you're talking about—a table, or not a table?
A: Both. I'm saying that this is, and is not, a table.
B: What does it mean even to say this? You first said it's a table; then in the next breath

you said it is not a table. Well, what *is* it then that you are talking about?

A: A table that is not a table.

B: But when you say it *is* a table, and then that it is *not*, you contradict yourself.

A: OK, so I'm contradicting myself. What's wrong with that?

B: What's wrong with it is that you can't communicate anything; your sentence is *unintelligible.* If it's a table you're talking about, then very well, it's a table, but it isn't at the same time *not* a table. If you say it's both, what is it you're trying to describe? Close your eyes and imagine a table; now close your eyes and imagine anything that's *not* a table. But can you close your eyes and imagine something that's at the same time *both* a table *and* not a table?

A: Whether or not I can imagine it is irrelevant; I can't imagine a million-sided polygon either.

B: There could *be* a million-sided polygon, whether you can visualize it or not. There's no contradiction in saying there is. But this case is different. You have to decide what it is you're talking about. If it's a table, then it's a table you're talking about, not something else. How could you communicate to someone clse, or even think to yourself, such a contradiction? Suppose I invite you to dinner at 7 o'clock and you say 'I'll come,' and a minute later you say, 'No, I'm not coming.' What is it that I'm supposed to expect? Am I to prepare dinner for you or not? I can't both prepare dinner and *not* prepare dinner. There's no way you can get around it. The Law of Noncontradiction is a necessary truth.

Few would want to say that a table can also be not a table. A more usual stance is to deny that these principles are about reality, and to assert that they are only "conventions of language"—just as the word "triangle" is a word established by conventional usage to mean the same as "any plane closed figure bounded by three straight lines." Here there is a disagreement between the "realist" who holds that the laws of thought are truths about the real world, and the "conventionalist," who holds that they are conventions of language. Let's consider a hypothetical dialogue between them:

CONVENTIONALIST: All the Laws of Noncontradiction is, is an explication of the meaning of the word "not." Let's classify all of reality into two categories: chairs and not- chairs. The chairs we put in one box, and the other box includes everything in the world other than chairs. Now, what is it that prohibits me from calling this thing both a chair and not a chair? Nothing but the way we use the word "not": "not-chairs" by definition include everything *other* than what's in the box labeled "chairs." That's the way the word "not" is used in our language: It's meant to *exclude* everything that isn't placed in a certain class. If we want to talk about A, then we exclude everything that isn't in class A and we *call* that not-A. What we mean by not-A is everything other than A. So this much-vaunted truth of yours, that something can't be both A and not-A only explicates (brings out) nothing more than the way we use the word "not."

REALIST: The verbal convention would not be possible unless the laws of thought were true. A convention is a convention, and a convention cannot at the same time be a non-convention: Without those truths your statement about verbal conventions, or indeed any other statement, couldn't get off the ground. Aristotle's "laws" state a fundamental truth about the *nature of things*. It's such a general truth that most people don't care about it, and it doesn't even occur to them; they are interested in acquiring *specific* information, such as which diseases are curable. But at the moment we're not engaged in any such practical activity, but in philosophy. Philosophy asks, what are the fundamental truths about reality? And among these are Aristotle's three "laws." We didn't make them up—we *formulated* them in words, to be sure, but they were true independently of that formulation. The sentence "Nothing is both A and not-A" reports a fact *not of our own making*:

That the desk I am writing on is either a desk, or not may be admitted to be a most unhelpful truth and one in which nobody but a philosopher would take the slightest interest. Does it say something true, however? Try to deny it and see. Does it say something about this particular desk? Yes, and this is not controverted by pointing out that what it says holds equally of all desks, clouds, and lamp-posts. We must repeat that a statement does not say nothing simply because it applies to everything.[2]

C: It applies to everything because, by definition, "not-A" applies to everything that isn't already covered by A. How after all do we learn the meaning of "not"? If someone said, "This is both a table and not a table," I would conclude that she hasn't learned what "not" means. I'd have to explain to her that whatever isn't included in A is *called* not-A. Once you understand what "not" means, you understand why it's a mistake to say "This is both a table and not a table."

R: I say the Law of Noncontradiction is a fact of reality; you say it is not. You will admit then that we disagree: That one of our statements contradicts the other. And if two statements contradict one another, one of them must be false. *That* is no convention. A convention can be changed. For example, it is a convention in the English language to use the word "cat" to refer to a certain kind of domesticated quadruped.

But that convention could be changed; indeed, other languages have different conventions for talking about cats. But the Law of Noncontradiction is not a convention, and we *cannot change* it. We can change the *words*, but not the *fact*. Is it just a convention that if I say there's a mouse in the room and you say there isn't, we contradict one another and one of us is mistaken?

But if the law of contradiction is really only a convention with alternatives, why should we be expected so firmly to take this contradictory as false? If there really is an alternative to the law, *both* sides of a contradiction may be true, and to insist on either to the exclusion of the other is dogmatism.[3]

In a realm where no proposition excludes its contradictory, nothing could be asserted as true rather than its opposite; assertion and negation would vanish . . . To us the source of this constraint seems clear. If it came from our own will, as conventions do, we could change it, whereas we cannot. If it came from experience, the law would be only probable, and positivists agree that it is more. To say with Kant that it comes from some uncontrollable region of our own minds compels us to say that though the contradictoriness of the real world may be unthinkable, it may nevertheless be true. Our own view of the source of constraint is presumably that of the "plain man." We accept the law and must accept it, because "nature has said it." If we hold that a thing cannot at once have a property and not have it, it is because we *see* that it cannot. The law of contradiction is at once the statement of a logical requirement and the statement of an ontological truth.[4]

C: Let's make up a language. There will be one word for each situation, and the negative of the word for the absence of that situation. Give any situation a name, such as "A," and give a second situation a different name, such as "B," and so on indefinitely. Just be careful to keep the names distinct, so we know what situation we are identifying with each name. And since we

---

[2]Brand Blanshard, *Reason and Analysis*, (LaSalle, IL: Open Court Publishing Co., 1962), p. 427.

[3]Ibid., p. 275.
[4]Ibid., p. 276.

want a name for the *absence* of situations as well as their presence, we will use "not-A," and "not-B," etc. for the absence of each situation. These are the basic rules of our language-game. It someone were to say, "This thing is both A and not-A," we would say to him that he has violated the rules of the game, since we have used "not-A" as the name for the *absence* of the very situation we had used "A" for the presence of. There now, do you see what a simple move in the langauge-game this is?

R: An inevitable move, I would say. We must adopt these rules because "A is A" and "not both A and not-A" are true antecedently to the adoption of the rules.

C: No, we need not have *these* rules. The rule about "not" is useful as long as we want to refer to the absence of situations as well as their presence. If we had the same word for A as for B, or for A as for the absence of A, communication would be impossible, for nobody would know, when we used the word "A," *what* we were talking about: A, or something else, B, or the absence of A (not-A), etc. Let me use an analogy: When you get a claim check in the baggage room, you have a number on the claim check and that same number on your suitcase. The person next to you will have a different number, but his number will be the same as the one on *his* suitcase; and so on. It is more useful to have it that way, so that each of us can retrieve and identify our own baggage without confusion. We *could* have a different convention: Everyone might have the same number on his or her claim check. But then there would be no point in having claim checks at all, for their utility lies in each person being able to retrieve his or her own baggage, without confusion in identification. The same consideration applies to the principles of logic. They are the prerequisites for useful communication.

R: They are the prerequisites of all commu-nication, because their truth is presupposed in every assertion we make. Again, our verbal conventions are rooted in the nature of reality.

C: Here we go again. If you mean what we now mean by "not," then there is no alternative to the Law of Noncontradiction. We mean to exclude all alternatives by saying that "not-A" will cover all the territory other than what is covered by "A." But this very fact helps to make it clear, doesn't it, that it is *not a fact about reality* that is being stated by the law? It doesn't tell you anything about "how reality is" or "the way reality goes." It doesn't tell you "Reality is *this* way," for there is no specifiable other way. Why not? How do we know there isn't? Is it that you know exactly what other way is meant, but know that it will never come about? No. You aren't told what the other way is. And if you were told, how could you possibly be sure that it will never occur? But if the principle doesn't tell you which way reality is (from among other possible ways), how are you to be taught what is meant by the expressions "A is A" or "not both A and not-A?" What else is it to teach the meaning of an expression that purports to represent a state-of-affairs than to show *when* we are to use it and when we are not? For example, we use the word "snow" under certain circumstances, and not under all other circumstances. We are always taught the meaning of a sentence by being shown cases of its truth ("This is snow") as distinguished from other cases when it is not true, when the expression does not apply. You can't be taught the meaning of "This is snow" by being told when it is *not* true but never when it *is*; and in the same way you can't be taught the meaning of an expression only by being shown when it *is* true or *does* apply to reality but never when it is false or does *not* apply. Now, "A is A" and "Not both A and not-A," I'm sure you would say, cannot ever be false. So how can you say they refer to some fact of reality? "This is snow" *does* refer to a fact of reality, for I know when the expression should be used in reference to reality—and when it should not. But you can't show me what fact of reality "A is A" refers to because there is *no possible case* of its falsity—there is no conceivable case to which it *does not* apply. But if I know when to apply an expression, I must also know when to refrain from applying it. And when am I to refrain from applying this one?

R: Never, of course. It applies, necessarily, to everything. You have given a good description of contingent truths: this could be an A, or it could be a not-A. But in the present instance we have a necessary truth. In the case of a necessary truth, there *is* no alternative. No matter what possible world you may try to describe, if there's something in it, A, that A is an A and not something else, and it can't be both an A and not an A, and it must be either an A or not an A.

Criticisms of the "Laws of Thought"

The laws of thought have been attacked, however—as being either not necessarily true or not true at all. On the whole these are misunderstandings, and rather elementary ones at that; but let's run through a few of the criticisms.

1. "A isn't always A. Sometimes it's something else, B." Sometimes a man is not a man, say when he's a coward.

But this is simply a play on words, in this case the ambiguity of the word "man." He's still a man in the sense of being an adult male; he may not be a man in the sense of living up to the requirements expected of men, such as being courageous. Here the meaning of the word "man" has shifted in midsentence. The Law of Identity never said that what is A in one sense of the word is also A in a different sense of the same word. The "law" holds only as long as the word "A" is used both times with the same meaning. When it isn't, we call the argument an *equivocation*. ("When is a sailor not a sailor?" "When he's aboard." Here again there is a play on words—"a board" versus "aboard." But the sailor is a sailor, not a board.)

2. "'A is A' isn't always true. Sometimes A is not A, for what was A becomes B. Tadpoles become frogs and are no longer tadpoles." But just as in the case of arithmetic, "A is A" does not say anything about what A may become or turn into: It tells you nothing about what the processes of the universe are like. It only tells you that when you have an A, then it is an A that you have and not something other than A. The next moment that A may turn into a B, and then it is a B and no longer an A.

3. "The Law of Excluded Middle doesn't always hold true. Suppose I say, 'This unicorn is either white or it's not-white.' But neither of these alternatives is true, for there is no unicorn at all."

But to use the phrase "this unicorn" presupposes that there is a unicorn here; if you say that this unicorn is white, your statement consists of two separate propositions: (1) there is a unicorn here, and (2) it is white. The second proposition presupposes that the first is true. But it is not. Let us restate the matter. Either there is a white unicorn here or there is not. And that statement *is* true; there is not a white unicorn here. Similarly it is true that either there is a black unicorn here or there is not. If we state the matter so as to avoid the tricky formulation, in which there are two statements posing as one, the difficulty is overcome.

4. "Something need not be either hot or cold, nor need a car go either fast or slow. The

liquid may be lukewarm, the car may travel at a medium speed."

But this objection is a confusion of *negatives* with *opposites*. The Law of Excluded Middle does not say that the car is going either fast or slow. Nor does it say that a given temperature is either hot or cold, or that an examination must be either easy or difficult. Each of these is a pair of opposites, and there may be a middle ground between them. The temperature of a liquid may be neither hot nor cold but lukewarm; an examination may be neither easy nor difficult; a car may go at a medium speed that is neither fast nor slow. The Law of Excluded Middle does not say that there is no middle ground between *opposites* (hot and cold), for of course there is. It only says that there is no middle ground between a term and its *negative* (hot and not-hot). Wherever you draw the boundary line between hot and not-hot, there is no middle ground between them—the law, true to its name, excludes any such middle ground: Any temperature that isn't hot is not-hot, but of course the not-hot includes *both* lukewarm and cold.

5. "According to the Law of Excluded Middle, Jones must be either at home or not at home. But what if Jones is dead? Then he's neither at home nor not at home; so the Law of Excluded Middle doesn't hold true in this case."

But here is another double-barreled proposition. According to the statement quoted, (1) there is a man named Jones, and (2) he is either at home or not at home. The second statement presupposes the truth of the first. If the first is false, there is no person for the second statement to apply to. Let us take each one separately. Either there is a live man Jones or there is not (true). And if there is, he is either at home or not at home (also true). The trouble comes if we take the double-barreled assertion at its face value, without analyzing it.

We are often confronted with double-barreled questions: Have you stopped beating your wife? Have you shed your horns? Have you stopped using your roommate's toothpaste? We are supposed to answer these questions with a "yes" or a "no." You have stopped? Then you did do it! You haven't stopped? Then you are still doing it! Many people fall into this trap. The trap is the failure to separate the double-barreled question into its components. Ask first: *Did* you ever use your roommate's toothpaste? And only if the answer is yes, does the second question arise: Are you still doing it?

6. "You either believe that the Abominable Snowman exists or you disbelieve it." "Not so. Skeptics *neither* believe nor disbelieve it—they suspend both belief and disbelief. They don't say yes, they don't say no; they may not think there is reason to believe either one."

But of course the Law of Excluded Middle doesn't say that you either believe *p* or disbelieve it. It doesn't even say that you exist. It says that either it is true that you believe it or it is not true that you believe it. Possibly you are a skeptic who doesn't believe it but doesn't *dis*believe it either; or you may never have thought about it one way or the other. Or possibly there is no "you" to believe *or* disbelieve it.

7. "Here is an expanse of color. At the right, it's 100 percent red ("fully saturated" red). As you proceed toward the left, it gets less red (less saturated), until at the left it has only a trace of redness in it—it's gray with a little red, or white with a tinge of red, and so on. Now take a certain sample in the middle; is it true that it's red? Well, it's true *to a degree*, but not to as high a degree as in the sample on the right. Don't say it's either red or not red; say rather that as you go from left to right it becomes *truer* to say that it's red."

There are degrees of redness, but it doesn't follow that there are degrees of truth. You can draw the line between red and not-red wherever you like; if you don't count something as red unless it's entirely red (unmixed with any other color), then only the sample at the right will count as red, and all the others are not-red. Or you can say it's red as long as it's 50 percent red, and in that case every sample from the middle to the right will count as red, the others being not-red. Draw the line wherever you like, but on one side of the line the color is red and on the other side not-red. Either the term "red" applies to a given sample, or it does not. That's what the Excluded Middle Law says—and it's a lot clearer than talking about degrees of truth. Redness can be a matter of degree, but truth is not.

8. "The Law of Noncontradiction doesn't always hold. For example, a man may love his wife and also hate her. A person who is asked, 'Do you like oysters?' may repy, 'I like them and I don't'—and isn't that often true? These are examples of a familiar phenomenon that is called *ambivalence*."

A man may feel both love and hate toward his wife, even at the same time. Love-hate feelings are very common. He may love her in respect of her character and her tolerance, yet hate her for her irritating mannerisms and repeated unpunctuality. But how does this violate the Law of Noncontradiction? To have one attitude with respect to one quality and another with respect to a different quality is no contradiction. Indeed, the law is often stated, as Aristotle did, "Nothing can be A and not-A at the same time *and in the same respect*." He loves her in some ways (respects) but not in others. And a person may like oysters in some ways but not in others.

What if a person claims to like and dislike something in the same respect? Can a person simultaneously like and dislike a casserole with respect to its taste? It would seem so: "I sort of like it," people say, or "I like it and I don't." Such remarks invite the reply, "Then you like it with respect to one aspect of its taste, but not with respect to another." Per-

haps so. But how do we know this? Aren't we inventing a new "respect" in order to save our principle? How can we be sure that we can always resolve "I like it and I don't" problems by specifying some new "respect"? What exactly is to count as *being* a respect? Critics are quick to point out that we can always manufacture a new "respect" in order to save the Law of Noncontradiction.

One is tempted to wonder, however, whether we need to find a new "respect" every time this kind of situation arises. Why not just say that the love is not total—the man has mixed feelings toward his wife (partly love, partly not), and that the guest has mixed reactions to the new casserole? Is there a violation of "Not both A and not-A" in having mixed reactions? Or one could say "The feeling isn't both *all* love and not all love," and if one put it this way, wouldn't the statement be true?

The problem of proof. How would you prove to someone that A is A, or that if no As are Bs then no Bs are As? One might say that we just *assume* it, or posit it; but that doesn't seem strong enough. Don't we *know* that it's true? Indeed, doesn't *all* argument and all discourse presuppose it? If A isn't A, then no argument can get off the ground. And how would you prove "if no As are Bs, then no Bs are As"? You can draw two circles, one labeled "A" and the other labeled "B", and try to show the person that if something is inside circle A it can't also be inside circle B, and vice versa. But what if the person denies it, or claims that he "just doesn't see it"? You might say that if a person's intelligence is that limited, there's not much you can do. The statements are necessary truths whether he concedes this or not.

Propositions as basic as this are not capable of proof, since proof requires bringing in *other* propositions from which these are deduced. And in the case of the basic ones, no others can be brought in which are more clearly true than they are. You can't prove "A is A" by means of other propositions: In fact every attempted deduction would *presuppose* the truth of "A is A" (the proposition "*p* is *p*" would be just another case of "A is A").

You can't prove "A is A" by means of itself: That would be arguing in a circle (assuming the very thing you're trying to prove). And you can't prove it by means of something else, because everything else rests on it. Even if we could deduce "A is A" or some other basic necessary truth from other propositions, we would then be faced with the problem of proving those other propositions. And if we deduced these from still others, we would then be asked to prove those.

Even if it could be done, it would not help us. Suppose we could deduce principles of logic, L, from a body of other statements, K. Then how would we prove K? By something else, J? And how prove J? The question here in infinitely self-repeating. We are caught in an *infinite regress*. We cannot establish the principles by means of themselves; we cannot establish them by means other than themselves; therefore, we cannot establish them at all. (Even in saying this we are using a principle of logic, though a slightly more complex one: "If *p*, then *q* or *r*; not q; not r; therefore not *p*.")

If proof is not to go on infinitely, it must stop somewhere. But we are so accustomed to being barraged with the request "Prove it" that we tend to think that this is required also of the very bases of proof themselves. "If you can't prove it, you can't know it." But proof is always by means of something *else*, which in turn demands proof by something else, and so on *ad infinitum*. What we *can* do is exhibit the consequences of denying them.

Still, the uneasiness may persist. We want every statement to rest on another one. We are in the position of the lady and the rock. She asks what the earth rests on and is told: The earth rests on an elephant. What does the ele-

phant rest on? A rock. What does the rock rest on? Another rock. What does that rock rest on? Another rock . . . , and so on, ad infinitum. The lady in the audience keeps asking this question over and over again; finally in exasperation the speaker says to her, "Lady, it's rock *all the way down!*" All the way down—to what? The speaker can stop her endlessly repeated question only by teaching her a little astronomy and curing her of naive notions of up and down—though perhaps she will never quite overcome a feeling of dissatisfaction with the explanation. You too may remain dissatisfied with our conclusions about proof unless you get over the idea that the ultimate principles of proof must themselves be proved. What we can do is attempt to *justify* our acceptance of these statements: For example, in the case of "A is A," we could justify it saying that all argumentation and discourse would be impossible without it.

Let us turn now from necessary truths to contingent truths—what would you say if someone said to you, "Prove to me that you're now feeling anxious"? What could you do? You could say, "You know I generally tell the truth; I'm not known to be a liar. Also, I'll tell you some things I have reason to feel anxious about." But most of all you are inclined to say, "I can't prove to you that I feel that way; I just *do*, that's all. It's true, but there is no way I know of that I can prove it to you. But I know how I feel, and I do not need to prove to myself that I do feel that way. I do feel anxious; to you I can present no proof of this (though perhaps some evidence), and as for myself, I need no proof."

3. ANALYTIC STATEMENTS

A is A, says the Law of Identity. One could select examples of it at random: Cats are cats. Chairs are chairs. Eating is eating. The examples may be as trivial as you please, but they are all true. They are called *analytic* statements.

"AB is A" would also count as analytic. Black cats are cats. Folding chairs are chairs. Their truth is guaranteed by the fact that there is nothing in the predicate of the sentence (B) that was not already contained in the subject (AB). By contrast, "A is B" is not analytic: for example, snow is white, lions are fierce, arsenic is poisonous. These statements are called *synthetic* statements; a synthetic statement is any statement that is not analytic.

Many synthetic statements are false: for example, "snow is purple." But a false analytic statement has a special feature: It contradicts itself, that is, it is self-contradictory. If you deny that cats are cats, you are saying on the one hand that they are cats and on the other that they are not. Indeed, an analytic statement has been defined as one whose negation (denial) is self-contradictory. Analytic statements have also been defined as statements that are true by virtue of the meanings of the words they contain; that is, to discover their truth you don't have to go to the world and observe whether they are true, you only have to examine the sentence itself. "Flubjubs are flubjubs" is analytic, even though you may never have heard of flubjubs. Just looking at the sentence tells you; you don't have to examine flubjubs or even know what they are.

Not every statement that looks analytic actually is, depending on how the words are used. "Business is business" sounds like a simple case of "A is A," but as it is actually used it means something like "In business, anything goes," which is not analytic at all. "Boys will be boys" is usually intended not to assert that young males are young males, but rather that young males can be expected to do a certain amount of mischief.

A statement may also appear to be analytic when the use of a word shifts from one sense to a different one. Consider our earlier example: A sailor is a sailor. But someone says, to create a puzzlement in his hearers, "Some-times a sailor is not a sailor." "How is that possible?" "When he's a board." On the basis of a pun (aboard, a board) our speaker seems to deny the Law of Identity. But of course a sailor is a sailor and a board is a board; and when the sailor is aboard he's aboard. When the meaning of "A" is changed to something else, B, in the statement "A is A," then it has actually come to be "A is B," which of course is not analytic at all.

On the other hand, many statements that don't seem at all to be analytic on first inspection actually turn out to be so. (1) Someone says, "If you study this long enough, you'll understand it." You study it five times, ten times, fifty times, and still don't understand it. The persons says: "Well, that just shows you haven't studied it long *enough*." And how long is long enough? Till you understand it. In other words if you study it until you understand it, you'll understand it. Perfectly true, and perfectly analytic. Or, (2) "People always act from the strongest motive." And how do you tell what the strongest motive is? Whatever they act from; whatever motive that is, that's the strongest, by definition. There is no way to falsify the statement, because the strongest motive *just is* the one they act from. The statement sounds as if it's saying something informative, but actually it just repeats itself, like every analytic statement. People are not always aware of this when they utter such statements, and they may consider their utterance to be some kind of profound truth. But the so-called profound truth turns out to be merely an analytic statement in disguise.

Definitions

"A father is a male parent." "A circle is a plane figure all points on whose circumference are equidistant from the center." "A bachelor is an unmarried man." These are all *definitions*—usually simple definitions, in fact; most words aren't as easy to define as these.

Aren't these all analytic? Aren't definitions analytic statements?

That all depends on what we mean by a definition. There are different kinds of definitions.

1. First of all, there are *stipulative* definitions. You stipulate that you will mean so-and-so by a word that you use. "What shall I call 10 to the tenth power?" asked the mathematician Kastner of his little grandson. "Googol," the grandson replied. And so 10 to the tenth power came to be known as "googol." Often a scholar, to convey a precise meaning, will either invent a new word or take an old word and stipulate a new meaning for it.

A stipulation is more like a suggestion than like a statement; it says, "I hereby propose to use this noise to mean . . . " or "Let's use this word to mean so-and-so." Suggestions, unlike assertions, are neither true nor false. You can say the suggestion "Let's use this word this way" is a good one or a bad one, fruitful or unfruitful, and so on, but not true or false. But to be analytic it must be a statement; if it's not a statement, it can't be an analytic statement.

2. Most of the definitions we use, such as those we find in dictionaries, are *reportive* definitions. They are reports of how persons in a certain language group use a certain word. "English-speaking people use the word 'father' to mean the same as 'male parent'" is a sentence that expresses an *empirical* statement—a report about how English-speaking people use a certain word, a report that can be confirmed by observing how other people who speak the English language use the word. As an empirical statement, it is not analytic either.

3. What is it that makes people call definitions analytic? Only this, that once you *assume* or *presuppose* that "father" is used to mean the same as "male parent" (which is an empirical fact about how words are used in the English language), that is, that you can

substitute the phrase "male parent" for "father" without change of meaning, *then* and only then can you say that it is analytic, an instance of "A is A." (*Without* that presupposition the phrase "Fathers are male parents" is not a case of "A is A.") Or one could put it this way: Once you introduce the *rule* that the word "father" is substitutable for the phrase "male parent," then, against the background of that rule, you can say they are identical in their meaning, that is, that the statement "Fathers are male parents" is an instance of "A is A."

As with definitions, so with *defining characteristics.* "A triangle is a plane closed figure bounded by three straight lines"—that's the usual geometrical definition of the word "triangle," and, assuming the truth of this report of English usage, we can say that the word "triangle" can be substituted for the phrase "plane closed figure . . . " etc. Thus we can turn it into "A is A," which is analytic. But we can do the same with the statement "A triangle is bounded by three straight lines." This isn't the *whole* definition of the word "triangle," but it's part of it; it states a *defining characteristic* (or property) of triangles, one without which something would not be called a triangle; in other words it's a logically necessary condition for being a triangle. Another example: A plane closed figure bounded by three straight lines is a plane closed figure—A B is A. And this again is analytic. It states a part of a definition, not the whole definition. You wouldn't call something a triangle unless it had this characteristic: To be a triangle it has to be (among other things) a plane closed figure.

Characteristics that are not defining are called *accompanying* characteristics. For example, "All swans are white" is not a statement of a defining characteristic of swans. When black swans were discovered in Australia, it was quite clear that it was not necessary for something to be white in order to be a swan. Of course, someone could have said,

"But they're black, so they're not swans." Such a person would be using whiteness as a defining characteristic of swans, so that he wouldn't call anything a swan that isn't white. He would be using a somewhat different definition of "swan" than others do. And he could, of course, have called the Australian birds by another name. But since the Australian birds were like swans in every *other* way, differing from them only in color, it seemed most convenient and less misleading to call the Australian birds swans also. Birds are usually defined in terms of their bone structure, and the bone structure was the same for the Australian bird as the others. That system of biological classification was already operative. Besides, color is usually a variable characteristic among creatures: some dogs are white, some black, some brown, etc., and there seemed no point in calling them all by different names just because they are different colors. And so, instead of calling the Australian birds something else, they came universally to be called black swans, thus making it clear that being white was *not* to be considered a defining characteristic of swans. A defining characteristic, remember, is a *sine qua non* (without which not)—a characteristic in the *absence* of which the word would not be applicable to the thing in question. Being white, in the case of swans, was not one of those characteristics.

In many cases it is easy enough to tell which characteristics are defining and which accompanying. "Steel is an alloy of iron" tells us, at least in part, what is meant by the *word* "steel"—it tells us how to identify something as being steel; but "Steel is used for purposes of construction" tells us nothing about how the word "steel" is used; it assumes that we already know what we mean by the *word* "steel," and tells us something about the *thing* already defined, that it is used for construction. But the latter of course is not a defining characteristic; steel might one day come to be used for different purposes, or not used at all.

Gold is an element, a metal, atomic number 79 on the periodic table of the elements; it is heavy, yellow, malleable, and combines with almost no other elements to form compounds, but it does dissolve in *aqua regia*. These are all characteristics of gold; but which ones are defining characteristics? Propectors of former days who knew little about chemistry identified gold by means of easily recognizable characteristics: the color, the weight, the noncombinability with most other elements. For them, gold was anything that had these characteristics. But chemists, who use atomic numbers (and atomic weights) as invariant characteristics distinguishing elements from each other, came to use these features as defining. Thus most chemists would probably say today that gold is anything that has atomic number 79; this would be its sole defining characteristic, hence its complete definition. Thus the definition of "gold" changed somewhat through time—the same word was used, but in a somewhat different way. As far as chemistry today is concerned, a sample of gold could be purple in color and still be gold. To find a sample of gold that was purple would be surprising, but it would be like the Australian black swans: It wouldn't keep something from being gold as long as it still possessed the features now considered defining.

No dispute about what is gold and what isn't would arise between the modern chemist and the old-time prospector as long as every sample of gold continued to have *all* the characteristics (as it does, thus far)—color and malleability as well as atomic weight and number; as long as this correlation continues, there is no particular need to say which characteristics are defining and which are not. But the moment you had one characteristic (atomic number) *without* the other (yellow), then a dispute could arise ("Is this really gold?'') just as it did when black swans were first discovered.

Often people refer to a defining characteristic as an *essential* characteristic. Being a bird is essential to being a swan; being an alloy of iron is essential to being steel; having a certain atomic weight is essential to being gold. But this language can be misleading: It makes many people believe that there is some "essence out there in the world" which people *discover*, whereas in fact what happens is that we select certain characteristics of things and *make* them defining, that is, we refuse to apply the word to the thing if the thing lacks that characteristic. And we could change this if we wanted to, especially in the light of new knowledge. The definition of "gold" was changed in the light of modern chemistry, and the definition of "whale" changed when it was discovered that those creatures were not fish but mammals, and being mammalian was incorporated into the definition. However, in both cases, the word continued to *denote* the same things—that is, to have all the same instances.

In all the aforementioned cases it has been quite easy to distinguish defining characteristics from accompanying characteristics ("Swans are birds" is analytic; "Swans are white" is not). That is because we have selected unusually clear-cut cases for purposes of illustration. The use of words in mathematics and the sciences is fairly precise. But the words of common life are not. It is not always easy to say exactly what we mean by words like "chair," "dog," "tree," "run," etc. It is not easy to say which characteristics of these things or processes we could count as defining—those in the absence of which we would not call it a chair, etc.—and those which are only accompanying. (Is a disposition to bark defining of dogs?) The reason for this is the vagueness of most of the words in our language; and because of this vagueness we cannot easily say whether a property is or

is not defining. Thus, we are in doubt whether to call statements mentioning those properties as analytic or synthetic. It is important, then, before we explore further the subject of necessary truths, that we first give some attention to the all-pervasive phenomenon of *vagueness*.

Vagueness

Why is it often so difficult to define a word? The ambiguity of a word is not what makes it difficult to define. We need only list a different definition for each of the senses of the ambiguous word. A much greater difficulty is a pervasive feature of language called *vagueness*. "Vague" is the opposite of "precise," and words and phrases that are vague are accordingly lacking in precision. But there are various ways in which words can fail to be precise.

1. The simplest form of vagueness occurs when there is *no precise cutoff point* between the applicability and nonapplicability of the word; in some situations the word is clearly applicable, in other situations it is clearly not applicable, but between these there is a no-man's-land of meaning in which one cannot say whether the word is applicable or not. Red shades into orange, and orange into yellow. A task that was easy becomes progressively less easy until it is no longer easy but difficult. You may drive every so slowly, but if you drive one mile per hour faster each day, the time will come when you are driving fast; but there is no clear boundary line between the two. If a person is driving at 60 mph in a residential zone, he is clearly going fast, and at 15 mph he is going slowly; but what if he is going 30? One could, of course, arbitrarily define "fast" (in this context) as "in excess of the posted speed limit in that area"; if that speed limit is 25, he is going fast, but if he continues the same speed into a 35 mph area, he is not. But as the word "fast" is used in ordinary dis-

course, it is not precise but vague: There is no one point of increasing speed at which one stops going slowly and starts going fast. There is a considerable "area of indeterminacy" in which one would not be able to say whether he is driving fast or not. (Note that the application of the word also depends on the context: A speed that is fast for a bicycle is slow for an automobile; one that is fast for an automobile is slow for an airplane; and one that is fast for an automobile in a business district is slow for the same automobile on the open highway. The term, then, is relative to context—but it is still vague in *each one* of these contexts.)

Vagueness is not always an unfortunate feature of language; in fact, vague words are quite indispensable. If you know exactly at what speed someone was driving, you do not need to use the words "fast" or "slow"; you simply state the speed. But if you don't know exactly, you might say, somewhat vaguely, "around 65," or, more vaguely still, "pretty fast." We have indeed a whole series of vague words, such as "slow," "medium," "pretty fast," "fast," "very fast," which we need to use when our information is not precise; but imprecise information is usually preferable to no information at all.

Countless words are vague in this way. The "polar words" are obvious examples: fast, slow; easy, difficult; hard, soft; light, dark; hot, cold; large, small; and so on indefinitely. Each of them shades gradually into the other, and there is no one point where you can draw the line and say, "At this point the object stops being small and starts being large." Or consider the word "between."

Going from A to B in a straight line, you would cross C; C without doubt would be said to be *between* A and B. But would D be between A and B? We might feel more hesitation here. "Well, not *directly* between. But close enough. Let's say it is between." Ordinarily, for example, we would say that Cleveland is between New York and Chicago, even though it is not on a straight line connecting them. (In that strict sense, *no* city would be between New York and Chicago, for a straight line between them would pass through the interior of the earth. Even if you choose some other strict sense of "between," such as "on the arc of a great circle connecting them," probably there is no city right on the line traced by this arc.)

Suppose our answer then is yes; now what of E? Is it between A and B? Well, if D is, you can hardly say that E is not—after all it is so close to D, it would be a bit arbitrary to say that D is but E is not. Then what of F? The same principle would apply again: E is between A and B, and F is right next to E, so F must be too . . . and so on until we have a point ten thousand miles away still between A and B!

Well, *that* point—call it X—isn't between A and B, surely. Yet E is, by our own admission. What can we make of this? Drawing the line between E and F seems unjustified: E would be between and F wouldn't, and they are so close together. But so is the line between F and G, between G and H, and so forth. There is *no* place where it is satisfactory to draw a boundary line. This is the "difficulty of the slippery slope": You want to go down from the top (you want to admit more than just C as being between A and B); but once you start down the slope, you can't seem to stop short of the bottom; yet you don't want

A   C   B

. ———————————— . ———————————— .

                            .D

                            .E

                            .F

to land *there* either. Set the boundary line anywhere you like, but you will fly in the face of common usage of the word.

You might say that this particular source of difficulty is nature's fault and not ours. We cannot draw a boundary line, except very arbitrarily, for the area of application of a word, simply because nature has presented us with a continuum which makes it impossible to do it satisfactorily.

Sometimes, for one special purpose or another, we have to do it, even though we feel uncomfortable about it. We have to draw the line between passing grades and failing grades, say, at 60, even though there is not much difference between a grade of 59 and a grade of 61—certainly far less than there is between the two passing grades of 61 and 100! But we are required to draw it somewhere. Ordinarily we do not distinguish sharply between the area of application of the word "city" and that of the word "town," but for statistical purposes the Bureau of the Census has to draw it somewhere, so it draws the line at 2500. In a town of 2499 a child is born, and lo, we have a city. In common usage, however, we do not draw such a sharp line, for we can see no justification for it. Thus in common usage these terms remain vague.

The kind of vagueness we have been considering is quite simple: There is one line or axis, at one end of which the word in question definitely is applicable, at the other end of which the word is definitely not applicable, but in the middle of which we can't say (unless we set up a new and arbitrary usage) whether it is applicable or not. But what if there is not one line, but many lines, all intersecting?

2. There may be *multiple criteria* for the use of the word. By this phrase we do not mean multiplicity of senses. A word may have many senses and yet each sense may have a precise criterion for its application; ambiguity is not vagueness. Nor do we mean that in order for a word to be applicable, a multiplicity of conditions must be fulfilled, as in the case of "tri-

angle." Several conditions have to be fulfilled in order for something to be a triangle, and yet this word is not vague. What we mean here is that there is *not any one definite set of conditions* governing the application of the word. The word lacks precision because there is no set of conditions (as there is in the case of "triangle") to enable us to decide exactly when the word is to be used. There is no set of conditions each of which is necessary and which are together sufficient, for the application of the word to the world.

Consider for example the proceedings that we call "games". I mean board-games, card-games, ball-games, Olympic games, and so on. What is common to them all?—Don't say, "There *must* be something common, or they would not be called 'games',"—but *look and see* whether there is anything common to all.—For if you look at them, you will not see something that is common to *all*, but similarities, relationships, and a whole series of them at that. To repeat: don't think, but look!—Look for example at board-games, with their multifarious relationships. Now pass to card-games; here you find many correspondences with the first group, but many common features drop out, and others appear. When we pass next to ball-games, much that is common is retained, but much is lost.—Are they all "amusing"? Compare chess with noughts and crosses. Or is there always winning and losing, or competition between players? Think of patience. In ball games there is winning and losing; but when a child throws his ball at the wall and catches it again, this feature has disappeared. Look at the parts played by skill and luck; and at the difference between skill in chess and skill in tennis. Think now of games like ring-a-ring-a-roses; here is the element of amusement, but how many other characteristic features have disappeared! And we can go through the many, many other groups of games in the same way; we can see how similarities crop out and disapear.[5]

There is a group of characteristics C_1, C_2, C_3 . . . C_n that games typically have. Among these characteristics are the following: C_1, there are rules

[5]Ludwig, Wittgenstein, *Philosophical Investigations*, trans. G.E.M. Anscombe (New York: The Macmillan Company, 1953), §66.

that govern the activity; C_2, there is the possibility of winning; C_3, it is pleasant diversion; C_4, the players need to exercise certain skills; and so on. If *all* games had all of these characteristics, and *only* games did, then the word "game" would have a unitary meaning; the statement of its meaning would consist of a statement of the characteristics C_1 to C_n. One game may have only C_1, C_2 and C_7; another may have only C_1, C_3, C_6 and C_7; another only C_2, C_5, C_6; and so on. All that is required in order for something to be a game is that it have *some* of the cluster of game-characteristics C_1 to C_n, not that it have *all* of them. Not every combination of game-characteristics will do, of course: for example, it is not enough that something have only characteristic C_2 (the possibility of winning) in order to qualify for gamehood. In wars and duels and debates, there is the possibility of winning, but none is a game. There is no way of specifying ahead of time and in the abstract just how much *is* enough; it would be absurd to suggest, for instance, that in order for an activity to be properly counted as a game, it is a necessary and sufficient condition that the activity have some combination of four or more of the C_n game-characteristics. It might well be that some activities that have only three game-characteristics are without doubt games, and that others which have five are not.[6]

Try for a moment to define the word "dog." What are some typical dog-characteristics? Dogs have four legs and fur; they typically have long (or longish) noses in relation to other mammals; they are able to bark, and sometimes do so; they wag their tails when pleased or excited; and so on. Clearly one or more of these characteristics could be absent: A three-legged dog would still be a dog as long as it had the *other* dog-characteristics (all of them? not necessarily); a dog that couldn't bark would still be a dog—there are whole species of "barkless dogs"; and so on. There is clearly one defining characteristic: being a mammal; doubtless the creature would immediately be disqualified from being called a dog if it were not mammalian. But this doesn't get us far, for there are countless mammals that

aren't dogs. When we go on to the other "doggish" characteristics, we may find one or two that we could consider defining, but for the most part we find a *cluster* of characteristics associated with the word "dog," not all of which have to be present; in fact, each of them can be absent (and therefore the characteristic is not defining) and the creature be still a dog as long as all, most, or some (this varies too) of the *other* characteristics are there.

Let us see now how our picture of language has changed. We began with the picture of a word designating all of a definite number of characteristics, let's say A, B, C, and D; unless a thing had all four of these, it would not be an X. But now we find that in the case of many words (most words?), it can be an X and have only A, B, and C, or A, B, and D, or A, C, and D, or B, C, and D; thus none of the four is defining. Indeed, it might be an X and have only A and B, or A and C, or A and D, or B and D, etc. In other words:

a. Among a definite set of characteristics, *no one* characteristic has to be present as long as all or even some of the others are present; but it cannot do without all of them. This might well be called the *quorum* feature of definitions. A quorum of senators must be present before the senate is officially in session, but no particular senator has to be there; there isn't one senator who cannot be dispensed with, as long as a minimum number of *other* senators is there. Enormous numbers of words fall into this pattern.

b. But what constitutes a quorum varies from one group to another, and from one word to another. It isn't necessarily "all the X-ish characteristics but one"; nor need it be "the majority of the characteristics—anything over 50 percent." The more of the X-ish characteristics there are, the more confidently we apply the term; but we can't say that any given percentage of the entire set has to be there. One can't say it's a game if four or more game-characteristics are present, and not if there are fewer than that. The word is *vague*

---

[6]George Pitcher, *The Philosophy of Wittgenstein* (Englewood Cliffs, NJ: Prentice-Hall, Inc., 1964), p. 220.

with respect to the percentage that must be present in order for the word to be applicable.

c. Thus far we have assumed that there is at least a definite number of X-ish characteristics in the set, and that the only difficulty was in settling on the percentage. But this is not so: Often there is no definite number of X-ish characteristics constituting the set—at least we can't be sure that there are. It's not only that we can't settle the matter (of applying the word) by finding the percentage of the X-characteristics that constitutes a quorum, but also that we can't settle on any definite number of characteristics as being *the* set of X-characteristics. Consider the word "neurotic": Is there any definite set of X-characteristics here? Perhaps a person is extremely nervous and irritable; perhaps he bursts into a temper at the slightest provocation; perhaps he always has guilt feelings in very strange circumstances (such as when touching glass) or lacks them when others have them; perhaps he is unstable and can't be depended on even in the most ordinary nonconflict situations; perhaps he can never make up his mind about anything and always vacillates; and so on. None of these things is defining of being neurotic; he could do without one or more—even all—on this list and be neurotic in spite of it. But is there a definite set of characteristics to choose from? Who could make such a list, and if one did, could she be quite sure that it was complete, that nothing could ever be added to it as part of the X-cluster for "neurotic"?

d. Not all the characteristics carry the same *weight*. Some may count more heavily than others: Thus A alone may count more heavily toward something being an X than B and C do together. Inventiveness counts more heavily in estimating one's intelligence than does sheer memory.

e. Some characteristics are not merely absent or present but present in *varying degrees*, and the higher the degree to which the characteristic is present, the more it gives weight to

calling the thing in question an X. Everyone has *some* degree of memory, but the greater the degree, the greater the intelligence (other things being equal). In most cases one cannot state in mathematical terms how much weight is added by how much greater the degree of presence has to be; one can only say, vaguely, "the greater the degree to which characteristic A is present, the more confidently we can say that this is an X."

All this gives us some idea of the multiplicity of ways in which a word can be vague. Vagueness is such a pervasive feature of language that it infects even the most technical scientific terms. You may have thought that "mammal" meant any animal that suckles its young; but if you look in the *American Dictionary of Biology,* you will note *eight* characteristics associated with this word, together constituting the X-set for it, of which an indefinite quorum must be present, and each one carrying a different (but not precisely specified) weight. Or consider the word "gold." A number of characteristics are associated with this word: Gold produces certain spectral lines, has a certain atomic number (79), a certain atomic weight, a characteristic color, a certain degree of malleability, a certain melting-point, and enters into certain chemical combinations and not others. Many chemists would say that the atomic number alone is enough to define the term—that this is its defining characteristic, and the only one needed. Yet chemists themselves would be quite nonplussed if something with that atomic number occurred that was *not* yellow, not heavy, not malleable, and had a different melting-point and produced a different series of spectral lines. Would they call it gold? Some doubtless would; others would not. Some would doubtless consider *all* of these characteristics to be defining—"it wouldn't be gold if it lacked even one of them"—but this is a dubious position in view of the fact that an isotope has a different weight from that normally characterizing the element, and yet chemists call it X ("X, but an isotope of X") as long as it has the *other* characteristics of X. Indeed, it is far from clear *what* chemists themselves would say if something like this occurred; they are so accustomed to seeing all the characteristics occur together that they have not given thought to the question of what they would call a thing that turned up which lacked one or two of them.

We simply have not anticipated what we would say if various kinds of new and unexpected developments were to arise. Would we still call something an X if unforeseen events E, F, G occurred? We may have made no provision for this possibility one way or the other. Consider, for example, when we do, and when we do not, use the word "cat." This word is certainly subject to what we have called the quorum feature of language: There are a number (not a very definite number) of characteristics associated with this word, such as being four-legged, bearing fur, having whiskers, stalking its prey and eating it, purring, meowing, and so on. No *one* of these characteristics seems to be necesasry: There could be a cat that never meowed, a cat that never purred, a cat that was a vegetarian, etc. A quorum of features must be present, for it couldn't be a cat and have *none* of them; and doubtless some features count more heavily than others. The more of them there are (particularly the ones that count most heavily), the more we are inclined to call something a cat. But now suppose that, in the presence of numerous witnesses as well as recording machines, the creature uttered a few lines of English poetry. What would we do then? Would we still call it a cat, or would we say it was a human being that *looked* like a cat? Or what if, before our eyes, it suddenly expanded to a hundred times its normal size?

. . . Or if it showed some queer behavior usually not to be found with cats, say, if, under certain conditions, it could be revived from death whereas normal cats could not? Shall I, in such a case, say

that a new species has come into being? Or that it was a cat with extraordinary properties?

Again, suppose I say "There is my friend over there." What if on drawing closer in order to shake hands with him he suddenly disappeared? "Therefore it was not my friend but some delusion or other." But suppose a few seconds later I saw him again, could grasp his hand, etc. What then? "Therefore my friend was nevertheless there and his disappearance was some delusion or other." But imagine after a while he disappeared again, or seemed to disappear—what shall I say now? Have we rules ready for all imaginable possibilities? . . .

Suppose I come across a being that looks like a man, speaks like a man, behaves like a man, and is only one span tall—shall I say it *is* a man? Or what about the case of a person who is so old as to remember King Darius? Would you say he is an immortal? Is there anything like an exhaustive definition that finally and once for all sets our mind at rest? "But are there not exact definitions at least in science?" Let's see. The notion of gold seems to be defined with absolute precision, say by the spectrum of gold with its characteristic lines. Now what would you say if a substance was discovered that looked like gold, satisfied all the chemical tests for gold, whilst it emitted a new sort of radiation? "But such things do not happen." Quite so; but they *might* happen, and that is enough to show that we can never exclude altogether the possibility of some unforeseen situation arising in which we shall have to modify our definition.[7]

The point is that we cannot foresee all the possible circumstances which, *if* they arose, would lead us to doubt whether or not the word should be applied to the thing in question. No matter how clear we may think we are in our use of the word, situations could be imagined in which we simply would not know what to say. We can try to block off doubt in certain directions by saying, "Well, if it did *that*, it wouldn't be a cat," but then what of countless other directions that we have never thought of?

Try as we may, no concept is limited in such a way that there is no room for any doubt. We introduce

---

[7]Friedrich Waismann, "Verifiability," in *Logic and Language*, 1st series, Anthony Flew (ed.), (Oxford: Blackwell, 1953), pp. 119–120.

a concept and limit it in *some* directions; for instance, we define gold in contrast to some other metals such as alloys. This suffices for our present needs, and we do not probe any farther. We tend to *overlook* the fact that there are always other directions in which the concept has not been defined. And if we did, we could easily imagine conditions which would necessitate new limitations. In short, it is not possible to define a concept like gold with absolute precision—i.e., in such a way that every nook and cranny is blocked against entry of doubt.[8]

Are all words imprecise in this way? No, but probably most of them are. Many words in mathematics (including geometry) are defined with absolute precision, such as "triangle," "plus," and "cosine." We know exactly when to apply these terms and when not to, without any penumbrae of doubt arising from unexpected or unthought-of situations. It is a triangle if it fulfills all the three conditions, and if it doesn't it isn't, and that's that. But virtually all the words we use in daily life, at least those we use to talk about things and processes and activities in the world, lack this precision.

3. There may be *vagueness in the words by which we define.* This one final aspect of the subject of vagueness must still be drawn to our attention. Let us examine a word that is vague on one or more counts already discussed, and then show how it is vague in still another way. Consider the term "inhabitant."

Under what conditions is a person to be counted an inhabitant of a community? It is clear that a person who resides and works within the boundaries of a community is an inhabitant; and it is clear that one who has never set foot within it is not an inhabitant. But what if he owns a residence in the community that he occupies only in the summer, renting it out and living elsewhere the rest of the year? What if he attends college in the community, living in a dormitory while the college is in session but living outside the community while the college is not in session? What if he is living and working in the community for a fixed two-year period, but owns

a home in another community which contains most of his belongings and to which he plans to return after this assignment is complete? Is he an inhabitant of the community during this two-year period?[9]

But now suppose that we have settled all these problems by stipulation of new and more precise meanings. Even after this is done, another problem arises:

Even if we could decide just which combination of conditions was necessary and sufficient for the application of the term "inhabitant," the *terms in which these conditions are stated are themselves more or less vague.* For example, we made use of the term "works in the community." No doubt, there are many cases in which the applicability or inapplicability of this term is unproblematic, but there are problematic cases as well. What of a salesman, the home office of whose company is in the community, but who, by the nature of his work, spends most of his working hours elsewhere? Or, conversely, what of a man whose employer is elsewhere but who spends most of his working hours in the community in question, as a consultant or lobbyist? And what of a writer who happens to do most of his writing within the boundaries of the community? Does he "work in the community"? The term "occupies a home" is also subject to vagueness. If a person owns several houses, does not rent any of them to others, and spends part of his time in each, does he occupy all of them or one or more of them? And so it goes.[10]

The point is this: When we define words by using other words—as we do in all except ostensive definition—these other words are usually vague themselves. We can define "X" in terms of characteristics A, B, and C, but it may not be clear what exactly constitutes the possession of characteristics A, B, and C. A dog is a mammal of a certain kind—but what exactly is a mammal? A mammal has four legs—but what exactly is a leg? (Is it a leg if it

[8]Ibid., p. 120.

[9]William P. Alston, *Philosophy of Language* (Englewood Cliffs, NJ: Prentice-Hall, Inc., 1963), p. 90.

[10]Ibid., p. 91. Italics mine. The word "community" itself is similarly vague.

is microsopically small? if the creature can't walk on it? if it looks like the things we call legs but protrudes from the top or side of the body? if its circumference is more than twenty times its length? and so on.) A dragon is a fire-breathing serpent—but when exactly is something on fire (what of possible cases in which some of the characteristics of fire are present but not others?), when can it be said to breathe (many borderline possibilities here), and when it is a serpent? Killing is taking a life—but when exactly is a life being taken? When you leave a person to die of exposure, not shooting nor poisoning him but just letting him lie there as you found him, can you be said to have killed him? If you drive your wife to suicide, is that killing? If a pedestrian dies because you didn't stop your car in time, and you didn't stop in time because the brakes unexpectedly didn't work, is that killing? And so on. The same vagueness that we find in the original term is likely to crop up again in the terms we use in defining it. Every time you think you have an airtight rule for applying word "X," it may turn out that the very constituents of the rule are not airtight themselves; the plugs that have been put in to fill the gaps have to be filled themselves.

All these aspects of vagueness characterize the way in which any living language is built. As long as words are defined by means of other equally imprecise words, and those in turn by others, there is no alternative. These words are learned by ostensive definition, but ostensive definitions are also imprecise: They point out *instances* of the application of a word, but no amount of ostensive definition will tell us what the exact boundary lines are, particularly when the vagueness occurs in many directions at once. Mathematical terms are the least subject to vagueness; and second, perhaps, the words devised for special purposes in the various sciences. But even here, as we have seen, considerable vagueness appears. The only way to avoid this difficulty would be to invent an artificial language and not use a "natural language" like English at all. In an artificial language we would start with a few words left undefined ("primitive terms"), and then would define others entirely in terms of these, and so on, being sure at each stage not to use any words that had not been explicitly defined before by means of the primitive terms. But however amusing a game such an artificial language might be, it would be of little help in the analyses of meanings in a living language—and it is precisely the words in a living language that give rise to most of the problems we discuss in philosophy, as well as in most other disciplines.

The Definition of "Human Being"

What is it to be human? What is the nature of man? ("Man" here is used in the generic sense, including men and women, children and adults.) There are so many statements about human nature bandied about as if they were profound philosophical mysteries that we would do well to pause for a moment to ask ourselves what can be made of such questions.

Questions beginning with "What is the nature of . . . " are typically vague. What are we asking for when we ask for the "nature" of something? We may be asking for that feature or those features by means of which we *define* something—that is, the defining characteristics. Thus, it is the nature of steel to be an alloy of iron, but not to be used for purposes of construction. Of course, different people can define something in different ways while still using the word to refer to the same things. One person will define "circle" as "a plane closed figure all of the points on whose circumference are equidistant from the center," and another will define it as "the plane figure whose circumference encloses the maximum area." Each definition mentions different characteristics, though both "amount to the same thing" in the sense that all the figures described by the one definition are also described by the other.

But when one asks "nature of" questions it is not always defining characteristics that are being asked for. If someone says, "It's the nature of cats to meow, and of dogs to bark," she is surely not saying that a creature wouldn't be a cat if it didn't meow or a dog if it didn't bark; after all, some dogs never bark. We say that it's "the nature of dogs" to eat meat, to hunt quarry when hungry, to wag their tails when pleased, and so on: In this case we are speaking of certain *dispositional properties* that dogs have—certain dispositions to act in certain ways under certain circumstances. (A dog might have a disposition to growl when threatened, but never actually growl because it never felt threatened.) Nor would it be required that *all* dogs do this, only that it is a rather general *tendency* of dogs to do these things. Similarly, when we speak of "human nature" we may be speaking of some general tendencies (dispositional traits) that human beings have, without assuming that all human beings without exception have them, and without assuming that we would define human beings in terms of these characteristics. At any rate, any feature that we would call a part of the "nature" of man or animals would be a fairly *pervasive* trait (not a rarity or a freak manifestation). Thus we may say, "I used to think of Bob's extreme hostility toward everyone as just a passing phase, but now I think it's part of his nature."

But when we say that all human beings do such-and-such things or have such-and-such tendencies, to what are we referring in the subject of the sentence? What do we mean in the first place by the word "man" or "human" to whom we attribute these various characteristics? "All Xs have characteristic A"—but what is the meaning of the "X" of which we speak?

Aristotle defined "man" as the rational animal, the animal possessed of reason. Whatever we may mean by "reason"—whether the

power of reasoning, or the capacity to form concepts and abstractions, or any other definition based on mental powers—an obvious objection arises. What about infants? They can't reason. But infants' capacities haven't yet been developed; to say that one is rational doesn't mean that all persons *do* reason but only that they have the capacity to do so. Since children have potential, they, too, count as rational animals. But what then of human vegetables, so brain-damaged that they can't even recognize their own family and lie there kept alive by tubes? Or what of people with advanced Alzheimer's disease, whose mental powers are irreversibly failing or gone entirely? These people no longer have even the *potential* for rational activity. Aristotle, sticking by his definition, would not call these creatures human beings at all; he would say they have lost their distinctively human characteristics; they may be organisms in the form of human beings, but are no longer really human since they no longer possess distinctively human characteristics.

"Man is the laughing animal," said Henri Bergson; but doesn't laughter presuppose a sense of humor—an ability to *understand* that which gives rise to laughter? And doesn't this require rationality? That's why a parrot doesn't "really" laugh, nor does a hyena; they just make laughter-like sounds. Similarly, one could define a human being as "the artistic animal," since only humans can make, or for that matter appreciate, works of art. But this again requires an ability to abstract, which is a part of rationality. The dog doesn't appreciate the symphony, not because it can't hear the sounds, but because it can't integrate them into a coherent pattern. So defining humans in terms of ability to understand humor or art would be a definition in terms of less *fundamental* features. If A explains B but B doesn't explain A, it is preferable to define in terms of A.

Another time-worn definition of "human being" is "featherless biped." This distinguishes people from birds, who have two legs but have feathers, and from most mammals, which don't have feathers but have four legs. Still, might you not say of some mammals that the back two limbs are legs and the front two are arms, as in human beings? What some people would call forelegs, others might call arms; and in that case a human is not the only featherless biped. Moreover—and more important—even if a human is the only featherless biped, should we define human in terms of these features? What if we discovered, either on earth or on another planet, a creature with two legs and no features that didn't look like human beings at all? By this definition, we would have to say these creatures are human. (Would you call a plucked chicken a featherless biped?) The fact seems to be that we just don't mean "featherless biped" when we call something a human being—there may be extensional equivalence (same denotation), but that's all. (Would we really call a featherless creature with two legs who looked like a walrus, a human being?)

Some biologists have tried to make the meaning of the phrase "human being" more precise. For example: Humans are creatures that at birth have the greatest weight in relation to adult body weight. Humans are creatures with the largest brain in relation to the rest of the body's size. Humans are creatures with the highest total number of vertebrae. Humans are creatures with the longest thumb in proportion to the length of the hand and so on.[11] But all these proferred definitions are likely to make us uncomfortable: Are these really ways of *defining* human beings? Aren't they just interesting *facts* about human beings—a creature having already been identified as human in some other way? We certainly don't *recognize* people this way: We don't say "this creature has the greatest

weight at birth, relative to her weight in adulthood, of any species, therefore I conclude that this creature before me is a human being." We already classify her as human, and these are just empirical facts about the creature thus classified.

Similar remarks could be made about attempts to define "human being" in terms of mental endowments: "A human is an animal capable of using tools." But some vultures use rocks to help them break open ostrich eggs; aren't the rocks tools? (Much depends on what counts as a tool.) Chimpanzees use lots of tools quite spontaneously. We might say, "Well then, human beings are the only animals that can *make* tools, though other animals can use them once they're there." But chimpanzees have been observed to modify sticks and other objects so as to make tools out of them, so that won't do either.

"Humans are the only animals that possess *language*." But other animals can *understand* at least single words, and some primates can make noises that seem clearly to signify definite objects. "Well, then, it's the human's ability to form *sentences*, not individual words, that distinguishes human beings from the other primates." But chimpanzees do appear to understand whole sentences, not individual words, though they don't seem to be able to form new ones; they have no conception of linguistic structure or syntax. But all this is treading on dangerous ground. If we do find a chimpanzee or other creature that can form new sentences, should we say that it is a human being? If we came across Martians who could do this, should we call them human beings, even though as far as their appearance was concerned they looked like cuttlefish, as H. G. Wells imagined?

"But the other animals don't feel the distinctively human *emotions*." This again can easily be doubted. After all, how do we know this? Recent investigations have concluded that gorillas and chimpanzees at any rate feel a pretty wide range of emotions—humor, de-

[11]See Don D. Davis, *The Unique Animal* (London: Pyrtaneum Press, 1981), pp. 21–22.

votion, grief, feeling of abandonment, enduring affection, even pity—but human beings were late to recognize this because these creatures don't communicate these feelings in the same way (by human gestures or human noises). But in view of their physiological differences from us, why should we expect them to?

In daily life we customarily use *biological* criteria for identifying creatures as human and distinguishing them from all other creatures. We call a creature human if it has two eyes, two arms, two legs . . . and then we go on to further description. But this won't do as a definition. Some people—that is, some creatures we call human—don't have two arms (either one has been cut off, or the person was born without it). We recognize other creatures as human beings by their *general overall appearance*—by how they look, as opposed to other kinds of creatures. But when we try to list exactly what those features are, we find it difficult to describe them; and even if we can describe the features, we seem to find creatures we'd call human beings who lack one or more of them.

Thus the phrase "human being" is vague in a double sense: (1) There is no one set of conditions that are each necessary and together sufficient for a creature to be considered a human being, but rather there is a *family* of characteristics, some of which have to be there, but not all of which have to be. (2) Between the human and the nonhuman there is no sharp dividing line. Is Neanderthal man human? Is Australopithicus human? We recognize some "human characteristics" in diagrams of these creatures; we don't want to say that they are *not* human (they look more like a human than like a gorilla or a chimpanzee) but on the other hand we don't exactly want to say that they *are* human either—rather, we say they're *like* human beings, more like human beings than like anything else, perhaps enough to be called "humanoid."

We should remember also that "what is"

questions are not requests for the same thing. For example, people had seen lightning for centuries, but only after Ben Franklin did they know "what it is." In one sense they always knew what lightning was: They could recognize the luminous bolts from the sky as well as we can, and they had no more trouble identifying a certain phenomenon as lightning than we have. What they did not know was the *scientific explanation* of this phenomenon; in *that* sense they didn't know what lightning was. Similarly, one sometimes hears people say, "Everyone can use electricity, but no one knows what it is." Yet don't we all know? We can test voltmeters, feel electric shocks when we touch an unshielded wire, and so on, but know nothing about what causes those things. But in another sense only the scientist knows what electricity is. It has to do with the attraction and repulsion of negative and positive "particles" (electrons and protons). (Once upon a time people could say that "nobody knows what it is," but hardly today.) And if someone were to say "No one knows what a human is," this would simply be a confusing piece of mystery-mongering (uttered as a rule to impress or mystify others). A human being is a mammal of a certain description (here we could describe the main characteristics), typically with certain dispositions and mental powers (here we could describe these). Very well, that's what a human is. Of course, there are plenty of things about humans that we don't yet know, such as their exact line of descent from other primates, and what exactly impels the activity we call "play," but this is a far cry indeed from saying that no one knows what a human *is*. In the most familiar sense of "what is," to know what X is we need only be able to distinguish X from all other things; we don't have to know everything there is to be known about X.

What has all this to do with the issue of analytic statements? If the Aristotelian definition of man as a rational animal is accepted, then that statement, being a definition of the word "man," is analytic, and other statements (such as "Man is a biped") are synthetic. On the other hand, if another definition is adopted, such as "Man is the creature capable of devising a language," then that statement, with that rather different usage of the word "man," is analytic, and other statements about man are not. In what seems to be our actual usage of the word in daily discourse, there is no one set of defining characteristics, but rather a family of characteristics, any of which may be absent as long as others are present; and if most members of the family are present we are inclined to call the creature a human being. But in this case there is no one statement with the word "man" or the phrase "human being" as the subject, which is analytic.

Problems with the Analytic-Synthetic Distinction

One reason, then, for being unsure whether a given statement is analytic, is the vagueness of meaning of most terms in a natural language like English. The meanings attached to the terms in a natural language often aren't clear-cut enough to permit us to say whether the statement is analytic or not. "The best players are those who win the most games," someone ways. But is this to be taken as a complete or partial *definition* of the phrase "best players"? If so, then it is a case of A is A, or AB is A, which is analytic, and the statement is a necessary truth by that definition. On the other hand, one might have another meaning of "best players" in mind—such as those possessing the most skill, dedication, imagination, tenacity, or whatever—and the statement could be interpreted as meaning that players who have those characteristics *also* win the most games—in which case the statement is not analytic (it's not A is A, but A is B). It all depends on what is meant by "best players," and most people don't say

what they mean by that phrase, indeed they don't even know—they haven't even thought about it, they just utter the phrase. How can we possibly classify statements that are used as sloppily as this?

But there *are* clear ones, surely, that we *can* classify as analytic or not. Surely our old friend "Bachelors are unmarried men" is analytic (again, assuming that that's what the word "bachelor" means in English). However, even a seemingly crystal clear word like "bachelor" is still somewhat vague—as most terms are in a natural language when we start to think of when we would apply them and when we would not. What exactly is a man? When does a boy become a man? You wouldn't say that a small child was a bachelor; would you say that a boy of 15 is? of 20? And what of a male adult who had a wife who died? We would probably call him a widower but not a bachelor. What if his wife left him years ago and he never remarried? We might call him simply a divorced man, but sometimes we call him a bachelor, too.

None of this affects the analyticity of "Bachelors are unmarried men," however. "Unmarried man" is vague, but that same vagueness carries over into the term "bachelor." They can have the same meaning, even though both of them are vague—indeed, *because* they are vague. If one of them was vague and the other not, they would not have the same meaning.

Let us consider the meaning of the term "analytic" itself:

1. Some philosophers have defined "analytic" as follows: an analytic statement is *one that is true by virtue of the meanings of the terms it contains.* "A bachelor is an unmarried man" is not analytic as it stands. It is of the form "A is B" not "A is A." But if you accept the definition of "bachelor" as "unmarried man," then by substitution you get "An unmarried man is an unmarried man," and this is analytic—it's simply an instance of "A is A." The statement is analytic only if the

definition is *presupposed*—when you assume that "bachelor" and "unmarried man" *have the same meaning*. But now comes a somewhat surprising question: How do you tell when two terms have the same meaning? One suggestion is that two terms have the same meaning if they apply to the same instances. Thus, every person who is a bachelor is an unmarried man, and every person who is an unmarried man is a bachelor. You never have the one without the other. They have the same *extension*.

But there is a problem about identifying "same extension" with "same meaning." Two terms may have the same extension and yet seem quite clearly to have different meanings. Assume that every creature that has a heart has a liver, and that every creature with a liver has a heart. Yet having a heart is a different property of a creature than having a liver. It just happens that the two always go together, but the two terms surely don't have the same meaning. It everything in the world that was round was also red, and everything that was red was also round, roundness and redness would have the same extension: They would never be found apart. Yet "round" is a word for a shape, and "red" is a word for a color—the two are clearly different properties and would remain quite different even if they had the same extension.

What is it, thcn, beyond "same extension" that constitutes "same meaning"? We may say, "I know *what it would be like* for a creature to have a heart but no liver; even though no such creature exists I can easily imagine one. And I surely know what it would be for something to be red but not round, even in a world in which everything red was round. Even if they do always occur together, I can easily conceive of them as occurring apart. But I can't conceive of a man being a bachelor and yet being married, or a circle that was also square. Not only can I not imagine it, it could never happen, because calling someone a bachelor already implies that he is unmarried;

that's what "bachelor" *means*. But now we are in a fix. What is it, we are asked, for two terms to have the same meaning? Apparently it isn't enough that they have the same extension. We can try to *imagine* one occurring without the other, and if we don't succeed we will say they have the same meaning. But is this a reliable procedure? If I can't imagine it, perhaps another person could?

Perhaps then we just do some intellectual exercising and think of all the examples we can, real and imaginary, and ask in each case "Would I *call* this an A if it weren't also a B"? We decide whether we would ever be willing to call something an A without its being a B. Suppose that after going over many possibilities we say "not only are all As also Bs, but nothing *could be* an A that didn't also have B." But can we be sure in advance whether we would do this? Perhaps in some far-out case we had never thought if we *would* call something an A that wasn't a B. How do we know we won't change our minds somewhere along the way? We might consider the statement "All creatures that give birth to others are females" to be analytic until zoologists tell us that in certain varieties of sea horse, it is the male who gives birth to the young. So what we first thought was analytic turned out to be just an empirical statement. How can we be sure? Every physicist probably believes that everything that is a physical body (A) also exerts gravitational attraction (however slight) on surrounding objects (B); physicists would grant no instance of an A that does not have B—so confident are they of Newton's law. Yet no one supposes that such a statement is analytic, or that "is a body" and "exerts gravitational attraction" are synonymous; the idea of a physical object is something people had long before anything was known about gravitation.

"Analytic" was a standard and accepted term before W. V. Quine and other philosophers raised many probing questions about synonymity (or synonymy, sameness of meaning). And these questions seemed to pull the rug out from under the term "analytic." Quine, who along with others who have pursued this question, wrote: "I do not know whether the statement 'Everything green is extended' is analytic. Now does my indecision over this example really betray an incomplete grasp of the 'meanings' of 'green' and 'extended'? I think not. The trouble is not with 'green' or 'extended,' but with 'analytic.' "[12]

2. But there is another definition of "analytic" that has often been used: An analytic statement is *one whose negation (denial) is self-contradictory* (or implies a self-contradiction). To say that a rectangle is round is self-contradictory, for it is to say that something is both four-sided and not four-sided. To say that bachelors are married is self-contradictory, for it is to say that a person who is married is also not married. In some cases we can't be sure, because the terms involved are too vague. Is "dogs can fly" (not merely false, but) self-contradictory? It's hard to say, as long as we don't know whether inability to fly is supposed to be a defining feature of dogs.

When people argue with one another, they are usually satisfied if they have shown that their opponent's statement is false—"It's false that all swans are white, here's a black one." But if they can show that their opponent is contradicting himself or herself, this is an even greater triumph: "You've just said that everyone is selfish, and now you say that someone you know isn't selfish, so you contradict yourself." When one philosopher can show that another has caught himself in a contradiction, this is often considered the greatest triumph a philosopher can achieve; it completely devastates the opponent's position— the opponent has to pick himself up and start

all over again. (A is A, and the opponent has said or implied somewhere along the line that A is not-A.) Is there a contradiction in saying that if you throw a stone into the air it will continue upwards into the clouds? No, the statement is false, but contains no contradiction. Is there a contradiction in saying that the stone *falls* upwards? Yes, because "falls" at least means going downwards (an object wouldn't be falling if it weren't going downwards), and it's self-contradictory to say that an object goes downwards upwards (notdownwards). When you describe a state-of-affairs, and its description involves you in a contradiction, that state-of-affairs is said to be *logically impossible*; all other states-of-affairs are logically possible, no matter how absurd they may be, such as a wasp turning into a dragon.

Logical Possibility

If it seems strange to say that a wasp turning into a dragon is logically possible, this is doubtless because we don't ordinarily use the word "possible" in the sense of *logical* possibility or impossibility. Usually, by "possible," we are referring to the state of being incompatible with laws of nature, that in the world as we find it "things just don't happen that way." A state-of-affairs is said to be *empirically* possible when it is compatible with laws of nature, empirically impossible when it isn't. Thus, it is empirically, not logically, impossible to have friction without heat, or for a person to jump out of a tenth-story window and float upwards.

As far as we know, laws of nature do not change. Stones fall when you let go of them, dogs beget dogs and not cats, argon and helium combine with no other chemical elements, all particles of matter exert gravitational attraction. Apparently what is empirically possible at one time is empirically possible at all times. What we *thought* a hundred years ago to be empirically impossible may

---

[12]W. V. Quine, "Two Dogmas of Empiricism," Section 4. In Thomas Olshewsky, ed., *Problems in the Philosophy of Language* (New York: Holt, 1969), pp. 398–417.

have turned out to be empirically possible, such as vehicles traveling faster than sound; but those who thought this were mistaken about the laws of nature. Nature works in ways which even now we are far from knowing completely, which only indicates that more things are empirically possible than we now know.

What does change with the passage of time is *technical* possibility, which has to do with people's ability to *utilize* laws of nature in practical activity. A hundred years ago the construction of jet aircraft was not technically possible, but today it is; what has changed is not the laws of aerodynamics but the ability of human beings to utilize them. To cross the Atlantic Ocean in one minute is not now technically possible, but as far as we know it isn't empirically impossible; there is nothing in the workings of nature to prevent it.

It *is* empirically impossible, as far as we know, for people to travel faster than light; this is a limitation imposed by nature, not by human abilities. But traveling faster than light is not *logically* impossible; if someone claimed to be able to exceed the velocity of light, his claim would be false, but not self-contradictory. The velocity of light is an empirical discovery, which might (logically) have been other than it is—for example, 200,000 miles per second rather than 186,000. It would be self-contradictory, however, to claim that you traveled from one place, A, to another place, B, without moving—to travel *is* to move. Travel without motion, then, would be an example of logical impossibility. To claim what is logically impossible is to violate the Law of Non-contradiction (pp. 108–10)—what is A cannot also be not-A.

Logical possibility, then, is far more inclusive than empirical or technical possibility:

Logically possible	Logically impossible
Empirically possible	Empirically impossible
Technically possible	Technically impossible

These three senses of the word "possible" are not exhaustive. When we say "It's possible that my aunt will visit us tomorrow," we are not saying merely that it's logically possible (that there's no contradiction involved) or that it's empirically possible (surely her coming to visit is compatible with laws of nature) or that it's technically possible (presumably she's able to come). What we are saying is more like "I have some reason to believe that she will visit us tomorrow."

It is for the empirical sciences, such as physics and chemistry and biology, to tell us what is empirically possible. It is for the applied, or practical, sciences, such as medicine and engineering, to tell us what is technically possible. Our chief concern here is what is logically possible. The others are introduced here only to distinguish them from logical possibility. The question that will confront us many times in the coming pages is, "Is or is not this or that state-of-affairs logically possible?" In doing this, we must be careful not to give a premature answer of "No" by confusing logical with other types of possibility. For example, it is *logically* possible for objects to fall faster or slower depending on their color; for you to chin yourself 6 million times in quick succession; for a man to live to the age of a million years; for dogs to give birth to kittens. As far as we now know, none of these things is empirically possible. When we say that they are logically possible, we do not mean that we expect them to happen, or that we think there is even a remote *empirical* possibility that they will happen; we only mean that if we asserted that they did happen, or would happen, our assertion would not be self-contradictory, even though it might be false.

Conceivability. If some state-of-affairs is logically possible, is this the same as its being conceivable? It might easily seem so: "It's logically possible for you to jump out of a tenth-story window and not go downward" would then be equivalent to "It's *conceivable* that you might jump out of a tenth-story window and not go downward'' (even though of course we don't expect it to happen). Of course we *can* define ''conceivable'' so that it means the same as ''logically possible''; this is indeed one of the most common usages the word ''conceivable'' has in philosophy.

''Conceivable'' is ambiguous, however. It may also mean ''imaginable,'' and in this sense it is *not* equivalent to ''logically possible.'' A thousand-sided polygon is surely logically possible; I cannot imagine one (form the image of one); what I am tempted to call my mental image of a polygon with 1000 sides is no different from that of a polygon with 999 sides, but I would not want to deny categorically that somebody, somewhere, can form the image of a thousand-sided polygon. People's powers of imagination vary. What is imaginable depends on who is doing the imagining. You may be able to imagine things that I cannot. What is logically possible does not have this variability. Whether I can imagine it or not, a thousand-sided polygon, an animal that's a cross between a walrus and a wasp, and a color different from any we have ever seen, are all logically possible; we need not stop to ask whether we can *imagine* them. Something can be logically possible and yet unimaginable (by you or by me, or even by everybody) because of the limitation of our powers of imagination.

On the other hand, if a state-of-affairs is really logically *im*possible, it is not imaginable by anybody: no one can imagine a tower that is both 100 and 150 feet high, or a circle that is square. If someone says he *can* form the image of a square circle, he is probably forming the image of a square, then of a circle, then of a square in rapid succession. But he can hardly imagine a figure that is both circular and not circular. (If he still says he can, let him draw one on the blackboard.)

''Conceivable'' is used in other senses as well. Whether or not a certain state-of-affairs is conceivable will then depend on the sense of ''conceivable'' which is being employed at the time. But until the sense is clearly stated, one should not be satisfied with the simple equation ''The logically possible = the conceivable.''

It is logically possible for a cat to give birth to pups? Biologically impossible—and biological impossibility is one form of empirical impossibility—but logically possible. It is a fact of nature that species reproduce their own kind, but there is no logical necessity about this.

''But isn't anything that a cat gives birth to necessarily a cat?'' Not if it barked, wagged its tail, looked like a dog, and was unhesitatingly identified as a dog by those who knew nothing of its origin. The headlines would not read ''Dog produces dog'' but the much more spectacular ''Cat produces dog.''

''But if a pup was the offspring, the mother must not have been a cat!'' Not even if it looked like one, meowed, purred, and had all the other characteristics which cause us to call it a cat? Would you have hesitated to call it a cat *before* the strange birth took place? Must you wait to see what the creature's offspring look like (if it has any) before being able to identify it as a cat? Cats are distinguished from dogs and other creatures by their general appearance, and it is logically possible for something with all the feline appearances to give birth to something with all the canine appearances. That nature does not operate in this way, that like produces like, is a fact of nature, not a logical necessity.

''Is X logically possible?'' may yield two different answers, because one or more of the words is ambiguous and thus the same sentence disguises two different propositions. Is it logically possible to remember something that never happened? In one sense, yes: You can have ''that feeling of recollection'' about something you believe has really happened, though it didn't (see p. 43) people often remember (that is, seem to remember) what never happened. On the other hand, if it's said that you don't remember something unless it really happened, then in that meaning of ''remember" you don't "really remember" X unless X really occurred. Does this show that the same thing is both logically possible and not logically possible? No, only that if the sentence is used to state one proposition, that proposition is self-contradictory, and if we use it to state another proposition, it is not. Logical possibility is not itself definition-relative; what is definition-relative is the word(s) we use for expressing or stating these propositions.

Time travel. Let us now apply the concept of logical possibility to an important and controversial kind of case: The alleged possibility of "traveling backwards in time." Most people would be inclined to say, "Time travel may never occur," and maybe it is empirically impossible and will remain forever a science-fiction fantasy. But surely it is *logically* possible—after all, can't we conceive of it? And haven't writers from H. G. Wells onward written stories about it? Granted that *if* there is a contradiction in it (A and also not-A), it can't possibly be; but is there? How do we find this out? Perhaps we are confusing different problems with each other:

We can proceed backward and forward in space; you can put your car into reverse as well as into forward gears. But if you speak of going forward or backward in time, isn't this just a metaphor taken over from space? What would it mean to move backward in time? If today is Tuesday January 23rd, how could tomorrow be the 22nd?

Nevertheless, many people say it's easy to imagine going back in time. We can imagine hydras with a hundred heads, horses like Bellerophon that fly through the air, and strange creatures such as no one has ever seen. Isn't it just as easy to imagine ourselves going backwards in time, say to the seventeenth century?

Imagine that tomorrow morning you wake up and you find no cars but lots of buggies and covered wagons, and people dressed as they were a century ago. The next morning you wake up and find the environment of a century before that—Indians roaming the plains, and so on. The question is, would you then *be* in the nineteenth and eighteenth centuries, or would you still be in the twentieth century (January the 23rd, January the 24th, etc.) surrounded on *successive* days, for some strange reason, by the physical environments of earlier eras? If what has just been described happened to you, would you say you had gone back in time, or that you were still "going forward" in time but for some unexplained reason it was *as if* you were living in earlier eras?

There *is* a contradiction in saying that you could be living in the twentieth century and also be living in the eighteenth century *at the same time*. These are two different times, and you can't simultaneously be living in both of them. (You can live in the twentieth century and be in the seventeenth century in your imagination, or read books or see movies about the eighteenth century, and so on—that is not in question; the question is only whether you can now *be* in the seventeenth century and also in the twentieth century.) The contradiction would be in the statement that you could be in the twentieth century and at the same time *not* in the twentieth century.

But, of course, this may not be what is being asserted. One could say: "I didn't mean that I could be in both centuries at the same time; what I meant was that I could literally go back in time, so that I am *no longer* in the twentieth century but am back in the seventeenth century." What's wrong with that? one may ask.

But now there is another problem: Those centuries have passed; they've happened; they're over—and they happened *without you*, since you weren't even born till the twentieth century. If you say you can go back to the seventeenth century and live among the Indians, aren't you faced with a contradiction? You would be saying *both* that the seventeenth century passed without you being in it (and it did, didn't it?), *and* that you are in it and participating in its activities. How could both of these claims be true? In H.G. Wells' *The Time Machine*, the hero is propelled forward to the fortieth century, meets a girl, and marries her, and by setting the machine backward brings her back into the twentieth century. But how can this be? Can someone that isn't born until the fortieth century "go back in time" and have a child in the twentieth century? What if that child became dictator of the planet, causing the whole planet to blow up, and in that case there wouldn't *be* any fortieth century? Isn't something very wrong here?

The crux of the matter seems to be this: the past is *what has happened*. And what has happened cannot be changed; the future can be changed, but the past is already "in the bag" and nothing can change it. Not even God could make *not* happen what already *has* happened. If it has happened, it cannot be made *not to have happened*. This seems about as clear a contradiction as we could encounter. And isn't this contradiction involved in "going into the past"? Let's say the population in 1700 was 2 million; but if you could literally go back in time and exist in America in 1800, then the population in 1700 would have been 2 million and one. And how could it be both 2 million and 2 million and one (that is, 2 million but not 2 million, A but not-A)?

Here, then, we seem to have a clear contradiction. You can fly about space as you wish, but you cannot cause what has already happened to have happened differently. You can wander around in a spaceship, and if you approach the speed of light you will age more slowly, so that when you return to earth you will meet your grandchildren (this at any rate is one consequence of Einstein's theory); but you cannot go back in time, *if* this means *being* in an era that has already passed. You couldn't go back to ancient Egypt and help the Egyptians build the pyramids, because they were already built once *without you*—you weren't there, you weren't born yet. You can imagine a replay of the whole process with one difference, that this time you *are* there—

but that would be history repeating (with the one difference) in the late twentieth century a series of events identical to those that took place in Egypt around 2000 B.C. The second would be a rerun, not the *same* events that took place long ago *without* you being there.

What has happened, has happened. You can't change the past; you can't make what has happened not have happened. This much at least, *is* a logical impossibiltiy, for it involves contradictions: You were there, you weren't there; you helped build the pyramids, and you didn't; the population was 1 million, and it was 1 million and one; you didn't yet exist, but you did; and so on).

In spite of all these arguments, there are those who say that time travel is not *logically* impossible. For example (1) they may say it on the same *linguistic* grounds that Quine used in criticizing the concept of meaning: "A is A" is analytic as long as "A" has the same meaning on both sides of the equation, and "A is not-A" is self-contradictory only if "A" has the same meaning both times. But many philosophers would say that the idea of meaning has not been sufficiently clarified (see pp. 18, 131–32), and thus any concept that depends on sameness of meaning (synonymy) is also suspect. We are trying to get beyond language, but we have to state what we mean in language, and once we are involved with a language, talk about "meaning" and "same meaning" is still suspect. And since logical possibility depends on the concept of incompatible meanings (A and not-A), it too is suspect.

What happens then? We may have good reasons for saying that something is impossible—for instance, a person jumping over the moon or flying to Saturn in 2 minutes—but not for saying it's self-contradictory: the concept of self-contradictoriness is suspect because the concept of sameness of meaning is suspect. Thus, falling upwards and dying before you're born may be impossible, but there maybe no difference in *kind*—only perhaps in degree—between these examples and "It is impossible for two trains approaching each other at 100 miles per hour on the same track, and now 20 feet apart, not to collide." Perhaps, some say, the alleged impossibility of time travel is like that.

Or (2) they may say it on factual grounds. We have been assuming, they say, a "linear" conception of time; that time always goes forward in a straight line (whatever we may mean here by the metaphor of a "straight line"). But what if progress through time is not unidimensional, like a straight line, but like a line moving in a plane, which may turn and curve back upon itself? But if that is so, then time may also turn back upon itself and return to its starting point.[13]

Is this, however, anything more than an interesting mental picture? Can day 1 be followed by day 2, day 3, etc., but turn back again to day 1—not the day that follows but to the day that *precedes* it?

> There was a young lady named Bright
> Who could travel faster than light.
> She eloped one day
> In a relative way
> And returned on the previous night.

And what if on the previous night she decided, in the light of an unpleasant nuptial experience, not to elope at all? (But she already had!) Can any amount of talk about time "turning back upon itself" change on jot or tittle of your childhood, which has already occurred and been completed?

4. OTHER NECESSARY TRUTHS

Philosophers who believe that all necessary statements are analytic have traditionally been called *empiricists* (judgment empiricists, to

---

[13]See, for example, the essays by Jonathan Harrison and David Lewis in *Puzzles, Paradoxes, and Problems*, Peter French and Curtis Brown (eds.), (New York: St. Martin's Press, 1987), pp. 222-243.

distinguish them from concept empiricists, p. 33-35): Synthetic statements, they say, must be known (if at all) empirically, by observation of the world, and observation can tell us only what *is* the case, not what *must* be the case; nor can it tell us that what has held true thus far will continue to hold true in the future. Philosophers who believe there *are* necessary statements that are not analytic, but rather are synthetic, have been called *judgment rationalists*. If there are nonanalytic statements that are necessarily true, we must know this not through observation of the world (this can never tell us "what must be"), but through some kind of "rational insight" into the nature or structure of reality.

The analytic-synthetic distinction, however, has received so much criticism that many philosophers have abandoned it—sometimes using it only for simple cases like "Bachelors are unmarried" and "If an object falls, it must go downward." At any rate, it hasn't turned out to be of much use in the most philosophically interesting cases, such as, Can there be colors without extension? Can there be minds without organisms? Can there be a thought without a thinker? Some have said that belief in thoughts without thinkers is self-contradictory, and therefore "When there's a thought there's a thinker" is analytic. Others have denied this.

But there are still many statements that seem to be necessarily true—whether or not they are analytic, whether or not the analytic-synthetic distinction is even accepted. Let us turn to a few of them and try to discern whether they are necessarily true, and if so why one is justified in asserting this.

1. It seems obvious to us that two things can't be in the same place at the same time, and that one thing can't be in two different places at the same time. Is this a necessary truth, or a contingent truth, or perhaps not a truth at all?

Suppose I see you come in the door. While you are standing there, you come in at another door. Impossible, we say—logically impossible. But why? "If you are here, you can't be there. It might be an optical trick, like reflections in a mirror; perhaps a magician might make me see something like this. (Then it would be you *and* your reflection—these *could* be in two different places.) Or perhaps you come in one door and your identical twin came in another door. But *you* can't be in two places at the same time. If the figure is in two places, it's two people, not one." But why are we so sure of this? One answer: "It's the nature of people, and things in general (defining characteristic?), that they can't occupy two places simultaneously; this is necessary truth about matter." Another answer, however, is: "The figure's in two places, therefore they're two people, not one. If they're in two different places, we would *call* them two people, not one. That's just the way we just language."

Two cars are often at the same place at two different times, perhaps just a split second apart. They can also be in two different places at the same time, perhaps right next to each other. But one thing is sure, two cars can't be in the same place at the same time. When they try, there's a collision. And if they collide, then a *part* of one car may be in the place a split second before a part of the other car. But the space occupied by a part of the one car cannot at the same time be occupied by a part of the other car.

Is this a contingent truth or a necessary truth? One might suggest that it isn't a truth at all. "Suppose you have two 1-liter containers of gas and you release both liters of gas into one 1-liter container. Don't you now have two liters of gas occupying one space (the 1-liter container)?" Let us begin (but not end) a dialogue between the conventionalist and the realist:

REALIST: Gases are mostly empty space, and of course it is possible for the molecules of gas that formerly occupied 2 liters of space to occupy 1 liter. I supose you could *call* this a case of two things being in the same

place at the same time. But that would be speaking very loosely. Take any one molecule of the gas; whatever space it occupies cannot be occupied by another molecule at the same time.

CONVENTIONALIST: But how do you know this? You've never seen any individual molecules, yet you seem so sure of your statement.

R: It's a necessary truth about space—that it cannot simultaneously be occupied by more than one thing (or one particle, etc.).

C: Your "necessary truth about reality" is no more than an empirical truth about how we use language. If there are two objects, we'd *say* that they occupied two different places; and if anybody said "if there are two molecules," you'd say without any investigation of the case that they had to occupy two different portions of space. How could we ever *learn to use* the sentence, "There are two things in the same place at the same time"? To what possible situation could such a sentence ever apply? Surely the point is clear—we can never cite an instance of two things being in the same place because the very admission that there are *two* objects is sufficient to entitle us (as we now use language) to *describe* their location as two places, not one.

R: Of course we so describe it; and we so describe it because it's *true* that the same thing can't be in two places (or two things in one place). This is just a fact of reality. We don't *define* an object in terms of not occupying two places; but it's a *fact about them* nevertheless that they can't—not just don't, but can't. And the use of the word "can't" warns us that we have on our hands another example of necessity—a necessity that exists in nature, not merely in our minds, or in our usage of language.

2. Everything, and every property of things, is perfectly *determinate*. For example, this piece of paper doesn't have just shape in general, not even rectangular shape in general, it is a perfectly definite (determinate) shape—

approximately rectangular and a specific size. This blade of grass is not just green in general, but a perfectly specific (determinate) shade of green. Everything in the universe has perfectly determinate properties; these properties can be classified into types (rectangular, circular, elliptical and so on), but each single one, regardless of what type it belongs in, is perfectly determinate in all its qualities. We couldn't imagine it any other way—can you imagine a balloon that's red but no specific shade of red? And it's not only that we couldn't imagine it: It's that it couldn't *be* anything other than perfectly determinate. Is this a necessary truth about reality, or is it only a contingent truth about the world as thus far experienced?

3. An object can't have two different colors over its entire surface at the same time. A marble can be striped, checkered, mottled. It can be covered with paint which is mixed in equal proportions of green and red. None of this is denied; what is denied is that it can be all red and all green over its entire surface at the same time. But why can't it be both red and green? It can be both red and square, both red and hard, both red and heavy; why can't it be both red and green?

There is a traditional principle in metaphysics, the Principle of Determinables. Determinables are general categories into which specific (determinate) properties fall. Color, shape, size, weight are all determinables; there are different shades of color, different specific shapes, and so on. A specific shade of red is a determinate under the determinable color; weight six pounds and ten ounces is a specific determinate under the determinable weight; being an equilateral triangle is a determinate under the determinable shape. Something can't weigh six pounds and also ten pounds, though it can weight six pounds and be malleable; it can't be both red and green, since these are determinates under the same determinable, but it can be both red and hard, since these come under different determinables. That it can't be all red and all green at the same time surely seems to be a

necessary truth. But whence comes the necessity? Consider this dialogue on the subject:

CONVENTIONALIST: If you understand the meaning of the word "red," you'll understand why something can't be all red and all green at the same time. "Red" means, among other things, not-green.

REALIST: The word "red" means red and nothing else, not green, not hard, not square, not schizophrenic. "Red" means red and "green" means green. Neither of them is the name of a shape or a size. So what else is new? "Red" doesn't mean hard any more than it means green. Still, something can be both red and hard, but not (all over) both red and green. Why the difference?

C: The difference, of course, is that as we use the word "red," being red *excludes* being green, but it does not exclude being hard. Being red is just *different* from being hard; but being red not only is different from being green, but *incompatible* with being green. That's just the way we use these words in our language.

R: It's a linguistic rule that we refer to unmarried men as bachelors; it's a linguistic rule that we use "annoyed" and "vexed" to refer to certain disturbed mental states, but "aggravated" to refer to an intensification of the conditions mentioned (thus we say "The course of the disease has been aggravated")—this is a linguistic rule that many people violate, when they used "annoyed" interchangeably with "aggravated." Linguistic rules can be changed, and they do change over time as our language changes. But the one you mention seems to be unchangeable. And this is because it reflects reality. The fact of reality is that something can be all red and all hard, but not all red and all green. *That* is the fact of reality that underlies what you call the verbal convention about the use of "red." But if verbal conventions are arbitrary and changeable, why do we have one that entitles us to say "Red, therefore not green" rather than one that says "Red, therefore not hard"? The Principle of Determinables is a law of reality, not a convention we set up that we could change if we wanted to.

Mathematics

The most prominent class of necessary propositions constitutes *mathematics*. Mathematical statements don't seem at all to be contingent. They seem to be eternally true and necessarily true. No matter what happens in the world, "2 + 2 = 4" and "9 × 8 = 72" remain true. Aren't we quite sure that they are true regardless of time or place? How could they be false on Mars, or on Sirius?

We may not know anything about what conditions exist in these far places, but can't we be sure at any rate that if there are two things and then two more things, then there are four things? And can't we be just as sure that this was true a million years ago or will be true a million years from now as it is true today? Surely such a proposition is not like "All crows are black," which you couldn't really know to be true until you had examined al the crows there are.

It has sometimes been held that such statements as "2 + 2 = 4" are not necesasry but contingent truths—that they are really no different from "All crows are black" or "Water boils at 212° fahrenheit under standard conditions." No exceptions to these last two statements have ever been found, and similarly no exceptions to the statements of arithmetic have ever been found; we have never come across any case in which two things plus two things did not equal four things. The mathematical laws are more *general* than are the laws of physics and chemistry and biology, for they apply to everything—not only to physical things but to thoughts, images, feelings, and to everything one could possibly think of. It is true of absolutely everything that two of it and two more of it make four of it. The math-

ematical laws are also better established than even the laws of the physical sciences. For thousands of years before anything was known of the laws of physical science, people had found that statements such as "2 and 2 makes 4" always hold true; it had been found to be true countless times, without one single negative instance. Nevertheless, according to this view, the laws of the physical sciences and those of arithmetic are of the same fundamental kind: they are both contingent. Both can be known to be true only by observation of the world, and both can be falsified by observation of the world. Just as it is logically possible that we might find exceptions to well-established laws of physical science (it is logically possible that we might find water when heated turning into ice instead of boiling), so it is also logically possible that we might find exceptions to the laws of arithmetic (2 plus 2 equaling 5, for example). We never have, of course, in spite of countless observed cases throughout history, and that is why we are so sure that these laws always hold true. But if we are more certain of "2 plus 2 equals 4" than we are of the proposition about water and crows, it is only because human beings have had evidence to support the arithmetical propositions many times a day for thousands of years, while our experience of crows is more limited and intermittent.

Virtually no one today holds this interpretation of arithmetical statements. In whatever ways people may differ about arithmetical statements, they all agree that they are necessary (necessarily true), unlike the statements of physical sciences. There might be white crows on Mars, or even on the earth; but always and everywhere, 2 plus 2 equals 4. There may somewhere exist creatures so different from ourselves that we cannot even imagine them; the biological laws that would describe their function and operation might be far different from those in our biology textbooks, but this much is sure, if there are two of such organisms, and then two more, then there are four. Could anything be more certain than this? Is there any danger whatsoever that the next time we have two and then two more we may *not* have four?

One might say, "But isn't even such a simple statement as '2 + 2 = 4' a generalization from experience? Don't we *learn* its truth from experience? And isn't it based on instances? I first learn about 2 and 2 houses, then about 2 and 2 apples, and so on. How is its being learned from experience compatible with it being analytic?"

Of course I *learned* that 2 and 2 makes 4, and probably we all learned it as children, using examples such as houses and apples. But what is it that we learned? Has it anything to do with apples and houses? No, it is simply that 2 and 2 when added together makes 4; all the business about houses and apples was just window-dressing. What we learned was that the symbol "4" is equivalent in meaning to the symbol "2 and 2"—that *these two expressions can be used interchangeably.*

We do indeed learn the meanings of words through experience—how else? But this does not have anything to do with whether the propositions in which they occur are necessary. Indeed, many people would call them analytic. To say that 2 and 2 does *not* make 4 would be to say that 1 and 1 and 1 and 1 does not make 1 and 1 and 1 and 1, which is self-contradictory.

When we put two pennies into our new piggy bank, and later two more pennies, we learned to say that we had put in four pennies, simply because "putting 4 pennies in" means the same as "putting 2 pennies and 2 pennies in." We learned to say it as a result of our experience—our experience of learning language—but *what* we said was a necessary truth, and analytic. But we *also* learned to predict that if we should open the bank later we would find four pennies in it. In this case what we learned was not an arithmetical truth about the world that we might call the *conservation of pennies*—that the pennies would re-

main undisturbed in the piggy bank; and, unlike "2 + 2 = 4," this proposition might have turned out to be false. But "2 + 2 = 4" could never turn out to be false.

Even this, however, could be questioned. One might argue: "The propositions of arithmetic aren't always true. Two and two doesn't always make four. For example, if you add 2 quarts of water to 2 quarts of alcohol, you ought to get 4 quarts—but you don't; you get a little less, owing to the interpenetration of molecules of the two substances. If you put together two lions and two lambs, and turn your back for a moment, you will not have four things, but only two—two lions. When two amoebas subdivide, they become four—what was two is now four! How can arithmetical propositions be necessary at all if they aren't even true in all cases—when reality often shows them to be false?"

But these objections are the result of misunderstanding. When we say that 2 + 2 = 4, we do not deny for a moment that what *was* two can *become* four (the amoebas), or that you can have four things at one time and have only two things at a later time (the lions having eaten the lambs). It says only that *if* you have two and two, then at that moment you have four. Arithmetic does not tell you anything about natural processes—how two things can become four things, or how what was four can become two things. Arithmetic doesn't even tell you that there are four of anything in the world at all, or even that there *is* a world in which such distinctions can be made. It says only that *if* there are two and then two more, *then* there must be four: that to say there are two plus two and to say that there are four is to say the same thing. When there are two lions, and two lambs, then there are four things; when there are only two lions, then there are only two—that is, one plus one—things. If two things give rise to a million things this would not violate "2 + 2 = 4" or any other proposition of arithmetic. Two rabbits soon become a million rabbits;

and if two things exploded into a million things, or into nothing at all, this occurrence would not refute any law of arithmetic. What turns into what, what becomes what, how one thing changes into another—all these are matters for the physical sciences to investigate; these are all a part of what happens in the world, and propositions about these things are all contingent. But the propositions of arithmetic say nothing whatever about the changes that go on in nature; they say nothing at all about the kind of world we live in, nor would they be changed in the slightest if the world were quite different from what it is, for the laws of arithmetic do not describe what the world is like. Arithmetic doesn't even tell you that the number 4 applies to anything in the world, but only that *if* it applies, then "2 + 2" also applies, because the two symbols mean the same thing.

Now consider the example of adding the water and the alcohol. It is a proposition in chemistry, not in arithmetic: It tells you what happens when you do something to something else. The formulation of the example, in fact, is quite misleading: We speak of "adding" water to alcohol. But adding is an arithmetical process; It is an operation we perform with numbers, not with physical things. Strictly speaking, we do not *add* water to alcohol; we *pour* some water into a vessel of alcohol. (Or if you do want to call it adding, it is adding in a very different sense from the one we use in arithmetic.) Only by observation of the world can you discover what happens when you pour something into something else. If you pour water into gasoline, you get no mixture at all. If you pour water into pure sodium, you get an explosion, with neither water nor sodium left at the end of it. What happens when you do something to something else is a matter for the physical sciences to investigate, but nothing thus discovered can refute any law of arithmetic, since they have nothing whatever to do with arithmetic.

Suppose you are counting trees: 2 trees to your left, 2 trees to your right, but every time you tried to count them all together you got 5 as your result instead of 4. What would we say if this kept on happening? Would it refute any of the laws of arithmetic? Would textbooks of arithmetic have to be revised, saying "Sometimes 2 and 2 makes 5"? Not at all; "2 and 2 makes 4" would remain true *no matter what happened in the counting process.* If you kept on getting 5 trees as a result, you might decide that you were systematically miscounting; or that in the very act of counting, another tree was created, or just popped into existence. But the one thing you would *not* say is that 2 and 2 sometimes makes 5. If you found an additional tree every time you tried to count them all together, you would say that 2 trees plus 2 trees plus 1 tree that seems to pop into existence when you count, together makes 5 trees. So the arithmetical laws would not be refuted after all.

A dialogue on this topic might go something like this:

A: Granted that it wouldn't, I still insist that it's a necessary truth. Not merely "2 + 2 = 4"—that is only a generalization of "two trees and two trees makes four trees," "2 apples and 2 apples makes 4 apples," etc. The arithmetical law says that two *of anything* and two more *of anything* makes four, and this is a law about reality, not about the manipulation of symbols. The law that 2 and 2 makes 4 *does* hold true of apples, as of everything else; it holds true *of reality.*

B: I think you are confusing two different things. It's easy to see that "2 + 2 = 4" as a proposition of pure arithmetic simply entitles you to use "4" equivalently with "2 + 2." It's easy to see that "If you add 2 quarts to 2 quarts (pour into, that is), you get almost 4 quarts" is not a proposition of arithmetic at all. But if you say "2 apples and 2 apples makes 4 apples," it isn't clear which side of the fence this statement is on.

It sounds *both* like a statement of pure mathematics *and* like a statement about physical objects, apples. But no wonder, for the statement is ambiguous; "2 apples and 2 apples makes 4 apples" is a "straddling" sentence. To find out how the speaker means it, one has to ask, "Is it of importance whether it's *apples* that are being talked about?" Suppose it were 2 ccs of sodium being poured into 2 ccs of water, would that make a difference? Well (1) if it's a statement of pure (unapplied) arithmetic, then it doesn't matter whether it's apples, elephants, grains of sand, or thoughts about Thursday—what the statement is about is numerical quantities, and the rest is merely illustrative. Such statements are all necessary truths. But (2) if it *does* matter that it's apples that you're talking about, then the statement is not about arithmetic at all but about apples—and may not even be true. We are easily misled about this, because apples, unlike water and sodium, normally sit quietly side by side and don't interact with each other. So if that's what it means—that apples when put together remain apples as they were before—then it is true, but it is a contingent truth about physical reality, not a truth of mathematics. It is logically possible that when they are placed together the four apples would all coalesce into one huge apple, or spawn a thousand little apples, or disintegrate or explode in one another's presence.

What happens when you put apples together is a matter for observation of nature; any statement that is about apples in which it matters that it's apples *and not something else* is a contingent statement. It all depends on which of these you mean. But if you just say "2 apples and 2 apples makes 4 apples" and squint a bit, forgetting about these distinctions, you may think that you have achieved the necessity "2 + 2 = 4" together with the

factual content of the other. But you haven't. You have the same sentence expressing two different propositions—the one necessary and analytic, the other synthetic and contingent.

Philosophers who do not eschew the analytic-synthetic distinction have often held that arithmetical statements are analytic as well as necessary. They say that "4" just *means* "1 + 1 + 1 + 1." It's true that a person can *think* of 2 + 2 without thinking of 4, and as Kant pointed out one can surely think of 7 + 5 without thinking of 12 (one might not even have learned that 7 + 5 = 12), but this makes no difference: I can think of Harold as my brother even though I don't think of him as my male sibling (I may never have heard the phrase "male sibling"), but he is my male sibling nonetheless, and the expressions "brother" and "male sibling" are interchangeable whether I know it or not. And some philosophers have held that *all* arithmetical statements—not to mention algebra and calculus—are analytic, in spite of the great complexity of many of them.

Still, this doesn't seem particularly obvious. Consider the following statements:

1. 2 is the only even number that is also a prime number.
2. 12 is the only number lower than 20 that is divisible by at least four other numbers (1, 2, 3, 4, 6).
3. Every multiple of 3, has as the sum of its digits a number divisible by 3.
4. 2 is the only number whose square and whose double are the same number. (4)
5. 1 is the only number whose square root is the same as itself.

None of these looks remotely like an analytic statement. That's not a sure test, of course, but whether analytic or not, they are all necessarily true, aren't they? Surely they aren't contingent truths, which we would have to revise if unexpected events occurred in the world? That every multiple of 3 has as the sum of its digits a number divisible by 3—surely this is a truth *about* 3, not a part of the definition of "3"; but if so it is a truth that *necessarily* holds—and it holds of 3, not of 4. (16 is a multiple of 4, but the sum of its digits, 1 + 6, is not divisible by 4.) Don't we have something more on our hands here than analytic statements?

"The foundations of mathematics" is a subject on which much has been written during the last century. Bertrand Russell and A. N. Whitehead, in their monumental three-volume *Principia Mathematica*, attempted to show that the truths of mathematics are all special cases of the truths of logic, but others have denied this. The subject is far too technical to permit exploration here. But the central idea is that one can consruct a system of *axioms*—much like those of geometry, which we considered on pp. 107—from which the truths of mathematics can be logically derived. The Italian mathematician Giuseppe Peano (1858–1932) constructed the following series:

1. 0 is a number.
2. The successor of any number is a number.
3. No two numbers have the same successor.
4. 0 is not the successor of any number.
5. If P is a property such that (a) 0 has the property P, and (b) if a number *n* has P, then the successor of *n* has P.

Using three undefined terms—"number," "0," and "successor"—he was able to generate an infinite series of numbers from these axioms; the axioms yield the entire system of integers. Given the series of axioms, the propositions of arithmetic follow from them as necessary truths.

Many problems, however, remain. Consider the statement "Every even number is the sum of two prime numbers" (Goldbach's theorem). Thousands of even numbers have been listed and in every case two prime numbers have been found which when added yield that number as their sum. But how do we know that the theorem holds true for all cases? Might we not come across an even number that is not the sum of two primes? There seems to be no reason why every even number *has* to be the sum of two primes; it has merely turned out that way thus far. Maybe some day someone will be able to prove that the theorem is true. And if it is true, surely it will be a *necessary* truth, not a contingent truth like "All crows are black." Doesn't all mathematics lie "in the realm of necessity"?

One philosopher who believed that mathematical propositions are necessary but not analytic—that they are synthetic necessary truths—was Immanuel Kant (1724–1804). He believed this not only of mathematics, but of many other statements which seemed to others to be analytic. But to make clear the reasons why he believed this, we must examine the outlines of his philosophical system, perhaps the most elaborate metaphysical system ever devised, without which we cannot understand his position on the realm of necessity.

5. KANT AND THE SYNTHETIC A PRIORI

What the world is like—that is, the facts of nature we observe, the uniformities we discover in nature's workings, what experiences we have and when—all of these we must either observe (in the world outside) or introspect (in our minds) to discover. These statements are not necessary truths; they are contingent—we must simply wait for experience to inform us of what goes on. We have also, it would seem, knowledge of necessarily true statements, such as 7 + 5 = 12 and "If A is larger than B, then B is smaller than A" and a host of others such as we have already considered. Many philosophers have held that synthetic statements are all contingent and that necessary statements are all analytic. That, at any rate, is the view of *empiricism*. (The word "empiricism" has been given many meanings, but most of them, such as "We should rely on experience" and "All knowledge comes from experience," are too vague to be useful.)

Yet there are philosophers who have held that in addition to contingent statements which are synthetic, and necessary statements which are analytic, there is a third class of statements, those which are *both* necessary and synthetic. These philosophers have been called *rationalists*. (Again, the word is susceptible to many meanings, mostly vague ones such as "emphasizing the use of one's reason." But since one's powers of reason seem to be employed equally by rationalists and empiricists, it has become customary in philosophy to define "rationalism" in this more precise way.)

But to many people the very idea of necessary truths which are nonanalytic has seemed like chasing after phantoms:

I have no clear notion of what it would be like to justify by reflection alone the truth of *p* when *not-p* is consistent [not self-contradictory] . . . But this *may* be only a fact about *me*. I cannot see how, of two equally consistent alternative propositions (*p* and *not-p*), reflection alone will determine which one describes the facts. But to say this does not *prove* that there cannot be synthetic [necessary] propositions.[14]

Indeed, one may ask, how can there be statements which hold true of the world but cannot be refuted by observation of the world, no matter what we discover in it? How can something be true of the world and yet not subject to refutation by any possible experience of the world? Isn't one trying to have the best of both worlds—or trying to have one's cake and eat it at the same time?

Now, however, we must consider still another pair of terms thus far unmentioned, *a priori* and *a posteriori*, which were introduced

by Kant along with "analytic" and "synthetic." A truth is said to be knowable a priori when we can know it to be true independently of experience—not that we didn't have to learn it at some time, or that we don't need experience of the world in order to understand it, but rather that we do not need to *verify* it through experience the way we do "All crows are black" or "Lightning is always followed by thunder." A posteriori truth, by contrast, is one that we do have to verify or confirm through sense-experience or introspection, as we do most of the truths we utter, such as "I am now sitting at a desk" and "I am now unhappy." "A priori" and "a posteriori" are *epistemological* terms—they have to do with how we can *know* propositions to be true; "necessary" and "contingent," on the other hand, are *metaphysical* terms having to do with the kind of propositions in question, whether they are known a priori or not.

It has often been assumed that all necessary truths are knowable a priori and that contingent truths are knowable only a posteriori, and that the extension (even if not the meaning) of the two terms is the same. This is indeed a very plausible view: If something is a necessary truth, we don't need to verify it empirically, we can know it without going through that process; and if it's a contingent truth, we do have to go through that process.

But if a priori truths are those that it's possible to know independently of experience (whether we do know them or not), we can ask, "Possible for whom? For God? For the Martians? Or just for people with minds like ours?"[15] Consider Goldbach's theorem: If it's true, it is necessarily true—nothing contingent about it. Yet we do not know at present whether it's true or whether it isn't. We can get some *evidence* by running through a lot of even numbers and finding that each of them is the sum of two primes—which is much the way

[14]Norwood R. Hanson, "The Very Idea of Synthetic A Priori," *Mind*, 1962, p. 523.

[15]Saul Kripke, *Meaning and Necessity* (Cambridge, Harvard University Press, 1972), pp. 34–35.

we get evidence for "All crows are black." "It's not trivial to argue on the basis of something's being something which maybe we can only know *a posteriori*, that it's not a necessary truth. It's not trivial, just because something is known in some sense *a priori*, that what is known is a necessary truth.[16] Consider the statement "This table is composed of molecules"; it certainly sounds like a contingent truth. Yet,

might it not have been composed of molecules? Certainly it was a scientific discovery of great moment that it was composed of molecules (or atoms). But could anything be this very object and not be composed of molecules? Certainly there is some feeling that the answer to that must be "no." At any rate, it's hard to imagine under what circumstances you would have this very object and find that it is not composed of molecules.[17]

It seems to be an empirical truth about matter. Is it then knowable only a posteriori?

Or try this one: Might you have been born a year earlier than you were? ten years earlier? You are inclined to say yes, it's a contingent truth that you were born when you were: you might have been born a bit earlier (if your mother had given birth to you prematurely). Might you then have been born a century earlier? or among the ancient Greeks? But then would it have been *you* that was born then, of a different mother? Then it would have been someone else, perhaps with your personality traits, but it couldn't have been *you* that was born in ancient Greece. That you were born when you were seems at first contingent, but now it looks more like a necessary truth. To be you, you had to be born when you were. Is this true? If so, could you have known it a priori?

The thrust of Kant's thought, however, was

in an entirely different direction from these examples. He was a philosophical system-builder, and his entire system rested on the notion of synthetic (nonanalytic) truths knowable a priori. Indeed, the question he asked himself was not "Is synthetic a priori knowledge possible?" but *"How* is synthetic a priori knowledge possible?" His philosophy was an attempt to answer that question.

We ordinarily believe that our knowledge must conform to "the way things are," but, said Kant, it is equally true that "objects must conform to our knowledge." At first this sounds highly implausible. How could the nature of our faculties determine what is true of the world? Does the world accommodate itself to our demands? No, said Kant, but the world as we perceive it with our senses and understand it through our reason, must be adapted to *our* mode of perception and cognition. To take a crude example, if we always looked at the world through green glasses which we couldn't take off (and never knew we had on), everything would look green. It's not that everything would *be* green, but that it would always *appear* to be so. In Kant, the real world is "filtered" through our human senses and understanding, and it is only as thus filtered that we can be aware of it. Thus it is that the world as we know it must "conform to our faculties." The world as it is, and the world as it appears to us, are not the same.

What reality is like in itself, apart from human perception and cognition, said Kant, is completely unknown and unknowable to us. This is what he called the *noumenal* world, of whose nature we have not the slightest conception. Everything we perceive, everything we think, is filtered through (1) the human senses and (2) the human mind. Our senses and our intellect are not like spectacles which we can remove and then "see reality as it is." They are always with us, and all we can have any knowledge of is the world as "filtered" through the sense organs and minds which we possess.

[16]Ibid., pp. 38–39.
[17]Ibid., p. 47.

Kant called the world of ordinary sense-perception and of science the *phenomenal* world. The phenomenal world is *spatial*—one thing is bigger than another, one thing is at a certain distance removed from another; the phenomenal world is also *temporal*—one event occurs before another, one occurs after another, one occurs simultaneously with another. But space and time—filters through which we are aware of anything and everything—are simply the "forms of our intuition," the way that reality inescapably appears to us. Space and time belong to the phenomenal world only, not the noumenal. They are the molds into which our experiences are cast, and without which we would not have them at all. We cannot even think of any object that does not occupy time or space. But this fact reflects the nature of the human mind, not the nature of reality. Phenomenal space has three dimensions (length, breadth, height); could it just as well have had seven or twenty-seven dimensions? We never doubt that there is only *one* space; nor can we imagine anything different. But our imaginations are limited to what is "filtered" to us—to the phenomenal world. We also assume that time is everywhere the same, and that if A precedes B and B precedes C, A will precede C; and this *is* a necessary truth about the phenomenal world; that is the way time presents itself to us in the phenomenal world.

There are other categories, too, by which our minds synthesize the data of experience (we shall not attempt a complete list). One of these is *substance*: We perceive the phenomenal world in terms of things (such as iron) and their properties (such as heavy, magnetic). Another is *causality*: we speak of events causing one another, being bound by a relation of cause and effect. Another is *number*: We say there are a certain number of things, and we count them—but this category (number) exists only in the phenomenal world.

If we caught fish in nets, and the reticulations in the net were 2 inches square, we would catch no fish less than two inches long, for they would slip through the net; but if the nets were underwater and we couldn't see the small fish slipping through, we might report that there are no fish in the sea less than 2 inches long. But this would not really report the contents of the sea—it would only reflect the nature of the nets. We might think that we were making a true statement about the fish in the sea, but we would not. So it is, according to Kant, with our knowledge of the phenomenal world, which we mistakenly believe to be knowledge of the real (noumenal) world.

Of the noumenal world we can make no statements at all, having no conception of it. But of the phenomenal world we can make many statements: not only specific statements such as about the number of trees in the yard, but general statements about what always occurs in our experience. (That we shall never catch fish less than 2 inches long will be true as long as the nets are as described.) Examples of such statements would be: Everything that exists is in time and space. Every event has a cause. Everything that has shape has color.

Kant believed the propositions of mathematics and of geometry were both synthetic and a priori. They are synthetic *a priori* truths about the phenomenal world. Anything nonspatial, nontemporal, noncausal, would "slip through the net" and never be knowable by human beings. It is the nature of our mind that determines the nature and scope of our knowledge, rather than the nature of reality itself. Objects must conform to our knowledge, not our knowledge to objects. This was Kant's "Copernican revolution" in philosophy: whereas Copernicus had created a revolution in astronomy, believing that the earth goes round the sun rather than the sun round the earth, so Kant created a revolution in philosophy, holding that what we see and think depends on the nature of our minds rather than the "objective reality" of which we think we have knowledge.

Surely, one may think at first sight, it is quite fantastic to assert that "objects must conform to our knowledge"; for how could it possibly be that the nature of our faculties should determine, or even influence in any way, what is the case in the world? Surely we are simply obliged to take the world as we find it; it would be a gross absurdity to suppose that it must somehow accommodate itself to our needs or our demands. Now, Kant feels the full force of this objection and to meet it he draws and insists upon a vital distinction between the world as it is *in itself* and as it *appears to us*. What exists, exists: its nature simply it what it is; with that, we ourselves can have nothing to do. It is, however, equally certain that what exists *appears* to human beings in a particular way, and is by them classified, interpreted, categorized, and described in a particular manner. If our sense-organs had been radically different from what they are, certainly the world would have appeared to us as being radically different; if our languages and modes of thought had been utterly different, the descriptions of the world that we should have been given would also have been different from those that we now give. Thus, though our faculties and capacities make no difference at all to the nature of what exists in itself, they do partly determine the character of the world as it appears; they determine the general *form* that it has; for whatever the world may be in itself, it appears to us in the way that it does because we are what we are. It is, then, with the world as appearance that Kant is concerned; it is objects as *phenomena* that must "conform to our knowledge."[18]

Since Kant, as well as the rest of us, was a human being with a human mind and human senses, how could he know that there was a noumenal world, and how could he have discovered that we can know nothing about it? He could not observe it, of course; he *inferred* it (correctly or incorrectly) from certain contradictions, which we encounter when we try to reason about general concepts such as space and time, on the assumption that they are real. If you arrive by valid reasoning at proposition *p*, and also arrive by valid reasoning at

proposition not-*p*, something has gone wrong; if the reasoning is valid, one or more of the premises must be mistaken. Contradictions do not exist in reality; *p* and not-*p* cannot both be true of reality. Contradictions occur only when we reason incorrectly. Kant believed that if we assume space and time to be real (noumenal) we encounter certain contradictions, which he called *antinomies*.

Consider time. Can we conceive of a beginning of it? One second there was no time, and then all of a sudden—pop!—time began. But this is unintelligible. A second is a measure of time, the interval between two ticks of a clock. Saying "before time began" already presupposes that there was time—time before time? "How long a time was there before time began?" is a self-contradictory question; time didn't begin if there was time before it. But if time began at time t-1, can't we always ask what happened *before* t-1? And if we can, then time didn't begin at t-1.

Let's say, then, that time had no beginning. It "always was"; time goes infinitely back into the past and infinitely forward into the future. When we say that the number system is infinite, we mean that you can always get a bigger number by adding 1; when we say that time is infinite, we mean that you can always ask, "And what happened before *that*?" even if we don't know the answer. But can we really conceive of something that occurs but never began, and will continue to occur but will never end? If time is infinite, said Kant, then up to any given moment an infinite period of time has completely elapsed; but "is it not indeed a contradiction to speak of the history of the universe up to the present as both completed and not finite?"[19]

Or consider space. If space is finite (bounded), then if we travel far enough we could reach the end of it. But no matter how far you went, couldn't you stick your

[18]G. J. Warnock, "Kant," in D. J. O'Connor, (ed.), *A Critical History of Western Philosophy* (New York: Free Press, 1964), p. 300.

[19]Ibid., p. 306.

hand out and always encounter *more* space? Couldn't you keep on doing this forever? Well then, space is infinite, unbounded. But doesn't any distance, however great, have to be some specific distance? What would the sentence "These two things are separated from each other by an infinite distance" mean? We can utter the words, but what would we be asserting if we did so?[20]

Or consider causality. We believe ourselves to be free and autonomous (self-determining) beings; we can deliberate, choose, and act, helping thus to determine our own future. Yet if determinism (universal causality) is true, whatever we think or do is the inevitable consequence of preceding events, and freedom is a delusion. We are both free and not free; here is another contradiction. If we restrict ourselves to the phenomenal world, thought Kant, the contradiction is irresolvable. Belief is a noumenal world is required to resolve it. (We shall consider this problem in detail in Chapter 5.)

There are only a few examples of the Kantian antinomies. Many philosophers since Kant have argued, in many hundreds of books, that the reasoning leading to the antinomies is faulty, and that recourse to a noumenal world is unnecessary, unjustified, and (some say) meaningless. Let us consider just a few.

1. "What!" we may say. "In the real world, as opposed to the phenomenal world, is an elephant *not* larger than a mouse? Is New York *not* north of Miami? Am I *not* sitting six feet away from you?" If space is not real, then none of these statements are true: they are true only of *appearances* (the phenomenal world), but not of *reality* (noumenal world). Do all these statements describe only appear-

ances, the underlying reality "behind" which is radically different, and forever unknown?

The same kind of objection could be raised about time. "Do you mean there's really no before and after? Aren't the crops planted before they are harvested? Didn't dinosaurs exist on the earth before human beings did? Wasn't I born after my parents were born? Don't I have a definite life span? Am I not uttering the last part of this sentence *after* the beginning of it? Even if, as Descartes thought, I am not a body but a mind that thinks and perceives, doesn't thinking and perceiving occur in time, with some thoughts occurring before other ones?" And again the reply would be the same: all these statements are true of the phenomenal world only; the noumenal world is non-temporal. We know ourselves only as inhabitants of the phenomenal world, but the phenomenal world is not the real world.

2. One could go further and question the meaningfulness of sentences like "Time is not real." How did we ever *learn* the meaning of temporal words if there is no time? We do speak of real versus imaginary time, or objective versus subjective time: "The dream seemed to last for hours, but it was only a few seconds"; "The lecture lasted 20 minutes, it seemed like a whole morning." Thus do we contrast real and apparent time. But what are we to make of the assertion that *all* time is unreal? In everyday life we can distinguish the real from the unreal in varying contexts. "The coin appears elliptical but it's really round" presents no problem, for we have ways of contrasting its real shape with its apparent shape (see pp. 2, 54–56). But what are we to make of "Everything we could ever perceive is nothing but appearance"? Whatever we say about this, don't we still have to go on to plan our future, to eat lunch and do countless other things—all in time?

Kant would be the first to say, however, that he was not making "ordinary language" distinctions. We learn all the things we do

[20]This account is greatly oversimplified, and lacks the elaborate terminology required to give an accurate account of Kant's views. For more extended discussions, see for example Jonathan Bennett, *Kant's Analytic* (Cambridge: Cambridge University Press, 1966) and Henry E. Allison, *Kant's Transcendental Idealism* (New Haven: Yale University Press, 1983).

learn, including how to use words, in the phenomenal world, the only world we know; but the phenomenal world still isn't the real world. Of the real world we have no conception, for it is ever "behind the veil." But we are led to believe in it, however, by considering the contradictions that confront us if we do not.

3. These alleged contradictions, however, have been questioned. Does our reasoning inevitably lead to them? Most philosophers don't think so. Consider space. Space may be infinite in one respect but finite in another. No matter how far you go, you never come to the end of space. But if you traveled far enough you would finally reach the point where you started, and then start repeating your journey—which is what happens when you travel around the world. As to time, many astronomers and philosophers of science today believe that the Big Bang was indeed the first event in time, though others believe that it arose from some presently unknown prior state. If the Big Bang was when the universe began, was it also the beginning of time? Many would reply "Yes, time is the measure of motion, and if there is no motion one cannot meaningfully speak of time. Don't say that before the Big Bang there was a prior period of time during which nothing happened; say rather that the concept of time *does not apply* here, any more than the concept of redness applies to theories." This point, however, is a subject of continuing controversy.

4. What, finally, of synthetic a priori propositions? As long as the reticulations in our net are 2 inches, we can know a priori that we shall catch no smaller fish in the net. As long as the structure of the human mind is as it is, everything known to us will be "filtered" through the "screens" of time, space, and causality. But, one is tempted to ask, how do we know that the structure of the human mind will not change? Can we know *that* a priori? It is a tempting question, which Kant apparently never considered.

The synthetic a priori truths, Kant held, hold true only of the phenomenal world. That time is one-directional and can only proceed "forward"; that space is three-dimensional; that only one line can be drawn through a point parallel to another line (Euclid's Axiom of Parallels) and many other statements of classical geometry—all these Kant believed to be synthetic and known a priori. It seemed plain to Kant that they could be known to be true prior to testing individual cases, and also that they were not analytic; his question was not "Are there synthetic a priori propositions?" (the answer, he thought, was clearly yes) but "*How* are synthetic a priori propositions possible?" His entire critical philosophy, developed at length in his *Critique of Pure Reason*, was an attempt to answer that question. In view of the science and mathematics of his day, his conviction that these judgments were synthetic a priori was highly plausible. But it seems much less plausible today. In Kant's time there were no competitors to Euclidean geometry; today, with the rise of non-Euclidean geometries, it has become clear that physical geometry is an *empirical* inquiry that cannot be settled a priori no matter how obvious the Euclidean geometry may seem to us. The deductive part of geometry may be analytic, but the premises (axioms) on which it is based are not: they are synthetic, but not a priori.

Kant also believed that the propositions of arithmetic, such as "7 + 5 = 12," are not only a priori but synthetic (non-analytic). His reason for saying this was that we can think of 5 and 7 without thinking of 12 (we may not even know that 12 is the sum of 5 and 7). But many philosophers have pointed out that this is a psychological, not a logical, consideration. What we can think of without thinking of something else depends on the individual who is doing the thinking, and is simply irrelevant to the question whether or not the statement is analytic. Kant, however, believed that the concept of number belongs just as squarely in the phenomenal world as space, time, and cause, and the the considerations that led him to the synthetic a priori in those areas applied also to mathematics.

Some philosophers today—those that do not reject the analytic-synthetic distinction altogether—believe with Kant that at least some mathematical propositions are both synthetic and a priori.[21] But the prevailing view is that the propositions of mathematics have

... the same unquestionable certainty which is typical of such propositions as "All bachelors are unmarried," but they also share the complete lack of empirical content which is associated with that certainty: the propositions of mathematics are devoid of all factual content; they convey no information whatever on any empirical subject-matter.
... Mathematical as well as logical reasoning is a conceptual technique of making explicit what is implicitly contained in a set of premises . . .
In the establishment of empirical knowledge, mathematics (as well as logic) has, so to speak, the function of a theoretical juice extractor: the techniques of mathematical and logical theory can produce no more juice of factual information than is contained in the assumptions to which they are applied; but they may produce a great deal more juice of this kind than might have been anticipated upon a first intuitive inspection of those assumptions which form the raw material for the extractor . . . [22]

Whichever of these views of mathematics one accepts, on one thing all parties are in agreement: The propositions of (pure) mathematics are not empirical statements, that is, statements one can verify or confirm by observation of the world. Mathematical truths are necessary truths—even though, in the complex regions of higher mathematics, it may

take a lot of calculation to determine which ones are true at all. In this respect mathematics is quite different from the empirical sciences—physics, chemistry, astronomy, geology, biology, psychology. In the sciences, the most elegant theory can be swept aside by a few new discoveries about "how nature works." Scientific propositions are subject to disconfirmation by observation—not usually by a single observation, as we shall see in the next chapter; but nevertheless observed facts of the universe can cause one scientific proposition after another to bite the dust, as the history of science amply testifies. Nature is loath to divulge her secrets easily, and scientists have no choice but to go where nature leads. In science, unlike mathematics, you have to get your hands dirty.

EXERCISES

1. "What is an apple?" " An apple is a fruit that grows on a tree." "I didn't ask you what classification it falls under; I only asked you what it *is*." "Well, an apple grows . . . " "I didn't ask you what it *does*; I asked you what it *is*." "Well, an apple is something composed of the following chemical elements . . . " "I didn't ask you what it is made of, or what I'd see if I looked at it under a microscope. I asked you, quite simply, what it *is*." What is wrong in this interchange?

2. Fifty years ago it was considered so certain that schizophrenia was incurable that if any case of mental disease was cured, it was automatically concluded that the diagnosis of schizophrenia had been mistaken. Today incurability is no longer taken as a defining characteristic of schizophrenia. Does this show that the definition of 50 years ago was false?

3. Consider the following dialogue:

A: A definition of "X" tells us what properties all members of the class X have in common.

B: No. All tables are solid objects, yet that isn't a satisfactory definition of "table." The definition is too broad, for it doesn't distinguish tables from all the non-tables that are also solid ob-

[21]See, for example, Alfred C. Ewing, *The Fundamental Problems of Philosophy* (New York: Macmillan, 1951).

[22]Carl G. Hempel, "On the Nature of Mathematical Truth," *American Mathematical Monthly 52*(1945): 543–556. Reprinted in Herbert Feigl and Wilfrid Sellars (ed.), *Readings in Philosophical Analysis* (New York: Appleton- Century-Crofts, 1949), passage quoted on p. 235.

jects. You have to know not only what is common to all tables, but what is *peculiar* to them.

A: Very well; suppose you know something peculiar to Xs, something that nothing else has. For instance, only elephants have trunks used to draw up water. This tells us what is peculiar to elephants. Is this then a satisfactory definition?

B: No, for it may not tell us what is common to all elephants, but only what is peculiar to them. A satisfactory definition must include both.

A: Very well, but now suppose that all elephants have trunks: All elephants have them, and only elephants have them. Now, at last, we have a satisfactory definition of "elephant."

B: No, not necessarily, because . . .

You fill in the rest. Why may the definition fulfilling both requirements still be inadequate?

4. "Is this a fox or a wolf?" Is this question about words, or about facts, (a) when you see the creature in the forest at some distance in the early morning mists you cannot make it out distinctly? (b) when you have the creature before you, examine it in detail, make chemical tests, and so on, and after doing all these things, still ask the question?

5. Which of the following propositions would you classify as analytic? State why.

    a. All swans are white.
    b. All swans are birds.
    c. All aunts are female.
    d. All aunts are blood relatives.
    e. All human beings are mortal.
    f. All human beings are selfish.
    g. Normal persons behave like the majority.
    h. Circles never contain straight lines.
    i. All minks are fur-bearing.
    j. Water at sea level boils at 212° F.
    k. All fish live in water.
    l. When large numbers of people are out of work, unemployment results. (Calvin Coolidge)

6. Could anything refute the following statements? If not, are they therefore analytic? Explain.

    a. If you study this book long enough, you'll understand it.
    b. Unless I'm mistaken, I'm now in Baghdad.
    c. Some day there will no longer be conflict among nations.

    d. Time cannot go backwards.
    e. Everyone acts from the motive which (at the time of acting) is the strongest.
    f. The best runner in this race is the one who will win.

7. Are the following logically possible? Justify your answer in each case.

    a. To jump 10,000 feet into the air.
    b. To see a sound.
    c. To have an unconscious desire.
    d. To see something that doesn't exist.
    e. To read tomorrow's newspaper today.
    f. To cross a river and be on the same side you started from.
    g. To see without eyes.
    h. To be knocked into the middle of next week.
    i. For a solid iron bar to float on water.
    j. For a sound to exist that no creature in the world can hear.
    k. For a table to eat the book that's on it.
    l. For a box to be pure red and pure green all over its surface at the same time.
    m. For Thursday to follow Tuesday without Wednesday in between. (Assume that you remain in the same spot, not crossing the International Date Line.)
    n. For no world to exist at all.
    o. For a part of space to move to some other part of space.
    p. For a thought to occur without someone to think it.
    q. For a straight line not to be the shortest distance between two points.
    r. For someone to have experiences after he or she no longer has a physical body. (More on this in Chapter 6.)

8. Is it logically possible for there to be a bird which

    a. lays its eggs upwards through a hole in the bottom of the nest?
    b. flies about in smaller and smaller concentric circles until, with a wild scream, it disappears up its own anus?

9. Comment on the following assertions:

    a. "He's in the room or he's not in the room"—an instance of the law of excluded middle; but suppose he's half in and half out? Or suppose he is dead? Or suppose we were mistaken in thinking that he ever existed? For such cases the law of excluded middle doesn't hold true.

b. A man may love his wife and hate her at the same time, even with respect to the same characteristic. So the law of noncontradiction doesn't hold true in such a case. Similarly for "I'm with it yet not with it," and so on.

c. A isn't always A—a boy becomes a man, a tadpole becomes a frog. The universe is dynamic, not static—and Aristotle's law of identity cannot take account of the dynamic character of the universe.

d. In deducing conclusions from premises, we may learn in the conclusion things we did not know when we stated the premises. So we have drawn new knowledge out of the situation. Accordingly, they cannot be analytic.

e. It is impossible to prove that A is A, or that something that's a table isn't also not a table. It can't be proved by means of something other than itself, and to prove it by means of itself would be arguing in a circle. So it can't be proved at all. Therefore, there is no basis for believing it.

f. "Either A or not-A." For example, either ideas are green or they are not-green. But that's ridiculous. They are neither green nor not-green: The concept of color simply does not apply to ideas at all. To do so is to be guilty of a category mistake.

g. "This can't be both a table and not a table" is a statement absolutely empty of content. It tells us nothing whatever about the table; it conveys no information, has "no factual content."

h. The so-called laws of logic are nothing but rules of inference—and rules, of course aren't true or false, though they can be useful or not useful.

i. When parents teach children the meaning of a word, "A," they teach them when "A" is applicable to reality and also *when it is not*. The same holds for teaching the meaning of a sentence, such as "Snow is falling." In that way, children can learn what situations in reality the sentence refers to. But how can children learn the meaning of "Not both A and not-A," since it can never be false? Since there is no possible situation to which it does *not* apply, how can children learn its meaning?

10. In each of the following examples, is the proposition a necessary truth? Is it a truth at all? Justify your answer.

a "Everything that has color has shape." But what about the sky?

b. "Everything that has shape has color." But what about an ice cube?

c. Everything that has shape has size." What about a rainbow or the round spots in front of your eyes?

d. "Everything that has shape has volume." What about a triangle? (Is the statement true if three-dimensional shape is meant?)

e. "Everything that has volume has shape." What about the water in a glass or gases released into a chamber?

f. "All matter is either solid, liquid, or gaseous." What about a single molecule?

g. Events in nature can't contradict one another; only propositions can.

h. True propositions cannot contradict one another.

11. Classify each of the following propositions as

(1) necessary but not synthetic,
(2) synthetic but not necessary, or
(3) both necessary and synthetic

Give your reasons in each case.

a. Everything that has shape has size.

b. Everything that has volume has shape.

c. Everything that has shape has color. (Note: Does "colored" include transparent?)

d. Every sound has pitch, volume, and timbre.

e. Every color has hue, brightness, and saturation.

f. Everything that has shape has extension.

g. Everything that has extension has shape.

h. $40694 + 27593 = 68287$.

i. No mammals grow feathers.

j. Every particle of matter in the universe attracts every other particle with a force varying inversely with the square of the distance and directly with the product of the masses. (Newton's Law of Universal Gravitation.)

k. A straight line is the shortest distance between two points.

l. Given any line L and any point P not on that line, only one line can be drawn through P parallel to L.

m. If *p* is true, *p* is not also false.

n. Either *p* is true or *p* is false.

o. It is right to do your duty.

p. If A is north of B and B is north of C, then A is north of C.

q. If A is east of B and B is east of C, then A is east of C.

r. If San Francisco is east of Tokyo and Tokyo is east of London, then San Francisco is east of London.

s. A person cannot be born 3 months after the death of his mother.

t. A person cannot be born 3 months after the death of his father.

u. All cubes have twelve edges.

v. If A occurs before B and B occurs before C, then A occurs before C.

w. If A hires B and B hires C, then A hires C.

x. There cannot be, at the same place and time, two different determinates (such as red and green) under the same determinable (such as color).

y. Every even number is the sum of two prime numbers. (Goldbach's theorem.)

z. If A is indistinguishable from B, and B from C, A is indistinguishable from C.

SELECTED READINGS

ALLISON, HENRY E. *Kant's Transcendental Idealism.* New Haven: Yale University Press, 1983.

BENACERRAF, PAUL, and HILARY PUTNAM, eds. *Philosophy of Mathematics.* Englewood Cliffs, N.J.: Prentice-Hall, 1964.

BENNETT, JONATHAN. *Kant's Analytic.* Cambridge: Cambridge University Press, 1966.

BERGMANN GUSTAV. *Logic and Reality.* Madison: University of Wisconsin Press, 1964.

BLACK MAX. *Models and Metaphors.* Ithaca: Cornell University Press, 1962.

BLANSHARD, BRAND. *The Nature of Thought.* 2 vols. London: Allen & Unwin, 1939.

BLANSHARD, BRAND. *Reason and Analysis.* LaSalle, IL.: Open Court, 1963.

BROAD, C. D. *An Examination of McTaggart's Philosophy.* Cambridge: Cambridge University Press, 1938.

FEIGL, HERBERT, WILFRID SELLARS, and KEITH LEHRER, eds. *New Readings in Philosophical Analysis.* New York: Appleton-Century-Crofts, 1972.

FLEW, ANTONY, ed. *Logic and Language.* 2 vols. (including Douglas Gasking, "Mathematics and the World," and David Pears, "Incompatibilities of Colors.") Oxford, Blackwell, 1953.

FREGE, GOTTLOB. *The Foundations of Arithmetic.* Oxford: Blackwell, 1953.

HARMON, GILBERT. *Thought.* Princeton: Princeton University Press, 1973.

HARRIS, JAMES and R. STEVEN. *Analyticity.* Chicago: Quadrangle Books, 1970.

HUME, DAVID. *Treatise of Human Nature*, book I, part 1, 1739.

HUME, DAVID. *Enquiry Concerning Human Understanding.* Section 2. 1751.

KANT, IMMANUEL. *Critique of Pure Reason,* 1781. Norman Kemp Smith ed., London: Macmillan, 1929.

LEWIS, H. D., ed., *Clarity Is Not Enough.* (including, A. C. Ewing, "The Linguistic Theory of the A Priori" and William Kneale, "Are Necessary Truths True by Convention?") London: Allen & Unwin, 1963.

LEWIS, CLARENCE I. *Analysis of Knowledge and Valuation.* LaSalle, IL.: Open Court, 1946.

HEMPEL, CARL G. "Geometry and Empirical Science" and "The Nature of Mathematics" in Herbert Fiegl and Wilfrid Sellars, eds., *Readings in Philosophical Analysis.* New York: Appleton-Century-Crofts, 1949.

KRIPKE, SAUL. *Naming and Necessity.* Cambridge: Harvard University Press, 1972.

McTAGGART, J. E. M. *The Nature of Existence.* 2 vols. Cambridge: Cambridge Univ. Press, 1921.

MUNITZ, MILTON. *Contemporary Analytic Philosophy.* New York: Macmillan, 1981.

NAGEL, ERNEST, and RICHARD BRANDT, eds. *Meaning and Knowledge.* New York: Harcourt Brace, 1965.

NAGEL, ERNEST. *Logic Without Metaphysics.* New York: Free Press, 1956.

OLSHEWSKY, THOMAS, ed. *Problems in the Philosophy of Langauge.* New York: Holt, 1969.

PAP, ARTHUR. *Semantics and Necessary Truth.* New Haven: Yale University Press, 1958.

PLANTINGS, ALVIN. *The Nature of Necessity.* Oxford: Clarendon Press, 1974.

PUTNAM, HILARY. "The Analytic and the Synthetic," in *Minnesota Studies in the Philosophy of Science*. vol. 3, ed. H. Feigl and G. Maxwell. Minneapolis: University of Minnesota Press, 1962.

QUINE, WILLARD V. *From a Logical Point of View.* Cambridge: Harvard University Press, 1953.

QUINE, WILLARD V. *Word and Object.* New York: Wiley, 1960.

RAMSEY, F. P. *Foundations of Mathematics.* London: Routledge & Kegan Paul, 1931.

ROBINSON, RICHARD. *Definition.* London: Oxford University Press, 1950.

RUSSELL, BERTRAND. *Introduction to Mathematical Philosophy.* Allen & Unwin, 1919.

WAISMANN, FRIEDRICH. *Principles of Linguistic Philosophy.* London: Macmillan, 1965.

WAISMANN, FRIEDRICH. "Analytic-Synthetic." *Analysis.* 1949–1952 volumes. (In six parts.)

WITTGENSTEIN, LUDWIG. *Remarks on the Foundations of Mathematics.* Oxford, Blackwell, 1958.

CHAPTER

4

SCIENTIFIC KNOWLEDGE

1. LAW, THEORY, AND EXPLANATION

By means of sense-experience we learn many things about the physical world—we perceive countless physical things, processes, and events, as well as the interaction of our own bodies with these things in nature. But if our knowledge ended there, we would have no means of dealing effectively with the world. The kind of knowledge we acquire through the sciences begins when we notice *regularities* in the course of events. Many events and processes in nature occur the same way over and over again. Iron rusts, but gold does not. Chickens lay eggs, but dogs do not. Lightning is followed by thunder. Cats catch mice, but cows don't. (Even to speak of a cat or a cow is to have noted some regularity—that some characteristics regularly recur, or go together.) Amidst the constant diversity in our daily experience of nature, we try to find regularities;

we trace what George Santayana (1863–1952) called "the thin red vein of order in the flux of experience."

If we were as interested in discovering *ir*regularities in our experience as we are in regularities, the task would be much easier. Some rocks are hard and some soft, some heavy and some light. Some rains are helpful, some ruinous. Some people are tall, some short. If *all* experiences were like this, we would not know what to expect next. Each new situation would confront us as if no past situations had ever occurred, and years of experience would give us no hint about the way future events would occur. But nature is not like this; nature does contain regularities, difficult though they sometimes are to find.

Why are we interested in tracking down these regularities? Not, as a rule, because we enjoy contemplating them for their own sake but because we are interested in *prediction*. If we can rely on it that when we see a twister in the sky a tornado is approaching, then if we see one we may be able to take precautions by finding shelter before it strikes. If people who are in proximity to others who have colds get colds themselves, we may keep Johnny from getting a cold by keeping him temporarily away from Billy, who has a cold. We want some basis for prediction, so that we will not always be taken by surprise at the next series of events with which nature confronts us. And often when we can predict, we can also *control* the course of events; at least we are in a better position to control if we can first make a reliable prediction. We can reliably predict eclipses, but we cannot control their occurrence; but in many cases we can control as a result of our prediction. If we can predict reliably that after heavy rains the river will flood, we can get out of the way of the flood, or even (if it happens repeatedly) build a dam.

Most of the regularities that we find have many exceptions: they are not *invariants*. There is a certain regularity to children getting colds when they play with other children who already have colds, but it doesn't always happen that way. Chickens lay eggs and never cans of sardines, but how many eggs they do lay and at what intervals is extremely variable. Trees are more likely to fall during a severe storm, but they don't always: some do and some don't. The scientific enterprise could be described as the search for genuine invariants in nature, for regularities without exception, so that we are enabled to say, "Whenever such-and-such conditions are fulfilled, this kind of thing *always* happens." Many times we think we have found a genuine invariance, but we have not. We may have been sure that water always boils at 212° F., since we have tried it many times and it has always happened. But if we try it on a mountain top, we discover that the water there boils at a slightly lower temperature, so our hope that we had found a true invariance is upset. We try some more, however, and find that the temperature of water boiling depends not on the moisture

in the air, not on the time of day, not on anything except the pressure of the surrounding air. We are thus able to say, "Water at the pressure found at sea level boils at 212°." Here at last we have a statement of genuine invariance; and behold, we have a *law of nature*.

Prescriptive vs. descriptive laws. The word "law" is ambiguous, and the ambiguity can be extremely misleading if we are not aware of it.

1. In daily life we most often use the word "law" in the context of "passing a law," "the law prohibits you from . . . ," and so on. Law in this sense is *prescriptive:* It is a rule of behavior imposed by a monarch or passed by a legislative body, and enforced by the legal machinery of the state. Laws in this sense are not propositions, because they cannot be false (it is, however, true or false *that* certain laws have been passed); they are, rather, imperatives, in effect "Do this," "Don't do that." The law does not state that anything *is* the case; rather, it issues a command, a *pre*scription, usually with penalties attached for failure to obey. But this is not the sense of "law" that is involved in speaking of laws of nature.

2. Laws of nature are *descriptive:* They describe the way nature works. They do not prescribe anything: Kepler's laws of planetary motion do not prescribe to the planets that they should move in such-and-such orbits, with penalties invoked if they fail; rather, Kepler's laws *describe* how planets actually *do* move. Laws in this sense describe certain uniformities that exist in the universe. Sometimes, for the sake of simplicity, they describe only what would happen under certain ideal conditions: Galileo's Law of Falling Bodies describes only the velocities at which bodies fall in a vacuum. But such a law is still descriptive: It describes our universe (not any logically possible universe), and it prescribes nothing. Only conscious beings can prescribe, since only they are capable of giving orders. But the

uniformities of nature would still occur even if there were no human beings to describe them.

Several confusions can be avoided if we keep this distinction in mind: (1) "Laws should be obeyed." Whether or not you should obey all the laws of the land is a problem in ethics. But a law of nature is not the sort of thing you can obey or disobey, since it is not an order or command anyone has given. What could you do if someone said to you, "Obey the law of gravitation"? Your motions, along with those of stones and every particle of matter in the universe, are *instances* of this law; but since the law only tells us how matter *does* behave, and doesn't prescribe how things *should* behave, you cannot be said either to obey or disobey it. A prescriptive law, moreover, could still be said to exist even if it were universally disobeyed. (2) "Where there's a law, there's a lawmaker." Again this applies clearly to prescriptive law: If a course of action is prescribed, someone must have prescribed it. But laws of nature are not prescriptions; they only describe how nature works. (The workings of nature may have been designed by God, but this is another issue, to be discussed in Chapter 7.) (3) "Laws are discovered, not made." This applies, again, only to descriptive laws. We *discover* how nature works, we do not make it work that way. But statute laws are made, devised, passed by human beings in positions of authority. Such laws would not exist but for human beings, but laws of nature would—that is, the uniformities of nature would exist whether human beings were there to observe them or not, although the *formulation* of these uniformities is the work of human beings.

Laws of nature constitute a smaller class of propositions than empirical statements in general. Any statement whose truth can be confirmed by observation of the world is an empirical statement. "Some chickens lay eggs," "World War I lasted from 1914 to 1918," "She fell ill with pneumonia yester-day," and "New York City contains approximately 8 million residents" are all empirical statements. Indeed, most of the statements we utter in daily life are empirical statements. But none of these is a law of nature: Laws of nature are a special class of empirical statements. Since laws of nature are at the very core of the empirical sciences—physics, chemistry, astronomy, geology, biology, psychology, sociology, economics—it is important that we be clear about what a law of nature is.

The meaning of "law of nature." What, then, is a law of nature? What requirements must an empirical proposition fulfill in order to be a member of that select class of propositions which we call laws of nature?

1. It must be a true *universal* empirical proposition. To say that a proposition is universal is to say that it applies to *all* members of a given class without exception. That all iron rusts when exposed to oxygen is a universal proposition, but that *this* piece of iron rusts, or even that *some* iron rusts, is not a universal proposition.

a. A proposition about a single thing— "This piece of rock is metamorphic"—may be *material* for a law of nature, but it is not a law. Science does not consist of such singular propositions. Books on physics, the most developed of the empirical sciences, make no reference (except by way of example) to the motions of particular bodies, nor do chemistry books tell us about this piece of lead or that vessel of chlorine. But one does find many such references in psychology books (psychiatry division), for example in case histories of patients. In this area few genuine laws have yet been discovered, so the psychologist must rely on individual case histories as a means toward finding laws of human behavior. In this sense, psychology is still very much in a prescientific stage, a stage physics had already left behind three centuries ago. But physics is in an advantageous position in that its laws are *simpler*—not in the sense of "easier to understand," for physics is probably more difficult for most students than any of the other empirical sciences, but in the sense that a law of physics can be stated in terms of the smallest number of conditions. In stating the velocity at which objects fall, one can ignore most of the universe: One can ignore the color of the object, its smell or taste, the temperature of the environment, the number of people watching the event, and so on for thousands of factors. By contrast, in dealing with human behavior it would be difficult to say what might *not* turn out to be relevant. A trivial event that occurred in your childhood, which neither you nor anyone else may remember, may still influence your behavior today and cause you to react differently to a given stimulus. The best we can do, usually, is to state certain general tendencies of human behavior, allowing for many exceptions. In psychology we hardly have laws at all, only tentative blueprints for laws; laws about human behavior that are both true and exceptionless have seldom been found.

b. Even true propositions about *some* members of a class are not usually considered laws of nature, though sometimes they are called "statistical laws." If 90 percent of the As that exist are Bs, there is a considerable regularity between the two, and the statement is far from useless as a basis for prediction. But, we are led to ask, if only 90 percent of As are Bs and the remaining 10 percent are not, why are the 90 percent Bs and not the others? What we want to find is some uniformity of a universal character underlying the statistical one. In daily life, however, we are constantly confronted by such regularities that are not universal. People with a cold usually have the sniffles, but not always; if one person hits another in the nose, the second person often gets a nosebleed, but not always. No one has yet formulated any universal statement about the precise conditions under which people get nosebleeds when struck on the nose, though we have a fairly adequate

idea on what factors it depends. There is some regularity here (the harder you hit him, the more likely he is to get a nosebleed, and so on), but no invariant relationship.

2. These universal propositions are hypothetical in form. Universal propositions, both in logic and science, are usually interpreted *hypothetically*—that is, as propositions of the "if . . . then . . . " form. "All iron rusts when exposed to oxygen" would thus be translated as "*If* there is iron, it will rust when exposed to oxygen." Thus formulated, the proposition does not tell us that there *is* any iron (it makes no existential claim), but only what happens under certain circumstances *if* there is. "All bodies freely falling in a vacuum accelerate at the rate of 16 feet per second per second" does not imply that there actually were or are any bodies falling in a vacuum.

3. There are many true, universal propositions that do not pass as laws of nature. Suppose I were to say, "All the dogs in this kennel are black," and that my statement were true: It would still not qualify as a law of nature. It is limited to a definite area in space and time—this kennel today. Even if its scope were broader ("All the dogs I've ever had in my kennels are black"), it still would say nothing about *all* dogs, or even all dogs of a certain breed. But if I say that all crows are black, I mean that all crows, *wherever* they may be, and *whenever* they may exist or have existed or have yet to exist, are, were, and will be black. (Blackness is not here considered defining of crows, else the proposition would be analytic.) The law is "open-ended": it has an unlimited range, both in time and in space. This does not mean that there is an infinite number of crows—nor indeed that there are any crows at all—but that it is an open class, with no strictures of time and space operating to limit the scope of the law. There is no time or place at which the law will not hold true: considerations of when and where are irrelevant to the application of the proposition. By contrast, the proposition about the dogs in my

kennel will not pass as a law because (1) though universal in form, the universality is restricted to a specifically delimited time and space; (2) the number of things covered by the proposition is not only finite, but this finiteness may be inferred from the terms in the proposition itself. This is not so for Kepler's laws of planetary motion; for example: though there are a finite number of planets, this fact cannot be deduced from the law; and (3) the evidence for the proposition exhausts its domain of application—the proposition is simply a summative report of what *has been* observed to be the case.

Since laws of nature apply to all places and all times, their claim extends into the future. This is perhaps the most important single feature of laws, for it enables them to be made the basis for prediction. If the proposition merely read "All crows thus far have turned out to be black," one might say "So what?"—we could not derive any predictions from it; but if we say that *all* As, no matter when or where, are Bs, we can deduce from it, plus the proposition that this is an A, that it will also be a B. But unfortunately we are not in a position to be sure of the first premise, that all As are Bs. Thus the argument, though it is valid, is not sound, since the truth of at least one premise is not known.

5. Even when all this has been said, many propositions that satisfy all these criteria are often denied the status of laws. The difference seems to lie in the proposition's degree of *generality*. "All metals are good thermal conductors" and "Silver is a good thermal conductor" are both universal propositions, since both apply to all members of the given class; but the first statement is more general than the second, for it covers a wider scope. Universal propositions whose degree of generality is greater are more likely to pass as laws; thus the statement about metals is considered a law, but the statement about silver is not. While "All rare-earth metals have higher melting points than the halogens" may pass as

a law, one would not likely hear the fact that tungsten melts at 3370° C referred to as a law but only as a fact.

6. An important feature of laws is one that may come as a surprise: no single observation is sufficient to undermine a law. If you say "That's a sparrow" and it isn't, your statement is refuted by sense-experience; if you say truly "That's an albino crow," you have refuted the generalization that all crows are black. But this is called a generalization, not a law. Laws do not have the same direct relation to experience as generalizations do, even the generalization, "All crows are black," which certainly looks law-like. This point will become clearer as we proceed.

To discover invariants in nature is only the beginning; we also want to *explain* them. That altitude makes a difference to the boiling of water is explained by the theory that air consists of billions of tiny molecules, and the more molecules of air there are above you the greater is the pressure; accordingly water boils more quickly at high altitudes, where the air pressure is less. "If there is friction, there is heat"—this seems to be a true invariant in nature, without exceptions. But we can explain why the invariance holds if we accept the theory that heat is the motion of molecules, and the greater the motion of molecules the greater the heat: Rubbing two things together induces molecular motion, hence heat. We use the molecular theory to explain why the law holds. (There is a close relation between laws and theories: As we shall see, many laws involve theories in their very formulation.)

Let us, then, examine the two other concepts that have emerged: theory and explanation. Without theories, most of nature's workings would remain unexplained. Without them, biology would still be in the classificatory stage (taxonomy), modern advances in genetics would be impossible, and physics would still be very nearly where it was three centuries ago. First, then, let us consider explanations, and second, scientific theories.

Explanation

When we don't understand something we ask to have it explained. "Why is the door open?" needs no explanation on a hot summer day, but does when the winter wind is blowing into the house. "Why are there no midterm exams here?" might elicit the response, "Because this university doesn't require them." "Why is there a small swinging door here?" "So the dog can get in and out." "Why wasn't she at the meeting last night?" "Because she had a conflicting engagement."

In requesting an explanation we are often asking for different things. "Explain that obscure passage in the poem"—that is, clarify it, paraphrase it so that I can understand what it means. We may say to the child, seeing the mess she has made on the floor, "Explain what you are doing." Most frequently we demand explanations in answer to questions beginning with the words "how" and "why." You can explain *how* you built the house without explaining *why* you built the house. (In answer to how, you explain the process by which you built it; in answer to why, you state the reasons why you built it.) But sometimes you can answer a why-question by explaining *how* something happened: "Why did that domino fall?" "Well, there were twelve dominoes standing near to each other. I pushed the first one, and it fell; in falling it hit the second one and made it fall . . . and so on, till the eleventh pushed over the twelfth one, causing it to fall; that's *why* it fell."

The question "why?" is itself ambiguous. When you ask me why I *believe* a certain statement is true, you are asking me to give *reasons* in support of my belief. Reasons for *p* are propositions that are given in support of other propositions, and if they are good reasons they do make *p* more probable (that's why we call them good reasons). On the other hand, when *why* is asked in a different context, not to justify a belief but to find out why something happened as it did, we are asking for an explanation of some event or process (or type of process) in the course of nature: why tides come and go, why carbon monoxide kills, why helium won't combine chemically with anything else.

If a person is rational, the reason she holds a certain belief also explains why she holds it; she wants to believe what is true, so the explanation and the reason coincide. It is not always so, however; the reason a person gives for belief in God may be various arguments, such as we shall consider in Chapter 7; but this may not explain why she really has the belief—perhaps the explanation is that she wanted a father-substitute or a protector in a cold harsh world.

When we ask why events in nature occur as they do, we may ask why a specific event occurred (Why did the pipes in the basement burst last night? Why did the window break?) or why a certain *kind* of event always occurs as it does (Why do balloons rise? Why does iron rust?).

When we ask for the explanation of a particular event, such as "Why did the pipes burst?" the explanation includes (1) certain *laws* of nature (such as that water expands when it freezes) and (2) certain particular facts (such as that the temperature dropped below the freezing point in the basement last night). We have to have both of these in order to explain the event. The laws and particular facts involved may be numerous: We need to know not only that water expands when it freezes (law) but that the pipes were filled with water (particular fact), that the strength of the expanding ice was greater than that of the resisting pipes (particular fact), and that when this happens the retaining vessel breaks since its contents must have someplace to go (law). The particular facts may be known from direct *observation* or may be a *hypothesis:* If we were in the basement and watched the thermometer and felt the cold, we can be said to have observed the particular condition for ourselves; but if we were sleeping soundly upstairs all the while but noticed how cold it was when we got up in the morning, the below-freezing temperature of the basement during the night was a hypothesis. The hypothesis alone (it was freezing in the basement) does not explain the event (pipes bursting) without the law (water expands on freezing), nor does the law alone explain the event without the particular fact (observed, or inferred by hypothesis) that the temperature in the basement dropped to below freezing during the night. In the same way, the breaking of the window requires reference to a particular fact or condition (someone threw a rock at it) and a law (about the fragility of glass and the mass and velocity of the object striking it).

But sometimes it is not particular events that we wish to explain, but laws of nature themselves. Why does sugar dissolve in water? Why does water expand when it freezes? We explain these laws by means of other laws and theories. Why do balloons rise in air if they contain hydrogen or helium? Because hydrogen and helium are lighter than the mixture of oxygen, nitrogen, etc., constituting our atmosphere (fact), and a gas that is lighter per unit of volume than another gas will go upward (law). Why does water, unlike most liquids, expand when it freezes? Because of the crystalline structure of the water molecule (theory). Why does iron rust? Because molecules of iron combine with the oxygen in the air (theory), and the resultant compound iron oxide forms (law). Both theories and laws are normally involved in explaining laws; we cannot go far in explaining laws without invoking theories.

Whether we explain particular occurrences or laws, reference to laws or theories is always involved in their explanation; and the law or theory must be one we already accept, else we will not accept the explanation. "Why doesn't the red liquid mix with the transparent liquid?" "Because the red liquid is colored water, and the transparent liquid is gasoline." The law involved here is that water and gasoline do not mix, and our acceptance of the explanation depends on our acceptance of this law. If the answer "Because it's red" had been given instead, we would not have accepted it as an explanation, because we know of no law of nature according to which transparent liquids will not mix with red ones.

Sometimes an explanation that we accept involves laws only in a very loose sense—a rough-and-ready generalization that is true much of the time but does not hold true for all cases. "Why does Billy have a cold?" "He's been playing with Bobby, and Bobby has a cold." It is not a law that those in contact with others who have colds always get colds themselves; but there is some degree of uniformity here, sufficient to make us accept the explanation. We could, of course, go on to say, "But Johnny also played with Bobby, and Johnny didn't get a cold," and then we would have to try to find some statement of the conditions under which people always get colds. Meanwhile, we tend to accept the generalization as an explanation of the facts. Similarly, if we ask, "Why were so many of the members absent from the meeting tonight?" and are told, "There was a conflict with a meeting of another organization to which most of our members also belong," we accept this as an explanation, although there is no law here, merely the necessary truth that people can't be in two places at the same time and the generalization that people who preferred meeting B to meeting A, or felt a stronger obligation to go to B, would tend to go to meeting B.

We are often presented so-called explanations that explain nothing. "Why do these pills put people to sleep?" "Because of the soporific power." This may sound impressive until we realize that "soporific power" means nothing more or less than the power of putting people to sleep. The so-called explanation does not tell us what we presumably wanted to know: what there is in this pill that causes it to put people to sleep. "Why does hydrogen combine with oxygen to form water?" "Because hydrogen has an affinity for water." But an affinity for X is only a tendency to combine with X, and the explanation does not tell us why hydrogen has this tendency. It has only repeated the question in other words. "Why does the mother cat take care of her kittens?" "Because she has a maternal instinct." This response is not entirely empty, for it tells us something, that the behavior is of the mother cat not learned; but apart from that it tells us nothing. No matter what an animal does, we can say that the creature has an instinct for that type of behavior. But the important question remains unanswered: what is there in the physiological constitution of the cat that causes it to exhibit this maternal behavior? Something about its genes and chromosomes, perhaps? This is an extremely difficult question, but at any rate we should be clear that the reference to instinct tells us virtually nothing. Maybe robins have a "migratory instinct"—that is, they do migrate—but this does not tell us why robins do and not sparrows. Instead of information, we are given merely words: "instinct," "affinity," "power," "faculty," and so on.

Teleological explanations. Throughout most of human history it was customary to explain natural events in terms of purpose. Storms and earthquakes were explained as manifestations of the wrath of the gods. Spirits inhabited the winds and the waves. Sometimes the gods were believed to be in conflict with one another. In other cases one god would vent his wrath on a certain person or group of persons; another god might disapprove and retaliate by felling that person's enemies. The Trojan War as described in Homer's *Iliad* would not have lasted half so long had it not been for the constant intervention of the gods on one side or the other.

Today we dismiss such explanations as childish fantasies; but many people still attempt to explain a natural catastrophe as a manifestation of God's wrath (such as the destruction of Sodom and Gomorrah) and to explain their own survival from a natural catastrophe— or a human-made one such as an airplane crash—when many others have died as "by the grace of God," who has a special purpose in letting them survive.

Such explanations are not empty like the explanation of the pill that puts you to sleep because of its dormitive power; if true, a statement such as "it's an act of God" would explain why the events occurred. Nevertheless such explanations do not fall within the domain of science. There seems to be no way of discovering empirically whether they are true, and science considers only those explanations that are empirical in nature, that is, which can be confirmed or disconfirmed by observation of the world. What is deemed "unscientific" is that they are not confirmable, not that they are *teleological* (from the Greek *telos,* end or purpose).

In fact, many teleological (purposive) explanations are very familiar and universally accepted. (1) We explain why a person did what he did by saying what his purpose was in doing it. "I wanted to go shopping" explains why he was at the store, and "I decided to take a short walk" is accepted as an explanation of why you were seen at the beach at midnight. Stating the purpose you had in mind is not enough for a complete explanation: Your body had to be functioning in such a way that you could do what you set out to do. You couldn't take a walk if you had suddenly had a paralytic stroke. And sometimes some mechanical aids are also required: "I wanted to go to the moon" doesn't by itself explain your being there. But since it is so generally true that people do what they choose to do, provided they have the ability and the means to do it, a statement like "I chose to do X" is considered a satisfactory explanation of why one did X. And that is an explanation in terms of purpose just as much as is an explanation like the gods bringing on an earthquake to teach a sinful populace a lesson. Explanation in terms of purpose is acceptable if there was someone (a purposer) to have the purpose.

(2) Sometimes we ask for the purposes of inanimate objects, particularly those made by human beings. If asked "What's the purpose of that stone?" we would be nonplussed: As far as we know it doesn't have a purpose, it's just there. But answering "To pound nails" in response to the question "What's the purpose of the hammer?" is quite satisfactory. The hammer itself has no purpose—it is an inanimate object, incapable of having purposes or designs. But the persons who designed and made the hammer *did* have a purpose in making it, as with all tools and objects of manufacture. The tool has no purpose in itself, but its makers had a purpose in making it, and this is what we are talking about when we speak of its purpose.

(3) Sometimes we speak of purpose in a different context, where the term purpose is so attenuated as to be quite misleading. For example: "What's the purpose of the heart?" "To pump blood through the body." We don't mean here that the heart itself is conscious and that it is determined to pump blood through the body. Nor do we mean that people had that in mind in making hearts, for people do not make them (except artificial hearts). Do we mean then to ask what purpose God had in mind in making the human organism, including the human heart? If a person is speaking in a theological context, and believes in a God who has purpose in everything, he may well be asking just that: what purpose did God achieve in making this? But ordinarily physicians and medical researchers, even those who devoutly believe in God, are not asking this question when they talk about the purpose of the heart. They are asking a different question, namely how the organ *functions* in the body, what part it plays in keeping the body alive and functioning. When they identify an organ or appendage to the body, such as the appendix, and ask what its

purpose is, they are asking how it contributes to the functioning of the organism as a whole. And strictly speaking this is not a question about purpose at all, but about natural function, even though the word "purpose" occurs in the question.

When some feature of an organism is explained in terms of its evolutionary survival value, is this an explanation in terms of purpose? No, it was not the purpose of the wolf to have a keen nose and binocular vision, though these features do help the animal to stalk its prey and hence to survive. The Arctic animals whose fur turns white in winter did not do it *in order to* survive (they did not *do* it at all). Having these features helps to explain the survival of the species that has such features, whereas other species, lacking these features, have long since died out. It does not explain how such features developed, but it does explain how once such features developed (for example, through a mutation) the creatures possessing the faculties in question were better able to survive and, via laws of genetics, were able to pass such features on to their offspring.

Scientific Theories

"Why did I get a shock?" "Because you touched an unshielded copper wire." "But why would doing that give me a shock?" To explain this, we must leave the familiar world of things we see and hear and touch and turn to the theory of electricity, involving atoms, electrons, and ionization. The word "theory" is used, somewhat loosely, to explain certain events or phenomena that cannot be observed with our senses, but which are believed to occur because they explain what is observed.

It is not always clear what is to count as being observable. We observe the iron filings changing their position as a result of a nearby magnet, and we say they are acting in a magnetic field; shall we also say that we see the magnetic field, or only the iron filings? We say we observe objects with our eyes, with glasses through windowpanes, through mirrors, through telescopes, through microscopes, and through electron microscopes. Or do we only observe images of these things? When it is said that we can observe extremely large molecules such as proteins through electron microscopes, is this like seeing them through spectacles? Saying that one "sees a molecule through an electron microscope" involves so much theory itself, that if certain current theories of atomic structure were abandoned we would no longer count what we see as a molecule (perhaps only its effect—just as you don't see electrons in a cloud chamber, only the presumed effects of their motion). "The line between the observable and the unobservable is diffuse, [and] it shifts from one scientific problem to another, and is constantly being pushed toward the 'unobservable' end of the spectrum as we develop better means of observation."[1] Nevertheless, most of these so-called particles are agreed by all to be genuinely unobservable by human beings.

Let us consider several examples of theories.

1. The most comprehensive theory in science, without which modern physics and chemistry could not exist, is atomic theory. Atoms, protons and electrons, neutrons, neutrinos, quarks, and all the rest of the burgeoning progeny of subatomac "particles," are theoretical entities in the sense that we cannot observe them in the way we observe trees and houses. The study of the nature of atoms, and the tests which have led scientists constantly to modify their conception of atomic structure through the years, are highly technical subjects which cannot be briefly explained to

those who have not familiarized themselves with the physical sciences for a considerable time.

Nevertheless, the central idea is simple enough. The early Greek philosopher Democritus, who lived around 460 B.C., had already developed an atomic theory based on very common observations that could be made by anyone.

For example, stone steps wear away bit by bit, year after year. Put a few drops of berry juice into a glass of water, and in a moment the entire liquid has become red. Or put some sugar into it, and immediately the sweet taste pervades the entire liquid. How can these and countless other things be explained unless by the existence of very small particles, invisible to the unaided eye? The stone steps are composed of these particles, which wear away gradually one by one until after years of wear we can fianlly notice the difference. The berry juice is composed of very small particles that spread throughout the entire liquid and color it red. The same with the sugar we dissolve in water, which makes the entire liquid taste sweet. Besides, the things we observe must be composed of something. I can cut this piece of chalk in half and rub against it with my fingers, with the result that pieces of it color my fingers white. But these small bits (it was reasoned) must in turn be composed of smaller ones, and these in turn of still smaller ones. At the end of this process, however, there must be particles that cannot be split any further, and these, as we have seen (p. 89), he called atoms. All the things we see and touch are composed of these very small particles that can no longer be subdivided. We cannot see them or touch them; but if we assume that they exist, we can account for an enormous number of different things that we do observe.

So went the reasoning of Democritus and Lucretius (ca. 96–55 B.C.). Their atomic theory was primitive, but the principle involved was no different from modern theories: The

[1] Grover Maxwell, "The Ontological Status of Theoretical Entities," in Herbert Feigl and Grover Maxwell (eds.), *Scientific Explanation, Space, and Time* (Minneapolis: University of Minnesota Press, 1962), p. 13.

unobserved was invoked to explain the observed. More refined atomic theories today have explained countless phenomena undreamed of by the ancients: why element A combines with elements B and C but not with D and E (and some with none at all), why certain elements and compounds have the properties that they do, why they evaporate or ignite at the temperatures they do, freeze at other temperatures, and so on. Virtually all the facts of modern chemistry have been explained in terms of atomic theory. But it is theory, not observed fact. And the introduction of this multitude of unobservable entities—particles, waves, energy, fields of force—ushers us into a whole new world of physical reality undreamed of less than a century ago.

Behind the world of appearances, the everyday world of common sense and ordinary human observation and experience, there is a reality of a different order which sustains that world and presents it to our senses. Now it is precisely such a reality that science reveals—a world of unobservable entities and invisible forces, waves, cells, particles, all interlockingly organized and structured down to a deeper level than anything we have yet been able to penetrate.[2]

Physicists sometimes describe the ultimate constituents of matter as particles, though the word hardly seems appropriate, since there is no way of perceiving them.[3] But that *something* is there, though far too small to be seen, is almost unanimously agreed. If they were merely convenient fictions, how is it that the tremendous variety of observable things they explain always occur as they do? Don't the things we see and touch have to be made of *something*—smaller constituents? Why would things behave just *as if* they were composed of these constituents if no such constituents

exist? (This is analogous to the question we asked in discussing Berkeley: why should things always behave as if they existed unobserved if they do not actually exist unobserved?)

2. In historical geology and evolutionary biology, it's not that the entities involved—such as rocks and living organisms—are too small to be observed, but that the events that are alleged to have occurred happened so long ago that there were no human beings around to observe them. Thus we speak of the *theory* of biological evolution, the geological theory of tectonic plates, and so on. We cannot, of course, observe now these events and processes long past; all we have now is the "evidence of the rocks" and the fossil remains of ancient organisms. We do not observe—rather we *infer*—that there was a Cambrian era, a Jurassic era, and so on, and that complex organisms evolved from simpler ones. A tremendous amount of evidence has been amassed in favor of these theories. To take but one example of thousands, why should we find different species of organisms (and remains of other species) in Australia that are utterly different from those we find elsewhere on the earth? The fact that Australia has been cut off from any mainland for many eons suggests that organisms evolved there in isolation from the development of organisms elsewhere, and that is why they are conspicuously different. A reading of Charles Darwin's *The Origin of Species*—or a recent work such as Ronald W. Clark's *The Survival of Charles Darwin*—gives some idea of the massiveness of the evidence and the minuteness of detail in the testing of one theory after another, rejecting some and revising others, elucidating in painstaking detail the observations (often minute and seemingly trivial) on which is built the edifice of evolutionary theory which we now possess.

We can observe some aspects of the evolutionary process going on now—for example, in the case of fruitflies as well as microorganisms that pass through many generations in

---

[2]Bryan Magee, *Philosophy and the Real World* (LaSalle, Ill.: Open Court Publishing Co., 1985), pp. 34–35.

[3]See J.J.C. Smart, *Between Science and Philosophy* (New York: Random House, 1968), pp. 158–159.

a day, and whose gradual evolution and mutations we can presently observe. Most of the evolutionary process, however, including most of the data on which the theory is built, cannot be observed in any one human lifetime, and we cannot observe past events *now*. (We can observe some events from the past indirectly through motion pictures, but unfortunately there are no filmed records of the remote past.) Nor were evolutionary events observable by any human beings at any time—not because of the events' minuteness in space but because of their remoteness in time.

3. In another discipline, psychology, we encounter still another kind of unobservable, the unconscious. Wishes and fears and jealousies had always been considered to be conscious. Indeed, the expressions "unconscious wish" and "unconscious fear" were taken to be a contradiction in terms. Isn't a wish like a pain? To speak of having a pain you don't feel is to contradict yourself, because to have a pain *is* to feel it (under anesthetic you feel no pain, and have none); in the same way, it was said, a wish is something you experience, and an unconscious wish is a contradiction in terms. When Sigmund Freud (1856–1939) wrote about unconscious wishes, then, wasn't he guilty of self-contradiction?

What Freud said, however, was that unconscious wishes were *like* conscious wishes except that one wasn't conscious of them. But isn't that like saying that there is an invisible intangible chair in this room which is just like the chair I'm sitting on except that it can't be seen or touched? And how is that different from no chair at all? What Freud pointed out, however, is that what he called an unconscious wish had something very important in common with the ones we consciously experience, namely, that they affect *behavior* in the same way. They do the same work; they're like the automatic telephone exchange instead of one in which one has to go through the operator. They function similarly in one's life, though they're not consciously experienced. For example: (1) A person may not consciously wish to be hurt or abused or beaten, but if the person constantly propels himself into situations where this is likely to occur, and seems always to seek them out, then, said Freud, the person has an unconscious wish to be hurt or abused. This wish was probably "repressed" into the unconscious because it was difficult to live with in the conscious state—it was "pushed into the unconscious" where the person, by not experiencing it consciously, would not have to deal with it. (2) A woman complains that she has had to take care of her alcoholic husband year after year; consciously she gets daily pain and distress from this experience; yet she sticks with her husband in spite of opportunities to leave. Why? The "earth-mother" type unconsciously *wants* to be a mother to a man rather than a wife; she is not aware of this desire, but she acts on the basis of it nonetheless. In this way we can understand her repeated refusals to get out of the situation she complains about. (3) Consciously a man wants to keep his job, to get along well with friends and fellow employees; why then does he always tell off the boss (of all people) instead of keeping his thoughts to himself, and end up losing his job? Why does he always "say the wrong thing at the wrong time" so as to alienate friends and acquaintances? Unconsciously he enjoys reveling in this sense of loss, so that he can prove to himself how bad other people are and how badly the world is treating him. He is conscious of their hostility, but he always blames them because he is totally unconscious of the fact that he himself always provokes it. There are so many thousands of examples of this sort of behavior that psychotherapy today would be as much at a loss without the unconscious as physics and chemistry would be without atoms.

But it is not merely such special cases of theory that characterize the sciences; science is theoretical throughout. We use observations we make by means of instruments as evidence in science, yet our trust in the reliability of these instruments is based on the acceptance of theories. When we use a telescope to glean information about distant stars, we presuppose certain theories of optics and the principle that light travels in straight lines. Even to understand what is meant in talking about voltmeters, spectrographs, oscilloscopes, and cloud chambers presupposes a great deal of scientific theory. Virtually every statement we take as evidence for another in science is *theory-laden.* Even the acceptance of photographs as evidence presupposes the acceptance of a theory of optics.

Should we speak of the *law* of gravitation or the *theory* of gravitation? We could slice it either way. Whichever we call it, you can't just go out and confirm Newton's law of gravitation the way you would observe whether swans are white. You don't test it by going outdoors and just looking around. You could see apples fall from now till doomsday without thereby testing Newton's law of gravitation (you would only be confirming the existence of *gravity,* the tendency of heavier-than-air objects to fall toward the earth). When you talk about Newton's law of universal gravitation, as well as his three laws of motion, you are already in a Copernican universe, and there is a background of assumptions being made about that universe—for example, that the stars are not (as Aristotle thought) fixed on the interior surface of a huge revolving sphere but are themselves in motion. There is a wealth of theory presupposed at every stage. Mass, for example, is a fairly sophisticated theoretical concept: You can't just go out and perceive the mass of an object; you can weigh it on a scale (and the use of the scale as a measure of weight already presupposes some theory) but the same object that weighs 10 pounds on the earth will weigh less than one-fourth of that on the moon (because of the moon's weaker gravitational attraction) though the mass remains unchanged. Mere observation wouldn't get you far in confirm-

ing Newtonian mechanics, without a considerable background of theory.

When we attempt to confirm one law or theory, in doing so we assume that others continue to hold true. When we say that an object has a certain temperature, because of an observed thermometric reading, we assume the correctness of the molecular theories underlying the use of the thermometer, for example that the height of a column of mercury in a tube is a good indicator of degree of heat (molecular motion). When we try to determine the age of rocks by the method of the rate of disintegration of uranium into lead, we assume certain atomic theories according to which this rate is absolutely uniform and uninfluenced by any outside factors. When we check the distance of various stars by the method of parallactic displacement, we assume the correctness of the method of triangulation. We can't test everything at once, so we assume as true the continued operation of theories (themselves already confirmed) in the process of performing the present test. Thus, there is a high degree of *interconnectedness* in scientific theories. Each theory is part of a fabric in which any doubt concerning one part reverberates throughout the system and affects other parts. As Pierre Duhem wrote in 1906:

People generally think that each one of the hypotheses employed in Physics can be taken in isolation, checked by experiment, then when many varied tests have established its validity, given a definitive place in the system of Physics. In reality, this is not the case. Physics is not a machine which lets itself be taken apart; we cannot try each piece in isolation, and in order to adjust it, wait until its solidity has been carefully checked; physical science is a system that must be taken as a whole; it is an organism in which one part cannot be made to function without the parts that are most remote from it being called into play, some more so than others, but all to some degree. If something goes wrong, if some discomfort is felt in the functioning of the organism, the physicist will have to ferret out through its effect on the entire system which organ needs to be remedied or modified without the possibility of isolating this organ and examining it apart. The watchmaker to whom you give a watch that has stopped separates all the wheel-works and examines them one by one until he finds the part that is defective or broken; the doctor to whom a patient appears cannot dissect him in order to establish his diagnosis; he has to guess the seat and cause of the ailment solely by inspecting disorders affecting the whole body. Now, the physicist concerned with remedying a limping theory resembles the doctor and not the watchmaker.[4]

Confirmation of Theories

A scientific theory is far from being a mere summary of the facts to be explained. It is much more comprehensive than the empirical facts that gave rise to it; it is a kind of leap in the dark. But as such it serves to connect many facts hitherto not seen to be related, and many others unsuspected and unknown at the time the theory was set forth.

Devising a theory is a process of creative imagination, much like a work of art. And like a work of art it may be arrived at by careful research followed by a sudden flash of intuition: "Eureka! I have found it!" Intuition may be how the theory is *arrived at,* but of course intuition does not ensure its *truth;* its truth must be tested in the crucible of experience, in which the most brilliant and imaginative theories may be found wanting.

Since a theory encompasses so many more things than it was originally designed to explain, some of the events will probably be future events. And thus one function of scientific theories is to offer *predictions.* The "acid

test," according to many scientists, of the success of a theory is its ability to make detailed and accurate predictions. When a scientist is able to predict, on the basis of a theory, something that would not have been predicted (or perhaps even suspected) without it, the scientist's theory receives the ultimate "Bravo" from his or her peers. "By their fruits shall ye know them"—and the fruits of science, it is often said, lie in the successful predictions which a theory makes possible.

One of the most dramatic illustrations of this is the discovery of the planet Neptune. When the planet Uranus was discovered through telescopes in 1721, it was carefully observed; as time passed its orbit was charted—which turned out to be somewhat surprising. According to Newton's laws of motion, it should have been at position X at a certain time, but instead it was at position Y. Astronomers might have used this as evidence against Newton's theory. But the theory already explained such a wide range of phenomena that they were hesitant to do this—it seemed preferable to bet on a theory that already explained much rather than scrap it in the face of seemingly contrary evidence. Two astronomers, Adams and Leverrier (acting independently of one another), looked about for an explanation of the peculiarity which would be compatible with Newton's theory: namely, that there was a hitherto unobserved planet that was exerting a gravitational pull on Uranus. The two astronomers assumed the truth of Newtonian mechanics, and on the basis of it, plus their observations of Uranus, calculated the position of the hitherto undiscovered planet. Using maximum telescopic power (for that day) and gradually observing its change of position against the background of the stars, they observed the planet Neptune, which had hitherto seemed like just another dim star; they observed, over many months, its motions relative to the stars. The success of their prediction gave a tremendous

[4]From Pierre Duhem, *Aim and Structure of Physical Theory,* Chapter 6, (Princeton: Princeton University Press, 1953). Reprinted in Herbert Feigl and May Brodbeck, eds., *Readings in the Philosophy of Science* (New York: Appleton-Century-Crofts, 1953), pp. 235–252. Passage quoted is on pp. 240–1.

boost to Newtonian mechanics (the law of gravitation and the three laws of motion). Newton's theory ruled the day and was unchallenged until the twentieth century.

But in Einstein's theory of relativity a new theory emerged, not replacing Newton's but leading to different observable consequences at some points. If Einstein's view was correct, that light must be attracted by heavy bodies, then light coming from a star of the earth, if traveling close to the sun, must be deflected by the gravitational pull of the sun. This could not normally be confirmed because the light of the sun makes it impossible for us to see stars in the daytime. But during a total eclipse of the sun, the difference in position should be observable. The stars near the sun were photographed in the total solar eclipse of May 29, 1919, and the observations confirmed Einstein's theory. Again a prediction had been made on the basis of the theory, and its success was among the factors that led to its acceptance.

What you see when you look at the sky is the sun by day and the stars by night, both of which appear to be going around the earth; this has seemed so obvious throughout most of human history that anyone who suggested that actually the earth was going round the sun was considered quite mad. If the evidence of our senses showed anything, it was (or seemed to be) that the sun, moon, and stars go round the earth, which is in the center. It was observed in ancient times that the sun, moon, and planets (the Arabic word for "wanderer") moved about among the stars, which never showed any apparent motion in relation to one another. (It was not until the twentieth century that it was discovered through spectroscopy that the stars themselves moved, often at hundreds of miles per second.) But this fact was accounted for, quite plausibly, by the theory that the sun and moon and planets each was set in the interior surface of a hollow crystalline sphere, each moving around the earth somewhat differently from

the others; beyond these spheres was the sphere of the "fixed stars," which also revolved around the earth, but only one sphere was required for the stars because they had no apparent motion relative to each other; they all moved together across the night sky. This theory appeared much more commonsensical than the far-out modern theory, which seemed to be utterly refuted by the senses, that the earth itself moved round the sun. Indeed, the hypothesis of the Egyptian astronomer Ptolemy (second century A.D.)—which charted and predicted the course of the planets as well as the occurrence of eclipses of the sun and moon—seemed the last word in astronomical theory.

Ptolemy and his contemporaries were puzzled as to why the planets moved in the sky (against the background of the "fixed stars") in the way that they do. For example, Jupiter may move slightly eastward among the stars for some time, and then temporarily turn back and move westward (retrograde motion). Why should this be? Ptolemaic astronomy believed that all the heavenly bodies moved in circles, but if you imagined them traveling in little circles around the big circles (these were called epicycles), then you would account for the apparently erratic retrograde motions of the planets. Every time that more careful observation showed another variation in the motion of a planet, it could always be explained by another epicycle (a small circular orbit around a larger one, around the still larger main orbit). No general theory could have predicted that the planets would move in epicycles, but *once the theory was accepted* it became possible by means of it to track the path of the planets through the years and—since the variation over a period of years was regular—to predict their future location.

If you assumed with Copernicus that the earth went around the sun, and the same for the other planets, you could account for the retrograde motions very simply. The earth, being closer to the sun than Jupiter, moves in

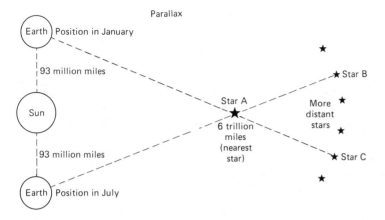

The earth is 93,000,000 miles away from the sun. Since it orbits around the sun, its position in January will be 186,000,000 miles distant from its position 6 months later. Hence the nearer star A will be seen in January against the background of more distant star C, but in July it will be seen against the background of more distant star B.

its orbit more rapidly, and when it is rounding a bend in its orbit the more distant planet will appear to be going in the opposite direction, just as to the driver of the fast race car on the inner track the slower driver on the outer track appears for a short time to be going in the opposite direction. The retrograde motion was just *what you would expect* if the Copernican theory was correct. However, the Copernican theory had no more predictive value than the Ptolemaic, since the Ptolemaic theory with its cumbersome epicycles could predict the future course of the planets among the stars just as well.

There was one observable consequence of the Copernican theory that would not occur under the Ptolemaic: If the earth was going round the sun in an orbit, in June it would be 186,000,000 miles distant from the position it was in in December; therefore, there should be a slight difference in the apparent position of the nearer stars in relation to more distant ones (parallax)—just as if you look at a nearby tree from one window, then from another window, the tree will seem to be in a different position in relation to the distant hills in the background. But in spite of careful telescopic observations no such parallax was observed, and this was taken as evidence against Copernicus' view. Copernicus did not

abandon his view, and held that the stars must be so distant that no parallax could be detected, but in this he had no observational evidence to back him up. It turned out that he was right, but Copernicus died in 1543 and the first parallax was not discovered until 1838. No one had suspected that even the nearest star was 6 trillion miles away. Thus, as far as the empirical evidence was concerned in Copernicus' own day, he had no more confirmation for his view than Ptolemy had for his, though his account had no need for the burdensome epicycles that had to be introduced *ad hoc* into the Ptolemaic theory.

If the two theories both explain the same set of observed facts, the theory which is simpler, in the sense of requiring fewest general principles, is the one likely to be accepted. If the evidence indicates that one man robbed the house, no one is likely to take seriously the theory that a dozen men did it. Of course, the simplest theory may not account for all the facts. If several different people's fingerprints are found, the solo-robbery theory cannot account for it. And the simple theory, though it may explain all the observed facts at the time, may turn out to be inadequate to explaining facts later discovered—and then the simple theory must be scrapped. (The simplest theories of atomic structure have long been abandoned.) But if a simple theory will indeed explain all the facts to be explained, it is (other things being equal) the simple theory that wins the day—as Copernicus' did long before the confirming evidence of parallax. Simple theories are neat, tidy, elegant, aesthetically pleasing—and it has long been an ideal of scientists to explain as much as possible by means of as little as possible.

Many of the theories in the natural sciences are unable to yield definite predictions at all. Seldom is there the dramatic and specific prediction that comes true on the basis of a theory, such as in the case of the discovery of Neptune. Darwin's theory of natural selection and the survival of the fittest does explain why some species survive and not others, but that alone does not enable us to predict which will survive and which will not. (That depends on a variety of conditions, such as scarcity of food, climatic changes, amount of moisture in a region from year to year; these are largely unknown factors over long periods of time.) We know a considerable amount about the conditions on which earthquakes depend, such as what happens when masses of rock collide (for the most part these are fairly simple mechanical laws), but we still can't predict earthquakes very well because we don't know exactly what's going on miles below the earth's surface. We have some well-confirmed meteorological laws, but we still can't predict next week's weather with much accuracy, because we don't know in detail what's going on in the upper atmosphere of the earth. Scientific theories, first and foremost, *explain*—the wider the range of phenomena the better; accurate prediction does not occur until the particular conditions are known in great detail, and most sciences have not yet reached this stage.

Science is most successful when it achieves a body of *unified* theory.

Newton was no opportunist, using one batch of assumptions to cope with Mercury, and then moving on to new devices to handle Venus. Celestial mechanics was a remarkably *unified* theory. It solved problems by invoking the same pattern of reasoning, or *problem-solving strategy,* again and again. From a specification of the positions of the bodies under study, use the law of gravitation to calculate the forces acting; from a statement of the forces acting, use the laws of dynamics to compute the equations of motion; solve the equations of motion to obtain the motions of the bodies. The single pattern of reasoning was applied in case after case to yield conclusions that were independently found to be correct.

At a higher level, celestial mechanics was itself contained in a broader theory. Newtonian physics, as a whole, was remarkably unified. It offered a strategy for solving a diverse collection of problems. Faced with *any* question about motion, the Newtonian suggestion was the same: Find the forces acting, from the forces and the laws of dynamics work out the equations of motion, and solve the equations of motion. The method was employed in a broad range of cases. The revolutions of planets, the motions of projectiles, tidal cycles and pendulum oscillations—all fell to the same problem-solving strategy.[5]

When a body of unified theory has been established, another valued feature emerges: *fecundity,* or fruitfulness in opening up hitherto unsuspected areas of investigation. A new theory leads us to ask new questions, gives us new ways of viewing the world, and in time leads to new "paradigms" from which future discoveries and new predictions may flow.

The unity of the sciences. These points are well illustrated by an example from current scientific theory.

The fossilized bones of many large reptiles, including dinosaurs, have been dug up for many years in various places on the earth. According to various methods of determining the age of rocks, these reptiles flourished until about 65 million years ago and then disappeared quite suddenly. Why did they suddenly

---

[5]Philip Kitcher, "Believing Where We Cannot Prove," in his *Abusing Science* (Cambridge: MIT Press, 1982), p. 46–7.

disappear? Biologists and paleontologists have long sought an explanation.[6]

As frequently happens in science, a clue was found that seemed to have nothing to do with the problem. A thin layer of clay was discovered in a deep gorge in Italy, in strata of rock at the boundary between the Cretaceous period and the Tertiary period—laid down during the period in which the dinosaurs became extinct. "So what?" one might ask. But in this layer large quantities of iridium were found—a metal rarely encountered on the earth's surface, but 10,000 times the normal amount was found in this layer. Iridium is heavy and would tend to go downward while the earth was still molten; perhaps it was spewed out through volcanic activity. Or perhaps it fell to earth in a collision with an asteroid or a comet. Here were two theories, each of which would explain the presence of the iridium. But which theory was correct?

Other deposits of iridium from the same period were discovered, and on sifting through the clay geologists found grains of quartz that looked cracked and strained. No such thing had been seen before other than near meteorite craters, at nuclear bomb test sites, and on the moon (collected during the Apollo mission). Geologists could figure out only one way in which quartz with these features could be formed, namely when subjected to enormous heat and pressure from a powerful explosion.

Meanwhile biologists had been busy compiling lists of animals that had become extinct during the last half billion years. Tremendous amounts of data were fed into computers, and to the scientists' surprise, the extinctions showed a recurring pattern—continuous long periods of evolution, then a brief period when they disappeared. There was a definite periodicity to these extinctions—recurring cycles of about 26 million years.

And how was *that* in turn to be explained? Ice ages were much too short. Astronomers now got into the act. Perhaps the explanation was extra-terrestrial—solar flares or supernovae. But each of these theories was tentatively rejected for lack of evidence. Then it was pointed out that most stars are double stars, not visible through telescopes or photographs but detectable by their gravitational effect on other stars. Let's assume, they said, that the sun too is a double star with an invisible companion star; and let's assume that, like comets, it has a highly elliptical orbit. During the thousands of years that it's far away it has little effect on the solar system, but when it nears the sun it moves much faster, as comets do when they approach the sun.

One could still say, "So what? What has that to do with dinosaurs?" But now a fairly recent astronomical discovery becomes relevant. Outside the boundaries of the solar system—beyond the orbit of Pluto, the furthest planet from the sun—is a vast array of comets, called the Oort Cloud (after its discoverer). When the sun's invisible companion, astronomers hypothesized, intersects the Oort Cloud, about every 26 million years, it carries with it through gravitational attraction, many of these comets, some of which are drawn into the earth's orbit. The dust from these impacts obscures the light of the sun, causing plants to die, and causing in turn the death of the creatures that feed on them.

The 26-million-year cycle has now been repeatedly confirmed. The missing link in the puzzle is still the sun's dark companion, which has never been detected. Millions of such stars exist in our galaxy, and to locate one of them, through its gravitational effects alone, would be a task of tremendous difficulty. If it were achieved, however, the principal missing piece in the puzzle would be supplied, and the cometary theory would be much more highly confirmed. At the moment, no one can be sure.

---

[6]For a detailed account of the cometary theory, see Jonathan Weiner, *Planet Earth* (New York: Bantam Books, 1986).

New theories still unthought of may be devised. There must be, we are convinced, *some* explanation of the destruction of most living things on this planet every 26 million years.

This account illustrates, first of all, how empirical science is a vast interconnected network of facts, laws, and theories. The system must be coherent: if any inconsistency is found within it, it must be removed. Perhaps what was thought to be an observed fact was an observational error; perhaps a fact was misinterpreted; if neither of these things has happened, and an inconsistency remains, something will have to give way—some theory will have to be abandoned or revised. If one theory cannot explain certain facts, perhaps another one can. If more than one theory can, we prefer the one that is most highly confirmed.

Second, the testing procedures are interdependent. When we try to determine the temperature of an object, we assume that there is a correlation between rise in temperature and the rise of mercury in a tube. This of course is not a mere assumption, and has been confirmed countless times for several centuries. In trying to determine the age of rocks, the correctness of certain testing procedures— such as the carbon–14 test, the rate of disintegration of uranium into lead—are assumed, but these in turn have also been confirmed (each for different time spans). If evidence turned up that the methods of dating were inaccurate, doubt would be cast on the figure of 26 million years. Any proposition in science can be revised in the light of new evidence; none is forever beyond dispute.

Third, let us notice what assumptions we are willing to make if they are coherent with an already confirmed theory. When perturbations in the orbit of Uranus were noticed, a choice had to be made: was Newtonian mechanics inaccurate, or was there a hitherto unobserved planet exerting a gravitational effect on Uranus? The latter was chosen, because Newtonian mechanics was already highly con-

firmed. A tried and tested friend may betray you, but the more you know him the more evidence of betrayal you will require. The astronomers opted for Newtonian mechanics. When the planet was observed, the choice turned out to be correct. In the far less confirmed cometary theory, an assumption is also made, that the sun has a dark companion star. If such a star exists, it may never be discovered. Even with current computer technology astronomers have estimated that there is about one chance of three of ever finding it. If it is never found, will that count against the cometary theory? It would surely be a gap in the total explanation, which would leave an enduring question mark around the theory. If years pass and no dark companion to the sun is discovered, some will say "It must be there; the entire explanation—including iridium and extraterrestrial objects and Oort clouds—fits together so well as an explanation of what we have observed, that we should continue to accept the hypothesis rather than discount it just because we haven't found one link in the chain, a link that in any case would be extraordinarily difficult to discover." But others will say, "Don't let your passion for closing gaps run away with you. The fact is that one important link in the chain is missing. There is no independent evidence of the existence of a companion star to the sun—we simply *postulate* it in order to make it fit in with the rest of the account."

Such differences will probably always remain—the difference between the cautious temperament that won't accept the hypothesis until all the links in the chain are discovered, and the adventurous temperament that says "It fits in with everything else we know—and nothing else does, so we should retain it even if we never discover any companion star." Shall we say that the treasure is buried where the map says it is, because the map has turned out to be correct thus far, or shall we disbelieve it until we discover it? The degree of confidence that is justified is difficult indeed to determine; what is not difficult to see is that scientific temperaments differ. Some will take the leap, even though they must do it in semi-darkness, and others will not leap until they are confident that they can see the goal and that they can make it to the other side.

Finally, let us notice in all this how far we have come from the everyday world perceived with our senses. The cometary theory involves primarily biology, geology, and astronomy, with no mention of the subatomic particles of physics. Yet even so there is a large body of theory involved in every step. It is involved in the assertion that there is a 26-million-year cycle. It is involved in every reference to gravitation, as if that were observable through the senses (as opposed to the moving bodies). It is involved in the speculation about quartz. It is involved in every reference to photographs and telescopes (both presuppose theories of optics). It is involved even in speaking of the *orbits* of planets and comets. We tend to import theory into our observation statements, speaking casually about the orbit of Uranus, as if we could ever see, even with telescopes, Uranus circling around the sun. What we see through telescopes is Uranus at various successive places in the sky, but never circling the sun as in a diagram or an orrery. Even this—that planets revolve around the sun—is theory, albeit highly confirmed theory. We have sent Voyagers and space probes to Uranus and beyond, and the calculations that made these achievements possible are all embedded in this theory.

Confirming and Falsifying

No matter how successful a theory may be in explanation and prediction, its success does not prove that it is true; it may be revised or even scrapped in favor of another one at a later time. Its acceptance is always *provisional,* never final. If one were to argue "All dogs are mammals; this is a mammal; there-

fore this is a dog" everyone would see the fallacy at once—it is the elementary logical fallacy called "affirming the consequent." But this is precisely what happens in scientific theory: "If Einstein's theory is correct, the observed position of the stars near the sun (seen during a total solar eclipse) will be altered; the position was observed to be altered; therefore Einstein's theory is correct." If one were to argue thus, the fallacy would be exactly the same as in the example of the dogs.

If scientific reasoning commits this elementary logical error, what then can be said in defense of theories? Only that they are never proved (validity deduced from known premises), only confirmed. Is *confirmability* then the test of the adequacy of a scientific theory?

Because they are unrestricted in scope—in both time and space—laws and theories can never be verified. There is no way that you or I or any group of people could verify even such a simple generalization as "All crows are black." Each black crow we find adds a bit of confirmation of "All crows are black," but no complete verification is possible. (Even if we had examined all the crows in the universe, how could we know that we had examined them all? And of course we could not examine all future crows, or those long past.)

But there is a problem even with confirmability. You could sit at sea level and confirm over and over again that water boils at 212°F (or 100° C); you could do this millions of times and yet the statement would not be true. You would have to conduct the experiment only once at a higher or lower altitude to discover this; but if you never bothered to *vary the conditions* you would never become aware of the inaccuracy of your proposed law.

Thus some philosophers, such as Sir Karl Popper, suggested that the test of a law is not confirmability but *falsifiability.* We can never observe all crows to see if they are black, but the discovery of *one* albino crow would be enough to refute the statement that all crows are black. "All dogs are mammals; this is not a mammal; therefore it is not a dog" is a valid argument; if something is not a mammal, the statement that it is a dog is *falsified*.

We would have to make sure that our exception was genuine, of course. The crow must not just *look* black in an odd light; and the person who claimed that he found that water didn't boil at 212°F at sea level would have to make sure that he had not made an observational error, and that his thermometer was in good working condition. If a chemistry student claimed that her sample of sodium didn't react when exposed to water, her teacher would probably dismiss this as an observational error (it wasn't really sodium, etc.), and with good reason. The teacher would consider it more likely that the student made an error than that all the chemistry books (based on thousands of previous experiments) were mistaken. Nevertheless, one genuine exception would be enough to refute the generalization.

Falsifiability then, has been put forth as the criterion for what distinguishes scientific theories from nonscientific theories. Any scientific law or theory has certain empirical consequences, and if those consequences fail to occur, the law or theory must be scrapped or revised. If the purported law says that all water boils at 212° F, and water boiled on a mountaintop doesn't, then the law will have to be abandoned or revised in such a way as to accommodate the new finding. In other words, scientific laws are always subject to *empirical testing,* and when a test turns out negative the law cannot stand as it did before.

"A is A" is always true, but since it is not falsifiable it is not a scientific law; scientific statements must be empirical (hence synthetic), never analytic. The statement "Every event occurs as God wills, and since this car accident occurred, God must have willed it" is a valid argument. The view that God willed the accident might indeed be true as far as science is concerned, and yet the argument is not a scientific proposition, because nothing that we could discover could falsify it. If there is an automobile accident, God willed it; if there isn't, God willed that also. There is nothing which if it happened would prove the statement false.

There is a recurring danger of unfalsifiability in psychoanalytic theory. For example, if a person constantly acts aggressive, she is aggressive; but if she is unduly passive, she is unconsciously trying to hide her aggressiveness. Or one could play it the other way: If he acts passive, then he is; but if he acts aggressive, he is only trying to conceal his passivity. No matter what data you come up with the theory professes to explain it; nothing that happened would falsify it. However, we should not be premature in judging psychoanalytic theory; it is mostly amateur psychologists who argue in this manner. The theories of psychoanalysis are quite complex, and it is easy to caricature them. The internal dynamics of human beings are extremely complicated, and it may well be the case that some people exhibit "normal" aggression while others hide their passivity under a facade of aggressiveness; trained therapists can tell the difference. There are countless events in the human psyche which, if they occurred, *would* falsify a psychoanalytic theory and force us to revise it. Indeed, the history of psychoanalysis since Freud has been a history of revised and abandoned theories in the light of new and complex data. For example, the division between neurotics and psychotics has been revised to accommodate a personality-type, called "borderlines," which doesn't fit either theory, even though many attempts were made to make the observed behavior fit the traditional theories.

But there is a problem with falsifiability also. Simple generalizations like "All crows are black" and "All white tomcats with blue eyes are deaf" are falsified by one negative instance—but some are not. If a hundred seemingly identical wineglasses had broken upon impact with a brick fireplace, but one didn't, you would not say that this fact refuted the generalization "Glass is fragile"—you would say something like "This piece of glass is stronger than the others."

There is no single observation which by itself would falsify a wide-ranging theory such as Newton's. If the table in front of you rose from the floor and remained poised in the air for 10 minutes before settling back on the floor, would that refute the law of gravitation? Not at all. Even if the event were photographed and observed by many witnesses, so that the occurrence couldn't be put down to observational error, we could say that some powerful magnet on the floor above was attracting it, or some other force that we didn't yet know anything about was affecting it. After all, the fact that balloons rise and airplanes can fly is no refutation of Newton's law—but at least we have explanations for these occurrences. Is it just that we will invent any theory we can think of in order to rescue the law? No, it's that other factors—sometimes unknown—can also act on an object. Every occurrence is a kind of *intersection* of many laws; and each law has implicitly a *ceteris paribus* (all other things being equal) clause. The apple will fall to earth *unless* some other more powerful natural force (perhaps not yet known) interferes. For example, why doesn't the table simply collapse in a heap on the floor, rather than standing as it does on its legs? If the force of gravitation is so strong, why doesn't the whole building collapse onto the ground? Because in addition to the gravitational force that pulls objects downward, there are electrostatic forces with positive and negative charges. Protons have a positive charge and electrons a negative charge, which usually balance one another approximately. These forces are ever so much stronger than those of gravitation, and as long as these forces are in operation, the table and the building will retain their shape and not fall directly toward the earth's center—which they would do if gravitation were the only force operating. It is only "freely falling bodies"

that will aim directly downward—and even then, not if the object is a feather which will float about in the wind rather than plummet directly downward. In every case, there are many forces at work, and knowledge of gravitation alone won't tell you what will happen or which force will be stronger on a particular occasion. Again, shouldn't the interior of the earth be liquid because of the extremely high temperature (far above the melting point of the elements it contains)? Yes, but there is a countervailing factor: The pressure on the elements in the interior of the earth are so enormous that this keeps them in a semi-solid state.

All this is found acceptable because other laws, already confirmed, are also operative. If we explain the failure of something to occur by the action of another force, we can't just pick the other force out of a hat. We have to have some independent evidence for its existence. If we merely hypothesize some unknown force, this may suffice for a while, but if we try repeatedly and never discover evidence for it, then we may doubt its existence and thus come to doubt the original theory—at least in the form in which it was stated. A hypothesis that is invoked simply to rescue a law or theory, with no independent evidence in favor of it, is called an *ad hoc* hypothesis, but if it can be supported only by *ad hoc* hypotheses a theory will in time be abandoned.

The theory of organic evolution is extremely well confirmed, and nothing discovered thus far has falsified it, but only changed it in details. But what *could* falsify it? Suppose we discovered, through carbon–14 dating techniques or other means for discovering the age of rocks or fossils, that all of the rocks and all the fossils therein all turned out to be about the same age, say 6000 years. If we could be sure about the accuracy of the dating technique, this would falsify the theory that life on earth has gone on for millions of years. Would it falsify the theory of evolution? No, we might say that the various organisms had evolved very quickly because of special conditions occurring at that time. But if we could not, after investigation, identify those conditions we would probably come to doubt that evolution had taken place at all. Perhaps we couldn't exactly *falsify* the theory, but we would consider this surprising new evidence as *disconfirming* a theory. To disconfirm it is to find evidence against it, while not yet going so far as to falsify it completely.

What would be required to disconfirm the special creation theory—that God created all creatures, as well as the earth they dwell in, in a relatively short period, perhaps six days, about 6000 years ago? The carbon-14 test and lots of other tests concerning the age of the earth—all the evidence amassed concerning the Cambrian era versus the post-Cambrian eras and so on—would seem to count decisively against *that* view. If the age of the earth is billions of years, it can't be 6000 years. But a related theory escapes that objection: That the entire process of organic evolution was ordained and designed by God, that life arose and evolved through supernatural means. *That* is surely compatible with any theory of evolution we have. Evolution could have been the *method* used in creation. No scientific theory could disprove that, nor could any scientific theory prove it either—or confirm it, or disconfirm it. Why? Because there is simply no way of discovering it; it is not studied by scientists, not because they believe it is false (though many do), but because the theory has no empirical consequences whatever. However life developed on earth, whether gradually or suddenly, slowly or all at once, one could say it was the result of God's design. There is no *handle* of empirical evidence by which we could test it in any way, as there is in any genuinely scientific theory. We know what it would be to confirm that life has continued for millions of years (that's what we do now); we know what it would be to confirm that life existed for only 6000 years (that's what we'd confirm if all the dating tests

turned out the same). But in neither of these cases would we be confirming that "the invisible hand of God" was responsible for the process; there is just no way to confirm *that*. Since it is not subject to empirical tests pro or con, it is simply not counted as a scientific theory at all. Scientific theories must have *some* empirical teeth in them.

Suppose your watch doesn't work and a friend suggests that there's a gremlin in it that is messing up the inner parts. "But I don't see any gremlins," you say as you take apart the watch. "But they're invisible gremlins," she says; "no wonder you can't see them."

A: But how is an invisible, intangible gremlin different from no gremlin at all? If you said there is an invisible elephant in the room that no sense organs or instruments could detect, I know what this comes to— it is no different from saying that there is no elephant in the room, or perhaps there is an imaginary elephant in the room. An invisible gremlin is no gremlin at all. Suppose I said it wasn't an invisible gremlin but an invisible elf. What difference would that make? How would you distinguish between the two theories? If you could see them you could tell the difference; but since they are invisible there's no way. Isn't it a matter of what label you want to paste on the back of the watch to remind you of the very same characteristics of the watch? If you ask me whether I'd rather have a watch run by a gremlin or one run by an elf, I'd say, "You choose." It wouldn't make any difference, since what happens is the same.[7] And I suppose you can't touch or photograph the gremlins either, and that they're immune to x-rays, radar, infrared photography, and the rest?"

B: Of course. They don't wish to be detected.

---

[7] For extended and fascinating discussions along this line, read John Wisdom, *Other Minds* (Oxford: Basil Blackwell, 1949).

A: But how is such a gremlin different from no gremlin at all? An invisible intangible undetectable chair is no chair at all. So is an invisible, etc. gremlin.

B: You can't really say the invisibility is proof against its existence. Your science is full of invisible entities and otherwise unobservable ones, such as electrons.

A: But the electron theory is at least empirically fruitful; we can explain on the basis of it why elements combine as they do, and many other things.

B: And I say that the gremlin theory explains why your watch doesn't work.

A: Your so-called explanation is no explanation at all. With it you can predict nothing; you can't even say that if it's an elf then if I chant some mumbo jumbo the watch will work again—none of these things makes any difference. The watch still sits there, not functioning. But if I replace the spring, the watch works again; so the broken-spring hypothesis has proven value. The gremlin hypothesis has none.

B: A theory need not have predictive value; many don't. But mine does have *explanatory value*. If there is a malicious little gremlin in the watch, it won't work. That does explain the watch not working.

A: An invisible gremlin is a contradiction in terms; you first say it's a gremlin and then that it's undetectable. You've taken away with the one hand what you've offered with the other. The theory you suggest is no theory but only a *word*—a word that in mythology *has* meaning, for gremlins in mythology were believed to be visible, and *that* belief was just *false;* but as you now use the word it is meaningless. You are just playing games with words.

B: Not at all. This gremlin happens not to be visible to human eyes. That something is unperceivable is nothing against it—science is full of such entities. That the gremlin has no predictive value may be true (I can't predict when the gremlin will enter the watch), but lots of scientific theories have no predictive value either. What they do offer is an explanation—and I am giving you one. It may also be that the watch has a broken spring, and that by replacing the spring you can make the watch work again; but even that doesn't *falsify* the gremlin theory. The gremlin may be what broke the spring.

A: The spring is broken, and putting in a new spring enables the watch to work again.

B: I can't offer you such a prediction in the gremlin case. I can't say "Get rid of the gremlins and the watch will work," because I never know where the gremlin is or what it will do next. But it *is* an explanation, an explanation in terms of unobservable entities, just like a thousand others in science. I may not be able to prove that the gremlin theory is *true;* but you can't prove that it's *false* either.

A: I can say an invisible gremlin is not a gremlin at all, any more than an invisible elephant is an elephant. Your so-called explanation is empirically *meaningless*. What's meaningless can't be true or false, any more than "Green ideas sleep furiously" is true or false.

B: It's not meaningless like "Walking sat eat very" (which isn't a sentence) or "Pirots carulize elatically" (these aren't even words), or "Green ideas go to sleep" (category mistake). It's a perfectly meaningful theory, what bothers you about it is that you just can't confirm or disconfirm it. I say it is no more meaningless than any other theory which invokes unobservables to explain what we observe.

A: But scientific unobservables are empirically fruitful. The gremlin theory doesn't fit in with any of the rest of scientific theory. Science is a vast web of interconnected theories and laws, each related to the other, each affected somewhat if another is in jeopardy. Your gremlin theory just sticks out like a sore thumb, isolated, unconnected with the rest.

The preceding dialogue may seem trivial or frivolous. But now let's examine a more "realistic" case:

It was once believed that certain women who acted peculiarly were witches, inspired of the devil. Almost no one believes this any more; but has the theory been falsified? or even disconfirmed? Even at the time no one believed that if you performed autopsies on the women you would find little devils inside; *that* could have been falsified by observation. No, the theory was that an invisible being, Satan, was causing them to act as they did. You couldn't see him, but that didn't mean he wasn't at work in them—the behavior of the women seemed to confirm that he was very busy indeed. The women were studied and questioned very carefully before the determination was made whether they were witches; the evidence-gathering process was detailed and prolonged. People were either released or condemned as witches on the basis of careful observation of their behavior. Yet in a relatively short time the entire witch theory was abandoned. Was the theory of Satan-infestation disproved? No, it was simply *abandoned*. Why was it abandoned? Not because Satan wasn't observable; science is full of unobservables. It was because another theory took its place, in the development of psychology. Behavior that had previously been given a supernatural explanation was now considered a perfectly natural phenomenon. The tremendous burden of guilt feelings on so many people living under stern Calvinistic ethics, the impossibility of fulfilling their expected duties to God and to their husbands, the psychological release found in confessing—these came to be recognized as factors that could explain why these women behaved as they did. But was the new theory any better? The new theory made these phenomena a part of the fabric of scientific explanation, a huge network of interconnected laws and theories. It was seen to conform to the pattern of the scientific explanation. The devil theory was abandoned, not because it had been refuted, but because it was *superfluous*. If you believed in the psychological causes of neurosis, then you *didn't need* the other explanation. Moreover, the scientific explanation fits in (coheres with) a vast amount of other information—from physiology, from biology (genetics), and from chemistry.

We seem to have moved gradually from talking about *falsifying* a theory to talking about *disconfirming* it (discovering something that would count against it, but not throw it out entirely), and from that to simply *abandoning* it. The theory of Satan-infestation was abandoned because a more comprehensive theory replaced it; but was the earlier theory thereby refuted? or even disconfirmed? One can abandon a theory if it no longer fits in with what one wants to believe, or which doesn't fit in with one's cherished presuppositions or prejudices. It might be abandoned because you wouldn't *permit* anything to count against it—just as a paranoid will not permit anything to disconfirm his theory that everybody is plotting against him. If people act hostile, that only confirms his view; and if they act friendly, they are only trying to trick him so that they can cheat him in the end. He would not accept anything as disconfirming his view about universal hostility. We call him irrational because he won't accept any evidence, however convincing to the rest of us, as counting against his pet theory. But surely scientific theories aren't in the same boat as the paranoid? The paranoid doesn't accept disconfirming evidence, not because it isn't there, but because he won't recognize it as disconfirming. Surely science is more "objective" than that?

It is and it isn't. Science does recognize disconfirming evidence, and constantly abandons and revises theories. On the other hand, there is such a thing as holding on to theories in the face of what at least looks very much like disconfirming evidence. Let us examine a couple of cases:

1. What would it take for Newton's laws to be scrapped? If all the planets in the solar system were suddenly to crash into the sun, would that constitute evidence against Newtonian celestial mechanics? No, we could say that something not yet known had occurred to make the sun, with its enormous gravitational attraction, "pull them all in." Even if this "something else" were never found, we could say it was nevertheless there, but undiscovered. Or consider the following: If Newton's theory is correct, the close approach of another star to the sun would exert enormous gravitational attraction on the sun. One theory of the origin of the solar system is that a larger star approached the sun, pulling huge amounts of matter out of it before proceeding on its way, and this matter later condensed into the planets. (The attraction was greatest when the star was nearest, presumably in mid-approach, hence the largest planets, Jupiter and Saturn, are in the middle, and the smallest ones, Mercury and Pluto, at the ends.) But now suppose that a larger star approached the sun and we watched this through telescopes and so on, but it had no effect on the sun at all: Suppose it acted for all the world as if no massive object was nearby, and went on in serene independence just as before. Wouldn't this cast some doubt on the Newtonian theory?

It could be so taken, but thus far it need not. Remember the *ceteris paribus* clause: There must be no "conflicting forces" at work, or they must be so small as to be negligible. One could say that there were other forces at work, whose nature was as yet unknown, but whatever they were they were far from negligible. And thus one could still salvage the Newtonian's view. One could always

put the blame not on Newtonian mechanics but on something else.

Individual scientific claims do not, and cannot, confront the evidence one by one. Rather . . . "Hypotheses are tested in bundles." . . . We can only test relatively large bundles of claims. What this means is that when our experiments go awry we are not logically compelled to select any particular claim as the culprit. We can always save a cherished hypothesis from refutation by rejecting (however implausibly) one of the other members of the bundle.[8]

2. In the nineteenth century the law of conservation of matter was universally believed to be true: Matter may change its form, but the amount of matter in the universe is always the same. But with the discovery of transformation of matter into energy in the twentieth century, the law of conservation of matter was abandoned. But a similar law, the law of conservation of energy, remained: The energy in the universe may change its form, but the amount of energy in the universe remains constant. This is still largely accepted in the scientific community. But what would it take to falsify it?

It is found that, if we take certain material systems, e.g., a gun, a cartridge, and a bullet, there is a certain magnitude which keeps approximately constant throughout all their changes. This is called "energy." When the gun has not been fired it and the bullet have no motion, but the explosive in the cartridge has great chemical energy. When it has been fired the bullet is moving very fast and has great energy of movement. The gun, though not moving fast in its recoil, has also great energy of movement. The gases produced by the explosion have some energy of movement and some heat-energy, but much less chemical energy than the unexploded charge had. These various kinds of energy can be measured in common units according to cer-

[8]Philip Kitcher, "Believing Where We Cannot Prove," in his *Abusing Science* (Cambridge: M.I.T. Press, 1982), p. 44.

tain conventions. To an innocent mind there seems to be a good deal of "cooking" at this stage, i.e., the conventions seem to be chosen and various kinds and amounts of concealed energy seem to be postulated in order to make the principle come out right at the end . . . [9]

In other words, if we cherish a scientific law or theory, and it has a high degree of confirmation thus far, we will do what we can to protect it from refutation or disconfirmation. We shall interpret our observations in such a way, or hypothesize new kinds or amounts of energy, so as to make the law come out unscathed; in all the sciences there is a considerable amount of this "cookery" going on. A law or theory has become accepted in the scientific community because of the large amount of confirming evidence; and once we have the evidence we accept the law, and a natural psychological inertia, we then tend to protect its truth against attack and assume that the trouble lies somewhere else in the system. Once a theory has become established, a large amount of disconfirming evidence is required before it is questioned.

3. When sound travels through air, the air particles move: Sound waves are alternating condensations and rarefactions of air. Sound can be transmitted only through a medium—air, water, or something else. But light and heat travel from the sun to the earth (when the sun rises, the temperature rises), yet there is nothing at all between them to transmit the light and heat. How could there be "action at a distance"—A here affecting B there, with nothing in between? How is this possible? Scientists were puzzled about this, so they devised the theory of the *ether:* The ether was a transparent weightless medium through which light and heat and gravitation were transmitted from one place to another; this ether pervaded all space. It was undetectable, but, it

was argued, there had to be *some* medium to transmit these forces from one place to another. For a long time attempts were made to find some traces of ether's existence: some friction, some lessening of energy, anything to indicate that there was "something out there in so-called empty space" to do this work. But no traces were found. The Michaelson-Morley experiment of 1872 was devised to detect any such traces, and its results were entirely negative. And so gradually the theory of the ether was abandoned—not disproved, though some claimed it was, but abandoned. Those who wanted to protect the principle of "no action at a distance" could hold onto it if they chose, but in time most scientists preferred to discard it. It was an unnecessary appendage in the mutually coherent network of propositions that constitute science.

2. CORRESPONDENCE AND COHERENCE

1. Correspondence. We are now in a position to return to our earlier discussion of truth and develop it further (p. 10). "A true statement," one is inclined to say, "is one that corresponds to reality. And a false statement is one that does not." This is at once the simplest and seemingly most obvious of the accounts of truth. But many complex problems appear as soon as we try to dip beneath the surface of this apparently innocuous statement. What is meant by "correspond," for example? Is it something like the following? The names of the colors on the first page of a chart correspond with the samples of the colors on the second page: That is, if color number 15 is labeled "magenta," then the sample numbered 15 on the next page is an actual sample of the color magenta. There is a one-to-one correspondence between the names on the first page and the colors on the second page. Is truth like that? If so, what kind of correspondence is it? And what is the

[9]C. D. Broad, *The Mind and Its Place in Nature* (London: Routledge & Kegan Paul, 1925), 103–104.

correspondence between? Is it between sentences and real or alleged situations or states-of-affairs in the world? or between propositions and facts? (And what are facts? In one sense, a fact is a state-of-affairs that actually occurs or exists—my sitting at my desk now is a fact; in another sense, a fact is a true proposition—"It's a fact *that* I was out of town last night.") Controversies have raged as to what the alleged correspondence is all about.

Let us draw two pictures. At the left of the page we draw a picture of a room with nothing but a table and chair in it. At the right we draw a picture of a room with nothing but a table and two chairs in it. Below these two pictures we write two sentences: (1) "There is a table and one chair in the room," and (2) "There is a table and two chairs in the room." Now, doesn't the first sentence describe the state-of-affairs pictured on the right side of the page? And so we could go on, comparing thousands of pictures with thousands of sentences. Some of the statements will be true, because they assert the existence of what is pictured, and others will be false, because what they assert is not what is in the picture.

Suppose now that on the left side we draw a picture of an elephant, and that the picture on the right has nothing at all in it. The first sentence would then be represented by "There is an elephant in the room," and the second would be represented by "There is no elephant in the room." But the second picture would be equally well described by "There is nothing in the room" or "There is nothing visible in the room." Someone might try to describe it by saying "There is an invisible elephant in the room," but then we would have to ask him how this is different in meaning from the sentence "There is no elephant in the room."

Of course, the adequacy of pictures soon comes to an end: What if you couldn't see the elephant but could touch it, or that it made noises and left droppings, and so on? Abandoning pictures now, we would have to *imag-ine* a state-of-affairs—after all we can imagine smells and sounds as well as sights, though we can't draw them. Next, we compare what we imagine with the sentence we wrote on the paper. "There is an acrid smell in the room" would then correspond, not with a picture, but with some situation or state-of-affairs which we can imagine. The smell either is there or it isn't; we might say: "There is an acrid smell in the room" is either true or false, depending on whether it corresponds to the situation we are imagining.

Nor need we be able to imagine it. If there is a strange creature in the forest unlike any we have every seen or been able to imagine, the statement reporting its presence would "correspond" with the fact that it is there. If it was there and we denied it, our statement would be false. The statement and the existing situation would fail to "correspond."

2. Coherence. But we seem to get into trouble when we turn to theoretical concepts. In Locke's day, light was believed to consist of corpuscles ("the corpuscular theory of light") and after Newton it was believed to consist of waves ("the wave theory of light"), and today light is believed to be somewhat like waves but also somewhat like corpuscles—but these are only mental pictures; light, we are told, isn't quite like either of these; it is "wavicles," and we may as well give up trying to imagine it. What is there then for us to imagine? Anyway, whether the one theory or the other is accepted depends not on what we imagine but whether the theory "fits in" with many *other* scientific beliefs which we have. In that case, the criterion for acceptance is not correspondence but *coherence.*

A body of beliefs is said to be coherent when (1) none of them is inconsistent with any others—that is, a system of beliefs including both "Wood burns" and "Wood does not burn" would not be coherent; and (2) when they mutually support one another—that is, each belief adds some probability to the others. We constantly use this coherence test in daily life, even though we may not know that it goes by this name. Suppose we wonder whether Smith was the murderer; if we believe she was, our belief may be true ("correspond to the fact"), but we have no way of knowing this, since there were no witnesses. However, detectives place the time of the murder at 11 P.M.; a neighbor saw Smith leaving the murdered man's house at 11:05 P.M.; blood of Smith's blood type was found on the murdered person's clothing; the fingerprints on the furniture exactly resemble Smith's fingerprints; Smith was absent from her house between 10 and 12 as her husband noticed; and so on. We have a pretty good case against Smith, and it consists largely of a number of observations that cohere, or *fit in* with each other; we can explain them all on the hypothesis that Smith was the murderer. Juries often convict on evidence such as this. The evidence consists largely of mutually cohering bits and pieces.

Suppose that I can't find my pen, which I used just half an hour ago. I look everywhere that I have been in the last half hour, but can't find it. Still, I say, it must be somewhere. Perhaps someone stole it; perhaps I haven't looked thoroughly enough and it is still somewhere under or between the pillows of the couch—but I am sure that it's somewhere. Now suppose someone says to me, "Maybe it just disappeared. I don't mean merely that it disappeared from *your* sight, but that it is gone forever; it doesn't *exist* any more, and that's why you can't find it. Once in a while things just disappear; it's not that they are hidden somewhere, but that they *no longer exist*. One moment they're there and the next moment, presto! they're gone." Why don't we believe this last statement? Certainly I can't discover any *evidence* that the pen still exists. I have tried and failed utterly. But over the centuries we have come to hold certain beliefs about nature and its workings; one of

them is that material things such as pens don't just cease to exist; matter is not annihilated. To believe that my pen was annihilated in the last half hour is not *coherent* with the vast body of beliefs we have come to have about material objects. And for that reason we accept the first alternative (the pen is still somewhere) rather than the second (it no longer exists). If someone suggests the second alternative seriously, we might dismiss it with a contemptuous sneer or as a bad joke.

Or suppose that someone suggests that it wasn't Smith who committed the murder, but a stranger who flew through the air down the chimney of that house at the very moment the murder occurred. We reject this suggestion without even checking it out, because it is utterly incoherent with our beliefs about how material things behave. People don't just fly through the air, go up and down chimneys, and so on. If we believed that, we would have to revise many other beliefs we have about gravitation and so on. The suggestion is so utterly incoherent with the main body of our beliefs that we don't give it a moment's thought.

We have already used the coherence test in this book. Aren't dreams the experiences that don't fit in, don't cohere, with the rest of our experience? And isn't that why we believe that dream-experiences don't inform us of reality whereas waking-life experiences do? And don't we dismiss an apparent physical object as a hallucination because it doesn't cohere with the rest of our experience—for example, the pink rats we think we see disappear, can't be photographed, can't be observed by someone else, and so on?

But let us return again to Smith and the murder. Suppose that several other people came in to testify that they were with Smith at a party 10 miles away that same night from 9 P.M. til 2 A.M., and that some pictures taken at the party showed Smith among the guests; another person remembers talking with Smith on her way to the party, headed in the opposite direction from the place where the murder occurred, and so on. We would now have some bits of testimony that are quite incompatible with the testimony by which the prosecution hopes to obtain a conviction. Both sets of testimony cannot be true, for they are incompatible with each other. We have two systems of beliefs, at least one of which must be rejected. What do we do now?

This seems to be the main problem with coherence if it is taken as the sole test of truth: There can be two systems of beliefs, each one internally coherent, but each incompatible with the other. Can't you have a coherent body of beliefs that is nevertheless *false?* It was not many centuries ago that women were tried as witches and put to death if their judges at the witchcraft trial decided that they were guilty. There were many tests to determine whether they were in fact witches: If certain questions were not answered in just the right way, they were considered impostors and not genuine witches. There was a highly coherent body of beliefs (mostly forgotten today) on which these questions were based; women were not just taken out and burned at the stake at random. If a woman was not genuinely infested by devils, there was no point in "burning the devils out." And if she was not really a witch, her death would not set an example for other witches; to kill her would then only be an act of wanton cruelty, and the judges considered it so just as much as judges would today. And yet, however mutually coherent their beliefs, we no longer believe any of the witchcraft tests or theories because we believe that at least one of the beliefs in the system, that people can be infested by devils, is *false.*

Practicing Christians today have a fairly coherent set of beliefs. God made the sun, the stars, the earth, and all things on it, and finally humans. God put the animals on the earth for human use. The purpose of humanity is to serve the God who created all people.

The world was made according to God's plan, and if some things in the world repel us, that is only because we do not fully understand the plan. If we sincerely desire something, we pray to God; if our desire is not granted, that is because God knows better than we do what is best for us. If we obey God's commandments we shall be rewarded in a life hereafter. On the whole this is a coherent system of beliefs, which has sustained millions of human beings through the centuries. But although highly coherent, many people doubt this system of beliefs; they ask the question, "Is it *true?*" And truth now cannot mean just coherence.

A system, however coherent, must be rejected or revised if it contains just *one* false proposition. But false by what standard? Not the standard of coherence, for a belief system may fulfill that. We seem driven back to correspondence: If even one of the statements in the system ("There is a benevolent God who created us") does not describe reality, then the whole system must be scrapped, or revised so as not to include the false proposition.

We do not believe that the pen "just disappeared" (was annihilated) because, we said, this belief is not coherent with our other beliefs. But this would not be a decisive consideration unless we had reason to believe that these other beliefs were *true.* If a statement is incoherent with a set of *false* beliefs, this incoherence would not count against it; it is only because we believe that the statement "material things don't suddenly cease to exist" is *true,* and in fact that we have massive evidence for it, that we dismiss the assertion that the pen just disappeared "into nowhere." And how did we arrive at the belief that pens and other material objects don't just disappear? Presumably on the basis of observing thousands of cases, in which we were in a position to say that the statement *does* state the facts (correspond to them?) because we observed those facts.

It is when we have no direct evidence as to what is true—as in the murder case—that we resort to coherence as a test of truth. Most trials are decided by circumstantial evidence, since the judge and jurors were not present at the scene of the murder for which the defendant is being tried. But if the murder had occurred in full public view, like Jack Ruby's killing of Lee Harvey Oswald after the John F. Kennedy assassination, then there would have been no question of coherence. Our eyes were all glued to the television sets and we all saw Ruby pulling out the gun and shooting Oswald. In that case we *saw for ourselves* what happened; there was no question about our belief (that Ruby killed Oswald) *cohering* with other beliefs. It didn't have to; didn't we see the event occurring ourselves? If such a sure belief doesn't cohere with other beliefs, we might say so much the worse for those other beliefs.

Let us consider these two aspects of the situation:

A: But scientific theory is different. There we have no *independent test* of truth, such as watching Ruby shoot Oswald. The existence of subatomic particles is something we can never discover directly and thus test their "correspondence with fact"; and we can't go back 60 million years to see for ourselves what killed the dinosaurs. We have to test these beliefs, then, by coherence with *other* well-established beliefs.

B: Well established. Not just *any* beliefs, but well-established beliefs. But established *how?* Through observation, where we can match the statement to the fact by correspondence. Where we can't, we do resort to coherence. But coherence is no proof of truth. In spite of mutual coherence of beliefs in biology, geology, and astronomy, it is still possible that the comet theory is *false*—false not because it doesn't cohere with other theories, but false because the events described never happened; the statement that it happened doesn't correspond with the facts.

It would seem, then, that the coherence theory is applicable to situations in which no direct evidence is possible; however, "coherence with a body of belief" is acceptable only if it is coherence with a *true* body of belief—and the word "true" in this last occurrence then means something like "correspondence with the facts." An entire body of belief, in fact, or a system of beliefs, may be false and it may take just one uncomfortable but undeniable fact to show this. There may be an entire mass of evidence pointing to the conclusion that Smith committed the murder, until Smith's twin sister turns up and admits to the deed; and now we accept a conclusion totally at variance with the coherent body of beliefs we had before.

The importance of coherence in our daily lives, however, should not be underestimated. Suppose someone tells you that World War II broke out in 1938. You look it up in history books which said the war began in 1939; you go to the library and read newspapers of the period, reporting that it was September 1, 1939; you ask your parents, who say they remember that it was 1939; and so on—the mass of evidential material is enormous. And so without further ado you say that your "informant" was wrong, it was 1939 and that's that. The fact that you weren't yet born in 1939 to observe for yourself whether the statement corresponds to the fact does not disturb you in the slightest; you would bet your life that it was 1939. You are just as (or almost as) sure of it as if you had witnessed the event yourself. It may not be coherence with all this evidential material that *makes* the statement true, but the coherence can be strong evidence of truth just the same.

Still, one may say, "scientific theory is different." It is like the situation in the Smith murder case where one can never observe the act for which Smith has been accused, since it occurred without witnesses. In scientific theory, there are not witnesses to neutrons, and what other test is there than coherence? The atomic theory in physics is a complex and highly coherent body of belief which explains virtually every observed fact of chemistry. Don't all the empirical sciences together form one vast body of beliefs with a high degree of coherence? Consider our example of the disappearance of the dinosaurs. We brought in biology, geology, astronomy, chemistry—and if the hypothesis had failed to fit in with *any* of these, or any *part* of any one of these, we would have had to discard the comet-hypothesis or reexamine some of the other theories of science to see whether they could be accommodated to it. What we want is the *most inclusive* possible body of coherent beliefs, and science seems to give us precisely that; isn't that why we have more respect for scientific theories than devil theories or tea-leaf theories or magic? When an incoherence occurs, we bend every effort to remove it by revising one or another of the theories.

"But," one may ask, "doesn't our belief that the hydrogen atom has one electron correspond with the *fact* that the hydrogen atom has one electron?"

We may *say* this if we like; but how will we discover whether such a correspondence exists? It's not like the books on the table which we can see for ourselves. What we do is watch various chemical combinations in a laboratory, see what combines with what, what happens when we put some of this with some of that, and so on; and then we devise a theory of different kinds of atoms, each with different numbers of electrons, and we devise it so as to be consistent with everything we know (or believe we know). It is coherence that does the trick, for in the realm of unobservables the correspondence test is useless.

3. The pragmatic theory. "The truth is what *works*." This view represents what is sometimes called the pragmatic theory of truth. The first question to be asked of this curious view is "What does it mean?"—especially with regard to the word "works."

You know very well when your car works. You turn on the ignition one morning and the car fails to start. You check the battery, the carburetor, and so on, and everything looks all right, but the car still won't start. A friend of yours, a mechanic, appears on the scene, makes a few changes under the hood, the car starts, and you drive it to school. There is no doubt now that the car "works." Contexts such as this provide the "home base" for the use of the word "works."

But what does it mean for a *belief* to work? Does your belief that the car works, itself work? What does it mean to say this? Suppose you want to go on a diet, and there are thousands of books on dieting, each with a different formula. After trying several you finally conclude, "This one works for me." That is, it is successful, it causes you to lose weight without too much exercise of will power. It is the *program* that works, not the proposition. Or suppose someone says, "Christianity works for me." Does that mean merely that it makes her feel better? That she is now happier or more contented than before? That her relations with other human beings are no longer ridden with conflicts? Depending on what you mean by "work" in this context, you may indeed say the belief "works," at least for you. But what has that to do with its truth? Can a belief work without being true? Can it be true and not work? What is the connection between being true and "working"? Whatever it is, you can hardly say that being true and "working" are the *same thing*. Don't some falsehoods "work"?

One might say, "Science is true because it works." Perhaps "works" here means that on the basis of scientific laws and theories one can now make predictions of events which come true. But wouldn't it be more accurate to say "The laws of physics are true, and that's why they work (enable me to understand nature, make successful predictions, and so on)" rather than to say "They work, and therefore they are true"? Indeed, one might say that if they didn't "work" in this sense, they would not even be accepted as science; scientists would investigate some more until they did come up with laws with predictive value. But surely it is because the law of gravitation and other laws *are* true descriptions of nature, that they enable us to make the regularly successful predictions that we do.

Perhaps the word "true" is too crude to do the whole job. If something works, we may say it is *useful*. If a statement correctly reports some aspect of the way the world is, it is *true*. And if it is coherent with a body of true statements, it is to that extent *justified,* although a body of beliefs may be coherent and yet not true.

3. THE PROBLEM OF INDUCTION

"If all the people aboard that ship were drowned, and Mabel was aboard that ship, then she was drowned." This is a simple example of deductive reasoning: if the premises are true and the reasoning valid, which it is in this case, then the conclusion is true. We also engage, however, in *inductive* reasoning: we have thrown a stone into the air a thousand times and it has always fallen back to the ground—it has never gone floating through the air or dissolved into ashes or changed into a centipede. So we conclude that in the future if we throw a stone into the air it will again fall to the ground. We can't validly deduce "It will fall to the ground" from "It has always done so," but we consider the fact that it has always done so as *evidence* that it will do so in the future.

We don't expect all past regularities to continue. In the past, people's principal mode of transportation was on the backs of animals, but now more people travel by car. In past centuries, people's lifespans were quite short, being terminated by starvation, disease, or attack by predatory beasts; but now, when most infectious diseases have been conquered and one machine can do the work of a hundred people, thus enormously increasing the production of goods, the lifespan of human beings is much longer—again the past uniformities did not continue. There are many things we do not expect to be the same in the future as in the past; but we still do expect stones to fall and not float.

In the case of some events that have occurred with some regularity, we would be surprised if the regularity continued. If you have tossed a coin and it has turned up heads twelve times in succession, you would not on that account be confident that it would turn up heads the next time (unless the coin was loaded). It was just "a run of luck," and the chance of it turning up heads the thirteenth time would be exactly the same as it was the previous twelve times, namely 50 percent. Or: If every president in this century who was elected during a year ending in 0 died or was assassinated in office, we would not be likely to lay odds that the next president elected in a 0-year would meet the same fate. If it has happened that way so far, we say this is a coincidence: two events or conditions that are not causally related, at least so far as we can determine. We say "It's a fluke," and would be rather surprised if this regularity continued.

Many regularities are conditional upon certain other events occurring or not occurring. Steel doesn't float on water but steel needles do (surface tension). Heavier-than-air objects tend to go downward, but airplanes fly. We don't expect iron filings when thrown out of a bag to form a clear pattern, but they do if there is a magnet nearby. And so on. Genuine regularities often involve many qualifications, such as "other things being equal"; this tree fell eastward when the west wind blew it down, but the tree next to it might not fall eastward—it wasn't leaning in the same direction, and so on.

Nor do we argue that it will happen so-and-so in proportion to the frequency of past regularities just because it has happened uniformly in the past. For example, if a man of 20 argued "Every time I've gone to sleep at night, I have awakened the next morning; so it is highly probable that I shall awaken tomorrow," and if a man of 90 arued "I have 70 more years of uniformity to go on, and so it is much more probable in my case than in yours that I shall probably wake up tomorrow," we would say that the mere frequency of past occurrence isn't what entitles us to be confident: In fact it is less probable, not more, that the man of 90 won't wake up tomorrow, because we know something about biology, and laws of cellular deterioration.

There are some regularities, however, which we fully expect to continue. When there is friction there is heat; when a metal is heated it expands; when dry paper is heated to a certain temperature in the presence of oxygen it bursts into flame; and so on. These we believe to be *unconditional:* they occur no matter what other conditions are present. We think of such regularities as *laws of nature.*

But how do we know that these regularities will continue to occur? We might well admit at the outset, "We don't really *know.* We don't know any statement about the future; we can't be sure until it happens, and then it is no longer future. If you are speaking of knowledge and not just reasonable belief, don't take future events as examples. Let's face it, we don't *know* that gravitation will operate tomorrow or that stones will fall; we just believe it on good evidence. It is *probable,* but not *certain.*"

Let us then rephrase the question: not "How do you know that tomorrow stones will fall?"—let's admit that we don't—but "Why do you say we have *evidence* that they will? What entitles you to say that it is even *probable?*"

Surely we believe it because we believe that these are laws of nature, and that when we discover them we are discovering the ways in which nature always works. It is *laws of nature,* not the tossing of coins or the death of presidents, which we are confident will continue to operate in the future as in the past. Particular future events, such as the sun rising tomorrow, are confidently expected only if they are taken as instances of the operation of laws of nature, such as gravitation. If another large stellar body were to strike the earth and smash it to bits or sent it reeling out of the solar system, then the sun would *not* continue to rise—and this would involve no violation of laws of nature; it would only be another illustration of them. No, it is the laws themselves, not the recurrence of particular events, that we project confidently into the future and say, "As they have operated, so they shall continue to operate."

"But of course," one may say, "laws of nature do operate in the future as well as in the past and present. They wouldn't be laws of nature if they didn't. Any regularity that stopped at 1987 would not be a genuine law." But we cannot settle this matter by defining "law": We can't say, "Laws are *defined* such as to include future events, therefore they will occur." We do define laws independently of spatial or temporal position, and so include future as well as past—so it's true that if a law no longer operated in 1987 we wouldn't call it a law. But then our problem merely shifts to "How do you know that there are (in this sense) any genuine laws of nature at all?" We can define terms howsoever we will, but this doesn't show that anything exists in the world to correspond to the definition.

The skeptic, however, says, "You project the past operations of nature into the future, and by what right do you do this? You show me the record of the past, and I agree. But what has that to do with the future? Why do you have such conviction that the operation of the universe in the past gives us any clue as to its future operations? What evidence have you that the past workings of nature are any guide to the future workings of nature?"

This problem has been called the *problem of induction.* The problem was set forth with piercing clarity by David Hume:

The bread which I formerly ate nourished me; that is, a body of such sensible qualities was, at that time, endued with such secret powers. But does it follow that other bread must also nourish me at another time, and that like sensible qualities must always be attended with like secret powers? The consequence seems nowise necessary. At least, it must be acknowledged that there is here a consequence drawn by the mind that there is a certain step taken, a process of thought, and an inference which wants to be explained. I *have found that such an object has always been attended with such an effect,* and *I forsee that other objects which are in appearance similar will be attended with similar effects.* I shall allow, if you please, that the one proposition may justly be inferred from the other; I know, in fact, that it always is inferred. But if you insist that the inference is made by a chain of reasoning, I desire you to produce that reasoning. The connection between these propositions is not intuitive. There is required a medium which may enable the mind to draw such an inference, if indeed it be drawn by reasoning and argument. What that medium is I must confess passes my comprehension . . .

That there are no demonstrative arguments in the case seems evident, since it implies no contradiction that the course of nature may change and that an object, seemingly like those which we have experienced, may be attended with different or contrary effects. May I not clearly and distinctly conceive that a body, falling from the clouds and which and in all other respects resembles snow, has yet the taste of salt or feeling of fire? Is there any more intelligible proposition than to affirm that all the trees will flourish in December and January, and will decay in May and June? Now, whatever is intelligible and can be distinctly conceived implies no contradiction and can never be proved false by any demonstrative argument or abstract reasoning a priori.[10]

One may say, ''True, we can't validly deduce propositions about the future from propositions about the past; that's deduction, and we don't have that in this case. But the evidence here is *inductive:* Induction gives us probability, not certainty, but it does tell us that if stones have always fallen there is a probability, not certainty, that they will fall tomorrow.'' But this, of course, is just what Hume is questioning: He is questioning the entire acceptability of inductive argument. To say that there is inductive evidence that induction will continue to be reliable, is to beg the very question at issue.

You say that the one proposition [about the future] is an inference from the other [about the past]; but you must confess that the inference is not intuitive, neither is it demonstrative. Of what nature is it then? To say that it is experimental is begging the question. For all inferences from experience suppose, as their foundation, that the future will resemble the past . . . If there be any suspicion that the course of nature may change, and that the past may be no rule for the future, all experience becomes useless and can give rise to no inference or conclusion. It is impossible, therefore, that any arguments from experience can prove this resemblance of the past to the future, since all these arguments are founded on the supposition of that resemblance. Let the course of things be allowed hitherto ever so regular, that alone, without some new argument or inference, proves not that for the future it will continue so.[11]

And thus Hume lays down the challenge: How do we get out of this impasse?

We might try to get out of it by laying down a general principle, sometimes called the *Principle of Uniformity of Nature:* ''As the laws of nature have been in the past, so they will be in the future.'' We are referring not to particular events, or series of events like the coin always turning up heads, which could change utterly without a change in the laws; rather, we are referring to the laws themselves; and one should perhaps say ''presumed laws,'' since a genuine law of nature by definition does operate in the future as well as in the past and present. Armed with this principle, one can argue, ''Law X has held in the past,

---

[10]David Hume, ''Skeptical Doubts concerning the Operations of the Understanding,'' *Treatise of Human Nature,* Part II. 1736.

[11]Ibid, Part II.

therefore law X will hold in the future." The argument is a valid one:

Those uniformities (that we believe to constitute laws of nature) that have occurred regularly in the past will continue to occur regularly in the future.
This uniformity has occurred regularly in the past.
Therefore, this uniformity will occur regularly in the future.

But how does one know that the major premise (the Principle of Uniformity of Nature itself) is true? Isn't that the very thing we were trying to prove? But if you're trying to demonstrate the truth of a proposition you can't assume its truth in the very process of trying to demonstrate it: this is "begging the question." You can't lift yourself up by your own bootstraps. And if the Principle of Uniformity of Nature is something we merely *posit,* then what is our assurance that what we posit is true? Positing is easy; demonstrating is something else again, and any attempt to demonstrate the Law of Uniformity of Nature seems to land us in a circle.

One could try another tactic: "In the past, when I predicted that water would freeze at 32°F (at sea-level pressure), it did so; my prediction was always fulfilled. Doesn't this provide evidence that in the future when I made the same prediction, it will also be fulfilled? In the past, when I predicted the future, I was always right; so this time also I will be right." But this argument only begs the question again. In the past, the future turned out as predicted; therefore, in the future the future will turn out as predicted. (As past futures were, so future futures will be.) As Hume would put it, by what reasoning do we get from the success of past predictions to the success of future predictions? It's the same problem all over again.

Human beings are "naturally" inductive creatures. We trust those friends who have been true to us in the past, rather than someone who had double-crossed us. Even animals are friendly to those who have been kind to them in the past rather than to people who have hurt them. Induction seems genetically built into us. You might say: "All this may well be true, but it doesn't answer the fundamental question of *what entitles* us to use past uniformities as a basis for predicting future uniformities? I grant that in the past when you predicted that the pencil would fall, it always did. But that doesn't show that *now,* when you predict that it will, it will—or even that it's probable that it will. You predicted it in the past, and you turned out to be right. What you predicted was *then* in the future. But now it has all happened, it's past; and what evidence have you that *future* futures will be like *past* futures? Prove to me that as past futures were, so future futures will be—even probably be! The fact that the prediction of the future was fulfilled in the past—what has this to do with what is *now* future?"

Hume gives an account of why we come to expect the workings of nature in the future to resemble those in the past, by saying that it is the result of *custom* or *habit*—the "indolence of the mind" by which we come to expect in the future what has gone before:

After the constant conjunction of two objects, heat and flame, for instance, or weight and solidity, we are determined by custom alone to expect the one from the appearance of the other. This hypothesis seems the only one which explains . . . why we draw from a thousand instances an inference which we are not able to draw from one instance that is in no respect different from them.[12]

We have a "natural" inertia which leads us to expect that as nature has worked in the past, so it will work in the future. But this, at best, gives a *psychological explanation* of why we are inductive creatures; it does not provide

_____

[12]Ibid.

what is required—a *philosophical justification*. It does not answer the question "What is our evidence for inferring, from the fact that nature has operated in a certain way in the past, that it will operate that same way in the future?" That justification Hume confessed himself unable to provide, and he challenged anyone else to provide it.

Attempts to Solve the Problem of Induction

Is there any way out of these difficulties? Several solutions have been suggested. Much of the controversy on this issue that fills the philosophical journals is far too technical to explore here, and even the outlines of many solutions can be presented only by means of elaborate mathematical formulas. We can only present a brief discussion of some of the lines of argument here:

1. Some philosophers have presented what may be called the *linguistic* solution. "There is no *evidence*," says the skeptic, "that as the uniformities of nature have been in the past, so they will be in the future." No evidence, we may say? A thousand times in the past I let go my pencil and it has fallen; never once has it flown into the air. This, and all the things I know about the behavior of physical objects, lead me to believe that the pencil will fall when I let go of it this time. Is this *no* evidence at all? If not, then what *could* count as evidence? Surely we have here the very paradigm of "good evidence"; if the facts just mentioned are not evidence, what is? What could be?

We may ask the skeptic, "What is it you are saying does not exist when you say that good evidence does not exist in this case? What is it that we lack? What are you waiting to have supplied?" And the answer seems obvious: There is nothing that the skeptic would count as evidence, nothing that is now missing that he would consider evidence, other than the occurrence of the future event itself—and

when it has occurred the event is no longer future, and he repeats the same story with regard to the events that are still future. There is nothing available *now* that he would count as evidence one way or the other for the future, whereas the rest of us *do* count the past behavior of the pencil as evidence that it will fall this time. It is not as if the skeptic were awaiting some magical rabbit to be pulled out of the hat, some momentous empirical discovery that, if we only had it, would allay his skepticism; there is *nothing* that would allay it, nothing that we could confront him with *now* that would convince him, for the simple reason that anything we can show him now is *now* and not the future, and he won't consider anything that happens now as in any way evidence for the future. What he demands it is logically impossible to supply.

But doesn't the logical impossibility of the skeptic's demand defeat his cause? If he raises a logically impossible demand, how can we be expected to fulfill it? He says we have no evidence, but whatever we adduce he refuses to count as evidence. At least *we* know what we would count as evidence, and we show him what it is. But he only shakes his head and says it isn't evidence. But then surely he is using the word "evidence" in a very peculiar way (a meaningless way?), so that nothing whatever would count as a case of it. Is he then using it in some new and special sense, like a new stipulative definition? Apparently not, for he has not supplied us with any such sense; he simply reiterates, no matter what facts we adduce, that he doesn't count these as evidence. As what? As evidence. And what is evidence, as he uses the term? He doesn't say. Isn't he then using it meaninglessly? "There is no evidence." Might he not just as well say "There is no glubglub"? What are we to say of someone who repeatedly tells us that there are no Xs, but refuses to tell us what he would count as an X?

The skeptic's situation is no different if we substitute related words for "evidence."

"There is no *reason* to believe that the pencil will drop if I let it go." But there is, we reply, every reason to believe it—the very reasons we have given. What more reason could there be other than the pencil actually dropping, in which case we could speak of an observed fact rather than of a reason to believe something that hasn't yet happened? If the skeptic says that there is no reason to believe it, what *would* he count as a reason? Let him describe something that in his opinion there *would* be a reason for believing. If there is none, it is not because he refuses to attach any meaning to the word "reason" in this context? He says there is no reason. No what? Reason. And what does it mean to say so, since nothing would count as being a reason? Again, his claim seems to reduce to meaninglessness, since he has not told us what he means by one of the crucial terms ("reason to believe") in it. But surely we need not respond to a meaningless charge. That the pencil has fallen to the floor every time we dropped it, no matter how often, is surely the very paradigm of a *good reason* for thinking it will continue to do so in the future. If that isn't a good reason, what is?

But the skeptic may reply: "I do not deny that there are good reasons for making statements. If I see bear tracks in the snow, I consider this good evidence (good reason to believe) that a bear has been here. That is an example of a good reason. But for beliefs about future uniformities we don't have good reasons. The fact that the pencil has always fallen, so far as I can see, provides no good reason to believe that in the future it will continue to do so. We simply have no reason to believe one way or another about the future. We do so believe, but this is just a blind faith. There simply *is* no evidence that the future will be like the past."

"You may, of course," the skeptic continues, "use the word 'evidence' in such a way that you will count the past as evidence for the future. But I ask you how you know that the past *does* constitute evidence. What has it to do with the future? What makes you so confident that future uniformities will occur as in the past? You haven't shown me the slightest reason to believe in any *connection* between past and future, or between observed cases and unobserved ones. If you could explain to me some such principle of connection, you might convince me. But you have shown me nothing at all, except things like the Principle of Uniformity of Nature, which simply *posits* that the future will resemble the past, without going one step toward establishing this assumption. Your arguments haven't even established that it is *probable* that the future will resemble the past; for how do you judge probability? By past performance—and it is precisely the relevance of this that I am questioning. In the usual sense of 'probability,' probability is relative frequency; if over the years there's been a 90 percent record of warm weather on July 1, then it is considered a probability that July 1 will be warm this year. The estimate is drawn entirely from *past* relative frequency, which I contend simply has nothing at all to do with future relative frequency."

We might counter: "But scientific predictions are based on the best possible evidence." But the skeptic replies: "Of course—if you count as evidence those propositions that scientists have found rendered other propositions more probable *in the past,* thus begging the question once again." "We go by laws, not by guesses," scientists say. But this again begs the question: "What entitles you to have faith that past uniformities will continue? It is precisely *your counting this as evidence* that I am questioning. I agree that what you call evidence is commonly *called* evidence. But that proves nothing. Hume's problem is unknown to most people, so it never occurs to them to question whether data from the past *should* count as evidence for the future. Maybe past data shouldn't—and then your inclination, or tacit assumption, that it should count, is simply a matter of faith."

2. Let's try another strategy. We might say: "In the past, when we predicted that stones would fall in the future, we turned out to be right. We reasoned inductively from past to future, and our use of induction paid off. Doesn't that give us some *reason to believe* that today, when we say that stones will fall in the future, we will be right again? Induction is like a tried and true friend who has never let us down. In the past, the future was predicted successfully (at least this segment of it); so we have every reason to believe that our present prediction of the future (the same segment of it) will also turn out to be correct."

But the skeptic responds: "But this is the same problem over again. In the past, the future turned out as predicted. How does this give you any reason to believe that in the future, the future will turn out as predicted? How can you make an inference from past futures (now past) to future futures? Such reasoning is worthless unless you assume that the future will be like the past—and that's all it is, an *assumption*."

Can we try to get out of this impasse?

Suppose that there was somewhere in the world an enclosure beyond which it was impossible for anyone ever to go or to make any observation. Nothing could be seen, heard, or in any other way perceived beyond the border. The territory beyond the enclosure, forever barred from human perception, is the land of the Future. The territory within the enclosure is the land of Present and Past, but since it is overwhelmingly the latter, it all goes under the name of Past.[13]

Suppose now that someone inside the enclosure is interested in the way things behave beyond the enclosure—such as that dogs that procreate will produce puppies and not kittens, or that stones when thrown will fall. And she wonders what evidence can be produced for believing this. She can't, of course, ob-

serve it; she has to base a hypothesis on her observations in the Land of the Past.

Now, there is one big difference between arguing from the past to the future and arguing from the observed enclosure to the unobserved one and it is this: in our imagined realm the border between Past and Future is constantly moving, revealing the territory that *had* been future but *now* is present and then past. As the boundary-line moves from future to present to past, we can see for ourselves what was in the land of the Future and check whether our predictions were correct. One would have thought that the receding border was a matter upon which the inhabitants of the Past may legitimately congratulate themselves . . . If the future had not yet begun to recede they would indeed be in an unfortunate position for securing such knowledge. But happily this is not the case. The border is constantly receding.[14]

And this gives us an opportunity to test whether our inductive inferences about the future were correct.

But does the future ever come to pass? If a prediction is made in 1986, and is confirmed in 1987, then what was future in 1986 has become present in 1987—thus whether the future will turn out as predicted in 1986 can be tested if one waits till 1987. But if "next year" always means the year *after* one is speaking, then it never comes, never could come. There are *two senses* of "future" being bandied about here.

In the sense of future-1, when one speaks about the future he is speaking of events which have not occurred, of things which do not exist, but of events and things which, with the constant movement of the line of the present, may sometime occur or exist. In the sense of future-2, when one speaks about the future he is speaking of the time which is always beyond the line of the moving present, of a time which never comes, which, by definition can never come, no matter how far the line of the present moves.

Interpreted in the sense of future-1 there are beliefs about the way the future will be like the past,

[13]Frederick L. Will, "Will the Future Be Like the Past?" *Mind 56*(1947):221–237.

[14]Ibid.

which have been and are being confirmed constantly by the uniform experience of countless positive instances in everyday life and in vast areas of science. Because they have been thus confirmed they constitute a vast set of assumptions with which scientists and laymen approach their problems in the various areas to which the confirmation applies. It is when these beliefs are interpreted in the sense of future-2 that the skeptics are able to produce a plausible argument to show that these beliefs are not empirically confirmable and are hence unknowable. But when these are so interpreted, the argument has no bearing whatever, favorable or unfavorable, on the soundness or success of any inductive inquiry . . . That one cannot produce empirical evidence for the statement that at a time which never comes and when no events occur, events will occur in these rather than other ways, may be readily admitted. But this is no good reason for skepticism. No skepticism is entailed by this admission so long as it is made with the understanding that there is evidence about the other kind of future, the kind which will come and in which events do occur. And it is this latter kind of future only, of these two kinds, with which our functions are concerned. It is this kind of future alone about which our inductions predict, and this kind alone which will ever confirm or refute our assertions. It is, therefore, not sensible for anyone to worry, in his inductive reasoning, about the character of a future which by definition can never come.[15]

3. Some philosophers have adopted yet another line of defense for induction. They admit that introducing a principle of uniformity of nature is useless, since this principle itself would have to be defended. We cannot deduce any statement about the reliability of induction from any other statement known to be true. Nor can we render it inductively probable, since this would be begging the question (assuming the point at issue): We cannot use induction to justify induction. But we can do something else: We can give a *pragmatic justification* of it—not of the principle itself, but of our *adoption* of it. We can interpret the principle as a kind of *rule* of the scientific enterprise—not attempting to defend the *truth*

of the principle, but only to justify our *adoption* of it as a rule of procedure. We justify the adoption of a rule of baseball only if the rule makes the game more interesting or challenging. We justify the adoption of the uniformity of nature principle in terms of the goals that would be realized by such adoption: the understanding of nature's workings, and the ability to *use* that understanding to predict and (sometimes) to control.[16]

We do not know of course that there *is* a uniform order of nature that extends from the past into the future. But *if* there is, then the method of scientific discovery—observing the data, noting apparent uniformities, discovering possible exceptions to these uniformities, devising explanatory hypotheses, testing the hypotheses, and so on—is our best bet for discovering the things which as scientists we want to discover. Guessing, armchair philosophizing, crystal gazing, having intuitions or mystical seizures won't do it; only painstaking observations can achieve this. True, we then extrapolate from past to future, but *if* the future is like the past (as far as basic uniformities are concerned), inductive methods will enable us to discover and predict this future. We are rather in the position of a patient who is told by his physician, "I don't know whether an operation will save you, but if you don't have an operation you will die." So we submit to the operation as a "best bet" although we do not know whether even after having it we shall survive.

Still, we cannot help but wonder: *In the past* the painstaking method of observation, experiment, and devising theories to explain what we find has yielded tremendously impressive scientific results. Crystal gazing and mystical experiences have not. But what is the assurance that this will remain so in the future? What if tomorrow morning more of na-

---

[15]Ibid.

[16]See Hans Reichenbach, *Experience and Prediction* (Chicago: University of Chicago Press, 1953), p. 349.

ture's secrets were unlocked by one of the "unscientific" methods now considered unfruitful—by doing auguries, or crystal gazing, or chanting incantations, or going into a trance? If the course of nature were to change abruptly, how do you know that what we now call "scientific method" would be a better basis for prediction than these other procedures which we now discount? If the course of nature changes, our "scientific method" might be entirely useless as a predictor of the future. How could one tell *which* method of prediction, if any, would work in such an altered state of affairs?

4. Still others have taken the position that we make the unreasonable demand of induction that it follow the pattern of deduction. True, we can't validly deduce conclusions about the future from premises that don't mention the future; so what else is new? Induction isn't an inferior form of deduction; it isn't deduction at all—it is something quite different. There is no point in blaming a dog for not being a cat.

It has been argued, accordingly, that there can be no such thing as *general* justification of induction; the whole quest for it is a mistake. What we can do is to justify certain *particular procedures* which are instances of induction to discover which ones yield reliable results. We can ask, "Is random sampling reliable?" But we neither can nor need to justify induction in general.

It is generally proper to inquire *of a particular belief,* whether its adoption is justified; and, in asking this, we are asking whether there is good, bad, or any evidence for it. In applying or withholding the epithets "justified," "well founded," etc., in the case of specific beliefs, we are appealing to, and applying, inductive standards. But to what standards are we appealing when we ask whether the application of inductive standards is justified or well grounded? If we cannot answer, then no sense has been given to the question.

Compare it with the question: Is the law legal? It makes perfectly good sense to inquire of a partic-

ular action, of an administrative regulation, or even, in the case of some states, a particular enactment of the legislature, whether or not it is legal. The question is answered by an appeal to a legal system, by the application of a set of legal (or constitutional) rules and standards. But it makes no sense to inquire in general whether the law of the land, the legal system as a whole, is or is not legal. For to what legal standards are we appealing? The only way in which a sense might be given to the question, whether induction is in general a justified or justifiable procedure, is a trivial one . . . We might interpret it to mean "Are all conclusions, arrived at inductively, justified?" i.e., "Do people always have adequate evidence for the conclusions they draw?" The answer to this question is easy, but uninteresting; it is that sometimes people have adequate evidence, and sometimes they do not.[17]

This is doubtless a position which will appeal to our "common sense." Yet the controversy aroused by Hume's question has not died down. Has Hume really been answered? Has anyone presented any evidence that in ten minutes the course of nature will not radically change? And then all bets are off—it's "deuces wild." And if this should happen, wouldn't we have been mistaken in believing that "what is commonly viewed as evidence" really *is* evidence? Scientists may go on believing that nature will continue to work as it has in the past, but *is* this any more than a "scientific faith"? Scientists continue their activities, never giving thought to this question; but the question has continued to fascinate (and plague) philosophers.

EXERCISES

1. Why are astrology, alchemy, and phrenology not considered sciences? Should geography be considered a science? (Does it have laws?) What about engineering and medicine?

2. Which of the following are theoretical con-

---

[17]P. F. Strawson, *Introduction to Logical Theory,* (London: Methuen & Co., 1952), p. 257.

cepts, and which refer only to things that can be observed? (a) gravitation (in physics); (b) mass (in physics); (c) light waves (in physics); (d) convection currents (in physics); (e) quasars (in astronomy); (f) cosmic rays (in physics and astronomy); (g) magnetic fields (in physics); (h) isotopes (in chemistry); (i) genes (in biology); (j) the average American voter (in sociology); (k) IQ (in psychology); (l) pent-up aggression (in psychology).

3. Keeping in mind the distinction between descriptive laws and prescriptive laws, evaluate the following comments:

a. We shouldn't disobey laws of nature.

b. Laws of nature have preordained what I shall do tomorrow.

c. When there's a law, there must be a law-giver.

d. We don't make laws, we find them.

e. Laws of nature control the universe.

f. Our behavior must conform to psychological laws.

4. Which of the following propositions would you consider to be laws of nature? Why?

a. Iron rusts when exposed to oxygen.

b. Gold is malleable.

c. All human beings are mortal. (They die at some time or other.)

d. All white tomcats with blue eyes are deaf.

e. When organisms reproduce, the offspring is always of the same species.

f. All the crows in the United States are black.

g. All oceans contain water.

h. One-third of American voters belong to the Republican Party.

5. Which of the following why-questions are requests for a reason, and which are requests for an explanation? Can any of them be construed in both ways?

a. Why did the water boil? Because I lighted a burner under it.

b. Why did you flatter the boss? Because I wanted to get a raise.

c. Why do you think it will rain this afternoon? Because dark clouds are gathering.

d. Why do you think there won't be another world war in our century? Because with present nuclear weapons no nation would dare to risk it.

6. Evaluate the following as explanations. In the case of unsatisfactory explanations, show what makes them unsatisfactory.

a. Why do birds build nests? Because they want to have a place to lay their eggs and bring up their young.

b. Why do birds build nests? Because it's their instinct to do so.

c. Why do most creatures lay more eggs than can possibly develop into full-grown offspring? Because they want to protect the species from extermination by competing organisms, cold, storms, and other destructive agencies.

d. Why did the Allies win World War II? Because they wanted to, and people generally do what they want to do.

e. Why does this substance become lighter (per unit of volume) as it becomes hotter? Because it contains an invisible substance, phlogiston, and the more of this it contains, the hotter it becomes; phlogiston is so light that an object is heavier for losing it.

f. Why did he arrive last night? Because God willed it so, and whatever God wills happens.

g. Why did that object sink in water? Because it is made of iron.

h. Why did you and I happen to meet downtown today? Because we both wanted to be at the same store when it opened this morning.

i. Why does this watch stop several times every day? Because there is a devil in it.

j. Why did you win the thousand-dollar prize in the lottery? Because some people have all the luck.

k. Why did that door open just now? Because some door-opening force caused it to do so.

7. "Why did she stab him?" Answer #1: "Because she hated him intensely and wanted more than anything else to see him dead." Answer #2: "Because, as a result of the motion of certain particles of matter in her brain, electrochemical impulses were discharged along certain neuronic pathways, stimulating certain efferent nerves, activating the muscles in her hand and arm, causing them to move in a certain way . . . " Do these two explanations conflict with each other? Does purposive explanation necessarily conflict with such "mechanical" explanations as given in Answer #2? How do you conceive the relation between them?

Are they both parts of the whole explanation? (To be discussed in Chapter 6.)

8. Examine the following dialogue, noting what you consider to be its good points as well as its bad points.

A. Did Newton discover any hitherto undiscovered empirical facts?

B. Yes, he discovered gravitation.

A. But we didn't need Newton to tell us that apples fall.

B. He explained *why* apples fall. They fall because of gravitation.

A. But gravitation isn't an explanation of *why* they fall. It is simply a fancy word stating a familiar fact, namely that things *do* fall. It is not an explanation, but simply a redescription in more general terms of the familiar fact that they do fall. (Compare the physician's statement that you are in this physical condition because you are run down.) What *is* gravitation but the fall of apples and the like?

B. Ah, you have admitted my point: Gravitation is, indeed, much more than the fall of apples—it is the fall of apples *and the like*. Newton connected apples in orchards with stars in heaven. He brought seemingly disconnected events together under a general law, and to do this is to have explained them. Of course, if you think animistically of gravitation as a pull exerted as if by some super-giant, you are mistaken. Gravitation is not a pull; the word is simply a name for the fact that matter behaves in a certain definite and specifiable way. But the law that it does behave in this way is a genuine explanation, and it explains a vast number of phenomena, including the revolution of planets and the fall of apples.

9. What is theory and what is observed fact in the account of the cometary theory (pp. 173–74)? How much of what is called "observation" or "observed fact" presupposes theories in its very formulation?

10. "Laws of science are *discovered,* but theories of science are *devised.*" Does this distinction hold up? Was the law of gravitation discovered or devised?

11. "All crows are black" is not verifiable, but falsifiable (by finding one albino crow). What would it take to falsify the following?

a. Somewhere in the world there is a lavender duck.

b. There is a solution to this problem, could we but find it.

c. The law of conservation of energy.

12. Would you consider the following to be *scientific* theories, and why?

a. Everything has expanded to double its former size during the night—including all our measuring instruments. Could we ever know the difference? What if anything would it mean to say that everything had expanded?

b. Is it meaningful to talk about other people, perhaps conscious beings on Mars, having senses that enable them to perceive in ways of which we human beings have no conception?

c. "Imagine a community of men living on a cell in the blood stream of one of us, but so small that we have no evidence, direct or indirect, of their existence. Imagine further that they themselves are provided with scientific instruments of the type we use, and possess a method of science and a body of scientific knowledge comparable to ours. One of the bolder of these thinkers proposes that the universe they inhabit is a Great Man. Is this hypothesis admissible on scientific grounds or is it to be laughed down . . . on the gound that it is 'metaphysical'? . . . Why at our own level cannot a similar hypothesis be raised: namely, that *we* are parts of a Great Man, the whole of our known universe being perhaps but a portion of the Great Blood Stream?"[18]

13. "If you were to include statements about *everything* in the universe, as one vast body of statements, then coherence would be a complete and sufficient test of truth."[19] Evaluate.

14. Assess the claim that it is meaningful to request a justification for individual inductive procedures but meaningless to request a justification for induction in general.

15. Induction is similar to deduction in that there are unprovable basic principles in both. We can't prove the law of identity or the law of noncontradiction, yet we accept them. Why can't we do the same with the Principle of Uniformity of Nature?

---

[18]Charles W. Morris, "Empiricism, Religion, and Democracy," *Conference on Science, Philosophy, and Religion,* p. 219.

[19]See Brand Blanshard, *The Nature of Thought* (London: Allen & Unwin, 1939).

SELECTED READINGS

BLACK, MAX. "Pragmatic Justifications of Induction," in *Problems of Analysis*. Ithaca: Cornell University Press, 1954.

BROAD, C. D. *Scientific Thought*. London: Routledge & Kegan Paul, 1923.

BRODBECK, MAY, ed. *Readings in the Philosophy of the Social Sciences*. New York: Macmillan, 1968.

CAMPBELL, NORMAN. *What is Science?* London: Methuen, 1920.

BURTT, E. A. *Metaphysical Foundations of Modern Science*. New York: Harcourt Brace, 1932.

D'ABRO, A. *The Evolution of Scientific Thought from Newton to Einstein*. New York: Dover, 1927.

FEIGL, HERBERT, and MAY BRODBECK, eds. *Readings in the Philosophy of Science*, part 6. New York: Appleton-Century-Crofts, 1953.

FEIGL, HERBERT, and GROVER MAXWELL, eds. *Minnesota Studies in the Philosophy of Science*. 3 vols. Minneapolis: University of Minnesota Press, 1957–1962.

FEIGL, HERBERT, and GROVER MAXWELL, eds. *Current Issues in the Philosophy of Science*. New York: Holt, 1961.

FIELD, HARTRY. *Science without Numbers*. Princeton, NJ: Princeton University Press, 1980.

FLEW, ANTONY, ed. *Logic and Language*, 1st series. (including, Paul Edwards, "Bertrand Russell's Doubts about Induction") Oxford: Blackwell, 1951.

GOODMAN, NELSON. Fact, Fiction, and Forecast. Indianapolis: Bobbs-Merrill, 1955.

HANSON, NORWOOD. *Patterns of Discovery*. Cambridge: Cambridge University Press, 1958.

HEMPEL, CARL, *Aspects of Scientific Explanation*. New York: Free Press, 1966.

HEMPEL, CARL. *Philospophy of Natural Science*. Englewood Cliffs, NJ: Prentice-Hall, 1966

KATZ, JERROLD. *The Problem of Induction and Its Solution*. Chicago: University of Chicago Press, 1962.

KITCHER, PHILIP. *Abusing Science*. Cambridge: MIT Press, 1980.

KUHN, THOMAS. *The Structure of Scientific Revolutions*. Chicago: University of Chicago Press, 1970.

MADDEN, E. H. *The Structure of Scientific Thought*. Boston: Houghton Mifflin, 1960.

NAGEL, ERNEST. *The Structure of Science*. New York: Harcourt Brace, 1961.

NEWMAN, J.R. *What Is Science?* New York: Simon & Schuster, 1955.

PAP, ARTHUR. *Introduction to the Philosophy of Science*. New York: Free Press, 1962.

POPPER, KARL. *The Logic of Scientific Discovery*. London: Hutchinson, 1959.

PUTNAM, HILARY. *Mind, Language, and Reality*. 2 vols. Cambridge: Cambridge University Press, 1975.

REICHENBACH, HANS. *Experience and Prediction*. Chicago: University of Chicago Press, 1953.

RESCHER, NICHOLAS. *The Coherence Theory of Truth*. Oxford: Clarendon Press, 1973.

SALMON, WESLEY C. *The Foundations of Scientific Inference*. University of Pittsburgh Press, 1967.

SALMON, WESLEY C. "An Encounter with David Hume." in Joel Feinberg, ed., *Reason and Responsibility*. Belmont, CA: Wadsworth, 1981.

SELLARS, WILFRID. *Science and Metaphysics*. London: Routledge & Kegan Paul, 1968.

SKYRMS, BRIAN. *Choice and Chance*. Belmont, CA: Dickensen, 1966.

SMART, J.J.C. *Problems of Space and Time*. New York: Macmillan, 1964.

WILL, FREDERICK L. *Induction and Justification*. Ithaca, NY: Cornell University Press, 1974.

WOODFORD, ANDREW. *Teleology*. Cambridge: Cambridge University Press, 1976.

5

CAUSE, DETERMINISM, AND FREEDOM

Most laws of nature make no reference to causes. The Law of Gravitation states that the gravitation between two bodies varies inversely with the square of the distance and directly with the product of the masses. It says nothing about what causes what. Boyle's Law states that the temperature of a gas varies with the pressure. A uniform relation between two things or processes is stated in each case, without reference to causality. Yet many laws, and especially generalizations in ordinary discourse, do make reference to causes: Alcoholism causes cirrhosis of the liver; the joint action of moon and sun cause tides; striking a match causes it to light; ingestion of arsenic causes death. We use causal words constantly—not only the work *cause* itself, but verbs that contain the concept of cause: "to cut" is to cause a cut to occur, "to lift" something is to cause it to go higher than it was before, "to break" a twig is to cause it to

break, and so on. Our language is shot through with causal words.

1. WHAT IS A CAUSE?

But what precisely is it to cause something? At first the answer seems easy; to cause something is to *produce* it; to cause something is to *bring it about*. But these are all synonymous expressions, not much more useful than saying that an asteroid is a planetoid. To give such answers only leads to another question, What is it "to bring about," or "to produce"? Giving synonyms doesn't give us an *analysis* of what the causal relation is between C, a cause, and E, an effect. What exactly are we saying or implying when we say that C causes E? It is on this point, not the giving of synonyms, that philosophers have given answers that sharply disagree with one another.

We observe many things by means of our senses—that there is a desk here, that there are five books on it. We can also observe that some events occur before or after other events: for example, that intoxication follows the consumption of alcohol and does not precede it. But do we also observe that the first *causes* the second? If so, what exactly are we observing when we observe this? We observe that someone scratches a match, and that the match lights; but what do we observe in addition to this when we observe, if we do, that scratching the match *causes* the match to light? Perhaps the cause occurs *earlier* in time?

Saying that C causes E is not merely saying that C precedes E in time. Many events occur before others without causing them. A moment ago the president of the United States sneezed; but this is in no way a cause of the fact that I am now eating lunch. And if I ate breakfast at 7:30 this morning and you, miles away and quite unknown to me, ate breakfast at 7:31, my eating did not cause yours.

Indeed, one could argue that C preceding E is not even necessary for C to cause E: C and E might occur simultaneously. Your standing in front of the mirror is the cause of your reflection appearing in the mirror: aren't the two simultaneous? Not quite. Light travels at 186,000 miles per second, so the cause of your reflection appearing in the mirror at time t_2 would be your standing in front of the mirror at time t_1, a very small fraction of a second earlier. Is it so in all cases? If you jump on one side of the seesaw, the other end of the seesaw flies up. Does the other end fly up at the *same* moment or a moment slightly after your jumping on the first side? Doesn't it take time for the motion to be imparted from one end of the board to the other? If the answer is again yes, what about other cases? There is a time-lapse in the case of light and other forms of radiation, but there is no known time-lapse in the case of gravitation: If a star in its course approaches another star, isn't the second star gravitationally affected by the first without any time-lapse in between? Indeed, one could argue that once the entire set of causal factors is complete (as we shall see, most causes are complex, and consist of numerous components), the effect must occur simultaneously with it: If all the causal factors are in place, there is nothing left that has yet to occur before the effect occurs.

To be safe, then, let us say that the cause at least does not occur *after* its effect. Swallowing poison on Tuesday doesn't cause a person to die on Monday of the same week. Rain falling today doesn't revive the crops yesterday. It may seem at first that even this seemingly obvious statement has exceptions. Suppose I have a goal (such as passing an examination next week); doesn't this future goal cause me to do certain things in the present (such as study)? No, the future event (passing the exam) has not yet occurred and is not yet there to do any causing; in fact, it may never take place at all. What causes you to study—or to do anything else in the area of goal-oriented behavior—is your *present* thought of that future goal and your *present* desire to attain it. These states exist now, though the fulfillment of the goal does not; if it existed already, you would not have to strive to attain it.

But saying that causes don't come after their effects has not taken us very far. There are many events that precede others, or occur simultaneously with them, without causing them. What then distinguishes C causing E from C simply occurring before (or at the same time that) E does? At this point we enter a major arena of controversy.

Necessary connection. Deeply embedded in our ways of talking and thinking is the idea that when C causes E, if C occurs then E *must* occur. This is sometimes expressed by saying that there is a *necessary connection* between C and E, and only when we know this are we entitled to say that C causes E.

But what does it mean to say that E *must* occur? What is the meaning of the word "must" in this sentence? The word "must" is used in various ways, and in our discussion of causality it is of some importance—as well as an interesting bit of philosophical analysis on its own—to pause before going further and try to nail down the principal ways in which this word is used.

1. "You *must* be in by midnight or else. . . ." This is the *imperative* sense of "must," the sense appropriate to commands and laws. A person is told that if he does not do a certain thing, certain punishments will be forthcoming. But this cannot be the sense of "must" appropriate to events in nature. When we say that wood must burn or water must flow downhill, the wood and the water are not being commanded.

A close variant of the first sense occurs when we say "I *must* return the money, since I borrowed it," even though no penalty is attached to failure to do so. Here we mean merely that we believe we are morally obliged to return the money.

Or when someone says, "You *must* come to my party tonight," she is not implying that the person is morally obliged or that there will be penalties if she does not. Her statement comes to something like this: "This (*x, y, z*) is what you'll be missing if you don't come. You must come; that is, if you don't come, you'll be missing *x, y, z*."

Another variant is still weaker: "It simply *must* be nice weather for tomorrow's picnic." Nature is not being commanded. About all that is expressed by this form of words is wishful thinking: "I wish very much that it would be nice weather tomorrow."

2. Often "must" is used in the context of *inference*. "If *p* is true, and *p* implies *q,* then *q must* be true." Here we mean that *q* is logically *deducible* from the premises given. We are not saying that *q* by itself must be true: We are saying that *q* must be true *if p* is true

and *p* implies *q*. The "must" here is not contained *in* any one of the statements, not even in the conclusion; the relation of "mustness" (logical necessity) lies in the *relation* between the premises and the conclusion. The conclusion should not be stated as "Therefore *q* must be true" but rather "Therefore it must be the case that *q* is true."

In the case above, the inference is deductive, and the "must" is one of logical necessity. But sometimes we use "must" even if the inference is inductive: "He must have been the killer," we say, somewhat loosely, meaning only that we inductively infer it, that the evidence points to it.

3. Often "must" is used to indicate a *necessary condition*. A is a necessary condition for B when, in the absence of A, B never occurs. Oxygen is a necessary condition for human life—that is, in the absence of oxygen human life would be impossible. The heat and light of the sun are necessary conditions for life on the earth—that is, if the earth did not receive heat and light from the sun, there would be no life on the earth. We often use "must" to express this empirical relation: For life to exist, there must be oxygen, there must be heat and light from the sun. We shall have much more to say about necessary conditions shortly.

What is the relevance of these senses of "must" to our discussion of causality? There are several confusions involved in our use of "must" in talking about the processes of nature. We would do well to dwell on these confusions before proceeding, for if we are not thoroughly acquainted with them our discussion of causality may be riddled with these confusions.

1. Confusion of causality with logical necessity. If the premises are true, and the argument is valid, then the conclusion *must* be true. This, as we have seen, is the "logical necessity" sense, or more simply the logical sense, of "must." This relation holds between propositions. There are also statements that by themselves are necessary: the necessary (necessarily true) propositions, such as "A is A," "Whatever is red is colored," and "Nothing can be red and green all over at the same time." But statements about causality are not logically necessary. "Friction causes heat" is not a logically necessary statement. It is logically possible that friction might have produced magnetic distrubances instead. It is only by empirical observation that we discover what causes what. "Moisture, warmth, and soil cause crops to grow," "Getting one's feet wet causes colds," "Pneumonia is caused by a virus," "The cause of the car's breakdown was a faulty generator"—these and countless other statements about what causes what are empirical statements, which we can know to be true only a posteriori, often after years of investigation. Detailed answers to the questions "What causes cancer?" "What causes the aurora borealis?" "What causes quasars?" and so on are to be found only after prolonged empirical investigation. We cannot get the answers by sitting in an armchair and figuring it out, as we do in mathematics. We must "dirty our hands" in the complex empirical world to discover what causes what.

Yet if we are not careful we shall find ourselves smuggling in the "must"-language just the same. Let's see how this can happen. Consider the statement, "Johnny is taller than Billy." This is, of course, an empirical statement, we must observe Johnny and Billy to discover whether it is true. The same is true of the statement, "Billy is shorter than Johnny." But the statement "*If* Johnny is taller than Billy, then Billy is shorter than Johnny" is a logically necessary statement—indeed, we would be contradicting ourselves if we said that Johnny is taller than Billy but that Billy is not shorter than Johnny. (What state-of-affairs could possibly answer to such a description?) Thus, we can say that *if* Johnny is

taller than Billy, it *must* (logically) be the case that Billy is shorter than Johnny. It is the hypothetical proposition that "must" be true, not either of its two component propositions.

Now let us consider the statement, "Whenever friction occurs, heat occurs." This is a law of nature, discovered to be true by empirical observation (at least in the cases thus far observed). That friction occurs (at a particular place and time), and that the temperature of the substance rises, are also discovered by observation. But if these two statements are accepted as premises of a deductive argument, the conclusion—"Therefore heat occurs"—logically follows from them: If the two premises are true, the conclusion *must* (logically) be true. None of the three statements is a necessary truth; what is necessarily true is the entire statement: "*If* when friction occurs heat occurs, *and* friction occurs, *then* heat occurs"—that is, *if* the premises are true, then it (logically) *must* be that heat occurs. But we are all too tempted to abbreviate this by saying heat *must* occur, forgetting that the "must" refers to the deductive *relation* between premises and the conclusion, not to the premises or the conclusion by themselves. We put in the "must" and then forgot about the empirical premises from which the conclusion is deduced. Thus we say, "Stones must fall," "Water must go downhill," "Organisms must sooner or later die," and so on, forgetting that these are not logically necessary statements at all, but only that they can be deduced from general laws about nature, which themselves are empirical rather than necessary truths.

But in the "real world," don't we indeed observe that water must flow downhill, that stones must fall? No, what we observe is that water *does* flow downhill and that stones *do* fall—just as we observe that Johnny is taller than Billy; there is no "must" about any of these statements.

"But" one could easily object, "water must flow downhill because that is a part of its *nature.''* This statement requires that another term be clarified, namely "nature." (See pp. 125–26.) If it were a defining characteristic of water (part of its definition) that it flows downhill—and wouldn't be water if it didn't—then of course the statement is necessarily true, like any statement of a defining characteristic, such as that all unicorns have one horn. But defining a term in a certain way imposes no restrictions on the world. If the definition were accepted, then, if the liquid we thought was water and was composed of H_2O did flow uphill, it wouldn't be water by that definition. We do observe that water, defined as H_2O, does flow downhill, though this is not a part of its definition. Thus, what we observe is that it *does,* not that it *must.* (Indeed, does it always? Some water evaporates into the air.) Water is heavier per unit of volume than the air above it, so it stays below the air; and its flowing downhill is simply one aspect of gravity, that things tend to reach their lowest possible point because of the pull of gravity. But none of these facts are necessary truths: Water could easily be conceived to evaporate *in toto,* or to freeze immediately and not flow at all, or for that matter to disappear entirely; we have to rely on empirical observation to discover what it actually does. What it does is not a matter of logical necessity but of empirical fact.

2. Confusing laws of nature with prescriptive laws. As we have seen, the term "must" is often used in connection with commands. Prescriptive laws (pp. 157–58) are of this kind. Certain modes of behavior, such as refraining from murder and theft, are prescribed by law under pain of penalty if they are disobeyed. But laws of nature are not prescriptions: Nature is not being commanded. Laws of nature are discovered by human beings, not devised by them.

The laws of celestial mechanics do not prescribe to the planets how they have to move, as though the planets would actually like to move otherwise, and

are only forced by these burdensome laws of Kepler to move in ordinary paths; no, these laws do not in any way "compel" the planets, but express only what in fact planets actually do.[1]

Historically, the two senses of the word "law" were not distinguished. The uniformities of nature were conceived as the expression. of the will of the gods, or of God. God *commands* the forces of nature to operate in certain ways, *compelling* every event to occur. Since he is far more powerful than any government, his laws are inviolable. Moreover, since God is good, his laws are so also: the laws of nature are the expression of a *moral order* supernaturally imposed upon the universe. The workings of this order *must* be as they are because they are the expression of divine will. Effects follow causes much as punishment follows forbidden acts and reward follows approved acts; they follow necessarily, because the laws are enforced by an all-powerful Deity. With this conception of the universe, it is no wonder that words such as "must" and "necessary" came to be attached to statements about causes and effects.

It is not relevant at this point to discuss whether this view of the universe is true; the question is whether the truth of this view is presupposed in every statement we make about causes or effects. When we say "Friction causes heat" or "The appearance of the lion caused the antelope to flee," do we really mean to imply this view of nature, so that if this view of nature were not true, we would not be entitled to make any statements at all about causality? Surely this is not the case. Whether we view nature as a manifestation of divine will or not, this is *no part of what we mean* when we make causal statements in everyday life. We would have to argue this view of nature *separately:* We would first utter the causal statements (about friction, the antelope, or about anything else) in any case,

---

[1]Moritz Schlick, *The Problems of Ethics* (Englewood Cliffs, NJ: Prentice-Hall, Inc. 1938), p. 147.

and then go on, *in addition,* to assess this view of nature. "The question which must be put to those who speak as if there were necessity in nature is whether they really mean to imply that the laws of nature are normative rules, enforced by a divine will. If they do not mean to imply this, their talk of necessity is at best an unfortunate metaphor."[2]

3. Confusion resulting from animistic use of language. One may object that the view of nature just described does not literally make sense. Do not words like "command" and "compel" and "necessitate" have meaning only within the context of human beings, beings who have wills and can thus be made to do things against their will? Stones and waterfalls have no wills, and therefore they can hardly be said to be *commanded* or *compelled.*

This, of course, is true, *unless* stones and watefalls *are* conceived as having wills. In the primitive view of things called "animism," this is precisely the case. Animism is the tendency to confer upon inanimate objects characteristics which belong only to animate beings.

Today people are no longer animistic in any literal sense. We do not believe that the mountains and trees are spirits, nor even that they contain spirits; we do not believe that the tree feels pain when it is cut down or that the stone is animated by a desire to get to the center of the earth; we do not believe that water is compelled to do anything, because only animate beings can have compulsion exerted upon them and water is inanimate. Nevertheless, we often talk *as if* we believed these things. We "read our feelings into nature." We speak of the sky as gloomy, though it is we who feel gloom and not the sky; we speak of the chasm as yawning, of the earth as smiling, of the train as "steaming away impatiently." Poetry is filled with animistic language, and the

poetic quality is often enhanced by it. But in philosophy, it is important that we be careful about this way of using language. Animistic language can be misleading, as a few examples will show.

Originally the word "resistance" stood for a certain kind of feeling people had, for example when trying to move a boulder or hold a heavy door open. Now we speak of resistance even when no animate beings are involved— We say that the object resists pressure, resists our attempts to move it, and so on, although we do not mean that it *feels* resistance. The word "resistance" has become transferred from the feeling to the thing which occasioned the feeling. We impute resistance to the doorstop that holds the door open because if *we* were in the position of the doorstop we would feel resistance. "Resistance," "force," "energy" and other animistically tinged words are constantly used in the physical sciences. Here, however, they are comparatively harmless, for they are given special and precise meanings within these fields.

You push a large ball and start it rolling toward the place where you want it. On another occasion you see another ball strike it, thereby imparting the motion to it. The work done is approximately the same. But since on the first occasion you pushed to get the ball where you wanted it, you incline to say, when you see the other ball doing the same work, that the first ball *pushed* the second, or *forced* it to go in the path it took, or even *compelled* it to go. This language is, of course, misleading. If these expressions refer simply to what you observe, namely that one ball makes contact with another and the other starts moving in a certain direction (what a motion-picture camera would record), then you have not gone beyond the empirically observable facts. But the words you use to describe the situation *seem* to import into the situation something that is not there at all; they seem to imply that the first ball had a feeling of effort or strain in "pushing" the second

[2]A. J. Ayer, *Foundations of Empirical Knowledge,* London: Macmillan, 1945. p. 198.

one, and that the second felt "resistance" to the motion of the first. We do not really believe this, but our language leaves the impression that we do.

The same is true even when we say that the first ball *makes* the second one move. If this means merely that when the first ball hits the second the second moves, and that this regularly occurs, then we are merely describing what we observe. But there is an animistic ring about the word "makes," which seems to hint at some kind of compulsion. In using all these words, let us remember that what we observe is simply that when the first ball strikes the second the second moves, and that this regularly happens. There is no more. We probably do not seriously demand more; but our linguistic habits, a carry-over from primitive times when animism was literally interpreted, do not render this instantly evident, and they are apt to confuse us. Probably there is no objection to using this kind of language, provided that we are clear about what we are doing; but our language is so full of animism that unconsciously our thought becomes so, and we are left with verbal expressions which we have the impulse to defend even though we cannot seriously take them literally. That is why we often resist the tendency to describe causal relations exclusively in terms of what we can observe. We want to say, "The first billiard ball *compels* the second one to move," and "When the first hits the second, the second *must* move," or even "When the first hits the second, the second *can't help* moving" (as if it were a conscious being that could avoid doing things if it wished to) or "The first ball *forces* the second to move" (note the implicit comparison with a quite different kind of situation, such as a robber forcing you to give up your money). These are the ghosts of animism which haunt our everyday language. We have been so accustomed since childhood to talking in these ways that we come to feel we have lost something when we have translated "The first

ball caused the second one to move" into "When the first ball contacts the second, the second regularly moves." We do not feel quite so much at home with this straightforward, nakedly empirical, studiedly nonanimistic language; and so we feel that we mean more than this, even though we cannot discover what the more is. When we have reached this stage, we are ready to begin using such terms as "necessary connection," whether they stand for anything or not. Such terms "have the right kind of sound," they fill the vacuum created by the removal of the animistic overtones from our everyday causal language.

Hume on Cause

What we observe, then, is not that C must be followed by E but that it *is* followed by E. Yet more is required to establish a causal relation than this. What is it, Hume asked, that entitles us to say that increasing temperatures cause a column of mercury to rise in a tube, that the sun's rays cause the earth to be warmed, that pouring water on sodium causes an explosion? The difference between mere temporal sequence and a genuine causal relation, said Hume, is that in the latter case there is not only temporal sequence but *constant conjunction*.

As we observe the world around us, at any given moment we find coutless events occurring. But as we observe more carefully this shifting panorama of events, we begin to notice certain *repeating sequences:* some Cs which are *regularly* followed by certain Es. It is the *regularity* of the sequence that makes the difference. Some events are *constantly conjoined* with others in our experience; then we say they are causally related. One observation of sequence is never enough to entitle us to say that C causes E; the sequence must be regular, or constant. In the words of modern Humeans:

To say that the electric current causes a deflection of the magnetic needle means that whenever there is an electric current there is always a deflection of the magnetic needle. The addition in terms of *always* distinguishes the causal law from a chance coincidence. It once happened that while the screen of a motion picture theater showed the blasting of lumber, a slight earthquake shook the theater. The spectators had a momentary feeling that the explosion on the screen caused the shaking of the theater. When we refuse to accept this interpretation, we refer to the fact that the observed coincidence was not repeatable.

Since repetition is all that distinguishes the causal law from a mere coincidence, the meaning of causal relation consists in the statement of an exceptionless repetition—it is unnecessary to assume that it means more. The idea that a cause is connected with its effect by a sort of hidden string, that the effect is forced to follow the cause, is anthropomorphic in its origin and is dispensable; *if-then-always* is all that is meant by a causal relation. If the theater would always shake when an explosion is visible on the screen, then there would be a causal relationship.[3]

The difference between a mere temporal sequence and a causal sequence is the regularity, the uniformity of the latter. If C is *regularly* followed by E, then C is the cause of E; if E only "happens" to follow C now and then, the sequence is called mere chance. And since (as we just saw) the observation of the regularity was the *only* thing that was done, it was necessarily the *only* reason for speaking of cause and effect—it was the *sufficient* reason. The word "cause," as used in everyday life, implies *nothing but* regularity of sequence, because *nothing else* is used to verify the propositions in which it occurs.[4]

There is, then, no a priori knowledge of causes. We cannot know without observation what causes what. "There are no objects," wrote Hume, "which by the mere survey, without consulting experience, we can determine to be the causes of any other; and no objects, which we can certainly determine in

[3]Hans Reichenbach, *The Rise of Scientific Philosophy,* pp. 157–158.

[4]Moritz Schlick, "Causality in Everyday Life and in Science," in *University of California Publications in Philosophy XV* (1932).

the same manner not to be the causes." But we may ask, is this true? When we see two trains rapidly approaching one another on the same track, can't we say a priori that they will collide? Not at all, says Hume. Prior to experience of how solid objects behave while in motion, we could have no idea of what would happen when they approached one another. Without experience of what they do, we would be no more entitled to say that they will collide than that they will turn to mush or disappear into thin air. But all our lives we have been acquainted with the behavior of moving bodies; the regularity of sequence is well established, in thousands of cases and with no exceptions. It is this experience of regularity which entitles us to make the causal claim. A priori, any conjunction of events would be equally probable. Neither armchair philosophizing nor speculations about "necessary connection" will advance us one step toward discovering what causes what.

It may be, however, that for at least two reasons Hume's account is either inaccurate or (at best) unfinished in detail: (1) There seem to be many cases of constant conjunction that are not cases of causality. The green traffic light goes on, then the red, then the green, and so indefinitely, but the green doesn't cause the red to go on, nor vice versa. Night and day seem to be constantly conjoined, yet night does not cause day nor day night. The growth of hair in babies is regularly followed by the growth of teeth, yet the first does not cause the second. (2) There also appear to be many examples of causality that are not examples of constant conjunction. We say that scratching the match causes it to light; but scratched matches don't always light—the sequence is far from exceptionless. The heart attack, we say, caused a man's death, yet heart attacks aren't always fatal. I decide to walk to the door, and after I've decided to I always do—until I suddenly have a paralytic stroke and am unable to move no matter how determined I am to do so. It would seem that observing constant conjunctions may give us a reasonable suspicion that there is a causal relation "going on somewhere in the neighborhood," but that it is not accurate to say "C causes E" means no more or less than "C is always followed by E."

Mill on Cause

According to John Stuart Mill (1806–1873), Hume was on the right track but never fleshed out his account. There are indeed many cases of regularity that aren't causal, and of causes where there is no exceptionless regularity. The true answer, said Mill, is to be found in examining two concepts, that of *necessary* condition and that of *sufficient* condition.

1. Necessary condition. When we say that C is a necessary condition for E, we mean only that if C had not occurred E would not have occurred. Oxygen is a necessary condition for fire—that is, fires don't start in the absence of oxygen. The presence of oxygen isn't enough—fires depend on other conditions as well—but it is necessary not in the sense of "necessary connection" but merely in the sense that in the absence of C, E would not have occurred.

We do not ordinarily speak of a necessary condition as the cause. The cause of the street being wet is that rain has just fallen, yet rain is not a necessary condition for the street being wet; a water-sprinkler will also make the street wet. For you to be ill, it is necessary that you first be alive, but one would not speak of being alive as the cause of your illness.

At this point, however, we should make an important distinction. Thus far we have spoken loosely of C as causing E, as if C and E were particular events. But particular events are not repeatable. The fall of a stone is a particular event, and if we drop this stone again

this will be *another* event—an event of the same class or type, but not the *same* particular event. A more accurate formulation, then, would be: "In the absence of an event or condition of type C (presence of oxygen), an event of type E (combustion) does not occur." The examples of causation presented thus far have been of this kind. But we may also say, "In the absence of this particular event or condition C, this particular event E would not have occurred." For example, if the car she was driving had not been struck head-on by a speeding driver, she would not have been killed. What we mean is that if the speeding driver had not struck her car she would not have died at this time (or at least from this accident). We do not mean that having one's car struck by a speeding driver is a necessary condition for deaths in general. Death can occur from many causes, and car accidents are in no way necessary conditions for death. All people will die, but most of them will not die from car accidents. Still, it may be true that, but for being struck by this car, she would not have died at this time. Here what we are saying is that if this particular event (collision) had not occurred, this particular outcome (her death) would not have occurred at this time.

The legal profession often employs this "but for" test: *But for* the fact that she stepped into the road, she would not have been hit by the passing car; *but for* his being in the air terminal at the moment that the terrorist's bomb went off, he would not have been killed in the blast. Here we do not mean to imply that events or conditions of type 1 (bomb blasts) are always necessary for events of type 2 (death), but only that in the absence of *this* occurrence (bomb blast), the person's death would not have occurred when it did. And thus the bomb blast is called the cause of the death. Even the law, however, does not use this "but for" test in all cases: "But for the fact that my father conceived me and my mother gave birth to me, I would not have committed this crime; therefore my parents are the cause of my committing this crime.'' Having parents is a necessary condition for your existence, and thus for your being here to do anything; yet it would be considered ridiculous to say that just because having parents is a necessary condition for your committing the crime, therefore they are the cause of it.

When we do say that C is the cause of E because "but for this particular event, that particular event would not have occurred," how do we know this? What entitles us to say it? Such statements, it seems, are grounded in our general background knowledge of how nature operates. Bomb-blasts do injure people, often destroying vital organs or producing enough blood-loss to cause death. Bomb-blasts aren't necessary conditions for deaths in general (people die from other causes), but in this case we are justified in saying that but for the bomb-blast the death would not have occurred when and as it did, and we call the blast the cause of the death.

Sufficient condition. The cause of an event, said Mill, is that set of conditions upon which the event (that is, an event of this type) invariably occurs. "The cause, philosophically speaking," wrote Mill, "is the sum total of all the conditions, positive and negative taken together, the whole of the contingencies of every description, which being realized, the consequent invariably follows." To speak of the cause—the whole cause—is to speak of that set of conditions which, when they are all met, is invariably followed by an occurrence of the type described as the effect. To state what is the cause of an occurrence is to enumerate this whole set of conditions.

Thus, what is the cause of combustion? First, there must be a combustible material (not everything burns). Second, there is a temperature requirement; The substance must be heated to that temperature—which differs

from one kind of substance to another. Third, there must be oxygen. When all these conditions are present, the substance burns; these three conditions are sufficient. Each of the three conditions alone is necessary, but no one of them alone is sufficient. Only the three together are sufficient; and when all three occur, combustion occurs.

What about those cases which seem to exemplify Hume's conception of cause as constant conjunction, but which are not causes? Isn't there a constant conjunction between day and night? Yet we would not call day the cause of night, or vice versa. Mill says that day is not the cause of night because the occurrence of day is not dependent on the prior occurrence of night. If the earth did not rotate on its axis and always turned the same side to the sun, like Mercury, then on that side there would always be day and on the other side there would always be night. And if the light of the sun were to be extinguished, it would always be night all over the earth. The alternation of day and night depends, in fact, on the following conditions: (1) There must be sunlight; (2) the earth must rotate on its axis, so that there can be first night, then day, then night again; and (3) there must not be obscuring material between earth and sun so as to cut off the sun's light. If any of these three conditions were absent there would be no alternation of day and night; and when all three are present—as they now are—there is this alternation. Each of the three conditions is necessary, and all three together are sufficient. If we are to describe the whole cause, we must set forth the list of conditions which are together sufficient.

The cases just described are unusually simple; the effects in question depend on only a small number of conditions. Most cases are far more complicated. What is the set of conditions which are together sufficient for a car to operate properly? The wheels must be attached; the axles must not be broken; the motor, generator, distributor, and countless other parts must be functioning properly and be connected in certain ways, and so on. The list of necessary conditions would run into the thousands. And each one of these thousands would have to be listed as *part* of the sufficient condition, for anything less than *all* of them is not sufficient for the car to run. Yet this example is simple indeed compared with examples in the biological realm, and even simpler compared with examples in the human realm. What set of conditions must be fulfilled in order for a person to enjoy a philosophical discussion, for example? The conditions here are staggeringly complex, and even if we list many items, we probably do not yet have a sufficient condition. In general, it is much easier to list necessary conditions (conditions in the absence of which the event never occurs) than sufficient conditions (conditions in the presence of which the event always occurs).

The only conditions that are sufficient by themselves appear to be those for "negative events"—the *failure* of something to occur. For your electric radio not to work, it is sufficient to pull out the plug. It is also sufficient to remove a transistor. Here there are many conditions, each of which *alone* is sufficient. But for the positive event to occur—for the radio to function properly—there is no simple set of sufficient conditions; the list is long, but at least in this case the radio repairman knows the whole set of conditions on which the radio's working depends, for he *can* (usually) get a radio to work, and of course it would not work unless a set of conditions sufficient for its working had been fulfilled. In the case of preserving bodily health to the age of 100, no set of sufficient conditions is known.

It is not a single *event* that causes another event. What causes an event (the effect) is a whole set of *conditions,* of which some are events (like lighting the fuse) but others are states of a substance (the powder is dry) and still others are states of the environment (there

is oxygen in the air). Causation normally occurs in the history of enduring entities, which we call substances or, more popularly, things. (This may not be true in every case, however: Lightning may cause a man's death; but is a bolt of lightning a substance?) Thus does Mill attempt to circumvent the objection often made against Hume's view, that events do not by themselves cause other events. Hume never said that they did, but his constant reference to constant conjunctions between cause and effect, as if the cause were one event and the effect another, led critics to conclude that Hume thought that the cause of an event was always another event.

Mill was careful to say that the cause (sufficient condition) is that set of conditions on the occurrence of which the effect invariably *and unconditionally* occurs. This proviso was intended to eliminate those regularities that depend on other factors which we usually assume or take for granted. The alternation of red and green traffic lights will take place only as long as the mechanism is working properly, and as long as one of the lights hasn't gone out or the red glass broken. The paper will always burn when it has reached the temperature of combustion, but not unconditionally; it depends on another condition, the presence of oxygen; try doing the experiment in a vacuum and you will discover this for yourself. A condition which is always or usually present— a "*standing* condition"—is one which we tend to ignore, but it may play just as essential a role in causation as a "*differential* condition," such as throwing a lighted cigarette into a paper-filled wastebasket, a factor which distinguishes this fire from other fires.

Mill's "scientific" definition of "cause" is not quite the same as our usage of "cause" in daily life. In ordinary discourse we tend to call *the* cause the factor to which we wish to call attention, although it is not the only causal factor. Mill held that out of the array of conditions which are together sufficient, we refer to as "cause" either (1) the last condition to be fulfilled before the effect takes place—thus, we say that lighting the fuse caused the gunpowder to explode, although if the gunpowder had been wet there would not have been an explosion (the explosion depends on other factors besides lighting the fuse); or (2) we might cite the condition whose role in the affair is superficially the most conspicuous—thus, we say that the insulting remarks directed at her were what caused her to burst into tears, forgetting that she is the type of person who is easily hurt (if she had been more thick-skinned, she would simply have passed off the remarks without letting them wound her); or (3) the condition which we believe our hearer doesn't already know about—thus, we say that his injury was caused by falling off a ladder, though the continued operation of gravitation is also required for the effect to take place; or we say that his death was caused by the ingestion of arsenic, and do not mention the equally relevant fact that arsenic destroys human tissue, and that if one's stomach walls were composed of iron the ingestion of arsenic would have no ill effects.

Other accounts. Other philosophers have given different accounts of why we select certain of the conditions and call them "the cause" while ignoring others. Since we are interested not merely in understanding nature but in controlling it, we are most interested in those factors which we can control or manipulate; and thus,

. . . the cause of an event in nature is *the handle* so to speak, *by which we can manipulate it.* If we want to produce or to prevent such a thing, and cannot produce or prevent it immediately (as we can produce or prevent certain movements of our own bodies), we set about looking for its "cause." The question "What is the cause of an event?" means in this case "How can we produce or prevent it at will?" . . .

This is an extremely common sense in modern everyday usage. The cause of a bruise is the kick which a man received on his ankle; the cause of malaria is the bite of a mosquito; the cause of a

boat's sinking is its being overloaded; the cause of books going moldy is their being kept in a damp room; the cause of a person's sweating is that he has taken aspirin; the cause of a furnace going out in the night is that the draft door was insufficiently open; the cause of seedlings dying is that nobody watered them; and so forth. . . .

A car skids while cornering at a certain point, turns turtle, and bursts into flame. From the car driver's point of view, the cause of the accident was cornering too fast, and the lesson is that one must drive more carefully. From the county surveyor's point of view, the cause was a defective road surface, and the lesson is that one must make skid-proof roads. From the motor manufacturer's point of view, the cause was defective design, and the lesson is that one must place the center of gravity lower.[5]

Mill would say that *all* these conditions are of causal relevance—they are components of that set of conditions which are together sufficient. Collingwood, by contrast, distinguishes between causes and conditions, and would not call the continued operation of gravity a cause at all.

A somewhat different view of the factors we select as being causes is given by H. L. A. Hart and A. M. Honore. They too distinguish causes from conditions, but suggest that we call "the cause" the condition(s) that constitute a *departure from normal functioning.* If there is a railway accident, we may say it was caused by a defective signal or a switchman going to sleep on the job, for these distinguish the case of the accident from the case of normal functioning. We do not mention the weight of the train and the laws of momentum, though these factors are just as essential to the occurrence of the accident, because they are present *both* in cases when accidents occur *and* when they normally do not. "The cause" is what made the difference between this and the usual cases. Different answers may well be

---

[5]R. G. Collingwood, "On the So-called Idea of Causation," *Proceedings of the Aristotelian Society* Vol. 38 (1938-9): 85–108.

given to the question, What was the cause?—depending on what we take the standing conditions to be. A man who has an ulcer eats spicy foods one day and has a painful attack. His wife may give as the cause of the attack the fact that he ate the spicy food, and the doctor may give ulcers as the cause. And both may be right. The wife is asking, "Given that he has ulcers, why did he have the attack today when he usually gets by without one?" And the doctor is asking, "What gave *this* man the attack after eating spicy food when other people don't get it even when they eat such food?" Each answer is correct, but which is selected as the cause depends on what the person takes to be the normal condition. To the wife, her husband's ulcers are "the norm," whereas to the doctor they are not.[6]

Both these views distinguish between causes and conditions, though in different ways. Mill, however, would have rejected both of them. The so-called causes and conditions are all components of a set of conditions which are jointly sufficient for the occurrence, and there is no difference between them as far as causality is concerned; the distinction is only one of practical convenience. Besides, don't we speak of causes even when there is no manipulation-handle? If the arctic seas melted, our coastal cities would be flooded; and the nearer a planet is to the sun, the warmer it is. Aren't there causal relations in these cases, though there is no way we can manipulate them to achieve the effects described? And as for deviation from the norm, we can ask for the cause of a deviation (What caused the train accident?) just as intelligibly as for normal functioning (Why didn't the train have an accident today?). If I am absent from class one day, students are more likely to ask "Why is he absent?" than to ask—when I meet the class as I'm supposed to—"Why is

he here today?" We can ask "How come she's healthy?" as well as "How come she's sick?"

Plurality of causes. Several conditions together make up a sufficient condition; but is each of these always a necessary condition? Perhaps conditions 1, 2, and 3 are together sufficient to produce E; but perhaps conditions 4, 5, and 6 are also together sufficient to produce E, even when 1, 2, and 3 do not occur. Then we have *two* sufficient conditions for E. Or perhaps there is an overlapping: 1, 2, and 3 may be sufficient for E, and 1, 2, and 4 are also sufficient for E. In that case, conditions 1 and 2 are necessary, for E does not occur without them, but conditions 3 and 4 are not, since sometimes E does occur without them.

It certainly seems as if the same effect may occur from a different set of conditions. If we want to remove a stain from a garment, we can do so by using gasoline or carbon tetrachloride or any of a number of other chemical reagents. We can produce certain organic compounds either by inducing chemical reactions in living organisms or by synthesizing them out of their elements or simpler compounds. You can get expelled from school by writing inflammatory material in the college newspaper, by planting a bomb under the president's desk, and so on.

On the other hand, it often happens that the plurality of causes is only apparent. (1) Sometimes *too much* is included in the statement of the sufficient condition. If pulling the plug is sufficient for the radio not to play, then pulling the plug *plus* the moon being full is also sufficient; every time you pull the plug and the moon is full the radio stops playing. But we do not consider the moon a causal factor because the radio stops playing when you pull the plug whether the moon is full or not. In this example the irrelevance of the moon is easy to see, but other examples are not quite so obvious. Thus we may say that billiard ball

[6]H. L. A. Hart and A. M. Honore, *Causation in the Law.* Oxford: Clarendon Press, 1964.

B is caused to move in a certain direction not merely by being struck by billiard ball A but by being struck with your elbow, or by jiggling the table, or by a slight earth-tremor. But this can hardly be considered a genuine case of plurality of causes. What is necessary and sufficient for the movement of the ball in this direction is that a certain degree of force be applied upon it in that direction; it does not matter who or what wields the force, and therefore no mention of these particulars need be made in a list of the conditions on which the event depends. Thus, in the numbered conditions we considered two paragraphs earlier, to include 3 and 4 as conditions may be including too much; what really does the causing is a component, C, that 3 and 4 have in common. If this is so, plurality has been eliminated, because the total set of conditions is in both cases 1, 2, and C. (2) Sometimes the same *general type* of effect can be brought about by different means: a house may burn down as a result of lightning, an overheated furnace, arson, and so on. If "house burning down" is the effect, then it can certainly be brought about by different sets of conditions. But the insurance inspector who examines the ruins after the fire can often detect the difference between fire-from-lightning and fire-from-overheated-furnace through a careful examination of the ruins. The effect *is* somewhat different in the two cases, and "destruction by fire" is a blanket term that covers many different specific effects. Perhaps if we broke down the effects as carefully as we do the causes, we would end up with no plurality of causes at all.

We shall not attempt any verdict on the issue of plurality of causes. This is a matter for scientists to decide empirically; our only concern is to be clear what the term means. We shall leave open the question of plurality of causes. When we say that C, the cause, is sufficient for E, the effect, we shall not be committing ourselves about whether it is the only set of conditions that is invariably followed by E.

Other Aspects of Causality

Several objections have been suggested to the definition of "cause" as sufficient condition other than those already considered.

Causation and contact. "But C can't cause E unless C *acts on* E. We don't say that the first billiard ball striking the second causes the second ball to move just because the one event is regularly followed by the other. We say it because the first ball *hits* the other, and thus *acts on it,* imparting its motion to it. When you pour hot water in a vessel of cold water, the temperature of the water in the entire vessel soon becomes uniform, because, we believe, millions of tiny molecules are constantly striking each other, and the faster-moving (hot) ones impart their motion to the slower-moving (cold) ones until the temperature reaches an equilibrium. You can't have causation unless one entity acts on another. Regularity is not enough."

But what of cases in which we don't know whether there is such action by contact? That it occurs in the case of molecules is after all theory and not observed fact. The transmission of sound through air or water can be explained in a similar way, by molecules striking each other. But what about light and heat? These are transmitted without any air particles at all, or any other kind of particles that we know of. When the part of the earth exposed to sunlight becomes warmer, surely there is a causal relation between the sun being above the horizon and earth becoming warmer; but what strikes what to achieve this? There are "photons of light," we say; but since the photons are not matter, should this be described as striking? The fact is that the sun rises and the earth becomes warmer; is there any doubt of a causal relation between these two? We may hypothesize an "ether," a medium through which the sun's light acts on the earth (see p. 182), in order to *explain* the causal relation, but isn't there clearly a causal relation, whether we know there is contact of particles or not?

Again, there is surely a causal relation between the near approach of another planet and the perturbation of the first planet in its orbit. Neptune was discovered as a result of the perturbations in Uranus' orbit. But gravitation seems to operate in empty space even if there is nothing at all between the bodies gravitationally affected. Are we still as sure that all causation operates by contact as we are that there is a causal relation between the presence of Neptune and the perturbations of Uranus? Perhaps then the "acting on" requirement is an unnecessary restriction.

Cause vs. explanation. Can we know that C causes E without knowing *why* C is followed by E? Scientists are not content with discovering that there is a causal relation between C and E; they want to know exactly how the causal relation operates—to give an explanation of it in terms of laws or theories. In fact, one might question whether we can be said to know that a junk-food diet causes low tolerance to disease and diminished energy unless we know *why* it does: how the ingestion of some foods, and the lack of other (nutritious) foods, operates in the body to bring about such undesired effects. Do we know that C causes E if we don't know how C operates to produce E? Unless we know (as we already do to a large extent) how a high-sugar high-fat diet affects the arteries and so on, do we know that the bad diet causes the malaise? Don't we have just an apparent constant conjunction which leads us to suspect a causal relation, without yet having shown that there *is* a causal relation?

But surely, one may say, we do. Don't we know that gravity acts on stones to make them fall to earth, even though the whole phenomenon of gravitation is still something of a mystery? And it would seem that there are many cases in which we can say with assurance that C causes E without knowing the whole mechanism by which it works. Physicians have extensive evidence that lithium cures depression, but it is (to date) not clear why. If a person has clairvoyant powers and can always tell detectives where a lost child is, isn't there a causal relation between where the child was hidden and the clairvoyant's vision of where the child is—even though, assuming that this happens, we really have no idea *how* the clairvoyant is able to do this (and neither does the clairvoyant herself)? In the light of such cases it would seem that to discover that C causes E is one thing, and to give an explanation of the process is another—and that sometimes we can assert the first with confidence even though we may know little or nothing about the second.

Causes and correlations. Sometimes one phenomenon is highly correlated with another, and we suspect that there may be a causal relation but can't be sure. For example, when above-ground nuclear tests were conducted in Nevada in the 1950s, their effects were not widely suspected; but 20 years later an unusually high incidence of leukemia occurred among the residents of southern Utah, downwind from the blasts. Did the radiation from the tests cause the leukemia? We tentatively answer yes, although many people get leukemia without much contact with radiation and other people absorb much radiation and don't get leukemia. Statistical correlations may be signposts pointing to causal relations, but they may also be false leads. In the leukemia example we would be inclined to say that the radiation *plus* other factors *X, Y, Z* (having to do mainly with the physiology of the individual) cause leukemia; that in other cases where *X, Y, Z* are not present the leukemia does not develop because the radiation alone is not a sufficient condition; and that in still other cases (plurality of causes?) leukemia develops in the absence of radiation.

Sometimes having typhoid fever causes a patient's death and sometimes not; having the typhoid germ inside one is not a sufficient condition for death. Whether one survives also depends on many other factors, such as how badly one was infected, whether one was in good physical condition (with more resistance to the disease), and even such things as one's mental attitude. Again, singling out a single causal factor is much easier than stating the entire series of conditions which are together sufficient—something nobody is yet in a position to do with regard to effects such as diseases.

Person-to-person causality. Some of those who agree with Hume on "necessary connection" do not share in the Hume-Mill analysis of cause. From what impression, asked Hume, is the idea of cause derived? His answer was that it was derived from impressions of regularity in our experience (constant conjunction). But others have alleged that the impression is of a different sort altogether: the inner impression (experience) of *power*—power to act, to move our limbs, to act on our decisions, to influence others by our action. Suppose I talk you out of an investment you were about to make; don't I know, from just this one instance, that there was a causal relation between my suggestion and your subsequent action? I don't have to experience any regularities or constant conjunctions to know this. Or, I decide to eat a sandwich that you have placed before me; don't I know that the presence of the sandwich, plus my desire to eat it, is the cause (or at least two causal factors) in my actually eating the sandwich? Do I have to eat lots of sandwiches which you place before me, and thus establish a constant conjunction, in order to know this? When it comes to volitions—actions of my will—I don't need any correlations or conjunctions.

And the fundamental, primordial, root idea of causality derives from my inner experience of power to influence.

Still, aren't these attributions of causality all based on certain generalizations—not about anything as specific as sandwiches, but generalizations found to be true in countless previous instances, such as that if I am hungry and there is food I will usually eat it? And as for the power of my will to influence the motions of my body, don't we have to *observe* what my will can achieve? I may climb on the roof and decide to fly through the air like a bird, but my inner feelings of power to do this (which many children have) is soon undermined by the facts: I take a nasty fall. Don't I have to discover through experience that I can bend my legs backwards (from the knee) but not forwards? Don't we have to discover what our powers are by the same methods of trial and error that we use to find causal relations in external nature? How do I discover that I can cause my arm to rise? Only by trying and succeeding. When I decide to raise my arm, it goes up; but if I decide to move my liver, it doesn't budge. I can jump 3 feet but not 300 feet; I can discover only by experience that I have the power to do the one but not the other. Children often have the sense of immense power or ability—"I can do anything"—but only experience will reveal to them whether they actually do have that power or ability. It would seem, then, that volition is simply just another example of causality in terms of necessary and sufficient condition. Hume wrote,

A man, suddenly struck with palsy in the leg or arm, or who had newly lost these members, frequently endeavours, at first to move them and employ them in their usual offices. Here he is as much conscious of power to command such limbs, as a man in perfect health is conscious of power to actuate any member which remains in its natural state and condition. . . . Neither in the one case nor in the other, are we ever conscious of any . . . necessary connexion. We learn the influence of our will from experience alone, And experience only teaches us, how one event constantly follows another.[7]

2. UNIVERSAL CAUSATION

Does every event that occurs—past, present, future—have a cause? Since we don't yet know what the future will bring, and we are acquainted with only a tiny portion of the present and past of our own world, the earth (not to mention the universe), it would seem that the answer to this question would be a simple "I don't know." We would seem to be in the position of someone who, confronted with a huge bag of a million marbles, is asked after examining five of them and finding them all black, whether all the marbles in the bag will turn out to be black.

And yet, in this scientific age, most people would be inclined to answer a confident yes to this question. Of course, they would say, everything has a cause—it's just that we don't know what all the causes are; but that doesn't mean that they don't exist. Is there anything of which we would be inclined to say that it had *no* cause at all? What would medical researchers trying to find the cause(s) of cancer say to the suggestion, "Perhaps it has *no* cause"? Wouldn't such a person be laughed out of the medical profession?

The view that every event is the effect of a prior set of conditions is called *determinism*. Strictly speaking, determinism says only that everything that happens has some cause or other—it doesn't say what kind. *Theological* determinism says that everything is caused by God. *Scientific* determinism says that everything is caused by prior events and conditions in the natural world, thus excluding supernat-

ural causes. *Mechanistic* determinism is still narrower, saying that everything is caused by prior events and conditions in the *physical* world, thus excluding mental causation.

Scientific determinism acquired its plausibility first in the disciplines of physics and astronomy. With the formulation of Newton's Law of Gravitation and his three laws of motion, the motion of the stars and planets were shown—or so it seemed—to be totally determined by prior conditions. If you knew the positions of every particle of matter, and the laws of their operation, you could predict the subsequent positions of every particle. Their present configuration was entirely determined by their past configurations, in accordance with Newton's laws.

Determinism, or course, is not the same as predictability. For example, (1) you might offer a prediction which turned out to be right, but without any scientific basis for the prediction. Or (2) you could believe all events were determined and yet not be able to predict future events because many of the causal factors are still unknown. This indeed is the position of most scientists. We can predict eclipses thousands of years in advance, but we can't predict with reliability next week's weather (but—we say—that's because we don't know all the relevant causal factors, such as what's occurring right now in the upper atmosphere). Nevertheless, if our predictions are borne out time after time, and if they are made on the basis of observation and calculation, we become increasingly convinced that we have hit upon the relevant conditions.

The laws of chemical combination have come to be viewed as deterministically as physics. Indeed, all of chemistry came to be reduced to physics, being explained in terms of atomic theory. The causes of chemical combinations (what happens when you combine what with what) are now as well established as anything in science, and atomic theory explains why they occur as they do.

In biology determinism was less obvious, as

---

[7]David Hume, *An Enquiry Concerning Human Understanding,* part VII.

long as the changes occurring in organisms were not understood. Darwin's epoch-making work *The Origin of Species* (1859) went a long way toward filling the gap in our understanding of the determining factors in biology: mutations, the struggle for survival, the survival of the fittest. What Darwin outlined in considerable detail were the causes of the *survival* of living things, not their *arrival.* The origin of life in a world that previously contained no organisms was still a mystery. In this century, however, there have been enormous strides in molecular biology. The gene is simply a large molecule whose changes occur entirely in accord with laws of chemistry, and more causes of hereditary conditions are discovered every year.

Determinism has also become dominant in psychology. Behavioral psychology has made great progress in discovering and predicting how animals and even human beings will behave, given certain stimuli. Countless psychological events—which seemed either causeless or of unfathomable cause, such as the many varieties of "abnormal" behavior, from the psychopathic to the psychotic—have been explained in terms of repression, sublimation, displaced aggression, and other forms of unconscious motivation. By such means psychiatrists can separate out these various conditions and, to a large extent, predict how a patient will behave under given circumstances. All the above phenomena were a seemingly impenetrable mystery a century ago. In human behavior the causal factors are extremely numerous, so no exact predictions are possible as in Newtonian physics; yet progress made in tracing the causes of human behavior has been enormous. It would seem, then, that determinism has pretty much won the day—that where we do not yet know the cause of something this is not because no cause exists, but because it has not yet been discovered. Determinism—the Principle of Universal Causation—would seem, then, to be an *empirical truth* about "the way the world works."

Is it immune to disproof? But now let us notice something that may have escaped our attention. As more and more causes were discovered, we gradually came to view the Principle of Universal Causation in a different light. It started out as an empirical law, a law that might be true or might not, depending on the outcome of investigations. But increasingly it has come to behave more like a *necessary truth.* If we find a cause, we say that this discovery further confirms the principle; but if we fail to find a cause, we say that this is only because we haven't looked hard enough—it's there to be found, but we have not yet unearthed it. But if we can always say that, how could the principle ever be disproved? Isn't it a strange principle which every positive instance confirms, but which negative instances *fail to disconfirm?* No matter how long we fail to find the causes of something, we can always say—and usually do—not that it is causeless but that it has a cause which is thus far unknown to us. If the principle is an empirical one this should arouse our suspicions. We are in danger of running with the hare and hunting with the hounds.

Consider an ordinary empirical generalization like "All crows are black." If we discover only *one* albino crow, this refutes the generalization. But the Principle of Universal Causation doesn't seem to operate in this way. Finding causes confirms the principle, but failure to find them does not disconfirm it—we only take refuge in saying, "The cause is there, it is just not yet discovered." Empirical discoveries count in favor of it, but no empirical discoveries count against it. What kind of principle is it that can be confirmed by empirical observation but not disconfirmed by them?

For example: If two sets of causal factors are identical, we say the effects will be identical. Two nonidentical causes could of course lead to nonidentical effects: If, for instance, you set up a laboratory experiment differently the second time, it might have a very different outcome. But if you set it up *exactly* the same way—with all the factors identical—then, we say, the outcome of the experiment would be the same.

But how do we know this? Suppose that the causal factors in our imaginary experiment were, to the best of our knowledge, exactly the same both times, but the effects were markedly different, and even after repeated checking we still found no difference in the causes. The two laboratory setups were identical; yet the experiments turned out differently. Would we now say, "Well, I suppose the principle has been refuted in this case, just as the discovery of black swans refuted the belief that all swans are white"? It is very unlikely that we would say this. Instead, wouldn't we say, "There is a difference in the causal factors somewhere, to produce such different effects—some subtle difference we haven't discovered. But there *must have been* a difference, otherwise the effects wouldn't have been different." And what justifies this *must?* Why do we say that if causes are the same, effects *must* be the same—why don't we even admit the possibility that unlike effects could originate from like causes?

No matter what happens, it would seem that no exceptions need be admitted to the Principle of Universal Causation. But then, aren't we treating the principle as if it were a necessary truth, rather than an empirical truth refutable by observation? If you thought that two clocks—in the same room, in the same atmospheric conditions, of the same make and construction—were identical in every respect, and it developed that one kept perfect time and the other started to run fast, you would conclude that there was some difference in the causal conditions; and, supposing that you found it, that difference would be perhaps in some detail of their construction which you had previously overlooked. After some experience with this we say—even without further evidence—that if there is a difference in the effects there must have been a difference in

the causes. *We take the very fact of difference in effects as proof of difference in causes.*

Although we may never find identical causes, do we not believe that *if* identity in the causes were attainable, there would be identity in the effects too? A girl is bouncing a ball against a wall, catching it, and bouncing it back again. The ball never lands at the same spot on the wall twice; nor does it ever bounce back to her in quite the same way on any two occasions; every time the direction, speed, and distance are slightly different. But do we not believe that *if* on any two occasions the conditions could be made exactly the same (identical)—speed, direction, point from which it is thrown, etc.—then it would bounce against exactly the same spot and rebound back to her in exactly the same way? Or, if you could only throw the dice tonight in exactly the same way you did last night, with each die in exactly the same position, then surely the same sevens you threw last night would turn up again. If something else turns up this time, isn't it because some of the conditions are different? The conditions are so intricate that we cannot be sure that they are even approximately the same on any two successive throws; but *if* they were exactly the same would not the same thing have happened?

Suppose now that we have submicroscopic eyes which can peer into every atom of matter involved in the cause; there is not a single aspect of the cause which is not visible to us. This being done, we find that the causes are identical; yet the effects are different. Would we not have to abandon the principle?

No, we could say, "All *these* conditions are identical in the two cases, but the fact that the effects are different only shows that we haven't included enough conditions. Some hitherto unconsidered factor was different in the two cases, and this difference accounts for the difference in the effects. So we must look around, outside the circle of factors we examined so exhaustively before."

Suppose now that we do this; we look outside the factors we originally considered, and still find no difference. So we look outside this in turn, to still other factors, hoping to find a difference there. Still we find none. We continue this process indefinitely.

Where must we stop in investigating this ever-enlarging circle of conditions? Only with the whole universe. And you could never find the universe as a whole to be in an identical state on any two occasions; *you* at least would be different on the second occasion, since you would remember that the universe had been like this on the previous occasion.

But even waiving this, even assuming that the total state of the universe (you included) is identical on the two occasions, and two non-identical events nevertheless followed, need you take this to be an exception to the principle? You would not have to, even then. One thing would be different, namely that the events took place at *two different times*. And this difference could never be overcome. We could always hold that the mere fact that time had elapsed, and nothing else, was responsible for the difference. (If the two events are imagined as occurring at the same time but at two different places, the same objection can be made about space: The fact of being in two different places, even if all the other conditions were the same, was what made the difference.)

This is not a sort of thing which has ever been held, because in formulating scientific laws it has never been found necessary to introduce such a factor. Always when events were different, some differences could be found (or assumed to exist) in the conditions themselves, *other* than the mere fact of the passing of time. Nevertheless, it is logically possible that the time factor would have to be considered in formulating laws; it is conceivable, for example, that water might boil at 212° in 1990, at 213° in 1991, 214° in 1992, and so on, not because of any difference in the conditions other than the lapse of time. This would be a highly peculiar state of affairs, and would excite much surprise simply because as far as we now know nature does not work this way; scientists would cast about desperately in search of conditions to account for the difference in the boiling point *other* than the time factor. But if they were forced to the wall, if they had to abandon the one principle or the other, the universal-causation principle or the time-makes-no-difference principle, they might well abandon the time-makes-no-difference principle. They would rather say that *the mere fact that time had elapsed* caused the difference between E_1 and E_2 than say that E_1 and E_2 were different although there was *no* cause for the difference.

What, then, is the status of the principle? Let us consider some alternatives open to us on this issue.

1. "The principle is analytic." But this won't do. "Every *effect* has a cause" is analytic, because an event that had no cause would not be the effect of anything. Effect *logically* presupposes cause. But this is not so with the statement that every *event* (every happening) has a cause; it only says that every event is the result of prior conditions—and there is nothing analytic about this; it seems to be a straightforward statement about the world, about reality.

2. "The principle is a synthetic necessary truth." At last, a real authentic case. But suspicions persist about this alternative; how can something be true *of* the world and not be refutable by experience of the world? Many philosophers have believed (with Kant) in such propositions, and will feel quite comfortable with the addition of this one to the list. But others will try to avoid this alternative if they can. They only feel pushed into this corner because the principle doesn't seem to be empirical but doesn't seem to be analytic either.

3. "The principle is merely an a priori *assumption*"—something which we assume without knowing, something to which we will *admit* no contrary evidence. Consider the case of a patient who says to a physician, "Doctor, I'm dead." "Well, dead men don't bleed, do

they?" "I guess not." The physician pricks him with a pin, and blood flows. The patient replies, "Doctor, I was wrong; dead men *do* bleed." Nothing will interfere with the patient's assumption that he is dead; this remains unquestioned, immune to all contrary evidence.

But surely the universal causation principle is more than mere assumption, something we refuse to deny just out of stubborness. Aren't there good reasons why we came by this principle rather than another one? Aren't there empirical reasons for accepting it—namely, our success in finding causes? Can it be merely an irrational prejudice, or something which we simply refuse to part with even in the face of contrary evidence?

And yet, though empirical observation led us to formulate the principle in the first place, it seems that no amount of empirical evidence would force us to reject it. We might keep on embracing it no matter what we found in nature. Suppose that tomorrow morning things began to happen very differently from the way they do now—that sometimes stones fall and sometimes they just disappear into the air; sometimes drinking water slakes our thirst and sometimes it kills us; sometimes cats bark and dogs meow; sometimes tables turn into frogs and wasps into pillowcases, with no apparent rhyme or reason. Would we now have to abandon the principle? No, we could say, "Even when the effects seem to be the same, they don't seem to depend on any uniform set of causes that we can locate—but don't worry, they're there, they're just too complex or subtle for us to discover them any more." Even in a chaotic universe we *could* still hold on tenaciously to the principle.

The principle as a rule of scientific procedure. In the light of apparently contrary evidence, we could *preserve* the principle, or we could *abandon* it. Such language makes it seem to depend on what we choose to *do*, not on what the world is like—and isn't that what we

were trying to discover. Isn't it a matter of what is *true,* not a matter of what we choose to adopt?

But let us consider the possibility that the principle is precisely that—not something true or false, and thus not a proposition at all; not something we learn from the world, but something we *bring* to the world; something that it is up to us to adopt if we choose, and to abandon if we choose.

Adopting is something we *do*. We can adopt, for example, a rule of behavior, a practice, a method of doing things. An accepted rule of baseball is "The batter may not have more than three strikes." Presumably it was adopted because its inclusion among the rules of baseball made baseball a more interesting or challenging game. The rule could be changed—as some rules are for various reason—but in any case the rule itself is neither true nor false. The Principle of Universal Causation might then be considered a kind of *rule of the scientific game,* a rule whose adoption makes the game more fruitful, or yields some other desired result. What we justify is not the rule itself but our *adoption* of the rule; and the rule can be adopted (not as true, but as fruitful) or rejected (not as false, but as not worth the trouble to continue with it).

There are numerous occasions on which this kind of thing is done. When a psychiatrist is speculating on why a patient consistently indulges in certain types of self-damaging behavior, he may suspect in case after case that in spite of what the patient says, in spite of all her protestations of how miserable her behavior makes her, she is getting something out of it, some psychological payoff for herself. She is attracted only to men who are helpless in some way, whom she has to take care of; she doesn't find appealing men who are capable and self-assured, but only those who provide the opportunity for her to assuage her guilt at not caring for her late mother. This confirms the therapist's initial suspicion that "she's getting something out of it, in spite of her denials.'' Next he has a patient who every week or so inflicts severe cuts on himself with a knife. The result is painful, yet he keeps on doing it. Why engage in such self-destructive behavior? The patient, an adopted son, found in childhood that the father preferred his natural children to his adopted one, and hated and resented the father for this. The father tried his best to be impartial, but his actual attitude came through to the boy nonetheless; and his father's advice about how to be a good citizen and respected member of the community was (so to speak) turned on its head: As he grew up, the adopted son became the neighborhood rebel, setting fires, throwing constant fits of temper, upsetting the household, anything to displease his father. Now in adulthood the self-mutilation serves two purposes at once. It becomes a way of "getting even" with the father by doing something of which the father strongly disapproved, and at the same time it becomes a way of making expiation for his juvenile pranks that he caused his father so much grief. Instead of his father punishing him, he now punishes himself, in a manner that still turns the tables on his father's advice and training. Thus, the psychiatrist thinks to himself, "So there was a payoff—deep down he gets a satisfaction from it, he is simultaneously expiating his sins and hurting his father at the same time." And so, with one case after another, the psychiatrist arrives at the generalization, "There's always some psychological payoff to the behavior—and until I've discovered what it is, I haven't cracked the case."

The psychiatrist, having arrived inductively at this psychological principle (one version of "psychological egoism"), may accept it as true; since, in his view, it has turned out to be true in so many observed cases, he believes it is also true of the unobserved cases. If there appear to be exceptions, these can be explained away. If some self-sacrificing person helps a stranger out of moral conviction ("It's my duty to do so"), many moralists would hold that this is a victory of duty over desire—

that duty does sometimes win; in this case there is no psychological payoff, only a victory of moral principle. But the psychiatrist, with his successful background using the principle of psychological egoism, will still look for a psychological payoff, and even if he doesn't find it he will say there is one that he hasn't yet discovered. At this point he has deserted the empirical grounds with which he began: Psychological payoff has now acquired the status of an a priori truth. Or perhaps he is simply *positing* it as a basic principle on which he can fruitfully analyze all future cases: "I consider this basic," he may say, thus making it immune to refutation by experience, interpreting every case in terms of it. Or he may simply *adopt* it as a rule of his therapeutic practice: a rule whose adoption is justified by his past successes in using it—not an arbitrary or capricious rule picked out of a hat, but a rule whose adoption is justified by its fruitfulness in "cracking cases." The psychiatrist may not know—he may not have asked himself—which of these things it is; they are, after all, closely related, and he is not a philosopher who has learned to make fine epistemological distinctions. But at some point or other he has come to consider his principle *immune to refutation*— either as a necessary truth, or as an axiom of his psychological theory, or as a rule of procedure in his practice.

Something like this may have occurred in the case of the Principle of Universal Causation. Heady with its success, scientists may have come to consider it immune to refutation—an a priori truth, or an unquestioned axiom, or a procedural rule in their investigations. And perhaps there are still more factors involved—a *suggestion* ("Let's find more causes") or a *hope* that more conditions will be found on which events depend, or even a bit of *wishful thinking* (whistling to keep your courage up when investigations repeatedly fail to reveal causes). Whatever the admixture, the universal-causation principle has been adopted not as a true description of the universe (which would have to be retracted if the universe turned out to be different), but as a kind of rule which one can continue to employ no matter what kind of phenomenon comes along.

A rule, of course, can be *abandoned* if it no longer appears worth preserving: Suppose that one time you let go of your pencil and it drops to the floor; you do it again, but the second time it flies in to the air; the third time it changes into an elephant; the fourth time it disappears completely without a trace; the fifth time it hits you in the nose and rebukes you for letting it go; and so on. Suppose this happened not only to the pencil but to countless other things as well, so that you could no longer discover any uniform conditions on which events depended. It would still be open to you to say, "There are still causal conditions for each one of these events, but they are so tremendously complex that I haven't found them. Causes still exist; they have just become hard to find." But we could also *abandon* the principle—not that we would now say it was false (as a procedural rule, it is neither true nor false); we might simply abandon the game as not worth the effort. Causes would no longer be worth tracking down. We would abandon the principle as we might abandon a mine—not because we were convinced that it contained no more gold but because of a conviction that, whether it did or not, the gold was so minute in amount or so thinly scattered or so hard to reach as to make it not worth the mining. Our abandonment would then express the resolve, "Let's give it up."

A return to the empirical interpretation. We have just described a transition that can, and sometimes has, been made regarding the universal-causation principle (as well as other principles employed in science). The move from a straightforward empirical interpretation, to an a priori interpretation, to some nonpropositional interpretation is usu-

ally made without full awareness of how the status of the principle has gradually shifted.

But, of course, we do not have to take these steps. In spite of the temptation to make the principle immune to empirical refutation, we *can* stick to our guns and maintain the original empirical nature of the principle. We believe, for example, that there are causal conditions for a lightbulb going on or off, and we believe we know what they are. We press the button and the light goes on; we press it the other way, and it goes off. But this of course isn't the sole causal condition, since it doesn't always happen this way. Sometimes we press the "on" button and the light doesn't go on—but then we find that the bulb has burned out, we replace it with another bulb, and it goes on. Or the "on" button is pressed, the bulb is *not* defective, but the light still doesn't go on. So we examine the wiring and find a short somewhere or a disconnected wire; we repair this and the light works again. There is a finite set of conditions on which the functioning of the bulb depends. But now suppose that, starting immediately, the light went on and off with no apparent dependence on these conditions. Sometimes the bulb lights up and—just as unpredictably—sometimes it goes off again, and we can't find any conditions on which it depends. Sometimes it suddenly shines even when the wires are disconnected, or when all the electric power has gone off in the neighborhood during a windstorm. Puzzled and astonished, we try other means of control: Maybe it depends on the time of day, or the moisture in the air, or the temperature of the room, or whether there are living organisms within four feet of it, and so on; a group of electrical engineers is called in, and they can make no sense of it. The bulb goes on and off quite unpredictably, in serene independence of any conditions we can think of. At first, guided by the past, we would say, "It's got to depend on *something*," or "There's got to be a cause, but I have no idea what it is." Yet if it continued to happen—not only to the light-bulb but to many other things—we might start to question the Principle of Universal Causation. We haven't refuted the principle, as was done in the black swan case, but still, we might come to cast some doubt on it—not only on its utility (as the "disease of chaos" spread through the environment), but on its truth. We might well question, in view of such developments, that every event in the universe depends for its occurrence on a definite set of conditions.

Something like this has actually happened in our own century in the science that has most successfully exploited deterministic assumptions, physics. The details are so technical, the equations so complex, that even students of physics do not usually understand them. But the upshot is that certain atomic and subatomic events appear to occur without being determined by any set of prior conditions. Certain atoms, for example, when shot between the poles of a magnet, will be deflected either up or down, but there is no way of predicting which way a particular atom will go. "But that," we might say, "is only because we don't yet know the cause—surely there is one." This, however, is exactly what modern physics (Heisenberg's Principle of Indeterminacy) denies; It is nature that is indeterministic on the subatomic level; it is not merely our knowledge of it that is incomplete. Some physicists have resisted this conclusion—Einstein, among them, said that God does not play dice with the universe—and the matter is still in dispute. But the mere fact that the possibility of a noncausal "particle physics" is admitted, or even considered, indicates that physicists today do not consider the Principle of Universal Causation a necessary truth, nor even a rule-of-the game to be adopted or abandoned.

Perhaps one should conclude that the principle is an empirical one after all, and that science now considers it a false description of nature. Or perhaps one could argue that inde-terminancy on the subatomic level need not mean that such events have no cause, but only that we must conceive of causality in a different way. Every event has a sufficient condition; of any event (call it E) if conditions sufficient for its occurrence had not been present, then E would not have occurred. But when Mill defined "cause" as sufficient condition, he meant that the same conditions that were sufficient to bring about E on one occasion would also be sufficient to bring it about *on all other occasions*. But what if this were not so? What if causes were such that, granted a certain set of conditions, a different outcome occurred each time, or half the time? Then there would be no predicting what kind of E would ensue. And we would no longer be able to *discover* causes, for we can discover causes only by tracing the uniformities in the conditions leading up to the events. We might say, then, that every event has a cause—a set of conditions sufficient to produce it—but that "Same cause, same event" would not be true: the same causal factors might on different occasions lead to very different events. One time the electron goes this way, another time it goes that way—not because its moving in this direction has no cause, but because the same set of conditions doesn't always produce the same effect.

Strictly speaking, this would not be indeterminism—indeterminism is a *denial* of cause (at least for some events); it would be an assertion of universal causation combined with a denial that the same cause always leads to the same effect. This may be a very different kind of universe from the one we are familiar with, but perhaps it is the kind suggested to us in subatomic physics.

It may be that the best that can be done, even in theory, is to formulate *statistical* laws: Forty percent of the time the particle goes this way, 60 percent that way. Scientists have tended to assume that if 40 percent of A is B and 60 percent of A is C, this difference itself must have a cause. If 25 percent of the people with the AIDS virus in their blood come down with AIDS, and 75 percent do not, we believe there is a causal factor present in the one group of cases but not in the other—even though this difference has not yet been discovered. But perhaps in the case of subatomic particles, statistical laws are really the bottom line, and even a complete knowledge of the conditions would reveal no reason for the difference.

These hints of irregularity in the universe— that it is the universe itself that is like this, and not merely that our knowledge is limited—have been a humbling experience. No longer need physicists accept the timeworn view that if you knew all the laws and all the initial conditions you could predict all the future states of the universe. This is not possible if some laws are statistical rather than deterministic. Whether this will ultimately turn out to be true, only the future of science can decide. Meanwhile, that the question is asked at all shows us that—in the science of physics, at least—the Principle of Universal Causation has not after all lost its empirical character. As Nancy Cartwright has put it, "God may have written just a few laws and then grown tired. We do not know whether we are in a tidy universe or an untidy one."[8]

3. DETERMINISM AND FREEDOM

The fascination of determinism for most people lies not in whether it will be accepted as true or false in modern physics, but in the belief that it is incompatible with human freedom: that if people's acts are determined they cannot be free. Since the word "determined" sounds as if what is determined is somehow foreordained or "in the cards" no matter what we do, it is preferable to substitute the

more neutral word "caused." Determinism, however, is simply the belief that everything that happens is caused, including human decisions and choices; and the conclusion often drawn is that if this is so, no one is ever free, because what a person does and thinks and feels is the inevitable result of prior causal factors.

The Idea of Freedom

But this conclusion is highly controversial. Determinism is often confused with another view, *fatalism,* according to which our efforts are always futile because whatever happens will happen regardless of what we do; our own efforts never make a difference in the outcome. Thus, one might argue, "If I'm fated to pass this exam, I'll pass it whether I study or not; if I'm fated not to pass it, I'll fail it whether I study or not; therefore there is no point in my studying." Besides being an excuse for inaction, the argument is quite clearly mistaken. That human efforts *do* make a difference is as plain an empirical fact as found anywhere. Some students pass courses because they study for them, and if they didn't study they wouldn't pass; whether they pass or fail depends on their efforts. Whether you drive the car downtown depends on whether you take the wheel; whether a person lives or dies may depend, in a crisis, on what you do or don't do. Such plain facts of experience can hardly be denied.

Determinism, by contrast, only says that whatever happens has a cause. *You* are the cause of many things—your studying helps you to pass the course. That you decide to study doubtless has a cause, too, but in any case the outcome does depend on you—if it weren't for you, the outcome would be different. And in that sense, surely, we are free. We are often free to do X or not to do X, as we choose. And what more freedom (one may ask) could we desire to have? You prefer to do

---

[8]Nancy Cartwright, "The Truth Doesn't Explain Much," in *How the Laws of Physics Lie* (Cambridge: MIT Press, 1983), p. 49.

X and, as a result of the decision, you do X; isn't that a clear case of being free? So what is the threat that determinism is alleged to present to human freedom? It can hardly be doubted that we make choices and act on them, and that we often do so as a result of deliberation, and that we can walk to the window if we want to or stay seated at the desk if we want to. Isn't this freedom?

The words "free" and "freedom" are not very clear-cut in their meaning. (1) Freedom is most often opposed to *coercion*—as when someone in a position of power tries to impose his will on you by force or threat of force. If someone hits you over the head, that is his act and not yours. But if he robs you at gunpoint he is using coercion to make you do what he wants; you would not have given up your money but for his threat. Ordinarily one would say in that situation, "I didn't give up my money freely—I was coerced." Even so, however, another person might say, "When presented with the threat, you freely chose to give up your money rather than your life; all the gunman did was *restrict* the choices open to you, but *you* still chose."

As a rule we would adopt the first of these usages; but the limits of coercion (hence lack of freedom) are somewhat vague. Has a man coerced his wife if he gradually drives her mad? Has someone coerced you when he exerts psychological pressure on you but doesn't lay a hand on you? Is a woman coerced when a man of powerful personality turns her to jelly and "she just can't say no" to whatever he commands? Has a person been coerced when she has been conditioned without her knowledge by the contents of a tape, continuously played while she was asleep? Are you coercing someone when you know "what buttons to press" to make him do your will, against his own better judgment?

There are many shades of meaning here, on the basis of which the distinction between freedom and coercion can be drawn. Never-

theless, everyone recognizes some difference. If a judge in divorce court asked a woman, "Did you freely marry this man?" and she said, "No, he threatened me with violence if I didn't," this would be accepted as a case of coercion. But if she said, "No, I married him because I had a strong desire to do so," the judge would say, "Then you married him of your own free will." If a philosopher then said, "No, she lacks freedom in both cases because all events are determined, and there is no such thing as free will," everyone would sense that some mistake was being made, a distinction ignored—a distinction which is of great practical interest and importance. The law usually excuses you from doing an illegal act if you were coerced, but not if you weren't. All actions may be caused, but not all of them are coerced.

(2) Some would say that you are free if there are no *external* constraints on you—no one is forcing you or threatening you, no one is making you act contrary to your own judgment. But what of *internal* constraints? A drug addict is sometimes called the "slave of his own impulses"; although no one is forcing him to take drugs, he finds the taking of them irresistible; it is as if some irresistible force or power had taken hold of him, forcing him to do what he does. Coercion is from the outside, compulsion is from the inside; isn't compulsion also lack of freedom? Some would say that a powerful compulsion constitutes lack of freedom; others would say that you are still free, but some things are (for you) extraordinarily difficult to do.

Consider the following possible situations. (1) A hypnotist says to his subject, "When you come out of your trance you will say 'It's hot in here,' go to the window and open it." And this is exactly what the subject does when she comes out of her trance. To her, her action seems as free as any she has ever performed; but to all onlookers it is obvious that she is acting under posthypnotic suggestion, and they would not call it free. (2) If someone unknown to you is manipulating electrodes attached to your brain, causing you to have desires you would not otherwise have, this also would be tampering with your freedom. The causal influence did not come from you; your desires did not manifest themselves freely because your decisionmaking process was not involved. Your brain was manipulated by others, and so your actions were not free. (3) What would one say of a person who was born and raised in Catholicism, who had been heavily indoctrinated all her life, was pressured by her parents to enter a convent, and later chose to become a nun? Was this a free choice on her part? Some would say yes, it was *her* decision. Others would say no, it was not a free choice (perhaps a "semifree" choice?) because of the constant and powerful influence exerted on her by others, and because of the consequences (in grief to her family, and so on) of her failing to do as they had constantly entreated her to do. Enormous and unremitting family pressures led her to make the decision, perhaps almost as inexorably as if she had been forced at gunpoint. Some persons, though far from all, would say that her decision wasn't "really free." Where the pressures are so great as to almost forestall (render impossible?) any other decision, some persons would call this a lack of freedom, even though the person herself did make the decision.

(3) Thus far we have described only *negative* freedom—freedom *from* those causal factors which interfere with deliberative and choice-making faculties which in daily life we call "the exercise of freedom." In this sense, we are free if no such interference occurs. But we also speak of freedom *to* do certain things—this is called *positive* freedom. You are free to walk, but not to fly in the air like a bird. You are free to bend your legs backwards from the knee—that is, you can do it if you choose to—but not free to bend them forwards. In this sense, freedom has to do

with *ability*. The two senses are related, of course. If you are free *from* your chains, you are free *to* walk about as you weren't before.

Some philosophers have deplored this double sense of the word "freedom," especially the confusion that results from not distinguishing them from one another. For example, (1) one may object, "It's true that you aren't free to fly through the air like a bird, but is *that* a restriction on your freedom?" To which others would reply, "Yes, it is—it's something I am not free to do, no matter how much I want to. It's true that nobody is forcing me against my will, but just the same I do not have the ability to do something I would very much like to be able to do—just as a person whose legs are paralyzed is not free to walk, and isn't *that* a lack of freedom?" (2) Am I free to spend my winters in the south of France? I am, in the sense that nobody is stopping me, nor threatening me, nor holding a gun to my head. But I am (at least at present) not free *to* do it, because I don't have the money. Others would respond that this is not really lack of freedom, only lack of ability. "Everyone has a limited range of choices," they would say. "What do you want, freedom to do without air and water and fly through the galaxy like a space ship? Having a smaller number of alternatives open to you isn't lack of freedom. You lack freedom only when someone (including perhaps your own unconscious impulses) is trying to make you do something against your will."

It is important that these senses at least be distinguished. When the dictator of a totalitarian nation promises his people freedom, they normally take this to mean freedom from dictatorial control over their lives. If he promises them wealth, which involves the ability to do things they couldn't do without wealth, that at least is a very different kind of promise. "I'm more free if I'm wealthy" is true in the sense that with wealth I am able *to* do things that I couldn't otherwise do; but even with wealth I may not be free *from* the dictator's orders; I would like to make my own decisions without interference, but I cannot do this because he coerces me—he stops me from doing things (like speaking my mind) which, if left to my own free choice, I would do.

Nor is this the end of distinctions that can be made about freedom. Isn't a dog free to roam about when it is not chained? "Animals like to roam about freely," we say. On the other hand, many persons would say creatures that are incapable of thought and deliberation cannot be said to possess freedom. Being free involves not only doing things you want to do (first-order desires) but also being able to reflect and change the wants that you have (second-order desires). The addict desires drugs, but he may also desire *not* to desire them; whereas the animal has no capacity to desire any change in its desires.

This is far from being a complete list of the senses of the word "freedom"—or, we may prefer to say, of ways of talking about freedom. There is some basis for all of them in our common usage of language. We need not choose among them, saying "This is freedom but that is not"; what is needed is to keep the various meanings clearly in mind so that we don't confuse them with each other. In all the cases we have discussed, there is a difference between being free and not being free, and we can point to cases of the one and to cases of the other. Volumes have been written on this issue without ever mentioning the Principle of Universal Causation. Indeed, numerous philosophers have said that the issue of causation is simply irrelevant to the issue of freedom.

Suppose now that someone has had a course in philosophy and says, "I don't mean anything of these things when I talk about freedom. What I mean by 'freedom' is *lack of causation*. If everything we do has causes, we're not free. Freedom exists only to the extent that some of our actions are not caused."

Indeterminism is the view that not every event is caused. What impact should this view have on the idea of freedom?

Indeterminism

Indeterminism does not say that *no* events have causes; such a view would be too obviously false to consider. Most events do have causes—possibly everything in the nonhuman realm. Even in the human realm, most events are caused by prior conditions: Your knee injury was caused by a fall. Likewise, the motion of your knee in response to a tap (the "patellar reflex") was also caused—as are all the things that *happen to* you, as opposed to the things that you *do*. It is only in the realm of *human action* that the indeterminist presses his case. In the actions that I initiate—in which I am active (not in the "reflex actions" in which I am passive)—I may be *influenced* by causal factors which act upon me, but I am not *determined* by them. I am free to act in accordance with my considered choice, and my choice is not completely determined by prior conditions.

In situations of moral choice, says the indeterminist, I may be called upon to choose between good and evil. I can do the good, or I can do the evil; and whichever I do is *up to me*—it is not the inevitable outcome of the huge array of causal factors acting upon me. I can, if I choose, act *contrary* to the sway of these factors. A person who had complete knowledge of my past would not be able to predict what I would do in this case, because this is a choice that I initiate, and in which I can transcend the sway of causality upon me. To say anything else would be to make nonsense of moral choice. If what I do is the inevitable outcome of the entire set of prior conditions, then I deserve neither praise nor blame for what I do, no more than a stone deserves praise or blame for rolling down a hill. In moral choice at least I *transcend causality*. I initiate something new in the world, which is not totally a product of prior conditions. I make the choice. I initiate my own actions. And I can be praised or blamed accordingly. Inderterminism is a moral requirement, if moral concepts are to have any meaning. Morality presupposes freedom, specifically the freedom to transcend causality.

In the situation of moral conflict, I (as agent) have before my mind a course of action X which I believe to be my duty; and also a course of action, Y incompatible with X, which I feel to be that which I most strongly desire. Y is, as it is sometimes expressed, "in the line of least resistance" for me—the course which I am aware I should take if I let my purely desiring nature operate without hindrance. It is the course towards which I am aware that my *character,* as so far formed, naturally inclines me. Now, as actually engaged in this situation, I find that I cannot help believing that I *can* rise to duty and choose X; the "rising to duty" being effected by what is commonly called "effort of will." And I further find, if I ask myself just what it is I am believing when I believe that I "can" rise to duty, that I cannot help believing that it lies with me here and now, quite absolutely, which of two genuinely open possibilities I adopt; whether, that is, I make the effort of will and choose X, or, on the other hand, let my desiring nature, my character as so far formed, "have its way," and choose Y, the course "in the line of least resistance.[9]

Determinism as Compatible with Freedom

The determinist, however, presents some serious objections to the indeterminist's account.

1. In the first place, is there any evidence that some human actions are uncaused? We can't be said to *know* that all events, including human actions, are caused, but doesn't all the evidence point in that direction? Is there any evidence at all for indeterminism in human events? There are no events *known not* to be

caused; there are only events *not known* to be caused—which is quite a different thing. As long as some events are not known to be caused, indeterminism has not been disproved; but on the other hand, where is the evidence in its favor? What evidence we have for indeterminism in the case of submicroscopic entities seems to have little indeed to do with the causation on a macroscopic scale, where billions of molecules are involved, and in this area there is no evidence for indeterminism whatsoever.

2. One may "feel free" and conclude that indeterminism is true, but feeling that something is true is no guarantee that it is. "I feel that we'll have snow next week" is no guarantee that we will. Feeling in this sense is simply no guide to knowing what goes on in the world. Anyway, such a conviction involves no denial of determinism. It really *is* up to me whether I get up from this chair right now or whether I remain sitting down. It's *my* decision; who would deny this? But does this show that my getting up is uncaused? On the contrary, pursues the determinist, your having the feeling of "it all depends on me" *itself has causes.* Do you really want to say that having that feeling at a certain moment in your life is causeless, was brought about by nothing—or more accurately, was not *brought about* at all?

3. We constantly assume the truth of determinism in our relations with other people, including our attempts to change their behavior. When you attempt to correct your child's behavior, you hope that the corrective measures you take will *cause* a change in that behavior. If your child's actions were really *causeless,* then you couldn't possibly cause a change in them, which after all is what you hope to do. When attempts are made to rehabilitate a criminal, the attempt is to *cause* a change in the person's behavior, so that he will not repeat his crimes. If he had indeterministic free will and his actions were causeless, there is no way you could influence (cause a change in)

---

[9]C. A. Campbell, "Is 'Free-will' a Pseudo-Problem?" *Mind* (1951): 463.

them. Even if only one percent of his actions were uncaused, there would be that one percent which would be totally beyond the influence of you or anyone else. Is that really what you want?

A person's actions grow out of her character and dispositions; they are the manifestations of that character. There is a causal relation between character traits and resulting actions. How else would we wish it to be? Here is a friend whom you have known for years. Suppose now that this friend were suddenly struck by an attack of indeterministic freedom—that is, the person performed actions which had no cause whatever. They were like bolts from the blue—except that bolts from the blue do have causes. Such an action—or would it even be an action? wouldn't it be just an event that *happened* to her?—would have no roots in her past nature, her formed character, her settled dispositions to action. A reliable and trustworthy friend, performing one of these uncaused "actions," might behave like a fiend. After all, her acts would now (in indeterminism) have no causal basis in her character, and it is for her character that you like and respect her. If the act just popped into existence from nowhere, it would not even be *her* act; it would not originate in *her*. Would *that* be freedom? It seems that indeterminism, a doctrine which was devised for the sole purpose of rescuing freedom, is actually the greatest enemy of freedom. Any attempt to describe an uncaused act is an attempt to describe an act that did not issue from you, had no basis in you, was not caused by you, and for which you could be neither praised nor blamed because it wasn't *your* act at all! Freedom presupposes determinism and is inconceivable without it.[10]

But, we ask, if everything is caused, aren't our own actions caused? Certainly, the deter-

minist replies, they are; one may indeed be grateful that they are, else we would be stuck with the indeterminist's causeless actions. Indeed, the determinist says, our actions *are* caused—*by us.* "*I* cause my actions" (active voice) and "My acts are caused by *me*" (passive voice) say the same thing. "I caused my actions" is the motto of freedom; "My actions are caused by me" is that of determinism. Determinism is not only compatible with human freedom, according to the determinist, but human freedom is possible only on the assumption that determinism is true.

4. Predictability is no barrier to freedom. Suppose I know you well and you have always been honest in every detail. Suppose that now you are offered a bribe. I predict that you will not accept the bribe, and my prediction turns out to be correct. This doesn't in any way interfere with your freedom: You are still free to accept the bribe or not to accept it—my prediction in no way interferes with *that*. It's just that I know you so well that I will take bets that you will not accept the bribe. This ability to predict that you will act in accordance with the character I have always known you to have, doesn't compromise your freedom in any way. The choice is still yours; all I am doing is predicting which choice you will make.

It's true that I cannot predict all your future actions; I don't know enough about the complex causal factors in your nature, and some hitherto unsuspected aspect of your character might lead you to do something I would never have predicted. But as we have already seen (p. 216), determinism in no way implies predictability. Complete predictability will doubtless never be attained.

Let's assume that Black is killed in a car accident in which Brown, speeding from the other direction, crossed the center lane and crashed into him at 100 miles per hour. Black would not have been at that spot on the highway at that moment had he not been late for lunch because of a misunderstanding about the time he was to see a client. Had he passed

---

[10]On this subject, see the classic essay by R. E. Hobart, "Free-will as Involving Determinism and Inconceivable without It," *Mind* (1934).

at that spot at the usual time he would not have been anywhere near Brown's car. As for Brown, he happened to come home early and overheard what his wife said on the telephone to her secret lover; this infuriated him, and he stamped out of the house and into his car. Ordinarily he would not have been on the highway at this hour, and ordinarily he would not have been careless in driving, but on this occasion his anger took possession of him and he hardly knew what he was doing; he didn't even see Black's car until a split second before he hit him. Even so, the accident wouldn't have occurred if the highway had been crowded—that would have slowed Brown down so that he wouldn't have reached the fatal spot at that moment. But since the highway was fairly clear, he pushed the accelerator to the floorboard, arriving at the spot just in time to collide with Black's car. When you consider the multitude of factors involved, you begin to see all that would have been required to predict the accident: You would have had to know (1) that Brown would come home early and at just the moment when his wife was on the telephone, and (2) that his reaction would be to get into his car and speed—as well as (3) which way he would go and how fast (a couple of seconds' difference in the timing, and the accident wouldn't have occurred). You would also have had to know that Black's secretary would mix up an appointment so that Black's client would come in late, resulting in Black's leaving late for lunch. Not only that, but you would have had to know the position of every car on the highway, for any change in this could have made a difference in the outcome. The number of factors that had to cooperate to produce this event is mind-boggling—what human being could ever be able to predict them all? And yet all of the factors described had causes. Could one really allege that any of the events involved was *un*caused? Could one deny that given the total cause, the effect in question would occur? Couldn't an omniscient being who knew the factors unknown to us—such as Brown's state of mind when he made the discovery about his wife—have predicted the outcome with just as much accuracy as that of which astronomers are now capable in predicting solar eclipses?

"But human beings, unlike inanimate objects and organisms, can act in such a way as to flout other people's predictions. If I predict the occurrence of a solar eclipse, the sun and moon cannot act in such a way as to refute my prediction—that is, they cannot change their behavior *in order to* refute me. Neither can your pet dog or cat do so. But other people can. Thus, if I predict that you will leave the room during the next 5 minutes and tell you of my prediction, you may stay in the room—although you intended to leave—just to prove me wrong." This of course is quite true; only human beings seem to have this ability. But the determinist is not fazed by this fact. "Among the causes of your staying in the room," he will say, "is the fact that I made the prediction that you wouldn't. Knowledge of my prediction was a causal factor influencing your subsequent behavior. In fact, if I knew you much better than I do, I might have been able to predict that you would act as you did just to refute my prediction."

5. Nor is indeterminism a "moral necessity," or a "presupposition of morality"; on the contrary, the determinist considers it but an invitation to chaos. Causeless events would be events which have no roots in the past; causeless events could not be an expression of your will, your temperament, the outcome of your deliberation. They would be "morally meaningless"—no fit subject for praise or blame, or for attribution of good or evil intentions or motives. They would be cut off from all the grounds of moral evaluation that exist. Something that is not *your* act is not something that I can praise or blame *you* for. It is determinism, not indeterminism, that is the prerequisite for morality.

Indeterminism was introduced to provide a

place for freedom in a causal universe. Indeterminists believed that "people are free, and if determinism is true, freedom is impossible." But now we seem to have reached an opposite conclusion: that if *in*determinism is true, freedom is impossible.

Chance

"We all speak of events occasionally happening by chance. Don't chance events imply indeterminism?" The determinist replies that chance events imply no such thing. However, the word "chance" is ambiguous:

1. Coincidence. It was a coincidence that two fires occurred in the same neighborhood on the same afternoon—that is, there was no causal relation between them, and one fire would have occurred even if the other had not. Nevertheless, each of the separate fires had a cause. Similarly, you and I met at a certain supermarket yesterday by chance—that is, neither of us had gone there with the intention of meeting the other. But this in no way shows that there wasn't a cause for your going or for my going.

2. Ignorance of causes. When biologists said that mutations occur by chance, this did not imply that mutations have no causes, only that their occurrence could not be predicted because the causes were not known. When we say that it's a matter of chance which way the football game will turn out, again we do not mean that the outcome of the game will be causeless, but only that we are ignorant of at least some of the many thousands of factors on which its outcome depends.

3. Mathematical probability. If there are 52 cards in the deck, the chances of your drawing the ace of spades is one in 52. Since there are only two faces to a coin, heads and tails, the chance of the next throw being heads is 1 in 2, or 50 percent. We say this even if we are quite ignorant of the actual past behavior of such throws. In mathematical probability we enumerate the possibilities (52, 2), and use that figure as the denominator of a fraction of which the numerator is 1 (assuming that there's just one drawing or one throw). When we say that the outcome of the toss of a coin is a matter of chance, we are not implying that there's no cause for its turning up heads or tails, but that we are ignorant of the relevant factors: the direction of the throw, the energy in the upthrust, how many times the coin will turn over before it hits the table, and so on. But ignorance of causes is not causelessness.

4. Statistical probability. Statistical probability is based upon past frequencies. If 50.2 percent of past human births have been male, the chances of the next child being male is 50.2 percent. If the coin has turned up heads 50 percent of the time, we say that the chances of its turning up heads the next time is 50 percent. This, however, is not the same as mathematical probability, for if the frequency had been different our estimate of the chances would be different. If the coin has always turned up heads in thousands of throws, we would strongly suspect that the coin was "loaded" and use statistical probability to place our next bet—not mathematical probability, which we can estimate even in total ignorance of the qualities of this coin.

5. No cause. Does "chance" ever mean no cause at all? In ordinary life the answer is undoubtedly no. If someone were to tell us that the outcome of the football game or of the next toss of the coin had no cause at all, most people would regard such an assertion with disbelief. But there does remain our previously discussed case of noncausal events on the subatomic level (which we never run into in daily life), the so-called Principle of Indeterminacy. In this rather unique case a physicist might say—asked whether the electron will go to the right or to the left—"it's a matter of chance." And in this rather unique case the reference to chance may be indeterministic—though as we have already observed (pp. 223–24), the correctness of such a statement is a matter of dispute.

Determinism as Incompatible with Freedom

The dispute, however, is far from over. Let us follow an imaginary conversation between a determinist and an indeterminist.

INDETERMINIST: But if everything is caused, then every human action is also caused.

DETERMINIST: Of course. My actions are caused by my choices. I do not say my preferences (I often do what I don't prefer to do) nor even my desires (I sometimes do what I don't desire to do—for example, an unpleasant duty that I hate doing, but do anyway).

I: But if determinism is true, your desires are also caused. The causes no doubt are extremely complex, and often people don't know why they have the desires they do, but (you would say) they are caused anyway. Do you know why you like blue more than green, or why you are irritated by certain kinds of coughs? Isn't what we desire pretty much out of our control? I can *do* as I please, but I can't *please* as I please.

D: Some desires seem to be fairly unchangeable; others are not. A person who has a strong desire for alcohol may not be able to alter this desire in a moment. But he can work on it—sometimes by turning down one drink and then the next until he gets out of the habit; more often by joining Alcoholics Anonymous—until finally, perhaps after years, he no longer has the desire. People do have some control over their desires, and often succeed in changing them over time.

I: But some people have the ability to exercise such a degree of will power, and some don't. You never know till you try, but some people try for years and still don't succeed; they simply lack the ability to change their own fundamental drives, which they didn't choose to have, didn't ask to have, but just find themselves with. They have no more choice in the matter than they had in being born male or female. If their desires determine their choices, and their choices determine their actions, how are they free with regard to their actions if they aren't free with respect to their desires? It looks as if their actions are just "going through the motions"— they think they act freely, but in fact they don't. They feel that they are originating their actions, but in fact (if determinism is true) they are no more free than the hands of the clock are to move over the face of the clock. Their acts are the inevitable product of prior conditions, which in turn are the inevitable product of still prior conditions, and so on. And very soon in this chain of events we reach conditions over which they had no control at all. You couldn't change the conditions in which you were brought up, or which shaped your subsequent personality, or which determined whether you were born male or female and countless other aspects of your genetic makeup and predisposition. Yet all these things shaped you into the person you are now. Your deterministic view is incompatible with freedom after all. William James was right when he wrote:

What does determinism profess? It professes that those parts of the universe already laid down absolutely appoint and decree what the other parts shall be. The future has no ambiguous possibilities hidden in its womb: the part we call the present is compatible with only one totality. Any other future complement than the one fixed from eternity is impossible. The whole is in each and every part, and welds it with the rest into an absolute unity, an iron block, in which there can be no equivocation or shadow of turning.[11]

And Edward Fitzgerald described determinism correctly in *The Rubaiyat of Omar Khayyam* when he wrote,

> With earth's first clay they did the last man knead,
> And there of the last harvest sowed the seed.
> And the first morning of creation wrote
> What the last dawn of reckoning shall read.

D: Such words create a powerful mental picture, which tempt to dominate one's mind when one thinks of determinism. But it is full of mistakes. "Appoint," "decree"— and who does the decreeing? I agree that *if* there is a decreer—God, who makes everything happen as it does, including human action—then your point is well taken. But what you are describing is a special case, theological determinism, in which God causes everything that happens. All I am defending is that everything has *some cause or other.* Nothing need have been "decreed."

Here is another error. In daily life when we say someone is free we never mean "free from causation"—we always assume that events have causes, and nobody in practical life is an indeterminist unless he has been corrupted by bad philosophy. When we say that a person's act is free we mean only that these acts are caused *in a certain way,* for example, not coerced. If I'm able to walk to the door, I'm free to do so, but if I'm paralyzed, I'm not. We distinguish between free and unfree actions constantly, and everybody makes the distinction even though they may not be able to articulate it. I fear that you blur this important distinction entirely.

Similarly, you say that events are an "in-

<hr>

[11]William James, "The Dilemma of Determinism," in *The Will to Believe* (London: Longmans, Green, 1897).

evitable product" and so on. But "inevitable" means *unavoidable.* Death is inevitable, because we cannot avoid dying at some time. But death by a certain disease is avoidable if we don't get exposed to that disease. And by taking care of our health we can usually avoid dying prematurely. Some things can be avoided, some cannot. You lump them all in the same category by calling them all "inevitable." By these semantic maneuvers you caricature my position.

I: I am still right. According to determinism, if E is the effect of D, and D is the effect of C, and you weren't free with respect of C (some fundamental desire), you aren't free with respect to E either.

D: Not so, E is the effect of D *and* lots of other causal factors; D is the effect of C *and* lots of other causal factors. That's why in one person a strong desire to commit a crime still doesn't result in that crime being committed, whereas in another person the same strong desire does result in the crime. Will power, for example, is a factor, and this is something that can be developed with practice and self-discipline. Lots of kids from the slums turn to a life of crime, but some of them also become college presidents and famous writers. You are deluded by this mental picture of a causal chain, with C connected with D and D with E, so there's no escape from E once you have C. But it's not like that at all. It's not like a string of dominos, where, by pushing the first domino, you knock over all the other ones. Human causation is a much more complex affair than that. There is multiple causation at every step. Encouragement, praise and blame, advice, and attempted influences offered by one person can often be causally effective in changing what the other person does—what the other person chooses, and even what the other person desires; but sometimes not—it depends on a huge concatenation of causal factors.

I: But if determinism is true, don't you have

to admit that if a certain complex of causal factors C-1, C-2, C-3, occur, then E, the effect of these factors, will inevitably (and I do mean unavoidably) occur?

D: Not at all. My desire *not* to have E occur may well be a causal factor in E's not occurring. I may not feel like studying, but I wish to avoid failure (E), and so I study anyway. My desires, my strength of will, and countless other things that are, to varying extents, under my control can *change* the outcome. *My will is a causal factor too.* So the outcome is *not* inevitable.

I: But what your strength of will is going to be at a given moment, isn't this, too, determined by various causal factors which aren't under your control? And even if some are in your control, aren't they the effect of prior factors which are *not* under your control? And so, either way, your actions are the effect of a complex of factors which, in the final analysis, you couldn't help. You are what you are because of the causal factors playing on you during your entire preceding life. If determinism is true, your every action, every choice, every desire, is the effect of a host of those prior conditions on which they depend. *Given* those conditions, you *couldn't* have done anything *other* than you did. What you did, you (causally speaking) *had* to do; there was no alternative, if determinism is true.

D: You are misusing words again. First, I didn't *have* to sit down just now; I chose to, and I did so freely, that is, without coercion. If I had really been compelled to do so (for example, by someone pushing me into the chair), then I would admit that my sitting down wasn't done freely. Being coerced is one form of causation, one way of being caused; all coerced acts are caused, but not all caused acts are coerced. I was not coerced just now, my act was free.

Second, neither is it true that I *couldn't*

have done other than I did. I stayed in my chair, but I could have gone to the kitchen to get a drink instead; I almost did, then decided not to. Is there any doubt that I *could* have done it? I couldn't if I were suddenly paralyzed, but since I wasn't, I could have gone. I could at this moment discontinue my conversation with you, but I probably won't. There are lots of things that I *could* do even though I don't do them. Don't say that according to determinism I could never have done anything other than what I did. That is simply not so. To say I can do X is to say I have the ability to do X; I can walk to the kitchen but not fly to the moon. I do have the ability to walk to the kitchen—want to try me out and see? Do you want to take bets on it?

I: I am merely saying that, if your determinism is true, you couldn't have done anything other than what you did in fact do. The past being what it was, you had no choice in the matter; you couldn't have done anything else.

D: Not even if I wanted to? Nonsense. If I'd wanted to open the window, I would have done so. If I'd wanted to stop talking with you, I would have done that. Ordinarily when we say "I could have done that" I mean that I *would* have done that *if* I had chosen to do so. The fact that I didn't choose to doesn't show that I couldn't have done it, if I had chosen to.

I: You could have done it if you had chosen to, I admit. But whether you were going to choose to, was already determined, if your theory is correct.

D: Determined? Determined in spite of me? (That's the misleading overtone that "determined" often carries.) No, determined *through* and *by* me. *I* am a causal factor too! I am not free to have different parents or a different childhood environment (if I could, I might select different ones). But I am free with regard to my *choices*. I chose to do X, and my choice doubtless had causes; but I chose X and as a result I did X. What else would you want? Do you want me to choose X and find myself doing Y instead? Is *that* your idea of freedom? If so, I'm glad I don't have it. I'm glad that choosing X leads to X, and choosing Y leads to Y—and that *my choosing makes a difference* in whether it is X or Y that occurs. What more freedom do you want than that?

I: You keep on evading the consequences of your position. Being just what you are at the moment, with just the factors operating on you that are operating (whatever they are), your deliberations as to what to do could have no other outcome than the one they did (that is, if determinism is true). You only think the outcome could have been different, but that is a delusion.

D: But it could have had a different outcome, if I had wanted it to. That is my freedom.

I: No. You don't see the implications of your own view. Given just *this* set of conditions, you could have done only *this* particular act. If the set of conditions had been somewhat different (for example, if you had desired Y rather than X), then you would of course have done some *other* act. Either way, if determinism is true, you could have done only what you *did* do.

D: You are once again being confused by a misuse of words. You want to say that I *could not* have done anything other than X, the next time, if *all the conditions* leading up to X the second time had been exactly the same. But you forget that one of those conditions is what I choose to do; so I still say, if I had chosen X I would have done X, and if I had chosen Y I would have done Y. I *could have* done either one. What I decide makes the difference. What you want me to admit is something self-

contradictory. You want me to say that I couldn't have acted differently if *all* the conditions had been the same; but you forget that if I had made a different choice, that would have changed the conditions so that they would *not* all be the same the second time. If I had chosen differently, then one of the conditions of action, the choice, would have been different, and so not all the conditions *would* have been the same.

I: Would you be happier if I said, "If all the conditions were the same the second time, you *would* have done the same"?

D: Of course, because "couldn't" implies "wouldn't even if I had chosen to." Sure, if *all* the conditions had been the same the second time I *would* have done the same. When we say, "I wouldn't lend him money a second time, since he didn't return it to me the first time," this may well be true, because not all the conditions are the same; the second time I have the unpleasant memory of his not having honored the loan the first time. But if *all* the factors were the same the second time (which of course they never are), then I don't deny that I'd do the same. Same cause, same effect. If the circumstances were exactly the same, and *I* were the same, I'd do the same thing as before. So what else is new?

I: Do not make light of what you have just admitted. "If I had been different, I would have done something different" is doubtless true. "If the conditions had been different, the outcome would have been different" is true and unexciting; so is "If I had been a different sort of person, I would have acted differently." But what about "I would (or could?) have done something different *even if all the conditions had been exactly the same?*" There are certainly many indeterministic writers who consider this to be the essence of freedom, or at least a necessary condition for it. "We can only retain the ideas of obligation and guilt as properly ethical ideas, if we can also believe in actions which could have been other than they were *although everything else in the universe had remained the same.*"[12] "Moral responsibility requires that a man should be able to choose alternative actions, *everything in the universe prior to the act, including his self, being the same.*"[13] And yet you as a determinist cannot grant this condition and remain a determinist. Given just this set of circumstances, determinism commits you to saying that only this desire will ensue; and given just this desire (plus other conditions that may vary from case to case), just this choice will ensue; and given this choice (plus accompanying conditions), just this action will ensue. Each step is a sufficient condition for the next step. You are still caught in a web of cause and effect, each step being a sufficient condition for the one that follows. And if C is sufficient for D and D for E, then each *will* invariably follow upon the other. That is what "sufficient condition" means. In espousing determinism you are commited to what I have just said.

Determinism and Fatalism

But now we seem to have come back to fatalism—not the superficial brand of fatalism we began with, which said that no matter what you do the outcome will not be different. *That* view, as we saw, is empirically false; Your efforts often do change outcomes. But what if the fact that you choose to exert effort is itself determined by previous conditions?

A: Well, you *made* yourself into the kind of person that exerts effort: You developed the habit in early life, so that you now have the "intestinal fortitude" to do difficult things and not shrink from them. Some people have developed habits of slovenliness, and as a result they are unable to exert effort effectively when the need arises.

B: This is probably true enough; but the fact that in your earlier years you developed the habit of exerting effort and doing difficult things you didn't want to do—this itself had causes, didn't it? And you don't have to go back very far in time before you reach a point where your decisions, your will, your formation of habits, had nothing to do with the matter at all—you had no control over your early environment, and certainly none over your heredity, and that is where the causes of your desires, your habits, your acts of will, ultimately come from. Every event in your life, together with input from the environment, is a sufficient condition for the next event; and that in turn is sufficient for the next one, and so on. And if C is sufficient for E, and C occurs, then E *will* occur—not of logical necessity (for there is no contradiction in saying that C occurs but E does not), but of what we might call *causal* necessity: that the laws of the operation of the universe being what they are, and the initial conditions being what they are, given a certain C, *no outcome other than E is causally possible.*

We already know that the area we ascribe to freedom is quite small; we had no control over when we would be born, or where, or to what parents, rich or poor, or what our early childhood environment would be like, or who lived next door or who our playmates would be, and so on. Given our hereditary makeup and the countless environmental influences playing on us in early childhood, were we really free to be other than we were, to form

---

[12]H. D. Lewis, "Guilt and Freedom," in Wilfrid Sellars and John Hospers, eds., *Readings in Ethical Theory,* 1st edition (New York: Appleton-Century-Crofts, 1953), p. 616.

[13]J. D. Mabbott, in *Contemporary British Philosophy,* 3rd series, H. D. Lewis (ed.), (New York: Humanities Press), pp. 301–302.

habits and decisions other than those we did? Is it not more plausible to believe that if we still think otherwise this is because we are ignorant of the highly complex causal factors to which we were subjected early on in life? But surely they were there, and psychologists are constantly learning more about what these factors are. These causal factors (largely in the early environment) that cause a person to become a criminal, for example, have been quite thoroughly studied and are now fairly well known, and this knowledge is likely to become much more detailed in the future. Psychologists have known for a long time that one's basic personality pattern is pretty well set by the age of five. The personality of the criminal-to-be is like a time bomb, only waiting to explode. The future is already, so to speak, "in the cards." You don't know all the outcomes because you don't know all the causal factors. But if you did know them, you could know all these outcomes.

A: "If you knew all, you could predict all." This statement is utterly vacuous. When would you say you knew all? Only when you could predict all. If you couldn't predict all, then of course you would *say* you didn't know all; so there is no way the statement could be refuted. "If you studied this book long enough, you'd understand it." You've read it fifty times and you still don't understand it? Well, that just shows that you haven't studied it long *enough*. And when will you say you've studied it long enough? Only when you do understand it. "If you study it till you understand it, you'll understand it"—that is what the statement comes to. In the same way, if you weren't able to predict everything you'd automatically say that you didn't know *enough* of the causal factors. What kind of empty utterance is this?

B: No—I can say everything I need to say without falling into that trap. All I need to say is that for any event E, there is a set of conditions sufficient for its occurrence (it had to be sufficient, or else the event wouldn't have occurred); and for each of these conditions, there was in turn a set of conditions prior to that, sufficient for *their* occurrence—and so on indefinitely back. There was a set of conditions sufficient to produce your determination to perform a difficult act; and for that set of conditions, whatever it was, there was a set of conditions sufficient to produce *that;* and so on. Each event is the outcome of its past, and is pregnant with its future.

Indeed, the fatalist takes much the same attitude toward the future as the rest of us do toward the past. We cannot change the past; it has already happened. We do not know the future, however, as we do the past, so we cannot predict it with accuracy. But if we did, the fatalist says, our attitude toward the future would be the same as it is toward the past. We can do things now that will change the future, but *that* we were going to do them was already determined in the past. Had we but known all the causal factors (which an omniscient God does), we would have known this.

Suppose you were to pick up a book in the library which, to your surprise, is the story of your life. The book was published before you were born, yet it contains accounts of events in your childhood which you had forgotten but now remember had occurred. You turn to the page which describes March 7 of the very day and year in which you picked up the book; and the book says that on March 7 you picked up the book and started to read it. Then you read in the later chapters, which say what you are going to do on March 8 and next week. And finally you look to the last chapter, which describes how you will die in an automobile crash ten years hence. You don't yet know, of course, whether these statements about your future will turn out to be true, but all the statements about your past and present did, and this gives you pause. Perhaps only

God could have written (or dictated) such a book; but there it is, and at least concerning those events you are acquainted with, the statements are all true.[14]

Of course there is no such book. If God knows your future, he apparently keeps this knowledge to himself. But that doesn't really matter. What matters is that *there exists* a series of true statements about you, and those you don't yet know to be true may turn out to be so. Surely you have considerable inductive evidence that they will, in view of the author's record of complete accuracy thus far.

What can be said of this "deeper" brand of fatalism? Let us resume the dialogue.

A: Human beings can act so as to refute predictions; inanimate objects can't. If I read in that book that I was going to keep on reading the book till 4 P.M. on March 7, I would close it by 3:45, thus rendering one statement in it false; or if it said I would close the book at that time, I would keep it open. I might read on and find the book saying that I closed the book after all in order to refute the book's prediction; but then I would open it in order to refute *that* prediction.

B: But the book would anticipate anything you might do to refute its predictions. Whoever wrote it would know exactly what you were going to do, when you would act to refute its predictions and when you wouldn't.

A: There are some predictions I could definitely avoid. If the book said I would die of a heart attack in 10 minutes, I might not be able to do anything about it. But if it said I would die in an air crash, I would from that point on *never* travel by air. Or if it said I would one day take a gun and kill someone, I would never under any cir-

cumstances have a gun in my possession; that way I couldn't possibly act in accordance with the prediction. Or if I wanted to refute the prediction badly enough, and the book said I would die 10 years hence, I could take matters into my own hands and commit suicide right now, thus refuting *that* prediction.

B: But all that assumes that the author of the book is *not* omniscient. An omniscient being knows everything you are going to do, so if an omniscient being wrote the book he wouldn't make any of those mistaken predictions.

A: And what if there is no evidence that there *is* such an omniscient being?

B: It doesn't matter. What matters is that there is a set of true statements all about you, and all written in that book. They are so numerous and unerringly accurate that you can't say it's just coincidence. Surely the fact that every statement thus far put to the test has turned out to be true provides good evidence that all of them are true.

A: The fact that even an omniscient being knows what I will do doesn't mean that I am not free to do it or not. I am still free to cheat (I have that choice), even if he knows I won't.

B: But he knows, not by guesswork, but because he knows (1) all the initial conditions and (2) the relevant psychological laws. The laws of psychology are just as ironclad as those of physics. We think they are not so, but we are caught up in the causal stream. We delude ourselves that we are anything but chips on the causal current being carried along on it just as inexorably as the log is carried downstream by the current of the rushing river.

A: You are now assuming that there *is* a complete set of psychological laws on which these unerring predictions can be made. And of course you don't know that there is.

B: True, but the fact that the predictions are

---

[14]This example is adapted from Richard Taylor, *Metaphysics* (Englewood Cliffs, N.J.: Prentice-Hall, 1981).

always right is good evidence that there are such laws, and that the author of the book knows them.

A: But let's remember a point you seem to have forgoten: *there exists no such book.*

Thus we are led to consider once again the Principle of Universal Causation. What *is* its status? (1) Is it an empirical truth? If so, the evidence for it is extremely incomplete, and the Principle of Indeterminancy, if true, shakes it (at least on the subatomic level) to its foundations. (2) It's surely not a necessary truth, though it is often treated as if it were: If you haven't found a cause yet, never fear, it's there anyway—and you keep on saying that even if you never find it. You treat it as if it were immune to refutation, and *that's* why you simply *assume* the truth all the while. (3) Or, it may be a kind of rule of the scientific game—in which case it's not subject to refutation but only to abandonment. But the deterministic arguments thus far have assumed the *truth* of determinism, and indeterministic arguments have assumed its *falsity*—not taking into consideration the possibility that it's not a proposition at all, and therefore *neither* true nor false.

We began (p. 156–57) by saying that we are trying to find regularity and order in a universe in which not very many regularities are obvious. The Principle of Universal Causation is one such statement of complete regularity: Every event, no matter what, is related to a set of conditions such that if the conditions were to be repeated the event would be repeated. One might ask, what does this express but the fact that we are determined to find a universe that is orderly through and through? If we were as interested in finding disorder as order, we could formulate a Principle of Disorder, which might go something like this: "No matter how uniform this sequence appears to be, it actually is not."

Perhaps then events don't entirely depend on prior sets of conditions. True, certain *types*

of events (burning) seem to depend on certain types of conditions being present (oxygen and so on); but even when this is so, the actual details of combustion in each case are quite different: We haven't described the whole situation in all its concreteness when we have described just these few aspects of it. No two cases of combustion are exactly alike. Within the orderly shell (if C-1, C-2, and C-3, then E), there is still a vast amount of diversity which our statement of uniformity does not take into account. There is plenty of "loose play" in the universe in spite of the statements of uniformity which we have managed with difficulty through the centuries to wring from nature. But philosophers, once they've hit upon something of value, always seem to carry it to the extreme. Instead of just admitting that regularity does occur in the universe, before long they've wrapped the whole universe into one tight system which involves absolutely everything, no matter how minute, in one huge seamless web. This may be aesthetically satisfying to some people; but the question remains: Do we have here a *description* of the universe, or something that we bring *to* it—something that belongs, not to it, but to the lenses through which we examine it? Kant took the second position, and there are some philosophers who believe that his was the more insightful of the two.

Other philosophers, however, characterize the tension somewhat differently.[15] They take determinism to be a true account of the world, but only from one aspect. Viewed "from the inside," we are all actors on the drama of life, and we are real *initiators* of novel sequences of events. We think, we deliberate, we have reasons for what we do, and sometimes we act in accordance with these reasons (good or bad). From this "inside" view, freedom is the most important, and indeed obvious, fact

---

[15]For example, Thomas Nagel, in *The View from Nowhere* (New York: Oxford University Press, 1986).

about us, something we all know from first-hand experience. Alternatives are open to us, and it is for us to choose which path we shall tread. On the other hand, when we adopt the "outside" view, we are flotsam on a causal stream that passes through us and around us. One set of conditions produces this event; another produces that event; and if your decision or mine is among the conditions, that too was caused by some prior events or conditions in the causal stream, which could eventuate in no outcome other than the one that occurred. Thus far, there has been no reconciliation between these deeply conflicting points of view.

EXERCISES

1. How is the word "must" being used in the following examples?

   a. You must do as you're told or you'll be punished.

   b. It simply must be nice weather tomorrow or our picnic will be ruined.

   c. If I had $10 yesterday and haven't lost or spent any or received any since, I must still have $10.

   d. In order to catch a walrus, there must first be a walrus.

   e. If we want to understand topic B, we must first discuss topic A.

   f. If you want this cake to turn out well, you must have three large well-greased cake pans.

   g. Why must you say such things?

   h. He must have been pretty thoroughly intoxicated or he never would have done it.

   i. You must be a mind reader.

   j. You must have your yard looking quite beautiful by this time.

   k. Everything is disarranged—there must have been someone in the house while we were gone.

2. In each of these examples the relation of A to B is that of necessary condition. State whether it is a *causally* necessary condition, such as we have been examining in this chapter, or a *logically* necessary condition, such as we discussed in Chapter 3.

A	B
a. Presence of oxygen	Occurrence of combustion
b. Having three angles	Being a triangle
c. Having extension	Having shape
d. Existence of sodium	Existence of salt
e. Presence of moisture	Growth of crops
f. Presence of nonopaque object	Looking through that object
g. Presence of heat	Occurrence of flame

3. In the following examples, is the relation of A to B that of necessary condition, sufficient condition, both, or neither?

A	B
a. Overeating	Illness
b. Deciding to raise your hand	Raising your hand
c. Writing an essay	Reading that essay
d. Running	Feeling fatigue
e. Plug pulled out of socket	Radio not working
f. Plug inserted in socket	Radio working
g. Rock hitting window	Window breaking
h. Occurrence of friction	Occurrence of heat
i. Rain falling on the street	Street being wet

4. In what way is *too much* being included in the statement of the cause in these examples? In what way *too little*? (Assume the correctness of Mill's account.)

   a. Scratching the match caused it to light.

   b. Eating the poison caused him to die.

   c. Throwing the lighted match into the pile of paper caused it to ignite.

   d. The cause of the dart hitting its target was its being wielded by a man in a blue suit.

   e. The flood in the river was caused by heavy rainfall upstream.

5. Do you think there is genuine plurality of causes in the following cases?

a. Headaches can be caused by many things: eyestrain, emotional tension, etc.

b. The same message can be communicated by telephone, telegram, letter, etc.

c. The stone can be moved by your lifting it, by my lifting it, by a pulley, etc.

d. A woman can bear a child by sexual contact or by artificial insemination.

e. There are many causes of death: heart disease, cancer, pneumonia, automobile accident, drowning, poisoning, stabbing . . .

f. Many different chemicals will take a stain out of a garment.

g. There are various possible causes of erosion: wind, rapid drainage of water, failure to adopt contour plowing . . .

6. Analyze critically the following expressions; if you find them faulty, indicate how they could be amended.

a. The first billiard ball *compelled* the second billiard ball to move.

b. When the first ball hits the second, the second one *can't help* moving.

c. The motion of the second ball is *inevitable* when the first one hits it.

d. The first ball hitting the second *made* the second one move.

e. The first ball hitting the second *produced* the motion of the second one.

7. According to the regularity ("constant conjunction") view of cause (for example, that of Hume, Reichenbach, Schlick), "there would be no more special connection between the striking of a match and the flame which followed it than between the striking of a match and an earthquake which might also occur just afterwards. It would merely be that the striking of a match is usually followed by a flame and not usually followed by earthquakes, and that would be all. We could not say that the striking *made* the flame follow. . . . On this view to give a cause . . . does not in the least help to explain why the effect happened, it only tells us that it preceded the effect."[16] Evaluate this passage sentence by sentence. (For example: Does the regularity interpretation of "C

caused E" render it impossible to explain why C caused E?)

8. What would you say is the cause in these cases?

a. The fire would not have spread to the neighboring house without a normal breeze, yet we say that lightning and not the breeze was the cause of the disaster. Would it be different if someone deliberately fanned the embers, or if just as the fire was dying out a leaking gasoline can fell from the back of a jeep?

b. We say that the flowers died because the gardner neglected to water them. But couldn't we just as well say that they died because you or I or the president of the United States neglected to water them?

c. A pushes B off a skyscraper; during his fall, C shoots him from a window halfway down. What is the cause of B's death?

d. A ship engaged in convoy duty in wartime is insured against marine perils other than war. Under orders, the ship pursues a zigzag course and dims her lights, meets unexpected high waves, is driven off course and onto rocks in a fog. Should insurance be collectible?

9. "Suppose someone claimed to have discovered the cause of cancer, but added that his discovery though genuine would not in practice be of any use because the cause he had discovered was not a thing that could be produced or prevented at will. . . . No one would admit that he had done what he claimed to do. It would be pointed out that he did not know what the word 'cause' (in the context of medicine) meant. For in such a context a proposition of the form 'x causes y' implies the proposition 'x is something that can be produced or prevented at will' as part of the definition of 'cause'."[17] Do you agree or disagree? Give your reasons.

10. "I do not need to examine more than one case to know that C caused E. If someone bribes me into doing something, I know from this one case alone that the bribe caused my action; I do not need any further examples, nor is any predic-

---

[16]Alfred C. Ewing, *The Fundamental Questions of Philosophy* (New York: Macmillan, 1951) p. 160.

[17]Collingwood, "On the So-called Idea of Causation," *Proceedings of the Aristotelian Society*, Vol. 38 (1938–39), p. 87.

tion implied that I would ever respond to a bribe again. If you persuade me to attend a concert, I know that your persuading has caused me to go to the concert; I may never respond to your persuasions again, but from this one instance alone I know that your persuasion caused me to go to the concert this time. I know that it was the unannounced arrival of my sister from India (whom I hadn't seen in 30 years) that caused me to be surprised—although if she were to appear again, I wouldn't be surprised at all." Assess this view.

11. Do you agree or disagree with the following reasoning: "The cause and the effect must be simultaneous, for the effect occurs at the very moment that the last condition (of a sufficient condition) is fulfilled. If there is even the slightest waiting period between it and the effect, there must be something *else* that has yet to occur before the effect can occur; otherwise, why wouldn't the effect occur immediately?"

12. Evaluate this statement: "That C is regularly followed by E is our means of knowing that C causes E. But this is not what the causal relationship consists in; it is the mark but not the essence of the causal relationship."

13. "I said that because it's true." Can the truth of a statement be the cause (or a causal factor) of your uttering it? (Remember that the truth of a statement is a nontemporal fact, while a cause is always a temporal event or condition.) What change of formulation would make the statement more accurate?

14. Is there a point where you are justified in saying that there is not only a statistical relation between A and B but a causal relation?

15. "What significance is there in my mental struggle tonight whether I shall or shall not give up smoking, if the laws which govern the matter of the physical universe already preordain for the morrow a configuration of matter consisting of pipe, tobacco, and smoke connected with my lips?"[18] Evaluate.

16. Evaluate the following statements.

a. Determinism can't be true, because I *feel*

that I'm free; I know this by introspection. This is a much better proof than any arguments.

b. Freedom is incompatible with determinism.

c. Freedom is incompatible with fatalism.

d. Freedom is incompatible with indeterminism.

e. Laws of nature make everything happen the way it does.

f. My background compels me to behave as I do.

g. If I had been under different influences I would have acted differently; and if the set of influences acting upon me on two occasions had been exactly the same I would have acted the same way the second time as the first—I couldn't help doing it. So I'm not free.

h. I couldn't have acted differently from the way I did act. No matter what the act was which I contemplated doing, there was only *one* road open to me (though I didn't know it at the time), only *one* thing that under those peculiar circumstances I *could* have done: namely, the one I did do.

i. It is true—at any rate, more obviously true than any theory about determinism—that human beings *deliberate*. Now, deliberation involves a genuine choice among alternatives, with the outcome in doubt at the time of the deliberation. But if the outcome is already "in the cards," it's not a case of genuine deliberation. Since there is deliberation, determinism must be false.

j. "According to determinism," it is said, "every desire, every impulse, every thought, is the inevitable consequence of antecedent conditions." But the word "inevitable" here is misused. "Inevitable" is synonymous with "unavoidable"; and it is not true that everything is unavoidable. Some things can be avoided. The fallacy here is the usual one of taking a word that is applicable to some things and extending its meaning so that it becomes applicable to everything.

k. Heisenberg's Principle of Indeterminancy is now fairly well accepted in physics. If indeterminism is operative in the realm of inorganic nature, why not in man also? In that case, we have freedom after all.

---

[18] Arthur E. Eddington, in *Philosophy* (January 1933): 41.

SELECTED READINGS

AYER, A. J. "Freedom and Necessity," in *Philosophical Papers*. London: Macmillan, 1963.

BEROFSKY, BERNARD, ed. *Free Will and Determinism*. New York: Harper, 1966.

BLOCK, NED, ed. *Readings in the Philosophy of Psychology*. London: Methuen, 1980.

CAMPBELL, C. A. *In Defense of Free Will*. Glasgow: Jackson & Co., 1938.

CAMPBELL, C. A. "Has the Self Free Will?" in *Selfhood and Godhood*. London: Allen & Unwin, 1955.

DUCASSE, CURT J. *Truth, Knowledge, and Causation*. London: Routledge & Kegan Paul, 1968.

ENTEMAN, WILLIAM, ed. *The Problem of Free Will*. New York: Scribner's, 1967.

FRENCH, PETER, and CURTIS BROWN, eds. "Backward Causation" in *Puzzles, Paradoxes, and Problems*. New York: St. Martin's Press, 1987.

HOBART, R. E. (Dickinson Miller). "Free-will as Involving Determinism and Inconceivable without It," *Mind,* Vol. 43, 1934, pp. 1–27.

HOLBACH, BARON DE. *The System of Nature,* vol. 1; chapters 11 and 12. 1795.

HOOK, SIDNEY, ed. *Determinism and Freedom in the Age of Modern Science*. New York: New York University Press, 1957.

HUME, DAVID. "Of the Idea of Necessary Connection," in *An Enquiry concerning Human Understanding*. 1751.

JAMES, WILLIAM. "The Dilemma of Determinism," in *The Will to Believe*. New York: Longmans Green, 1897.

LEHRER, KEITH, ed. *Freedom and the Will*. London: Macmillan, 1963.

MACKIE, J. L. *The Cement of the Universe*. Oxford: Clarendon Press, 1974.

MILL, JOHN STUART. "Are Human Actions Subject to the Law of Causality?" in *A System of Logic*. 1843. (See also Book 3, Chapter 5, and Book 6, Chapter 2.)

MOORE, G. E. *Ethics*. London: Oxford University Press, 1912. (Chapter 6.)

MORGENBESSER, SIDNEY, and J. WALSH, eds. *Free Will*. Englewood Cliffs, NJ: Prentice-Hall, 1962.

OPPENHEIM, FELIX. *Dimensions of Freedom*. New York: St. Martin's Press, 1961.

PEARS, DAVID. *Freedom and the Will*. London: Macmillan, 1965.

RASHDALL, HASTINGS. *Theory of Good and Evil*. 2 vols. London: Oxford University Press, 1924. (Chapter 3 of Book 3.)

REID, THOMAS. "Of the Words Cause and Effect, Action, and Active Power." in *Essays on the Active Powers of Man*. 1788. (Essay 4, Chapter 2.)

RYLE, GILBERT. "It Was to Be," in *Dilemmas*. Cambridge: Cambridge University Press, 1954.

SALMON, WESLEY, "Determinism and Indeterminism in Modern Science"; ELIZABETH BEARDSLEY, "Determinism and Moral Perspectives"; and J. HOSPERS, "Free-will and Psychoanalysis" in JOEL FEINBERG, ed., *Reason and Responsibility*. Belmont, Ca: Dickensen, 1981.

SELLARS, WILFRID, and JOHN HOSPERS, eds. *Readings in Ethical Theory*. Englewood Cliffs, NJ: Prentice-Hall, 1970. (Part 7.)

STACE, WALTER T. *Religion and the Modern Mind*. Philadelphia: Lippincott, 1952. (Chapter 6.)

TAYLOR, RICHARD. *Metaphysics*. 3rd ed. Englewood Cliffs, NJ: Prentice-Hall, 1983.

WATSON, GARY. *Free Will*. London: Oxford University Press, 1982.

6

MIND AND BODY

1. PHYSICAL AND MENTAL EVENTS

There are minds, and there are bodies—human and animal. Or so it seems. We constantly use expressions such as "My mind is made up." "Have you lost your mind?" "My mind is confused today." "It's all in your mind." We think, we feel, we deliberate, we make decisions. Can bodies do these things? We can't do these things without bodies, of course; we can't think without brains. But that is only to say that having a brain is a necessary condition for thinking; it is not to say that the brain thinks or feels or decides. What then thinks and feels and decides? Some would say, "The mind does these things." Others would say, "*You* do these things—but you couldn't think if you didn't have a mind to think with."

There seems, then, to be something else at work here, not just physical bodies—not even just physical organisms. Living things are different from nonliving things such as stones, but they are still material things, composed of matter—organic matter. They are material objects which do things that other material objects don't do; they grow, they assimilate food, they reproduce, they die. Do they have minds? There is much disagreement about this: Perhaps dogs and cats don't think, but what about chimpanzees? Don't chimpanzees figure out solutions to problems? Perhaps animals don't deliberate and make decisions, but they do perceive the world and they do experience pain and pleasure; the yelping dog whose foot has been cut off by a mowing machine surely feels pain as much as you or I. It is not clear how far down the scale of life we must go before we can no longer say that organisms have minds; we don't attribute minds to plants, nor to some animals such as amoebas or viruses. In any case, it seems clear that human beings do have minds. And so we appear to have a problem: What is the relation of minds to bodies? How do we "bridge the gap" between them?

Materialism is the view that there is no gap to be bridged: There is only matter. "All that exists is matter; all that occurs is motion," said Thomas Hobbes (1588–1679). No one today would believe in such a crude form of materialism. There is energy and gravitation and electrical fields and magnetic fields and fields of force, and matter itself may be reducible to quanta of mass-energy. Hobbes' view would have to be restated to say that all that exists is *physical* in nature—a part of the publicly observable world studied by the physical sciences. Does this imply that there are no such things as thoughts, feelings, and sensations? No, that would be absurd—"I think that there are no thoughts" would be a self-refuting statement. It implies only that even thoughts, feelings, and sensations are physical, part of the physical universe studied by physics and chemistry and biology.

But how can this be? Consider what happens when you hear a noise. Something first happens outside your body: sound waves, alternate condensations and rarefactions of the air, cause air particles to strike repeatedly on your eardrum, so that it vibrates. The eardrum is connected by three small bones to a membrane that covers one end of a spiral tube in the inner ear. The vibration of your eardrum is transmitted through this chain of three bones to the membrane at the end of the tube. The tube is filled with a liquid, perilymph, so that the vibration in the membrane attached to these bones causes a corresponding vibration to pass through this liquid. Inside the first tube is another one, filled with a liquid called endolymph; vibrations in the perilymph cause vibrations in the membranous wall of the inner tube and waves in the endolymph. Small hairs stick out from the membranous walls into the endolymph, which are made to vibrate by the vibrations in the endolymph. The auditory nerve is joined to the roots of these hairs. The vibration of the hairs causes impulses to pass up the auditory nerve to a part of the brain called the auditory center. Not until the auditory center is stimulated do you hear a sound.

So far all the events described have been physical; they have been minute changes going on inside your head. They are extremely difficult to observe, even with cleverly devised instruments, since people's heads are not transparent and it is difficult to open a person's head while the person remains alive with his brain functioning as usual. Nevertheless, many such minute physical changes have been observed and measured.

The entire process just described takes only a small fraction of a second; but now, when the auditory nerve has carried the stimulus to the appropriate portion of the brain, something new and different occurs: you *hear a sound,* you have an *auditory sensation.* This is "something new under the sun." It is something quite different from anything that went on earlier in this brief but complex process. The auditory sensation is a *mental event,* not a physical event like the preceding ones. It is an *awareness,* a state of *consciousness.* The same holds for visual sensation and all other kinds of sensation: kinesthetic sensations, smell-sensations, taste, touch, heat, cold, pain, and so on; and also for states of consciousness not directly associated with the senses, such as thoughts, memories, images, emotions. Let us see in what ways they are different from physical events.

1. We can always locate physical things, events, and processes in space. They take place some*where.* The sensory and neural processes associated with sensation take place inside the person's head. But where is the sensation? Suppose you hear a bell ringing; where then is your auditory sensation? It is not in the physical sound-waves—these are in space outside your body, between the bell and your ears. Still less is it in the bell, which is a phys-

ical object which you can locate in space. But the auditory sensation—where is it? Inside your head somewhere? Would a surgeon cutting open your head ever find it? If your skull were transparent and a surgeon with a powerful microscope could see what was going on inside it, she might see the stimulation of the auditory nerve, but would she see or hear your *sensation?* (And if she did would it not be her sensation rather than yours?)

Or take the case of vision. Light waves impinge upon the retina of your eye, producing there an inverted image of the object seen. This is physical; the inverted image can be observed (though it is not what *you* are seeing). The optic nerve is stimulated, a chemical-electrical impulse passes along it, and finally, in a very small fraction of a second, the occipital lobe of the brain is stimulated; then a *visual sensation* occurs. Up to the occurrence of the sensation, every step of the process can be located in space, somewhere inside your head. But supposing you are looking at a solid green wall, where is your sensation of green? Is it in your head, inside your brain somewhere? If so, where? Would someone opening your head or looking at it through a super-x-ray microscope find the green you were seeing? Would it make sense to say that the green was 4 inches behind your eyes? It *would* make sense to say of a neural process that it was going on 4 inches behind your eyes.

Similar considerations apply if the sensation is not caused by objects outside your body. Suppose you are, as we say, seeing red spots before your eyes. Where are the spots? Before your eyes, literally? Six inches in front of your eyes perhaps? You cannot locate them there, and neither can anybody else. These spots don't appear to exist in physical space at all. You may say, "They aren't real; they don't really exist at all." But don't they? They don't exist as physical spots, like the spots on a dog, but you *do* see spots and that is an inescapable fact of your experience, just as inescapable as your visual sensation of the dog's

spots. By saying that they are not real you may mean that they do not form part of the physical world, but they do certainly exist—you are seeing them right now. Perhaps they exist only as mental events, but they still exist. Because they are not physical, however, you cannot locate them in the physical world, in front of your eyes or behind your eyes *or anywhere else.* Mental events are nonspatial; physical events ae spatial. It makes no more sense to ask "Where (in space) is this mental event occurring?" than it does to ask "Where is the number 4?" (as opposed to the *numeral* "4" which I have just written on the blackboard and which certainly *is* located in space). Do not assume that because it is false that a mental event occurs outside one's head it therefore occurs inside one's head. A physical event or process would have to go on in the one place or the other, but not a mental one: The category of space, or spatiality, just does not apply to them at all. That is one thing that distinguishes them from physical events and processes.

If mental events (states of consciousness), then, are not locatable in space, then neither are they *extended* in space. You cannot meaningfully ask how much space they occupy. How much space do the red spots before your eyes occupy? Two inches? Three feet? (And if you did make some such assertion, how would you go about verifying it?) Suppose you form an image of the Empire State Building, or, more precisely, an image shaped to represent the Empire State Building. How tall is—not the Empire State Building itself—but your image of it? What is the tallness of the image as compared with the tallness of the Empire State Building itself? Is it one-tenth as tall, perhaps? If so, how could it possibly be squeezed into your brain, whose dimensions are only a few inches? If you constructed a *model* of the Empire State Building, you could meaningfully say that your model was one-tenth as tall, or one-thousandth as tall, as the building itself, for your model is a physical object located at a definite place in the physical world. But the image you have in your mind is not like the model you have before you on the table: The image is not inside your head (no one opening your head or looking at it from the outside would ever find it there), but neither is it outside your head, say on the table. It is not in physical space and has no extension in physical space.

2. Physical objects, physical events, and physical processes are publicly observable; but mental events (states of consciousness) can be experienced by only one person.

It may be technically impossible now (though possibly not fifty years from now) for me to observe in microscopic detail what is going on inside your head, say at the midpoint of a straight line connecting your two ears. But whatever it is, it is some physical process taking place in your brain.

Indeed, we can imagine a machine, called an "auto-cerebroscope," by means of which you yourself could see what was going on in your own brain. With an ingenious series of mirrors you could see the surgeon cutting away at the cerebral cortex of your brain, while you were under a local anesthetic. You could see just which nerve pathways were stimulated when you had each experience; for example, you could see exactly what happened in the occipatal lobe of your cortex when you experienced the green of the tree. What the example illustrates is that the green you see, and whatever is going on in your brain when you see the green, are two different things. Your brain is available to the surgeon's inspection as well as your own through the auto-cerebroscope; but the experience of green is yours. If a law of psychophysical correlation could be established about what was going on in your brain whenever you had the experience of seeing green, the surgeon would be able to say, "Aha! You must be seeing green, for that little ganglion is wiggling in that funny way again," but he would never be able to have your experience of green. Doubtless he could have an experience of green by looking at something green himself, but that green would be correlated with *his* brainstate, not yours. You and the surgeon could observe one another's brainstates, but you could not have one another's experiences.

But don't you experience thoughts as going on in your brain? To say this is to import our knowledge of physical science into our phenomenological reports. Aristotle thought the brain was there only to cool the blood, and that the seat of mental activities was the heart. You experience your thoughts as occurring not in any *place* at all. What of the spots before your eyes after you've been dealt a blow on the head? They are experienced as being in front of your eyes. They are in *phenomenal* (apparent) space, though no one would ever find them in physical space, say 6 inches in front of your eyes.

However, other examples seem to give a different result, particularly in the case of pain. Don't you feel a pain in a place—in your toe, in your head, in your tooth, in your stomach? It would be strange indeed to say you felt a pain but it was not anywhere in your body. Pains, then, are experienced as being in a definite location. Still, a physician tapping various places in your body and asking "Where's the pain?" would see only your body, she wouldn't feel your pain (she would only infer it from where you said the pain was). Indeed, people locate pains in limbs that have already been amputated. We must distinguish, again, between physical space and phenomenal space: Your pain is experienced as being in a certain location, and thus is said to be in phenomenal space; but it is not in physical space, like your ear. Also, many philosophers would distinguish between your pain and your *awareness* of the pain: Your awareness of the pain, unlike the pain itself, is *not* in your head or your tooth or your toe.

3. There is still a third characteristic of mental events, something often called *intentionality*. Used here in a special sense, the

word does not mean intentions but what is called "aboutness." I don't just think, I think *of* something or *about* something; I don't just see, I see *something;* I don't just feel anger, I feel anger *toward* something or someone. (The objects of these states may be imaginary: I may think of a unicorn, or have a hallucination of a unicorn, or feel angry at someone who doesn't exist.) Nowhere in physical nature does this aboutness occur. A molecule or a mountain is not *about* anything; it does not direct its attention at any object—indeed, it has no attention to direct. (It may be that not all mental states are intentional in this sense. You may feel depressed, but not about anything in particular; and a toothache is just a toothache, not directed toward any real or imaginary object.)

In view of these distinctions, can anyone still say that there are no distinctively mental events, or that they exist but are really physical like a molecule or a tree? Isn't it obvious, one might ask, that there is a distinction between physical and mental events? The contemporary philosopher C. D. Broad described is as follows:

Let us suppose, for the sake of argument, that whenever it is true to say that I have a sensation of a red patch it is also true to say that a molecular movement of a certain specific kind is going on in a certain part of my brain. There is one sense in which it is plainly nonsensical to attempt to reduce the one to the other. There is a something which has the characteristic of being my awareness of a red patch. There is a something which has the characteristic of being a molecular movement. It should surely be obvious even to the most "advanced thinker" who ever worked in a psychological laboratory that, whether these "somethings" be the same or different, there are two different *characteristics.* The alternative is that the two phrases are just two names for a single characteristic, as are the two words "rich" and "wealthy"; and it is surely obvious that they are not. If this be not evident at first sight, it is very easy to make it so by the following considerations. There are some questions which can be raised about the characteristic of being a molecular movement, which it is nonsensical

to raise about the characteristic of being an awareness of a red patch; and conversely. About a molecular movement it is perfectly reasonable to raise the question: "Is it swift or slow, straight or circular, and so on?" About the awareness of a red patch it is nonsensical to ask whether it is a swift or a slow awareness, a straight or circular awareness, and so on. Conversely, it is reasonable to ask about an awareness of a red patch whether it is a clear or confused awareness; but it is nonsense to ask of a molecular movement whether it is a clear or a confused movement. Thus the attempt to argue that "being a sensation of so and so" and "being a bit of bodily behavior of such and such a kind" are just two names for the same "characteristic" is evidently hopeless.[1]

Behaviorism

It won't do to say that experiences such as thoughts, feelings, and sensations *are* behavior; we can often think for hours without exhibiting any behavior at all. ("I wish I knew what you're thinking as you sit there so quietly.") One theory, usually called *behaviorism,* holds that thoughts are *tendencies* to behave in certain ways, or *dispositions* to behave. When I see a red traffic light, I have a tendency to press on the brakes (even if I don't actually do so); when I am in a sour mood, I have a tendency not to act friendly to others; and so on. Even when I am quiet and trying not to react, subtle cues in my facial expression and body language may give me away.

What is the brittleness of glass? It is a disposition of glass to break easily when subjected to forces that are quite small. A piece of glass may never shatter at all, but it is still brittle—it is still true that it *would* break if struck with a hammer, and so on, even if it never does. But this is not the whole story; The glass has this tendency because of a certain *state* it is in, namely having a certain kind

---

[1]C. D. Broad, *The Mind, and Its Place in Nature* (London; Routledge & Kegan Paul, 1925), pp. 622-623.

of molecular structure (which is familiar enough to chemists). It is because of that *state* of the glass that it has the *dispositional* property of brittleness.

A similar suggestion has been made about mental states.[2] A person with the tendency to become easily angered possesses this dispositional trait as a result of a certain inner *state*. And this inner state, so runs the theory, is a state of the person's *brain*. As long as a person has that kind of brain-state (about whose details we know very little), characterized for example by an excess of adrenalin, the person will exhibit the disposition to become easily angered, even if nothing actually occurs to anger him.

The tendency to become easily angered is clearly a dispositional property of a person; and the anger he feels is, equally clearly, some inner state. The question is, is it a state of the *brain?* The anger doesn't seem to occur in physical space, but the brain events do. The state of your brain and the state of my brain are equally accessible (or inaccessible) to brain-probing surgeons; but I feel anger only when *my* brain is in that state, not when yours is. Why the difference? My physical states, including brain-states, are observable by others; but my anger is not experiencable by anyone but myself. Before going into the relation between feelings of anger and brain-states, it is important that we consider what has traditionally been called "the problem of other minds."

2. THE PROBLEM OF OTHER MINDS

When my finger is cut and bleeding, I know that I have a pain in the most direct way possible: I feel it. I do not *infer* from my behavior or anything else that I feel pain, I am *directly aware* of it—what philosophers sometimes call "immediate acquaintance." But when *your* finger is cut and bleeding, I do not know in the same way that you are feeling pain. I *infer* it from the fact that I see the blood and hear you saying that it hurts, and so on, but I do not feel your pain. (I may feel great empathy toward you, and feel distressed at the thought that you are in pain, but that still isn't feeling your pain in the way I feel my own pain when my finger is cut.) It seems to be impossible for me to feel your pain, or for you to feel mine. We are each aware of our own experiences, and no one else's.

This is not to say that I cannot *know that* you are in pain. Probably I do know it, at least in the weak sense of "know." I have strong evidence that you are in pain, and no evidence against it; on the whole I have good reason to believe you are in pain, just as I am when my finger is cut. Thus, I may know both propositions to be true: "I am in pain" (in the strong sense of "know") and "You are in pain" (in the weak sense of "know"). But even if I know *that* you are feeling pain, I do not know it by *feeling it myself*. That direct means of access is available only to me. I may look at your face and say, "I'll bet you're feeling worried today," and you may confirm what I say. But in my own case I don't need to look in the mirror and say, "My face looks tense and worried today, so I must be feeling worried." In my own case, I don't have to make such an inference: I know right off whether I am worried or not. (The only doubt would be whether the *word* "worried" correctly describes what I feel; perhaps the word "tense" would describe it better. I feel what I feel, but it may not be easy to describe in words what I feel.)

Thus, even if it is granted that I can know you're in pain, I still can't *feel* your pain, or think your thoughts, or experience your worry. If you tell me what you're worried

[2]See for example, David Armstrong's "The Nature of Mind" in C. V. Borst (ed.), *The Mind-Brain Identity Theory* (New York: St. Martin's Press, 1970), pp. 67–79; and in Armstrong's *A Materialist Theory of Mind* (London: Routledge & Kegan Paul, 1968).

about ("There's a hurricane on the way"), I too may feel worried; but even so, I feel my worry and you feel yours. There are two worries going on here, yours and mine, and I can't experience yours any more than you can experience mine. In fact, it would seem to be a necessary truth that I can't experience your experiences and you can't experience mine.

But is it a necessary truth? Suppose that the laws of physiology were different, and that we consider two persons, A and B. When A is cut with a knife, B feels pain, and when B is cut, A feels pain. Wouldn't that be a case of A feeling B's pain, and B A's pain? We might *say* that it is; if "my pain" means "the pain felt in my body," the answer would be yes. But in another sense the answer would be no. A might feel pain when B's body is injured and B feel pain when A's body is injured; this would be a very peculiar kind of world: I might say to you, "Don't get hit over the head today, I don't want to have that headache again." Still, wouldn't I be having *my* pain— but feeling it when your body was injured— just as you would still be feeling your pain when my body was injured? The causal conditions of having pain would be different in such a world, but I would still have my pain and you would have yours. "My pain" is *the pain I feel*—regardless of the causal conditions under which it was felt; even if I feel the pain when your finger is cut, it would still be my pain, because I am the one who *has* the pain.

It seems, then, that "I feel your pain" and "You feel my pain" are not just empirically impossible—contrary to biological laws—but logically impossible; it would involve saying that I feel a pain that is not mine but yours. Experiences, including pains, are essentially private; I could not have your pain any more than a circle could be square. In that case, however, I cannot possibly *verify* that you are in pain; I can verify only what your facial expression is and, if necessary, supplement that with a lie-detector test and a brainscan. But I cannot feel your pain myself. By such means I may be able to discover what thoughts or feelings you are having—even to know (at least in the weak sense of "know") *that* you are feeling so-and-so. But knowing *that* you are having a certain feeling is not at all the same as feeling it myself. If I know you well I may be able to say truly, "I know just what you're going through," but that's not the same thing as feeling it myself. I may emphathize strongly with you and even feel pain when you are in pain, but the pain I feel is still mine and the pain you feel is yours.

Can I verify the proposition that you are feeling pain? Not if verifying means having all the evidence, or even the best possible evidence, which would be feeling it. At best I can verify that you behave in a certain way, and respond in a certain way to a lie-detector test.

Perhaps then all I mean by saying that you are in pain is that you behave in a certain way and respond to lie-detector tests and so on. But this view is absurdly implausible. If you have just cut yourself badly and I see your agonized behavior, do I, in saying that you feel pain, mean only that you behave *as if* you felt pain? Surely I mean that your behavior is an *indication* that you feel pain—and when I say that you are in pain I mean to say exactly the same thing about you that I am saying about myself when I say that I am in pain. The only difference between "I am in pain" and "You are in pain" is the personal pronoun. *What* I am saying about me and about you is exactly the same in the two cases. The question is, How can I verify the pain in your case, as I can do so immediately in my own?

"Well, at least I can *confirm* that you are feeling pain." Surely the fact that you cry out after having been cut is a good *confirmation* to me that you are in pain. Sometimes when you cry out you may be play-acting, but with careful observation I can confirm that too.

Many would be content with confirmation rather that verification. But a skeptic can pursue the question further: How do I know that you have pains or any other experiences at all? How do I know that you experience pain or pleasure or have sensations or thoughts or feelings of any kind? Could you not be a cleverly rigged-up automaton, wound up like a top every morning to go through certain complicated motions every day, but all the while experiencing nothing at all? True, you give answers to mathematical questions faster than I do; but so do computers when they have been programmed to do so. How do I know that you are not a fancy computer, having no more feelings or thoughts than the computers scientists build? If you were one, programmed to go through just the motions that you do, how would I ever know the difference? You would do the same things, say the same things, every bit of your behavior would be the same—so how could I tell? I can tell that you feel pain only from the symptoms from which I make the inference—but what if the symptoms were the same? If I don't believe that a computer has feelings, and if you behaved just as a computer does (the computer too can exhibit pain behavior and even say that it is in pain), what reason would I have for saying that you experience pain but the computer doesn't? Your behavior is all I can confirm, and I have no evidence that there is anything else beyond that. I have never even once felt your pain; for all that I know, your pain may be a myth.

To counter this alarming possibility, the *argument from analogy* is often invoked. When my finger is cut (A), I feel pain (B); therefore, I infer that when your finger is cut (A′), you feel pain (B′). That doesn't confer certainty on the statement that you feel pain, but doesn't it make your feeling quite probable? After all, you behave as I do when I feel pain; you too are composed of skin, bones, nerves, and blood vessels—just as I am. So can't I infer by analogy (similarity) that if I feel pain when cut, so do you?

The trouble is that as an argument from analogy, this seems a weak one. Suppose I see a set of boxes stored in someone's garage. I open one box and find that it is full of books. I don't open any of the rest, but I say, "Since all the boxes look pretty much alike, I infer that they all contain books." Admittedly this wouldn't be a very safe inference, and you wouldn't bet much on it. The boxes might contain anything—trinkets, papers, children's toys. If you open only one box, you're not in a very good position to say that they all contain books. Your position would be much better if you had opened all the boxes but one, found that they contained books, and then inferred that probably the last box would contain books also. An argument from analogy based on only one case is a pretty poor argument.

But isn't that exactly the position we are in with regard to other minds? In my own case, I have (1) my behavior and (2) my feeling pain. But in every other case, I have only the behavior to go by. So am I not in the position of the person who concludes that all the boxes contain books, on the slender basis of finding that one box contains books?

Yet I am much more confident that you feel pain when your finger is cut, than I am that all the boxes contain books after examining the contents of only one box. Why is this? Is this just an irrational conclusion, a prejudice? Or is it my belief that you have feelings based on something other than a weak argument from analogy?

Consider the following three statements:

1. I ask you, "Where is the book I lent you?"
2. You understand my question and think for a moment.
3. You utter the words, "I'm sorry—I forgot it, I left it at home."

The first statement is a report of words emanating from my mouth; these I not only utter but can hear myself uttering. The third statement is also something I can hear; your lips move and you utter the words. The problem is with the second statement. How do I know it is true, since I can't experience your thoughts? John Stuart Mill wrote,

I conclude that other human beings have feelings like me because, first, they have bodies like me, which I know in my own case, to be the antecedent condition of feelings; and because secondly, they exhibit the acts, and other outward signs, which in my own case I know from experience to be caused by feelings. . . . In the case of other human beings I have the evidence of my senses for the first and last links of the series, but not for the intermediate link. I find, however, that the sequence between the first and last is as regular and constant in those other cases as it is in mine. In my own case I know that the first link produces the last through the intermediate link, and could not produce it without. Experience, therefore, obliges me to conclude that there must be an intermediate link; which must either be the same in others as in myself, or a different one; I must either believe them to be alive, or to be automatons; and by believing them to be alive, that is, by supposing the link to be of the same nature as in the case of which I have experience, and which is in all other respects similar, I bring other human beings, as phenomena, under the same generalizations which I know by experience to be the true story of my own existence.[3]

Particularly impressive is the fact that I ask someone a question and then from that person's lips emanate words which answer the very question I asked. How would this be possible if the other body doesn't have a mind that understands the question? To understand the question must he not have consciousness like me? Surely, the belief that he has consciousness like me is *the best explanation* of his ability to answer my questions.

Many would rest content with this answer, believing the problem of other minds to be solved. But there are a few bothersome questions that have been raised about this account.

1. How did we ever learn to use words like "pain" and "anger"—and other words we use—in talking about our "inner states"? As children we learned to use words by having them uttered by parents, accompanied typically by acts of pointing: "That's a chair," "That's a car." But of course you can't point to pain or anger. So how does the child learn to use the language of sensations and feelings? How did we ourselves learn to use the words correctly? How did words like "pain" become part of a *public language?*

Suppose you have some special feeling whenever you see, say, a mountain gorge. You might give a name to that peculiar sensation, and use it again if you had that same peculiar sensation another time. But thus far the name would not be part of a pbulic language; you could use it only in "communing with yourself." You might try to communicate this special feeling to others, but others might be quite uncomprehending as to what you meant. But the word "pain" is not the same. You learned to use that word from seeing your parents and other people use it: And to use it correctly you didn't need to feel their pains, or even to feel pain yourself. It was only necessary to observe the occasions on which they used the word—what their behavior was like when they used it, and by doing so you became able to use it yourself. If your father cut his finger and said that it hurt, and later you cut your finger, you could say the same thing of yourself—and presumably the feeling you had when this happened would be one you would identify as "pain."

This is not to say, then, that you have no "inner episodes" such as sensations of pain, but that you can learn to identify something as pain only by observing behavior that accompanies the use of the word. The child did not begin with her own case, as the argument from analogy seems to assume. She learned it as she learned any word in a public language, by observing the contexts in which other people used it. Thus, even though you can feel only your own pain, as a child you could learn how to use the word "pain" without having felt it. And you would recognize what you feel

³John Stuart Mill, *An examination of Sir William Hamilton's Philosophy,* 6th ed. (London: Longmans Green, 1889), pp. 243–244.

as being pain because of the similarity of the context to that of others when they spoke of pain. How else, it would be asked, would we learn the meaning of terms like "anger," "hope," "dread," and countless others?

2. We have argued thus far that you can know that you are in pain, and that your pain report is about as certain as a statement can be. But this too has been questioned.

Suppose that an encephalograph was constructed to test whether your reports that you are in pain are true; the machine is designed to test your pain level. What if you sincerely report that you are in pain, but this report conflicts with the evidence of the encephalograph? Should it be concluded that you are not telling the truth when you say you are in pain?

"Not at all," one might well exclaim, "I *know* whether I feel a pain. If the machine says I'm not, then it's the machine that's making the mistake. After all, *I* know whether I have a pain or not—I feel it! The machine only provides an indirect test—one that can be mistaken if the machine malfunctions."

However good the evidence may be, such a physiological theory can never be used to show the sufferer that he was mistaken in thinking that he had a pain. . . . The sufferer's epistemological authority must therefore be better than the best physiological theory can ever be.[4]

But wait: How does Jones know that he is using the word "pain" correctly? Has he any *criteria* for the use of the term? He feels what he feels, but perhaps he is misdescribing what he feels in calling it a pain. Or perhaps he can describe it rightly once it is recognized for what it is, but he doesn't recognize it for what it is, in much the same way that a person may think she sees someone else in the room when she is only seeing her image in a mirror.

The encephalograph says that the brain-process constantly correlated with pain-reports occurs in Jones's brain. However, although he exhibits pain-behavior, Jones thinks that he does not feel pain. . . . Now is it that he does not know that *pain* covers what you feel when you are burned as well as what you feel when you are stuck, struck, etc.? Or is it that he really does not feel pain when he is burned? Suppose we tell Jones that what he feels when he is burned is *also* called "pain." Suppose he then admits that he does feel *something,* but insists that what he feels is quite *different* from what he feels when he is stuck, struck, etc. Where does Jones go from here? Has he failed to learn the language properly, or is he correctly (indeed infallibly) reporting that he has different sensations than those normally had in the situation in question?[5]

If the certainty of a sincere pain report is thus cast in doubt, some alarming skeptical possibilities now confront us. Would one sincere pain report—if at odds with the machine report—be enough to break down at one blow well-confirmed scientific theories? Can our certainty about our pains possibly be shaken by such questions as "Does she really know which sensations are called pains?" and "Is she a good judge of whether she is in pain or not?" Can the truth of a pain report *never* be overridden by evidence from other sources?

Consider another kind of case. You say, "It's hot in this room." But you look at the thermometer and it reads 55°; you check other thermometers and they all say the same. Are you sure you are right and the thermometers wrong? In this case we say the thermometers are right and that it isn't hot in the room, you just *feel* hot; perhaps you have a slight fever. Here we trust the thermometer and not your individual judgment. Why not do the same in trusting the encephalogram rather than your individual pain report?

"But this is different," one might say. Instead of saying it's hot in the room, you should say that you *feel* hot—no one will

[4]Kurt Baier, "Smart on Sensations," *Australian Journal of Philosophy* (1962): 57.

[5]Richard Rorty, "Mind-Body Identity, Privacy, and Categories," *Review of Metaphysics 19* (1965): 24-25.

doubt that this is true. You do have a heat experience, no one is doubting the truth of your report that you *feel* hot; it's just that this time your heat experience doesn't correspond to the actual temperature. But in the case of the pain report, how can we deny that the person is feeling pain? If *you* are the one who has the pain, won't you say without hesitation that the encephalograph is mistaken? Aren't *you* the final judge of whether you feel pain? Isn't this one case that's absolutely clear and unshakable?

But some philosophers have questioned even this. We learn the word "pain"—like other words—in certain behavioral and environmental contexts; that's how we come to recognize pain when we feel it, and to name it correctly. However,

Now suppose that these public criteria (for "knowing how to use 'pain' ") change as physiology and technology progress. Suppose, in particular, that we find it convenient to speed up the learning of contrastive observation predicates (such as "painful," "tickling," etc.) by supplying children with portable encephalographs-cum-teaching-machines which, whenever the appropriate brain-process occurs, murmur the appropriate term in their ears. Now "appropriate brain-process" will start out by meaning "brain-process constantly correlated with sincere utterances of 'I'm in pain' by people taught the use of 'pain' in the old rough-and-ready way." But soon it will come to mean, "the brain-process which we have always programmed the machine to respond to with a murmur of 'pain'." . . . Given this situation, it would make sense to say things like "You say you are in pain, and I'm sure you are sincere, but you can see for yourself that your brain is not in the state to which you were trained to respond to with 'Pain,' so apparently the training did not work, and you do not yet understand what pain is." In such a situation, our "inability to be mistaken" about our pains would remain, but our "final epistemological authority" on the subject would be gone, for there would be a standard procedure for overriding our reports.[6]

The question is, however, whether such first-person reports can be overridden in this

way. The person reporting the experience may be lying, or may be misreporting the experience by using words incorrectly, as we saw on pp. 77–78. But if neither of these things is taking place, how can the person be mistaken? Some would contend that the first-person report is not coherent with the physical evidence, and that if the physical evidence is considerable, the first-person report, lacking coherence with the other propositions, must be rejected. But others would contend that if the physical evidence is not coherent with the first-person report, then it is the physical evidence that should be rejected and the first-person report that should be maintained.

3. THE RELATION BETWEEN MENTAL AND PHYSICAL

If mental events occur as well as physical ones, what is the relation between them? How, if at all, do they affect one another?

1. Interactionism. The commonsense view most people seem to take for granted is called *interactionism:* that is, the theory that mental and physical events mutually influence one another. Physical events affect mental events: Food poisoning can give you sensations of extreme pain; sirens blowing cause you to feel distress or pain; you receive good news in a letter and feel joy. Mental events also affect the physical: You feel anxious or afraid and your heart beats faster; you decide to take a short walk, and your body begins to move, responding to your decision; you have a "positive attitude" and this helps you to work efficiently and hold your head high. A thousand daily events in your life and everyone else's seem to confirm the interaction—in fact the mutual dependence—of physical states and states of consciousness. A patient's mental state has a great deal to do with whether she will recover from cancer; and aren't cases of psychosomatic illness examples of "the mind affecting the body"?

---

[6]Ibid., p. 25.

But *how* do physical states cause mental ones, or mental states cause physical ones? When you look at the table, what happens? The perceptual process is extremely complex, but familiar to students of physiology: It is the old story of light waves, retina, optic nerve, and brain. Much of this is still not fully understood (how do lightwaves get "translated" into electrophysical impulses leading to the brain?), and there are many technical difficulties in discovering exactly what goes on in the brain of a person who is alive and conscious. But physiologists aren't particularly worried about this—"the difficulties are merely technical." The worrisome moment occurs when the state of consciousness comes into being. There is the "tree"; the light waves from it reach your eye; the inverted image hits the retina; impulses race along the optic nerve to the brain; and then, presto, there is an experience of green which—unlike all the previous events—doesn't seem to occur inside the head and is private to the individual who has the experience. If a retinal image carrying a special "message" along the optic nerve is mysterious, at least the series of events can be charted in space. But state of awareness is "something really different," inaccessible to physiologists or brain surgeons. And yet it seems clear that this series of physical events has caused the experience—seeing the "tree" depends on light waves, retinal image, optic nerve, occipital lobe, and brain. Isn't this as clear a causal relation as can be found?

Even more mysterious, yet seemingly undeniable, are states of consciousness influencing the physical world—by means of your body, of course, which is also in the physical world. You deliberate what to do; you are not sure whether to resume your reading or go to the kitchen first and prepare a snack; finally you make your decision and your body moves accordingly. Surely you would not have gone to the kitchen unless you had first thought about it and then *decided* to walk to the kitchen. Yet this too is quite mysterious. How did what

goes on in your consciousness—deliberating and deciding—affect what goes on in your brain, get communicated through your efferent nerves, and move the muscles of your body? We may be quite confident that there *is* a causal relationship, yet be totally mystified as to how it operates.

The brain seems always to be the "point of connection" between the two; the physical never causes the mental nor the mental the physical except through processes going on in the brain. But this fact does not "close the gap" between mental and physical events, for the brain is itself a physical thing that can be perceived like any other physical thing and has a determinate size and weight. The "gap" between physical and mental events can't be bridged by something which is itself physical. When the final event in the brain occurs before an experience, how does that cause the experience to come about? Descartes thought that the pineal gland in the brain (one of the few nonpaired parts of the brain) was the connecting link; but as his critics pointed out, the pineal gland is a physical thing, and how *it* can cause an experience to occur is as mysterious as ever.

This fact need not prevent us from saying there *is* a causal relation. If a series of physical events regularly is followed by a mental event, we can conclude that the first causes the second, even though we may not know *how* the first causes the second. Surely even in the physical realm there are occurrences which are not understood. A piece of wood is heated until it bursts into flame. Could anyone have predicted, when first certain objects were heated, that besides becoming hotter there would be this new phenomenon—weightless self-luminous tongues of flame? Is this not, in its way, as unique and mysterious as the occurrence of mental events when certain physical events in the cerebral cortex occur? Many persons would find this no more surprising—perhaps less so—than the fact that after countless millennia of inanimate objects existing on the earth, certain molecules came into existence that could grow and reproduce themselves. For that matter, isn't gravitation—a force being exerted by every particle of matter in the universe, even when the objects are billions of miles apart—as mysterious as anything?

Why we should have that peculiar sensation we call "red" when light waves of one length strike the retina, and the peculiar sensation we call "orange" when light waves of a slightly different length strike it, is indeed unexplained. We are mystified by these psychophysical correlations because we do not see *why* the one physical impulse should cause one kind of sensation and not another. But if we are made uncomfortable by the unexplained, should we not be made equally uncomfortable by unexplained events within the physical realm, such as the appearance of living organisms on the earth when there was no life before?

"But when C causes E, C *acts on E* in some way." It's true that we can see how billiard balls act on each other. But the billiard-ball theory of causation can't handle phenomena like magnetism and gravitation, or any kind of "action at a distance." And if one says that a star a thousand light-years away does "act on" the sun—even though at a great distance, so that its influence needn't involve contact—well then, why can't one say also that the body acts on the mind, the physical on the mental, without contact of particles?

"But body and mind can't act on each other, because they're in two different realms. A physical process or event is always 'in the public domain,' potentially observable by many observers; but a state of consciousness is available only to the person who has it. This is a gulf far greater than any we ever find within the physical realm." This may indeed be so, though this fact alone does not show that there can be no causal relation between the two so-called realms. But to many people the difference seems so immense as to preclude any causal relation. Such is the position of psychophysical parallelism.

2. Parallelism. According to parallelism, there is no causal relation between mental and physical events: It is as if the two kinds of events took place along parallel tracks without ever affecting each other. For every state of consciousness there is some corresponding physical event in the brain. If you are thinking about Paris, there is some event in the brain uniquely correlated with this thought; and if you are thinking about London, there is another event in the brain uniquely correlated with that thought. And so on, for every thought and every mood, feeling, and sensation.

No such correlations, of course have yet been discovered; the correlations physiologists are fairly confident of are very rough-and-ready ones, such as between having emotions and having a certain undamaged section of the cerebral cortex. No neurophysiologist has ever found a difference in your brain when you think of London as contrasted with when you think of Paris. That there is such an exact correlation is more a matter of faith than of discovery.

For every mental event there is a corresponding brain event, say the parallelists; but the reverse is not true. Many physical events occur—indeed most of them do—without any mental correlate at all. Before sentient creatures appeared on the earth, physical processes occurred without anyone present to be aware of them; and even after sentient creatures appeared, most physical processes still went on without any corresponding mental events. Mental events occur *only* when certain events occur in the cerebral cortex of a brain. So the parallelism is one-sided: For every M (mental event) there is a corresponding P (physical event), but it is not the case that for every P there is a corresponding M.

What then of the fact that "mind affects matter"—that one's mental state may affect the outcome of a bodily disease, for example? It isn't anything mental that does this, say the parallelists; the actual causing is done in the physical realm. Corresponding to a "good mental attitude" is a brain state (presently unknown) which can affect things like recovery from diseases. We speak loosely when we say "Mind can affect matter"; the truth is that only matter can affect matter, but corresponding to some brain states are mental states which we experience.

According to parallelism, is not the mind in the position of a mere passive spectator of the physical, unable to *do* anything in the physical world? No, says the parallelist, not if the situation is properly understood. For suppose that the chain of physical events described in the previous paragraphs is labeled P-1, P-2, P-3, and so on. This chain of physical events is uninterrupted. Now, at a certain stage, namely when brain events of a certain kind occur, mental events occur simultaneously with them. Suppose this starts at P-12. Then corresponding to P-12 we have M-12; corresponding to P-13 we have M-13; and so on. The relation between M-12 and P-12 is invariable: If P-12 were to occur again, M-12 would occur again simultaneously with it. (Probably this outright repetition would never occur, because memory traces in the brain would make the second brain state different, even if the external stimulus were exactly the same; and the consciousness of previous occurrences of the same kind of event—memory—would make the mental event different the second time.) Now let us assume that P-25 is the legs moving, or more precisely one event in that process; and that M-15 is the volition (act of will) and P-15 its corresponding brain event, about which at present we really know nothing. Now P-15, a brain event, *is* in the causal chain of events leading up to P-25, and without it P-25 would not have occurred. M-15 is not in this causal chain; P-15 is M-15's *representative,* as it were, in the causal order; it is only by means of P-15 that any effect is caused in

the world. Nevertheless, M-15 is essential to the process: P-25 would no more have occurred without M-15 than it would have occurred without P-15. In other words, M-15 is just as much a *necessary condition* (and part of the sufficient condition) of P-25 as P-15 is.

No house was ever built, no book was ever written, without the occurrence of mental events. The parallelist does not deny this, but only insists that what did the actual *work* in the physical world was never the mental event itself but its representative in the physical realm, not M-15, but P-15.

If this is so, what is the difference between saying that M-15 is a necessary condition but *not* a cause, as the parallelist does, and saying, as the interactionist does, that it *is* a cause, at least *one* causal factor in the occurrence of P-25? There does not seem to be any. If M-15 always occurs before P-25, and P-25 never occurs without M-15, then is not M-15 just as much a cause of P-25 as P-15 is? Isn't the difference between parallelism and interactionism a difference of language—in other words, a verbal difference, the one applying the word "cause" in a situation where the other declines to do so? According to both views, a physical stimulus is part of a sufficient condition (and in most if not all cases, a necessary condition as well) of a mental effect; and according to both views, a mental event such as a volition (act of will) is part of a sufficient condition (and in most cases at least, a necessary condition as well) of a physical effect, or series of physical effects such as building a house. The interactionist calls this a *causal* relation, as indeed we do in ordinary life.

Isn't the parallelist then being merely obstinate in refusing to call it causal? Seeing red depends on a multitude of factors in the physical world, including the brain; what is the point, or even the sense, in saying "It's dependent all right, but not causally dependent"? Perhaps the parallelist still has "in the back of her mind" the idea of causality as necessarily involving action of one physical entity upon another—and since this is not present in the physical-mental case, she refuses to call the relation causal. But we have already seen that there are many events and processes, even in the physical world alone, in which causation does not involve one thing acting upon another. Why then insist upon it here? The main reason that parallelism has tended to drop out in twentieth-century discussions of the mind-body relation is that once the dispute over the meaning of "cause" has been straightened out, there does not appear to be any difference between it and interactionism. The kind of relation that exists between the mental and the physical would be called causal in any other context, so why not here?

3. Epiphenomenalism. Yet there is a certain strangeness in saying that physical events, such as events in the brain, are caused by other events that are not physical at all. "On the basis of what we know already, it would be quite extraordinary if it were to turn out that a physical event, such as one particular brain cell firing off an electrochemical impulse to another, sometimes has no physical cause. It would be even more extraordinary if this event were to prove to be, not random, but caused by something nonphysical. The existence of nonphysical causes of physical events would require us to recognize whole new species of causal relations and causal laws."[7]

Thus, one may say, "The mental event is just an *accompaniment;* it is like a shadow that always accompanies you as you walk, but has no control over the direction in which you walk." And thus we are led to a third theory, *epiphenomenalism,* according to which the relation of the physical to the mental is like that of the shadow to the person or the smoke to the locomotive. The causation is one-way. The physical causes the mental, but the mental never in turn causes the physical. Brain events cause mental events, but mental events never cause brain events. Thomas Henry Huxley (1825–1895) put it straightforwardly:

All states of consciousness in us, as in [animals], are immediately caused by molecular changes of the brain-substance. It seems to me that in men, as in brutes, there is no proof that any state of consciousness is the cause of change in the motion of the matter of the organism. . . . Our mental conditions are simply the symbols in the consciousness of the changes which take place automatically in the organism. . . . The feeling we call volition is not the cause of a voluntary act, but the symbol of that state of the brain which is the immediate cause of that act. *We are conscious automata. . . .*[8]

How then is epiphenomenalism different from parallelism? Only in that physical events, according to epiphenomenalism, do cause mental events, but mental events do not in turn cause physical events; Mental events are only the *by-products* of physical events ongoing in the brain. They occur, and they are caused by brain events, but they have no effects in the world. "The brain secretes thought as the liver secretes bile." My thoughts and feelings never affect my behavior; It is always events and processes in the brain, acting through the efferent nerves and muscles, which cause my behavior. The mental events by themselves are as unable to cause anything as your image in the mirror is able to cause you to move—as unable as the smoke that issues from the locomotive to cause a change in the direction of travel of the locomotive. Indeed, it would appear that the whole of human history would have been the same as it is now even if there had been no mental events at all; as long as there are brain events there is no need for mental events—they do no work, they have no causal efficacy.

[7]Peter Carruthers, *(Introducing Persons),* (Albany, NY: SUNY Press, 1986) pp. 133–134.

[8]Thomas Henry Huxley, "On the Hypothesis that Animals are Automata and Its History," in *Methods and Results* (London: Appleton, 1874). Emphasis added.

"Why are there mental events at all," one might well ask, "if they *do* nothing in the world?" But what is the meaning of the word "why" in this question? (1) The world is full of unexplained correlations of events; perhaps the fact that brain-event X is followed by mental event X′ (and that this happens regularly) is about all the knowledge we can get. When we ask "Why, when A happens, does B always happen also?" we are requesting an *explanation of the correlation* between A and B. In many cases, like water expanding when it freezes, we do have an explanation of this, but in many cases, like vinegar causing the experience of a pungent smell, we are left with an unexplained correlation. (2) We could also take the "why" as a request for a teleological explanation, an explanation in terms of purpose, such as "Why did you go to Chicago?" But in this sense, as we have seen (pp. 163–64), a purpose requires a purposer; and we can hardly say it was our *purpose* to have pain when our nerve endings were stimulated. (3) In biology, when we ask why an organ of the body is there, we are asking what function it fulfills, what role it plays in keeping the body alive and functioning. It is in this way that we explain why red blood cells do what they do: not that they have been placed there by a purposer, but that by acting in a certain way they help to keep the organism alive. Thus, the organs, processes, and pervasive tendencies of organisms do not usually survive for thousands of generations unless they serve some purpose in this sense—unless they increase in some way the organism's chances for survival, or promote or enhance its life. But may we not say the same of consciousness? For example, we may ask: "Doesn't consciousness serve a purpose? If you feel pain you may become aware that your foot is burning, and by removing the foot from the fire you may save your foot. The pain you feel may alert you to the danger and cause you to get out of danger's way. And so on. So consciousness *does* achieve a biological purpose." The epiphenomenalist, however, will not deny that pain serves a purpose in this sense, but he will allege that it is not the state of consciousness (pain) *itself* that does the work of removing your foot from the fire, but the brain state which causes the pain and also causes the nerves and muscles to be stimulated.

Epiphenomenalists do not deny that putting your hand in the fire causes you to feel pain; but they do deny that feeling the pain is the cause of—or even a causal factor in—removing your hand from the fire. Why affirm causation in the first case, yet deny it in the second? The interactionist affirms causation in both cases, the parallelist in neither case. Isn't the epiphenomenalist stuck with the worst of both worlds?

The epiphenomenalist, however, proceeds from the conviction that mental events by themselves are impotent—that if any causing is to be done, it must proceed from something in the physical world, whether brain-states or something else. Only physical causation is believed to be compatible with science. Others respond that this is only a dogma, which the epiphenomenalist seems to be clinging to as a kind of a priori assumption. Shouldn't science follow wherever the truth leads? And if it is just as plausible to say that feeling the pain causes you to take your hand out of the fire, as it is to say that putting your hand into the fire causes you pain, then this should be admitted, and one should let theories of causation fall where they may.

But the grip of physical causation is a strong one, and those who trace causes in biology and psychology may find it irresistible. Epiphenomenalism flourished in the nineteenth century, with its analogies about the object and its shadow, and the locomotive and its smoke. These are only mental pictures, of course, and though they may have strong psychological impact they prove nothing about the aptness of the picture. Other variants of epiphenomenalism have been given, both before the nineteenth century and since: for example, "The mental is a *function* of the physical"—the motion of a wheel is not the same thing as the wheel itself, but if there were no wheel there could be no motion-of-the-wheel. Motion is one way a wheel functions, and throwing off mental events (like sparks?) is one way a brain functions. There are numerous variations of this view, called "functionalism," with brain-activity, not mental activity, as their causal center and (so to speak) their "base of operations."

4. The Double Aspect Theory. Still others—such as Benedict Spinoza (1632–1677)—have said that both physical events and mental events are only aspects of something different from them both; there is a third "something" of which the physical is the "outer" aspect and the mental is the "inner" aspect. The physical is one manifestation, the mental another manifestation, of this more fundamental reality.

Now, however, we seem to have another mystery on our hands: What is this third entity of which the physical and the mental are manifestations? Whatever it is, it doesn't *cause* physical or mental events; these are only its "ways of appearing" to us. Can it be perceived? No, it cannot even be imagined. How is one supposed to know that it exists? Only (like Kant's noumenal world) as the solution to a problem. But does it solve the problem or only present us with a mystery? It gives us a mental picture of a person walking through a hall paneled with mirrors—one mirror-image to the right (mental) another to the left (physical). But we know what a person is apart from his mirror-image. Do we have any idea of what the "third thing" is of which the mental and physical are "aspects"?

One may say, as it has recently become fashionable to say,[9] that physical and mental

---

[9]For example, see P. F. Strawson, "Persons," Chapter 3 of his book *Individuals* (London: Methuen & Co., 1959).

states are both aspects of entities called *persons*. The physical and the mental are "brought together" in persons.

What is it to be a person? First of all, persons are conscious beings; but this is not enough—dogs, cats, and countless other animals are also conscious. Second, persons are *self*-conscious: They have a conception of their own past and future; they can plan ahead and can evaluate their present states and dispositions and attempt to change them; so far as we know, no other animal does this. Third, persons are rational agents; they form concepts; they arrive at knowledge; they use that knowledge to plan their future course of action. (Some of the higher mammals also have a limited capacity for this.) Fourth, persons have feelings—happiness, grief, doubt, empathy; they are moved by suffering and by great music.

There are some human beings who are not persons by this definition—for example, irreversibly unconscious patients in hospitals ("human vegetables"), the feeble-minded, those in the last stages of Alzheimer's disease. And there could well be others who are persons but not human beings, such as rational beings from another planet who biologically resemble no earthly species.

Let us agree, then, that it is persons who think and act, and persons who have both mental and physical characteristics (not bodies alone, not minds alone). But it is far from clear how this helps us with the mental-physical problem; How are the mental and physical related to one another? To say that they both emanate from persons, or are both aspects of persons, leaves the relation between them unresolved.

5. The Identity Theory. And so we come to the *identity* theory. According to this view, mental states are *identical with* physical states of the brain. When you say that you are "having a thought" you are really saying that something (you may not know what) is going on in the cortex of your brain. It is not that mental and physical events are uniquely correlated, or are distinct events causally related to each other, but that the two are quite literally *the same event*.

This may seem to be simply a return to materialism, ignoring all the distinctions between physical and mental events that have already been discussed. And yet, in full knowledge of this, the identity theory arose and has been developed largely after those theories were formulated. How can any theory asserting the identity of mental and physical events be plausible in the face of the arguments already given?

First, it is important to be clear about the meaning of the ambiguous word "identical." (1) When you say that this cube is identical with that cube, you are saying that the two cubes have exactly the same qualities—they are *qualitatively* identical: Both are square, both are red, both weigh the same, and so on. There may not be two exactly identical cubes in the world, but if there were, this would be an example of qualitative identity. If, however, position in space and time were to count as a quality, then it would be logically impossible for two cubes to have all the same characteristics, since if they were in the same place at the same time they would not be two cubes but one. Usually when we speak of two things as qualitatively identical we mean all their qualities *except* position in space and time. (2) But when you say that A is identical with B, you can also mean *numerical identity*—that they are not two things but one, that they are literally *the same* thing or quality. It is this sense of "identical" that is intended in the identity theory.

The planet Venus sometimes appears in the eastern sky before dawn and sometimes in the western sky after sunset. In ancient times it was thought that they were different stars, the Evening Star and the Morning Star (Hesperus

and Phosphorus). The supposed two stars, however, are one and the same object, the planet Venus—they are numerically identical. Or again, two explorers may be mapping unknown territory, and each one, approaching a mountain from opposite directions, may give a different name to a newly discovered mountain, only to discover later, when they have compared their maps and charts, that what they thought were two mountains were actually one and the same mountain, approached from different directions. The identity theory says that mental states and physical states are numerically the same—they are quite literally the *same* state.

This may seem wildly implausible; and perhaps it is. Identity theory, however, attempts a few clarifications to enable us to understand what is being asserted:

1. How can words describing mental events and words describing physical events have the same meaning? They don't; they clearly have very different meanings. When I say that I have an after-image, I mean something different from saying that my brain is in a certain state. I may know nothing about my brain, but I *can* describe my after-image. And if they don't mean the same, how can the two possibly be numerically identical?

The identity theorist, however, does not say that words for experiences *mean* the same as words for physical states. The phrase "human being" does not mean the same as the phrase "featherless biped," and yet the two phrases do, or at any rate may, *denote* the same things. The phrases "vice-president of the United States" and "president of the United States Senate" do not have the same meaning, but they do denote the same individual. The word "lightning" does not mean the same as "electrical discharge," though every flash of lightning is in fact an electrical discharge. That this is so is of course an empirical discovery unknown before the rise of modern physics. But so is the identity theory, if true, an empirical discovery—the discovery that what we previously thought were two events are in fact one.

"I see lightning" does not *mean* "I see an electrical discharge." Indeed, it is logically possible (though highly unlikely) that the electrical discharge account of lightning might one day be given up. Again, "I see the Evening Star" does not *mean* the same as "I see the Morning Star," and yet "The Evening Star and the Morning Star are one and the same thing" is a contingent proposition. . . . [10]

Nor do the words "somebody" and "the doctor" mean the same, but the somebody whose office I was in this morning is nevertheless numerically identical with the doctor. Similarly, when I say "I have an after-image" I do not *mean* the same thing as when I say "I have such-and-such a brain process." Yet what is going on is a brain process just the same.

2. "But A cannot be numerically identical with B if there are things you can know about A without knowing them about B, or vice versa."

But this is not true, says the identity theorist. We believe that a flash of lightning is an electrical discharge, and yet we may know that something is a flash of lightning without knowing that it is an electrical discharge. We may know that someone is vice-president of the United States without knowing that he is also president of the Senate; yet the person who is vice-president is the same person who is president of the Senate. I may know that the object I see is red but not know that it is a balloon; yet it is a fact that the red object I see is a balloon; the red thing I see and the balloon are the same object. A person may be able to talk about her thoughts, feelings, and sense-experiences without knowing anything

about her brain processes, just as she can talk about lightning without knowing anything about electricity. X may be identical with Y, although we may not know that it is, and therefore we may not know that the qualities we attribute to X are also qualities of Y.

3. "If X and Y are identical, then if I expect X to occur I should also expect Y to occur. But I don't: I can say that I expect a certain after-image when I have looked at an intense color on a screen, but this is not the same as expecting that my brain will be in a certain state: I have no knowledge, and hence no expectations, about that."

This is true enough, but the identity theory does *not* claim that when we use a mental word, "after-image," we can substitute a physical word describing a brain-state without change of meaning. The two do have different meanings. It is not a *meaning*-identity between two sets of *words* that is claimed but an *empirical* identity between two *things*. I can expect a flash of lightning without expecting an electrical discharge, if I know nothing about electrical discharges; but when lightning flashes, it is an electrical discharge just the same. I can expect an after-image without expecting a brain process, since I know nothing about brain processes; but what is happening is a brain process just the same. It is possible for two things, A and B, to be numerically identical, and yet for a person to *expect* A without expecting B. It is possible for the words "A" and "B" to have different *meanings* even though they have the same *denotation,* and our expectation is directed toward a certain meaning (I may expect the vice-president but not the president of the Senate). Thus the fact that I can expect a certain experience without expecting a brain process does not prove that the two are different things but only (what was already granted) that the meaning of the words "experience" and "brain process" are not the same.

But another objection arises out of this one:

---

[10]J. J. C. Smart, "Sensations and Brain Processes," in V. C. Chappell, ed., *The Philosophy of Mind* (Englewood Cliffs, NJ: Prentice-Hall, 1962), pp. 147–148.

4. "But isn't it logically possible for experience to occur without brain states, even if in fact they never do so? And how can this be logically possible with the identity theory, which says they are numerically identical?"

It *is* logically possible, says the identity theorist—but *not actually true.* If there *were* a case of an experience occurring without a brain state, this would immediately disprove the theory, just as the occurrence of a flash of lightning which was not an electrical discharge would disprove the hypothesis that flashes of lightning are electrical discharges. The claimed numerical identity between mental and physical events is not a *logical* identity, such as we express in the statement that A + B is identical with B + A. Rather, it is an *empirical* identity; the identity in question is an empirical discovery. An identity theorist would say that the experience is *in fact* (not as a matter of logical necessity) numerically identical with a brain process. It is indeed logically possible for experiences to occur without brain processes, but if it actually happened it would disprove the identity theory. However, says the identity theorist, *this never in fact happens.*

The brain, along with the rest of the body, "returns to dust" after death. Thus, if a person had experiences after his bodily death—a possibility we shall examine in the next section—the identity theory would have to be rejected. Or again, if living persons actually received communications from persons already dead—showing them to be alive and having experiences even after they were "brain-dead" and their bodies in the grave—this too would wreck the identity theory. Like any empirical hypothesis, there could be facts that would count against it. Any evidence that there is consciousness after death would be evidence against the theory. The identity theorist is simply saying that there are no such facts, and that until there are shown to be such facts the identity theory can stand.

But is the occurrence of such events— which many people have strongly disputed— the only way the identity theory can be attacked? Must we wait for such events as messages from the dead to be established? Isn't there a more obvious way to criticize the identity theory: Consider:

5. "We agree that the phrases 'morning star' and 'evening star' do not mean the same, although they both denote the same object. but now I would remind you that *if* the morning star has any characteristics that the evening star does not have, or vice versa, then they cannot be numerically identical (the same object). We can, of course, *believe,* or even know, that the evening star has them without knowing that the morning star has them (we may not even know that the morning star exists), but if they are *in fact* numerically identical, then it must *in fact* be true that every characteristic of the first is also a characteristic of the second, and vice versa. Now the mental has characteristics that the physical does not have, and vice versa; and if this is so, they cannot be numerically identical." Thus:

(a) "A brain process always occurs at a certain *place*—in the brain. Does the mental event occur there?"

No. B-processes [brain-processes] are, in a perfectly clear sense, located where the brain is, in a particular region of physical space. but it is not true that C-states [conscious states] occur in the brain, or inside the body at all, for that matter. To be sure, l may have a pain in my leg or in my head; we do locate sensations in the body. but that is not to say that we give location to the *state of consciousness* that I have when I am having a sensation. The pain is in my leg, but it is not the case that my state of being-aware-of-a-pain-in-my-leg is also in my leg. Neither is it in my head. In the case of thoughts, there is no temptation to give them location, nor to give location to the mental state of being aware of a thought. In fact, it makes no sense at all to talk about C-states as being located somewhere in the body. We would not understand someone who pointed to a place in his body and claimed that it was there that his entertaining of a thought or having of an after-image was located. It would make no more sense than to claim that his entertaining of a thought was cubical or a micrometer in diameter.

The fact that it makes no sense to speak of C-states occurring in a volume occupied by a brain means that the Identity Theory cannot be correct. For it is a necessary condition for saying that something is identical with some particular physical object, state, or process that the thing be located in the place where the particular physical object, state, or process is. If it is not there, it cannot be identical with what *is* there. Here we have something that distinguishes the mind-body case from such examples of identity as men with featherless bipeds, Morning Star with Evening Star, water with H_2O, lightning with electrical discharge, etc.[11]

Consider the following: Computers can now be constructed that spew out more information, and far faster, than any human mind can produce. Shall we say that computers also have thoughts, that they "figure things out," that they have mental states, possibly even pains and pleasures? Does the computer *know* the solution to problems we program into it? (1) There are those who say that it does—that if a computer can give us information and even advice, it has as good a claim to possessing a mind as any human being. It does the work of minds, so it's plausible to say that it has a mind; there is no logical necessity about minds being correlated only with the brain states of organisms. If so, however, there are mental events that aren't brain states; after all the computer has no brain. But the identity theorist could respond that such states are physical states of the computer, though not of a brain, but are physical states all the same. (2) In any case, most persons would deny that computers have thoughts; computers give information *as if* they had thoughts, but they are just complicated pieces of machinery that human beings have constructed to provide information; they do only what we program them to do. They do not go through thought

processes and they do not possess knowledge.[12]

(b) "A brain process is *publicly observable;* difficult though it may be to get at for technical reasons, those who probe brains with instruments can observe it, at least to some extent. But a pain or a thought is a private event; nobody can have your pain or your thought but you.

It may be replied that this is only a temporary matter owing to our comparative ignorance of brain states, and that if I had a complete knowledge of neurology, I could, by looking into your brain, know that you were having a pain and even what you were thinking about. This last remark may be true, but of course it does not meet the objection. The fact still remains that even if I *know* what you are thinking, I do not *have* your thought, and knowing that you are in pain is different from experiencing your pain. (Even believers in telepathy do not claim that I can *have* your pain but only that I can *know that* you are in pain, without observing you.) The experience of the mental event is still private, though the knowledge that you have it is not. The perfect neurologist could be just as sure as you are that you are experiencing a pain, but she still would not be having it.

The identity theorist may reply, "Until brain-process theory is much improved and widely accepted, there will be no *criteria* for saying 'Smith has an experience of such-and-such a sort' *except* Smith's introspective reports. So we have adopted a rule of language that (normally) what Smith says goes."[13] But even if there *were* criteria other than Smith's introspective report, such as examining Smith's brain at that moment, and even if everyone by taking a peep at Smith's brain

---

[11]Jerome Shaffer, "Could Mental States Be Brain Processes?" *Journal of Philosophy, LVIII*(1961): 815–816.

[12]See for example, John Searle, "Minds, Brains, and Programs," in *The Behavioral and Brain Sciences,* vol. 3 (Cambridge: Cambridge University Press, 1980), pp. 417–424.

[13]J. J. C. Smart, p. 152.

could tell exactly what Smith was thinking, it would still be the case that Smith alone is *having the experience;* and it is the having of the experience that is private, not the *knowledge* that Smith is having it.

It is not easy to see how the identity theory can convincingly meet this objection. The analogy that it presents with *other* cases of identity is more convincing than the conclusion that the mental and the physical are identical.

When we say the Morning Star and the Evening Star are identical, we mean that both names refer to one physical object at different times in different places. When we say that the president and the commander-in-chief of the armed forces are identical, we mean that both roles are assigned, by law, to the same person. What do we mean in the case of the Identity Theory? Do we mean (1) that certain *brain states are mental,* that they can be directly known by introspection, that someone without the slightest training in neurology can know without observation that certain incredibly complex events ae going on in his infero-temporal cortex? Do we mean (2) that *mental events are physical,* that the thought that today is a holiday, for example, has a shape, a size, a charge, or a color, that it can be photographed, or perhaps smelled? Both of these interpretations seem most paradoxical.[14]

The morning star *is* the evening star; lightning *is* an electric discharge; and heat *is* molecular motion. But these are only analogies with the mental-physical case. The mental-physical case is different from all the others:[15] Imagine God creating the world; what would he need to do to make heat identical with molecular motion? He would only have to create the molecular motion itself, and in doing so he would already have created heat: . . . they are identical. Having created molecular motion, he would not have to undertake a second

job, creating heat. (Creating the *feeling* of heat in conscious organisms would be a second job.) In the case of the mind-brain relation, would it be enough for him just to create brains? It would, if the identity theory were correct, for according to that theory the two are identical. But it would not be enough; he would first have to create organisms with brains, specifically with C-fibers that pain is supposed to be identical with; and having created these, he would then have to create the *felt* experience we call pain—he would have to make the creatures experience the C-fiber stimulation so that it was *felt* as pain, not as a tickle or a sweet taste. And this would be a second job. Indeed, it would be within God's power to make the brain state occur *without* the pain, or the pain without the brain state. Thus, the brain state is not the same thing as the pain. The connection between a brain state and a pain is not necessary but contingent.

When attempts are made to reduce thoughts and feelings to brain states, one thing is entirely left out: what the thought or feeling *feels like* to the experiencer. How can any description of the state of a brain reveal this—any more than a chemical description of ammonia will tell us what it smells like?

Suggesting that your thinking about the North Pole is "really" a physical event is similar to the hypothesis that matter is energy would have had if uttered by a pre-Socratic philosopher. We do not have the beginnings of a conception of how it might be true. In order to understand the hypothesis that a mental event is a physical event, we require more than an understanding of the word "is." The idea of how a mental and a physical term might refer to the same thing is lacking, and the usual analogies with theoretical identification in other fields fail to supply it.[16]

Indeed, we seem to have the same kind of situation here that we encountered in the determinism-freedom controversy: a differ-

---

[14]Jerome Shaffer, "Recent Work on the Mind-Body Problem," *American Philosophical Quarterly, II*(1965): 94.

[15]This description is adapted from Saul Kripke, *Meaning and Necessity* (Cambridge: Harvard University Press, 1972), p. 155.

[16]Thomas Nagel, "How Does It Feel to Be a Bat?" *Philosophical Review 83,* 4 (1974): 435-450.

ence between the "subjective" and the "objective" viewpoint, or "the view from inside" as opposed to "the view from outside." As ordinary human beings, and poets and novelists in particular, we concentrate on what things look like and feel like—something that requires no assistance from the natural sciences. But when we take the "objective" stance, we find only particles of matter in motion, including those in human brains. "Most of the neobehaviorism of recent philosophical psychology results from the effort to substitute an objective concept of mind for the real thing, in order to have nothing left over which cannot be reduced. If we acknowledge that a physical theory of mind must account for the subjective character of experience, we must admit that no presently available conception gives us a clue how this could be done."[17]

What is needed is something we do not have: a theory of conscious organisms as physical systems composed of chemical elements and occupying space, which also have an individual perspective on the world, and in some cases a capacity for self-awareness as well. In some way that we do not now understand, our minds as well as our bodies come into being when these materials are suitably combined and organized. The strange truth seems to be that certain complex, biologically generated physical systems, of which each of us is an example, have rich nonphysical properties. An integrated theory of reality must account for this, and I believe that if and when it arrives, probably not for centuries, it will alter our conception of the universe as radically as anything has to date.[18]

4. PERSONAL IDENTITY

What am I? A person; a conscious being; a self—all these answers seem sensible and obvious. But what is this self?

One answer to this question is, I am a body—a body that happens to be causally re-

lated to certain events and processes we call mental, such as thinking, but a body nevertheless. I begin to exist when my body is formed, and I cease to exist when my body dies.

When I say I am six feet tall, I mean that my body is six feet tall; and when I say I weigh 175 pounds, I mean that my body weighs 175 pounds. Still, am I not different from my body? I say "I have a body," and isn't this preferable to saying "I *am* a body"? Is the body something I have, or own, or possess, or is it what I am? There is surely a strong temptation to say that I *have* a body—in which case I am something more than my body.

In fact, sometimes when I use the pronoun "I" I don't seem to be talking about my body at all. "I am thinking about Paris" is surely not the same as "My body is thinking about Paris." My body doesn't do any thinking at all; not even my brain thinks—*I* think. I think with my brain—or more accurately, I couldn't think without a brain; having a brain is a necessary condition for doing any thinking. Still, it would be a mistake to say that when I think, my body (or any part of it) is what is doing the thinking. When I think, wonder, dream, believe, or hope, it doesn't seem to be my body that is doing any of these things. It is *I* who think. But what then is the "I", if not my body?

Plato believed that I am a mind which just happens to be associated with a body; I am "chained" to my body, until death unchains me from it. This strain of thought is also very prominent in the Christian tradition. The founder of modern philosophy, René Descartes, said that the self *is* the mind. It is not that I *have* a mind, but that I *am* a mind—a mind which exists in conjunction with a body, and which is causally related (in this life, at any rate) to the existence and activities of a body; but the real "I" is the mind. There is matter, and there is mind; and human beings are minds. Sticks and stones are matter only; God is mind only; and human beings are

---

[17]*Ibid.*

[18]Thomas Nagel, *The View from Nowhere* (New York: Oxford University Press, 1986), p. 51.

minds that are accompanied by, or possess, or always exist in conjunction with, bodies.

According to Descartes, the essence of matter is *extension*. To be extended is to be "spread out" in space, to occupy physical space. But the essence of mind, he said, is thought (which for Descartes included sensation and feeling). You cannot say that a mind is 5 inches wide (only that your brain is), or that it is any*where* at all. You cannot perceive it with the senses (the sense organs themselves are parts of your body); you cannot touch it or weigh it on a scale. Yet it is the essential you, and according to Descartes it would be possible for you to exist without any body at all. Bodies happen to be the means whereby we are enabled to identify other persons; we can perceive their bodies, and thus know that they exist. But the Jones whose body you see is nevertheless first and foremost a mind, "a thing which thinks," as well as feels, believes, doubts, dreams, and so on. In this life the body is equipped with sense organs whereby one can perceive the world, including other bodies; but that does not change the fact that one is a mind: The mind is "essential," the body "accidental."

Sometimes the word "soul" is substituted for the word "mind." but it is not very clear what this term means. The Greek term "psyche," which is usually translated as "soul," simply meant (to the ancient Greeks) life; anything that was alive had a soul in this sense. On the other hand, when Descartes said that the mind could exist independently of the body, this implies that consciousness can go on even after the body dies; and isn't this what Christian champions of the doctrine of the "immortal soul" have in mind?

But what *is* the mind? We have discussed mental events, but what is the mind itself? Is it a kind of container that contains all the mental events? But this seems to be merely spatial imagery; the mind, Descartes said, is nonspatial. Descartes and ensuing philosophers often talked about the mind as a *sub-stance,* only a mental substance, not a physical substance. But is is difficult to see what this comes to. Try to imagine such a nonspatial substance. Does it have parts? has it ingredients? what is it composed of? is it indivisible? is it really a *thing* at all?

The *word* "mind" occurs as the subject of a sentence, but that doesn't imply that there is a thing corresponding to the word; it is mistaken to believe that for every substantive (noun) there is a substance. "Something" is the subject of the sentence "Something happened to me today," but the word "something" does not name a substance. The word "mind" can be the grammatical subject of sentences, as in "My mind is very alert today," but it doesn't follow from this that there is a thing, mind, which has alertness as a quality. Still, isn't there something (or someone) that is alert?

Many times when we use the word "mind" we can substitute other terms. "I am not going to change my mind" means that I am determined to retain my present opinion. "It's all in your mind" means that you're only imagining it. "She has a mind of her own" means that she is independent, perhaps even stubborn. "He has a creative mind" means that he originates many new and original ideas. "She is of sound mind" means that she is sane.

But mind is not eliminated by changes of terminology. If she is of independent mind, she *thinks* for herself, she doesn't accept beliefs on the authority of others. But thinking is a mental activity—surely an activity of minds? (Brains don't think, they are only what you can't think without.) "I've changed my mind" means that I no longer think what I thought before. "What do you have in mind?" is a request for what you are thinking about. If a person says there is no such thing as a mind, would he welcome the suggestion that he is mindless?

Still, we tend to be uncomfortable with the suggestion that we *are* simply minds, minds that happen to be somehow connected with bodies. It would be more natural to say that we *have* minds. And the same with bodies; you aren't just a body, but you *have* a body. And having a body seems to be just as important to being *you* as having a mind. What would you, an athlete, be without a body? Does "I have a mind but not body" really make sense? You can say "I had my appendix removed yesterday," but what would it mean to say "I had my body removed yesterday?"

Perhaps then the word "mind" is simply a collective name for all your experiences, just as "society" is a collective name for a large group of individual persons. Perhaps the totality of your experiences throughout your life is what constitutes your mind. But then what is it that makes them *your* experiences? What distinguishes the host of experiences constituting your mind from the host of experiences that constitutes my mind? David Hume, introspecting as carefully as he could, concluded that there is no such thing as an "I" (or self) over and above the various experiences of thinking, wondering, perceiving, and so on. All I am aware of, he said, is these various experiences, and I never encounter *myself* as the owner of these experiences.

There are some philosophers who imagine we are every moment intimately conscious of what we call our *self;* that we feel its existence and its continuance in existence. . . . For my part, when I enter most intimately into what I call *myself* I always stumble on some particular perception or other, of heat or cold, light or shade, love or hatred, pain or pleasure. I never can catch *myself* at any time without a perception, and never can observe anything but the perception.[19]

This may not be so much a *denial* of the self as an *analysis* of what it means to talk about a self. The self, says Hume, is simply a "bundle of experiences." From birth to death our experiences occur in temporal succession,

and this entire series of experiences, in a succession of time-slices, is what constitutes the bundle. There is no self beyond the bundle, any more than there is a superperson over and above the individuals constituting a society. Hume's view is sometimes called the "bundle theory of the self."

But, one may ask, what unites the series of states in the bundle into the history of this person rather than that? Don't the various experiences in the bundle require an owner, or "haver," of the experiences? Thoughts and feelings don't float around with no one to have them. Thoughts require thinkers; there are no free-floating thoughts. Thoughts belong to someone; they are experiences in the history of some self or other. The thoughts I have are mine. My experiences throughout life form one series; your experiences constitute another series; and no item in my series is also an item in your series. (We may both think *about* the same thing, but my thoughts are still mine and yours yours.) No part of my bundle is also part of yours. In an ordinary bundle, however, say a bundle of sticks, a stick can be taken from one bundle and placed in another bundle; but this is not so with mental events, which belong exlusively each to its own bundle.

What is it then that ties the items in my bundle together? Isn't it just the basic fact—which we don't seem to be able to analyze further—that they are *mine;* they belong to my history, not to any one else's? As the Scottish philosopher Thomas Reid (1710–1796) put it, in response to Hume,

My personal identity implies the continued existence of that indivisible thing which I call *myself.* Whatever this self may be, it is something which thinks, and deliberates, and resolves, and acts, and suffers. I am not thought, I am not action, I am not feeling; I am something that thinks, and acts, and suffers. My thoughts, and actions, and feelings, change every moment; they have no continued, but a successive, existence; but that *self,* or I, to which they belong, is permanent, and has the

---

[19]David Hume, *Treatise of Human Nature,* book I, part 4, chapter 6.

same relation to all the succeeding thoughts, actions, and feelings which I call mine. Such are the notions that I have of my personal identity.[20]

Moreover, is it really true that, as Hume says, "I always stumble on some particular perception or other . . . I never can catch *myself*"? Am I just aware of the feeling? Am I not always aware of the feeling as being *my* feeling? Isn't it the awareness of the experiences as mine that unites them all together as the history of my self? It's not just that they occur in a certain temporal succession; the same is true of your experiences as well as everyone else's. Perhaps they are tied together by *memory*. But whose memory? Beyond temporal succession and memory there seems to be *ownership*. Am I not aware, not merely of thoughts and feelings, but of *myself* as the person who has them? Introspection would seem to answer yes to this question.

When Is it the Same Self?

How do we identify someone as being the same person as she was before? What is it that endures through all the changes, that entitles us to say that in spite of the changes it is still the same person or self? What changes would have to take place in order for us to be able to say that this is no longer the same person?

Things survive many changes. Someone scratched my desk yesterday, but still I say it is the same desk as it was yesterday, the same desk I have used for years. If I painted it a different color I would still say it was the same desk. If I put locks on the drawers I would still say it was the same desk. If I chopped it into kindling and burned it in the fireplace I would no longer say this—not only is it not the same desk, it is no longer a desk at all but a pile of kindling—it no longer has the fea-

[20]Thomas Reid, *Essays on the Intellectual Powers of Man* (1785), essay III, chapter 4.

tures that define something as a desk. ("That *was* a desk," I might say, watching it burn.)

The first and most obvious answer to the question, "When is it the same person or self?" is: "As long as it continues to be (or have) the same body. *Bodily continuity* is the criterion." Having the same body doesn't mean retaining all the same bodily features, however. You have changed a lot since you were a child—in weight and height and general appearance; yet you still have the same body you had then. It may be true as biologists tell us that not a single cell that is in your body today was there 7 years ago, but the general *structure* remains even though the cells have been gradually replaced by others—just as you say, standing on the bridge, that this is the same river that you crossed yesterday, even though the drops of water that passed under you yesterday are now far downstream.

How do I know that my friend whom I haven't seen for ten years is the same person I knew ten years ago? Well, he has changed, but still I can recognize him; there's a certain facial configuration that's similar. He looks older, he has scars and wrinkles he didn't have before. Also, he talks the same way—he may have developed a bit of an accent from his stay overseas, and he is more mature now in the way he talks, and a little fatter; but I still recognize him as the same person.

But do I *know*? Perhaps not; perhaps he had an identical twin I didn't know about, and this is the twin. But then if I asked him questions about incidents in our childhood shared only with him, he wouldn't remember them because he wasn't there, and that would alert me to the possibility that this isn't the same person. Yet he might have been told of them in detail by his brother, so I can't be quite sure (as in the book and motion picture, *The Return of Martin Guerre*). The way to be sure would be to follow him around with a movie camera every moment of his life, so that even if he changed gradually in physical and mental characteristics the film record would show that he had not been replaced by someone else; there was no moment at which this person did not exist, and the uninterrupted film record would show that this is indeed the same body I knew from ten years ago. There was not a split second between birth and death in which his body did not exist. And so, one might say, it's the same person as long as it's the same continuously existing body, even though the bodily characteristics change with time.

For example, (1) suppose the person is a woman who has amnesia and remembers nothing. That doesn't keep her from being the same person, as long as it's the same body; and the uninterrupted record of the movie camera would show this. (2) Suppose she has sudden personality changes—she is a Dr. Jekyll and "Mrs." Hyde. Still, she is the same person because she has the same body—she is still Sarah Smith although she is subject to sudden and surprising personality changes. (3) Suppose she is a multiple personality: Sarah sometimes calls herself Jane, and when she is Jane she is hostile rather than her usual friendly self, and she doesn't remember what Sarah has said or done; and sometimes she calls herself Betty, and then she is very different again and doesn't remember anything done by either Sarah or Jane *(The Three Faces of Eve).* We can now say, "She has three different *personalities,* but she's still the same person who was born on such-and-such a day and was raised in such-and-such a town, and so on." (4) Even if she has a car accident and becomes a human vegetable without consciousness of anything, she is still Sarah Smith lying there in the hospital bed, although she doesn't know that that's who she is. When someone has dual or multiple personality—or becomes an unconscious, merely breathing organism, we do sometimes say "She's not the same person she was"—but this can be taken to mean that her personality has altered, not that she is not the person who was born at such-and-such a date and place, and so on;

when we say "She's not the same person any more," don't we speak figuratively? It's still the same "she," is it not, and don't we imply this even when we say "She is not the same person any more"?

A boy runs away from home and joins a commune; he takes part in the group chants and other rituals, and his personality is so altered that people who knew him before are shocked at the change. He's still Doyle Darcy; though he has changed, it's still the same "he." The commune members claim that his "real self" has finally come out through his experiences in the commune; but his parents, when they find him, allege that he was his "real self" at home and that the commune leaders "brainwashed" him. Which is his real self? The answer would seem to be, both selves are; both represent aspects of his personality. What those around him call his "real self" depends on which personality they consider the most desirable one, and on this one they confer the honor of calling "real." Even so, in all this wasn't he the same Doyle Darcy the whole time, born on such-and-such day, and so on? We say that *he* has changed, not that someone has secretly spirited him away and substituted someone else, whom we now see.

Some philosophers have suggested that being the same person is a *matter of degree,* and that a person may be *partially* the same person he was before, though not entirely so. Since he still has the same body (in spite of changes continuously ongoing within it), the assertion seems to be that the personality changes are what entitle us to say "he's a different person" or (more literally) "he's a partially different person" (or a "very different person") from what he was before. He still has the body of Doyle Darcy, born on such-and-such a day, and so on, but his personality is so different now that it would be mistaken to call him any longer the same person he was before. His body may be the same, his name may be the same, people can still recognize him as Doyle

Darcy, but he is different; he is at least partially a different person.

"But can't we say truly that he isn't the same person after he joined the commune as he was before?" Yes, he is the same biological organism, born of such-and-such parents on such-and-such a date. But since he has changed so much, and now repudiates the boy that he was when he lived with his parents, can't we truly say that he's a different person now (as he himself says)? When a change is very marked or sudden, we often call an organism by a different name; a baby elephant becomes a grown elephant, but a tadpole changes overnight into a frog, and then we don't call it a tadpole anymore. Can't we say the same of Doyle, at least in regard to his personality traits? "He's a different Doyle now." Perhaps not *entirely* a different person—many personality traits and habits remain—but at least *to a high degree* a different person. Why can't "being the same person" be a matter of degree? Why not say "I am the same person I was at the age of ten, but also I'm a different person—I am mature now, have knowledge and emotions I lacked then, have been shorn of many delucions about life and the world, and I don't even feel like the same person I was then." In a psychological sense, isn't this true? When the changes are slow and gradual, there is no one point at which we would say we became different—but after a span of time we can nevertheless say we are, just as a person who has seen you every day for ten years doesn't notice the gradual changes in how you look, but a person who hasn't seen you for ten years is suddenly struck by them and may not even recognize you. "I can't believe this is you!" we may say to this person. Our remark, of course, presupposes that it really is the same person (we can hardly believe it although we know it's true). And yet, would it be incorrect to say "In many ways I am a different person now"—just as the song of which you have changed one note after another till it's hardly recognizable is no

longer the same song—or is it the same song, yet different? Does it matter which we say, as long as we are aware of the facts underlying our modes of verbal expression?

It is not entirely clear what is gained by this suggested change of nomenclature. No one doubts that Doyle now has different attitudes, beliefs, and goals; the question is whether these changes are sufficient to entitle us to refer to him now as a different person, or a partially different person. If they are, couldn't one say the same about a body? Couldn't one say, "It's sort of (or partially) the same body as he was born with—but he's bigger now, and older, and because of his war wounds no one would recognize him who knew him ten years ago," and so on. Wouldn't this, by the same criterion, entitle us to call him a different person because of the bodily changes, just as, in the previous discussion, we are entitled to call Doyle a different person because of his personality changes?

In all the examples thus far, the condition of bodily continuity has remained intact and has led us to say that it's the same person throughout a body's many changes. Now let's stretch the criterion of bodily continuity a bit.

Case 1. Professor Smith is teaching a class in New York and suddenly, at 11:06 A.M., in full sight of everyone, he disappears from view: One moment he was standing there lecturing, the next moment there's nobody there. We are at a loss to explain this: People may disappear by walking out of the room, but not just by vanishing into thin air. But now a friend in Seattle phones to tell you that just as he was expecting his regular professor to appear in the classroom, an entirely different person appeared and started to lecture, and this happened at 11:07 A.M. (Eastern time). He describes the newcomer, and the description matches exactly the description of the professor who suddenly disappeared from his classroom in New York: same appearance, same clothing, same scar on his face—and, it later turns out, same fingerprints. Could the disappearance from New York and the sudden appearance in Seattle be related? Might it actually be *the same person* who disappeared in one place and appeared in the other? How could you be sure?

Suppose various people interrogated him in Seattle and asked him how he got there, and he said "I remember lecturing to a class in New York, and then suddenly I blacked out and found myself here in Seattle, I don't know how." And suppose he remembered his life in New York, and mentioned numerous details that could be checked for accuracy. Wouldn't we now say that the same person who disappeared in New York appeared in Seattle? None of us know how he got there or what happened during that one minute between his disappearance in one place and his reappearance in another. Wouldn't we nevertheless be justified in saying it was actually the same person? What clinches the case is not merely that people recognized him as the same person—that is, the same body—but that he *remembered* his previous life. *Memory* seems to have a great deal to do with whether we take someone to be the same person.

In fact, if *you* were Professor Smith, and were in Seattle reminiscing about New York, wouldn't you *know* you were the same person, even though you didn't know how your body got to Seattle, and indeed even if you had a *different* body in Seattle? This last fact would make people more skeptical about its really being you, but wouldn't *you* know?

Case 2. What if you had an acquaintance who was visible only two minutes out of every three? She sits there in the chair talking with you, and then she disappears—she can't be seen, heard, or touched; then one minute later she reappears. Here the bodily continuity is clearly broken. For two minutes she is perceivable, then for one minute it is as if she didn't exist at all. *Did* she exist during that minute? Is it logically possible for a person's bodily existence to be *intermittent?*

How would we decide this matter? We might ask *her;* Has she any memory of that one minute of disappearance? If she says no, then perhaps she didn't exist during that minute (or was unconscious); but suppose she says yes, and tells us correctly what went on in the room while she was invisible—what then? Wouldn't we have to conclude that she did exist all the time? And if *you* were the person whose bodily appearances were intermittent—but as far as your mental life is concerned it went on as before—wouldn't that show that you existed even during the intervals when you couldn't be perceived by others? But now bodily continuity as a criterion of personal identity has quite collapsed. Now we are nearer the view of Descartes that I am a mind—who happens to be contingently related to a certain body.

In our examples thus far, the body, even if only intermittently existing (or at least intermittently perceivable), has been a recognizable human body. What happens if we change this condition?

Case 3. Suppose that you go to bed at night and wake up the next morning with a body you don't recognize; you were thin, now you are fat; you were light-skinned, now you are dark-skinned, and so on. You have *a* body, but not the one you had before—the one you have resembles much more the body of Mr. Brown, who disappeared last week without a trace. Could it be that you have his body? Could you *be* the person everyone knows as Mr. Brown? No, we would probably say, you are still you in spite of the bodily changes: You *remember* your previous life in the former body, and you have none of Mr. Brown's memories. Memory, not merely having the same body, seems to be a test of whether it is the same person as before.

Case 4. Let us extend this even further. In Franz Kafka's story *Metamorphosis,* the main character, Gregors, turns into a beetle. He can no longer speak (having no organs of speech), nor can he even move about in his former way, but he is still Gregors in the body of a beetle. He remembers his previous life and tries to communicate with his family, and finally—through taps and signs he learns to develop—he comes to make them realize that he is still their son Gregors. *He,* Gregors, still exists; and there is a body, but not a *human* body. Is he still the same person? Is he a person at all? Some would say, "No, he is no longer a person but a beetle"; but others would say, "He is a person in the body of a beetle." In any case, he has the *mind* of a person, and the memories of *this one* person; so surely he is still Gregors. There is still a body, but not a *human* body; yet there remains a human mind, and moreover it's the mind of one specific person, Gregors. Are we still sure that bodily continuity is the only acceptable criterion for continued selfhood?

Case 5. You can have your appendix or gall bladder removed and still be the same person. You can have a transplanted heart or an artificial heart and still be the same person. But what about a transplanted brain? You can exchange kidneys with someone else and remain the same person, but can you exchange brains with someone else? Assume that it is technically possible for surgeons to remove your brain and place it in another's body, and vice versa, with all the connections, such as efferent and afferent nerves, being made so that the brain functions in the unaccustomed body. Would it still be you?

At this point we would probably hesitate to say, "If it's your body, then it's you." If someone else's brain is implanted in your body, wouldn't you then have that person's memories, not to mention many characteristics which are brain-dependent, including your tastes and preferences, your tendencies to respond in definite ways to stimuli, your overall temperament? And if someone else had your brain in her body, wouldn't she have your memories too? And might this not indi-

cate that she is in your body and you in hers? After all it's your mind, isn't it, even though you no longer have the same body you did before? And if it's the same mind, isn't it the same self—namely you? Perhaps Descartes was right after all in saying that your mind is what is essential to being you, and that whether you continue to have the same body as before is a contingent matter, inessential to being you.

Case 6. Suppose that A's brain continues to function normally, but owing to a car accident he is a quadriplegic and has suffered such extensive injuries that most of his body is destroyed. B by contrast has a healthy body but has a brain disease that will soon kill him. A surgeon then removes A's brain and places in B's body, connecting A's brain with B's nerves and so on. Assuming that the operation is successful, and that the survivor is now alive and well, who is the survivor, A or B?

The law would doubtless say that the surviving person is B. What survives is the body of B, who was born at a certain time and place, and whose wallet still includes B's picture and credit cards with B's signature. The survivor would be liable for B's debts and traffic fines. The courts would consider B the survivor and A to be legally dead. Still, can we be sure that it *is* B who is the survivor? The survivor has A's brain, A's memories, A's habits, A's personality. The survivor remembers A's childhood, but not B's. The survivor's present experiences are connected with A's previous experiences, not B's. So isn't it A who has actually survived, even though he is now "in" B's body? (The film *Here Comes Mr. Jordan* presents a series of fascinating speculations on this possibility.)

Who is the survivor, A or B? We might suggest, "We both agree on what the facts of the case are. Now it's just a matter of what we choose to *call* it. If you use a bodily criterion, then B is the survivor; if you use a mental criterion, then A is the survivor. OK, *you* choose which to call it. It's just a matter of nomenclature.''

But *is* it just a matter of nomenclature? Suppose you were A, alert but mangled in body; or on the other hand, that you were B, with a brain disease but a body intact. And suppose you had been told, by an impeccable authority, that at a certain time in the future— say a month hence—you would experience a week of intense pain followed by a week of intense enjoyment. If you were A, would you have reason to anticipate the pain and the pleasure, or could you only anticipate extinction? And if you were B,. would you anticipate the pain and the pleasure, or could you only anticipate extinction? Which one, A or B, would be correct in anticipating these experiences?

Surely the fact that the *law* would say that B is the survivor (because of fingerprints, birth certificate, driver's license, etc.) would make no difference at all. If the survivor is A, then the law would be simply mistaken in saying that it's B. If it's B who would be having these later experiences, the decision of the law that ''it's really A'' would be simply irrelevant to the case.

Indeed, wouldn't it be more likely that we would come down on the other side? Since it's A's experiences, A's memories, and so on that now occur, isn't it A who has reason to expect the threatened pain and promised pleasure? But in that case, isn't what makes A and not B the survivor the fact that A still has (or is?) a mind, is a center of consciousness, an experiencer of pain and pleasure and anticipation? Isn't that what counts? If Gregors survived even in the body of a beetle, isn't it still A— in the present case—even though his brain is now connected to the body of B?

Case 7. A man comes into town who looks just like Abraham Lincoln in his last year of life. You mention the resemblance to him, and he says that he *is* Abraham Lincoln. You mention that he died in 1865 and that it is now

more than a century later, and he says that he is a *reincarnation* of Lincoln.

The first question to be asked is, exactly what does it mean to be the same person reincarnated? I once had a student who claimed to be the reincarnation of J. S. Bach. I pointed out that Bach's body had been buried in 1750. But this did not faze him; he did not merely allege that Bach's spirit lived on in him—that might be said of any serious music student, and in any case one could say that the influence of persons now dead lives on constantly in persons still alive; that kind of thing is perfectly familiar. What the student alleged was that he quite literally *was* Bach. Well then, did this mean that his life took on where Bach's had left off, that he composed Bach's contatas and concertos and oratorios that the original Bach had never had a chance to write because his career was interrupted by death? But no, that didn't seem to be the case either; the student wrote no such works, and his few feeble attempts at writing music were not at all like anything Bach ever wrote. One is inclined at this point simply to say that the student's statement was *false* (not necessarily that he was a liar—to tell a lie is to say what you believe to be false, and he sincerely believed it was true).

The question is, what does a claim of reincarnation mean? (It must be meaningful before it can be either true *or* false.) What would it be for someone to be a reincarnation of Bach? If he simply resembled Bach, then he would be just a twentieth-century lookalike. If he composed music like Bach's, we would be grateful for the music; but we would also view him as someone who had the uncanny ability to write like Bach—Bach was one person, who died in 1750, and this student was another, who was born in 1965. True, he could reel off a lot of facts about Bach's life, which he acquired from books, but so could any Bach scholar; that made him knowledgeable about Bach, but it didn't make him Bach. So what would it mean to say that he was a reincarnation of Bach? Why not just say that here was a twentieth century music student who admired Bach and tried to write like him? That is surely the way we would ordinarily describe this situation.

Back now to our twentieth-century Lincoln. He at least looks like Lincoln, but lookalikes are familiar enough, they barely rate headlines. Now suppose that he tells us many details of Linbcoln's life, some of which we have read but some of which we haven't heard before. We don't know if they are all true, but there are some that we are able to check. He tells us of a diary which he left in a metal case in a certain oak tree near Springfield in 1837; we go there and find it just as he said. We consult historians, none of whom knew of it. We consult handwriting experts, who declare unanimously that it is Lincoln's handwriting. And chemical dating tests all agree that the diary dates from 1837. We give him polygraph tests, and he passes them all. He gives us details of Civil War history which no historian has ever written, but of those details that can be confirmed, we always find them confirmed. He says he remembers being shot in Ford's Theater, and after that he remembers nothing until he awoke in a strange place just this morning.

If this happened, what should we say? Should we say that he *is* Lincoln, and that a person's existence (at least this person's) can be intermittcnt—interrupted for a while and then resumed as before? But Lincoln's body has been buried in Springfield since 1865; its presence was checked just a few years ago by various people before they finally sealed it in cement. Should we say that he *can't* be Lincoln—you can't have two Lincolns, one buried in Springfield and one alive here today? But that would be to identify Lincoln with his body, and perhaps that's a mistake. Here is a man who *remembers* countless details of Lincoln's life—and isn't memory a perfectly good test for being the same person, even in the absence of bodily continuity? And his memories

of Lincoln's life are so detailed that, it would seem, only the real Lincoln could possess them all.

But now a problem arises about memory. He must *really* remember Lincoln's life (1809–1865), not just *seem* to. And sometimes we think we remember when we really don't. Perhaps your mother recounted stories about how she bounced you up and down on her lap, and repeated the story so often that you really seem to remember this happening—in spite of the fact that she made it up and it never happened; yet now you say quite sincerely that you remember that she did this. Couldn't this be the case with our Lincoln? Well, he might have misremembered some things, but in every case that we can still check, his memories turn out to be accurate. Doesn't this show that he really remembers them, and not that he only seems to? We doubt his word when he tells us that he was photographed one day in 1862, but he tells us in what closet in a mansion in Maryland the picture was stored. So we go there, and there it is; all the historians we consult certify its authenticity. And so on, for every other detail which he mentions.

"Well, it could be coincidence." But coincidence can extend only so far. You may at first say it's coincidence that the tides rise when the moon is full, but when you see it happen month after month and year after year you can hardly any longer put it down to coincidence; you may still now know *why* it happens that way, but you do know that it regularly *does*. That the moon really does cause the tides is much more probable than that it always happens by coincidence (the occurring together of events that are not causally related).

Shall we say that he only *seems* to remember, or that he *really does* remember all these things? We would probably come down on the side of really remembering; he passes all the confirmatory tests, and there is no reason any longer to suspect that "he only thinks he remembers it.'' At this point we will have to conclude *something*. And what could be more reasonable that to conclude that this *is* Lincoln, that his mind is still very much alive although he now inhabits a different body (the dead one is buried in Springfield), and that his existence was for some reason interrupted for more than a century? This would certainly shake at least two of our most strongly held beliefs, (1) that a person cannot survive in a different body, and (2) that the existence of persons (both minds and bodies) is continuous and not intermittent. Still, wouldn't we now have reason to doubt these cherished beliefs? We could *call* it reincarnation, if we chose; or we could simply say that persons can survive the death of their bodies and continue to exist in different bodies. Wouldn't we have to admit the fact, even if we could offer no explanation of it?

Suppose for a moment that *you* were the Lincoln in question; you remembered Lincoln's life, including being shot and awakening this morning in a strange place. Even if others might be deceived, wouldn't *you* know whether you were the same person who was shot in 1865? It would seem that the answer must be no. Just as in the case of ''remembering'' that your mother bounced you up and down on her knee, you might think you remembered what really happened without actually remembering it (in the sense that you can't really remember what didn't happen). The test of whether memory is genuine cannot be introspection, which is fallible; the test must be an objective one, such as public confirmation of the details you claim to remember. But if this public confirmation occurred in case after case, would not our skepticism in the matter gradually dissolve into belief? If the events occurred as described, what alternative would we have? We would simply have to abandon our old beliefs and admit that persons can exist in the absence of the bodies that they originally inhabited.

Case 8. Suppose that

. . . a machine is built that will, when a person enters it, record the type and position of each molecule in his body and then disintegrate him. The process takes only a few seconds and ends with a pile of atomic debris lying on the floor of the recording chamber. The tape which contains the information about the molecular structure of the individual's body can then be fed back into the machine; and after the requisite raw mateials are added, the machine will fabricate a person who not only looks and talks exactly like the one who entered the machine in the first place, but also believes that he is that person.[21]

This example violates the criterion of bodily continuity, for there are a few seconds when ''you'' are only a pile of atomic debris on the floor. But it violates bodily continuity no more than the case of the professor who finds himself suddenly in Seattle. In the present case, the atoms that constitute your body are then reconstituted in the same order. Is it you that survives, or someone who is just like you? Well, it seems to be *you,* wouldn't you say? Not only are the atoms of your body reconstituted, but (more important) the person has your personality and (most important of all) remembers your past experiences up to the moment you stepped into the machine. It's surely you, isn't it? You remember your childhood, you remember stepping into the machine and stepping out of it again, and only 30 seconds have passed according to the clock on the wall—far less time than elapses during an ordinary sleep.

Case 9. You would probably give the same verdict with regard to the following ''Star Trek'' examples. To transport people from the Starship Enterprise to other planets, a machine is devised which breaks up the human

---

[21]From ''Personal Identity,'' by Charles B. Daniels, in Peter A. French and Curtis Brown, eds., *Puzzles, Paradoxes, and Problems* (New York: St. Martin's Press, 1987), pp. 49–50.

body into its constituent atoms and accelerates these particles in a high-energy beam; then the bodies are reconstituted exactly as they were on some faraway planet.[22]

Surely it's still you, living now on the distant planet?

Case 10. Let's change the example slightly:

Scientists tell you that instead of having to travel by rocket, which would take many years, you can step into their machine here on Earth and (so they claim) step out of a similar machine on the colonized planet a few hours later. What the machine does is conduct a complete scan of the state of every single cell in your body, recording all this information on a computer (the nature of the scan being such that the cells are all destroyed by the process). The information is then transmitted in the form of a radio signal to a machine on the colonized planet, which will build a replica of you which is exact right down to the last detail.[23]

The body that emerges on the distant planet has all your personality features as well as your memories of life on Earth. Since this is the case, isn't it still *you* who survives? True, there is a difference between this case and the previous one; the atoms constituting your body on earth have been left behind, to be replaced by entirely different ones on the distant planet; so the body is a new one, unlike the previous case of the "beamed-down trekkies." No material is transmitted by the machine. So the new body is (1) not continuous in space and time with the old one, and (2) not made up of the same atoms. Still, the body on the distant planet is qualitatively identical with your body on earth, with a consciousness that contains memories of your life on earth. And because of this, is it not you? You don't feel yourself in any way to be a different person; your existence on the other planet seems to you entirely continuous with your existence on earth. You may even go about fulfilling some of the plans you made for yourself on earth.

Surely we would be entitled to say that it is *you* who survives, not a reincarnation of you on some other planet. How does this differ from the Abraham Lincoln case? In that instance, too, the person looks like Lincoln, talks like Lincoln, and has Lincoln's apparently genuine personality and memories. Shall we say that this is Lincoln or a reincarnation of Lincoln in another body? One important fact is that this does look exactly like Lincoln; we are tempted to say that it is Lincoln, though we don't know what happened to him in the intervening years. If a man today had a terminal illness and decided to have his body frozen until a century later when there might be a cure for the disease, and a century later he did emerge complete with memories, surely we would say that it is the same person who survives into the 21st century. In this case, of course, the requirement of bodily continuity is satisfied. In the case of Lincoln, if something like that happened to him we would say it is the same man, Lincoln, who confronts us now after a period of suspended animation. But in the Lincoln case we don't know what happened to him between then and now; so perhaps we should say that this is a *reincarnation* (re-embodiment) of Lincoln—Lincoln's mind animating another body that resembled his.

Suppose now that there was no resemblance between this man and the original Abraham Lincoln; then we'd never recognize him as Lincoln. But suppose he had Lincoln's memories and could direct us to the same tree containing the old diary, and so on. The lack of physical resemblance might lead us to say that it wasn't Lincoln after all. But *he* doesn't think of himself as anyone but Lincoln. He remembers clearly giving the Gettysburg Address and so on. What we have here is the same mind in a different body—mental continuity without physical continuity.

---

[22]A description of this case is found in Peter Carruthers, *Introducing Persons* (Albany, NY: SUNY Press, 1986), pp. 191–192.

[23]Peter Carruthers, *Introducing Persons,* p. 198.

Even if the man before us did look like Lincoln, as in our original example, perhaps we should say that he too is not the original Lincoln but a *reincarnation* of Lincoln in a different (though similar) body. It wouldn't make any difference to *him* which we called him—Lincoln himself or his reincarnation; his recollections of Lincoln's life up to 1865 are the same either way. But if he lacked *both* the body *and* the recollections, there would be nothing to connect him with the historical Lincoln, and then, like the Bach student, there would be no point in saying that he was a reincarnation of Lincoln; indeed, what would it mean to say it? Anybody could *say* that he or she was the reincarnation of someone else, but how would you distinguish the real ones from the pretenders in the absence of criteria? And once we abandon both bodily and psychological continuity, what criteria for reincarnation could there be?

It may be that the difference between the atomic-transfer-machine case and the Lincoln case lies in our system of *background beliefs* about the way things happen in the world:

When we read the details of the machine case, we find they fit easily into a whole set of background beliefs we have about how things actually work in the universe. The people emerging from the machines have the characters, personalities, and beliefs they do *because* character, personality, and belief is determined by the position and type of certain molecules in one's body—at least that is what we believe about these matters. And when we realize that the people who emerge from the machines are not the ones who first entered, we are *still* able to give this explanation of why they act, talk, and believe as they do. We do not *have* to fall back upon such outlandish things as clairvoyance or queer rememberings to explain the phenomena (not that a thing cannot be explained by both the concept of molecules at work and by the concept of remembering). But if we didn't have the background beliefs we do have, the machine case might be on a par with the reincarnation case.[24]

---

[24]Charles B. Daniels, *op. cit.,* p. 55.

Case 11. In all these cases, the continuity of personality characteristics and, particularly, of memory survival lead us to say that in spite of all these drastic changes "it's still the same person" who survives. But now let's complicate the case still further. The machine disintegrates "Nancy"—leaving only a pile of debris on the floor—and the tape containing her molecular structure is then fed back into the machine: Nancy is reconstructed exactly as she was before, complete with memories. Now why can't the machine record this information on two or more tapes—tapes fed into separate machines, thus resulting in two persons who claim to be the same person? Which of *them* is Nancy? Are both of them Nancy? Can there be two persons, each of whom is the same person?

Clearly they are not the same person *now*. They can both see the duplicate of themselves and might even get into conversation with each other, discussing their memories of a time when they were the same person. They *were* one person (before stepping into the machine), but *now* (after stepping out, on the distant planet) there are two of them. If only one of them is Nancy, which one is it? Is there any way to tell, since they have identical personalities and identical memories? If you were the person stepping out of the machine—and remembered stepping into it earlier—you would surely claim that you were Nancy. But so does the other person, who also remembers stepping into the machine and later stepping out of it. You and the other Nancy are clearly two different persons *now,* but each of you has as good a reason to say that she is Nancy as the other. Still, you are here and the other Nancy is over there—how can there be two Nancys? There are two brains, two centers of consciousness, two sets of memories. Will the real Nancy please stand up? Or are they both Nancy? But how can two persons (which they clearly are now) be the same person—not qualitatively identical persons, but the same person?

"It's a matter to be decided by linguistic stipulation," we might finally say. "You can call one of them Nancy, or you can call them both Nancy. Since we've never encountered this kind of situation, we don't know [haven't decided] how we would describe it in words if it did arise." This seems like an easy way out of the mess. But if you were Nancy-1, with memories of Nancy on earth, you would certainly claim with good reason to be the same person as before. But exactly the same considerations apply to Nancy-2. Suppose that before stepping into the machine you were told that, after stepping out, you would have one hour of excruciating pain; and suppose that after stepping out Nancy-2—but not Nancy-1—suffers that hour of excruciating pain. Would that show that Nancy-2 was the real Nancy and not Nancy-1? It might seem so; but perhaps the person who predicted the pain was predicting it of the wrong one—he just made a mistake? What would be our criteria here for deciding?

Indeed, we need not go so far as this science-fiction example to make the point. Let's return to our Abraham Lincoln example. The man before us claims to be Lincoln, looks like Lincoln, says he remembers giving the Gettysburg Address and signing the Emancipation Proclamation, and gives us evidence that he is Lincoln, not just a lookalike. But just as we have decided that he is really Lincoln—come back after all these years—and are wondering what to make of this curious fact, another man comes along who also looks like Lincoln, talks like him, claims that he remembers giving the Gettysburg Address, and gives us recollections of his previous life, including data that can be authenticated—just as in the case we've already considered. Can we say that both these men *are*—the one and only—Abraham Lincoln? They both carry identical sets of memories, and both sets of memories are authentic. What are we to say now? In the case of inanimate objects like tables, it's easy: If they are in two separate places they are two tables and not one; and if they are in two separate places they are two *bodies* and not one—but what if there are two bodies but *identical* sets of memories? There are clearly two persons, two personalities—but each has the same claim to be considered Abraham Lincoln, the sixteenth president of the United States.

Viewed from the outside (in the third person), each of them has the same claim to the title of being Lincoln. Viewed from the inside (in the first person), Lincoln-1, with Lincoln's memories, "knows" that he is Lincoln and that the other is an impostor; but Lincoln-2 also considers Lincoln-1 to be an impostor.

We could say that there are two bodies but only one person. This would be contrary to anything we need to say in our present world, because we have never confronted cases of this sort. Or we could say there are two bodies and two persons, but that each of these persons have identical recollections. This too does not describe any situation we encounter in our present world, but if what has just been described did occur, the latter would probably be the least misleading way of describing it. Either description would constitute a denial of a fundamental belief ("If there are two bodies, it must be two people"; "If there is one person, there is one body"); some philosophers have held these beliefs to be necessary propositions. But a necessary proposition must be true in all possible worlds, and we have just described a possible world in which these things occur. The conclusion to be drawn, presumably, is that some propositions which were thought to be necessary are not. And that our language, embodying our conceptual schemes, is not set up in such a way as to decide between these alternative descriptions.

Immortality

1. Life in Another Body. Every human body dies and returns to dust. According to any bodily criterion of personal identity, therefore, the self cannot outlive the death of the body; consciousness ends when the body dies. But as our examples in the previous section developed, it came to seem more and more plausible that the history of a self is not merely the history of a body, and that it is at least conceivable that consciousness might continue in spite of bodily death. The examples did not pretend to show that this *does* happen, only that it *could* happen—that it is logically possible. Suppose, for example, that you are lying in a hospital bed and hear the physician whisper that you are dying, and then you lose consciousness; but you wake up again in an entirely different environment, and you remember your life in your earthly body. If you died and woke again, you would know, wouldn't you, that you had survived the death of your body? This would seem to be the decisive test; it would prove once and for all that at least one person survived bodily death. But of course we won't be able to perform this decisive test until we ourselves die. And if the result is negative, we'll never know.

If we can imagine these things, can we not take it a step further? Couldn't you awaken in an entirely different world altogether, yet remember your life in this world?

Mr. X, then, dies. A Mr. X replica, complete with the set of memory traces which Mr. X had at the last moment before his death, comes into existence. It is composed of other material than physical matter, and is located in a resurrection world which does not stand in any spatial relationship with the physical world. . . . Mr. X meets and recognizes a number of relatives and friends and historical personages whom he knows to have died; and from the fact of their presence, and also from their testimony that he has only just now appeared in their world, he is convinced that he has died. Evidences of this kind could mount up to the point at which they are quite as strong as the evidence which . . . convinced the individual in question that he has been miraculously . . . [moved to Seattle]. Resurrected persons would be individually no more in doubt about their own identity than we are now,

and would be able to identify one another in the same kinds of ways, and with a like degree of assurance, as we do now.[25]

Regardless of the kind of variations played on this theme, the constant element is the existence of a *body*. You awake in a new body; you recognize the (resurrected) bodies of others, and they recognize you. This can hardly be *the same* body you have in this life, which is now cremated or lies buried in a grave—and its continued presence in the grave can be checked by others, as is sometimes done in cases of exhumation. So it is a different body. How did the body you had in this life suddenly get replaced by a different one? Such a replacement seems so bizarre that only a supernatural power could perform such a feat—it is no wonder that belief in immortality is almost always accompanied by belief in God.

What kind of body would this be? Would it be identical with the one you had at the time of your death? But that body would be defective in some way, or else death would not have occurred. If one is to think of the "life of a new body" as something to be desired, as most religions do, would it then have to be a perfect body—whatever that is? It would surely have to be similar enough to our present bodies for others to *recognize* us, and for us to recognize them. The Christian tradition, for example, describes us as having life in a new body, not life without a body. This makes the resurrected life more familiar, more like the life we have now; it provides consolation for those who have lost loved ones in death— they will one day see their loved ones again, speak with them. Would an overweight person on earth still be overweight in heaven? Presumably a male on earth would still be a male in heaven; but would he have the same scar on

---

[25]John Hick, "Theology and Verification," in Anthony Flew (ed.), *Body, Mind, and Death* (New York: Crowell-Collier, 1964).

his cheek, the same protruding teeth, the same tic, the same waistline and height? Or would he be an invisible spirit? And what is that? A voice you can hear and recognize but not a physical form you can see? Once the connection with the senses becomes so remote that you can't see or touch others, much of the appeal of immortality disappears. The woman whose husband has just been killed in a car accident looks forward to seeing him again in another life—but what is it about this prospect that gives her consolation? Seeing him as he was just before he died? Communicating with him about shared memories? Having him sit at the dinner table while he eats his favorite dishes (hers) as he used to? (Do they eat beef in heaven?) Perhaps what she craves most is to have sex with him as she used to do; but could sex continue in an afterlife?

Thus far we have considered only the conceivability of individual consciousness after death; we have in no way considered its probability. If you yourself died and then awoke again as described, remembering your experiences on this earth, that would, as we said, constitute decisive evidence that at least one person had survived death. But of course you will not be able to verify this until after you die. Most believers believe it simply on faith, or on the basis of a scripture such as the Bible, whose assurances they trust. But aside from this, is there any scientific *evidence* for life after death, (not the decisive evidence we would get by surviving death ourselves, but indirect evidence)? Psychical research societies have investigated these matters for many years. It is alleged that there are

. . . numerous well-authenticated cases of apparition of a dead person to others as yet unaware that he had died or even been ill or in danger, [including those in which] the apparition conveys to the person who sees it specific facts until then secret, [such as] the apparition of a girl to her brother nine years after her death, with a conspicuous scratch on her cheek. Their mother then revealed to him that she

herself had made that scratch accidentally while preparing her daughter's body for burial, but that she had then at once covered it with powder and never mentioned it to anyone.

Another famous case is that of a father whose apparition some time after death revealed to one of his sons the existence and location of an unsuspected second will, benefiting him, which was then found as indicated. . . . Other striking instances are those of an apparition seen simultaneously by several persons. It is on record that an apparition of a child was perceived first by a dog, that the animal's rushing at it, loudly barking, interrupted the conversation of the seven persons present in the room, thus drawing their attention to the apparition, and that the latter then moved through the room for some fifteen seconds, followed by the barking dog.[26]

One wonders what to make of all this. Although the Society for Psychical Research makes every attempt to eliminate fraud and delusion, many people simply deny that such things occur: This may simply be dogmatism on their part, or inability to reconcile new discoveries with their present beliefs—like those who condemned Galileo for alleging that the earth goes round the sun.

Assuming that such apparitions occur (and apparently some have been photographed), what do they mean? Is the "apparition" the *same person* as the one recently deceased? Is it a person at all? If so, what can be the mode of existence of such a person? (What do ghosts do?) What kind of life is the life of an apparition? Has the "person" who appears after death in an apparition been living (and breathing, and eating?) during the time subsequent to his or her death? What kind of existence would this shadow existence be? The further we get from life in a familiar body that we can see and touch, the further our powers of imagination are strained in trying to determine, not so much whether statements about

---

[26]Curt J. Ducasse, "Is Life After Death Possible?" in Antony Flew (ed.), *Body, Mind, and Death,* pp. 226–227.

them are *true,* but (always a prior question) *what it means* to assert them in the first place.

2. *Disembodied Existence.*

Hume alleged that if two things, or qualities, A and B, always occur together, they can be imagined to occur separately (the one without the other), and it is a matter of empirical inquiry whether they do. As a general principle one could question this; can color occur without extension? can color occur without shape? But let us ask, in the present context, whether consciousness can occur without a body, even though all the instances of consciousness we are familiar with are related (causally or otherwise) to bodies.

Try to imagine yourself without a body. Imagine thinking thoughts, having feelings and memories, and even having experiences of seeing, hearing, and so on *without* the sense organs that in this life are the empirically necessary conditions of having these experiences. Having eyes is one thing; seeing colors is another. Isn't it conceivable—whether or not it occurs in fact—to see colors even though you lack the sense organs which in your present life are the *means* by which you see colors?

You go to bed one night and go to sleep, then awaken some hours later and see the sunlight streaming in the window, the clock pointing to eight, the mirror at the other side of the room; and you wonder what you will do today. Still in the bed, you look down where your body should be, but you do not see your body—the bedsheets and blankets are there, but there is no body under them. Startled, you look in the mirror, and see the reflection of the bed, the pillows, and blankets, and so on—but no *you;* at least there is no reflection of your face or body in the mirror. "Have I become invisible?" you ask yourself. Thinking of H. G. Wells' invisible man, who could be touched but not seen, you try to touch yourself; but there is nothing there to be touched. A person coming into the room would be unable to see or touch you, or to hear you either; a person could run his hands over the entire bed without ever coming in contact with a body. You are now thoroughly alarmed at the idea that no one will know you exist. You try to walk forward to the mirror, but you have no feet. You might find the objects near the mirror increasing in apparent size, just as if you were walking toward the mirror. These experiences might occur as before, the only difference being that there is no body that can move or be seen or touched.

Now, have we succeeded in at least imagining existence without a body? Not quite. There are implicit references to body even in the above description. You see—with eyes?— *no,* you have no eyes, since you have no body. But let that pass for the moment; you have experiences similar to what you *would* have if you had eyes to see with. But how can you *look* toward the foot of the bed or toward the mirror? Isn't looking an activity that requires having a body? How can you look in one direction or another if you have no head to turn? And this isn't all; we said that you can't touch your body because there is no body there; how did you discover this? Did you reach out with your fingers to touch the bed? But you have no fingers, since you have no body. What would you touch (or try to touch) *with?* You move, or seem to move, toward the mirror—but what is it that moves or seems to move? Not your body, for again you have none. All the same, we said, things seem to get larger in front of you and smaller behind you, just as if you were moving. In front of and behind what? Your body? Your body seems to be involved in every activity we try to describe even though we have tried to imagine existing without it.

Every step along the way is riddled with difficulties. It is not just that we are accustomed to think of people as having bodies and can't get out of the habit. This makes things more difficult, but it is only part of the problem. The fact is that you can't imagine doing things like looking in a different direction without turning your head, which is usually the result of a decision to do this—and of course you can't turn your head if you have no head to turn. If you *decide* to turn your head, you can't carry out this decision in the absence of a head, and so on. There seems to be a whole nest of difficulties—not merely technical but logical—constantly embedded in the attempted description.

There is no necessary, conceptual, connection between the experience we call "seeing" and the processes that physiologists tell us happen in the eye and brain; the statement "James can still see, although his optic centers are destroyed," is very unlikely in inductive grounds but perfectly intelligible—after all, people used the word "see" long before they had any idea of things happening in the optic centers of the brain. It therefore appears to be clearly conceivable that seeing and other "sensuous" experiences might go on continuously even after death of the organism with which they are now associated, and that the inductive reasons for doubting whether this ever happens might be outweighed by the evidence of Psychical Research.

I think it is an important conceptual inquiry to consider whether *really* disembodied seeing, hearing, pain, hunger, emotion, etc., are so clearly intelligible as is supposed in this common philosophical point of view. . . .

"The verb 'to see' has its meaning for me because I *do* see—I have that experience!" Nonsense. As well suppose that I can come to know what a minus quantity is by setting out to lose weight. What shows a man to have the concept *seeing* is not merely that he sees, but that he can take an intelligent part in our everyday use of the word "seeing." Our concept of sight has its life only in connection with a whole set of other concepts, some of them relating to the behavior of people who see things. (I express exercise of this concept in such utterances as, "I can't see, it's too far off—now it's coming into view!" "He couldn't see me, he didn't look round," "I caught his eye," etc., . . . [T]he exercise of one concept is intertwined with the exercise of others; as with a spider's web, some connections may be broken with impunity; but if you break enough the whole web collapses—the concept becomes unusable. Just such a collapse

happens, I believe, when we try to think of seeing, hearing, pain, emotion, etc., going on independently of a body.[27]

There is a whole web of meaning-connections between perceiving and having a body; when we try to break all the connections we appear to be reduced to unintelligibility. But perhaps we used a bad example; perhaps we can imagine thinking, wondering, doubting, and so on (mental operations) taking place without a body. *Where* do these operations occur? They occur, one might say, in a mind; and a mind, unlike a brain, does not exist at any physical *place*. But what do you think about? Surely about a world that is not your mind. And what causes you to have the thoughts you do? Not a brain process, because you have no brain. And once again the description begins to be suspect. What is the *you*? One can go back to Descartes and say, "I am mind which thinks." There is no organism any more, only a disembodied mind. All I can do is engage in these mental operations, and no one else can know I exist because there is no longer any body to perceive. Whether this satisfies anyone's conception of personal immortality is surely open to question. Whether it is even intelligible is an issue that is still hotly disputed.

EXERCISES

1. What does "in the mind" mean in these expressions?

a. You didn't really see it—it's all in your mind.

b. She has too many silly ideas in her head.

c. This strange idea kept cropping up in the back of her mind.

---

[27]P. T. Geach, *Mental Acts: Their Content and Their Objects* (London: Routledge & Keagan Paul, 1965), pp. 112-113.

d. She was a scatterbrain—her thoughts just went flitting this way and that through her mind.

e. Having so many responsibilities put too much pressure on his mind.

f. He changes his mind so frequently that no one knows what he really believes.

2. Evaluate each of the following assertions:

a. Mental events are nothing but brain events.

b. According to psychophysical parallelism, mind exerts no influence on matter.

c. The brain secretes thought as the liver secretes bile.

d. What I see is always something going on in my own brain.

e. Mental events and physical events are logically interconnected.

f. If mental telepathy is a fact, I can experience your pain directly.

g. If mental telepathy is fact, one's experiences are not really private, for other people can share them.

h. Mental events are not really private even now (without telepathy), since I can share your experiences (such as your suffering) by being with you and empathizing with you.

i. Some mental events *are* locatable in physical space; for example, I have a pain in my finger, or my tooth, or my leg (I can even have a pain in an amputated leg).

j. It is true that no surgeon, on opening someone's brain, has ever found any mental events, but perhaps that's because he has never looked hard enough.

3. According to Descartes *(Traité des passions de l'âme,* p. 34 ff.), an interactionist, the point of contact between mind and body lies in the pineal gland of the brain, by which physical stimuli cause states of consciousness and volitions are carried into action. "Let us . . . conceive of the soul as having her chief seat in the little gland which is in the middle of the brain, whence she radiates to all the rest of the body by means of the spirits, the nerves, and even the blood, which, participating in the impressions of the spirits, can carry them through the arteries to all the members. . . . " Evaluate this view.

4. "It is not the mind that survives death, it is the *soul* which survives death." What could be meant by "soul" if the word is not synonymous with "mind"? Is the soul a substance? a mental substance? Would a theory of the soul be different (and if so, how) from a theory of the mind?

5. Do you consider it logically possible, and why,

a. for one mind to affect another mind without the intermediary of matter?

b. for a mind to exist without a body?

c. for a mind to touch a body?

d. for one person to have two bodies?

e. for one person to have two minds?

f. for one mind to control two bodies directly? (e.g. by willing to raise its arm)

g. for one body to be controlled by two minds?

In each case, try first to describe a situation which would count as an instance of the kind of thing mentioned.

6. Do you believe that your dog or cat:

a. has desires?

b. has wishes?

c. has fears?

d. ever worries about anything?

e. dreads anything in the future?

f. thinks of you when you're absent?

g. wonders where you are?

h. loves you?

i. appreciates the food you provide?

j. has any concepts?

k. has any beliefs?

l. knows any propositions to be true?

Give reasons for your answer in each case.

7. Consider these two claims: (1) "Napoleon had a stronger power-impulse than most people do." (2) "No, it's not that he had a greater desire for power, it's that he had much *less* of a desire than the rest of us do for everything else." Is there any way to tell? Is there a difference?

8. If you anticipate being touched by a very hot object, you expect to feel a burning sensation—and you *do,* even if what touches you is ice. What does expecting to feel a burning sensation cause—a false belief, or a burning sensation?

9. "This desk before me would not be the desk it is if it were not made of wood; if it were of a different size and shape; if it didn't have just this particular scratch on it; if it didn't have just these books which are on it at this moment. Every property of this desk is necessary to its being this desk. Similarly, you would not be the person you are if

you had been born at a different time; if you had been born a different sex; if you didn't have the color eyes you do; if you didn't have the parents you do; and if you weren't reading just the book you are reading now.'' Discuss.

10. Is it logically possible to witness one's own funeral?[28]

11. What would you say about personal identity if the existence of the body was *intermittent*? Two minutes out of every 3 there is a body—you see it moving and hear words come from its lips— and the other minute there is nothing there at all: nothing that can be seen, touched, photographed, x-rayed, nothing fulfilling any of the tests for a physical object. What meaning (if any) would you attach to the hypothesis that he existed during the 1-minute intervals? What (if anything) would entitle us to say that what reappeared after the 1-minute disappearance each time was *the same* person as the one who existed before the disappearance? (Would he have to reappear in the same place, or have the same physical characteristics that he had prior to his disappearance? By what criteria would you decide whether it's ''really the same person''?)

12. Which of the following ways of speaking would you find preferable, and why?

''I am a mind'' or ''I have a mind''? ''I am a body'' or ''I have a body''? Can you give some basis for the preference? Which do you consider preferable, ''I am a mind which has or is associated with a body'' or ''I am a body which has or is associated with a mind'' or ''I am a person who has a mind and a body'' or ''I am a person who is both a mind and a body''—or some other formulation?

13. Would you still say ''It's the same person'' if

a. she loses her memory, completely and permanently, but her body persists?

b. she turns into a monkey, but retains her memories as a human being?

c. she turns into a monkey, and also loses her memories as a human being?

d. her body disintegrates before your eyes, but her voice (or one that sounds exactly like hers) continues to speak?

e. her body disappears before our eyes, returning (or another body just like it) 10 years later, complete with the woman's memories and personality traits?

14. Defend one of the following views: (a) that you can know that others have pains and can give evidence; (b) that you can have well-founded belief that others have pains, but belief short of knowledge; (c) that you do not have even well-founded belief in this matter.

15. If someone you had conversed with many times died, and if his skull was posthumously opened—revealing not bones and tissue but plastic tubes and electric wiring—would this discovery lead you to believe or suspect that he had never been a conscious human being at all but a mindless automaton? Why or why not? (If someone opened *your* skull and found only plastic tubing and complicated circuits, would that person be entitled to say that you had been an automaton all along without conscious states?)

16. Can computers feel pain? Assuming that they can present some of the same responses that human beings do, including saying that they're in pain, would this incline you (or disincline you) toward saying that computers can feel pain? Is pain necessarily a response to tissue damage in one's body, or is this only a contingent fact, which might be otherwise?

17. How would you go about finding out whether creatures from another planet, appearing on earth, felt pain? They don't withdraw their hands from the fire—but then perhaps fire doesn't hurt them as it does us. And so on.

18. Suppose that instead of one man with Lincoln's memories six men, all lookalikes of Lincoln, turned up, and each one of them could produce some piece of evidence like the diary in the tree, and thus each had an equal claim to be the real Lincoln resurrected. Would you say there were six genuine Lincolns now? all the same person? or all impostors? or what?

19. A man disappears suddenly from the chair opposite you where he was sitting; you can neither see nor touch him, but his voice continues to converse with you as before. Would you say he still exists? Only as long as the voice continues? If sight

---

[28]See two articles on this by Antony Flew: ''Can a Man Witness His Own Funeral?'' *Hilbert Journal* (1956); and ''Sense and Survival,'' *The Humanist* (London, 1960).

and touch are the means by which we recognize something as a physical object, what happens when we have neither sight nor touch but only sound? Would you say the person exists, or only the sound of his voice still exists?

20. Can you render the alleged concept of consciousness without a body plausible? Try to describe it. If you cannot, does this lead you to conclude that existence of mind without body is logically impossible? or merely that your powers of imagination (or that of every human being) are too limited to handle this concept? or that we have no such concept? or what?

SELECTED READINGS

ANDERSON, ALAN R. *Minds and Machines.* Englewood Cliffs, NJ: Prentice-Hall, 1964.

ARMSTRONG, D.W. *A Materialist Theory of Mind.* London: Routledge & Kegan Paul, 1968.

AUNE, BRUCE. *Knowledge, Mind, and Nature.* New York: Random House, 1970.

AYER, ALFRED J. *The Concept of a Person and Other Essays.* London: Macmillan, 1964.

BORST, C. V., ed. *The Mind-Brain Identity Theory.* New York: St. Martin's Press, 1970.

BROAD, C. D. *The Mind and Its Place in Nature.* London: Routledge & Kegan Paul, 1925.

BUTLER, JOSEPH. "Of a Personal Identity," in *The Analogy of Religion,* 1736.

CAMPBELL, KEITH, ed. *Body and Mind.* New York: Anchor Books, 1970.

CARRUTHERS, PETER. *Introducing Persons.* Albany: SUNY Press, 1986.

CHOMSKY, NOAM. *Language and Mind.* New York: Harcourt Brace, 1968.

DAVIDSON, DONALD. *Actions and Events.* Oxford: Clarendon Press, 1980.

DANIELS, CHARLES B. "Personal Identity," in Peter A. French ed. *Philosophers in Wonderland.* Sussex: Harvester Press, 1975.

DENNETT, DANIEL C. *Brainstorms.* Cambridge, MA: Bradford Book, MIT Press, 1978.

FEYERABEND, M., and GROVER MAXWELL, eds. *Mind, Matter, and Method.* Minneapolis: University of Minnesota Press, 1966.

FLEW, ANTONY, ed. *Body, Mind, and Death.* New York: Macmillan, 1962.

FODOR, JERRY. *Representations.* Cambridge: Bradford Books, 1981.

FULLERTON, GEORGE S. *A System of Metaphysics.* New York: Macmillan, 1904. (See Part 3.)

GLOVER, JONATHAN. *The Philosophy of Mind.* London: Oxford University Press, 1976.

HOOK, SIDNEY, ed. *Dimensions of Mind.* New York: New York University Press, 1960.

JAMES, WILLIAM. *Principles of Psychology.* New York: Longmans Green, 1890. (See Chapter 10.)

KRIPKE, SAUL. *Meaning and Necessity.* Cambridge: Harvard University Press, 1972. (See Lecture 3)

LEWIS, H. D., ed. *Clarity Is Not Enough;* Including A. C. Ewing, "Ryle's Attack on Dualism" and H. D. Lewis, "Mind and Body" London: Allen & Unwin, 1963.

LOCKE, JOHN. *An Essay Concerning Human Understanding.* 2nd ed., 1694. (See Book 2, Chapter 27.)

MALCOLM, NORMAN. *Memory and Mind.* Ithaca: Cornell University Press, 1977.

NAGEL, THOMAS. *The View from Nowhere.* New York: Oxford University Press, 1986.

ORNSTEIN, JACK. *The Mind and the Brain.* The Hague: Nijhoff, 1972.

PERRY, JOHN. *Personal Identity.* Berkeley: University of California Press, 1975.

PUTNAM, HILARY. *Mind, Language, and Reality.* Cambridge: Cambridge University Press, 1975.

RORTY, AMELIE, ed. *The Identity of Persons.* Berkeley: University of California Press, 1976.

RYLE, GILBERT. *The Concept of Mind.* London: Hutchinson, 1949.

SHOEMAKER, SIDNEY. *Self-Knowledge and Self-Identity.* Ithaca: Cornell University Press, 1963.

STRAWSON, P. F. *Individuals.* London: Methuen & Co., 1959.

STRAWSON, P. F., ed. *Studies in Thought and Action.* London: Oxford University Press, 1968.

VESEY, GODFREY, ed. *Body and Mind.* London: Allen & Unwin, 1964.

VESEY, GODFREY. *The Embodied Mind.* London: Allen & Unwin, 1965.

WIGGINS, DAVID. *Identity and Spatio-temporal Continuity.* New York: Oxford University Press, 1967.

WILLIAMS, BERNARD. *Problems of the Self.* Cambridge: Cambridge University Press, 1973.

WISDOM, JOHN. *Other Minds.* Oxford: Blackwell, 1949.

WITTGENSTEIN, LUDWIG. *Philosophical Investigations.* Oxford: Blackwell, 1953.

CHAPTER
7
THE PHILOSOPHY OF RELIGION

The word "religion" does not always carry the same meaning. Some people use it to mean belief in God (or gods); by this meaning, a person who does not believe in God or gods has no religion. For others, religion means total commitment or total dedication to something, not necessarily God. In this sense, a person who is totally dedicated to some humanitarian project is said to be religious, and the cause to which he dedicates himself is "his religion." "That's his religion," one may say, of someone who devotes his life to Marxism or to the preservation of endangered species. A person's religion has even been defined as "whatever a person does with his leisure time." The variations on the use of the word are virtually endless. A person may have a religion in any one of these senses, but it only follows from the first sense that the person has a belief in God.

Even a person who believes in God is not necessarily said to be religious. A person may give a kind of pro forma assent to belief in God: If asked whether she believes in God she will say yes, but it occupies no part in her life, and she seldom or never thinks about it, or acts upon it. To be religious, as opposed to professing a religious belief, involves such matters as prayer, membership in a religious organization, thought and meditation about spiritual matters, dedication to a way of life, and emotional involvement in the religious ideal—though not necessarily all of these.

Many aspects of religion are of no concern to us as philosophers. We are not concerned here with the psychology of religious believers, or matters of ecclesiastical organization; we are concerned, as philosophy always is, with the *justification of belief*. By what arguments, if any, can religious belief be defended or attacked? Moreover, we shall narrow this question to belief in God or gods, saying nothing about religions such as Buddhism which have ethical beliefs but profess no belief in

God, though Buddhism is almost always counted as a religion.

What kind of belief is belief in God? Belief in God is belief in a supernatural being, we might say. But what is meant by " supernatural being"? "Supernatural" means literally "above nature." But the word "above" cannot here be taken literally. The universe includes all space, so there is nothing literally above it. The believer in God holds that in addition to the material universe of planets and stars and galaxies, in addition to atoms and energy and the entities observed or hypothesized by the physical sciences, there is something else—a power (or powers) that created or sustains the universe, and that created the laws of nature and can suspend these laws at will—though this power did not necessarily do all of these things. In ancient Greek religion the gods did not create the universe, but only gave it new form; and according to *deism* God does not sustain the material universe but only created it and thereafter let it run by itself like a piece of machinery. According to *theism*, on the other hand, God both created and sustains or guides the universe. (Christianity, Mohammedanism, and Judaism are all theistic.) According to most religions, this power has *human* characteristics—is a personality with qualities such as benevolence, love, or vengeance. But there are also religions that believe in a supernatural power possessing virtually none of these human characteristics, other than the *power* to issue commands and punish those who disobey. In every case, however, there is believed to be something in reality *other than* the universe of matter and energy studied by physics and other sciences—perhaps a supernatural mind, a "cosmic consciousness"—but at any rate, a power that exists in addition to the universe perceived with the senses or investigated by science. A person who denies that any supernatural being exists is an *atheist;* one who withholds judgment either way is an *agnostic.*

A religion that holds there is only one such supreme power is called *monotheism*—for example, Mohammedanism, Christianity, and Judaism. A religion that holds there are many such powers is called *polytheism*—exemplified by the numerous gods of the ancient Greeks (Zeus, Apollo, Minerva, Poseidon, and so on) as well as of most ancient religions. Most of the arguments we shall consider are intended to establish monotheism, but we shall briefly consider polytheism as well. Moreover, virtually every argument *for* the existence of God is matched by arguments *against* it. We shall begin, accordingly, with a presentation and critical examination of the main arguments that have been presented for belief in God.

I. ARGUMENTS FOR THE EXISTENCE OF GOD

Where do such arguments begin—where do they get off the ground? As a rule, they take some feature or features of the world we inhabit and try to show how these features point to, or give evidence for, a being who exists "beyond" it. The only argument that does not begin with some feature of the empirical world, but is "an argument from pure reason," is the ontological argument, with which we begin.

A. The Ontological Argument

According to St. Anselm (1033–1109), who first propounded the ontological argument, God is that than which nothing greater can be conceived. We can conceive of God as existing, just as we can conceive of a unicorn as existing even though it does not actually exist. But God, unlike the unicorn, *must* exist; for God is the being than whom nothing greater can be conceived, and if God did not *actually* exist, our concept of God would be the concept of a being less great than of one who does exist. Therefore, God exists.

Unicorns, according to St. Anselm, exist "in the understanding only"—even though they don't exist in the physical world, it is easy to conceive of them as doing so. Why not the same with God? Why can't we just say that the *concept* of God is the concept of a being than whom nothing can be greater, but still leave open the question whether anything exists in reality corresponding to that concept? After all, we may say, *you can't define anything into existence*. I can define a unicorn as a horse with a horn protruding from its forehead, and thus I have the concept of a unicorn; but from this it doesn't follow that unicorns exist. If it did, I could populate the world with thousands of creatures just by imagining them. St. Anselm of course is aware of this; but the case of God, he says, is different, for God, being the greatest possible being conceivable, must exist *in order to be the greatest*. If God lacked existence—existed only "in the understanding" like unicorns—then God would not be as great as if he *did* exist, and thus would not be the greatest being conceivable. A being that is wholly imaginary cannot be as great as a being that is actually existent. A wholly imaginary God, a being that existed only "in the understanding" could not be as great as one that actually exists in reality.

It is not entirely clear what "greatest" means: greatest in power? in love? in justice? But it doesn't really matter for the argument. The point is that that which is the greatest conceivable being requires existence, else it would lack one necessary element of greatness and not be the greatest after all.

Yet, one may ask, what does this prove? Can't I imagine a perfect island—an island so perfect (in whatever respect one chooses) that no possible island could be more perfect? And by the same argument, might one not say that such a perfect island must exist, because if it did not exist it would not be as perfect as if it did? But again St. Anselm says no. You can imagine an island than which no greater (more

perfect) *island* is possible; but there may be many things greater than, even more perfect than, this "perfect" island (such as an imperfect human being). And the idea of God is the idea of something *than which nothing greater*, of any kind, is conceivable; and for that perfection to occur, actual existence is necessary. Between a maximally great God existing only in the understanding, and a maximally great God existing in reality *as well as* in the understanding, the latter is without doubt greater.

One could question, however, whether existence is a property that is essential to greatness or perfection. If something is perfect if it has properties A, B, and C, is it any more perfect if it has A, B, C, *and* exists? Isn't it the same "something" we're thinking of in both cases? This was the point of Kant's criticism of the ontological argument: Kant declared that *existence is not a property*. When you say that a unicorn is a horse with a horn, and then you add that such a creature actually exists, are you adding anything to the list of the unicorn's properties? Not at all, said Kant. You are not adding a property to the list, you are only saying that something which has all these properties *exists*. But to say that X *exists* is saying something of a different order from saying that X has certain *properties*. A perfect circle has the property of all points on its circumference being equidistant from the center, but it doesn't follow that any such figure exists anywhere; and if it did, this fact would add no properties to the circle already described. The question of *whether X exists* is one thing; the question of *what properties X has* is another. Kant held that the ontological argument made the mistake of assuming that existence is a property, and accordingly he rejected the argument.

Nothing that does not exist can fulfill the requirements for being St. Anselm's God. But, it seems, nothing follows from this about whether St. Anselm's God actually exists. You can define God as "an existing perfect being," so existence is by definition necessary for such a God. But what it does not show is that such a being actually exists.

The foregoing discussion gives only a hint of the wealth of philosophical literature that has arisen around the ontological argument. Volumes have been written about it. To appreciate the complex debate on the ontological argument, however, requires far more training in philosophy than can be expected of an introductory reader.

B. The Cosmological Argument

There are various forms of the *cosmological* argument, but they all have their starting point with familiar facts of experience: that things exist in the universe, events occur, causes operate, and they all require a cause or an explanation. And, it is argued, the only thing that can provide this is God.

St. Thomas Aquinas (1225–1274) and Samuel Clarke (1675–1729) were among the chief proponents of the cosmological argument. Of Thomas' five arguments for the existence of God, the first three are versions of the cosmological argument. (He rejected the ontological argument.) The first of Aquinas' five arguments attempts to explain the existence of motion: How did anything in the universe get moving? But this presupposes that "the natural state of things" is rest, and Sir Isaac Newton's view that motion was as "natural" a state as rest has made Thomas' first argument less acceptable today. Things already at rest tend to continue at rest, and things already in motion tend to continue in motion; why does motion require explanation any more than rest?

(1) The Causal Argument

The most popular form of the cosmological argument has always been Thomas' second one, the *causal* argument. Everything that happens, it is said, has a cause. (The causal argument assumes this proposition to be true.) But if everything has a cause, the universe too must have a cause, and that cause is God.

It is events, happenings, comings-to-be, that have causes. It is not strictly speaking a thing that has a cause, but the coming-into-being or transformation of that thing, namely an event or process. And the universe, of course, is not an event or process; in fact it is not even a thing. It is, one might say, the entire collection of things and events and processes that occur; "the universe" is a collective term for all of them together. Let's assume, then, that each of the events in the universe had a cause; does it follow that the universe as a whole had a cause? One might suggest that there are as many causes as there are occurrences, each with its own cause.

But still the question persists, Doesn't there have to be a First Cause to set the entire series of other causes in motion? Didn't there at least have to be a first event? God, however, is not usually referred to as a First Event, but rather as an enduring being who created the material universe and thus *caused* its first event to occur. In either case we face the same question—whether a first event or a first being, isn't God required to start the entire series of causes and events which constitute the history of the universe?

There is one very elementary consideration that is fatal to the causal argument as stated. If everything has a cause, then God too has a cause; and what caused God? Many children ask this question, to the embarrassment of their parents. But the question cannot be dismissed. If everything without exception has a cause, doesn't that include God too?

"But God is the cause of everything else, and himself has no cause." But if this is so, then the argument's original premise—that everything has a cause—is false. As it stands, the conclusion of the argument (God has no cause) contradicts its own premise (Everything has a cause). If the premise is true, the conclusion cannot be, and if the conclusion is true, the premise cannot be; they contradict one another. Most people do not see this because, as Arthur Schopenhauer (1788–1860) remarked, they use the causal argument the way they use a taxi; they use the taxi to get them where they want to go, and they don't care what happens to the taxi after that. They use the causal principle to get them to God, and take no thought of the fact that if the causal argument is true it applies to God also.

Let us then amend the statement to read that everything *except* God has a cause. God is the cause of everything, without being the effect of anything, that is, without himself being caused. But if God had no cause, was he the cause of himself? And how could that be—if X is already there, X doesn't need to be caused, and if X is not already there but doesn't yet exist, how can it cause anything? What does *causa sui* ("cause of itself") come to? Is it more than just a meaningless phrase?

"But we have to stop somewhere; causes can't continue backward forever; so why not stop at a First Cause, God?" But other philosophers have turned the question back on the questioner: "*Why* stop there? If you want to go further, and say that God too was caused, then what was the cause of God?" And so on. Or, if you want to stop the process, why not stop at the physical universe, and say that *it* had no cause?

If we stop, and go no farther, why go so far? Why not stop at the material world? How can we satisfy ourselves without going on ad infinitum? And after all, what satisfaction is there in that infinite progression? Let us remember the story of the Indian philosopher and his elephant. It was never more applicable than to the present subject. If the material world rests upon a similar ideal world, this ideal world must rest upon some other; and so on, without end. It were better, therefore, never to look beyond the present material world. By supposing it to contain the principle of its order within itself, we really assert it to be God; and the sooner we arrive at that Divine Being, so much the better. When you go one step beyond the mundane system, you only

excite an inquisitive humor, which it is impossible ever to satisfy.[1]

Some philosophers have pointed out that, in the midst of all this speculation, we are misusing the word "cause," carrying it outside the realm in which it has a use. Our knowledge of causes lies entirely within the realm of spatio-temporal things, processes, and events. Beyond that, we have no reason to speak of causes at all, for experience tells us nothing about any such causality. To extend the principle into some trans-empirical realm is to desert the empirical world in which all known causes occur. Indeed, one might well ask what *meaning* the word "cause" has apart from any references to events and processes going on in the universe. Kant wrote, "The principle of causality has no meaning and no criterion for its application save only in the sensible world. But in the cosmological proof it is precisely in order to enable us to advance beyond the sensible world that it is employed."[2]

Even if successful, however, the causal argument gives us only a first cause. It does not give us any of the deities of traditional religions. (And the same for the other arguments: For example, the ontological argument only gives us a that-than-which-nothing-can-be-greater, not the God of traditional religions.) But in most religions God is a personality, having human characteristics such as goodness and power and mercy, only in far greater degree. There is a pervasive human tendency to identify the first cause with a person whose volitions cause the universe and all that is in it. And yet if we are to go by the empirical evidence we have of causes, there is no evidence that mind or volition goes back that far

---

[1]David Hume, *Dialogues Concerning Natural Religion*, part IV, Norman Kemp Smith edition (Edinburgh: Thomas Nelson & Sons, 1935), pp. 161–162.

[2]Immanuel Kant, *Critique of Pure Reason*, Norman Kemp Smith (trans.) (London: Macmillan, 1933), p. 511.

in the history of the universe. As Mill pointed out.[3] (1) Many movements of matter, such as arranging pieces of wood into a house, are indeed the result of will, and without volition they would never occur. (2) But in no case are we entitled to say that the will *creates,* or brings into being, the matter; it merely changes the position of particles of matter which already exist. (3) The will does originate motion, for example when a bodily movement follows upon an act of will; but it does so only by means of innumerable brain-events, in which one form of energy is converted into another (energy of motion); physical energy itself the will does not create. Far from creating energy, the behavior of the brain-particles (which must occur if consciousness is to occur at all) is itself an instance of the law of Conservation of Energy. In all cases of which we have experience, energy is prior to volition and not the other way around; volition (or its bodily concomitant, depending on one's theory of mind) is just one of thousands of manifestations of energy. So volition is hardly in a position, in an empirical argument, to be an ultimate cause. (4) It seems quite certain that volition did not come into being for countless ages—during all of which the Law of Conservation of Energy was nevertheless in operation—until during the long evolutionary process it finally arose. Energy is, so far as we know, eternal; volitions are not, for we can trace their beginning in time.

None of this, of course, proves that mind— a conscious being who makes decisions—is not the first causal factor to have operated in the universe. One might say, "It could well have happened that way, only we have no empirical means of knowing it now." A conscious being, let us assume, caused the entire series of events and processes to begin; presumably this being not only created the material universe but also the laws of its operation.

But now another question confronts us: Did this act of divine volition which created the universe occur at a certain point in time, or did it not?

Suppose we say that God created the universe at a certain point in time. The Bishop of Usher determined from Old Testament genealogies that the universe was created in 4004 B.C., and many nineteenth-century Bibles contained marginal notes to this effect. Today, of course, the date has been pushed much further into the past. The origin of the earth alone apparently dates back more than four billion years, and that of the galaxies more than twice that far. But the actual date doesn't matter. The question is, *was* there such a date? Some advocates of the Big Bang theory allege that the first bang—the formation of the universe, followed by its explosive expansion to an area measuring billions of light years—was the first event; prior to that *there were no events.* Theologically minded scientists add that before this first *material* event there was God, who willed the Big Bang to occur. But in either case, did this first event occur at the first moment of time? Was there a time *before which* there was no time? And what would it mean to say this? ("There was time all right, but no material universe.") But how can there be time with "nothing in it," so to speak? What would it mean to say that for a million years there was no time and then suddenly time started? How could time *start?* Couldn't we always ask, "*When* did it start?" Was there time before the start? Remember our discussion of Kant, pp. 149–50.

However, it may not be necessary to posit a first moment of time. Perhaps, like the number system, time is infinite, with no beginning and no end. And if the series is infinite, where does God fit into the picture? God is no longer "first cause," for there was no first cause. If the universe has always existed, then God did not create it at a certain point in time. The universe had no *origin,* since the question "When did it originate?" is apparently the

---

[3]John Stuart Mill, "Nature," in his *Three Essays on Religion.* (London: Longmans Green, 1874.)

same question as "When did it begin?"—and according to the view now being considered it had no beginning at all. It was "always there"—a discomfiting phrase. We can speak of the number series as infinite because we can always get a higher number by adding one; but is infinite time like that? Can we really conceive what it means to say, "The universe didn't begin 12 billion years ago with a Big Bang; it didn't even begin with a divine act of creation; it was *always* there"?

Was it "always" there? Or did the universe have a beginning, before which there was nothing—not even time? (And did time, then, have a beginning *at a certain time*?) Physicists and astronomers now seem fairly well agreed on the Big Bang theory of the universe's origin, but it still leaves many questions.

On the far side of the Big Bang is a mystery so profound that physicists lack the words even to think about it. Those willing to go out on a limb guess that whatever might have been before the Big Bang was, like a vacuum, unstable. Just as there is a tiny chance that virtual particles will pop into existence in the midst of subatomic space, so there may have been a tiny chance that the nothingness would suddenly be convulsed by the presence of a something.

This something was an inconceivably small, inconceivably violent explosion, hotter than the hottest supernova and smaller than the smallest quark, which contained the stuff of everything we see around us. The Universe consisted of only one type of particle—maybe only one particle—that interacted with itself in that tiny, terrifying space. Detonating outward, it may have doubled in size every 10^{-35} seconds or so, taking but an instant to reach literally cosmic proportions.

Almost no time passed between the birth of the Universe and the birth of gravity. By 10^{-43} seconds after the beginning the plenum was already cooler, though hardly hospitable: every bit of matter was crushed with brutal force into every other bit, within a space smaller than an atomic nucleus. But the cosmos was cool enough, nonetheless, to allow the symmetry to break, and to let gravity crystallize out of the unity the way snowflakes suddenly drop out of clouds. Gravity is thought to have its own virtual particle (the graviton), and so the heavens now had two types of particles (carriers of forces and carriers of mass), although the distinction wasn't yet as clear as it is in the Universe today.

At 10^{-35} seconds the strong force, too, fell out of the grand unified force. Less time had passed since the Big Bang than it now takes for a photon to zip past a proton, and yet the heavens were beginning to split. Somewhere here, too, the single type of mass-carrying particle became two—leptons and quarks—as another symmetry broke, never to be complete again. The Universe was the size of a bowling ball, and 10^{-60} times denser than the densest atomic nucleus, but it was getting colder and thinner rapidly.

One ten-billionth of a second after the Big Bang, the firmament reached the Weinberg-Salam-Glashow transition point, and the tardy weak and electromagnetic forces broke away. All four interactions were now present, as well as the three known families of quarks and leptons. The basic components of the world we know had been formed.[4]

The foregoing narrative describes what is believed to be the first events in time. But it may be that we have been treading the wrong road in this whole question. Perhaps we should not ask whether we need to posit God as first cause of the series of events, but rather we should posit God as an *explanation* of the fact that there *is* a series at all.

(2) The Argument from Dependency

In St. Thomas' other formulation of the cosmological argument, he argues from contingency to necessity. The universe contains countless contingent beings. But, it is argued, a contingent being presupposes a necessary being; you can't have a series, ending or unending, of contingent beings.

This language sounds somewhat strange to modern ears; we speak of necessary *propositions* ("Dogs are dogs") and contingent propositions ("Dogs have four legs"), but what

---

[4]Robert Crease and Charles Mann, *The Second Creation* (New York: Macmillan, 1986), pp. 405-406.

would be a necessary or contingent *being*? It is easier to come to grips with the argument by speaking of *dependent* versus nondependent beings. Every person, every animal, every object in the world is a dependent being; it depends for its existence on something else without which it would not have existed. But how can you have a chain of dependent beings without, somewhere (at the end of the line?) having a being that does *not* depend for its existence on anything else? There must, it is argued, exist a nondependent, "self-existent" being; it relies for its existence on no set of conditions outside itself—and this being is God. The existence of a nondependent being is explained wholly from within ("from the nature of") that being itself.

But what is it that requires explanation— each dependent being or the whole collection? There is a difference between explaining *one* occurrence and explaining an entire group or collection of occurrences. If we have explained why each of five people are where they are at a certain time, haven't we done all the explaining we need to do?

Suppose I see a group of five eskimos standing on the corner of Sixth Avenue and 50th St. and I wish to explain why the group came to New York. Investigation reveals the following stories: Eskimo No. 1 did not enjoy the extreme cold in the polar region and decided to move to a warmer climate. No. 2 is the husband of No. 1; he loves her dearly and did not wish to live without her. No. 3 is the son of Eskimos 1 and 2; he is too small and too weak to oppose his parents. No. 4 saw an advertisement in the New York Times for an Eskimo to appear on television. No. 5 is a private detective engaged by the Pinkerton Agency to keep an eye on Eskimo No. 4.

Let us assume that we have now explained in the case of each of the five Eskimos why he or she is in New York. Somebody then asks: "All right, but what about the group as a whole, why is *it* in New York?" This would plainly be an absurd question. There is no group over and above the five members and if we have explained why each of the five members is in New York, we have ipso facto explained why the group is there. A critic of the cosmological argument would claim that it is just as absurd to

ask for the cause of the series as a whole, as distinct from asking for the causes of individual members.[5]

Or, as Bertrand Russell once remarked, the fact that every human being had a mother doesn't show that the human race in general has a mother.

But the argument persists. Don't we also need an explanation for *the whole series* of dependent things? Don't we still need a nondependent being to explain why the whole collection of dependent beings exists? Doesn't dependency have to be somewhere grounded in nondependency? Dependent beings require an explanation outside of themselves. Aquinas believed that the universe could not exist as a succession of dependent beings, and that the only alternative to saying that something requires explanation outside itself is to believe that it is explained *by itself alone*, or is its own explanation.

But this conclusion too has been challenged. (1) Some philosophers have held that there are "brute facts" in the universe—facts that cannot be explained by means of anything else. For example, it may be just a "brute fact" that when light waves of a certain frequency strike my eyes I see that particular shade of color I call yellow; I know of no explanation why I should have just *that* kind of sensation when just that physical stimulus occurs. It may be that certain laws of nature are also "brute facts," though we may not know which they are. We can explain laws of thermodynamics by means of laws of mechanics, and we can explain the laws of chemical combination by means of atomic theory. But there are other laws for which we know of no explanation. Perhaps gravitation is an example, though a "unified field theory" may yet explain gravitation in terms of something more fundamental still. But then that more fundamental law or theory would be a "brute

⁵Paul Edwards, in Paul Edwards and Arthur Pap (eds.), *A Modern Introduction to Philosophy* (New York: Free Press, 1959), p. 380.

fact"—unless, that is, it in turn was explained by something else. However far such explanations may go, don't we sooner or later end up at the level of "brute fact"—something that explains other things but is not itself capable of explanation? If we reach that stage (and we may never know whether we've reached it), don't we just have to say "That's the way things are," and then say no more about it?

(2) But other philosophers have insisted that the very request for an explanation at this stage is meaningless. To explain something is to place it within a broader context of laws and theories; and when there is no longer any such context, the request for explanation is meaningless, though we can of course keep on uttering the *words*. I can't tell you how a car runs without explaining it in terms of some laws of mechanics; nor can anyone explain the occurrence of gravitation without a wider network of laws or theories by which to explain it. But when that wider network is absent, because the question is about the whole network itself, hasn't the request become meaningless? "Why is there a universe?" one may ask; even children ask, "Why is there anything at all?" Almost everyone feels a sense of wonderment, and the question exerts a powerful psychological effect. But hasn't the rug been pulled out from under us in the attempt to answer such a question? "I want you to explain X, but the necessary conditions of explanation are absent"—isn't this what it comes to? To explain something is always to explain in terms of something else—but when there is no "something else" by means of which to do the explaining, what happens to the concept of explanation? Hasn't it lost its meaning, just as the concept of being above something else has lost its meaning light-years away in the midst of empty space when there is no star or planet as a reference-point for determining whether something is above something else? (Remember our discussion of the word "above," p. 15.) It's not that explanation comes to an end when we hit "brute facts," but that the very

term "explanation" has lost its meaning when it is torn out by the only context in which it has any meaning.

C. The Argument from Miracles

One argument for belief in God—or gods—that has had great popular appeal is the argument from *miracles*. According to this argument, miracles have occurred at various times in human history. And the occurrence of miracles is a proof of the existence of God, for only God could cause miraculous events to occur.

What exactly is required for an event to be miraculous? Suppose you throw a solid iron bar into water and it floats, or you hold a loaf of bread in your hand and it disappears before your eyes, or you pour someone a glass of water and it turns into wine. Are these events, assuming them to occur, miraculous?—and by what criterion?

1. We might agree that a miracle must be an unusual event; something that happened all the time or even once a year would not be considered miraculous, unless we extended the word to include such uses as "the miracle of sound," "the miracle of the new Chrysler," and so on. But a miracle can hardly be just any unusual event. The earth passing through a comet would be an unusual event, but it would not be considered miraculous as long as it could be accounted for (as it could) by known laws of nature. Perhaps an object may drop from an airplane and in falling strike a telephone wire outside your window and sever the wire, and the segment of wire on its way to the ground may strike a passing cat and electrocute it. This is surely unusual—"it wouldn't happen again in a million times"—but it would not be considered miraculous, since everything that occurred in this unusual sequence of events is explainable by known laws.

2. It would seem, then, that no event would

be called a miracle as long as it is an instance of some known law or laws of nature. But is this enough? Suppose that an event occurred which could not be accounted for on the basis of any *known* laws of nature. Would it then be a miracle? Probably it would make us suspect that there were some laws of nature we did not yet know, or that some of those we were already familiar with had been inaccurately formulated and must be revised or qualified in such a way as to admit the new occurrence. When it was first noticed that photographic plates were exposed although they had been in complete darkness all the time, this could not be accounted for on the basis of any known law of nature; but people soon came to realize that there were other laws they had never suspected which did account for this curious phenomenon, and in so doing the science of radioactivity was founded. When comets' tails were found to be repelled by the sun, it was not assumed that the universal attractive power of matter stated in the law of gravitation had gone berserk; other laws were discovered which accounted for cases like these.

3. Under what conditions *would* an event be considered miraculous? We cannot now say "when it isn't an instance of any *known* law"; shall we say "when it isn't an instance of *any law at all,* known or unknown"? This at least escapes the objection to the previous view. On this conception of a miracle, however, we could never definitely state that any event was miraculous. For how could we ever know that the event in question could never, even in millions of future years of scientific investigation, be explained on the basis of some law or theory, however complex and elusive? We could not, and therefore we could never know an event to be miraculous. If the iron bar suddenly floated, we would indeed be surprised; but who knows after all exactly what complicated sets of circumstances may cause matter to behave as it does? We judge what is probable or improbable by the kind of

behavior nature has exhibited in the past; but there may be a good many springs in nature's depths which only occasionally, or under very special conditions, bubble up to the surface. The surprising behavior of the iron bar might turn out to have something to do with the moisture in the air, or some law of radioactivity not now known, or even the mental state of observers. Such things would be unexpected because they are not in accordance with the way nature generally works (as far as our present knowledge goes), but they would certainly not be without precedent in the history of science. It was a surprise to learn that profuse bleeding could result from a mental condition and not from any of the physiological causes so earnestly sought for, or that a perpetual hand-tremor could result from a forgotten aggressive act committed in early childhood in which no physiological damage was done. Many persons are still suspicious of such phenomena because they feel that "nature just doesn't work that way"; but we should have learned enough by now in the hard school of scientific experience to know that nature has a few tricks up her sleeve that we never suspected, and which will certainly seem strange as long as we judge "how nature ought to behave" by laws which are already familiar to us.

On this definition of "miracle," then, we could never be sure that any event, no matter how bizarre or unusual or contrary to the regular course of our experience, was a miracle; we could never know that the event could not be subsumed under some laws. However, let us *suppose* that we could be absolutely sure that some such event was *not an instance of any law at all, known or unknown.* Would this show that God must be invoked to account for it? The answer seems inescapable: Of course it wouldn't; it would only prove that some events are not instances of laws. But to establish this and to establish the existence of God are, of course, two entirely different things.

4. According to others—for example, John Stuart Mill—an event cannot be considered a miracle no matter how strange it is, if it would occur again if the same set of conditions were repeated. In order to constitute a miracle, an event must take place *without* having been preceded by a set of conditions which are sufficient to make it happen again. The test of a miracle is: Were there present conditions such that whenever these conditions recur the event will recur? If there were, the event is no miracle. Once again, we could never be sure that an event was a miracle in this sense—we could never know for sure that if the same conditions were to recur, the "miracle" would not recur; at best we could only know that when the conditions were the same as *far as we knew* (and taking into account only those conditions which we thought to be causally related to the event—we have to add this provision or else the conditions to be included might be extended to cover the entire state of the universe, which of course can never repeat itself), the allegedly miraculous event did not occur. But there might always be other conditions that never occurred to us to consider, which were yet causally relevant, and if added to the set of conditions to be repeated, the event *would* occur.

Moreover, just as on the preceding definition of "miracle," even if somehow we *could* know that we had all the relevant conditions, and that they were all the same, but the event did not recur, what would this prove? Only indeterminism—that is, that two identical sets of conditions may yet be followed by nonidentical events. This might be a surprise, but would it force us to invoke God to account for it, any more than a completely deterministic state of affairs would do so? After all, one might ask, why can't the universe be indeterministic rather than deterministic?

5. There is also what might be called the argument from probability. Some events, it is said, are so vastly improbable that their occurrence must be miraculous. That molecules of

protein and amino acids—it has been said—should combine in such a way as to form a living cell that could reproduce itself is so vastly improbable that the origin of life can be explained only by the hypothesis that it was miraculous.

First, it seems that the occurrence of life in the universe *is* "vastly improbable"; at any rate we know of no place except the earth—of all the billions of stars and planets in the universe—where it exists. Life, at least as we know it, cannot occur for example on any of the planets in the solar system; extremely hot or cold temperature, the occurrence of poisonous gases like methane, and the absence of one or more of the necessary chemical elements (oxygen, hydrogen, nitrogen, carbon) on all of them appears to preclude the empirical possibility of it. There may well be life on other planets somewhere among the millions of galaxies, but its occurrence does require very special conditions which seem seldom to occur in the universe. But is it any more improbable than our previous example of the object dropping from the airplane and electrocuting the cat? Such an event might well occur only once in all history, but it is not counted as miraculous because it can be explained in terms of laws presently known. (And isn't the formation of living cells also in accord with laws of nature?)

Second, how do we *estimate* probabilities in cases of this kind? We can say that the collocation of events *plane-object-wire-electrocution* is improbable because we have considerable experience of the frequency of occurrence of the items in the series. But with the further progress of biology the origination of living things from inanimate matter may come not to be seen as "vastly improbable" but as "highly probable," indeed inevitable given certain complex conditions.

Finally, if we say that God caused the molecules to combine in these ways, we then have another mystery on our hands, just as we did in the case of the causal argument: What explanation can be supplied of the presence of a God who had the ability and intelligence to combine the molecules in these ways? Or shall we say that *this* is just "brute fact"?

6. There is still another meaning of the word "miracle": A miracle can be *defined* as an intervention of God into the natural course of events. Now if it is asked whether a miracle in this sense would entail (logically imply) the existence of God, the answer of course would be yes—an intervention of God would indeed entail the existence of a God that could intervene. But this definition, of course, begs the whole question. The question would now become "*Are* there any miracles in this sense? *Is* there in fact anything to correspond to this definition?" *If* these are miracles in the sense we are now considering, then of course God exists, but to say this is only to utter a single tautology; it is only to say "If God intervenes, there is a God." But what would establish the statement that God intervenes? The existence of unusual events, as we have just seen, would not prove it.

According to this definition miracles do logically imply the existence of God; but to say so is analytic; an intervention of God requires a God. But how is one to show that any actual event occurs or has occurred to correspond to this definition. Of all the other definitions of "miracle," on the other hand, the occurrence of the events described would not establish the existence of a God who caused them.

But this may not be the end of the matter. Suppose we said, "The occurrence of unusual events like solid iron bars floating on water would not prove that God caused them; but if we couldn't explain it otherwise, wouldn't it at least make the view that God caused these events more *probable*? Couldn't the occurrence of such events at least be reasonably explained as a direct intervention of God into the course of nature?"

Many such events have been alleged. It has been alleged that the sun stood still for Joshua in ancient Israel, and that it stood still once again before the citizens of the Portuguese village of Fatima in 1917. It has been alleged that water was turned into wine, that a small number of loaves and fishes was multiplied into enough to feed thousands, that people were raised from the dead, healed of their diseases, and so on—all through miraculous intervention. Of course, if these events can be explained by natural means, no recourse to miracles is required; this is often the case with the healing of disease, for example, in which cures are often possible by psychological means such as hypnotism, combined with a certain mental set on the part of the patient. But there is no way events like the multiplication of loaves and the sun standing still can be accounted for by present laws. So, it is argued, if they occurred, they must be interventions of God.

But did they occur? In his famous essay "On Miracles," Hume argued that our only guide to estimating the probability of these alleged events is our total experience of the existing order of nature. "No testimony," he wrote, "is sufficient to establish a miracle unless the testimony be of such a kind that its falsehood would be more miraculous than the fact which it endeavors to establish."[6] And in virtually every miracle ever recorded, it is more congruous with the course of our experience to believe that the miracle did not occur. That people are deluded (or even that they lie), that rumors spread and are wildly exaggerated when they have spread even a small distance from their source, that people will believe almost anything and broadcast it as true when it is something they *want* to believe and are already strongly conditioned toward believing—these are all facts well known to all of us and require no miracles for us to believe; we are acquainted with all these things in our

---

[6]David Hume, "On Miracles," in *An Enquiry Concerning Human Understanding* (LaSalle, IL: Open Court, 1938) Section 10,: p. 120.

everyday experiences. Most alleged miracles were reported by people in times long past whose stories we can no longer check, people moreover who were ill-trained in reporting exactly what they saw and were usually wishing for the occurrence of the miracles; and the wish was father to the belief.

Even when the miracle *was* attested to by many people, as was the case in Fatima, our reason for doubting it is much greater than our reason for believing it, since we know what would have to happen in nature in order for the account to be true. For the sun to stand still in the sky—that is, for the earth to stop revolving about the sun—would be contrary to the entire course of nature as we know it, and it would have many other consequences, such as objects flying off into space, which did not occur. It is more probable, said Hume, that the people were deluded in their reports of what happened than that the miraculous event actually occurred.

None of this, however, *proves* that the events reported did not occur. We may have no decisive evidence that they did; but neither have we (at least in many cases) decisive evidence that they did not. We are rather in the position of a Sherlock Holmes who has to solve a crime that was committed many years ago and in which most of the clues once available have now vanished. The fact is that people who *already* believe in God on other grounds will tend to believe in miracles as an added manifestation of God's handiwork but that people who see no reason to believe in God do not find the evidence sufficient to convince them. The argument from miracles does not constitute a strong enough argument by itself, but if one is already convinced by one or more of the *other* arguments for God's existence, he may accept this one as supplementary to it.

Belief or disbelief in miracles—in the events occurring as being manifestations of God—depends not nearly as much on the evidence in the particular case (in most cases we have

no evidence one way or the other) as on our antecedent beliefs. Many persons believe that most of the alleged miracles are in some way unworthy of an omnipotent being. If God wanted people to believe in him, why perform a few miracles in a remote area where few people could witness them? Would it not be just as easy for an omnipotent being to issue proclamations in loud tones emanating from the sky and simultaneously intelligible to all people in all languages? If the latter had occurred, many more people would be convinced of God's existence than they would from any present accounts, where most people have to go by hearsay. Instead of healing a few people of their disease, why not all sufferers? Instead of performing a miracle in Fatima in 1917, why not put an end to the enormous slaughter of World War I, which was occurring at the same time, or keep it from starting? Or, if this is tampering with man's free will, why not perform another kind of miracle that would also save lives, such as stopping the earthquake in Lisbon that killed 30,000 people as they were gathered in their churches to worship (the example repeatedly employed by Voltaire in *Candide*)? Why not stop or prevent a major catastrophe instead of a minor one, instead of an event like turning water into wine, which made little difference one way or the other compared with the vast misery of human beings at the same time and place, none of which was alleviated?

It is interesting to observe, also, that people are quick to accept as a miracle any unusual event, or an event that goes contrary to natural probabilities, as long as it works in their favor. A hundred people are killed in an airplane accident, but one survives. "It's a miracle!" say the survivor and his family. What the families of the nonsurvivors had to say about the matter is usually not recorded. Now suppose, instead, that there is an airplane accident in which one person dies but a hundred survive. The family of the one nonsurvivor does not say, "It's a miracle!" although the survival of a hundred when one dies is on a par with the survival of one when a hundred die. In general, people who already have some kind of theistic belief are apt to call miraculous any event that is improbable, whose causes they do not fully know, and that works in their favor. Those who reflect on this fact are not likely to put much stock in the argument from miracles—not because they have an alternative explanation for the event (though sometimes they do) but because they see that what people call a miracle depends very much on what they *want* to believe, more than on what the facts of the case are. One would not call a miracle the sudden death of all one's friends, no matter how much the event defied a natural explanation, though some might say it of the death of their enemies; the enemies, of course, would simply reverse the classification. Moreover, each religion has its own set of miracles; and the events that are classed as miracles by one religious group are denied to be miracles by the others.

Suppose, however, that these sources of doubt could be rectified; suppose a truly extraordinary event occurred today, witnessed by all of us, as well as photographed and tape-recorded. Suppose that at this minute we all heard a voice coming from somewhere in the sky, simultaneously intelligible in all languages, announcing that from this moment on whoever deliberately kills another human being will be struck down with a thunderbolt on the spot; and suppose that from that moment on this actually happens; every killer is immediately killed, as announced. Wouldn't *that* prove the existence of God?

We would at first want to disprove some obvious suspicions: that it was not some clever auditory trick, and so on. And if it was understood in all languages, in what language would it be transcribed on your tape-recorder? And from what point in the sky would the sound originate? Would the tape recording become louder as you approached a certain point (perhaps as recorded in a high-

flying plane)? And so on. We might have to change the description of some of the conditions; how, for example, could it be in all languages at once? But even if it were in one language—say ancient Sanskrit or Hebrew—there are enough scholars around to translate it for us and tell us what the announcement said. And if all killers were thenceforth executed by thunderbolts in accordance with the announcement, this would still be mightily impressive. "There's something out there we hadn't figured on," we might say; or more likely, "There's *someone* out there, a personality, a mind, someone with sufficient power to carry out threats." It would certainly be evidence for the existence of "a powerful being out there"—perhaps not a being who was omnipotent, or infinitely wise, or the cause of the universe, or a "necessary being"—but at least something for whose existence we had thus far had no direct evidence. But no alleged miracle in history has thus far presented us with anything like this kind of evidence.

This example, however, brings out a point about the allegedly miraculous. Even a very extraordinary event, one contrary to known laws of nature, wil not impress people as a candidate for the miraculous nearly as much as will occurrences with a "personal touch"—that appear to be the work of a will, a personality of some kind. Water changing into wine in a cellar would not be as impressive as someone standing before a crowd and changing it (assuming it could be tested as water beforehand and as wine afterwards), or publicly multiplying five loaves and two fishes into enough to feed thousands. Even raising someone from the dead might not be found particularly impressive—physicians have revived people after their heartbeat and brainwaves stopped; it would more likely be thought of as a medical triumph than a miracle. But suppose posters in various languages started to fall mysteriously from the skies announcing that the Antarctic ice cap will be made to melt (thus raising the sea level and flooding coastal cities around the world) unless all nations remained at peace; than suppose an Israeli-Arab war broke out and promptly the entire Antarctic ice sheet melted: This might well be counted miraculous because it would exhibit the manifestations of a will, backed up by *power*, which both are universally considered characteristics of a deity.

D. The Argument from Religious Experience

"You are looking for God in the wrong place," "You won't find Him by looking for cosmic tricks like voices from heaven, or in any way tampering with the laws of nature which He created in the first place. (What kind of mechanic is it who has to keep tinkering with the vehicles he services?) You will find God only in your *inner experience*. God reveals Himself to us in certain experiences we have, which are a manifestation of His existence."

What is meant by the phrase "religious experience"? Apparently such experiences vary enormously from individual to individual; it is not easy to draw the line between what counts as a religious experience and what does not. We could simply say that a religious experience is an experience of God, but this would be like our last definition of "miracle" (p. 298). By bringing the alleged source of the experience into the definition of the experience itself, it would raise the question of whether anything exists that fulfills the definition. What the experience is like is one issue; whether it has a divine source is another. If we include the existence of God in the definition, we are left merely with the assertion that experiences of God prove the existence of God—which indeed they would. But what we need is a conception of religious experience which distinguishes the content of such experiences from whatever external reality (if any) their existence may point to. Let us then try to characterize the experience itself.

There is such a profusion of religious experiences that it is difficult to find a formula that includes them all. William James describes them at length in his classic work, *The Varieties of Religious Experience* (1902). For the most part they are experiences involving at least the feeling that one is directly in contact or communication with God. Sometimes they are accompanied by the conviction of one's own divinely inspired powers and abilities; sometimes by happiness amounting to ecstasy; sometimes by a feeling of total security; sometimes by intense guilt at one's sins and shortcomings. Usually there is an inclination to worship, adore, revere, love, or fear the God allegedly revealed in the experience; but sometimes, as in religions that proclaim no independently existing God, there is no sense of a superior power outside oneself before whom one must prostrate. Sometimes the God is felt as benevolent and loving; sometimes only as powerful, even threatening.

The question is, what does the occurrence of such experience prove? Does it show that a divine source of such experiences exists, or only that the experience has psychological causes, such as the "need for a father," personal insecurity, or dread of mortality?

If you say that the occurrence of these religious experiences does prove the existence of God, then what kind of God do they establish? One person insists that her experience is definitely of the God of Christianity; another insists that his experience proves the existence of Allah and the truth of the Muslim religion. And so on. Persons raised in a certain religious tradition usually assume that their experiences to establish the belief in the God of their own religion. But then of course we have a problem. If experience A proves the existence of God A, does experience B prove the existence of God B? If we allow the inference in one case, how can we deny the same inference in the other cases? And then doesn't the argument prove too much—the existence of Yaweh, of Allah, of the Christian trinity, or for that matter ancient Egyptian gods such as Isis and Osiris? If the argument proves one of them, doesn't it prove them all?

Why not then admit them all? The trouble is that they all contradict each other at some point. Each religion claims to be the only true one and declares that the others are false claimants to the truth. If Christianity is true, then Jesus is God (or at least one aspect of God), but if Judaism is true, this is not so; and meanwhile the Muslim religion declares that Allah is the one true God and that Jesus was at most his prophet. Each religion has some truth claims that contradict the claims of the others. If James is the true ruler of England, then Cromwell can't be, and vice versa; one or the other (perhaps both) is a false claimant to the throne.

In order to ameliorate this situation, the following argument is sometimes used: All religious experiences are of the same being; people disagree only in the way they *describe* the object of these experiences, for this depends on their particular environment and upbringing. They are at a loss for words and use language in loose, misleading, and even contradictory ways, when they talk about it; but the God experienced is the same in every case—only the historical, "accidental" features are different. Purge the religions of their historical features, in which Mohammedanism and Christianity for example do contradict each other, and take only the essence or kernel common of each, and they do not contradict each other because they are one.

This may seem an easy way out of the situation; but there are several points that should be considered before it is adopted. (1) In this process you have taken away the God of every *particular* religion. Christianity declares, for example, that God is revealed in the Holy Scriptures, and manifested in Christ, and that any view which denies this is false. Remove these beliefs and you do not have "the essence of Christianity" left; you have something left that can hardly be called Christianity at all,

whatever else it may be. Purge Christianity of its historical features and you have purged away much of Christianity. Some may consider this all to the good, but we should not then say that we have "true Christianity" left when we have done this. (2) Let us try to imagine such a being as the God who is supposed to possess only the features shared by all religions and none of the peculiarities of any particular religion. Such a God could not be loving (for the gods of some religions are not), or brutal (for the gods of some religions are not), and so on; such a God could hardly possess any characteristics whatever, so few are the characteristics which the deities of all, or even a small fraction, of the religions of the world possess in common. About all such a God would have left is power. Strictly speaking, he would not even possess unity, for many religions are polytheistic—but at the same time he could not be multiple either, for some religions are monotheistic. What kind of God would it be that is neither one nor more than one? (3) Neither could such a God be given "more character" through the *addition* of certain characteristics—he could not be the God of various specific religions "all rolled up into one," as has sometimes been suggested; for then he would be loving like the Christian God, vengeful like Yahweh, demanding human sacrifice like Baal, prohibiting it like the God of Christianity, and so on. These characteristics are logically incompatible with each other. Clearly *some* of these beliefs must be mistaken; hence it would appear that religious experience alone cannot guarantee the truth of the God of any religion.

"But some religions much be excluded—the obviously barbaric ones, such as Baal-worship. . . . " Where, in this case, are we to draw the line? What kinds of religious experiences are going to establish the God in question, and which are not? What is the criterion? More important still, how is this criterion to be justified and defended against others? If the occurrence of one religious experience really establishes the existence of the deity believed in by this person, what is to exclude another from doing so? One may, indeed, employ some question-begging use of the term "religious experience," so that only the experiences of one religion or denomination are "truly religious," the others being "mere deceptions." But the opponent of one who argues thus can simply return the compliment. There, perhaps, ends the argument and begins the fight.

It would seem, then, that having a certain kind of experience is not *by itself* a guarantee that an objective thing corresponding to that experience exists. Let us compare the present situation for a moment with a situation encountered in perception. Suppose a person were to argue, "Of course ghosts exist; how else could I have seen one last night?" One need not deny that the person had a *visual experience* of a certain kind, which led him to declare the existence of ghosts; but having the ghost experience is perfectly compatible with having a hallucination. A traveler in the desert may "see" an oasis in the sense of having a visual experience which leads her to judge that there is an oasis not far off; but of course she can judge wrongly. The existence of the experiences is not denied—the persons in question are not deliberately deceiving others when they report thus, but what can be denied is that an objective ghost or oasis exists which is the object of these experiences.

Religious experiences are, of course, very different from these ghost experiences and oasis experiences. They are far more intense, more deep-seated, more valuable, and they "mean more" to the experiencers. As far as the inference from experience to object is concerned, however, the same consideration applies. One cannot, merely on the basis of having the experience, admit any one of the alleged objects of the experience without admitting them all. The fact of religious experience alone cannot guarantee the truth of a religious belief. (The subject of religious experi-

ence will come up again when we discuss the doctrine of mysticism, p. 325–27.)

E. The Argument from Utility

The *utility* argument could hardly be called philosophical, yet it is so popular that it should be mentioned in passing. It its most typical form it goes something like this: Belief in God is a great and indispensable moral influence; without it, human beings would be far less likely to live moral lives. Therefore, everyone should believe in God.

In this form, it is not an argument that pretends to prove the *truth* of its conclusion; it merely says that it should be believed because believing it has a good influence. The conclusion is a moral one ("one should believe") rather than one that alleges that the belief is true.

To examine the argument, we would first have to agree on what is meant by "living a moral life." Does it mean being honorable and truthful? Is it keeping one's promises and paying one's debts, as Cephalus said in Plato's *Republic*? Doubtless it is intended to mean much more, but exactly what? Is obeying the law part of what is meant by living a moral life? If so, all laws? any laws? Does it matter which? Some say that prostitution, fornication, and homosexuality are immoral; others find them perfectly moral. Are these to be included or excluded? And so on, for countless other kinds of actions.

Then, having agreed which kinds of actions are to be counted as moral, one would have to conduct a sociological survey to discover whether religious belief does in fact tend to make people live this kind of life. The answer would probably be, sometimes it does and sometimes it doesn't. Depending on the belief, sometimes it may even be harmful. Moreover, which religious belief is intended? Belief in the Christian God? in Mohammed? in the Greek gods and goddesses? in the Norse warrior gods?

Even if all this could be settled, what would it show? Not that the belief in question was *true*, and that is what arguments for God's existence are all about. ("You should believe *p* because *p* is true.") If belief in ghosts made people live better lives, this wouldn't make belief in ghosts true. The *effects* of a belief are a different issue from the *truth* of a belief.

There is another problem as well: Can you really believe something, sincerely, because believing it is useful, or ennobling, or has certain other effects? When you believe it, don't you believe it as something that is *true*? When religious belief is taught, must it not be taught as a belief that is *true*? Would the plea "It may not be true, but I want you to believe it anyway" be effective, even on children? Can you sincerely believe what you are not convinced is true?

Once a belief has been shown to be true, whether it is useful, has good influences, and so on is a *separate* question. That many biological innovations can be achieved with recombinant DNA is true, but much argument continues about its effects, even its morality. The question whether religious belief is useful, uplifting, and so on would hardly be likely to take place if there were not already some doubt about whether it was true, or could be shown to be so. As John Stuart Mill said,

An argument for the utility of religion is an appeal to unbelievers, to induce them to practice a well-meant hypocrisy, or to semi-believers to make them avert their eyes from what might possibly shake their unstable belief, or finally to persons in general to abstain from expressing any doubts they may feel, since a fabric of immense importance to mankind is so insecure at its foundations, that men must hold their breath in its neighborhood for fear of blowing it down.[7]

And in our own day, Betrand Russell has said:

I can respect the men who argue that religion is true and therefore ought to be believed, but I can feel only reprobation for those who say that religion ought to be believed because it is useful, and that to ask whether it is true is a waste of time.[8]

Many persons, indeed, have been much concerned to disengage morality from any dependence on religion. They have felt that it is a dangerous thing for religion and morality to be closely intertwined in the public mind, the survival of morality being made dependent on the survival of religion; for in that case, if the religious belief should ever collapse, the morality which has been made dependent upon it may collapse with it.

Pascal's wager. One variant of the utility argument should be mentioned because of its historical importance. Blaise Pascal (1623–1662) suggested that we should believe in God because if we do we will get to heaven, and if we do not we won't. If our belief turns out to be true, we'll be rewarded; if it is not, we'll never survive our death to know the difference. So the best bet is to believe.

One could object to this "wager" in several ways. First, there is nothing in it about the belief being *true*, only that if you believe, it will pay off handsomely in the after life. Second, it is not true that you've lost nothing if the belief is false; you may have given up many things in order to live the Christian life, and if Christian belief is false your sacrifice (if that's what is was) will be for nothing. So we had better have good evidence, before we do this, that the belief is *true*. Third, and most important, however, is this consideration: Can we really believe—sincerely believe—in something or someone if our only basis for doing so is to win a wager? Can belief be induced in this way? Isn't the whole thing a kind of cynical game? You can *pretend* to believe, but surely God will know that you're only pre-

---

[7]John Stuart Mill's essay, "The Utility of Religion," in his *Three Essays on Religion* (London: Longmans Green, 1874), p. 70 is a classic study of this question.

[8]Bertrand Russell, *Why I Am Not a Christian* (London: George Allen & Unwin, 1957), p. 172.

tending. Yet how can you sincerely believe unless you are convinced that the belief is *true*?

Besides, the argument can be carried further; one might say, "Protestants say that both Protestants and Catholics can go to heaven; Catholics have traditionally said that only Catholics can go to heaven. So it would be to your interest to become a Catholic, for if you become a Protestant and Catholicism is true, you may go to your reward, whereas if you're a Catholic and Protestantism is true, you'll be out of luck." To which some have offered this reply: "How do you know there isn't a God who is so impressed by sincerity of belief, and by adjusting belief to evidence, that he will consign to hell anyone who believes in him just to be on the winning side?"

F. The Teleological Argument (Argument from Design)

Of all arguments, the one with widest appeal is the teleological argument (from the Greek *telos*, purpose), or argument from design. More than any other it appeals to empirically observable features of the universe and attempts to infer from these that God exists— not necessarily God the creator, or God the first cause, but God as cosmic designer. Observe the world carefully, the argument runs, and you cannot help coming to the conclusion that it contains abundant evidence of order and design—evidence that a "master architect" has been at work. Not blind chance but order and purpose govern the universe, and evidence of purposiveness permeates it. And when there is purpose, there must be a purposer; where there is design, there must be a designer.

What kind of being must the designer of the cosmos be? Is he (or she, or it?) a person— a personality with intelligence, wisdom, and other human qualities? The advocate of the teleological argument replies in the affirmative: Design presupposes intelligence. But what *kind* of designer? Does the designer have unlimited power? Is he benevolently disposed toward the creatures he has designed? Although the usual answer given to these questions is yes, opinions as we shall see are divided on these last two questions. In all versions, certain features of the universe are taken as evidence for a designer, and presumably if the universe were very different from what it is, it would *not* provide such evidence (or would provide evidence for a different kind of designer). To that extent at least the argument has an empirical base.

If successful the argument does not establish the existence of a necessary being, a first cause, or even a creator-of-the-universe-out-of-nothing; it attempts to establish only the existence of a being with sufficient intelligence and power to shape the materials of the universe in accordance with a plan or purpose. The first-cause argument, had it been successful, would have yielded us only a first cause; the contingency argument would have yielded only a necessary being; the teleological argument—if successful—will yield us only a cosmic designer. Traditionally the name "God" has been given to all these things; but this assumes that that which is a necessary being or a first cause is also a cosmic designer. We should not insist that all of these must be the same being because we use the same word, "God," for each. When Plato discussed the hypothesis of a designer (or artificer) in his dialogue *Timaeus,* he never assumed—nor did any of the ancient Greeks—that the cosmic designer created the universe from nothing as people usually interpret the biblical account; in Plato, the cosmic designer took materials already present and shaped them in accordance with a plan, much as a builder takes materials already in existence and uses them to design and build a house.

Let us see, then, what forms the teleological argument can take, what kind of designer it can make a case for, and what evidence it can adduce. When we have done so, we shall examine the general structure of the argument in all its varying forms.

The universe, the argument begins, is *orderly*, and order is the result of design. The millions of stars in the heavens behave in an orderly manner, all exhibiting certain physical laws that hold equally for all of them; and so do the millions of species of life on the earth. How could all these things have come into existence except as the result of design? Pieces of clay do not come together of themselves to make bricks, or bricks to form a house; this requires the designing activity of human beings. In the same way, particles of matter cannot come together of themselves to form living cells, or cells to form the complex living organisms that inhabit the earth; such a result can be brought about only by a designer who fashions the materials in such a way as to form them.

But such arguments are subject to several objections: (1) The word "order" is not very clear: that which seems orderly to one person will not seem so to another. A painting that appears orderly to one observer will appear chaotic to another. (2) Nor is it clear that the universe is orderly in any specific sense. If galaxies are orderly, but drifting nebulae in the universe are not, then it must be pointed out that there are many nebulae in the universe; and so on for anything that might be considered not to be orderly. Yet if *anything* that the universe contains is orderly, no matter what, then what are the limits on the term "orderly"? What could count *against* a thing or arrangement of things being orderly? If you throw a bag of marbles on the floor, they must fall out in *some* order or other. In this sense, every arrangement of things must be orderly, so the statement that *this* universe is orderly tells us nothing distinctive about it. (3) Most important, what is the guarantee that order is always the result of design? Some examples of order are indeed the result of design, as in the case of mechanical objects (watches, wrenches,

automobiles); we know this because we ourselves (or other human beings) have taken the materials and put them together in certain ways to form objects that we can use and enjoy. The order is there as a result of designing minds—*ours*. But as Hume said, order is evidence for design *only* to the extent that order has been *observed* to result from design. And the order we find in plants and animals has *not* been observed to result from design. We have never seen any beings who form plants or animals, or for that matter stars, as a result of their design, and therefore we are not entitled to conclude that these things do exist as a result of design.

"But that's just the point," the defender of the teleological argument replies, "We have never *seen* plants and animals being designed the way architects design buildings and watchmakers design watches, but we must *infer* that they were designed, for how else could we account for their existence? Once again, stones don't come together on their own to form cathedrals, and neither can particles of matter come together to form organisms. This requires intelligence, and since the intelligence in the case of organisms is not human, it must be divine."

This comment, however, invites still another objection. What if the phenomenon in question can be explained without assuming the existence of a cosmic designer? Then we shall not, strictly speaking, have disproved the hypothesis, but we shall have shown that it isn't required in order to account for the facts. Can this be done, specifically in the case of organisms, which are the most striking example of order that invites the hypothesis of design?

In a universe composed chiefly of inorganic matter, the existence of life and mind seemed a mystery that could be explained only on the hypothesis of a cosmic designer. But for many thousands of years there have been theories of organic evolution attempting to explain the existence of organisms without recourse to the hypothesis of a designer. The early Greek philosopher Anaximander (611–547 B.C.), for example, argued that organisms originally sprang from the sea and evolved into land creatures. But no comprehensive theory with the full weight of detailed and painstaking empirical observation behind it arose until the publication of Charles Darwin's *The Origin of Species* in 1859. Darwin set forth a hypothesis according to which organisms gradually evolved, from the simplest amoebas to the most complex primates, through the struggle for existence and the survival of the fittest. As a result of his pioneering and the work of many biologists since, the hypothesis of organic evolution has become so well confirmed as to be universally accepted among biologists. It did not, to be sure, explain everything: It explained why certain species survived, but not how the first species originated. But this gap too has been gradually closing, beginning more than a century ago with the synthesis in the laboratory of uric acid (the first organic compound to be produced from inorganic ones) to the latest feats of genetic engineering. Gradually, by bits and pieces, the genesis of life (under conditions occurring during the pre-Cambrian era of the earth's history) has come to be explained without any recourse to design.

The designer hypothesis has not thereby been shown to be false. If a person believed in design before, he could do so after Darwin as well as before, even accepting all of Darwin's conclusions. He could say that, whereas it had previously been thought that God had created all the species instantaneously, he now believed that God had chosen the slow and gradual process of evolution as a means of executing his design. The method of design would have changed, but not the fact. Nevertheless, the teleological argument has lost most of its currency (among scientists, at any rate) since Darwin—not because Darwin disproved de-

sign, for he did not, but because there no longer seemed to be any necessity for having such a hypothesis. If you believed that a knock on your door was caused by the ghost of a departed spirit, you no longer need to believe this if you find that the knock was caused by a salesman making a call (though it is still possible for you to believe that the knock was caused by the salesman *and* a departed spirit).

But the impact of Darwin's theory cut deeper: It did not refute design in general, but it did appear to refute, or at any rate seriously to impair, belief in a *benevolent* design—yet the belief in a benevolent designer, one who cared about his creatures and did not wish them to suffer, has always been the mainspring of belief in design. People would not be so likely to be attracted to the argument from design if they thought that the cosmic designer was malevolent. Yet it was precisely the belief in a benevolent designer that was difficult to sustain in the face of belief in the evolutionary process, for the evolutionary process is a scene of continuous and endless strife, pain, and death. Life is a struggle for existence, in which many species die out and every individual inevitably dies—most often in agony, through starvation, cold, disease, or being eaten alive by animals. The individual life is expendable; millions of individuals of every species die every day (usually before they have lived out a full life), but life continues through their offspring, who in their turn die in pain and suffering. Does the designer inflict all this suffering merely to preserve the species, at the expense of the individual? If so, it is not much consolation to the individual; and of what value is a species if all the individuals in it must live a life of constant threat and insecurity and finally die in misery? Nor does nature appear to be any more careful of the species or type than of the individual; thousands of species have perished through starvation, changes in climate, being attacked by other animals, or because some new mutation arose that was swifter or more adaptable. Nature seems indifferent to individual and species alike.

> "So careful of the type?" but no.
>   From scarped cliff and quarried stone
>   She cries, "A thousand types are gone:
> I care for nothing, all shall go.
>
>   . . . .
>
> [Shall] Man, her last work, who seem'd so fair,
>   Such splendid purpose in his eyes,
>   Who roll'd the psalm to wintry skies,
> Who built him fanes of fruitless prayer,
>
> Who trusted God was love indeed
>   And love Creation's final law—
>   Tho' Nature, red in tooth and claw
> With ravine, shriek'd against his creed—
>
> Who loved, who suffer'd countless ills,
>   Who battled for the True, the Just,
>   Be blown about the desert dust,
> Or seal'd within the iron hills?[9]

Through countless ages innumerable species of creatures evolve; those that are able to adjust themselves to changing conditions, to find sufficient food and drink and shelter and safety, survive for a time; the rest are blotted out in the struggle for existence. Most living things, including all the carnivorous animals, can continue to live only by catching other living things as prey and devouring them as food. Even when they are successful in this (at the expense of the creatures they kill), the environmental conditions are so undependable, and the life of the organism so dependent on a vast multitude of conditions (they can live only within a narrow range of temperature, moisture, and nutritional supply), that even a comparatively small change in the environment or disorder in the functioning of the organism may cause their extinction. If nature is designed, the plan of the designer does not appear to be benevolent.

In sober truth, nearly all the things which men are hanged or imprisoned for doing to one another, are nature's every-day performances. Killing, the most criminal act recognized by human laws, Nature does once to every being that lives; and in a large proportion of cases, after protracted tortures such as only the greatest monsters whom we read of ever purposely inflicted on their living fellow-creatures. . . . Nature impales men, breaks them as if on the wheel, casts them to be devoured by wild beasts, burns them to death, crushes them with stones like the first Christian martyr, starves them with hunger, freezes them with cold, poisons them by the quick or slow venom of her exhalations, and has hundreds of other hideous deaths in reserve, such as the ingenious cruelty of a Nabis or a Domitian never surpassed. All this, Nature does with the most supercilious disregard both of mercy and of justice, emptying her shafts upon the best and noblest indifferently with the meanest and worst; upon those who are engaged in the highest and worthiest enterprises, and often as the direct consequences of the noblest acts; and it might almost be imagined as a punishment for them. She mows down those on whose existence hangs the well-being of a whole people, perhaps the prospects of the human race for generations to come, with as little compunction as those whose death is a relief to themselves, or a blessing to those under their noxious influence. Such are Nature's dealings with life. Even when she does not intend to kill, she inflicts the same tortures in apparent wantonness. In the clumsy provision which she has made for that perpetual renewal of animal life, rendered necessary by the prompt termination she puts to it in every individual instance, no human being ever comes into the world but another human being is literally stretched on the rack for hours or days, not infrequently issuing in death. Next to taking life . . . is taking the means by which we live; and Nature does this too on the largest scale and with the most callous indifference. A single hurricane destroys the hopes of a season; a flight of locusts, or an inundation, desolates a district; a trifling chemical change in an edible root, starves a million of people. The waves of the sea, like banditti seize and appropriate the wealth of the rich and the little all of the poor with the same accompaniments of stripping, wounding, and killing as their human antitypes. Everything, in short, which the worst men commit either against life or property, is perpetrated on a larger scale by natural agents. . . . [10]

---

[9]Alfred, Lord Tennyson, *In Memoriam*, LVI.

[10]John Stuart Mill, "Nature," in *Three Essays on Religion*, pp. 28–30.

There are countless facts that have been cited on both sides of the issues: (1) "Consider what a variety of conditions required for life to exist at all. There must be a basic minimum of elements—oxygen, nitrogen, carbon, and hydrogen—without which life cannot exist at all; there must be certain conditions of moisture, temperature, and soil that must be fulfilled; and just these conditions do exist on the earth. How could such a concatenation of conditions have come about except by design?" But on the other hand, one could argue, "Life requires a delicate combination of conditions in order to exist at all—true. But on the many planets that do *not* support life (and ours is the only one we know that does), this combination of conditions does not exist—is this to be taken as evidence against design? Moreover, the variety of conditions required for life on this planet works against us; when one such condition, such as sufficient moisture, is not met, the creature dies of thirst. The organism is an enormously complex structure, admirable to behold, and according to you a proof of design. But this complexity means that when one thing goes wrong, the organism does become ill and often dies; any of a number of things can extinguish his life; if life did not depend on such a delicate balance of conditions, it might not be so hedged on every side by threats to its existence and dangers of its extinction." (2) "What a marvelous design exists in living organisms: consider a young kitten, leaping and playing; its body, a vast network of tiny nerves and muscles and bones, regenerates with smooth efficiency. Surely such a complex system must have been designed." But on the other hand, "With what wonderful craftsmanship the pit viper is designed: It can both see its prey and sense it directionally in the dark by means of the heat that the victim's body emits; its tongue darts out, and with lightning-like speed its fangs with their deadly poison are infixed in the body of its victim, who swells up, undergoes the most indescriba-

ble pain, and within half an hour is dead." (If the victims were always rats or other creatures we do not like, we would probably not mind, but human beings are equally the victims. People want the design to be not only benevolent but benevolent toward *them*. A design that kept vipers going at the expense of people or even dogs is not one likely to appeal to most people.) (3) "What wonderful forces are at work in the human body, so complex that centuries of biological investigation have not yet enabled us to understand its workings fully. Every part is interdependent with every other part, one part assisting another when the organism's life is threatened, each part working together with others to maintain the health of the entire organism." "Ah, but not always. Because of this very interdependence, things are constantly going wrong, and often no cure is possible. Moreover, surgeons (not supplied by nature but by man's ingenuity) have to get at our internal organs as one would open a can of sardines, since the designer, if there is one, has seen fit to put these complex and vulnerable organs inside us without even the convenience of a zipperlike opening for easier access. Would it have been much trouble for the designer to make our arteries out of durable elastic tubing so that they would not harden with age? Wouldn't people be better off if brain power and energy lasted throughout a lifetime instead of reaching a peak at about 40 and then declining? Why should so many people, before they even start in life, be condemned by incipient weaknesses and congenital diseases, to physical agony or chronic illness or idiocy? Nor are the parts replaced in the course of nature when they go wrong; what would you think of a car manufacturer who failed to supply new parts even though his automobiles were constantly needing them? Observe too how a cancer works away at a vital organ, silently and unnoticed, as if to escape detection by anyone who wants to discover it before it is too late, making the victim suffer unremitting torments for weeks or months, passing through every stage of intense pain until death comes as a relief.'' The citing of examples on both sides could be continued indefinitely.

The Problem of Evil

The principal objection to the teleological argument, if that argument is intended to prove the existence of a *benevolent* designer, is the problem of evil. In ancient times Epicurus (342–270 B.C.) put the problem as follows: ''Is God willing to prevent evil, but not able? Then he is not omnipotent. Is he able, but not willing? Then he is malevolent. Is he both able and willing? Then whence evil?'' Hume put the argument in the form of a dilemma: ''If the evil in the world is from the intention of the Deity, then he is not benevolent. If the evil in the world is contrary to his intention, then he is not omnipotent. But it is either in accordance with his intention or contrary to it. Therefore, either the Deity is not benevolent or he is not omnipotent.''

The problem arises only if the hypothesis is that of a designer who is both omnipotent and benevolent. If he is not omnipotent, then the evil in the world can be attributed to the fact that he doesn't desire it but is unable to prevent it. If he is not benevolent, then the evil can be said to arise from the fact that he is able to prevent it but doesn't wish to. But if he is both benevolent and omnipotent (which most religions say that he is), then the problem arises in full force: Why evil?

Hume's dilemma is valid, as every student of elementary logic can work out for himself. But are its premises true? There have been a number of attempts to escape from it by questioning one or more premises in some way or other.

1. There is no evil in the world. One might deny that there is any evil at all and thus undercut the presupposition of the problem. But this solution is so implausible that it would take considerable gall to suggest it. People may not entirely agree on what things are evil (it would require a long excursus into ethics in order to become clearer about this), but they do agree that some things are. Who does not believe that some things are bad and to be avoided? Ordinarily, for example, we believe that pain and suffering are evil, and we exhibit this belief in our practice when we try to avoid them or to minimize them as much as possible; for example, we try to alleviate the pain of those who suffer from diseases. Nor is the suffering illusory; people do not merely *think* they are suffering, they *are* suffering. The fact of such suffering is, indeed, one of the principal reasons many persons find it difficult to believe in a God who is both all-powerful and benevolent. *We* would alleviate these sufferings if we could; yet God, who is supposedly all-powerful and benevolent, fails to do so.

2. Evil is a negative thing. St. Augustine advanced the idea that evil is not a positive thing but a lack, a privation, a negative. There is no evil, but only the comparative absence of good; evil is simply nonbeing. Sometimes it is added, as Augustine did, that to be real is to be perfect, and thus only God can be wholly real; his creation, being necessarily finite and limited, must necessarily involve incomplete goodness, and thus involve evil to some degree or other.

But to say that evil is negative seems to be primarily a play on words. Is war negative, the absence of peace, or is peace negative, the absence of war? Whichever way we classify it, the one is as real as the other—there is war and there is peace; there is happiness and there is suffering; there is good and there is evil. The facts of reality are not changed by being classified as negative or positive. Suffering exists, and is not alleviated in the slightest by the consideration that ''it is only negative.''

It may console the paralytic to be told that paralysis is mere lack of motility, nothing positive, and that insofar as he *is*, he is perfect. It is not clear, however, that this kind of comfort is available to the sufferer from malaria. He will reply that his trouble is not that he lacks anything, but rather that he has too much of something, namely, protozoans of the genus *Plasmodium*.[11]

3. Evil is necessary to the greatest good.
"Granted that there is evil in the world. But there *has* to be, since that is the only way good can be achieved. We are all familiar with instances of this: you cannot get back to full health without painful surgery, but you undergo the surgery (which is not as good when considered by itself—that is, you wouldn't do it *except* thereby to achieve recovery) to attain a goal. The pain and suffering incurred are worth it as long as they are the only means by which you can achieve recovery. And so on for countless situations. Even war is sometimes the only way a better world (or the prevention of a worse one) can be attained. Thus, though there *is* evil in the world, it is compatible with the goodness of God, since the evil that there is is the least possible required to get the greatest possible good. This is not a perfect world, but it is the *best* of all *possible* worlds."

It is true that people often have to suffer pain in order to recover health, our medical knowledge being what it is, and the laws of biology being what they are. But this consideration, which does justify a physician in inflicting pain on a patient in order that the patient may recover, applies only to limited beings who can achieve the end *in no other way*. Once we suspect, however, that the physician could achieve the goal *without* inflicting suffering on her patient, and that she is inflicting it anyway, we call her a cruel and sadistic

monster. God, unlike the physician, is omnipotent; he could bring about a recovery without making the patient go through the excruciating pain. Why then does he not do this? If it is objected that this would require a miracle and that it would upset the orderliness of nature to continually perform miracles, it can be replied that the laws of nature could have been so set up that no miracle would be required in each case. After all, who is the author of the laws of nature? Why did God set up the causal order in such a way as to require his creatures to die in agony? There is not the excuse in the case of God that there is in the case of the surgeon, who can bring about his patient's recovery *only* by causing suffering; for God, being omnipotent as well as benevolent, could easily bring about the recovery without such means; indeed, he could have kept the patient from being sick in the first place. What would we think of a surgeon who first infected his child's leg and then decided to amputate it, although a cure was within his power to give and the infection was of his own giving to begin with? But this would be precisely the position of an omnipotent God. A physician who is benevolent but not omnipotent can be excused for causing suffering only because the end can be achieved in no other way; but this is precisely what is not the case with an omnipotent God, for, being omnipotent, he does not need to use evil means to bring about a good end. Indeed, it is a mistake to use means–end terminology in talking about omnipotence at all: An omnipotent being could bring about the end directly, without embarking upon means to do it. Means toward ends are needed only by beings who are not omnipotent.

When I was in India, I was standing on the veranda of an Indian home darkened by bereavement. My Indian friend had lost his little son, the light of his eyes, in a cholera epidemic. At the far end of the veranda his little daughter, the only remaining child, slept in a cot covered over with a mosquito

[11]Wallace I. Matson, *The Existence of God* (Ithaca, NY: Cornell University Press, 1965), pp. 142–143.

net. We paced up and down, and I tried in my clumsy way to comfort and console him. But he said, "Well, padre, it is the will of God. That's all there is to it. It is the will of God."

Fortunately I knew him well enough to be able to reply without being misunderstood, and I said something like this: "Supposing someone crept up the steps onto the veranda tonight, while you all slept, and deliberately put a wad of cotton soaked in cholera germ culture over your little girl's mouth as she lay in that cot there on the veranda, what would you think about that?

"My God," he said, "what would I think about that? Nobody would do such a damnable thing. If he attempted it and I caught him, I would kill him with as little compunction as I would a snake, and throw him over the veranda. What did you mean by suggesting such a thing?"

"But John," I said quietly, "isn't that just what you have accused God of doing when you said it was His will? Call your little boy's death the result of mass ignorance, call is mass folly, call is mass sin, if you like, call it bad drains or communal carelessness, but don't call it the will of God. Surely we cannot identify as the will of God something for which a man would be locked up in jail, or put in a criminal lunatic asylum."[12]

Of course, if God too is limited in power, as the physician is, then the outcome may be the result of his inability to do better in spite of his good intentions. But such defense is not available in the case of a God who is both benevolent and omnipotent.

. . . did I show you a house or palace, where there was not one apartment convenient or agreeable; where the windows, doors, fires, passages, stairs, and the whole economy of the building were the source of noise, confusion, fatigue, darkness, and extremes of hot and cold; you would certainly blame the contrivance, without any further examination. The architect would in vain display his subtlety, and prove to you that if this door or that window were altered, greater ills would ensue. What he says, may be strictly true: the alteration of one particular, while the other parts of the building remain, may only augment the inconveniences. But still you would assert in general, that if the architect had had skill and good intentions, he might have formed such a plan of the whole, and might have adjusted the parts in such a manner, as would have remedied all or most of these inconveniences.[13]

A good architect would have designed the house in such a way as to avoid these disadvantages, so that one would not have to choose between a design that was bad and one that was worse. And if an architect was so incompetent that he could devise no such house, perhaps he should refrain from any more house designing. If the best universe that a designer could bring about is one as full of pain and suffering as this one, perhaps he should have refrained from universe designing and chosen instead some activity in which he had greater competence.

4. "Good often comes out of evil?" Out of hardship and adversity comes achievement. Out of suffering comes appreciation of the feelings of others. Out of poverty comes thrift. And so on. How else can these things come about?"

"In the first place, if God could not bring about any other outcome, he is not omnipotent. *We* perhaps cannot bring about another outcome, conditions being what they are, and the laws of nature being what they are; but an omnipotent God could. In the second place, the good that comes out of evil is often hardly sufficient to justify it. The causal order is so complex that there is probably no disaster to one person that does not work to the advantage of another. A hurricane kills a hundred people and destroys a hundred buildings, but it provides work for builders. Is it worth it? If you were God, would you be justified in bringing about all this death and destruction

[12]Leslie D. Weatherhead, *The Will of God* (Nashville: Abingdon Press, 1944), quoted in Harold Titus, *Ethics for Today*, 3rd ed., p. 539.

[13]David Hume, *Dialogues Concerning Natural Religion*, part XI, Norman Kemp Smith edition (Edinburgh: Nelson & Sons, 1935), p. 204.

in order to provide this work? Don't you consider the bombing of cities evil, in spite of the fact that some old buildings are destroyed, which enables new and better ones to be built on their site? Would *you* be justified in bombing a city to bring about this result? In the third place, if good sometimes comes out of evil, evil also sometimes comes out of good—probably just as frequently. For everything we thought evil at the time and later changed our minds about in the light of later developments, there is probably another event we thought good or beneficial at the time that in the light of later events we now consider disastrous or regrettable. The fact is that the most usual tendency is for good to produce more good and evil to produce more evil."

Health, strength, wealth, knowledge, virtue, are not only good in themselves but facilitate and promote the acquisition of good, both of the same and of other kinds. The person who can learn easily, is he who already knows much; it is the strong and not the sickly person who can do everything which most conduces to health, those who find it easy to gain money are not the poor but the rich; while health, strength, knowledge, talents, are all means of acquiring riches, and riches are often an indispensable means of acquiring these. Again, *e converso*, whatever may be said of evil turning into good, the general tendency of evil is towards further evil. Bodily illness renders the body more susceptible of disease; it produces incapacity of exertion, sometimes debility of mind, and often the loss of means of subsistence. All severe pain, either bodily or mental, tends to increase the susceptibilities of pain for ever after. Poverty is the parent of a thousand mental and moral evils. What is still worse, to be injured or oppressed, when habitual, lowers the whole tone of the character. One bad action leads to others, both in the agent himself, in the bystanders, and in the sufferers. All bad qualities are strengthened by habit, and all vices and follies tend to spread. Intellectual defects generate moral, and moral, intellectual; and every intellectual or moral defect generates others, and so on without end.[14]

---

[14]John Stuart Mill, "Nature," *Three Essays on Religion*, pp. 35–36.

5. *"The purpose of evil is not to make us happy but to make us virtuous.* The world is a moral training-ground for the building of character. Evils are put there to discipline and improve us rather than to punish us."

"But the order of nature is such as to frustrate the goal of making people virtuous as much as or even more than the goal of making people happy. Here is a person who, we believe, needs to know what suffering is like, so that he will not be so insensitive to it in others; and what happens? He is never made to experience it; but a person who already is borne down by the weight of suffering only has more of the same heaped upon him—the person who already has one disease, let us say, contracts another. This is the way of things in the actual world. Sufferings seem to occur hit-or-miss: They miss the person who (if anyone) should have them, and come constantly to others who already have more than they can bear, rendering them miserable and perhaps embittered for life. This is quite inconsistent with the behavior of a being who is both omnipotent and benevolent. Or to take a specific case: Here is a man who drives his car carelessly so as to be a danger to others on the highway. Short of changing his nature, the best way to make him more careful would be to have him involved in an accident in which he was slightly injured, just enough to scare him; but what actually happens, more often than not, is that he escapes scot-free while others are injured or killed, until that one last time when he himself is killed in an accident, when it is too late to improve him. If moral improvement was the aim, any reasonably intelligent 15-year-old who was benevolently disposed and had the power could effect a better distribution of good in the world than now exists.

If the Creator of mankind willed that they should all be virtuous, his designs are as completely baffled as if he had willed that they should all be happy; and the order of nature is constructed with even less regard to the requirements of justice than to those of benevolence. If the law of all creation were justice and the Creator omnipotent, then in whatever amount suffering and happiness might be dispensed to the world, each person's share of them would be exactly proportioned to that person's good or evil deeds; no human being would have a worse lot than another, without worse deserts; accident or favoritism would have no part in such a world, but every human life would be the playing out of a drama constructed like a perfect moral tale. . . . The world we live in is totally different from this; insomuch that the necessity of redressing the balance has been deemed one of the strongest arguments for another life after death, which amounts to an admission that the order of things in this life is often an example of injustice, not justice. . . . Every kind of moral depravity is inflicted upon multitudes by the fatality of their birth: through the fault of their parents, of society, or of the uncontrollable circumstances, certainly through no fault of their own. Not even on the most distorted and contracted theory of good which ever was framed by religious or philosophical fanaticism, can the government of Nature be made to resemble the work of a being at once good and omnipotent.[15]

6. God's goodness is different from ours. But now a different solution may be suggested: "Perhaps what we call evil is really good; what seems evil to us is in fact good when seen from the vantage point of omniscience. The goodness of everything is perceived only by God, but he after all sees everything while we see very little: That everything is good is seen by his infinite intelligence but is beyond our finite comprehension."

Considering the spectacle of the world as we find it, said Mill, there is no judgment of which we are more certain than that it is not perfectly good. If we distrust this judgment, we have no reason to trust *any* moral judgment, including the judgment that what is evil to us is good to God. Even if everything we think is evil is really good, the fact is that we still *think* it is evil—and this would be an error, an error hiding from us the perfect goodness of the universe. And since it would surely be

better if we did not commit this error, the existence of this error would be an evil.

But in fact the view that what seems evil to us is all good in God's eyes would require us to take a very curious view of God. This world is full of pain and suffering, cruelty and death, wars, plagues, floods, and droughts, and human beings who suffer and die when they occur. If there is a powerful being who considers all this to be *good*, what view must we take of the morality of such a being? Is such a being worthy to be worshiped? Would he not rather be like a dictator whom we might obey because of his power but whom we would never for a moment think of as *good*? We would not think of a physician as good who failed to prevent suffering of her patient even if she had the power to do so and yet effect a cure; but an omnipotent God would be in precisely this position: Why then should we call him good when we would throw a physician who did this out of the medical profession? Yet we are supposed to believe that a God who could prevent needless suffering and yet decline to do so is good.

When I am told that I must believe this, and at the same time call this being by the names which express and affirm the highest human morality, I say in plain terms that I will not. Whatever power such a being may have over me, there is one thing which he shall not do: he shall not compel me to worship him. I will call no being good, who is not what I mean when I apply that epithet to my fellow creatures; and if such a being can sentence me to hell for not so calling him, to hell I will go.[16]

So many of the things we are supposed to attribute to God are incompatible with anything we call goodness that we try to shift the meaning of "good" to accommodate the discrepancy. We are told that God is good, but infinitely good, and that of course we can-

---

[15]Ibid., p. 38.

[16]John Stuart Mill, *An Examination of Sir William Hamilton's Philosophy,* (New York: Henry Holt, 1865), p. 131.

not understand infinite goodness. But, of course, the same argument could support the view that either God or the world is infinitely *bad*: If some things look to us as if they were good, never fear, in the light of infinite knowledge we could see that they are all bad after all—the universe is the perfect epitome of evil. This argument is exactly on a par with the view that, although it sometimes seems evil, everything is really good.

Moreover, if God is infinitely good, the fact remains that infinite goodness must still be *goodness*, just as infinite space must still be space.

Among the many who have said that we cannot conceive infinite space, did anyone ever suppose that it is *not* space? that it does not possess all the properties by which space is characterized? Infinite space cannot be cubical or spherical, because these are modes of being bounded; but does anyone imagine that in ranging through it we might arrive at some region which was not extended; of which one part was not outside another; where, though no Body intervened, motion was impossible; or where the sum of two sides of a triangle was less than the third side? The parallel assertion may be made respecting infinite goodness. What belongs to it as infinite I do not pretend to know; but I know that infinite goodness must be goodness, and that what is not consistent with goodness, is not consistent with infinite goodness.

If in ascribing goodness to God I do not mean what I mean by goodness; if I do not mean the goodness of which I have some knowledge, but an incomprehensible attribute of an incomprehensible substance, which for aught I know may be a totally different quality from that which I love and venerate . . . what do I mean by calling it goodness? and what reason have I for venerating it? If I know nothing about what the attribute is, I cannot tell that it is a proper object of veneration. To say that God's goodness may be different in kind from man's goodness, what is it but saying, with a slight change of phraseology, that God may possibly not be good? To assert in words what we do not think in meaning, is as suitable a definition as can be given of a moral falsehood.[17]

The power of the deity, by contrast, is always interpreted in a completely human way: It is never thought to mean that we could not be killed or punished, in spite of the fact that the power of the deity is conceived of as far greater than ours. Greater power means more of the same thing that we call "power." Does not the same remark apply to "good"? But divine goodness is often spoken of, unlike divine power, as incomprehensible, perhaps because so many of its manifestations conflict so strongly with anything we would ever call goodness.

7. Human freedom as the cause of evil. "The evil in the universe is caused by human wickedness. Human beings are free, which means free to do evil as well as good. Even an omnipotent being could not make human beings free and yet not free to do evil. Evil is thus an inevitable consequence of humankind's freedom."

This is probably the most often cited attempt to get round the problem of evil. There is a distinction, however, between *natural* and *moral* evils. Natural evils are those that occur in the course of nature without human intervention: earthquakes, volcanic eruptions, floods, hurricanes, plagues, and so on. These catastrophes are not caused by human activity. Moral evils, however, are those inflicted by people upon other people, such as mental and physical torture, plunder, killing, war. The latter is the only class of evils that could be said to be the result of human freedom. Even if the argument is a valid one with regard to moral evils, it does not explain the existence of the natural evils.

But let us now concentrate on the moral evils.

A: Man, you will surely agree, is created a free being, which means that he is free to choose good or evil. His often choosing evil, then, is the result of his freedom. There is no way for persons to be free ex-

---

[17]Ibid., p. 101.

cept by having choices open to them, and the moment choices are open a person may choose the worse instead of the better alternative. From this fact very great evils may indeed follow: One person in a position of power may order millions of other people to be killed in concentration camps. But all this is a part of man's freedom; once you grant that man is free, you must go along with it *all the way*. If human beings are free, they are free, free to perpetrate the most extreme miseries upon other human beings.

B: But if this is so, is man's freedom worth such a price? If one person's freedom involves the power to have millions of other people exterminated, I'm quite sure the victims would wish the freedom of the dictator to be somewhat more limited. In order that *he* may have his freedom, *they* must be massacred. Isn't that putting rather too high a premium on *his* freedom, since his freedom requires that they give up not only their freedom but their lives? Is it any comfort to them, as the gas in the chamber is turned on, to reflect that this is the price they are paying for the dictator's freedom of decision? Could not that freedom be possible at a lesser price?

A: No, it couldn't. If man is free, he is free to commit evils. Otherwise freedom is a delusion.

B: But there are many things that man is not free to do now, such as fly like a bird or digest sticks and stones. I don't see why a few further limitations would not be beneficial. For instance, people might have a protective shell so that they would be immune to attack by other people, thus making murder impossible. People would still be free to make countless decisions, and they would still have many choices open to them, but at least they would not be free to take away the lives (and with them the freedom) of *other* people. There would still be many choices available that did not

carry in their train the destruction of other free agents. One of the greatest areas in which people can exercise their choice is in scientific or artistic creativity. There would be a large area of free choices here, without choices going so far as to involve murder. I would think that that would be a much better basis for the exercise of choice than we have now, for as things are now one person's choice may involve another person's destruction. And I would remind you that if God could *not* devise a system without evil in which human beings are free, then God is not omnipotent.

A: I dispute this. God's omnipotence does not imply that God can do what is logically impossible. God could not make a square circle, for example, because if it is a circle it isn't square. Nor could God make what *has* happened *not* have happened; the past is what has occurred, and no one, even God, could make what has occurred not have occurred. Omnipotence is the ability to do anything that is logically possible, such as suspend laws of nature.

B: I agree that saying God is omnipotent doesn't mean that God can do what is logically impossible. But what's logically impossible about creating human beings so as to give them choices, and yet limit those choices in some ways—as they already are in other ways? If people can't fly like birds, why should they be able to (for example) kill and maim other people so easily? There are certainly plenty of other ways in which free choice could be exercised besides taking away life (and with it the possibility for any free choices in the future) from other human beings. There's surely nothing self-contradictory about *that*.

A: The logically possible choices are limited:

A creator who is going to create humanly free agents and place them in a universe has a choice of the kind of universe to create. First, he can create a finished universe in which nothing needs improving. Humanly free agents know what is right, and pursue it; and they achieve their purposes without hindrance. Second, he can create a basically evil universe, in which everything needs improving, and nothing can be improved. Or, third, he can create a basically good but half-finished universe—one in which many things need improving, humanly free agents do not altogether know what is right, and their purposes are often frustrated; but one in which agents can come to know what is right and can overcome the obstacles to the achievement of their purposes.[18]

I suggest that God chose the third alternative, because only in such a universe could there be beings who through their decisions and actions can form their own character and be responsible for their own actions. It is *logically* impossible for God to *impose* a character on the beings he creates, and at the same time leave them *free* to develop their own characters by their own choices. Imposing a character on them would take away the creatures' power to develop their own. It's either-or; you can't have their actions guaranteed good because God created them so, and at the same time have them free to choose between good and bad alternatives. Their ability to act freely is *logically* incompatible with their characters being ''set in advance'' by God. The logical impossibility here is just as genuine as the impossibility of changing the past.

B: By the command of Stalin in the 1930s, seven million people in the Ukraine were systematically starved to death, and thus deprived forever of *their* freedom. Is Stalin's freedom to perpetrate such acts so precious as to be worth the destruction of the freedom of his seven million victims? You are certainly placing a higher value on *his* freedom than on *theirs*. And you are saying seriously that without this freedom people would not be free agents but only programmed automata?

_____
[18]Richard Swinburne, ''The Problem of Evil,'' in Stuart C. Brown (ed.), *Reason and Religion* (Ithaca, NY: Cornell University Press, 1977), pp. 81–102.

A: Yes. To the extent that a creator predetermines a person's character, to that extent the person is not free to develop it himself. You can't have it both ways. When it comes to moral decisions, a person must be free all the way—even free as Stalin was to condemn millions of people to death. That's a part of human freedom; you can't have moral freedom and not include the possibility of choosing evil, even a monstrous evil like this one.

B: Then I don't think the freedom you describe is worth it. Nor would I choose to create a universe in which such incalculable suffering could be inflicted by some persons upon others. If I did knowingly create such a world, I would be a cruel tyrant. I would refrain from world-making if the only kind of world I could make would be a world like *that*. If I couldn't control the causal laws of my world (though as an omnipotent being, I could), I would at least perform a few miracles and have Stalin die of a heart attack before he could do these things—or better still, never let him be born.

A: You *say* that human freedom wouldn't be worth it. But the things you condemn are inextricably connected with the ones you applaud. It is only if there are problems that they can be solved; only if there is conflict and difficulty can there be triumph over them; only if there is risk can risk be surmounted; and only if there is danger of defeat can there be victory.

Suppose, contrary to fact, that this world were a paradise from which all possibility of pain and suffering were excluded. The consequences would be very far-reaching. For example, no one could ever injure anyone else: the murderer's knife would turn to paper or his bullets to thin air; the bank safe, robbed of a million dollars, would miraculously become filled with another million dollars (without this device, on however large a scale, proving inflationary); fraud, deceit, conspiracy, and treason would somehow always leave the fabric of society undamaged. Again, no one would ever be injured by accident: the mountain-climber, steeplejack, or playing child falling from a height would float unharmed to the ground; the reckless drive would never meet with disaster. There would be no need to work, since no harm could result from avoiding work; there would be no call to be concerned for others in time of need or danger, for in such a world there could be no real needs or dangers.

. . . . .

. . . [In] such a world . . . our present ethical concepts would have no meaning. . . . If, for example, the notion of harming someone is an essential element in the concept of a wrong action, in our hedonistic paradise there could be no wrong actions— nor any right actions in distinction from wrong. Courage and fortitude would have no point in an environment in which there is, by definition, no danger or difficulty. Generosity, kindness, the *agape* aspect of love, prudence, unselfishness, and all other ethical notions which presuppose life in a stable environment, could not even be formed. Consequently, such a world, however well it might promote pleasure, would be very ill adapted for the development of the moral qualities of human personality. In relation to this purpose it would be the worst of all possible worlds.[19]

B: An omnipotent God could still create human beings in such a way as to have them develop moral qualities without massacring one another. It's true that the moral qualities are very valuable, the world being what it is *now*: Courage is valuable when one goes to war, but wouldn't a world without war be better? And couldn't human virtues still be exercised in other ways, for example in the self-discipline required to complete some worthwhile creative activity? Besides, we have already seen (pp. 313–14) that the world is not a very efficient training ground of moral virtues—that if *that* is God's purpose, the purpose is as much frustrated as if it were to make people happy. Many of the things we call virtues now are so only because of the evil of the world we live in,

and I would gladly do without them if the world were ever so much better—then we wouldn't need them. Those virtues that are contingent upon having an evil world we could well do without if the world were no longer evil. Besides, the *distribution* of these evils is far from what justice would demand. If the moral evils of the world are a punishment for humanity's wickedness, what of the innocent victims? The aggressors sometimes get away with what they do, but the victims never. For what is a child being punished when he is left alone in a room and burns to death on a hot stove, or when he is striken with poliomyelitis or spinal meningitis? For what is a whole people being punished when their country is invaded by a powerful foreign army and thousands of their citizens die to repel the invader? Is *this* your idea of a justly governed universe?

A: You can't know whether it's injust until you see the whole scheme of things—and that includes the hereafter, in which all injustices are rectified.

B: The fact that there are injustices in this world doesn't prove, of course, that another world exists to correct them—any more than the fact that people are hungry proves that they will always have food. But let's grant a hereafter; how can that possibly cancel out the evils of the present? A person slowly wastes to death of a debilitating and painful bone disease; does a happy hereafter really "make it up" to this person? In one of Dostoyevsky's many examples of the evil inflicted on human beings by one another, he considers a sadistic army officer who has a child torn to pieces by wolves. Maybe the officer will suffer in hell. But what good does hell do, since the child has already been tortured? That evil *has* occurred, and even omnipotence cannot make what has happened *not* have happened. Nothing that could ever happen in the future would be just recompense for

---

[19]John Hick, *Philosophy of Religion*, (Englewood Cliffs, NJ: Prentice-Hall, 1962), pp. 44–45.

this act. It remains a stain, a blot, on the history of the world, a blot that *nothing* can remove, not even eternal punishment for the person who committed the deed. The world is put together in such a way that this thing not only could have happened but *did* happen. Nothing that ever *will* happen can make it otherwise.

The "freedom argument" remains the most persistent attempt to circumvent the problem of evil. Whether it is successful will depend largely on how much value is attributed to the faculty of human choice over the range of choices that human beings now have.

Alternative Teleological Arguments

Meanwhile, there are other versions of the teleological argument which do circumvent the problem of evil.

1. An omnipotent being who is malevolent. This view has not been as popular as the belief in a benevolent being, perhaps because one's desire for justice to be done in an afterlife is not fulfilled by belief in a malevolent being. Such a being would be like a powerful but tyrannical dictator, different only in that he is all-powerful and one would be completely and forever in his clutches. No act, no thought could escape his attention, and noncompliance with his will, however evil his dictates, would result in endless torment. Many critics of Christian fundamentalism have believed that the Christian God is something like this in that he has devised hell—a place of never-ending torment for nonbelievers. Even the most hardened prisoner in an earthly jail may be released or paroled, but not so with the God who punishes his creatures forever without any hope of reformation, pardon, or parole. Such punishment would seem to be utterly pointless, since it could never lead to any good result, and, one might wonder, what

crime could possibly deserve *endless* punishment.

Or perhaps the Christian devil (Satan) comes closer to being omnipotent and malevolent. It could be argued that Satan has some virtures, such as persistence and patience, but even if he has none, at any rate he is not omnipotent. But if he were the perfect epitome of evil, and also omnipotent, he would be the kind of being suggested by the teleological argument in the present form. The support for this hypothesis would be found in the very facts that were difficulties for the previous view: the prevalence of pain and suffering, the helplessness of many people to face obstacles that they have to face, the facts of dying and that life can live only on other life, and so on. All such things could be easily explained on the hypothesis of a being who designed the whole scheme of things so as to maximize the suffering of his creatures.

On this view, the problem of evil would not exist, since the world was designed by a being whose sole interest was the creation and promotion of evil. Rather, there would be a "problem of good"; why is there any good at all if God is both evil and omnipotent? Then there could be various unsuccessful theories to get rid of the problem of good: Good is really nonexistence; good is a negative; everything is really evil, but some good is required to fulfill the deity's evil ends; and so on.

2. A benevolent but not omnipotent designer. There might be a cosmic designer who was benevolent but limited in power, like human beings only less so. On this view, there is no problem of evil; there is evil because God is limited in power and cannot help the evil that there is—he has to work with material over which he lacks complete control. It has sometimes been suggested that God is merely a fellow worker with human beings in the attempt to minimize the evil in the universe. This view not only encounters no problem of evil but also has inspired many persons to work for the elimination of evil, since it is now partly up to them; their efforts can make a difference. Yet the view has not been very popular, perhaps because people want a God who can present them with certain guarantees—for example that if they deserve their reward he will be able to deliver it, and that there will be no hitches in his plan. They want security more than incentive. (One problem for this view: If there is but one God, who or what could limit his power? Whence would come the competition?)

3. Ditheism. Since ancient times it has sometimes been suggested that there are two cosmic intelligences, each planning and executing his plans in the world, but whose plans work at cross-purposes. Obviously neither is omnipotent (if one were, the other would not be God), but one is benevolent and the other not. Thus the ancient Zoroastrians and Manicheans argued that the world is a battleground for conflicting deities, not the work of a single designer; that is why some things in the world really are good and others really are bad (they do not merely appear to be so). Nor is there any problem of evil; the evil is easily explained by the existence of the evil deity. In the Manichean view, the physical universe was designed by the good god and human beings were designed by the bad one—a doctrine perhaps better in accord with observable facts than any other we have encountered.

Sometimes, in Christian theology, it is as if there were two gods, Jehovah and Satan. But Christianity is not ditheistic, since one of the two is all-powerful. The conflict between them is a sham battle, since Jehovah created Satan in the first place, is guaranteed to win over him in the end, and could destroy him any time if he so desired (which raises the question why this has not happened). In a genuine religious ditheism, both deities must be limited in power, and the outcome of the struggle genuinely in doubt.

4. Polytheism. If two, why not more than two? Why not revive the polytheism of the Greeks, who believed in many gods, each with his separate sphere of influence, and each interacting with the rest? To be sure, Zeus was the kingpin; but he was by no means omnipotent, for his best-laid plans could be thwarted by other gods, and particularly by his wife Hera. Since the laws of nature operate uniformly and impartially, there must be a certain degree of cooperation among the gods, or perhaps Zeus reigns supreme in one department; but there is still much room for diverse influences, even for gods working at cross-purposes. Why, indeed, should there be only *one* cosmic planner? In the cases of design known to human beings, a plan usually was devised in a rather crude form by one person, then certain rough edges were removed by someone else, and further improvements made by a third, and so on through many generations, as in the case of shipbuilding:

If we survey a ship, what an exalted idea must we form of the ingenuity of the carpenter, who framed so complicated, useful, and beautiful a machine? And what surprise must we feel, when we find him a stupid mechanic, who imitated others, and copied an art, which, through a long succession of ages, after multiplied trials, mistakes, corrections, deliberations, and controversies, had been gradually improving? Many worlds might have been botched and bungled, throughout an eternity, ere this system was struck out; much labor lost; many fruitless trials made; and a slow, but continued improvement carried on during infinite ages in the art of world-making.[20]

And, one might add, even at the present moment the art of world making has been far from perfected; perhaps if the cosmic world designers pooled their efforts and got at the job more conscientiously, a world might be

[20]David Hume, *Dialogues Concerning Natural Religion*, part V.

brought about that is a considerable improvement over the present one.

5. A cosmic organism. Thus far we have considered only teleology in the form of design, or plan, in the mind of a designer. A being possessing a mind plans, and carries out his plan; this is the most familiar type of teleology known to us, since it goes on in ourselves; we design something, and it comes into existence as a result of our plan. But organisms also exhibit teleological behavior. The sunflower deepens its roots in the life-giving soil and turns its face to the sun, thereby making its continued existence possible. True, the sunflower does not consciously do this *in order* to preserve its existence, but (pp. 163–64) its behavior is teleological nonetheless: It acts in such-and-such a way, thereby making it possible for a condition (such as survival) to occur that would not have occurred without this activity. Instead of saying, then, that the universe is the result of a plan in a mind, why not say instead that the universe is the result of teleological activity on the part of a huge cosmic organism?

In like manner as a tree sheds its seed into the neighboring fields, and produces other trees; so the great vegetable, the world, or this planetary system, produces within itself certain seeds, which, being scattered into the surrounding chaos, vegetate into new worlds. . . . [21]

Or why not consider the ancient Brahmin hypothesis

. . . that the world arose from an infinite spider, who spun this whole complicated mass from his bowels, and annihilates afterwards the whole or any part of it, by absorbing it again, and resolving it into his own essence. Here is a species of cosmogony, which appears to us ridiculous; because a spider is a little contemptible animal, whose operations we are never likely to take for a model of the whole universe. . . . But . . . were there a plant wholly inhabited by spiders (which is very possible), this inference would there appear as natural and irrefragable as that which in our planet ascribes the origin of all things to design and intelligence. . . . Why an orderly system may not be spun from the belly as well as from the brain, it will be difficult . . . to give a satisfactory reason.[22]

"But this is ridiculous!" we may exclaim. Aren't these hypotheses absurd? Are they *all* wildly improbable? Must we admit them all as possibilities, and a thousand others like them? "What wild, arbitrary suppositions are these? What *data* have you for such extraordinary conclusions? And is the slight, imaginary resemblance of the world to a vegetable or animal sufficient to establish the same inference with regard to both?[23] But this, says Hume, is just the point; They *are* all wildly improbable; there is no justification for believing any of the versions of the teleological argument.

We have no *data* to establish any system of cosmogony. Our experience, so imperfect in itself, and so limited both in extent and duration, can afford us no probable conjecture concerning the whole of things. But if we must needs fix on some hypothesis, by what rule, pray, ought we to determine our choice? Is there any other rule than the greater similarity of the objects compared? And does not a plant or an animal, which springs from vegetation or generation, bear a stronger resemblance to the world, than does any artificial machine, which arises from reason and design?[24]

Argument from analogy. All the arguments in this group are arguments from analogy. An analogy is simply a comparison, and an argument from analogy is an argument from comparison. We begin with a compari-

---

[21]Ibid., part VII (p. 177 in the Norman Kemp Smith edition).

[22]Ibid., pp. 180–181.
[23]Ibid., p. 177.
[24]Ibid.

son between two things, X and Y, which are alike in certain respects, A, B, C, and conclude that they are also alike in another respect, D, in which they have not been observed to resemble one another. For example, a person (X) and a dog (Y) are alike in numerous respects; they have hearts that pump blood, they consume and digest food, and so on (A, B, C). Therefore, it is concluded, since a person has a liver (D), the dog will also have a liver. (Assume that the argument is presented before it has been discovered through dissection of dogs whether they have livers.) Since the human being and the dog are alike in numerous respects, the argument runs, it is likely that they will resemble one another in the other respect in which no such similarity has yet been discovered.

Arguments from analogy, of course, are never conclusive. That two things are alike in numerous respects never shows that they will also be alike in other respects. They may be, but even if they are, the argument from analogy does not prove it; only an investigation of the two things will enable us to discover whether they are alike in the new respect. If the two things are very similar in a large number of respects, it may be more likely that they are similar in the new respect; since lions and leopards are very similar in most respects, a characteristic of lions is quite likely to be true also of leopards—but not all characteristics; if all of them were the same, lions would be indistinguishable from leopards. Even in cases where the two things are very similar, the argument from analogy is still inconclusive.

The teleological argument in its various forms has usually been presented as an argument from analogy. Thus, there is a watch and a human eye. They have some characteristics in common—for example, the same apparent adaptation of means to ends. If we came across a watch without knowing what it was for, we would conclude that it had been designed by someone, for every part is linked to every other part in such a way as to fulfill one

function, that of keeping time. Similarly, in the human eye there is the same complex interconnection of parts, all serving one function, that of seeing. Since the watch is the result of design, we infer that the eye is also the result of design.

There is precisely the same proof that the eye was made for vision, as there is that the telescope was made for assisting it. They are made upon the same principles; both being adjusted to the laws by which the transmission and reflection of rays of light are regulated. . . . These laws require, in order to produce the same effect, that the rays of light, in passing from water into the eye, should be refracted by a more convex surface than when it passes out of air into the eye. Accordingly we find that the eye of a fish, in that part of it called the crystalline lens, is much rounder than the eye of terrestrial animals. What plainer manifestation of design can there be than this difference?[25]

The analogy between the eye and a manufactured object like a watch or telescope is fairly obvious. In both cases there is a complex structure that fulfills a function. (We must say "function" and not "purpose," for to say that the eye fulfills a purpose would assume the point at issue; opponents of the teleological argument would say that the eye, while it fulfills a function, seeing, was not the result of design, and hence not of a designer's purpose.) But in the case of the eye, as well as of organisms in general, no designing activity has ever been observed, whereas in the case of manufactured objects it has; and in addition, there is considerable other evidence that the eye, along with the entire organism of which it is a part, is the result of a slow and gradual process of evolution. Moreover, eyes are often defective.

To discover that certain forms and formations are adjusted for certain action has nothing to do with

---

[25]Bishop William Paley, *Evidence of the Existence and Attributes of the Deity* (1802). Passage reprinted in P. Edwards and A. Pap, *A Modern Introduction to Philosophy* (New York: Free Press, 1959), p. 412.

design. None of these developments are perfect, or anywhere near so. All of them, including the eye, are botchwork that any good mechanic would be ashamed to make. All of them need constant readjustment, are always out of order, and are entirely too complicated for dependable work. They are not made for any purpose; they simply grew out of needs and adaptations; in other words, they happened.[26]

What people do with the teleological argument depends largely on which features of the world they start with. If we start with ships instead of watches, we get the hypothesis that the universe was the result of many centuries of accumulated experience in world making. If we start with desert wastes, we get the hypothesis that besides being sloppy and inefficient, the designer did not have human well-being in mind. The universe contains so many things, each with so many different properties, that there is virtually no argument from analogy that we cannot construct, depending on which features we select at the outset. That is why Hume concluded that argument from analogy provides no basis for *any* conclusions concerning a designer, or for that matter multiple designers, "cosmic organisms," or (in Hume's words) "any system of cosmogony."

2. MEANING AND TRUTH IN RELIGION

Anthropomorphism. Most people, when they think of God or gods, conceive it (or them) in a highly anthropomorphic manner: They "conceive of God in the form of man" (*anthropos*, man, and *morphe*, form). People say that God is wise, benevolent, powerful; that he commands, hears our prayers, desires our welfare, forgives our trespasses. And when primitive people thought of God or gods, they thought of a "bigger and better"

human being out there somewhere in the sky or on a mountaintop, watching us, issuing commands, rewarding those who obeyed. Such gods were physical organisms, presumably having sense organs not entirely unlike ours. Having fashioned Eve out of Adam's rib, God met with Adam and Eve in the cool of the evening.

Virtually all religions, for example, refer to God as "he"; do they really believe that God is of the male sex—perhaps a saintly old man in flowing white robes wielding a scepter? If one says that God is not literally male, is one then to refer to God as "she"? But that would be to describe God as belonging to the female sex. (Perhaps calling God "he" is a relic of the days when the man was the undisputed head of the household.) The word "it" is impersonal—referring usually to inanimate objects—and seems to fit no better than the other two, because God is still conceived of as a person with a personality (benevolent or vengeful, forgiving or unforgiving, and so on). Yet "he," "she," and "it" are the only singular personal pronouns we have.

As religions become less anthropomorphic, they ceased to think of God as a physical organism occupying physical space; instead, God was a mind, a personality, with human qualities like love and wisdom. There are problems, as we have seen, of conceiving of a mind without a body; but let us ignore these for the moment and see what features a mind must have. A person thinks of A at time t–1 and of B at time t–2; a person deliberates, chooses, acts, sometimes changes his mind and regrets previous decisions. To think of God as a mind places God directly in the timestream. God does this and then does that. To attribute these human characteristics to God is still anthropomorphic, though there is an attempt to do without any crude physical anthropomorphism. Yet to say that God does things like create or design worlds, hear and answer prayers, and reward some persons and punish others, is still anthropomorphic. It is

[26]Clarence Darrow, "The Delusion of Design and Purpose," in *The Story of My Life* (New York: Charles Scribner's Sons, 1932), p. 413.

incompatible with saying, as some do, that God is nontemporal, not existing in time but *timeless*, having no history at all, like the number 2 (one cannot meaningfully say for example that the number 2 was a year old yesterday). A mind might be everlasting but not timeless; to have a mind involves doing things like thinking, willing, feeling, deliberating— all of which are processes that take place in time. (The word "eternal" is ambiguous: it can mean *timeless*—having no history—or *everlasting*—existing throughout all time.)

A mind, whose acts and sentiments and ideas are not distinct and successive; one, that is wholly simple, and totally immutable; is a mind which has no thought, no reason, no will, no sentiment, no love, no hatred; or in a word, is no mind at all. It is an abuse of terms to give it that appellation.[27]

Yet if we speak of a mind *without* thoughts, feelings, volitions, and other events in its history, and yet call it a mind, is this not to take away with one hand what we give with the other? It doesn't help to say that it is still a mind, but a mind of a very different kind from ours, such that we cannot really conceive of it; for if we cannot conceive of it, what entitles us to call it a mind at all? What entitles us to say that it is a *mind* rather than something else? It is much as if we were told that there exists a very special and unusual kind of book that has no pages, no cover, no print—in fact, it is a red liquid. But whatever it is, this is not what we mean by "book" when we use the word; it cannot be a book, since it lacks the defining characteristics of books. Just as surely, it would seem does "timeless mind" lack a basic defining characteristic of mind.

Moreover, many of the traits people attribute to God are inconsistent with other traits they attribute to him. God desires—but how

can a being who has everything desire anything? God changes his mind—he "repented himself" and he had made human beings. "God created the world to glorify his name" —which, Mill said, is to attribute to God "one of the lowest of human attributes, a restless appetite for applause." As we have seen, if God is omnipotent he need not adopt means to achieve ends; He can achieve the ends directly and therefore need never do one thing in order to achieve another (such as tolerating evil in order to promote good). To say such things about God is almost as crudely anthropomorphic as to say that God is a physical organism having bodily organs.

Nonliteral use of terms. But perhaps when we call God benevolent, wise, and so on, these terms should not be taken literally; perhaps we should not mean them, in describing God, in the same sense in which we mean them when we refer to human beings. (However, as Mill said, when people speak of God as powerful they always seem to mean power in its most literal sense, the power to save or destroy, the power of life and death.) Perhaps when we say God is just we should not mean justice in any literal sense; perhaps we should use such terms only in a *figurative* sense.

We constantly use words in figurative senses. When we call a man a weasel, we do not imply that he has four legs and fur, but that he has some characteristics of a weasel— at any rate, characteristics popularly (though often falsely) attributed to weasels—such as deceitfulness. The popular definition of an assistant dean, "A mouse training to be a rat," doesn't purport to be a biological description. We may call a person on various occasions a lion, a bear, a snake, an insect, a walrus, a toad. But in calling a person any of these names, we have certain descriptive characteristics in mind which we could name if asked. "What do you mean by calling him a snake?" And we could easily answer such a question. The figurative term is simply a quick short-

<hr>

[27]David Hume, *Dialogues concerning Natural Religion*, part IV (in the Norman Kemp Smith edition, p. 159).

hand way of referring to a group or collection of familiar characteristics. We can easily translate these figurative expressions into *literal* ones. But what happens in cases where we can't do this?

Suppose I am told of a new theological discovery, namely that Brahma wears a hat. And then I am told that it is a divine hat and worn infinitely, since Brahma has neither head nor shape. In what sense then is a hat being worn? Why use *these* words? I am told that God exists but in a "different sense" of "exists." Then if he doesn't exist (in the plain sense) why use *that* word? Or that God loves us—but in a wholly special sense of "love." Or God is a circle whose center is everywhere and circumference nowhere. But this is then to have neither a center nor a circumference, and hence not to be a circle. One half of the description cancels out the other half. And what is left over but just noise?[28]

Some theists have suggested other avenues, however. One is that of "symbolic truth." The truth about God, it is said, is far beyond any human powers of description, and words we use function not as descriptions but as *symbols* of a truth that is beyond our reach. Suppose someone says, "God is a hot fire," not meaning thereby that God is characterized by a high temperature; the phrase "hot fire" is only a symbol for a quite different property which we cannot express in words. There are problems, however. If the true property is unknown, how do we know that the word we use as a symbol correctly expresses it? Why is one word or phrase used rather than another one? Why is "God is a hot fire" preferable to "God is a cold sweat"? If it is, isn't this because *some* resemblance is believed to exist between the properties of God and the properties of fire? Why else would the one phrase be more apt than the other?

Still another gambit consists of saying that

the words do apply literally to God, but with an enormous difference in *degree*. The dog loves its master; the person loves God; God loves all human beings. The love that a dog can experience, while genuine, is only a pale shadow of the love that human beings can experience, yet there is enough similarity between the two so that the word "love" can be used in preference to other words. Similarly, God's love, though so great as to be incomprehensible to us, is still more aptly called love than anything else—we somehow "get closer to it" by calling it that than by using any other term for it. As a dog's love is to a person's, so a person's love is to God's. But in attributing love to God we are only hinting at something we cannot fully conceive and cannot adequately express in words.

Mysticism. The mystic, however, takes a far more radical turn, declaring that no language we can use is in any way descriptive of God's nature. If we say that God is loving or merciful, or that God is omnipotent, or even that God is powerful, we are saying something that is not true—not because God hates or is not merciful or not omnipotent, for this would be equally untrue, but because God *transcends* all such distinctions, and is *beyond* all attempts to encapsulate his characteristics in our human concepts (hence in our human words). We are trying to *conceptualize* God, and God cannot be conceptualized.

What then *can* be truly said about God? According to the mystic, nothing at all. One can only be silent. Anything we say limits God. To say that God possesses characteristic A is to say that he lacks characteristic non-A, and to say this is to limit God, who transcends all such distinctions—including, apparently, the Law of Noncontradiction. Even to say that God is limitless is inadmissible, for it would limit God by saying that God cannot also be limited; God transcends *all* distinctions, even this one. Even to say that God *exists* is to attempt to bring God under a concept, and this

---

[28]Arthur C. Danto, "Faith, Language, and Religious Experience," in Sidney Hook (ed.), *Religious Experience and Truth* (New York: New York University Press, 1962), p. 137.

concept cannot be applied to God anymore than any other.

How then is one to have any concept of God at all? One cannot, says the mystic; God is inconceivable by the human mind. What then does the mystic mean by the word "God" when he uses it? Doesn't every word, to be a word and not merely a noise, have to mean *something*? It does stand for something, says the mystic, something of which the human mind has not even the glimmerings of comprehension. But the mystic does endeavor to provide one pipe-line from the human to the divine, and this is mystical *experience*. Mystical experience is entirely unlike any other, and there are no adequate descriptive terms for it. But persons have had such experiences from time immemorial. The experience differs from case to case, yet it has certain recurring features in most or all of its manifestations:

1. *Ineffability*: The mystical experience; words are wholly inadequate to describe its nature.
2. *Conviction*: The experience seems to those who have it to be a revelation of a transcendent reality; it comes to experiencers as an insight into truths that the intellect cannot grasp.
3. *Passive intake*: One is passive in receiving it: The experiencer is the passive recipient of an experience which (she is convinced) comes from another dimension of reality, which the experiencer receives like a message from another world which comes to her without the involvement of her active intellectual or volitional powers.
4. *Unity*: "The usual duality of a subject reflectively beholding an external object, which stands in sundered relation to it, is overpassed. It is a moment of *fusion* like that which comes in the enjoyment of great music or of surpassing beauty or sublimity, or of perfect love, a moment when the soul, abandoning its conscious, successive, bit-by-bit manner of knowing, responds to its object by a single undifferentiated act, all of one piece."[29]

---

[29]Rufus Matthew Jones, *Pathways to the Reality of God* (New York: Macmillan, 1931), Chapter 2.

5. *Positive experience*: It is a positive experience, involving ecstasy, heightened consciousness, release from tension and conflict. It comes as an irresistible revelation from "something out there." The experience is often described as "oneness with God," "union with the infinite," "an infinite ocean of light and love flowing over the ocean of darkness." (This is a description of the *experience*, not of the *object* of the experience, which is *indescribable*.)

One could attempt to describe the experience in much more detail; but a philosopher is likely to ask some pointed questions:

PHILOSOPHER: So what? What makes you think the experience points to anything beyond itself? People have all kinds of experiences, very intense ones. Depression can be very intense, and doubtless it has *causes*, but it doesn't point to any depression-out-there which is being *cognized* in the experience. Mystical experience is a psychological phenomenon, that's all. It doesn't require therapy because it doesn't do anyone any harm, and apparently does the experiencer a lot of good; but it's just another abnormal psychological phenomenon for all that. Don't make any *claims* for it. Your error is in claiming that the experience is caused by union with God or 'oneness with the divine' or some such thing. The *experience* is real, and may be as wonderful as you say it is; but the *claims* you make for it are unintelligible. (How can you be *one* with something that is not you but something else?)

MYSTIC: Its abnormality is surely nothing against it. It may be that people have to be in an abnormal state of mind to tune in on a wavelength of reality which ordinary mortals cannot attain to.

P: But what is your evidence that there is a reality outside of yourself which you are experiencing in this case? When we both look at a tree we can confirm that we are having experience of an object outside ourselves, which we can see and touch and bump into. But what proof is there that in mystical experience the experiencer is making contact with an outside reality which is revealed to him only in the experience?

M: I cannot prove it to those who have not had the experience. But I would point out that mystics throughout the ages have tended to describe their experiences in much the same way, in spite of cultural differences, and in spite of not being influenced by each other. *They* understand one another's language, even though the rest of us don't. Suppose you found someone meditating or in a trance, repeatedly pronouncing the words "square circle." You point out that there aren't and can't be square circles, that the phrase is a contradiction in terms. He admits that it is, but that this is the phrase that his experience regularly leads him to utter. And now suppose we discover that in many diverse times and places we find people—in specially rhapsodic states of mind—uttering the phrase "square circle." Surely there is *something* they are all experiencing, even though the phrase "square circle" is not an adequate description of it. To outsiders, indeed, it appears gibberish; and taken literally it is. But the mystics themselves know what it is they mean by the phrase, even though they can't describe it in terms that others will understand—any more than a person who can see can describe the experience of color to a person who was born blind. The mystics seem to be tuned into a unique wavelength and for us who don't or can't tune into that wavelength, we can only stand and wonder what it's all about. But *they* know.

P: There is something similar in all their experiences. *That* much may be true—just as people who imbibe mind-altering drugs have similar experiences which sober people don't have. But don't confuse this with saying that there is some *object* of their experience "out there somewhere" which is the cause of the experience, and which their experience is proof of. That is no more true than the fact that drug users have similar experiences is proof that there is something "out there" that they are in tune with, when in reality they are just having similar physiological and psychological reactions to the drug. The cause of the experience is internal, not external. The fact that the mystic experience may be more wonderful than others doesn't change the epistemology of the situation. If something is (to use the usual phrase) "objective," then it must pass the tests of objectivity, as the tree out there does. If it doesn't, then you must admit that it is simply an experience, however ecstatic. You can't call something objective when it fulfills none of the criteria of objectivity, anymore than you can call something a dog when it has feathers and quacks like a duck.

What Kind of Hypothesis?

The mystical experience establishes no divine source of experience. But perhaps nothing that we can discover can establish it, or even give any hint of it, one way or the other. Is that not a possibility?

If gods were conceived as human beings, only bigger and better, when we should be able under certain circumstances to perceive them, and their existence would be an ordinary empirical hypothesis like the view that there are insects under that rock. If the Greek gods lived on Mount Olympus, one would only have to scour Mount Olympus for a long period of time to conclude that Zeus, Hera, Poseidon, and the rest do not reside there or anywhere else in or around Greece. But of course we no longer believe in gods with physical bodies. Many people do believe, however, that God has (or is) a mind—thinking, willing, deciding, blessing—but a mind without a body. In that case, however, God's existence cannot be detected by means of the senses, or for that matter by instruments such as x-rays, microscopes, and radar.

But aren't there many entities that scientists believe in which cannot be detected by the senses or even by instruments? Quarks and neutrons can't be seen, touched, or even seen in microscopes; they are, as we say "known by their effects." You can't see them, but their existence does make a difference. The entities themselves may be entirely inferences from experience, but scientists believe they are entitled to make the inferences, citing certain observable phenomena which, they say, would not have occurred unless the existence of these entities is assumed. Similarly, we "know God through his effects" in the world. We can't see God but we are entitled to infer God's existence from what we do observe in the world—just as with electrons. The teleological argument, for example, starts out with citing certain observable things and processes in the universe, and concludes that these are the effects of God's labors. Now perhaps the teleologist's inference is unwarranted—perhaps we can account for what we see without invoking a designer. But a bad scientific theory is still a theory within the domain of science— like the once-respected theories regarding ether or phlogiston. But scientists don't consider the existence of God a scientific theory at all—neither a good theory nor a bad one, but something not even within the domain of science. Why the difference?

One might say that this is because, with the God hypothesis, you can always reinterpret the evidence to get the conclusions you want. You can always posit some characteristic of God to reconcile his existence with the events you see occurring in the physical world. Ten thousand people are killed in an earthquake, yet God is perfectly benevolent and omnipotent; how can this be? Well, he has a plan greater than anything we can discern; or, his goodness is different from ours; or, these deaths are means toward some greater end. And thus we try to reconcile whatever facts there are—however unfavorable to our theory—with the view of God we want to preserve. We claim to go by the facts wherever they may lead, but in fact we tend to interpret the facts in such a way as to reconcile them with the theory we want to hold. In science it is said we can't do this; we have to respect the observable facts regardless of whether they may spoil our favorite theory.

But "saving a theory at all costs" is something that is familiar in science also; witness the lengths scientists were willing to go to in order to preserve the principle of no action at a distance, or the conservation of matter. In the end, of course, the theories had to go; but one could go a long way in preserving them as long as one was willing to pay the price of abandoning other theories.

But let's suppose that this defect is corrected. Suppose we take our stand (for example) in favor of an omnipotent and benevolent designer, and if the evidence goes against us we abandon the hypothesis; we don't try to think of ways to circumvent it. If X happens, our hypothesis is confirmed; if Y happens, it is disconfirmed; and if Y (for example, the facts brought forth when discussing the problem of evil) is what occurs, then we abandon the omnipotent-benevolent designer hypothesis. If we did this, would the teleological argument then be a scientific hypothesis?

Even so, the answer appears to be no. A scientific theory is accepted only if it can be made to "fit in" with the huge interlocking network of laws and theories that constitute science. It must have explanatory power (the more the better). And from this explanatory power must arise some ability to predict future occurrences on the basis of the theory. But the God-hypothesis is not connected with any body of laws and theories; it stands quite apart from them, apparently unrelated to any part of the network. Nor does it have any predictive power; no matter what happens, one can always say God willed it or it was a part of God's plan; one cannot predict what God is going to do next. If a thousand people die, then that was part of his plan; but if they do not, then it was part of his plan to keep them alive. We can predict nothing but can only say "after the fact" what the plan was. Such assertions of course are scientifically quite useless.

"But that doesn't disprove God's existence. There may indeed be a God who has the power to create or design the universe, and whose plan we cannot fathom, and therefore cannot predict what He will do. We might believe there is one God who created and also sustains the universe (theism), or one who, having created it, chooses to ignore it. Maybe we aren't in a position to know which is true, but one or the other may *be* true just the same.

The ancient Epicureans believed that there were many gods but that they had nothing to do with human life—they sat in the garden and chatted and drank ambrosia, but they eschewed all contact with human beings, so the fact of their existence made no difference to human experience. If human beings had wished to devise the hypothesis that such beings existed, and then looked to experience for confirmation of the hypothesis, they would have found none, since the gods had left no traces in the world. Still, one could urge, they might exist even though people looked in vain for traces of their existence.

A contemporary philosopher, John Wisdom, has presented a story that could be called "the tale of the invisible gardener":

Two people return to their long neglected garden and find among the weeds a few of the old plants surprisingly vigorous. One says to the other "It must be that a gardener has been coming and doing something about these plants." Upon inquiry they find that no neighbor has ever seen anyone at work in their garden. The first man says to the other, "He must have worked while people slept." The

other says, "No, someone would have heard him and besides, anyone who cared about the plants would have kept down these weeds." The first man says "Look at the way these are arranged. There is purpose and a feeling for beauty here. I believe that someone comes, someone invisible to mortal eyes. I believe that the more carefully we look the more we shall find confirmation of this." They examine the garden ever so carefully and sometimes they come on new things suggesting that a gardener comes and sometimes they come on new things suggesting the contrary and even that a malicious person has been at work. Besides examining the garden carefully they also study what happens to gardens left without attention. Each learns all the other learns about this and about the garden. Consequently, when after all this, one says "I still believe a gardener comes" while the other says "I don't" their different words reflect no difference as to what they have found in the garden, no difference as to what they would find in the garden if they looked further and no difference about how fast untended gardens fall into disorder. At this stage, in this context, the gardener hypothesis has ceased to be experimental, the difference between one who accepts and one who rejects it is now not a matter of the one expecting something the other does not expect. What is the difference between them? The one says "A gardener comes unseen and unheard. He is manifested only in his works with which we are all familiar," the other says, "There is no gardener" and with this difference in what they say about the gardener goes a difference in how they feel towards the garden, in spite of the fact that neither expects anything of it which the other does not expect.[30]

On such a view, there is no empirically discoverable difference between the universe as conceived by the atheist and the universe as conceived by the believer. There is no discernible feature of the world that the one would grant but the other would not. But one wonders also *what* exactly the believer is believing.

[30]"Gods," *Proceedings of the Aristotelian Society,* vol. 44, 1944-45. Reprinted in Antony Flew (ed.), *Logic and Language,* first series, pp. 192-193. Also reprinted in John Wisdom, *Philosophy and Psychoanalysis* (Oxford: Blackwell, 1949).

Is it that there *exists* an invisible gardener who leaves not the slightest trace behind? (If we kept a 24-hour watch, could we detect him? Or would we just see the plants moving and arranging themselves?) Or does the difference lie not in any view of "what's out there" but in the way two people *feel* toward the world—perhaps the second person doesn't really believe anything different from the first, but is only comforted or consoled by *thinking* of the observed changes as the work of an Invisible Gardener?

Some writers have suggested that belief in God is merely a disguised *ethical* belief, that uttering sentences like "God is good" is merely a way of stating one's commitment to a certain way of life, plus (perhaps) belief in certain historical events such as the life of Jesus. But if this is all the belief involved, it would better be considered under the heading of ethics. It smacks of intellectual dishonesty to take religious language, which most people employ to express genuine theistic belief, and use it to express something entirely different—moral views—especially if one continues to leave his hearers with the impression that he still intends the words in the former religious sense. We shall not dignify this mode of speaking by calling it *religious* belief.

Another possible view, however, is that although there is no difference whatever *in the here and now* between the belief of the atheist and that of the theist, there is the expectation of a difference to be discerned later, after death:

Two men are traveling together along a road. One of them believes that it leads to the Celestial City, the other that it leads nowhere; but since this is the only road there is, both must travel it. Neither has been this way before; therefore, neither is able to say what they will find around each corner. During their journey they meet with moments of refreshment and delight, and with moments of hardship and danger. All the time one of them thinks of his journey as a pilgrimage to the Celestial City. He interprets the pleasant parts as encouragements and the obstacles as trials of his purpose and lessons in

endurance, prepared by the king of that city and designed to make of him a worthy citizen of the place when at last he arrives. The other, however, believes none of this, and sees their journey as an unavoidable and aimless ramble. Since he has no choice in the matter, he enjoys the good and endures the bad. For him there is no Celestial City to be reached, no all-encompassing purpose ordaining their journey; there is only the road itself and the luck of the road in good weather and in bad.

During the course of the journey, the issue between them is not an experimental one. They do not entertain different expectations about the coming details of the road, but only about its ultimate destination. Yet, when they turn the last corner, it will be apparent that one of them has been right all the time and the other wrong. Thus, although the issue between them has not been experimental, it has, nevertheless, been a real issue. They have not merely felt differently about the road, for one was feeling appropriately and the other inappropriately in relation to the actual state of affairs. Their opposed interpretations of the situation have constituted genuine rival assertions, whose assertion-status has the peculiar characteristic of being guaranteed retrospectively by a future crux. . . . The theist and the atheist do not (or need not) expect different events to occur in the successive details of the temporal process. They do not (or need not) entertain divergent expectations of the course of history as viewed from within. However, the theist does and the atheist does not expect that when history is completed it will be seen to have led to a particular end-state and to have fulfilled a specific purpose, namely, that of creating "children of God."[31]

There is, then, a difference in their *expectations*. Suppose that the theist's expectations are fulfilled and, at the end of the road, he finds himself in a shining celestial city. Would that prove the existence of God? Would God be perceivable with his senses even then? (If so, what would God look like? Could a mind without a body present an appearance at all?) What would be proved is that there is a life after death (immortality), but that of course is not the same as proving God's existence. Even in heaven wouldn't belief in God still be an *inference*?

---

[31] John Hick, *Philosophy of Religion*, pp. 101–102.

"Yes, we still couldn't 'see God'—but being in heaven would be strong evidence for God's existence." But can even this much be granted? That a person can survive death bodily would be an interesting fact about the universe; that she could be transported after death to a heavenly place would be another; but what exactly would be the connection between immortality and God? How would the existence of the first prove the existence of the second? Indeed, what *would* prove the existence of the second? Could anything at all verify it or even confirm it? What would you have to see to confirm it? shining lights? an old man in long robes?

"But it might be true, even if no one could verify or confirm it; we would just have no *way* to confirm it one way or the other. Why should everything that exists be confirmable by human beings, even by resurrected human beings?" Such a view has been set forth, and it considers all the traditional arguments for God's existence to be *irrelevant*. God is utterly separated from the entire "natural order" of things.

The eternal order is not the natural order, and the natural order is not the eternal order. The two orders intersect, but in the intersection each remains what it is. Each is wholly self-contained. Therefore it is impossible to pass, by any logical inference, from one to the other. This at once precludes as impossible any talk either of the proof of disproof of religion.

When philosophers and theologians speak of "proofs of the existence of God," or "evidences of Christianity," what they have in mind is always a logical passage from the natural order, or some fact in the natural order, to the divine order. They may, for instance, argue in the following way. Here is the world. That is a natural fact. It must have had a cause. Other natural facts are then pointed out which are supposed to show adaptations of means to end in nature. Bees pollinate flowers. Surely not by chance, nor following any purpose of their own. Or the heart has the function—which is interpreted as meaning the purpose—of pumping the blood. This teleological mechanism was not made by us, and the purpose evident in it is not our purpose. Therefore the cause of the world must have

been an intelligent and designing mind. Doubtless I have much oversimplified the argument, and this version of it might not be accepted by the theologian as a statement of it which is to his liking. Certainly it is not a full statement. That, however, is not the point. The point is that, however the argument is stated, it necessarily starts from the natural order, or from selected facts in the natural order, and ends with a conclusion about the divine reality.

In other cases the natural fact from which the argument starts may be some very astonishing occurrence, which we do not yet know how to explain, and which we therefore call a miracle. This is evidence, it is believed, of a divine intervention.

In all cases we use some fact or facts of the natural order as premises for our argument, and then leap, by an apparently logical inference, clear out of the natural order into the divine order, which thus appears as the conclusion of the argument. The point is that the premise is in the natural world, the conclusion in the divine world.

But an examination of the nature of inference shows that this is an impossible procedure. For inference proceeds always along the thread of some relation. We start with one fact, which is observed. This bears some relation to another fact, which is not observed. We pass along this relation to the second fact. The first fact is our premise, the second fact our conclusion. The relation, in the case of the deductive inference, is that of logical entailment. In nondeductive inferences other relations are used, of which the most common is that of causality. Thus, although the sun is now shining, and the sky is cloudless, I see that the ground is wet, and the trees are dripping with water. I infer that an April shower has passed over, and that it rained a few minutes ago. My inference has passed along the thread of a causal relation from an effect as premise to a cause as conclusion. To pass in this way from facts which are before my eyes, along a relational link, to other facts which are not before my eyes—which are inferred, not seen—is the universal character of inference.

But the natural order is the totality of all things which stand to each other in the one systematic network of relationships which is the universe. Therefore no inference can ever carry me from anything in the natural order to anything outside it. If I start from a natural fact, my inferential process, however long, can end only in another natural fact. A "first cause," simply by virtue of being a cause, would be a fact in the natural order. It is not denied that it might conceivably be possible to argue back from the present state of the world to an intelligent cause of some of its present characteristics—although I do not believe that any such argument is in fact valid. The point is that an intelligent cause of the material world, reached by any such inference, would be only another natural being, a part of the natural order. The point is that such a first cause *would not be God*.

No such vast mind running the universe, or a part of the universe, however enormous, magnificent, powerful, intelligent, good, it might be, could be God. For it would be merely another natural being, a part of the natural order, or perhaps the whole of it. God so thought of is a superstition, a gigantic and perhaps benevolent ghost, an immense, disembodied, and super-earthly clergyman. And some such superstition is what is implied by all the supposed proofs of His existence.[32]

It is difficult to know what to make of this view. One is inclined to ask first, "How do you know that such a position is true?" And the answer might be, "There is no pipeline from the natural world to the divine, hence no way to confirm or disconfirm it. But of course, such a view might still *be true*, even though we have no way of knowing it. I can say it's true, and you can say it isn't, and there is no way either of us can discover which of us is right."

Problems of meaning versus problems of truth. Philosophers disagree on whether "the problem of God" is fundamentally a problem of meaning or of truth. Those who consider it a problem of meaning argue somewhat as follows: "After all this controversy I still don't know exactly what is referred to by the word 'God.' I know the meaning of 'Zeus lives on the top of Mt. Olympus'—that's an ordinary emprical statement and can be subjected to tests, like setting a 24-hour watch on Mt. Olympus and installing cameras and so on and finding out whether a team of observers ever discovers anyone of that sort. But when you become less anthropomorphic, the meaning-problem intensifies as the religious belief

becomes more 'sophisticated.' God is now invisible. Well, atoms too are invisible, but their existence is confirmed by a huge array of evidence; virtually nothing in modern chemistry would be explained without atomic theory. But there seems to be no such confirmation in the case of an invisible God. The traditional arguments, as we have seen, are all inadquate. Perhaps then we should conclude that the belief is false. But a false belief has to be as meaningful as a true one; If I know what "Snow is white" means, I also know what "Snow is not white" means. To be able to discover that something is so-and-so, I must also know what it would be to discover that it is *not* so-and-so. But what is there to discover in the case of God? God is a mind not connected with a body, people say; but does even this assertion make sense? A mind, but no brain, no neurons, no cerebral cortex? We have already seen (pp. 282–83) what problems confront us here. But even if we grant this, how could a pure mind, with no body, *do* things in the world, like creating and sustaining it? Close your eyes and try to imagine how this takes place. How can a pure mind manipulate the universe, make it move, or suspend its laws? And if you tell me that the mind is not like ours, but timeless like the integers in arithmetic, then how can I call that a mind at all (pp. 323–24)? The whole alleged concept is riddled with contradictions. All we have is just *words*. The minute I want the words to mean something, I'm told that the words are not applicable 'in the usual sense' and that 'goodness' doesn't mean goodness and 'mind' doesn't mean mind and even 'existence' doesn't mean existence. What am I to make of all this? As far as I can tell, it's noises without meaning—nonsense, gibberish."

On the other hand one might reply, "I don't think there is an insuperable problem about meaning. I know what it is for someone to be powerful, so I can carry this quality to the nth degree and imagine what it would be for someone to be all-powerful (to be able to

[32]W. T. Stace, "The Divine as Beyond Proof," in *Time and Eternity* (Princeton: Princeton University Press, 1952), pp. 136–38.

do anything except what's logically impossible, like change the past or make $2 + 2 = 5$). And the same with goodness, wisdom, and the other qualities. Although we have never observed minds without bodies, I cannot see any meaning difficulty in it; it seems to be logically possible—in this world minds depend on brains, but this need not be the case always and everywhere. I can imagine a mind much greater then human minds, who has the power as some human beings appear to now—powers of telekinesis—to create and move things simply by an act of will. Such a being may have brought the universe into being out of nothing —'Let there be light,' he said, and there was light—and also designed it according to his purposes. (But I can't answer the question 'How did *he* get there?') The world we inhabit may thus be a manifestation of the will of such a Being. This doesn't show that the belief is *true*, only that it is *intelligible*—and if it is intelligible, it *might* be true. There is no logical barrier to its being true."

Assuming that this second view is correct, what more can we say? There are different religions competing for our allegiance; each one points to its own God and its own miraculous occurrences and denies those of the others. Most people accept without question the one they were born into. If any of them is true, it is far from apparent which one that is. The Bible says that it alone is true and that the others are false religions, but the Koran says that too of itself. If a book says that what it contains is true, that doesn't prove that it *is* true; its truth is not self-authenticating. So we have the problem of competing candidates for the position of "the true God." Moslems believe that Allah is the true God, Jews believe that Jaweh (Jehovah) is the true God; and countless peoples and nations throughout history have each believed theirs was the only god (or gods). Or perhaps a god exists that doesn't have the specific characteristics of any of the traditional religions. Or perhaps none of them at all exists. Unlike science, where we learn to pick up the clues and know more with each passing generation, there are no clues here that we can trace, so we are left in the dark. Thus, such a person would say, "I have no problem with meaning in the case of religious belief, but there is an enormous problem about discovering the truth."

At this point, many persons would adhere to the religion of their choice simply as a matter of *faith;* if we don't know, we can at least have faith. But faith in exactly what? Christians hold to their belief by faith; Zoroastrians hold to their belief by faith; so do the others. Faith, of course, is no proof, nor even evidence; If faith in X proved X, then faith in Y would prove Y, and so on. Faith that I shall find my way out of the desert doesn't prove that I *will* find my way out; many people have faith to the end but still die of thirst in the desert. Having faith is a kind of mental attitude and doesn't prove that what you have faith in is *true*.

"But if there's no way of proving whether it's true or not, why *not* have faith in it, if having faith improves the quality of my life?" Here one might say, "Have faith in it if you want to—if you can really have faith in the existence of something you're not convinced is true. But don't confuse faith with *knowledge*. Be warned. You don't *know* that what you want to believe is true, and it may not be true. If you can still 'have faith' in it under these circumstances, be my guest, but don't expect me to have that same faith, since you have offered me no reason for having it."

"The belief may be true, or it may not be true. If it is true, my life will be greatly enriched by believing it, and I shall feel more secure. Lacking proof either way, why shouldn't I choose the more rewarding alternative, traversing one road even not knowing whether it's the right one?" Fitzjames Stephen wrote in 1874,

In all important transactions of life we have to take a leap in the dark. . . . If we decide to leave the riddles unanswered, that is a choice; if we waver in our answer, that, too, is a choice; but whatever choice we make, we make it at our peril. If a man chooses to turn his back altogether on God and the future, no one can prevent him; no one can show beyond reasonable doubt that he is mistaken. Each must act as he thinks best; and if he is wrong, so much the worse for him. We stand on a mountain pass in the midst of whirling snow and blinding mist, through which we get glimpses now and then of paths which may be deceptive. If we stand still we shall be frozen to death. If we take the wrong road we shall be dashed to pieces. We do not certainly know whether there is any right one. What must we do? "Be strong and of a good courage." Act for the best, hope for the best, and take what comes. . . . If death ends all, we cannot meet death better.[33]

But if we choose one of them, what exactly is it that we would be choosing?

EXERCISES

1. Would the following events, if they occurred, confirm the existence of the God of Christianity? Why or why not?

a. If Christians lived on the average 25 years longer than non-Christians.

b. If prayers of Christians were usually answered but those of non-Christians were not.

c. If the accounts written by Mark, Luke, etc., turned out to have been eyewitness reports rather than written a generation or so later.

d. If children started to quote the Bible as soon as they learned to talk, without having learned any of the statements in the Bible.

e. If Christians had fewer neuroses and psychoses than non-Christians.

f. If water was turned into wine at a ceremony in Jerusalem every Easter.

g. If professing Christians, after their death, disappeared from their coffins and flew upward through the air until they vanished from sight.

2. Evaluate the following assertions:

a. God was the first event.

b. God caused the first event.

c. There was no first event, but God is the explanation of why there was a first event as well as any subsequent events.

d. God was present before time began.

e. God created time.

f. God created time, then the world.

g. The universe came from God.

h. First there was a conscious being (God), a mind without a body, who then created matter (including bodies).

i. God created space before creating the matter which would occupy the space.

j. Only if one believes in God can one solve the mystery of why anything exists at all.

k. If you don't belive in a God who created and designed the universe, you must believe that everything that happens and ever has happened is one vast *accident*.

3. "Since the innocent often suffer and the guilty go unpunished in this life, there must be another life in which these wrongs are righted and each person judged by an impartial God according to his or her deserts." Evaluate this argument.

4. Describe the kind of universe (if any) which would make the following hypotheses (each in turn) probable.

a. There are two gods (one good, one evil) fighting for control of the world.

b. There are many gods, each with his own sphere of influence.

c. Everything in the universe tends toward good.

d. Everything in the universe tends toward evil.

e. Everything that appears to be bad in the world, will in the end turn out for the best.

f. Everything that appears to be good in the world, will in the end turn out for the worst.

g. There is one God, both omnipotent and benevolent.

h. There is one God, omnipotent but not benevolent.

i. There is one God, benevolent but not omnipotent.

5. Are there any occurrence, or series of occurrence, which if they were to happen would lead

[33]Fitz-James Stephen, *Liberty, Equality, Fraternity* New York: Holt, 1882), p. 353, first edition 1874.

you to say "It's miracle"? If so, describe them and indicate why you would label them miracles.

6. "My sick child recovered, and I take this fact as evidence for a benevolent God." "But my sick child did not recover, so I take this fact as evidence that there is not a benevolent God." Does either alleged fact confirm the hypothesis for which the fact is given as evidence? Justify your answer.

7. "Two hundred years ago the average human lifespan was only half what it is now. This increase is directly traceable to the advances in medical science. Medical science, not God, is the cause of the greater longevity today." "No, the facts you cite equally confirm another hypothesis: that God used medical science (perhaps even implanting ideas in the minds of medical experts) to fulfill his plan, that of lengthening the span of human life." Discuss.

8. We all know what it is to create a poem, or a disturbance, or an idea. But what is it to create out of nothing? Imagine yourself a conscious being, and no material universe exists. You say, "Let there be stars," and suddenly stars come into existence where there were none before. How would you know that your uttering these words was what brought the stars into being? (You take the medicine and feel better, but how do you know that taking the medicine is what caused you to feel better?)

9. "No scientific argument—by which I mean an argument drawn from the phenomena of nature—can ever have the slightest tendency either to prove or to disprove the existence of God."[34] Do you agree with this statement, and why? Discuss the general question of the relevance of empirical facts to religious belief. (Read Chapter 5 of Stace's *Religion and Modern Mind*, the chapter from which the above quotation was taken, for more material on this question.)

10. Which of the following statements could be taken, in your opinion, as literally true? When words or phrases in them cannot be taken literally, try to translate the sentences in which they occur into sentences which *can* be taken literally. Exam-

ine those that can be taken literally, for internal consistency.

   a. God is above the stars.
   b. God is above human concerns.
   c. God existed before time began.
   d. "And God said . . . "
   e. God exists throughout all space and all time.
   f. The earth is God's footstool.
   g. God caused the world.
   h. God is love.
   i. God is truth.

11. Discuss the criteria for the use of the word "exist" with reference to each of the following:
   a. "Tables exist."
   b. "Headaches exist."
   c. "Magnetism exists."
   d. "Ghosts exist."
   e. "God exists."

12. "God does not really possess the properties we attribute to him (masculine gender, existing in time, having will and intellect and feeling, and so on), but he possesses something *like* each of these things; the words we use to characterize God apply only *analogically*." Evaluate this view.

13. Which of the following would you accept, and which would you reject, and why?
   a. There is an elephant in this room, invisible and intangible.
   b. There are radio waves in this room, invisible and intangible.
   c. There are atoms in every bit of matter, invisible and intangible.
   d. There is a God in the world, invisible and intangible.

14. If the following events were to occur, what would they show? Would they establish (or render probable) a supernatural being?
   a. Someone who is about to kill another human being suddenly dies of a heart attack.
   b. Every adult human being in the world is simultaneously stricken with paralysis in one leg. In time people discover that if they read a few verses from the Gospel of St. Luke (concerning the miraculous healing of the sick), the paralysis of each person who reads it suddenly and permanently disappears.
   c. You die, and then wake up again, with a different body but all of your memories of earthly

---

[34]George G. Simpson, *The Meaning of Evolution* (New Haven: Yale University Press, 1967), p. 127.

life. You see around you a city of gold, a radiant sky, and white creatures with wings flying about. Someone in a long white robe approaches you and says, "You are in heaven now."

d. Someone appears on earth and says, "God is invisible, but I, who am visible, am God's representative." To show his credentials he changes water into wine and raises people from the dead.

15. Assume that you are creating a world, including human beings, and that you want to minimize or eliminate pain and misery but at the same time want to preserve people's freedom of choice. (1) What laws of nature or human nature would you change? (2) Without changing any laws, to what extent would you permit pain and misery in order to preserve freedom of choice? Consider the following cases:

a. A man regularly provokes his wife into fits of jealous rage. Her response amuses him. "I like to play with people's minds," he says; "that's *my* freedom."

b. A man who has raped and mutilated a girl later repents his deed. "I would never do such a thing again," he says. "But it was the only way I could learn."

c. By repeatedly distorting the news and suppressing items he dislikes, the head of a news-gathering agency povokes a dangerous international crisis. "We are all free to express our views," he says. "Whatever the cost, freedom is worth it."

d. Human beings have freedom of choice; no other animal does. In the interests of promoting maximum freedom for human beings, it is accordingly permissible to kill animals for food, for their hides, and for sport, as well as to use them for purposes of medical experimentation and to satisfy intellectual curiosity. The sacrifice of animals is a small price to pay for the enhancement of human freedom and increasing the range of human choices.

16. Should the teleological argument be considered a scientific theory? Doesn't it have empirical consequences which can be confirmed or disconfirmed?

17. "Whereof thou canst not speak, thereof thou must be silent" (Ludwig Wittgenstein). Must the mystic, to be consistent, remain completely silent?

18. Except for highly anthropomorphic religions like the polytheism of the Greeks, which are empirically false (no such creatures as the Greek gods have ever been found on Olympus or elsewhere), many philosophers find the tenets of the more "sophisticated" religions such as Christianity to be meaningless—to "make no sense," to be misuses of language parading as meaningful assertions. Others consider the tenets of these religions to be quite intelligible, though disagreeing on whether any of these tenets are true (many consider them meaningful but false, e.g., that a benevolent universe-designer exists). Discuss your position on this issue, with reasons.

19. Does the fact that the sciences employ a certain method ("the empirical method") to arrive at conclusions indicate that they deliberately *exclude* certain aspects of reality from their investigations? "The most successful scientific investigation has generally involved treating phenomena *as if* they were purely materialistic, rejecting any metaphysical hypothesis as long as a physical hypothesis seems possible. The method works. The restriction is necessary because science is confined to physical means of investigation and so it would stultify its own efforts to postulate that its subject is not physical and so not susceptible to its methods. Yet few scientists would maintain that the required restrictions of their methods necessarily delimit all truth or that the materialistic nature of their hypotheses imposes materialisms on the universe."[35]

SELECTED READINGS

ALEXANDER, SAMUEL. *Space, Time, and Deity.* 2 vols. London: Macmillan, 1918.

ALSTON, WILLIAM, ed. *Religious Belief and Philosophical Thought.* New York: Harcourt Brace, 1963.

ANGELES, PETER, ed. *Critiques of God.* Buffalo: Prometheus Books, 1976.

AQUINAS ST. THOMAS. *Summa Theologica.* Many editions.

---

[35]Ibid.

BLANSHARD, BRAND. *Readon and Belief*. New Haven: Yale University Press, 1975.

DEWEY, JOHN. *A Common Faith*. New Haven: Yale University Press, 1934.

FLEW, ANTONY, and ALASDAIR MacINTYRE. *New Essays in Philosophical Theology*. London: SCM Press, 1955.

FLEW, ANTONY. *God and Philosophy*. London: Hutchinson, 1966.

GEACH, PETER. *Providence and Evil*. Cambridge: Cambridge University Press, 1977.

GEACH, PETER. *God and the Soul*. New York: Schocken Books, 1969.

HICK, JOHN. *The Existence of God*. New York: Macmillan, 1964.

HICK, JOHN. *Faith and Knowledge*. Ithaca: Cornell University Press, 1957.

HICK, JOHN, ed. *Classical and Contemporary Readings in the Philosophy of Religion*. Englewood Cliffs, NJ: Prentice-Hall, 1964.

HOOK, SIDNEY, ed. *Religious Experience and Truth*. New York: New York University Press, 1961.

HUME, DAVID. *Dialogues concerning Natural Religion*. 1776. Norman Kemp Smith edition published by Thomas Nelson Sons, Edinburgh, 1935.

JAMES, WILLIAM. *The Varieties of Religious Experience*. New York: Modern Library, 1902.

KITCHER, PHILIP. *Abusing Science*. Cambridge, MIT Press, 1982.

LEWIS, C. S. *The Problem of Pain*. New York: Macmillan, 1962.

MACPHERSON, THOMAS. *The Philosophy of Religion*. Princeton: Van Nostrand, 1965.

MACGREGOR, GEDDES, ed. *Philosophical Issues in Religious Thought*. Boston: Houghton Mifflin, 1976.

MacTAGGART, J. E. *Some Dogmas of Religion*. London: Edward Arnold, 1906.

MATSON, WALLACE I. *The Existence of God*. Ithaca, NY: Cornell University Press, 1965.

MILL, JOHN STUART. *Three Essays on Religion*. London: Longmans Green, 1874.

MILL, JOHN STUART. *An Examination of Sir William Hamilton's Philosophy*. New York: Henry Holt & Co., 1865, Chapter 7.

MORRIS, HENRY M. *Scientific Creationism*. San Diego: Creation-Life Publishers, 1974.

MUNITZ, MILTON. *The Mystery of Existence*. New York: Appleton-Century-Crofts, 1965.

PIKE, NELSON. *God and Evil*. Englewood Cliffs, NJ: Prentice-Hall, 1964.

PLANTINGA, ALVIN. "The Free-Will Defense," in *Philosophy in America*, ed. Max Black. London: Allen & Unwin, 1965.

ROWE, WILLIAM. *The Cosmological Argument*. Princeton, NJ: Princeton University Press, 1975.

STACE, WALTER T. *Religion and the Modern Mind*. Philadelphia: Lippincott, 1952.

STACE, WALTER T. *Time and Eternity*. Princeton, NJ: Princeton University Press, 1952.

SWINBURNE, "The Problem of Evil," in Brown, Stuart C., ed., *Reason and Religion*. London: Royal Institute of Philosophy, 1977.

WARD, JAMES. *Naturalism and Agnosticism*. 2 vols. London: Black, 1899.

WISDOM, JOHN. *Philosophy and Psychoanalysis*. Oxford: Blackwell, 1965.

WISDOM, JOHN. "Gods," in Antony Flew, ed., *Logic and Language,* first series. Oxford: Blackwell, 1952.

8

PROBLEMS IN ETHICS

Many sentences we utter express nothing that can be classified as either true or false, because the persons uttering them are not asserting anything. "What time is it?" is a sentence, but it is neither true nor false, it merely asks a question. "Close the window!" is a command, and you would be misunderstanding it entirely if you responded, "Yes, that's true." "Let's get out of here" is a suggestion, and suggestions may be good or bad, appropriate or inappropriate, but not true or false. Similarly, exclamations like "What a day this is!" or "Whoopee!" (the latter is not even a sentence) aren't true or false. They indicate mood, and they appear to be declarative—to declare that something is or is not so. But if they are declarative, what do they declare? If one person says that population control would be a good thing, and another says it isn't, what is the first person asserting that the second is denying? Are there empirical facts

which could settle the issue? But what if both parties already know the relevant facts in the case?

1. THE NATURE OF MORAL JUDGMENTS

1. Expression versus assertion. A sentence may be in the indicative mood and give every appearance of making a statement and yet not do so. There are "purr-words" like "gorgeous" and "scrumptious" and "snarl-words" like "horrible" and "ghastly"—and perhaps we use sentences containing these primarily to purr or snarl: that is, we're really not *asserting* anything to be true or false, we are just "letting off steam"—we are *expressing* our feelings or attitude toward something but making no *statement* about it—not even the statement that we have the attitude. Some sentences we utter, like "Damn him anyway," serve to *express* our feeling rather than to state anything, much as Smith's closing eyelids and his tendency to drowse off after lunch express his sleepiness or his lethargy but do not assert anything about it; they reveal his sleepiness to us without his saying anything. Some sentences function much like gestures. We can often observe the person and infer how she feels without her saying a word. "What a bitch!" may express her feelings about another woman without her making any specific claims about her: The intent of her language is expressive rather than informational.

Much of the language we use in daily life is like this: We don't so much give information, or receive it from what others say, as express our feelings and attitudes and try, through our language, to work on other people's feelings and attitudes in order to change or control them. If you listen to the sentences uttered at many a family gathering, you might soon be convinced that expression of attitudes and the attempt to induce them in others is the principal function of language in practice, and that the communication of information is only incidental.

A serious question remains, however, as to what sentences should be considered non-informational. If someone says, "Killing your parents is wrong," is this simply the expression of an attitude? It may indeed be that—it probably does express the speaker's negative attitude toward that practice—but is that *all* it does? Can it not also state what the speaker sincerely *believes?* And may it not be that what the speaker believes is *true?* If so, there is such a thing as moral truth—a topic we have now to consider. To express an attitude is one thing; to state something (true or false) is another, and often the same sentence may perform both functions at once. It is this second function that now requires examination. We could say that "Murder is on the rise" is a statement of fact, and that "Murder is wrong" is an evaluation—but if we put it that

way, is it not still open to us to say that an evaluation may be true or false? or perhaps justified or unjustified? What *can* we say about it?

2. Statements of personal taste or preference. We might say that evaluations are statements all right, but that they only state what our *tastes* in the matter are. I prefer shrimp to steak, you prefer steak to shrimp; your statement of preference is true and so is mine— neither of us is likely to call the other a liar; each of us is informing the other of what our tastes in the matter are. You may even tell me that steak is *better,* but if you do so I will probably conclude that this is just another way of saying that you prefer it. (If you say it's better *for* you, that is a different issue entirely. Then we are talking about what foods are more healthful than others, an empirical issue on which we might ask the advice of nutritionists.) I am not likely to argue that shrimp *ought* to taste better to you than steak does or that there is something intrinsically preferable about the taste of shrimp.

Some people prefer fishing for recreation, others prefer tennis. This can be plausibly considered a difference in personal taste. But it should not be concluded that *all* statements of this kind are about differences in taste. Consider the sentence, "Killing the animal painlessly is better than letting it die slowly" —is it merely an assertion of personal preference? If someone says, "Killing animals at all is wrong" or "Letting animals die without our intervention is preferable to killing them outright," isn't this person *contradicting* what the first said? Yet the person who says she prefers shrimp and the other who says he prefers steak are not contradicting each other. If one person says, "Abortion is wrong," and another says it isn't, they surely *seem* to be contradicting one another. And if they are, aren't they stating propositions? And when propositions contradict each other, if one of them is true, the other must be false.

Thus not all sentences that we (very roughly) classify as evaluative are merely expressions of taste. In general when people make statements such as "I like this," "I don't like that," they are comparing notes on their autobiographies; such statements don't contradict each other. But statements such as "This is right," "This is wrong" do indeed appear to contradict each other. People surely *think* they are disagreeing when they say these things to each other. How could they argue if they're not disagreeing?

Disagreement occurs when there is a proposition which one person believes to be true and the other person believes to be false. The statements "I prefer shrimp" and "I prefer steak" do not represent a disagreement. We might loosely *call* them a disagreement about tastes, but all they state is a *difference* in tastes or preferences. A difference is not the same as a disagreement. Whether mercy killing of the terminally ill is right or wrong is a matter on which there has been much disagreement; if it were merely a difference in taste, it is difficult to see why people would argue about it as they do.

3. "Objective" versus "subjective." "All right, let's call them statements then, and not mere expressions of personal preference." But a common complaint is that such statements are too "*subjective.*" That the United States contains fifty states is an objective truth; but that sunsets in Hawaii are beautiful—is that also an objective truth? Isn't it much more a matter of how you respond to the sight of the Hawaiian sunset? Let's grant that it's a judgment by the speaker—but what sort of judgment is it? What is it that you are judging to be true? And how can you possibly discover whether or not it *is* true? Such are the problems that flood in upon us as we consider what are (again very roughly) called "judgments of value" as opposed to "judgments of fact."

Miriam is proud of her new hat and is trying it on in front of the mirror when her friend Dolores comes in. "What do you think of my new hat?" asks Miriam. Dolores takes an instant dislike to it, saying "My dear—the Taj Mahal." And suddenly Miriam too is aware of a certain domelike quality in the hat, which had escaped her notice; suddenly Miriam too dislikes the hat.[1] The resemblance was subtle enough so that it had to be pointed out to the ordinarily observant Miriam, yet it was enough to cause her to discard the hat. Was the resemblance to the Taj Mahal an "objective fact" about the hat? Was the statement of resemblance a true proposition? If no one else had noticed it, should we say that the resemblance was always there, though unnoticed, or should we say that the two women only imagined it or "just came to see it that way"? Does it depend on how many people say they see it? What is objective and what is subjective here?

"Paula looks more like her sister," says Aunt Marie. "No, Paula looks more like her brother," says her mother. How is this dispute to be resolved? Does Paula *really* look more like her sister? Is her mother then mistaken? Perhaps it's the high cheekbones that most impressed one and the jutting chin that most impressed the other. Or more probably each saw a different "total pattern," or *Gestalt,* in the girl's face, much as different people see very different shapes and patterns in the starry sky, or in an inkblot test. Are the features "really there"? Aunt Marie might convince the mother of her own position by carefully pointing out features of the girl's face; but if the mother still said "No, I still say Paula looks more like her brother," what is one to do? If the dispute is about "objective fact," surely it ought to be resolvable in some way. Yet aren't certain "objective facts" there—the high cheekbones and so on?

We might say that resemblance is a "to-you" or "to-me" characteristic, like "inter-

---

[1]The example is taken from John Wisdom, *Other Minds* (Oxford: Blackwell, 1949).

estingness": Consider the statement, "Calculus is interesting to me, but boring to you"—once you specify *to whom* it is interesting, there is nothing more to be resolved; in "Calculus is interesting (without saying to whom) one's meaning is incompletely specified. As to resemblance, one might say "A resembles B *to C*" and "A does not resemble B *to D*" and thus end the matter. But is resemblance like that? Don't two triangles *really* resemble one another in shape more than either of them resembles a circle? Resemblance isn't *that* subjective, is it?

Should we say then that resemblances are objective, but most people don't notice them? That's not quite accurate either. Two people may be very observant, each noticing every feature that the other points out, and yet they may come out with a different verdict: "A is more like B than like H" as against "A is more like H than like B." When each person has a different apperceptive background, and each sees in for example a face a different Gestalt, a total agreement on the individual characteristics need not yield agreement on general resemblance. "Yes, I see what you see, and I can sort of make myself see it that way—but yet as I look at her I am all the more convinced that she resembles her sister the most." Can resemblance be objective—"sort of"? Resemblance is not quite like "interestingness," which is entirely a matter of whether the subject appeals to the individual in question. If one person refers to a woman as "dainty" and another says no, is one of them mistaken? Is daintiness one of her qualities like her height or weight? If someone says, "She has mean lines in her face," is this true or false? Is the report "subjective" or "objective"?

If you paint a small room a light color the room looks bigger. "But that's just your subjective reaction." Still, it *looks* that way to everyone; dark colors make the room look smaller, light colors make it look larger. Is this *still* a subjective reaction, or an objective fact about the room—or an objective fact about human reactions? In a painting, warm colors tend to come forward and cool colors tend to recede into the background. Is this merely "a subjective reaction"? If it's a universal or near-universal reaction, are we still to call it "subjective"?

"Subjective" and "objective" are extremely vague adjectives, and their use is more likely to result in careless slogans than in careful thought. What, then, of the statement, "Barbara is a good person"? Is this like the examples just given? Or is it a "subjective evaluation" describing the way Barbara impresses the speaker? Or is it an "objective fact" about her? Perhaps, were the speaker to make clear what specific features he had in mind in calling her a good person, it would be strictly a matter of empirical fact whether Barbara is good or not. Yet no matter what features the speaker had in mind, was he—in calling Barbara a good person—*merely* pointing out those features, as he might point out her weight and height? Wasn't he also *commending* those features? Couldn't "She's a good person" be a statement of fact *and* a favorable evaluation of her at the same time?

Aesthetic Judgments

When we hear a certain melody—a passage from Tschaikovsky's *Pathetique Symphony* or from Chopin *Etudes,* or the slow movements of Handel *Concerti Grossi*—we are strongly inclined to say that these passages are sad, or plaintive, or suffused with gentle melancholy. They are all quite different of course: The sadness of the slow movement of Beethoven's *Eroica* symphony is more like "noble grief" than the soul-searching, inward turning sadness of certain Monteverdi madrigals. Still, the general characterization persists in spite of differences in detail. If someone said that these passages were joyous or tense or frantic, wouldn't she be just as mistaken as if she said snow was purple?

There is a tendency to say of aesthetic judgments that "They're only subjective" or "They just reflect the way the listener feels" —yet persons who say this will on another occasion defend a judgment ("This passage is sad") which they consider too obvious to permit disagreement. Nor is it that hearing the passage makes the person *feel* sad; it may do so, or it may not. We may have heard it so often that it no longer moves us; yet we may still consider the passage sad or melancholy. It's not that hearing it makes us *feel* sad, it's that we *recognize* it as sad—as having a sad quality; perhaps it moves slowly, with no sudden skips or jumps, the way people do when they are grieving the loss of a loved one. Perhaps sad music has some of the qualities of sad people, and if so this is hardly a mere "subjective reaction" but an empirical fact about the music.[2]

The statement "The music is beautiful" is a somewhat more difficult case. If one person says that the arias from Mozart's *The Magic Flute* are supremely beautiful, and another says they are not, how does one settle the issue? The second person, by hearing the arias over and over, may come to agree. But what if he does not? Is there anything more to be done? What kind of issue is this, anyway? It doesn't seem to be empirical, as in how many bars there are in the musical manuscript or what its key-signature is. Is it then just a "subjective reaction"—one person is moved by the music, the other is not? Or is it that one listener finds, or seems to find, a *quality*—which we might call beauty—in the music that the other fails to find?

Perhaps there *is* a quality—namely beauty—which is present in certain works of art (as well as in nature), and perhaps this quality can be present to varying degrees? If so, one person detects the presence of this quality and another may fail to detect it, just as a person may fail to find the prize in a Cracker Jack box. Beauty, according to this view, is an objective feature of things, like shape and size, and if the quality is there in the work and someone says it isn't, that person is simply mistaken, much as one can be mistaken about the size or shape of an object.

Perhaps beauty is a quality we can isolate in parts of a painting or a symphony; or perhaps beauty characterizes the object as a whole. In either case, however, it is far from clear just what we are looking for. What is the quality called "beauty" which we attribute to songs and pictures and poems and scenes in nature? Is it one quality or many? Is it a simple quality or a complex one? Is it the same in all its occurrences, or is a poem beautiful by virtue of features *different* from those that make a picture or a sonata beautiful? All these issues have been discussed at great length, with no agreed-upon answer.

Is beauty like a Lockean secondary quality, perhaps? The beauty in that case is not intrinsic to the object but is a disposition on the part of the object to produce certain experiences in us. (These are sometimes called "aesthetic experiences," but many aestheticians doubt that there is such a thing—it may be safer to say "experiences which dispose us to say 'That's beautiful'.") But there is a difference between being red and being beautiful, even if both are secondary qualities. People agree quite universally on which objects are red and which green, and so on, and if they disagree there are instruments to inform us of the wavelengths of the light emanating from the object. But in beauty there is no such "objective control." We can demonstrate to a color-blind person that he is mistaken when he claims there is no difference between red and green; for example, we place a stack of cards before him, some red and some green, and put each in a pile; he marks them in a way known

[2]See O. K. Bouwsma, "The Expression Theory of Art," in Max Black (ed.), *Philosophical Analysis* (Ithaca, NY: Cornell University Press, 1950); and John Hospers, *Understanding the Arts* (Englewood Cliffs, NJ: Prentice-Hall, 1982), chapter 4.

only to himself, shuffles them—so the red and green cards (indistinguishable to him) are now completely mixed up—and gives them to someone else; this third person then rearranges the cards back into separate red and green piles, as we did before: Thus, the color-blind person will have to conclude that there is *something* we are seeing that he is not. But what is there analogous to this in the case of beauty? Even if we agree that the view from Glacier Point is beautiful, how do we defend this view to those we consider beauty-blind? And they, whose judgments disagree with ours, will say that *we* are beauty-blind. The trouble with beauty as a quality of objects is that objects have a tendency to cause very different kinds of experiences in different observers.

Moreover, the *source* of the "beauty" experience seems not to be the same in all cases. If a poet is praised for the depth of her imagery, this can hardly constitute praise for a musical work, in which no words appear at all and hence no imagery; if a painter such as Gauguin is praised for his use of colors, this can hardly be a reason for praise of a poet or composer, since literary artists do not employ a visual medium. One usually finds the grounds of critical praise to be too *specific* to be usable in all works of art. Some attempts have been made to find a single source of beauty in all the arts, such as the concept of *organic unity*. In an organic unity, every part is such as to be so interconnected with every other that a change in one part would cause a deterioration in the whole. Change one note of a melody, and the whole character of the melody changes; change the words "to the syllable of recorded time" in Macbeth's speech to "to the last moment of recorded time," and the whole line goes flat. Organic unity has been a dominant criterion for works of art since Aristotle's *Poetics*.

Yet if organic unity is made identical with beauty, or even the main condition of beauty, it doesn't seem to work: (1) Organic unity is itself somewhat subjective in that different viewers or listeners will count certain parts as "necessary to the whole" whereas others will not; (2) some works with a high degree of organic unity can still be trivial (for example, only "formally correct," expressive of no deep emotion); and (3) in any case other criteria are always used besides organic unity, such as complexity, and what these other criteria are is a continuing matter of dispute. Thus, to equate organic unity with beauty, or even to consider it the principal criterion for the presence of beauty, appears to run into impassable barriers. The same considerations apply to every criterion that has been suggested for the presence of that special aesthetic quality called "beauty."

In light of all this, must we turn back to some kind of aesthetic subjectivism? Is anyone's aesthetic opinion as good as anyone else's? Many people may be inclined to *say* so, especially in frustration at being unable to defend their own aesthetic judgment against someone else's. "It's all a matter of opinion," they conclude, throwing up their hands. Of course one might say it *is* a matter of opinion, but whose opinion is better and why? We may be utterly baffled by such questions yet remain convinced that not all aesthetic judgments are of equal worth. Isn't a person who has studied the arts for years in a better position to judge than someone coming to it for the first time? Isn't a person who is sensitive and imaginative, particularly if she is a painter or poet herself, in a better position to pass judgment on matters of this kind than someone who has never paid much attention to the arts? People trained in physics will have a better "feel" for what is a good theory than outsiders who know little or nothing about it; why shouldn't the same be true of people attempting to judge value in the arts?

A person who has read Shakespeare even a little is usually impressed with his greatness as a poet. Those who have spent their lives studying literature will testify, one and all, to

Shakespeare's greatness compared with that of most other poets and dramatists, and will defend *Hamlet* and *King Lear* against most other dramas. Is this to count for nothing? One empirical fact is quite evident, that the work of some poets, musicians, painters, and sculptors has *stood the test of time*. One returns to them over and over again, always with greater personal rewards, whereas the work of many others quickly "wears out." One may *like* certain minor artists for various reasons, such as pleasant associations with early experiences ("That's the song that was sung at my honeymoon"), but we are able to distinguish those things we *like*, at least at the moment, from those that we consider *good* or *great*. That Homer was a good poet, or Bach a first-rate composer, and Cezanne a great painter, is about as considered a judgment as one can encounter anywhere. With contemporary artists we are less sure, for time has not yet completed the winnowing process; some work that is very fashionable today may be a "flash in the pan," and someone who works in a new idiom and remains unknown during his lifetime may be considered great in all subsequent ages. But the verdict of history on the greatness of artists is one which is borne out with every passing decade, and in view of the enormity of experience that molded the judgment it is hardly to be taken lightly. Neoclassical and Romantic critics may diverge in their judgments of *why* Homer and Vergil were great poets, but there has been little disagreement throughout the centuries *that* they were. There has been less disagreement on this than there has, probably, on any other subject: Scientific theories have come and gone, medical fads have been forgotten and replaced by others, and the weirdest views on virtually every subject have held sway for a time, yet judgments on "who are the immortals" in the arts have been, by comparison, astonishingly uniform. Views on the rightness or wrongness of moral practices such as infanticide, abortion, homosexuality, and euthanasia have

been extremely varying from place to place and age to age; and views as to who is the true God have been even more capricious through time. Time-tested aesthetic judgments have been models of uniformity by comparison.

Moral Judgments

Aesthetic value and moral value are the kinds of value most often discussed by philosophers, but they are not the only kinds; there are for example economic value, political value, scientific value, recreational value, and so on. There is a clear sense in which value is a "to-you" and "to-me" characteristic; a man who takes a day off to go fishing values that day of recreation above the income he could have earned by working that day; a woman who gives up her career to raise her children values the upbringing of her children above whatever rewards she could have had from pursuing her career. People indicate their values every day in the marketplace; if a merchant parts with an article at a certain price, she values the money above the article, or she would not have made the trade; and if the customer did not value the article above the money, he would not have parted with the money to buy the article. And of course what people value varies enormously from person to person and situation to situation. An Eskimo may place a high value on having an igloo, but a native of the tropics places no value on having one because he has no use for it. Most people place a high value on money because with it they can buy things they need and want, but to Robinson Crusoe alone on his island the gold he found had no value whatever.

"But there are things we *should* value, even if we don't." The drug addict values the drug above all other things, for he gives up everything else to obtain it. Yet we chide him for having such values. We say, "It would be of *more value* to you if you gave up drugs and tried to lead a constructive and fruitful life.'' And isn't this true? What some people value, they shouldn't, and what some people don't value at all, they should. But ''should'' for what purpose, toward what end? ''To stop using drugs would be *of value* to you even though you apparently don't *value* it.'' What sort of thing is meant by ''of value''—how can it be ''of value'' to you if you don't value it? It can be of value to the drug user in the sense that it would benefit his life; it would make him happier, give his life a focus again, give him self-respect. Almost all people do value those things. They may not be willing to undertake the *means* that will achieve these values for them, but they do value them; almost everyone wants to live a healthful and happy life. Even the addict values such ends, however unwilling or psychologically unable he may be to undertake the means. But what if he no longer cares about a long or healthful life, or the achievements he might have had, but only about his addiction? Then he no longer values either the means or the end. However, it would still be *of* value to him, in the sense that it would alter the quality of his life if he did change his values. That is still a true empirical statement. It is a statement he might even accept, though he does not act upon it.

But regardless of what things people *do* value, what *should* they value? Are there *good* values? Moralists have held forth very different values as the ones which all persons should pursue: living a life in the service of God; the pursuit of virtue; the pursuit of happiness; the pursuit of freedom—or of justice, or self-interest. How are we to judge which of these things are good? ''That's a good hunting dog'' is understandable because we know what hunting dogs are used for; but ''That's a good armadillo'' is not until we know what purpose the person had in mind; and ''Seven is a good number'' has no meaning at all until we know what the purpose of the ''seven'' is. (''What's it good *for*?'' we might ask.) When

we say, ''This is good *for* you,'' we mean that it improves your health or well-being—that is the purpose it serves. We also say, ''This food tastes good,'' though here no purpose is served other than simple pleasure to the palate. Thus we have no trouble with ''This food is good *for* you'' or with ''It tastes good *to* you. ''

''This is a good sports car'' is also a fairly straightforward empirical statement; we know what *criteria* people use in judging sports cars, and if a car fulfill the criteria, we call it good (of its kind). If a car can't go fast, sputters constantly to a stop, and needs mechanical attention every few days, and so on, we would say that a person was *mistaken* in calling it a good sports car—that such a person was guilty of a factual error. We know what the criteria are for judging sports cars—and hunting knives and jackhammers and other mechanical objects—because we as human beings have designed and constructed them for a specific purpose; they're good if they fulfill that purpose, not good if they don't. But human beings are not mechanical objects designed for a purpose; so what is meant by calling them good—what are the criteria of goodness for human beings? Theologians have an easy reply: Just as cars were constructed by human beings to fulfill a certain purpose, so human beings were created by God to fulfill a certain purpose; human beings are good to the extent that they fulfill God's purpose (such as honoring God's name). This reply, however, leaves all nontheological ethics out in the cold. Isn't there such a thing as a good life—or a bad one—quite independently of belief in God? Even different systems of theology don't always agree on what God's ideal for human life is.

The meaning of ''good,'' then, is a much more difficult question when talking about human lives and human actions than it is when talking about jackhammers and sports cars. ''That was a good thing you did,'' someone says after you jumped in the water and saved someone from drowning. What precisely is she saying about your act? Is there a quality, goodness, which she is attributing to you, and if so what does that quality consist of? This doesn't seem to be at all like the statement, "That's a good gun (for shooting)"; the gun can be good for that purpose even if it is used to kill people. So what exactly *is* being asserted when one says, "That was a good thing you did" or "That was the right thing to do"—other than just commending the person for the action? If one person asserted it and another denied it, how would we go about settling the issue between them? What *is* the issue? Is there any way we could put it other than simply to say, "The act was right?"

Many philosophers, called *ethical naturalists,* have been tempted by the idea that statements like "X is right" are really *disguised non-ethical statements;* if they were truly non-ethical it would be much easier to say what they mean. But attempts to interpret them in this way have been less than a resounding success: (1) It won't do to say that "X is right" merely means "I approve X." My approval might be mistaken or misplaced; besides, if another person says "X is not right" is he merely saying that *he* disapproves X? If so we are not disagreeing at all; he knows I approve and I know he disapproves, so there is nothing left to argue about. (2) Nor will it do to say "X is right" means the same as "Most people approve X." That is something you could find out by taking a poll; but if most people approve of persecution of minority ethnic groups, that doesn't show that such persecution is right, only that most people do approve it. (3) One might say that "X is right" means "Anyone who was fully informed as to all the facts of the matter *would* approve X." But many people, like judges and trial lawyers, are fully informed on the facts of the case and still disagree as to whether X is right. (4) Perhaps, then, "X is right" means that anyone who was fully informed on the facts *and* was impartial in his judgment would approve X. But who is to be the judge of whether someone is impartial? How is one to identify the impartial judge? And what exactly is impartiality? If one person says, "It was right of her to enter the burning house to save the child," and another says, "No, she only lost her life in the process, and there was practically no chance of saving the child or herself to begin with—what she did was just foolish," which judgment is impartial (if either is)? How does the impartial judge in a divorce court decide where a child of divorcing parents is to live? Does the judge primarily value the child's wishes (as to which parent to live with), or the mother's nurturing ("She is at home more"), or the father's ("He loves the child more" or "He could support the child better")? What will the "truly impartial judge" decide? People disagree even on the factors which go to determine impartiality.

In any case, however desirable impartiality may be, is that what calling an act "right" *means?* It surely seems as if trying to reduce ethical statements to ordinary empirical ones is only tempting a blind alley: that ethics is ethics and nothing else (certainly not empirical science), just as mathematics is mathematics and nothing else. You can't give an analysis of the one in terms of the other. Ethics is a separate discipline—an autonomous discipline, one might say (to quote the current jargon).

One theory of ethical naturalism ("naturalistic" even though it reduces ethical statements to statements about the supernatural) calls for special attention: that is, the view that "X is wrong" means the same as "X is prohibited by God." Some proponents of religious ethics believe that moral judgments are entirely reducible to theological judgments—that to call an act wrong just *is* to say that God condemns it, and no more than that. If this view is true, then if God changed his mind and said that deception was right, it *would* be right, since what is right is only what God condones and what is wrong is what he prohibits.

But, as Plato brought out 2500 years ago in his famous dialogue *Euthyphro,* this view leads to strange consequences. Is what is right or wrong merely a matter of divine whim? If one came to believe there was no God, would there then be no right or wrong acts? "If there is no God, all is permitted," said Ivan Karamazov in Dostoyevsky's novel—but permitted by whom? Plato's position on the matter was that if there is a God who gives moral commands, he has some *reason* for giving the commands that he does—a reason that could be accepted and acted on whether one believed in God or not. Believing in God may act as a *motivation* for some persons to behave morally, but it can hardly constitute the *meaning* of moral judgments, for this would make God's commands quite irrational and quixotic—indeed, from such a view people would do certain things because God commands them and *not* because what he commands is right. Thus, concluded Plato, right and wrong are, in their meaning, independent of God's will, even if there is a God who does issue moral commands. God sees what is right and commands us to do it, but it would be right even if God did not command it; murder would be wrong even if God did not prohibit it. This view seems even to most theologians to be the more plausible position.

The majority of moral philosophers have believed that ethical statements cannot be translated into empirical statements, theological statements, or any other kind of statements without utterly changing their meaning. How then *are* we to define ethical terms like "ought" in sentences like "You ought to do this"? Let us turn, then, to a consideration of ethical *non-naturalism.* According to this view, at least some ethical terms are indefinable by means of non-ethical ones. Even if "right" can be defined, as some have suggested, as "productive of the most good," at least "good" in its turn cannot be defined by means of non-ethical terms. There is no combination of non-ethical terms that will suffice

to render the meanings of *ethical* terms. As Henry Sidgwick wrote in his classic work *The Methods of Ethics:*

> What definition can we give of "ought," "right," and other terms expressing the same fundamental notion? To this I should answer that the notion which these terms have in common is too elementary to admit of any formal definition. . . . The notion we have been examining, as it now exists in our thought, cannot be resolved into any more simple notions; it can only be made clearer by determining as precisely as possible its relation to other notions with which it is connected in ordinary thought, especially those with which it is liable to be confounded.[3]

If you say that something has such-and-such consequences, you are making an empirical statement about it; but if you say that having such-and-such consequences is good, you are saying something quite different, and not translatable into any empirical statements. To say that X has such-and-such characteristics ("is enjoyed," "is desired," "is approved by the speaker"—or "by God" or "by the majority," etc.) is to say one thing; to say that X is good is quite another. To say that X is good is, indeed, roughly synonymous with saying that X is *desirable;* but then "desirable" is synonymous with "ought to be desired," and "ought" is again an ethical term. Ethical non-naturalism does not say that ethical terms cannot be defined by means of *other* ethical terms—for example "desirable" can be translated into "ought to be desired," and "right" might be translated into "ought to be approved" (which is very different from saying that it *is* approved); but this is only to define one ethical term by using another. What non-naturalism says is that one cannot define ethical terms exclusively by means of nonethical ones—anymore than one can define temporal words by means of others that make no refer-

---

[3]Henry Sidgwick, *The Methods of Ethics,* (London: Macmillan, 1878), p. 23.

ence to time, or words about magnitude by means of words having nothing to do with magnitude. "You can't get an *ought* out of an *is*" is the motto of nonnaturalism. Such words as "good," "right," and "ought" are so fundamental in ethics that there are no other words by means of which to define them; their own synonyms will not do, since these are ethical terms as much as the ones we are attempting to define.

G. E. Moore (1874–1958) attempted to refute all naturalistic theories by a famous device known as the "open-question technique." Regardless of what property of a thing you suggest as the meaning of an ethical term, he said, you are always open to the following objection: Someone can always meaningfully grant that X has the property, A, in question and yet deny, or doubt, that it is good. One can always say "I grant that X has this property (by which you endeavor to define 'good'), but nevertheless, *is* X good?" I know that this person is supremely happy but, nevertheless, is happiness always and everywhere good? I know that this man is honest, but is honesty good? Perhaps the answer is yes; but even if it is, one cannot answer this simply on the basis of a preferred definition of "good" with which others might strongly disagree.

Indeed, says Moore, "good" is verbally indefinable, just as other words in our language such as "yellow" and "pleasure" are verbally indefinable. To identify "good" with any "natural object" Moore calls the *naturalistic fallacy*.

Suppose a man says, "I am pleased"; and suppose that it is not a lie or a mistake but the truth. Well, if it is true, what does that mean? It means that his mind, a certain definite mind, distinguished by certain definite marks from all others, has at this moment a certain definite feeling called pleasure. "Pleased" *means* nothing but having pleasure, and though we may be more pleased or less pleased, and even, we may admit for the present, have one or another kind of pleasure; yet in so far as it is plea-

sure we have, whether there be more or less of it, and whether it be of one kind or another, what we have is one definite thing, absolutely indefinable, some one thing that is the same in all the various degrees and in all the various kinds of it that there may be. We may be able to say how it is related to other things: that, for example, it is in the mind, that it causes desire, that we are conscious of it, etc., etc. We can, I say, describe its relations to other things, but define it we can *not*. And if anybody tried to define pleasure for us as being any other natural object: if anybody were to say, for instance, that pleasure *means* the sensation of red, and were to proceed to deduce from that that pleasure is a color, we should be entitled to laugh at him and to distrust his future statements about pleasure. Well, that would be the same fallacy which I have called the naturalistic fallacy. That "pleased" does not mean "having the sensation of red," or anything else whatever, does not prevent us from understanding what it does mean. It is enough for us to know that "pleased" does mean "having the sensation of pleasure," and though pleasure is absolutely indefinable, though pleasure is pleasure and nothing else whatever, yet we feel no difficulty in saying that we are pleased.[4]

But to compare "good" with "yellow" also has its problems. We can pretty well agree on what objects are yellow; even color-blind people can agree on this (pp. 38–39, 342–43). But if people disagree on what is good, where can we turn to obtain agreement? What if one person says that the non-natural quality of goodness belongs to a certain action or motive or state-of-affairs, and another person denies it? Is there any rational recourse here? Or do we resort again to "Then ends the argument and begins the fight?"

Meta-ethics is the subject that deals with the meanings of ethical terms. In spite of many thousands of pages in books and scholarly periodicals in which meta-ethical issues are discussed, not much agreement on these issues has resulted. *Normative ethics* is the subject that deals with substantive issues such as what ends are *good*, what acts are

---

[4]G. E. Moore, *Principia Ethica* (London: Cambridge University Press, 1903), pp. 12–13.

right, what policies are *just,* and for what actions a person should be held *responsible.* It is worthy of note that many persons who are deadlocked on meta-ethical issues are often in agreement on issues of normative ethics, as if the results of investigating the meanings of ethical terms made no difference to their inquiries. We shall say no more here about meta-ethics, and turn instead to normative ethics.

2. NORMATIVE ETHICS

"The good for man." Many philosophers have set forth their conception of what kind of life is "good for" human beings. Aristotle, for example, held that human beings have several distinct capacities: the nutritive, which they share with all living things; the perceptual, which they share with other animals; and the rational, which belongs to human beings alone. "Man is the rational animal"; rationality is what distinguishes human beings from all other creatures. (Remember our discussion of the definition of "human being" in Chapter 3, pp. 126–30.)

What then is good for human beings? To "act in accordance with reason." It's not that God has created human beings and commanded them to live in a certain way, but rather that human beings have a *distinctive nature,* and human good is rooted in human nature. And human nature is the nature of rational beings.

Again, the word "rational" may cause trouble. Reason, we saw (pp. 44–45), isn't limited to reasoning, not even to deliberating. Is it rational of a person to risk one's life by trying to rescue a child from a speeding car? Is it rational to try to keep one's beloved alive even in constant pain and against all probability of survival? Is it rational to espouse a cause which looks hopeless? What precisely is rational and what is nonrational when exhibited in actions? Another problem presents itself as

well: Why should that which is *peculiar* to human beings have to be that which is *good* for human beings? Rational powers have enabled human beings to acquire knowledge and cure diseases, but they have also enabled human beings to construct nuclear bombs and plot the demise of enemies. Some have even contended that "having big brains" has been the curse of the human race.[5]

Instead of saying "Human beings are rational animals," wouldn't it be equally plausible to say "Human beings are volitional animals?" Human beings are the only animals capable of thought, deliberation, choice, and action based on that choice. Other animals do not deliberate and choose; only human beings do. And this is an indispensable factor in the life of human beings—*freedom.* Frustration and disappointment result when human beings are prevented from making choices and acting on them; if there is anything that can be counted on to make people miserable, it is being prevented from acting in accordance with one's choices. So the good for human beings should at least include maximum freedom to choose and to act.

Other animals do not have—and (being for the most part programmed to behave as they do) do not need to have—this freedom; but human beings do. That is why the good for human beings is not the same as the good for other animals. Animals can be happy—or at least content (that is, have no worries)—if they can eat, reproduce, and roam; this is the good life for animals in accordance with *their* nature. But more than that is required for *human* fulfillment. If human beings tried to live the life of pigs, the suppression of their human potentialities would make them miserable. Nor could human beings even survive on this planet if they tried to adopt the methods of animal survival.

---

[5]See for example, Kurt Vonnegut, *Galapagos* (New York: Dell Publishing Co., 1986).

Consciousness—for those living organisms which possess it—is the basic means of survival. For man, the basic means of survival is *reason*. Man cannot survive, as animals do, by the guidance of mere percepts. A sensation of hunger will tell him that he needs food (if he has learned to identify it as hunger), but it will not tell him how to obtain his food and it will not tell him what food is good for him or poisonous. He cannot provide for his simplest physical needs without a process of thought. He needs a process of thought to discover how to plant and grow his food or how to make weapons for hunting. His percepts might lead him to a cave, if one is available—but to build the simplest shelter, he needs a process of thought. No percepts and no instincts will tell him how to light a fire, how to weave cloth, how to forge tools, how to make a wheel, how to make an airplane, how to produce an electric light bulb or an electronic tube or a cyclotron or a box of matches. Yet his life depends on such knowledge—and only a volitional act of his consciousness, a process of thought, can provide it.[6]

The men who attempt to survive, not by means of reason, but by means of force, are attempting to survive by the method of animals. But just as animals would not be able to survive by attempting the method of plants, by rejecting locomotion and waiting for the soil to feed them, so men cannot survive by attempting the method of animals.[7]

"But suppose I accept all this," we may finally say; "it still doesn't tell me specifically what I should do in a given situation. How should I plan the course of my life? At what goals should my actions be directed? If I am to pursue the good, what is it exactly that I should do?" On this important issue there have been many kinds of suggestions. Let us now examine the main ones.

Theories of the Right

Two main pursuits of the branch of philosophy called *ethics* are: (1) the study of the *good*—which ideals and goals should be pursued and why; and (2) the study of *right*—which actions that a person does are right and which wrong, and why. The two pursuits are of course related; what ideals you believe are good will make a difference to what acts you consider right: (1) Theories for which the good is primary first set forth their concept of the good, and right actions are those that tend to promote that good; but (2) theories that begin with right (or duty) first set forth a view about what one should or should not do, and the achievement of the good will be either a consequence of such actions or incidental (or even irrelevant) to them. Theories of the first group are called *teleological* (because right action is a means to a *telos,* or end), and theories of the second group are called *deontological* (from the Greek *deon,* duty).

"What ought we do, and why?" This seems to most people the fundamental question of ethics. We shall now examine, only in barest outline, the principal answers that have been given to this question.

1. Ethical egoism. According to ethical egoism, the goal of each person's life should be his or her own self-interest. You should act in such a way as to promote your own interests. Normally these interests will include those things that most people desire, such as health, peace of mind, maximum freedom to choose, a measure of security, and most of all one's happiness. There are many different views as to how one should go about achieving this: Epicurus thought it could best be done through a life of placid contemplation, nonintervention in the affairs of the world, and noninvolvement in close relationships with other people; the Stoics thought it could best be done through having a minimum of wants and desires, so that one could never be hurt or disappointed; Aristotle thought it could be done through a life of moderation—nothing in extreme—tempering one's passions without extinguishing them, and through a balance be-

[6]Ayn Rand, *The Virtue of Selfishness* (New York: New American Library, 1962), p. 21.

[7]Ibid., p. 23.

tween the happiness of solitary activities like acquiring knowledge and that of interpersonal activities like love and friendship. The emphasis throughout was on how *you* could make yourself a happier or better functioning human being. ("Self-interested" does not mean the same as "selfish": If you are ill you see a physician to improve your condition—this is an example of self-interest, but one would hardly call it selfish; "selfishness" generally means having or doing what you want at the *expense* of the interests of other people.)

It is your *long-term* happiness or well-being you should aim at, your well-being over your lifespan. If you think only of today and ignore tomorrow or next year, you may have an enjoyable time today but be miserable thereafter. Planning ahead, then, as to the kind of life that maximally promotes your interests, is essential to the practice of ethical egoism.

Does ethical egoism advocate that you cheat, lie, steal, and otherwise do things that are ordinarily considered immoral? This would be short-sighted egoism: If you do not deal honestly with other people, once they realize what you are they will avoid you or not deal honestly with you in return. If you are not concerned for your friends and relatives, they soon will not be concerned for you either. If you betray your friends, they are likely to betray you in turn. If you seek to dominate them, they—who usually don't want to be dominated but to make their own decisions—will resent you and take some kind of revenge on you or at least ostracize you. If you don't pay your debts you are unlikely to get any more loans. If you commit crimes you are likely to land in jail sooner or later, and even before that you will dread the possibility of being caught—hardly an avenue toward long-term happiness. Each of these may have exceptions—in particular cases you might not be caught, might not be betrayed, and so on—but you can't usually be sure of this, and the usual tendency of such actions is for them to come back to you in some way (Karma), and

that you will be dealt with by others in much the way you deal with them.

Some have interpreted ethical egoism to mean that you are entitled to be cruel to other people, gain power over them, trample over them, and in general use them so as to fulfill your wishes. Would this, however, really further your own interests? In Plato's famous example in *The Republic,* the would-be tyrant obtains power over an entire people, and satisfies his wants by enslaving them, killing whom he chooses, and in other ways dictating the course of their lives. He thinks that the attainment and use of such power will bring him happiness. But this is an egoistic miscalculation; instead of happiness it brings him only misery; he no longer has friends, his enemies band together to kill him, his life is in constant danger, he never knows whom he can trust. His power-impulse has turned him into the most miserable of men. Plato believed that wrongdoing consisted not in the ideal of being happy but in the incorrect *means* that people use to attain it.

It should be kept in mind, too, that egoism is designed as a theory applicable to everyone; if you should be egoistic, so should everyone else. "Only I should be an egoist" is not an ethical theory at all, and the person who attempts to practice it, expecting everyone else to be self-sacrificing for *him,* is more properly called an *egotist:* an egotist could be defined as a person who feels and acts as if no one else existed. Such people are shunned by others, nobody likes them or wants to be in their presence, for other people are aware that the egotist doesn't have any care or concern for *them* (though he may pretend to) but is only interested in promoting himself. Nor does he want others to treat *him* as he treats *them;* he wants to be the Big Honcho, but doesn't want anyone else to also be the Big Honcho. But you can't have a hundred chairs each of which is the only chair in the room, and you can't have a hundred people each of whom is the only one who should be served by the others. The ethical egoist, then, must approve of other people also being ethical egoists. If he is to be left free to pursue his own interest, he must also leave them free to pursue theirs.

Indeed, concern for others, even generosity, far from being incompatible with egoism, flows naturally from it. It is a truth of psychology known to every therapist that you can't really love others unless you first love yourself—"love" in the sense of self-esteem, having a conviction of self-worth. If you don't have this, you will resent whatever good accrues to others.

It is one's view of oneself that determines one's view of human nature and one's way of relating to other human beings. The respect and goodwill that persons of high self-esteem tend to feel toward other persons is profoundly egoistic; they feel, in effect, "Other people are of value because they are of the same species as myself." This is the psychological base of any emotion of sympathy and any feeling of species solidarity. But this causal relation cannot be reversed. A person must *first* value him- or herself—and only then can he value others. . . .

To love selfishly does not mean to be indifferent to the needs or interests of my partner. When we love, our concept of self-interest embraces the well-being of our partner. This is the great compliment of love: to declare to another human being that his or her happiness is of *selfish* importance to ourselves. Do we wish to believe that for our partner the relationship is an act of self-denial and self-sacrifice? Do we want to be told that our happiness is *not* of selfish interest to our partner? . . . [Do] we want our lover to caress us *un*selfishly, with no personal gratification in the doing, or do we want our lover to caress us because it is a joy and a pleasure for him or her to do so? And let us ask ourselves whether we want our partner to spend time with us, alone together, and to experience the doing as an act of self-sacrifice. Or do we want our partner to experience such time as glory? And if it is glory that we want our partner to feel, if we want our partner to experience joy in our presence, excitement, ardor, passion, fascination, delight, then let us stop talking of "selfless love" as a noble ideal.[8]

Concern for the welfare of those one loves is a rational part of one's selfish interest. If a man who is passionately in love with his wife spends a fortune to cure her of a dangerous illness, it would be absurd to claim that he does it as a "sacrifice" for *her* sake, not his own, and that it makes no difference to him personally and selfishly, whether she lives or dies.

If one's friend is in trouble, one should act to help him by whatever nonsacrificial means are appropriate. For instance, if one's friend is starving, it is not a sacrifice, but an act of integrity to give him money for food rather than buy some insignificant gadget for oneself, because his welfare is important in the scale of one's personal values. If the gadget means more than the friend's suffering, one had no business pretending to be his friend.[9]

But what of persons who are strangers to us? If we care about their welfare, and if we are able, we can attempt to be generous to them in case of need, as we might wish them to be to us if we were in their situation. Even if we do nothing for them, however, we will not attempt to destroy their well-being: We will let them go their way in pursuit of their own interests, just as we ourselves want to be uninterfered with in the pursuit of ours.

What happens if there is a *conflict* of interest—if what one person wants or needs is also what another person wants or needs? Often both can attain it: One person being happy and successful doesn't preclude another person also being happy and successful. Unless I am consumed by envy, your being happy doesn't prevent me from being happy. But aren't there times when two people want the same thing and both can't have it, as when two men both want to marry the same woman? But even here, one might suggest, "Let her decide between them. If she married the man she does *not* prefer, then he would not have what he most wanted anyway—the woman who wanted him above all others." Should egoists then resort to open conflict and

---

[8]Nathaniel Branden, *Honoring the Self* (Boston: Houghton Mifflin, 1983), pp. 220–221.

[9]Ayn Rand, "The Ethics of Emergencies," in *The Virtue of Selfishness,* pp. 45–46.

fighting to settle such matters? But this solution would be counterproductive for both of them. One might be injured or killed, and the other might not have achieved what he most wanted anyway. A better solution for egoists in situations of conflict would be cooperation, or when that is not possible, compromise. If we are each engaged in peaceful competition, such as starting up a drugstore on opposite sides of the same street, we may agree that one or both of us should locate elsewhere (in case the market can't sustain two drug stores so near to each other), or we may agree to each compete to the best of our ability and "let the best man win."

In the economic arena, at any rate, concern with one's own success is far from incompatible with the success of others. Someone who invests time and capital to start a business is a risktaker who is risking her all on the public's desire to buy her product; if she succeeds, she will provide employment for others and a new choice of product to consumers. (She can't force them to buy her product; she can only offer it in the hope that they will buy it.) She may not *care* about their welfare, her motives may be entirely self-interested (to make money, to meet a challenge), yet the *effect* of her action is to enrich the lives of others.

In the sentimental folderol that characterizes so much social and political commentary today, we almost never hear the term "compassionate" applied to a business executive or an entrepreneur. Yet in terms of results in the measurable form of jobs created, lives enriched, communities built, living standards uplifted, and poverty healed, a handful of "compassionate capitalists" have done infinitely more for their fellow men than all the self-serving politicians, academics, social workers, or religionists who claim the adjective "compassionate" for themselves.

. . . Ernst Mahler was an entrepreneurial genius whose innovative ideas and leadership, over a period of about 30 years, transformed this once-small, insular newsprint and tissue manufacturer into one of the largest paper corporations in the world, which gives prosperous employment to more than 100,000 and produces products (which Mahler helped innovate) that are now used by more than two billion people. Mahler became enormously wealthy, of course. Yet his personal fortune was insignificant when compared with the permanent prosperity he generated, not only for his own company but for the hundreds of thousands who work for industries which his genius ultimately spawned and which long outlived him—not to mention the revolutionary sanitary products that have liberated two generations of women, or the printing papers that completely transformed international publishing and communications for fifty years.

I can safely predict that you have never heard of him up to this moment. Not one person in 100 million has. Yet his contribution has permanently uplifted the lives of millions and far exceeds in real compassion most of our self-congratulatory politicians and "activists" whose names are known to all. What is so troubleing is that those who cloak themselves in this "compassion mantle" are so often the very people who are hedging in the economic freedom that made Ernst Mahler's life and contribution possible.[10]

The objections to ethical egoism, even in the ameliorated form just described, have been vociferous and unremitting, and always of much the same kind: Why should you consider the interests, even the long-term interests, of only yourself? Don't other people count too? Isn't *their* well-being as important as *yours?* (1) I grant that if you are thrifty and industrious and take care of yourself, others won't later have to take care of you. But what if in spite of their best efforts some people can't take care of themselves and have no relatives or friends willing and able to do it? Shouldn't that be a concern of yours, and of everyone? (2) You have given interesting examples of one person's self-interested activity bringing about great benefits to others; but what about those cases in which one person's pursuit of self-interest brings about a lessened well-being for others? Often the cheater, the liar, or the bunco artist gets caught; but sometimes, through luck or the inefficiency of the

---

[10]Warren Brookes, *The Economy in Mind* (New York: Universe Books, 1982), p. 223.

police, they don't; and then it would seem perfectly to their long-term self-interest to continue defrauding others. "But they still have themselves to live with." That's true, but many people find crime extraordinarily easy to live with. The people who need a sense of guilt and remorse the most are usually those who have it the least. You can't deter them by appealing to *their* self-interest; their self-interest is nicely fulfilled by continuing in their criminal ways. You can appeal to them only by some moral principle that transcends egoism.

Egoists have attempted to get round these objections, but let's take a brief look at the other theories.

2. Utilitarianism.

In utilitarianism the emphasis shifts from the well-being of the individual to that of society as a whole. Each person should aim not at his or her own maximum happiness (or well-being, or fulfillment—the words differ in different descriptions) but in that of everyone. Utilitarianism doesn't say that you should act so as to promote everyone's well-being *except* your own; this view is called *altruism,* and would make each person a sacrificial lamb on the altar of the happiness of others: A considers only B's happiness, and B considers only A's happiness; to which many have replied that people are the best judges of their own happiness, not that of others. Utilitarianism, by contrast, says that you should consider your own happiness or well-being *only as one among many.* If happiness is good, then it is good no matter *who* has it; thus one should aim not at the maximization of one's own happiness, but that of everyone else as well. If I can benefit society by doing something that brings happiness to many others but none to myself, I should do it, because my happiness is outweighed by that of the many; similarly, another person should give up personal happiness if thereby he can increase that of myself and many others. On the other hand, if an ac-

tion a person could perform will bring more happiness (or less unhappiness) to himself or herself than to others, then one's own happiness should prevail. One calculates the total happiness and unhappiness to be achieved by one's action, counts happiness as a plus and unhappiness as minus, and then does whatever action will produce the most plus, after the minus has been subtracted. I should give up whatever goals and projects I had planned, no matter how happiness-producing for me, if joining someone else's project would be more happiness-producing for all concerned. If after a season of hard work I am on vacation but an emergency arises in which I could save lives, I should do this; indeed, if more total happiness for all concerned would be achieved by laboring to help the oppressed or feed the hungry, then I should take no vacation at all. The utilitarian theory is sometimes embodied in John Stuart Mill's slogan, "The greatest happiness of the greatest number."

The happiness which forms the utilitarian standard of what is right in conduct, is not the agent's own happiness, but that of all concerned. As between his own happiness and that of others, utilitarianism requires him to be as strictly impartial as a disinterested and benevolent spectator. . . . As the means of making the nearest approach to this ideal, utility would enjoin, first, that laws and social arrangements should place the happiness, or . . . the interest, of every individual, as nearly as possible in harmony with the interest of the whole; and secondly, that education and opinion, which have so vast a power over human character, should so use that power as to establish in the mind of every individual an indissoluble association between his own happiness and the good of the whole.[11]

The utilitarian principle is simple and easily stated, but its application in practice is enormously difficult, chiefly because in most cases we cannot anticipate accurately what the consequences of our actions will be. A mother may do things for the sake of her children's

_____

[11]John Stuart Mill, *Utilitarianism* (1861), Chapter 2.

happiness, yet only succeed thereby in making them unhappy; for example, if the parent is extremely permissive and always lets them do what they want, they may be happy at the time, but they will be very unhappy when they find later that the world is not so permissive and that employers don't usually employ "spoiled brats." Besides, many people sacrifice themselves uselessly; their sacrifice does nothing to stem the evil they were trying to prevent. Many people attach themselves to some "noble cause," but the means they employ to achieve it are ineffectual or counter-productive, and even if the cause succeeds it may do more harm than good (as with most violent revolutions).

Here are just a few examples: (1) You can make a murderer happy by helping him escape from jail, and without sacrificing your own happiness in doing so. Should you do it? No, for the likelihood is that after he is loose he will commit more crimes, thus causing far greater unhappiness in the community than the happiness he would have gained by escaping. (2) Should you give up going to college in order that your grandmother's hospital expenses can be paid? The consequences of the alternatives are difficult to estimate. Perhaps you would do better to postpone your education, if no other way is possible. On the other hand, your education may be more important, with greater potential good for your future and that of others, than having your grandmother receive the best possible care. (3) Should you risk your life by taking an experimental drug which—if successful—would save the lives of hundreds of people? Perhaps; this depends on the probability of a favorable outcome. You might be risking your life uselessly, or some other means might be found of testing the drug, or there may be no evidence that the drug would be successful anyway. "It all depends"—that is the kind of answer the utilitarian will usually have to give. To maximize happiness is an easily understandable ideal; but how to actively implement the ideal

in specific cases is difficult and often impossible, for the consequences of actions are complex and vary from case to case, so that each case would have to be judged individually with regard to its (usually very complex) consequences.

To describe utilitarianism so fully as to forestall the many possible misunderstandings of it would take many pages, and Mill himself devoted an entire book (*Utilitarianism*) to this task. Many objections, however, have been presented against the utilitarian theory, of which only a few can be stated here:

(1) The theory requires one to make *interpersonal* calculations of happiness and unhappiness. I can say in my own case that the gratitude of a friend makes me happier than receiving some expensive gift, but am I in a position to say that a gift of $100 makes me happier than it would make you or someone else? Can I even say that giving Susie an ice cream cone makes her happier than it makes Billy? When the number of people involved mounts into the hundreds, and the consequences of the action continue far into the future, can I have even a reasonable idea of what present course of action of mine will be likely to maximize the general happiness? (2) Suppose I come home from a long day of work and sit down to watch television. Am I doing wrong? Few people would say so, although there are many things I could be doing that would enhance human happiness much more than sitting at home watching television. (3) If some "squatter" families come to your house and demand to live there for a year rent-free, is it your duty to let them all occupy your house because—although you'd be worse off for their being there (you couldn't get your work done and couldn't enjoy any leisure in the house)—they would be better off if they could use your home? According to the theory of utility, perhaps. Yet wouldn't you be in the right if you said, "It's my home: I worked for it, I paid for it, and it belongs to me and my family. I have a *right* to it"? Here, utility is at odds

with rights, a concept we have not yet introduced. Utilitarians might counter that the general *practice* of people having exclusive occupancy of homes they've bought has maximum utility, yet there would probably be many exceptions, as when the happiness of the squatters outweighed the unhappiness of the homeowner.) (5) At the very least the ethics of utilitarianism is extremely demanding. Ordinarily we say things like, "How wonderful of you to do this! It's more than could be expected of you"; but there is no room in utilitarianism for *supererogatory* acts, acts "over and above the call of duty." If you have saved one life when by heroic effort you could have saved two, you have (according to utilitarianism) actually done *wrong,* because you have not maximized happiness.

3. Universalizability. The Golden Rule of the Gospels says, "Do unto others as you would have them do unto you." Do as you would be done by; treat others as you would wish to be treated. If you don't want others to be dishonest with you, or cheat or betray you, do not do these things to them. If you expect to be treated well by others, then do the same for them. (The Golden Rule does not say that by doing this you will promote your own interests, or even those of society.)

Some problems have been raised about the Golden Rule because what one person wishes may be different from what another person wishes. If someone said, "Help others in trouble, for you would wish to be helped if you were in trouble," another might respond, "I don't wish to help others, nor do I wish to be helped." A masochist might say, "I don't mind being beaten, and I don't mind beating others."

Immanuel Kant set forth a principle called the "categorical imperative," altering the Golden Rule to read, "Act so that the maxim of your action [moral directive exemplified by your action] could become a *universal rule of human conduct.*" "Everybody except me is

prohibited from initiating violence against others" could not be a universal rule of human conduct, for everyone who read it would be the "me" who is the exception, and thus everyone would be an exception to the rule; the result would be that the rule would have no application. The rule permits no exceptions in one's own behalf: If it's right for you to steal, it's right for others also; and if it's wrong for them, it's also wrong for you. The rule is absolutely impartial as between persons.

Yet there are many conflicting maxims that could be made into universal rules of human conduct: For example, helping others in trouble (and being helped by them) and *not* helping them (and not being helped by them) could both be adopted as practices by everyone. In neither case is one making an exception of oneself. The Categorical Imperative could then be amended to read, "Act so that you could *wish* the maxim of your action to be a universal rule of human conduct," but then again there is a difference in what different people wish. It is true that most cheaters don't want to be cheated, and most thieves don't want others to steal from them. This would indeed be incompatible with a universal rule. Still, might someone not say, "You are free to steal from me, and I am free to steal from you—I consider this a universal rule of human conduct that is preferable to the universal prohibition of theft." What one person might wish to have adopted as a universal rule of human conduct might be at variance with what another person might wish. Which one then should we follow?

There are many complexities involved in the analysis of Kant's principle. But one main thrust of the rule is important: Before you act, consider the implications of everyone doing as you are about to do. Before you lie, steal, or kill, contemplate a world in which everyone did this (including, of course, others doing it to you). And if you don't approve others doing it to you, then you shouldn't do it either, for the same rule is equally applicable to all. You cannot make an exception of yourself; the same considerations that apply in judging others apply to judging yourself.

Of course, you may be in a special position due to circumstances: If you are the president of the United States, you may sign bills and give commands that others may not. But that is equally true of anyone who is president; it isn't applicable merely to you. If you are a parent, you may command your child whereas others may not, but that holds true of parents in general, not only you. What you can or may do depends on your specific role, but then the rule applies to everyone in that role. The morally fundamental rules however are universally applicable to all human beings—simply because they are rational agents—and as such are committed to consistency of action. You may not injure others, just as they may not injure you.

Kant also presented a second version of his Categorical Imperative, which others have considered to be not merely a reformulation of the first version but a separate and distinct principle. "Every rational being exists as an end," said Kant, "and must never be treated as a means alone." You are an autonomous being who does not exist merely as a means toward other people's ends, nor do they exist merely as a means toward the fulfillment of your ends. Respect for you as a human being demands that you not be used merely to attain the ends (goals) of others, and you are obliged to treat others with that same respect.

What practical implications does this principle have? Can't you use others to achieve your ends at all? Is it wrong to buy something at a store, because you are using the merchant as a means to your end (getting the product) and he is using you as a means to his end (getting the money)? No, this is a voluntary mutual exchange to which both have consented, and neither party has been wronged; each has dealt with the other for mutual benefit—if he didn't prefer the money to the merchandise,

and you the merchandise to the money, neither of you would have made the exchange. An example of a practice that clearly *would* violate Kant's principle is slavery. A slave is owned by a master, and is treated merely as a means toward the fulfillment of the slave-owner's wishes. Thus slavery is *always* wrong. Utilitarians, by contrast, would not oppose slavery under all conditions—they would say "it all depends." Usually slavery does have prevailingly bad consequences, but *if* the well-being of the slave-masters outweighed the misery of the slaves, then in such cases slavery *would* lead to "the greatest happiness of the greatest number," and would be in accordance with utilitarianism. It would be acceptable (according to utilitarianism) when it maximized human happiness, although not of course the happiness of the slaves—the happiness of the slaves would be sacrificed to the greater happiness of everyone else.

Utilitarianism is a *consequentialist* theory of normative ethics, because the rightness or wrongness of an act depends entirely on its consequences. Kant's theory by contrast is *deontological* because the rightness or wrongness of an act does not depend entirely on its consequences; slavery, for example, is incompatible with respect for each person as an autonomous agent, and as such it is wrong quite independently of its consequences for society.

4. Other deontological theories. Numerous versions of deontological ethics have been proposed. Sir David Ross, for example, has defended various kinds of actions as duties, though they are not always compatible with utilitarianism. The following is a partial list: (1) You have duties to your children that you do not have to other persons; you should help your children even though you could help other people's children more by doing the same for them. Your own children are your special and unique responsibility; you brought them into the world and are responsible for their welfare until they can fend for themselves. You do not have a similar obligation to other people's children, even if they have more unmet needs than your own children do. (2) You should keep a promise, not only because promise keeping always has the best consequences (sometimes it doesn't), but because a promise once made is a binding commitment. There may be times when a promise may be broken, but not merely because more good may come of breaking it. If you hired someone to mow your lawn and the person did so and then demanded payment, and if you said, "Instead of paying you I'll give the money to the Red Cross, where it can do more good," you would be acting wrongly—not because you weren't maximizing good (you might well be) but because you were breaking your word, on which the other person relied. (3) If you have caused injury or damage to someone, you owe reparations to *that* person; your duty is to "make things right" to her by repairing her window which you've smashed, even though more good consequences might have ensued if you had given the money to a poor family to whom you had no such duty of reparation. (There have been many attempts to reconcile these examples with utilitarianism—involving novel versions of utilitarianism too numerous and complicated to be considered here.)

A particularly important concept in deontological ethics is *justice.* Justice means treating people as they deserve, that is, in accordance with their deserts. A teacher gives a student a just grade if he gives her the grade she deserves in the course; it might make the student much happier to get an A which she didn't deserve (and might not decrease the teacher's happiness at all), yet it would be wrong to do this because it would be an injustice. Sentencing a prisoner to 50 years for a traffic violation would be unjust, even if it were impartially imposed on every traffic violator, because no one deserves such a heavy penalty for a relatively trifling offense. De-priving a person of wages which he has earned is an injustice, because the treatment of the employee is not in accordance with his deserts; he did the work and has earned the wage. It is more important for people to be *justly treated* than for happiness to be maximized. Granted, treating people justly *usually* is also conducive to greater happiness on the whole. But this is not always so; and even if it were, the reason for treating people in accord with their deserts is not that it is happiness-maximizing but that it is just. Whatever punishment a killer deserves, it should be given *because* he deserves it, *not* because others would be happier (or in some way better off) seeing him punished.

Another concept that affects our judgment of the morality of actions is that of human *rights.* I have a right to something if I have a valid claim to it; and this claim protects me against those who would interfere with my exercise of my right. A right is rather like a "no trespassing" sign, saying, "So far you may go in interfering with my life and my choices, but no further." Your right to swing your fist ends where my nose begins. The formula often given is, "I have a right to act as I choose, as long as I do not thereby interfere with the equal right of others to act as they choose"—or, "I should be free to do whatever does not abridge the freedom of anyone else." Just as many actions that maximize utility are unjust, so many actions that maximize utility violate individuals' rights. If I assault someone whom I meet walking along the sidewalk, I am interfering with that person's rights—"he has a right not to be harmed"—but if I say no to his request for money, I may be failing to maximize utility, but I am not violating the other person's rights. If I give him money, this is an act of benevolence on my part, but if I don't I am not violating his rights, for he has no right to my income. I may be dying of a painful terminal disease and another person may be maximizing happiness (in this case, minimizing unhappiness) by putting me painlessly out of the way; nevertheless, if I have not consented to be killed, he has violated my right to life.

There is, then, a potential conflict between utility and rights. What about egoism and rights? The kill-and-be-killed type of egoist, of course, doesn't mind violating the rights of others. But the "rational egoist" described on pp. 350–54 finds considerable support in the concept of rights. She can "stand on her rights" even in the face of disutility. She has a right to her own television set, even though a passerby might make a convincing case that *he* would enjoy it more than she does. She has a right to sign a voluntary contract, even though the consequences of signing it may be unfortunate for her. A woman has a right to say no to a man, even though he would enjoy sex with her more than she would dislike it.

There can even be a conflict between rights and justice. If a person has invested his own money in a business enterprise, hasn't he the right to hire whom he pleases? (It's he who stands to lose if he makes the wrong choice.) Yet justice would seem to require that he not engage in racial and sexual discrimination in hiring—that he hire the best qualified applicant regardless of race or sex.

Neither justice nor rights is the whole of morality. If I break into your house in order to obtain some medicine to save my child's life, I have indeed violated your property rights; yet surely I haven't acted wrongly. An act *may* be right although it involves a violation of rights—and can be wrong even if it doesn't, as when I refuse to give someone money even if he needs it and I won't miss it.

How then are we to weigh these various factors against one another? Formulations such as the following have been suggested: If I go fishing I'll enjoy it—there's nothing against it as long as some duty doesn't override this enjoyment; but if it does, if for example I can do someone a great service instead of going fishing, then I shouldn't go. (*Utility*

overrides egoism.) If I can correct an injustice, if for example I can assign a student the grade she deserves instead of the grade I gave her, I should do this, even though the results might not maximize utility. (*Justice overrides utility.*) And if I am an innocent victim of attackers, I have the right to defend myself against them (the right of self-defense) even though one result of this is that a police officer is unjustly demoted from her job. (*Rights override justice.*)

But does it always work out that way? Do rights always "trump" justice and utility? I may be imprisoned for something I didn't do (violation of my rights), but what if my incarceration frees my wife to find solace elsewhere, and she finds a man with whom she is happier than she could ever be with me? (*Greater overall utility.*) It's a violation of a person's rights for him to be tortured, but what if the torture induces him to reveal where the bomb is hidden which would have destroyed an entire city? Can't counterexamples be given to any example of these suggested "overridings"? Doesn't it depend on the features of the individual situation (which differ from case to case), so that no inviolable general rule can be given? This is one of the wrenching "bottom-line" problems of ethics. Many arguments have been presented on this problem, but even among those who have reflected on these matters for years, no unanimous agreement has been forthcoming.

Rules and Relativism

The theories of normative ethics that we have just examined all set forth moral *principles*—that is, prescriptions for action designed to be applicable to every situation you might confront. The principles alone will not tell you what to do; for this you also need detailed descriptions of the situation and its context. But the principles provide the criteria you are to use in adapting your action to the situation—a kind of lighthouse that guides you through the troubled waters of moral decision, though the lighthouse alone cannot provide the directions for what to do when you approach a particular reef—that depends on the nature, direction, and distance of the reef, which you require empirical observation to determine.

Most people, however, unless they have read books on ethics, have never so much as heard of moral principles. They have been brought up on various *rules* of conduct, usually in a rather haphazard manner. They have been told not to lie, not to steal, not to cheat on exams, not to start fights, not to betray friends, and so on. Rules deal with specific types of behavior, which the rule either condones or prohibits. The Ten Commandments are a set of rules. The rules *may* be rooted in general moral principle, but usually they are not; they are just a collection of prohibitions which we are supposed to obey. "Thou shalt not steal," "Thou shalt not kill," and "Thou shalt not commit adultery" are rules; and to none is appended a qualification like "in order that thereby the greatest good of the greatest number shall be achieved"—that is, the rules don't seem to be rooted in a utilitarian principle, nor for that matter in any other. They are, as most rules are, a collection of do's and don'ts, with no reason given why one should observe just these rules and not others.

Often the rules conflict with one another. "Never break a promise once it's made," we are told; but what if some family crisis arises which seems to you more important than the promise—does the rule "Help your loved ones when they need your help" take precedence over the rule that prohibits promise breaking? Clearly you can't follow both rules in this instance. You are told never to kill, but also to defend yourself when you have to; if someone attacks you, which rule are you to follow? And why?

A collection of rules without basis is hardly a satisfactory situation for ethics. That is why philosophers have sought moral principles rather than simply a collection of rules. If you have an overall principle like that of utility ("the greatest happiness for the greatest number"), at least you have a lighthouse to guide you through the shoals; you know where you are going, even though you may mistake or misapprehend some facts along the way. And most general principles—all those we have described—will require that the vast majority of moral rules will have to be revised, or exceptions built into them, in order to conform to the principle. "Never take human life" will conflict with egoism (and other principles as well) when it is your own life that is threatened. "Never tell lies" will conflict with the utilitarian principle on those occasions when telling the lie will produce the most good overall. If you are the skipper of a ship with refugees aboard, who would be killed if caught, and the captain of a hostile ship boards yours and asks you, "Are there any refugees aboard?"—are you to follow the legendary advice of George Washington and say, "I must never tell a lie"? To do so would conflict with the utilitarian principle as well as with justice and respect for rights. Whether you should follow the rule in a particular case would depend on a variety of circumstances which differ from one situation to another, and these the rule never mentions.

Philosophers tend to be uncomfortable about rules hanging in midair; they want the rules to be rooted in some moral principle. Normative ethics has to do first and foremost with the justification of moral principles—and the point that is most worrisome is that the various *principles themselves* often conflict with one another. Egoism would never ask you to be an unwilling sacrificial victim; utilitarianism might. If your father and a distinguished medical researcher were in a burning building and you could rescue only one of them, deontologists would probably advise you to save your father, though utilitarians would say that you should rescue the medical researcher, since her continued life would produce the most good for the world. Each principle claims to provide the fundamental basis for ethics; but how are we to choose among the principles? It makes a great deal of difference to our actions which principle we accept.

1. The geometrical model. Some philosophers have conceived of ethics as a kind of a priori system, using geometry as a model of how an ideal system of ethics would function. Suppose, for example, we take the utilitarian principle as the basic axiom of our ethical system. Then any rule conflicting with utilitarianism will have to be abandoned or revised—for example the rule "Never break promises" will have to be revised to read "Never break promises unless doing so maximizes utility." And the same for every other rule: Each must take second place to the principle of utility itself. How does the principle relate, not to rules, but to specific actions? We would have a deductive argument, as follows:

All acts that maximize happiness (or well-being) are right.
This act would maximize happiness.

Therefore,

This act would be right.

The first premise of the argument is a statement of the general principle. The second premise is an empirical statement about the consequences of the action. From the two statements together we can validly deduce that the act in question would be right.

The second premise is likely to give us a lot of trouble. How can we know in advance which act will maximize happiness? The consequences of actions are far-flung, complicated, and often unexpected. Who can estimate them with confidence? Consider a particular case of divorce: Will the husband and wife be happier after the divorce? Will the

children? There are considerations against it; for example children usually are better off with two parents in the home than with only one. On the other hand, they don't live in a happy environment if the parents are constantly at one another's throats. A lot depends on whether the parents could "work it out" or whether the differences are irreconcilable. Sometimes it turns out one way, sometimes another. There seems to be no general rule; each case must be decided individually, since the circumstances differ from case to case. How can we be sure how the sum total of consequences, favorable and unfavorable, will balance out in this case? We may have some evidence one way or the other, but our judgment about the truth of the second premise ("This act would maximize happiness") must be hedged with caution. Very often the action is a "leap in the dark," and we can only hope for the best. And if this is so in a situation affecting just one family, how much greater are the complex calculations required in a case involving an entire society or nation, such as whether a certain bill should be passed by Congress? The calculations would become so complex as to boggle the mind.

What interests philosophers, however, is not so much the empirical difficulties involved in determining the truth or falsity of the second premise, but the justification of the first premise—the general principle itself. You can estimate the rightness of actions by the principle of utility, but is the principle of utility itself acceptable? (We can deduce certain properties of geometrical figures on the premises of Euclidean geometry, but it is a different question whether Euclidean geometry itself is a true description of the world. See pp. 107–8.)

Here the a priorist in ethics is likely to champion a view often known as *ethical intuitionism*. Just as we can know (according to sense-data theorists) that I see a spot of red in my visual field, and no further justification is either possible or required, so we can know that certain fundamental moral tenets are true. These may be principles, such as the principle of utility, or they may be specific rules ("It is always wrong to harm others"), in which case the principle will have to be revised if it conflicts with the rule. But there are certain moral convictions which are basic to the discipline of ethics and cannot be deduced from anything more fundamental—just as "A is A" is not provable by means of anything else, since every other proposition presupposes it. Thus, according to Sir David Ross, there are statements about right and wrong which are

. . . self-evident; not in the sense that it is evident from the beginning of our lives, or as soon as we attend to the proposition for the first time, but in the sense that when we have reached sufficient mental maturity and have given sufficient attention to the proposition, it is evident without any need of proof, or evidence beyond itself. It is self-evident just as a mathematical axiom, or the validity of a form of inference, is evident. The moral order expressed in these propositions is just as much part of the fundamental nature of the universe (and, we may add, of any possible universe in which there were moral agents at all) as is the spatial or numerical structure expressed in the axioms of geometry or arithmetic. In our confidence that these propositions are true there is involved the same trust in our reason that is involved in our confidence in mathematics; and we should have no justification for trusting it in the latter sphere and distrusting it in the former. In both cases we are dealing with propositions that cannot be proved, but that just as certainly need no proof.[12]

Ross' view attempts to ensure not only that the deductions made are valid, but that the major premise stating the moral principle is true. One problem with this view, however— as with all appeals to "intuitively known truth" (pp. 45–46)—is that different people do not all share the same basic moral intuitions. We have described various prin-

ciples, each of which is intuitively obvious to its proponents, but each of which conflicts with the others at some points. In cases of such conflict, what are we to do? It is easy to say, "My intuitions are right, and yours are mistaken." But the other person may return the compliment, and then once again "ends the argument and begins the fight." Of course we can hope that these intuitions can all be brought into harmony with each other through discussion and reasoning; but what if they are not?

2. The scientific model. Other philosophers have rejected this a priori-deductive model in favor of a different one, which is modeled upon the empirical sciences. We have seen (pp. 168–75) that science is a huge system of mutually coherent propositions, no one of which is sacrosanct, but in cases of conflict one or another item in the system must be scrapped or revised so as to maintain consistency within the system. One could say similarly of ethics that there are many "considered judgments" that we make with great confidence (such as the prohibition against intentionally harming others) and that in cases of conflict some adjustment must be made; sometimes a rule will have to be revised so as to conform to a "considered" principle, and sometimes a principle must be revised when it conflicts with a rule which we are more certain is true than the principle. "Never intentionally harm others" may seem an inviolable rule; but if a man followed this rule and stood by while terrorists raped his wife and tortured his children, would we consider his action right? We may not have had that kind of situation in mind when formulating the rule, but in this case we are more convinced that the man should repel the attacker than that the rule should be obeyed. The rule "Have consideration for all persons equally" might be accepted by many; but if a woman's husband has a painful disease requiring extensive and costly medical care, isn't she right to expend

---

[12]W. D. Ross, *The Right and the Good* (Oxford: Oxford University Press, 1930), pp. 29–30.

every effort in money and energy to get him the best medical care available, even though she *might* have spent the same money to alleviate the condition of several hundred hungry people? In that case, the utilitarian principle (assuming that it would maximize good to help the hungry) has to go, in favor of the more urgent duty to save her husband.

When conflict occurs, the system must be patched up at some point in order to avoid inconsistency within it. Sometimes it is a rule that gives way, sometimes a principle that must be changed or modified, sometimes a statement prescribing a particular action. Often the prescription of a particular action is so urgent ("Here I stand: I can do no other") that in order to accommodate it, a rule or even a principle must go. Ethics is a kind of "patchwork quilt" of various judgments—universal and particular—and one can't always tell in advance which is going to give way and which should be given priority in the circumstances—the particular action, the rule, or the principle. This conception of how ethics works is strongly analogous to the way science works—a network of interrelated laws, theories, and observations of particular phenomena, interdependent and forming together a coherent system of beliefs.

According to Sir David Ross, the moral duties we have are all *prima facie* duties—duties we have unless some other prima facie duty is stronger. Thus, we have a prima facie duty to make restitution for damages or injuries we have inflicted, though again there may be conditions in which this prima facie duty is overruled. We have a prima facie duty of gratitude to those who have benefited us, and in a situation of choice we should benefit our benefactor in preference to someone who has conferred no benefit on us. These prima facie duties may conflict with one another in a particular case, and these situations are ones of moral conflict (among competing prima facie duties). It is never certain, Ross says, what our actual duty is in a particular instance of such

conflict—the conflict may indeed be irresolvable—but what *is* certain is that we have these prima facie duties. Thus in Ross' system there is a mutual adjustment of rules to situations much as there is of observations to theories in the empirical sciences.

But of course there is a difference. In science empirical facts—however unpleasant to a general theory—must be somehow accommodated. Perhaps a well-established generalization has to bite the dust; perhaps an entire theory of atomic structure must be revised; or perhaps the theory can be kept intact if another theory is revised. What must be maintained above all is consistency within the system and maximum coherence of its parts. The same applies in ethics.

In science, however, we have empirical data that are publicly observable: These samples of water do not boil at 212° F, so the generalization that water always boils at this temperature is overthrown; we now observe that it depends on the air-pressure, and we must include that in the law. In ethics, by contrast, we do not have empirical data that *require* changes in the rules. A fanatic will not hesitate to defend his chosen rules even in the face of utter disaster for everyone (himself included) when he applies them. The hard data of the sciences become in ethics our "considered moral convictions." And such convictions are more vulnerable to denial than the empirical data of science; one can simply deny that the moral conviction being asserted is correct.

There is another familiar worry as well. A system may be fully coherent and yet not true. One could spin out systems which are complex webs of fantasy—like the peculiar, distorted but consistent world in the Tolkein books—and yet bear no relation to reality. Are we quite sure that a system of ethics based on entirely different values from those of Western civilization—such as reliability, honesty, justice, mercy, and liberty—could not be just as consistent and coherent? Shouldn't this be a disturbing thought for ethics?

Ethical relativism. Moral convictions, examined in the light of history, have exhibited a considerable amount of relativity from culture to culture. Mathematics is not relative in this way: Chinese mathematics and Chinese physics contain the same propositions as American mathematics and American physics. If there is any contradiction between them, one of them is mistaken. Neither the nature of numbers nor the laws of nature vary from culture to culture. But this feature is notoriously lacking in ethics. When we appeal to our moral intuitions or to our "considered moral judgments," who is included in the "our"? Should the moral code of the Sikh be the same as that of English gentlemen? If a person has made a mathematical error in calculation, we can show her the error no matter what culture she comes from; could we do this in the case of ethics?

Ethical relativism is the view that what is right at one time or place may not be right at another time or place, that what is right varies from culture to culture—not what is *thought* to be right (which clearly does vary) but what *is* right. What may be wrong in America might be right in Zamboanga, and so on.

But here an important distinction must be made. If anything is clear in ethics, isn't it that what you should do depends on the *context* in which you act? Circumstances vary from place to place—not only between America and Zamboanga, but between times and places in America, between communities, and between individuals in the same community. It would be difficult to deny that moral *rules* not only do but should vary depending on circumstances. In a desert society it might be quite mandatory to make the wasting of water a serious offense, since the wastage might cause death by thirst of many persons in the community. But in a water-affluent society, wasting water would be a matter of no great importance. Both the individual and the whole community would benefit from the rule in the desert society; neither would benefit from it in

an area where there was a large annual rainfall. A law requiring people to rescue others in danger may be desirable among Eskimos or in the Himalayas, but it doesn't follow that a law requiring motorists to help other motorists in distress would be desirable in America. (The helpful motorist might be rewarded with a blow on the head and the loss of her purse.) Surely moral rules (as well as legal ones) must be adapted to the conditions that exist at the particular time and place. This need not affect the *principle*. One rule, for example, might have high utility in one society and a quite different rule in another—so both rules would fall neatly under the principle of utility, or the egoistic principle, and so on.

The question for ethical relativism, then, is not "Should moral rules vary from place to place?"—for the answer seems to be clearly yes. The question is rather, "Are different moral *principles* applicable at different times and places?"—and the answer to this is far from obvious. Anthropologists describe in detail how the rules current in one society differ from those in others, but none of this indicates that these societies operate on different moral principles. Nor would it be easy to find out. Most of earth's inhabitants have no conception of moral principles at all. If we asked them, would they even understand what we were asking? Are most primitive tribes capable of that degree of abstract thinking? Who can tell what the underlying principle is in many cases—is it "The greatest happiness of the greatest number," or is it merely "Do what is conducive to the survival of the group," or is it "Do what your chief says, no matter what it is"? It would be difficult indeed to figure out from what moral principle, if any, the rules of a specific society stem.

One might believe that various tribal prescriptions exemplify very different principles. How could tribes who engage in constant intertribal warfare believe in the happiness of the individual or the group? Yet they might—they might believe that they would be rewarded in heaven for dying on the battlefield; or that fighting is the greatest "high" one can experience in life, in spite of the great risk; or that if you don't fight to get a woman she isn't worth it; and so on. We tend to forget that many people's actions are based on *beliefs* we don't share. (1) If members of a tribe believe they will enter the next world in the same body in which they leave this world, they will expect and even want to be killed before they are old and crippled. If we had that belief, might we not also think it right to kill our aged or middle-aged parents and relatives, for their own sakes and as a sacred duty? (2) The Thebans may have had as much pity as we would for Oedipus, aged and blind, but they believed that if they did not banish him from Thebes the gods would take vengeance on the entire city. That *religious* belief may explain why they felt obliged to act as they did; their *moral* views on abandoning the aged and helpless may have been much the same as ours. (3) If you believed that your welfare in the hereafter involved hourly prayer, you would doubtless believe that such frequent prayers were mandatory; but if you didn't have this belief about the hereafter, you would not. Both beliefs fall nicely under the mantle of ethical egoism; they are directed at your future welfare.

Ethical nihilism. The ethical relativist, at any rate, does not deny that there are justified moral principles, only that they vary from culture to culture. But this already concedes more than some persons would grant: that some moral principles *are* justified, albeit variable in their application. The ethical *nihilist* by contrast believes that there is no justification for *any* moral beliefs whether relativistic or not; moral convictions are simply opinions having no justification at all.

The ethical nihilist is like the skeptic about the external world who insists that you don't know you are now looking at a piece of paper (no matter how long you look, how many other people testify to it, and so on); or like the Humean skeptic about induction, who holds that no matter how often a law of nature has been confirmed there is not the slightest reason for believing it will continue to operate in the future. And if he sticks to his convictions, the skeptic cannot be *refuted;* he has the same evidence before him that we do, but he simply refuses to "make the leap" or draw the conclusions that the rest of us do. Given his denial of all your evidence, you can't prove him wrong. But it could also be added that his maneuver is *pointless;* he goes to lunch and to bed just as we do, he expects the stone to fall if he lets go of it just as we do (and would take bets on it just as we would), and he also tries to preserve his life and probably cares for his family just as much as we do. He is in some ways like the compulsive who is never sure he has locked the door; he goes back time and again to see if he's really locked it (each time he goes, the door is indeed locked, but this doesn't convince him two minutes later). The skeptic must make decisions just as we do; he must deliberate and decide what to do today, whether to go into this profession or that, whether to visit his aged mother, and so on—only he says there is no rational basis for choosing any moral ideal above any other.

He will not deny that there are *hypothetical* imperatives: "If you want to be rich and famous, cultivate 'important' people." "If you want to be healthy, eat nutritious foods." "If you want to help others, go to the Bowery with some money in your pocket." And so on. These are statements about what leads to what, and as an ethical skeptic he would not deny these empirical statements—though if he were also an epistemological skeptic, he might. "If you want to kill someone and escape notice, use a gun with a silencer" would be an equally good example of a hypothetical imperative. It all depends on what you want; but there is nothing that you *should* want, other than as a means to an end that you want to achieve. No moral judgment is passed by the nihilist on the end, because these are "incapable of justification." He probably values his life, but if someone were to use a gun with a silencer to kill *him,* he could not consistently say that this was immoral, or bad, or deserving of punishment. He might say, "It's immoral by your moral code, but then no moral code is preferable to any other." Whether he would, or could, consistently live on the basis of this position is another matter.

What does the ethical skeptic demand? Does he demand deductive proof of ethical beliefs, like the skeptic who will accept only deductive proof that the future will be like the past and, not attaining this, declares that no justification is possible? But how could one possibly deduce propositions containing such words as "good" from premises that do not contain these words? How, from any collection of nonethical statements, could one prove the statement that happiness is good or that it is preferable to pain and misery? To the ancient Greeks, the main task of ethics was to discover how to lead a happy life; they never asked for proof that being happy is a good thing. ("Have a good day," uttered even by a stranger, is taken as a favorable kind of greeting. What would we think of someone who said casually, "Have a lousy day" or "Have a nasty time"?) Isn't it better to enjoy life than not to enjoy it? Isn't it better to be free of pain than to be constantly tormented by it? Isn't it better to use our rational powers to understand the world, or some part of it, than to waste our days sipping martinis? Isn't a productive life better than an unproductive one, and isn't being at peace with oneself better than being constantly insecure and rent by inner conflicts? Isn't it undesirable to be always cold and hungry? And if so, isn't leading a life that helps to prevent such a condition (for oneself or others) preferable to a life that is aimless and achieves nothing? Isn't it with convictions like this that ethics must begin?

Once we have admitted this much, we have already gone some distance in showing that "anything goes" ("deuces wild") does not hold true in ethics. If we can believe with Kant that what is right for one is right for all (in the same circumstances), with Mill that happiness is preferable to unhappiness, and with egoism that self-improvement is preferable to self-destruction, then we have already committed ourselves to believing that some ways of living are preferable to others, and some actions as well. But since human desires differ, and human temperaments differ, and the circumstances of human life differ vastly from one time and place to another, a great deal of variation is inevitable; a lifestyle that is attractive to some will be repellent to others, and limitations on freedom that seem indispensable to some will seem inexcusable to others. As Aristotle said at the beginning of his *Nicomachean Ethics,* we should not demand anymore precision of a subject matter than that subject matter admits of.

To get a clearer picture of "ethics in action"—and the interaction of empirical data with rules and principles—we shall close this chapter with an examination of two special areas of interest: ethics and law, and ethics and society.

3. ETHICS AND LAW

Perhaps the best way to understand the intermixture of empirical facts, moral rules, and moral principles in actual practice is through the consideration of law. Unlike moral theorists, judges must make decisions; they cannot wait until ethical theory has been perfected to arrive at these decisions. And presumably the decisions have some basis: What judges decide depends at least in part on what the facts of the case are, although different verdicts are often based on the same set of facts. In examining several types of legal cases we shall see how such concepts as utility, justice, and rights interact.

A. Theories of Punishment

The criminal law operates by the motto "Do not injure others." Anyone who violates this rule is subject to punishment. But what considerations justify the practice of punishing? If one person has killed another, a wrong has been done; when the murderer is punished the victim cannot be brought back to life, yet the perpetrator is made to "pay for his deed," which involves still more pain and discomfort. Do two wrongs make a right? What justifies the law inflicting punishment on people against their will? There are divergent views on this question.

1. According to the *retributive* theory, criminals should be punished because they *deserve* it. The retributive theory is based on *justice,* and justice is the giving to each person of his or her *deserts.* One is punished *because* one has wronged someone else, and the degree of punishment should be proportional to the seriousness of the wrongdoing. Thus, a murderer should be punished more severely than an armed robber, and an armed robber more severely than a petty thief.

Opinions vary, however, as to what punishment a person deserves. Some say that a convicted murderer should himself be killed (capital punishment); others say that a term in prison is apt punishment. Most retributivists do not hold that the punishment should be a "mirror-image" of the crime ("an eye for an eye") but should be *proportional* to the seriousness of the crime. Not all, however, will agree as to which offenses are the most serious; is robbing banks, for example, a more serious offense than raping prostitutes? Many will say, "Sometimes yes, sometimes no—it depends on the facts of the individual case"— and indeed, the retributivist is committed to investigating the facts of each case separately in order to determine more adequately what each person deserves.

It is the person, not the act, whose desert is to be decided. In general the law assumes that each person is a moral agent who could have acted otherwise; he could have avoided killing his wife, robbing the bank, and so on, if he had chosen to (and moreover he could have chosen to). If a "hard determinist" were to say that no one could do otherwise than he did given the precise circumstances, the law would not be impressed; the law operates on the premise that persons are rational agents who could have avoided doing what they did. The law doesn't mind if the Principle of Universal Causation is true, as long as people can choose which actions they will cause. Only when special circumstances arise, so that it was not your will that was involved—for example if someone stronger than you forced your hand on the trigger of the gun—does the law view it as an act of the other person, and thus, in the eyes of the law, the other person deserves punishment, not you. The law does not consider such niceties as, "Could you have done otherwise than you did, even if *all the circumstances* had been the same?" (pp. 235-36); the law only asks, "Were you a moral agent who could have acted otherwise if you had so chosen?" For the law this is the norm; in special cases such as insanity, in which persons may have no idea what they are doing, then they are not moral agents and do not deserve punishment. If you were coerced, for example, or if a neurologist was "playing around with your brain," then he and not you is liable; but even so the retributivist would ask, "Could you have avoided placing yourself in such a situation?"

2. The *utilitarian* theory has an entirely opposite emphasis. Instead of asking about the past—"What do you deserve for what you did?"—it asks, "What can be done in the future to make things better?" This would include (1) *rehabilitation* of the criminal, so that he would not repeat his deed; (2) *deterrence* of others—the fact that A has been imprisoned for armed robbery may deter B, C, and D from committing similar crimes; and (3) *protection* of society by isolating dangerous

people in institutions so that the rest of us can walk the streets more safely. Unfortunately not all of these consequences are usually achieved at the same time. While a retributivist would give the maximum penalty to the worst of crimes, murder, the utilitarian would ask, "Will punishing this person deter others from crime?" and "Is this person a threat to society, against whom society requires protection?" Not everyone agrees which of these considerations is the most important. Some say that *dangerousness* is the principal criterion—that it is most important for us to be protected against people who commit violent acts; the point of imprisonment is to "isolate the dangerous." But many persons behind bars are not dangerous at all (at least not any longer), and many dangerous persons walk the streets who have committed crimes but never been convicted for them.

And thus the question arises, How should one balance these three kinds of utilitarian consideration against one another? Most persons would regard protection against dangerous persons as the strongest utilitarian reason for keeping them isolated from the rest of society. But what if a person has been convicted only for petty theft, but remains a constant danger to others—is full of hostility and far more dangerous than a one-time killer who killed his wife's lover but would never kill again? It is extremely difficult to estimate the consequences of any particular imprisonment. Will it have prevailingly good or bad consequences for society? Five years in prison is likely to make a criminal out of anyone; yet if the person is dangerous, and no attempt at rehabilitation changes this (which is the usual case), what can we do but keep such a person isolated? And in all this, must no attention be paid to the past—to the seriousness of the crime that was committed? Should one's eyes be only on future consequences, which are about as difficult to estimate as next year's weather?

3. The *restitution* theory has still a different emphasis. The victim should be compensated for the losses suffered, and the criminal is the one who should make the restitution. By "making it up" to the victim to help restore the status quo (or for the victim's family, in the case of murder). Restitution for murder of course is not possible; one can't bring the murdered person back to life. But one can make *some* kind of restitution, and to do this should be the purpose of punishment. It does the victim no good to have the aggressor behind bars; indeed, the victim has to pay taxes to help keep him there. It may even be that restitution can achieve both retribution and utility. Compensating the victim over a period of years—the punishment—may prove to be the criminal's just dessert and, at the same time, *may* also have the greatest utility, bringing home to the criminal the devastating nature of what he has done to the victim and family more vividly than any retribution could.

In practice we employ each of these theories—retribution, utility, and restitution—largely to suit our convenience. "Five years, for what he did?—He deserves at least that!" (retribution). "They should put such people away so that they can't commit more crimes!" (utility). "He was robbed and the robber spent the money, so what did the victim get out of the robber's sentence?" (restitution). The first two theories at any rate cannot be reconciled with one another: We may hope that criminals get what they deserve *and* that this will have the best possible consequences, but the reasons for the punishment are still quite different. One says, "He is punished because he must be made to pay for his crime" (retribution), and another, "He is punished because people need to know that you can't get by with murder" (deterrence). Though the effects may in some cases be the same, the *reasons* given by way of justification are quite different; retribution is "past-looking" ("You are punished because you did so-and-so"), whereas utility is "future-looking" ("You are punished in order to achieve so-and-so").

B. Responsibility

The law takes for granted that human beings are rational agents capable of voluntary action, and are thus responsible for their actions (except in special circumstances to be described below). If you deliberate whether or not do to something—weigh it pro or con—and then act, this is a paradigm of voluntary action. However, an action need not be premeditated in order for a person to be responsible for it. If a man in a fit of anger shoots someone and kills him, he is held to be responsible—both in morality and in law—in spite of the fact that he did not deliberate about it in advance. (Deliberate killing of another person is first-degree murder; killing without premeditation is second-degree murder.) It is enough that he was *capable* of refraining from doing it; he could have decided just beforehand not to do it, but did not so decide. The action was *avoidable,* yet he did not avoid it; and that is why he is considered responsible for doing it. (If a fatalist were to say that people are never responsible for any of their actions because "whatever happens is inevitable," the law would still draw a distinction between those actions they could have prevented themselves from doing and those they could not.) An action you could have avoided is considered a voluntary action, and both morality and the law hold you responsible for your voluntary actions.

What about the *consequences* of your actions? You can hardly be held responsible for *all* the consequences of your actions, for these may stretch indefinitely into the future and are impossible for anyone to anticipate. Should President Monroe be responsible for *all* the consequences of the Monroe Doctrine, which he signed, including those occurring centuries later in conditions no one could anticipate? If a teacher dismisses her class five minutes early and at that moment a bomb goes off in the hall, injuring some of them, the teacher is not held responsible for that consequence of her action, for she could not have foreseen it.

Shall we say then that people are responsible for the *foreseeable* consequences of their actions? But foreseeable by whom? A thoughtful person can foresee more than an unreflective person, a brilliant person more than a stupid one. In daily life we tend not to hold people responsible for what they couldn't help; but the law, aiming at somewhat greater precision, has developed the doctrine of the *reasonable* man, reasonable action, and reasonably foreseeable consequences. For example, if you hit a man in the nose it is reasonably foreseeable that you may bloody his nose but not that he may die of the bleeding (if he turns out to have hemophilia). If you roll the car downhill without applying the brakes, it is reasonably foreseeable that you may hit something on the way down. If you throw somebody off a roof it is reasonably foreseeable that he will fall and die. But if your roommate has an appendicitis attack and—before the doctor comes—you apply a heating pad not knowing that this will make it worse, are you responsible? Many people are aware that you shouldn't apply heat in this situation; but if you did not know this and applied heat, should you be held morally responsible for your ignorance? legally responsible?

1. Ignorance. Ignorance is one condition that often excuses a person from responsibility. The statement "I didn't know that the glass contained poison" excuses you from the charge of murder (you thought the glass contained only water, and someone else put the poison in). The statement "I didn't know you wanted to save these papers" excuses you from burning important papers in a wastebasket (you reasonably assumed they were no longer wanted); but it wouldn't excuse you if the papers had been arranged on the desk. "I didn't know she had an allergy" ordinarily excuses you from having served some dish to an acquaintance whose physiological peculiarities you did not know.

If you can easily avoid being ignorant, you are still held responsible despite being ignorant. If someone comes at you with a toy gun that looks like a real gun, you may defend yourself, for you reasonably believe that your life is threatened. But if a surgeon botched an operation because she hadn't read a medical book for 20 years, she would be held responsible for her ignorance. If a man tried to put out a gasoline fire with water, he might or might not be held responsible for the ignorance—it would depend on whether he could reasonably be expected to know that gasoline and water don't mix (in an industrial society he probably would, in a primitive society he would not). But if avoiding ignorance requires first reading numerous books or encyclopedias, the average person is not held responsible even though ignorance would be avoidable by extensive reading, because a person is not reasonably expected to be knowledgable unless he is in a profession or trade—medicine, pharmacy, fumigation—which requires him to have such knowledge. The first Indian who drank the white man's firewater was ignorant of its effects and would not be responsible for this ignorance; he had no way of knowing.

If a man with a gun shoots everyone in sight, in the belief that they are all enemies who are "out to get him," he is not excused because his ignorance of the facts is not considered reasonable. If a person throws another off a twentieth-story roof, sincerely believing that the victim will not fall but will go directly upwards to heaven, he is considered inexcusably ignorant of an obvious fact (that people fall down from heights and don't go upwards) and is not excused in law—it is treated as a case of inexcusable ignorance even though his

belief was sincere. (One might *morally* excuse such a person if one was certain that he meant the other person no harm and that he *sincerely* believed that the person would go directly to heaven. However, even in such a religiously oriented morality one would still be expected to ask the other person first whether he wanted to go to heaven in just this manner and at this moment.)

Whether ignorance of fact excuses a person depends on whether the ignorance is found reasonable under the circumstances. Common morality might also excuse a person for being ignorant of laws, such as some obscure requirement buried in the hundreds of pages of the Internal Revenue code. But the law does not consider ignorance of the law excusing: The statement "I didn't know there was a law against carrying a concealed weapon in this county" would not excuse a handgun offender, for if it did anyone who wanted to be let off could claim ignorance of the law; it would be suicidal for the law to admit ignorance of law as an excuse. *Disagreement* with the law is often considered an acceptable excuse in morality—even heroic or noble—if the law is considered a bad one. Yet as long as it is law, the law can hardly admit this as an excuse, and for the same reason; if all those who committed a crime claimed that they disagreed with the law that prohibited the crime, they would be let off and the law would become ineffective.

2. Mistakes. A mistake of *fact* is often excused in both law and morality, provided the mistake was reasonable in the circumstances. If a homeowner reasonably mistook someone entering her house at night for an intruder and shot him, she would ordinarily be excused from the charge of murder. A man would be excused from following oral instructions if he was deaf. If you take someone's book from a desk thinking it to be your own, you would normally be excused (if you returned it on discovering the error) because it was a reasonable mistake to make. But there is some disagreement about when mistakes of fact are reasonable. For example, suppose a man drives home late at night and all the tract houses look alike; he parks his car at the wrong house, enters, and gets into bed—in the dark—with a woman who is not his wife; is his mistake reasonable? Or is the woman justified in filing charges of attempted rape?

In mistake of fact, your mistake may be found "reasonable under the circumstances." In mistake of law, however, you are not likely to be excused for a reasonable mistake. If you sincerely interpret a statute in one way, but the court decides that a different interpretation is correct, you are still liable for "mistake of law." The reason for this is utilitarian: If any sincere interpretation of a statute were permitted (and how would anyone discover whether the interpretation was sincere?), it would be difficult for courts to reject any interpretation, however outlandish. Still, isn't such a practice unjust? Should a person be held responsible for not knowing the "correct interpretation" when the court has not yet decided which interpretation to accept? Is the citizen supposed to have powers of precognition? As often happens in the law, justice defers to utility.

3. Coercion. A robber points a gun at you and says "Your money or your life." This is a standard case of coercion, and when someone coerces you into doing something, it is (in both morality and the law) the coercer's act and not yours, even if you do something illegal—such as robbing a store—because of the threat. However, there are many twists and turns in the concept of coercion, as the following imaginary dialogue will illustrate.

A: How much of a threat must there be, for it to count as a case of coercion?
B: A threat of death or great bodily harm. The robber may take only your money, but what he threatens to take is your life.

A: I seem to see a slippery slope here. If a blackmailer threatens to expose you if you don't pay him hush money, is that coercion? If it is, then what about the mother who won't let her daughter leave the house unless she first washes the dishes? There's a threat here, isn't there? Can't you say she is coercing her daughter into washing the dishes? If a stranger threatens to take your coat if you don't give him five dollars, isn't that coercion too—even though the loss of a coat is far less serious than the loss of your life or limb? Well then, how about someone who says "Do what I say or I'll sneeze"? Or the mother-in-law who says "If you don't do what I want, I'll move out." (Is that a threat or a promise?)
B: None of these is coercion. I'd say "Go ahead and sneeze," and "Go ahead, take my coat." As for the blackmailer, he is offering a trade—his silence in exchange for your money, and you are free to reject the deal.
A: But you are also free to reject the deal offered by the armed robber. In every case of coercion, there *is* a choice. If someone just hits you over the head, that's the use of force against you (assault) but not coercion. In all the cases I've described, there is *some* threatened loss if you don't comply, and I can't help wondering where you draw the line with this. How serious must the threatened loss be? Is the threatened loss of a woman's chastity more serious than the threatened loss of her pocketbook?
B: I say it must be threat of death or bodily harm. What happens if she doesn't submit to him or give him her pocketbook? Then he may inflict death or bodily harm (rape), right? And that makes it coercion.
A: What if he never intends to carry out his threat? Or if he can't because (unknown to him) someone has removed the bullets from his gun?
B: Since the victim doesn't know that, it presents the same threat. He may have only a

toy pistol, but it looks like the real thing half concealed or in the dark, and is perceived as the real thing. The victim can't be expected to be omniscient.

A: Would you also say that the person must force you to do something you don't want to do?

B: Of course. I don't willingly give up my money to the robber, I do it only because I'm confronted by the threat to my life.

A: What if he makes you do something that, unknown to him, you wanted to do anyway?

B: I'm still not doing what I want. I want to dance and he makes me dance, but what I wanted was to dance without the threat of death, and when he threatens me I can't dance in the way I wanted to.

A: You have ignored another type of coercion—coercion by psychological means, not by the threat of a gun, but by working on your mind.

B: That's not coercion at all. How could he threaten me except by physical force? If there were no such threat, I'd just walk away from the situation. How could I possibly be coerced that way?

A: I'd say that many people are coerced by psychological means all the time. A man wants to pursue an affair with a woman, and he gradually and knowingly drives his wife crazy. Or, he knows just what "buttons to press" to get her to do just what he wants. Or, she's a passive type who's intimidated by men with a dominant personality or a deep voice; she loses all her resolve when she hears him, and always does what he says.

B: How can you call that coercion? In coercion you're made to do something against your will; in this set of examples the wife does something as a result of *her own* act of will.

A: So it is also when you give the gunman your wallet; *you decide* to give it up in view of the threat. Similarly, the wife decides to do what her husband says. If the case of the gunman is coercion, why not also that of the wife?

B: Because giving up your wallet is not doing what you *want*. The wife is doing what she (at that moment) wants when she capitulates to her husband.

A: Sure, the husband operates *through* her will rather than *against* it, when he cons her into doing what he wants. It's more subtle than threatening violence, but that's what con artists do. But both devices have the same effect; I call them both coercion.

B: No matter how he influences her, she defers to his wishes "of her own free will," as we say. There's no threat of violence against her, and she can choose whether or not to obey him, so she is not being coerced.

A: Sure, and you also decide "of your own free will" to give in to the robber's demands. That's even what you *want* to do under these circumstances; you want to keep your life more than you want to keep your money. And the wife is doing what she wants, too; if she doesn't obey she will feel very uncomfortable, perhaps guilty, perhaps afraid of loss of his love or attention. So she does it. The effect in the two cases is the same.

B: But the cause is not. He *influences* her, but influence isn't coercion. Who isn't influenced by other people all the time? If influence were coercion, then practically everything we do would be coerced. A teacher strongly influences a student to read more books, but it would be absurd to say that the teacher is coercing the student. The student decides to act in accord with the teacher's suggestion, that's all.

A: You underestimate how extremely powerful psychological coercion can be. The wife may be much too tired or sick to go partying tonight, but the husband cons her into it.

B: But at the time, she *does* want it.

A: Not necessarily. She really doesn't *want* to go partying, but he casts a kind of hypnotic spell over her and she does it. She hasn't necessarily even *decided* to do it—she's just putty in his hands and may not even go through a conscious decision-making process.

B: I'd say that's her problem. She is unduly suggestible, but she is not being coerced.

A: It's not a standard case of coercion, but neither is it entirely voluntary action. People respond to different kinds of psychological pressure—but the other person "presses the right buttons," and she does what she doesn't want to do. When Howard Hughes had been a recluse for many years, and didn't want anyone to see him, he looked out of his penthouse hotel window one day and said he thought he'd use that room because the view was so nice. His employees saw that if he started doing that he'd soon be in touch with the world again and they might be out of jobs. They knew he dreaded being photographed, so to get him back into his windowless room they said "If you sit there, someone might fly past in a helicopter and take your picture." That was enough; he returned to his windowless room and didn't come out again. They pressured him and it worked. And you don't think this is coercion?

B: Not at all. He could have said no. And when he was told about possible photographs, he *wanted* to get back into his windowless cell. They pressured him, but they didn't coerce him.

A: And I say that if the psychological pressure is strong and unremitting enough, it amounts to coercion. They're just two different ways of getting people to do what you want them to do.

This dialogue is at least the beginning of a philosophical analysis of the concept of coercion—as we also did with causation, freedom, and numerous other concepts. We turn now, more briefly, to the concept of compulsion.

4. Compulsion. Coercion comes from other people, compulsion from within oneself. How can one compel oneself? The phrase is not to be taken literally. Psychologists are aware of countless cases of what they call "compulsive behavior," in which no one is forcing you to do as you do, but you seem compelled by some "inner force" to do it. The pathological gambler can't stay away from the gambling tables and only quits when she's broke. The alcoholic and drug addict seem drawn by some irresistible force to consume these substances, and no power on earth seems sufficient to make them avoid it as long as it is obtainable. The child-molester knows severe penalties attach to what he does—and may also believe that what he is doing is wrong—yet is drawn powerfully toward it; it is his strongest desire, stronger than the desire for food if he were starving. To be literally a slave another person is to be coerced by the slavemaster; but one is also said to be a "slave of one's passions" or of "irresistible cravings and wants."

Common morality is not very sympathetic toward excusing persons on grounds of such compulsions, believing that such criminals "could have refrained if they had tried harder." Yet common morality may be uninformed. Take the strongest desire you have, then multiply it in intensity by a thousand; could you still refrain? That is probably what the alcoholic feels who says, in the language of Alcoholics Anonymous, that alcoholics are the victims of a disease which they are helpless to cure. (The alcoholic's cure is, however, often achieved by the consistent mutual support of alcoholics helping one another, and A.A. has a high rate of cures. So, though the act may be unavoidable by the person's own unaided will, there are things he or she *can* do which may achieve a cure nonetheless.)

There are crimes committed by persons in

such a state of "overpowering impulse" which divide the verdicts of courts and laymen alike. A person finds himself in a state of constant hostility and rage—he may not know against what, yet he carries this intense feeling with him always. What would be a minor annoyance to most of us becomes in him the occasion for intense rages which nothing apparently can control—he is, as it were, "inhabited by the devil." In such a state he may kill indiscriminately; or he may kill only when a special set of circumstances—such as seeing a girl who resembles his mother whom he intensely hates—triggers his hostility to a point where (so it seems to him) he "has no choice but to kill." He cannot understand why others condemn him; wouldn't they, too, behave like him if they had his personality? He seems to himself, as well as to many psychiatrists, to be a passive victim of an overpowering force, an unwilling instrument in the hands of an inner compulsion far more powerful than his "rational will."

Courts have sometimes excused such crimes on the ground of "irresistible impulse"; if it was irresistible, how could one resist it? How can you condemn a person for doing what he can't help doing? The problem with "irresistible impulse," however, is that you can never be sure whether you have encountered a genuine case of it. *Could* the person have resisted the impulse, if he or she had tried? *Could* he have stopped and thought for a moment before committing the deed? *We* tend to say that he could and should have, and thus that they are responsible. But many a psychiatrist will testify that in such a condition he was not responsible; he is no more to be morally condemned than a lion would be for killing an antelope; resistance was simply "beyond his power." Yet if courts let such people off, believing them genuine examples of irresistible impulses, how many fraudulent cases—often impossible to distinguish from genuine ones—would allow guilty criminals to go free?

Many such persons are exempted from criminal punishment—and often committed to mental institutions instead—under the label of "insanity." But "insanity" is one of the most slippery concepts of all. Is the person who kills another in a fit of rage to be called insane? Sometimes yes; but often, undoubtedly no. It all depends on what the vague word "insane" means, and no definition has been devised which even specialists in the field can agree on. Insanity is supposed to be "a disease of the mind"—but what is to constitute a disease of the mind as opposed to that of the body (where we know quite clearly what diseases are)? Is insanity an *inability* to act in a prescribed or lawful way? Is the sociopath—lacking any sense of right and wrong and who cannot be appealed to by any moral considerations—to be called insane? Suppose a man flies into a rage and kills. Is he "temporarily insane"? Is he insane at noon but not at 1 P.M.? If a man flies into an incoherent rage before a jury, is this evidence that he is insane? And what of the cool, collected, paranoid killer, who stalks his prey for years under the misapprehension that his victims pose a threat to him? The Swiss Penal Code gives a brief definition of insanity: being "incapable of appreciating the unlawful nature of his act, or of acting in accord with such appreciation." But does this brief definition encapsulate what we have in mind in calling someone insane? *Do* we have anything clearly in mind in calling someone insane?

Meanwhile, the existence of powerful inner compulsions, perhaps even irresistible ones, seems to be a fact. A retributivist would find such persons not responsible for what they do, and not deserving of punishment: "Forgive them, for they know not what they do." But a utilitarian would put them away nevertheless if they were dangerous to others, like mad dogs. What we should make of these powerful inner compulsions, and what we should do when the inner motivations are still so little understood, are matters that continue to plague morality as well as the courts.

5. *Consent.* If you consent to something, voluntarily and without coercion, the law as a rule considers you to have taken upon yourself the consequences of such consent, and you cannot then complain that you were forced. Consent is what distinguishes ordinary sexual intercourse from rape. Consent on the part of the owner is what transforms theft into a gift. A person who inflicts bodily harm on another person is guilty of assault and battery, but not if the other person consented to being injured.

Nevertheless, consent does not always exonerate. (1) You are drowning in quicksand; someone extends a rope to you but says, "I won't pull you out unless you consent to be my slave for life." You consent. Although you readily consented under the circumstances, no court will uphold such an agreement: The court will say that you did it under coercion (sometimes this is called "extreme duress"). (2) You consent to have your life ended by someone administering you a poison or a fatal gunshot; however, one's consenting to be killed is not (in most nations) excused by the law. The person who administers the lethal dose or fires the gun—even to save the other person a life of intense pain—is considered guilty of murder. (Here one's moral convictions may well conflict sharply with the law. If your life belongs to you and not to others, have you no right to end it if you choose?) (3) A child readily consents to the offer of a mind-altering drug by an adult, perhaps out of curiosity. But the child's consent does not save the adult from criminal charges. In general, children are not held responsible for their actions (including consent), because they are usually unable to foresee the consequences of these actions. (4) A patient consents to an operation on the advice of her surgeon and signs the required forms. But suppose the surgeon has not informed her that her chances of recovery are slight, and in fact that her chances would be as good or better without the surgery. No one doubts that the patient con-

sented, but it is not mere consent but *informed* consent that is required; the patient must be informed of "all the relevant facts" in order to make an informed decision. What is consent without the information on which to base it? (5) The consent of persons declared legally insane counts for nothing. They can sign no contracts, write no will, have no bank accounts; their property can be taken from them. Of all persons, those whom the court has declared *non compos mentis* have the fewest rights under the law. Although in our eyes they may be merely peculiar, eccentric, or irresponsible in some manner, once they are declared insane they lose the rights and privileges of other citizens (including those in prison). As far as their legal rights are concerned, they are the most helpless and oppressed of all citizens. This is doubtless one of the greatest injustices in the legal system; does the utility of incarcerating innocent persons against their will, when they have trouble fending for themselves in the outside world, do anything to make up for the violation of their rights as human beings?

C. Intentional Acts

If someone intentionally steps on your toe, you feel more offended than if she did so accidentally, even though the amount of physical pain is the same. The acts for which people are most severely punished—children, by their parents; lawbreakers, by the law—are those which are done intentionally. Murder is intentional killing; manslaughter is in general accidental killing; the sentence for the first is more severe than for the second.

But what is it for an act to be intentional? (1) In one view, you intend those consequences of an act which you *desire* to occur. If your only desire is to speed at 100 mph and as a result you run over a pedestrian, your act is intentional with regard to speeding but not with regard to killing the pedestrian, since you did not desire that result. (2) In another view, you intend those consequences you reasonably *expected* to take place, whether you desired them or not. If you could reasonably expect that someone's death would occur as a result of your speeding (the streets were thronged with people, etc.), then you intended that consequence even though you did not desire it. The two theories in practice sometimes have different results: If you are target practicing in a deserted area and you are a bad shot, but happen to shoot someone who unknown to you is passing by, you would not have shot him intentionally according to the second theory; but if you nevertheless *desired* his death, the improbability of the consequence wouldn't count at all according to the first theory, only the fact that you desired it.

A person's intention is future-oriented: "I intend *to* . . ." (followed by a description of some future act). A person's *motive,* by contrast, has to do with what led him to do what he did. He intended to kill his wife, but what was his motive—jealousy? money? desire to marry someone else? In morality we may praise or condemn people for both their intentions and their motives; both can be considered good or bad: "Her intentions were good, though her act was wrong" or "He did a good deed from a bad motive" (giving to charity so that others would remark on how generous he was). In law, by contrast, no amount of bad intentions will convict a person of a crime. In law, there must be an *act*. (Ask yourself: Is there a utilitarian reason for the difference?) If the act is intentional, the perpetrator will probably get a heavier sentence than if she accidentally caused damage or injury, but there must be an act. In Christian doctrine, "He who hath committed adultery in his heart" is just as much to be condemned as if he had actually done it—that is an enormously demanding aspect of Christian morality. But in law only acts can be prosecuted. (*Omissions* can count as acts, however: If par-

ents omit to take care of their children by starving them, they are liable to criminal prosecution even though they plead, "But we haven't *done* anything!" Omitting to do what one has a legal duty to do counts as an act.)

Attempting to do something is an act—you try to kill someone but fail. But the mere *intention* is no act and is not punishable. There is a reason for this, of course: If we were to be punished for our intentions, we would all be behind bars. In any case it is difficult to know what a person's intentions are unless the person acts (people often fail to act on their intentions). Nevertheless, some puzzling cases arise in which moral judgments may diverge sharply from legal judgments.

Lady Eldon, traveling on the Continent, bought what she supposed to be a quantity of French lace, which she hid, concealing it in one of the pockets of the coach. But the package was discovered by the customs officer at Dover. The lace turned out to be an English manufactured article of little value, and, of course, not subject to duty. She had bought it at a price far above its value, believing it to be genuine, intending to smuggle it into England.[13]

What was she guilty of? Intending to smuggle French lace? Yes—but the law can't arrest you for your intentions, only for your actions. She *intended* to smuggle it in illegally; what she actually *did* was to bring into England duty-free lace which had been made in England—an act which of course was not illegal.

Now change the example slightly: She really did bring in French lace, and the customs officer at Dover found it and said to her, "Lucky for you that you returned to England today rather than yesterday. They just changed the law this morning; French lace is no longer on the duty list." Again, she has

---

[13]Described in Graham Hughes, "Attempting the Impossible," *New York University Law Review 42,* 6 (1967): 1005–1020. Quoted in John Arthur and William Shaw, eds., *Readings in Philosophy of Law* (Englewood Cliffs, NJ: Prentice-Hall, 1984), p. 351.

done nothing illegal: She brought in French lace at a time when there was nothing illegal about doing so. She is guilty of nothing in law.

If you buy stolen goods reasonably believing they are not stolen, but later discover that they are, you nonetheless are required to return them to the rightful owner, even though you paid for them in good faith. But suppose you buy some goods you *believe* are stolen, though in fact—unknown to you—they are no longer stolen but have meanwhile been returned to their rightful owner? Buying goods that are in fact not stolen is surely no crime, is it? The intention may be what counts in morality, but isn't the fact what counts, and should count, in law? Isn't it like the Lady Eldon cases?

But here opinions are divided. Some courts have convicted people for intentionally buying goods they *thought* were stolen. If you think you are poisoning your wife but actually are administering to her a harmless liquid, are you innocent because in fact the substance was harmless? The courts would normally count this as a case of attempted murder.

At this point we may be inclined to say, "It's always what the person *reasonably believes* that counts, and the husband reasonably believed the glass contained poison." But Lady Eldon reasonably believed she was importing prohibited French lace. What are the limits of reasonable belief? Smith and an accomplice[14] were driving in a car, the rear of which was loaded with stolen goods. They were stopped by a police officer. Another officer, who had been on friendly terms with Smith, came round to the driver's side to speak to Smith. Noticing the goods in the back of the car, the officer told Smith to pull over to the side of the road. Smith started to

do so, but then accelerated in an attempt to escape. The officer was at first walking, then running alongside the car, then got his arm inside the open window on the driver's side and clung to the car. He managed to hang on as the car picked up speed. Traffic was heavy and Smith's car took an erratic course down the road, close to the traffic on the other side. They met four other cars coming from the opposite direction. The officer's body struck against the first three cars, but then he was shaken off and fell in front of the fourth car, sustaining fatal injuries. Smith then turned around, stopped, unloaded the stolen goods, and returned to the place where the officer lay. "I knew the man," he told the police who came. "I wouldn't do that for the world. All I wanted to do was shake him off."

Let's assume that what Smith said was true. He didn't want to kill or even injure the officer; he had no such intention. He believed, perhaps reasonably, that he could emerge from the situation without injuring the officer, who was his friend; yet the court found Smith guilty of murder—not because he intended to kill the officer, but because he intended grievous bodily harm, as a result of which the officer died. Ask yourself: How much should depend on what the facts were; how much on what the man believed; how much on what he had reason to believe? And how strongly should each of these factors be *weighed,* and why? Lifelong students of the law continue to disagree about these things. They might embrace the same moral principles, yet disagree on the particular case. The application of principles to cases, all of which differ from one another, makes the field of applied ethics bewilderingly complex.

The rule or the particular case? Once apprised of the detailed facts of a particular case, judges typically form a decision of what is right or just or fair *in that case,* and then employ whatever legal precedents will tend to support that decision. But to generalize from particular cases is hazardous, since each case

---

[14]Described in R. M. Curley, "Excusing Rape," *Philosophy and Public Affairs 5,* 4 (Summer 1976). Quoted in John Arthur and William Shaw, eds., *Readings in Philosophy of Law* (Englewood Cliffs, NJ: Prentice-Hall, 1984), pp. 370–71.

is different. Someone who invokes rule A may have cases 1, 2, and 3 in mind; another who invokes rule B may have cases 4, 5, and 6 in mind. And no rule is likely to do justice to the diversity of facts involved in the particular case.

"A man driving a 1939 Cadillac . . . toward Chicago runs into a Model T Ford, driven by a farmer who has just turned onto the highway from a dirt road, and demolishes the Ford but does not hurt the farmer. The farmer sues, and a judge . . . awards him $100."[15] The next week an almost identical accident occurs. Should the same decision be rendered? Not necessarily:

Maybe the first Cadillac was doing 60 miles an hour and the second one 30. Or maybe one was doing 45 but it was raining one week and clear the next. Maybe one farmer blew his horn and the other didn't. Maybe one farmer stopped at the crossing and the other didn't. Maybe one farmer had a driver's license and the other didn't. Maybe one farmer was young and the other was old and wore glasses. Maybe they both wore glasses but one was nearsighted and the other farsighted.[16]

Yet each of these details could well make a difference to the final verdict. How is one to determine which details are relevant, and how heavily to weigh each one? "The vital motivating impulse for the decision is an intuitive sense of what is right or wrong in the particular case."[17]

A judge's "sense of fairness" may thus lead to a diversity of opinions on particular cases; the slightest difference between them may be considered relevant. What is called the "law of attempt"—specifically, attempts to do

what is in fact impossible under the circumstances—is a particularly apt illustration. A man thinks he is shooting a deer out of season; but in fact the deer is stuffed, and it's impossible to kill a deer that's already dead. An old man tries to rape a girl, but he is no longer capable of the physical act of penetration required to constitute a case of rape. A voodoo doctor believes that her curse will cause her enemy's death, although on empirical grounds it is impossible—so the rest of us believe—to kill someone by that means. A man is intoxicated and thinks he is raping a girl, though it is only a corpse, or a model in a clothier's window. Is there any general rule we can elicit from these cases? Should they all be decided the same way? But aren't they all relevantly different from each other?

Let us see how attempts differ. Attempted murder is a crime, though not as severe as murder (it's not murder if the attempt doesn't succeed). Attempted rape is a crime too; we may believe that it too should be punished, as in the case of the old man. Is the pickpocket who picks an empty pocket guilty of anything? He has stolen nothing, but he has attempted to do so. A woman tries to kill someone, but she doesn't realize there are no bullets in the chamber. To kill anyone in such a circumstance is impossible; yet isn't she guilty of the attempt? Or perhaps attempts shouldn't be punished at all, since they produce no bad consequences (utilitarian argument)?

Yet there *is* a utilitarian argument for punishing attempted murder: If one attempt is not punished, the next attempt may be successful. If a man is a bad shot and tries to kill his enemy but misses, his failure is not from lack of will but only from lack of skill, and he may make sure that he exercises more skill in his next attempt. Consider the following cases:

1. A woman who believes in voodoo wants to kill her exhusband, whom she hates; but he is a thousand miles away. She pronounces a curse

---

[15]Free Rodell, *Woe unto You, Lawyers!* (New York: Pageant Press, 1957), p. 116.

[16]Ibid., p. 117. Discussed by C. Gordon Post in *Introduction to the Law* (Prentice-Hall, 1963).

[17]Judge Hutcheson, "The Judgment Intuitive: The Function of the 'Hunch' in Judicial Decisions," *Cornell Law Quarterly, 14:* 274. Discussed by Jerome Frank in his *Law and the Modern Mind* (New York: Coward McCann, 1949).

on him, which she believes will kill him; in her mind she is committing an act of murder.

2. A man shoots someone with intent to kill, but there are no bullets in the gun.

3. A man shoots at what he thinks is an enemy, but it's getting dark in the woods and the "enemy" turns out to be only a tree stump.

4. A man attempts to kill another by placing a time bomb in his bed, set to go off at a time when the man is asleep. But the man doesn't come home that night and the detonation doesn't kill anyone.

5. A woman sets out to poison her husband; she puts what she thinks is poison into his coffee and offers it to him. He drinks it, but—unknown to her—it's a harmless substance and has no ill effects on him.

Now, each and every one of these persons had *mens rea*—guilty intent. They all intended to kill their victims. Not only did they intend this, they all *attempted to,* each in his or her own way. Moreover, each one was quite sure that the *means* he or she used would cause the death that was desired. And yet the only person who would surely be exonerated is the first, the woman in the voodoo case. But why? She intended to kill her exhusband, she attempted to, and she thought she was succeeding; likewise, the means she used was one she thought would achieve her desired end. So far every one of the cases is alike.

The only significant difference seems to be that *we* know—or we think we know—that practicing voodoo doesn't achieve the desired end. As far as what she wanted to do and attempted to do is concerned, she was as guilty as all the others; it was not thanks to her that her exhusband didn't die. Morally she was as guilty as the rest. Why then doesn't the law consider her legally guilty? Because, we believe, voodoo doesn't kill anybody. She could practice it from now till doomsday and it would harm no one. What she *thought* was the means was *not* the means; she was simply engaging in a harmless pastime. Science doesn't believe in voodoo; so the law doesn't even hold her guilty of attempt. In all the

other cases, if the facts had been as the person thought they were, someone would have been dead; you *can* after all kill people by shooting and poisoning them. But because we believe you can't kill people by voodoo, the police would not even inquire whether she was engaging in it, even if her ex-husband died the next morning.

Let us compare the "unscientific" voodoo case with the following: Suppose a person has a flash of intuition at every court trial and claims to *know* whether the defendant is guilty or not. And suppose that person always turns out to be right; she has a much better track record than the judge's or the jury's. Even if the jury found the defendant guilty, she claims he is innocent, and sure enough, later someone else confesses to the crime. Her track record is perfect; but because we have no idea *how* she was able to be regularly right, we say she *lacked evidence*—and hence, by the standard definition of knowing (pp. 19–23, 30), she didn't *know*. Still, the disturbing thought occurs to us that if the purpose of a trial is for the guilty to be condemned and the innocent to be let go, she fulfills that purpose ideally. She has never made a mistake, which is more than one can say for juries. Shouldn't we then simply consult her for the correct verdict each time and not bother about a trial at all? The answer usually given is no, because of *procedural* requirements that would be unfair to omit: Defendants have to be confronted with evidence proving beyond a reasonable doubt that they are guilty; but all the psychic in our example has supplied the court is her unverified word. Thus the law must proceed by "scientific method," even though its track record is not as good as hers. A fallible record based on evidence is considered preferable to an infallible one presented without evidence.

D. Unintentional Acts

People are often condemned, both morally and legally, for acts they did not intend to commit and for consequences they did not foresee. *Recklessness* is intentional: You drive your sports car down a country road at 150 mph; you didn't intend to kill anyone but you did intentionally drive at that speed; you may not have considered the possible consequences, or more probably you did consider them and discounted them because you were anxious to drive at that speed. *Negligence,* on the other hand, is quite unintentional: Negligence is simply failure to take reasonable care in what you are doing. This failure to take reasonable care can cause injury and damage, and you are liable for it if it happens; the fact that you forgot or you "just didn't think of the possible consequences" doesn't legally excuse you. You may consider this unfair because you intended no harm, yet the victim has been harmed whether you intended it or not.

A teenager leaves his motorcycle on the sidewalk intending to put it into the garage, but he forgets about it; a blind man passes by, stumbles over it, and is injured. The teenager is negligent although what he did was not intentional. The manufacturer of a vaporizer may be found guilty of negligence because the vaporizer was faultily designed—it tips over too easily, or the steam isn't sufficiently sealed off, so that anyone who accidentally tips it over is burned. On the other hand, a product may be well designed but the *user* of it may be negligent in its use (or both). If you stick your head in the oven to see whether the roast is done, you are negligent in your use of the oven, and the manufacturer of the oven is not liable for your injury. But if you find a mouse in your Coca-Cola bottle, the company is liable for negligence. But how far should one go with this? Should the zoo have to put a sign on the alligator's jaw reading, "Caution—do not touch"? Should a person be able to sue the farmer because she had an allergic reaction when she ate his strawberries? Should the manufacturer of a water-slide be cited for negligence because he failed to place a warning

sign on the slide (for instance, because one out of a million users sustains a neck injury while sliding rapidly into shallow water)? In such cases, surely, it is the user who is at fault.

There are many borderline cases. (1) Suppose an employee is filling boxes with Coca-Cola bottles and disregards instructions; he handles the bottles by their necks, and a bottle explodes and injures him. Is it the employee's fault, or the manufacturer's? Ordinarily we would say it is the employee's fault for disregarding instructions; in fact, however, the company is usually found liable, not out of considerations of justice but (what is believed to be) utility—the company has the "deepest pockets" and is best able to pay. (2) A woman buys a weed killer containing arsenic (there are warnings with skulls-and-crossbones on the bottle) with which she kills weeds on her lawn. Several days later, having forgotten the incident, she decides to lie down on her lawn and get a tan; she becomes ill because her skin absorbs the leftover weedkiller. Who do *you* think is negligent? (3) A person buys a frying pan whose handle breaks when she uses it; but it is marked "Factory Second." Does this exonerate the manufacturer? (4) Should someone who slips and falls and is stabbed in the heart by a pencil he is carrying in his shirt pocket be able to recover against the pencil manufacturer? Common sense may say no, but courts sometimes say yes. (5) A plastic champagne cork flies out of a bottle when the restraining wire is partially loosened and hits the person opening it in the eye, causing loss of vision in that eye. Should the bottle contain a warning label, or should it be left to the "common sense" of the user that opening a bottle whose cork is facing you may be dangerous?[18]

Much depends in these cases (1) on how *useful* the object is (if there were as many fatal accidents with Tinker Toys as with cars, it may

---

[18]Some of these examples are taken from Arthur Miller, *Miller's Court* (Boston: Houghton Mifflin, 1982).

be that Tinker Toys would long since have been banned), but cars are of very high utility; (2) on how *dangerous* it is (standards of negligence in fumigating and in electrical wiring are very high); as well as (3) how liable the object is to *misuse*. (There must also be a causal connection between the product and its use: A car manufacturer is liable for selling a defective car, but it is not liable if the car breaks down on the road and the buyer is mugged while waiting for a tow truck.) But there is no unanimity on when a person (or a company) has failed to take "reasonable care."

Many students of the law are dissatisfied with exonerating a person who is innocent of negligence. Someone has been injured or her property damaged, and—even if the other party is not negligent—isn't it better that he pay for the damage than that the injured person be left without compensation? Thus, there has been a gradual transition in the law from negligence to *strict liability;* you are liable for the damage if you in any way caused it, even if your act was unintentional and even if you were not negligent in so doing. Accidentally stepping on someone's toe in a crowded department store may not be negligent on your part; yet you can be sued for it. In strict liability, you are found guilty if there was any causal relation between you and the injury, even though your act was neither intentional nor negligent. A person may take extraordinary precautions and still find himself at the receiving end of a lawsuit; he is *strictly liable* for the damage.

Here are a few examples of strict liability laws: (1) A merchant ships some corrosive liquid from New York City to Albany, reasonably believing that its route will be entirely through New York state. But the shipment is made over the George Washington Bridge through New Jersey, thus placing it under the interstate commerce regulations, which prohibit such shipments without a permit; he is fined. (2) A bartender serves a customer a drink, first examining the man's birth certificate to make sure he is over 21, as required by law. But the birth certificate is a cleverly forged one, and the customer is only 20. The bar owner can have his license revoked even though he was not negligent and reasonably believed the customer was over 21. (3) A woman remarries because her husband has been gone for 5 years and many people have reported to her that he is dead. She quite reasonably believes he is. But he shows up again, and she is guilty of bigamy, that is, of having more than one husband at one time; her reasonable belief to the contrary is no legal excuse. (4) A man elopes with a girl who appears to him—and to everyone else—to be of legal age; in fact she is under age, and he is guilty of statutory rape. The fact that he reasonably believed that she was a legal adult makes no difference. (5) A man reasonably believes that confidentiality laws between patient and physician which protect him in California also protect him in Arkansas; but Arkansas has no such statute, and he is not excused for failure to know this. (6) A pharmacist sells a bottle of medicine over the counter, not knowing that it is no longer legal to do this: A law was passed last month making the substance obtainable by prescription only. But the pharmacist has been sick in the hospital for the last month and didn't know of the change in the law, nor had time to find out about it, yet he is held strictly liable for his offense.

Strict liability often goes counter to utility. A fumigator who is liable for all damages, whether or not they are his fault, may decide to leave the profession, as many physicians do when they have to pay $100,000 and more a year for malpractice insurance (to cover the costs of damage suits in which the physician may not be at fault). But apart from utility, strict liability may be unjust, in that it requires a person to pay for damages and injuries which were neither intentionally caused nor the result of negligence.

Strict liability has evoked strong moral opposition. "If I took all reasonable care, in fact possibly extraordinary care, why should I be held liable? What more could I have done than my best? 'Ought implies can,' and I couldn't have been more careful than I was; yet by the law of strict liability I am held liable. That isn't fair!" That is a plausible contention by the defendant in the case. But a different case is made by the plaintiff: "I suffered injury, and even though the person who caused it didn't intend it, and even though she was careful and not negligent, I still was injured, so I should receive damages. My back was injured in the accident, though I realize the driver had to stop suddenly to avoid hitting a truck whose brakes had suddenly given out." Strict liability is a fair policy as seen from the point of view of the person injured. The two are on a collision course: It doesn't seem possible in every case to be fair to the involuntary injurer and *also* to the injured. This legal issue is, as usual, based on moral considerations. To penalize A who was not at fault doesn't seem fair or just to A; not to penalize A doesn't seem fair to B who sustained the injuries. There is no way in which both A's and B's demands can be met, and if both have valid claims, justice cannot be done to both parties.

Reasonable belief. Should a case be decided by what *was* in fact the case? or by what the person *believed* to be the case? or by what the person *reasonably* believed to be the case? Strict liability says: "You did it—what you thought or believed doesn't matter." This position seems morally unjust, however: Why should you be liable for what you couldn't help? Suppose someone says, "It's what *I believed* that counts—and I believed that the stranger I killed was a devil." Yet this doesn't seem satisfactory: People believe the strangest and craziest things, often with no evidence whatsoever. "I must have been hallucinating, but I thought it was my wife—and in this state sexually assaulting your wife isn't rape; so you

should let me go." But, says the court, this man's belief is not a *reasonable* belief. Ordinarily it is what one reasonably believes that decides the issue. Thus, (1) a man does not know that the drink he offers his wife has been poisoned; he reasonably believes it is just a martini and has no reason to think anything else; and the case is decided (he is declared innocent) on the basis that his belief was reasonable under the circumstances. (2) A conductor on a train is innocent of any offense after he ejected a passenger from the train if he reasonably believed the passenger hadn't paid her fare (she couldn't find her ticket). (3) A man kills another in the honest and reasonable but mistaken belief that it was necessary to preserve his own life; he is not guilty of murder. (4) A police officer may shoot a suspect if she reasonably believes that her life is threatened by the suspect's gun which is pointed at her.

In a famous British case, a man invited his friends at the club to have intercourse with his wife. "She'll pretend to resist," he warned them, "but it's only a pretense. She'll scream and kick and object loudly, but with her that's all part of the act. She loves to be forcibly attacked. So, have fun, be my guest." His four clubmates took him at his word; she did scream and resist, but they remembered what the husband had said and they all had intercourse with her anyway. The next day she charged them all with rape. The case went to the highest court in England, the House of Lords, and the House of Lords exonerated the men on the ground that, under the circumstances, they "reasonably believed" that she was a willing accomplice and therefore that they were not guilty of rape. The decision, which came to be known as the Morgan Rule, was extensively criticized in the papers as "the rapists' charter." It was only later that the Morgan Rule was reversed: The House of Lords reconsidered the matter and decided that rape is by definition sexual intercourse with an unwilling partner. This is in fact what had occurred, and the men's belief, however reasonable under the circumstances, had nothing to do with it. And thus the rapists' charter came to an end—and with it the view, in this case at least, that "reasonable belief is enough."[19]

Sometimes reasonable belief is sufficient, sometimes it is not. There may be no single underlying principle to account for the difference, but several considerations are relevant. (1) Sometimes the court feels that the matter is of such vital importance that no excuse of ignorance or mistake, even reasonable ones, should suffice. If the court believes that a woman should not have two husbands or one man two wives, then if that occurs it is automatically a crime; permitting excuses would only "weaken the law." (2) Sometimes, if the court permitted the excuse, there would be no practical limits to violation of the law. If the bar owner could plead, "But he *had* a birth certificate that said he was 21," or the eloper could say, "But she *looked* over 18," then virtually anyone could be let off. Even if the girl was under 15, he could always say that she looked over 18 *to him,* and who could deny it? (3) For the reasons already indicated on pp. 369–70, the court cannot permit ignorance of the law to constitute an excuse; if it did, everyone could plead ignorance. Thus, even though all laws of your state and nation would take lifetimes to read, if you violate one you are held responsible for the violation. Here there is a clear tension between morality ("Ought implies can—and I *can't* read all the law") and the law (the law cannot render itself impotent).

Generalizations in science often are true; but generalizations in law seldom are. Each generalization has a certain kind of case in mind, and may be rejected beyond the limited range of those cases. Hence the frustrating failure to find general rules in law: Each

one seems vulnerable to convincing counter-examples. Yet the study of law is of immense importance to ethics—not only for the great opportunities it affords to clarify our concepts (coercion, negligence, insanity, etc.) through careful philosophical analysis, but also for the great range of actual cases of human action which it requires us to consider, not merely as cases to be subsumed under general rules, but as examples of human action in all their uniqueness and individuality, challenging and baffling our best attempts to generalize from them.

Even when the law professes allegiance to a certain rule, the cases that fall under the rule can yield conflicting verdicts. On the one hand there is a diverse group of rules held with varying degrees of conviction; on the other hand there are particular cases, each one of which may be relevantly different from the next. The law attempts to produce a "fit" between the one and the other. But so numerous are the relevant differences among the cases that such perfect fits are seldom found.

4. ETHICS AND SOCIETY

Unless you are Robinson Crusoe alone on an island, there is no choice but to live in some society or other. What kind of society is best? No single kind of society is likely to suit everyone, but may there not be certain kinds of societies at which we should aim, and others we should do all we can to avoid? Even an ethical nihilist—who considers no value judgment to be preferable to any other—is likely in practice to consider one preferable to another, to work for or against one or another. Various kinds of societies have been set forth as ideal, and in surveying them we encounter a mix of various concepts: freedom, happiness, justice, rights. By surveying them we shall see how the emphasis shifts from one to another as various ideals of social organization are set forth.

Let us begin with specific types of legisla-

---

[19]E. M. Curley, *op. cit.*

tion which have been favored by some and strongly opposed by others. We shall consider only a small sample of the many proposals under the heading, "What kinds of laws should there be?" We shall not attempt to solve these problems—they involve complex issues that remain in constant dispute—but to give some indication of the *reasons* given for defending or opposing them.

Social Issues and the Law

1. *Euthanasia* (mercy-killing) is a controversial issue on which a variety of moral concepts have been employed. A dialogue on it might proceed as follows:

A. I want euthanasia legalized for egoistic reasons. If I were to become incurably ill, I would want to be put out of my misery.

B. Yes, but not everyone would; some persons want to hang on to life even though they are in great pain ("When there's life there's hope"). They would see the legalization of euthanasia as a threat. If euthanasia were legalized, the legalization would apply to everyone, including those who don't want it. Those persons would *oppose* it for egoistic reasons. If two egoists disagree on a policy which must be adopted for everyone or rejected for everyone, what is to be done? That's the problem with egoism; unless agreement can be reached, it is helpless to deal with matters of social policy.

A. Can't we assume at least that pain is an evil—at least pain that leads to no positive good? If your dog is enduring great pain from an incurable injury, it would be an act of mercy on your part to put the animal painlessly to sleep; you don't care much for your dog if you won't at least do that for him. Exactly the same consideration applies to human beings who are terminally ill; to keep them alive would be cruel and pointless.

B. Now you are speaking as a utilitarian. Very well, but there is a difference. Human beings can give their consent or withhold it. To kill a person, however ill, without that person's consent would be murder. The dog of course can't give its consent, or withhold it either; he depends on you to do your best for him.

A. True, people can consent and dogs can't; so let's say people must first consent. But when must the consent take place? A very ill person may no longer be able to give consent. Or she may give consent at one moment and withold it at another. Should you take what she says during a moment of discouragement that may soon pass, and use that as an excuse for getting her out of the way? Then greedy relatives would hover about waiting for that weak moment, so as to collect the inheritance early.

B. That could be taken caré of by having the patient sign a notarized form in advance, preferably even before becoming ill, and witnessed by three or more physicians, saying that if she should ever become terminally ill a lethal shot can be administered.

B. What if she changes her mind after she becomes ill, and is no longer physically able to communicate to others this change of mind?

A. That is a risk, to be sure—not a great one, because there's usually *some* way for a person to communicate. But it's preferable to a condition of needless suffering that can't be ended because anyone who tries to do the merciful thing faces a murder charge. Put in all the safeguards that you like, but at least make it possible for people to end their own misery.

A. I suspect that if this became a general policy, patients would be afraid to go to the hospital, fearing that they would be silently killed while they were there.

B. Not if the safeguards were present and enforced. Instead of dread, they might well feel relief, that if their suffering became too great there is a legal way to end it.

C. I think you are both mistaken. Every person has a right to his or her life, and this implies at least that this life cannot be taken away by others.

A. The right involved is not to be killed (or harmed, etc.) *without* the person's consent. You can surrender your right to your possessions by voluntarily giving them away. In exactly the same way you can surrender your right to life. If you want to give it up, no one *else* has the right to insist that you must hang on to it. Your life is not the property of others, so it is not for them to say when you should give it up. Even if you have a chance of recovering, you still have every right to say, with Marcus Aurelius, "The room is smoky, so I leave it."

2. The main reason why *abortion* remains so intractable an issue is that it appears to involve a direct conflict of rights. The mother has a right to her life; but the unborn baby also has a right to its life. If the mother has a right to the use of her own body, and thus a right to abort a fetus, what happens to the right of the unborn child? The conflict is particularly harrowing when the fetus' existence imperils the mother's life. The two main positions are: (1) abortion is wrong (except perhaps when the mother would die if an abortion were not performed); and (2) whether to have an abortion is entirely the choice of the mother, because (a) she is the owner of her own body and (b) the fetus is not a human being until it can exist independently of the mother.

The crucial issue, however, is when the fetus is to be counted as a human being: after the first trimester of pregnancy, or as soon as it exhibits brain waves, or movement, or response to injury, or even as soon as it is conceived? There seems to be no way to settle this last controversy, since it all depends on how one defines "human being." Arguments, more emotional than rational, rage around the question of when the fetus becomes a human being, even after all the relevant facts of

biology are known to both parties. At whatever point the fetus becomes a human being, at that point abortion is the deliberate taking of human life. But no recital of biological facts has succeeded in resolving this issue. What seems called for is a *stipulation* as to when human life begins. But a stipulation, of course, is neither true nor false; and a stipulation that is adopted by some may be rejected by others.

3. A child is born so disabled that its prospects for life are very dim, and its prospects for any "quality of life" are nil. The child can no more respond to the question "Do you want continued life under these circumstances?" than can a dog. Suppose the child is born blind, deaf, and totally disabled. It is already born, so there is no question of abortion—though there would be a question if it had been a fetus that seemed likely to produce a malformed birth. Here the question would be whether (1) to administer a painless death shortly after birth (active euthanasia); or (2) simply to let the malformed infant die through lack of nourishment (passive euthanasia); or (3) to keep it alive at all costs, regardless of the price in future pain and misery.

If one insists that *all* human beings have a right to life, and rights always override utility, then no further controversy arises: It should be kept alive—though it is still a question whether "extraordinary means" should be employed to do this, such as being constantly attached to an IV machine. One might well ask, however, what the chances are for such a baby's future well-being, as well as the well-being of parents and siblings: What if this baby's care consumed most of the waking hours of parents who already have other children, and would mean that the other children would suffer inattention and neglect, and possibly poverty, as a result of keeping the disabled child alive? Must the infant's right to life outweigh the right of the other children to a "decent *quality* of life"?

4. Consider a different social issue, *gun control*. Many arguments have been advanced

in its favor: (1) If no guns were available, fewer people would be killed in family quarrels and accidental shootings. (2) The majority of householders who use guns on intruders become victims of those same guns—thus the guns don't really protect them. (3) If guns were confiscated they would gradually disappear from circulation. All of these are undoubtedly good utilitarian considerations, designed to increase human happiness.

But against these arguments are others: (1) The guns would only go underground; criminals and the Mafia can usually obtain weapons anyway; the householder, forbidden to own one, would be a disarmed victim, unable to defend himself against a lethal weapon. (2) When it is known that the householder has a gun, as in Switzerland, fewer armed robbers think twice before attempting a crime. (3) When government itself is oppressive, guns provide the only defense against it. Thus, as usual, utilitarian considerations can be used to support both sides of the issue.

But now another argument is presented, based on rights. Don't we have a *right* to defend ourselves? The second amendment to the Constitution guarantees us the legal right to self-defense; have we not a moral right to this as well? And doesn't this transcend any considerations of utility?

However, it is far from clear what form that right should take. Does it entitle a person to own a machine gun? a bomb? a Saturday night special? only a butcher knife? Would the gun-control enthusiast ban butcher knives, even though they are needed in the kitchen? What if you have no weapon but practice karate and can kill an aggressor by knowing just what pressure-points to touch? If guns were prohibited, wouldn't you be subject to other kinds of attacks?

Many empirical facts can be used to support one position, and many to support another—and most people cite only the facts and statistics that support their own case. Moreover, even if *all* the relevant empirical facts were agreed upon by both sides, there would still be disagreement on which policy to pursue. Different people have different ideals; they interpret the same facts differently; and once people have developed a "mental set" in favor of a certain position, it gradually assumes the status of an a priori assumption, becoming virtually immune to refutation.

5. Should the law permit you to say or print whatever you want whenever you want (*freedom of speech*)? Utilitarians will say, "Freedom of speech should be permitted when permitting it maximizes happiness." And as a rule it will; one of the first acts performed by a police state is to censor speech and the press, and prohibit the dissemination of ideas contrary to that of the government. Take any example you like of such a nation and you will see that the people are oppressed, fearful, and in general less happy than they would be if these freedoms were granted. The First Amendment to the Constitution specifies that Congress may pass no laws "abridging the freedom of speech or of the press." Not only is freedom of speech—in general—in accord with utility, but we also speak of the *right* to freedom of speech as among our most basic rights. Human beings are not only rational animals as Aristotle said (capable of reason, though not necessarily always using it) but are also *volitional* animals: they are creatures who deliberate, choose, and act upon their choices. To take away freedom of speech would be to inhibit one of the most basic capacities that makes us distinctively human. To be forced to endure imprisonment or death for saying "the wrong thing" is one of the most dehumanizing situations human beings can endure. Human beings cannot live like animals, passively refraining from making decisions: and informed decisions require free exchange of information and opinion. Freedom of speech, then, seems to be a clear example of rights and utility being in accord.

Yet both common morality and the Constitution as interpreted by the courts have placed limits on the right to freedom of speech. (1) You are not permitted to make false and malicious statements about others; this is the law of defamation (libel and slander). If people could say or write whatever falsehoods they liked about you, causing you to lose your job and your reputation, the loss to you would be greater than the loss to freedom of speech on the part of the malicious gossips. Thus a utilitarian would probably approve such laws. But do you have a *right* to your reputation? Your character is what you are; your reputation is what other people think you are. Your reputation is not really your possession, is it? Can you really say you have a right to it? Don't others have a right to think and speak as they like of you? From the standpoint of rights, it is not so clear that this limitation on freedom of speech is justified. (2) You are not permitted to write words or display pictures which are judged "obscene." This is a sore point on which many volumes have been written. The utilitarian case is utterly divided, partly because the empirical data are incomplete. Whether pornography harms children, for example, remains a hotly disputed issue; and as for adults, the moralists who would ban it are countered by others who say that it is a "social safety-valve" which prevents sexual crimes like rape rather than causing them. Utility aside, one may claim the ability to buy literature of any kind, including pornography (in words and pictures), as a right. (3) Should one be permitted to speak in such a way as to incite others to crime? The law takes a dim view of such incitement. If the speaker says "Burn the place down!" to an angry mob, this act of speech may cause them to set a whole city block on fire—which would be contrary to utility, since far more harm than benefit would result. On the other hand, one could quite plausibly say that acts of speech alone do not cause burning buildings; each person is a voluntary agent, and it is his or her decision whether to participate in the arson. Thus only those who actually commit the deeds (not

those who merely emit words) should be held liable. The same goes for conspiracy: To conspire to commit a crime is itself (legally) a crime, but one of the parties is free not to assent to the conspiracy: If others rob the store it is their deed, not that of the person who suggested it or told them how to do it.

The issue of freedom of speech is bound up with an important related issue, that of property rights. You can be arrested for shouting "Fire!" falsely in a crowded theater (to take the standard example). But why shouldn't you be free to do this? Because people might be trampled to death in the scuffle, utilitarians say; the restriction on freedom is less harmful than the loss of life. But the argument from rights is quite different: The owner of the theater has certain rights over his property; he permits you to enter his property under certain conditions—that you watch the film or concert quietly, so as not to disturb others; that you not shout or write graffiti on the walls or spit on the floor; and so on. If it's his property, he has the right to make this condition, and if you do not abide by the agreement he has the right to throw you out. It's not so much a freedom of speech issue as a property-rights issue. For the same reason, you should not be permitted to shout obscenities in a cathedral, or to become drunk and destructive at someone else's party.

6. *Property rights.* Why is *property* important? Because without being able to control some portion of your environment, you cannot sustain your life. Since we cannot live as incorporeal spirits, but must gain food and shelter in the physical world, we must have a right to protect that portion of it on which we depend. If you own or rent a house or apartment, you should be permitted to reject unwelcome visitors. If a horde of people come along and occupy your kitchen and bedroom, saying, "It belongs to all mankind," you can eject them too; it is *your* apartment, you paid for it, your possessions are in it, and others are violating your rights by being there. (Utili-

tarians would add: It would also be utter chaos if everyone who wished could cook in your kitchen or sleep in your bedroom.) If you plant a garden, you must be free from trespassers and vandals who would trample on the plants and steal the harvest as soon as it was ripe. It was you who planted the seeds and nourished the crops, and by right the harvest is yours—you worked to make it possible—and it does not belong to those who did not.

Yet, as everywhere in applied ethics, it is difficult to stake out clear boundaries. Should you be permitted to put up a fence around your yard? Of course. An electrified fence? No, because this would endanger others; those who touched it would be killed. Should you be permitted to lure people in from the street, kill them, and bury them in the basement? Of course not, for this would violate their right to life. (A consequence of this would be that "no trespassing" laws cannot apply to police officers who have reason to believe a crime has been committed and might want to check your basement.) One limitation on property rights is that you cannot use your property in such a way as to do harm to others. You cannot build a factory with smokestacks emitting noxious smoke into the air, polluting the atmosphere and endangering your neighbor's health. You cannot throw garbage from your windows onto the front lawn, causing a rat problem in the neighborhood, or raise pigs in your back yard (at least in the city, where neighbors would have to endure the stench).

Perhaps you do things that don't really harm others but only *inconvenience* them, such as building a structure on your vacant lot which obscures your neighbor's view, or painting your house a color others find repellent. Is it your right to do these things? Yes, unless you've agreed not to: If you were prohibited from doing anything that merely inconvenienced others, there might be no limit to the prohibitions—depending on your neighbors. People might feel inconvenienced by the fact that you drove into and out of your driveway once a day, or by the sound of your normal voice. Or perhaps you do things that don't harm your neighbors but *offend* them—such as nude sunbathing in your back yard? Perhaps you have your radio turned on fairly loud at 10 P.M. and disturb your neighbors who go to bed at sunset. The line between harming them and inconveniencing them or offending them is not always easy to draw. Different jurisdictions draw it at very different places. Ordinarily you are allowed a "reasonable noise level," except at night when the rule is more stringent because most people sleep then. If your constant use of a water sprinkler reduces the water pressure in your neighbors' house, is that harming them or merely inconveniencing them? The lines here are far from sharp. A simple appeal to "property rights" will not solve it. And the appeal to utility, as usual, is inconclusive because no one may know whether the positive consequences outweigh the negative ones.

You have no right to violate the rights of others; for this reason you may not use your property in such a way as to interfere with others' exercise of *their* rights. Thus you, upstream, may not pollute the waters on which they, downstream, depend for drinking. But now the problems multiply as we get beyond the neighborhood level and turn to large regions of the earth. Far up in the Himalayas, the inhabitants of Nepal have left forests undisturbed for generations; but now, with industrialization, expanding population, more roads and homes and factories, forests are being cut down. Don't the Nepalese have a right to cut them down—it's their property, isn't it? But consider some of the consequences. Without forests, heavy rains in the monsoon season rush down slopes, carrying precious soil with them, and cause huge floods in the rivers of India followed by droughts on parched lands which no longer contain enough good soil to sustain agriculture. Aren't the Nepalese using their land in such a way as to harm others? Aren't Brazilians, by cutting down the

Amazon rain-forest to make way for "civilization," changing an entire eco-system, bringing about future deserts in other regions which have depended for their rainfall on the Amazon basin? Yet, don't the Brazilians have a right to cut down the forests if they want to? (One could argue of course that it isn't the Brazilians' land but that of the native Indians, who are being displaced by industrialization. This raises questions of original *title* to land which are too detailed to enter into here.) Without industry the increasing population of the earth will be more and more poor and unemployed; industry provides them jobs and articles that can be mass-produced cheaply, plus many they never had before. As world population grows, more technology is required to sustain it. At the same time, human interference with nature at one place may make living off the land impossible in other regions. How can people use any land at all and be quite sure that they are not harming someone, somewhere? Ecologists have long insisted that every part of the earth is interdependent with every other.

With sufficient technological advances, the earth could probably sustain a greater population than it now has. Whether we like it or not, the increase is occurring apace. The rise of population cannot be sustained above a starvation level without greater production of food, shelter, and other items—and these require more technology to make possible greater production from the amount of usable land that exists. Yet with the growth of technology comes land deforestation, diminishing water supplies, the turning of topsoil into wind-blown desert as more people try to eke a living from an increasingly hostile earth.

To many people it seems that the only solution is the one adopted in China, strict population control. "Better to have fewer people born and have them live comfortably, than to have twice as many living at starvation level." This might well be the solution adopted by utilitarians; it might not maximize the total *amount* of happiness, but it would raise the *average*—the amount available to each person. Yet population control is something that interferes with one of the most treasured and intimate aspects of human existence—the raising of children. "One of our basic rights is to have children, as we choose, without outside control. If the law requires us to have no more than one or two children, this is about as serious an interference of the law with our lives as there could be." If we insist on this as a right, and if we agree that *voluntary* limitation of childbirths has approximately a zero likelihood of succeeding (the peasant wants his sons to succeed him on his land and help him in his old age), then the future of the earth's population may be miserable indeed. Isn't claiming the right of unlimited reproduction in effect claiming that one has a right to harm others? Rights are rooted in human needs and geared to the fulfillment of those needs; but if unlimited reproduction is a right, doesn't that imply a right to *frustrate* human needs by making a vastly expanded population try to live on more than the earth can produce to sustain them? Do rights *always* trump utility? Or are we mistaken that the alleged right of reproduction is a genuine right? Or is it a prima facie right, like Ross' prima facie duties—a right unless there are sufficient countervailing conditions?

7. The problem becomes yet more complicated when one includes not only human beings but the *treatment of animals*. The expansion of the human race over the earth has caused the destruction of most of its animal life; entire species are becoming extinct at an increasing rate. Here is as clear a case as one could find of "either-or": Animal species cannot continue to exist and flourish as they did for thousands of years if human beings greatly increase in numbers and try to meet their own needs. Where buffalo once roamed there are farms, fences, a whole array of conditions incompatible with the necessities of life for buffalo, so that they are now confined

virtually to a few national parks. The eagle is a treasured national symbol, though vastly decreased in numbers, but to the farmer whose chickens are eaten by the eagles they are pests and threats to his livelihood. In central and southern Africa, where millions of animals once grazed, only small regions remain where people have left them alone. The demands of an increased human population render these regions smaller each day. Lions and giraffes, already limited to ever-smaller areas, now encounter fences between their hunting and grazing areas and the water they need to survive; the fences stop them, and they die. But people want the fences in order to mark off their property lines, for they raise cattle where once the antelope roamed, and the sale of beef is more profitable on the international market than the sale of venison. These people choose to grow imported cattle on their own land; isn't that a part of their property right? But now we confront not only our first problem—that many uses of one's property may inadvertently harm others—but a second problem: that the animals who have roamed this land for generations seem doomed to gradual death and extinction. Don't animals have rights too?

On this controversial question several positions have been taken. The first is that human beings are the only species that counts—only human beings have rights, and it is only the well-being of human beings that should be considered. This conviction is based to a large extent on the biblical dictum that the animals were placed on earth for use by human beings. But animals as well as human beings can suffer injury and pain, and can also be happy, or at least content—they can enjoy such well-being as befits their own species, just as human beings can have the kind of well-being that befits the human species. If racism is to be deplored, why not also "species-ism"? But animals cannot speak to present their case.

Thus we are led to the second position, that animals too count—they must be included in our calculation of consequences. Cruelty to animals—trapping them, killing them, clubbing baby seals to obtain their hides, and so on—is morally wrong, utilitarians would argue, just as the deliberate torture and killing of human beings is wrong. Most champions of animal preservation have taken this position.

But another and still stronger position has also been taken: that animals have rights as well as human beings. Animals are not moral *agents* (they do not make moral choices), but they are moral *patients*—they can be mistreated and killed, which is a violation of their rights as sentient beings as much as it would be a violation of human rights to mistreat and kill a person. Now, it may well be that human beings (at least most human beings) are repositories of greater value than animals are, so that if a bear or poisonous snake threatens your life, it is permissible to kill the threatening animal. Nevertheless, an animal has a right to live, just as you do. Cattle and pigs should not be raised for slaughter, not only because of inhuman conditions in slaughterhouses (a flaw that utilitarians point out), but because animals are living sentient beings whose rights you are violating by killing. The final consequence of accepting this view is that one may not eat meat of any kind, or kill animals for their hides, or use animals as experimental guinea-pigs in medical laboratories.[20] If rights are extended to include animals, the changes required in the habits and lifestyles of human beings would be enormous.

There are few issues in ethics on which controversy remains so rife as this one. In many issues, once the facts of the case are clear to everyone, agreement is reached. But on this case, even if all the participants to the argument knew all the facts about slaughterhouses and crowded conditions in which fowl are raised for market, and that animals can die in

---

[20]See Tom Regan, *The Case for Animal Rights* (Berkeley: University of California Press, 1983). Stephen R. Clark, *The Moral Status of Animals* (Oxford: Clarendon Press, 1977); Peter Singer, *Animal Liberation* (New York: Avon Books, 1975).

pain just as people can, some would still say that *human* beings are justified in killing animals for food and others would not. The difference lies not so much in knowledge of the facts as in *appreciation* of them, a *feeling* for them. Even those utilitarians who object to cruelty to animals and wanton kiling of them would go only so far as to say that we have a duty not to be cruel to animals (a part of our general duty to maximize the happiness and minimize the pain and misery in the world), but not that animals have rights. The advocate of animal rights, however, insists that even if all cruelty to animals were avoided it would still be wrong to kill them painlessly because doing so would violate their right to life. Much of the difference in these positions doubtless arises from people's different degrees of *empathy:* Persons who champion animal rights try to put themselves imaginatively in place of suffering creatures, and consider how they would feel if they were victimized and their lives ebbing away as a wild creature's might. The advocates of animal rights interpret "Do unto others as you would have them do unto you" to include animals among those "others."

But don't animals kill with as much cruelty as people? Few animals in the wild attain old age, for they are eaten by predators or die of starvation, thirst, or disease (see pp. 308–10). But none of this is relevant to *human* action; the question is what human beings should do. And what human beings can do is not mistreat animals, not raise them in conditions leading to cruel treatment (growing them in crowded pens, etc.), and not kill them and violate their equal right to live, the same right human beings have. Such changes are likely to be brought about only by legislation.

The Role of the State

Once social policies are decided upon, they are usually implemented by the government of a nation; no one else has the power to enforce them. The state is the only institution that possesses a monopoly on the use of physical force within a defined geographical area. You cannot be arrested for refusing to buy a Ford but you can be arrested for disturbing the peace. All the policies discussed in the previous section, except in the very unlikely event of everyone voluntarily adhering to them, must be enforced by governments. One of the main questions of social ethics, then, has always been the proper nature and scope of government.

Most governments throughout history have been dictatorships by one person or a small group who impose their will on the entire population. Such governments are certainly inimical to *freedom;* people are forced to forego their own voluntary decisions and under threat of punishment to obey the edicts of the wielders of political power. Such governments are also inimical to *human rights:* If you have a right to life, liberty, and the pursuit of happiness, a totalitarian state constantly gets in the way of them; it tramples on them ruthlessly. It is also of rather low *utility:* Human misery is multiplied when people are slaves or vassals; moreover, the level of production necessary to decent standards of living declines when people are forbidden to pursue their own chosen professions and to trade the products of their labor in the marketplace. *Justice* is also unlikely to result when decisions are arrived at by the whim of a tyrant or his henchmen. Yet, apart from dictatorships, there is a diversity of opinion as to what kind of government is most desirable, largely because of differences over what is the proper function of government in the first place.

Democracy is the form of government almost universally advocated today. Even tyrannical governments advertise themselves as "people's democracies." Individuals can participate in government by voting, and this is one exercise of their freedom. When they can participate, they are more likely to be interested in what government does. Yet democracies have great shortcomings. The legislators who are elected are often more interested in their reelection than in their constituents' long-term well-being. And as for the voters, the ignorant, the short-sighted, the champions of special interests are so numerous that they usually out-vote the intelligent and fore-sighted, who have a much clearer idea of the long-term consequences of the measures the majority favors. Egged on by citizens who want more and more economic advantages from government, the legislators (who need their votes to be reelected) enact more and more legislation which appropriates money to various pressure groups. But people usually are as unwilling to pay higher taxes as they are willing to accept the subsidies; thus an in-creasing gap develops between what the gov-ernment spends and what it takes in. The na-tional debt increases, and finally, the only way legislators can think of financing these huge expenditures is to print more money (infla-tion), which leads to sharp increases in prices: Our wages no longer buy what they used to. Price controls are then enacted, making it il-legal to charge more than a specified amount for a product. But since producers can't af-ford to produce the product at that price, it is no longer produced, and the stores become emptied of supplies, and massive want and starvation ensue. This has happened in de-mocracies time and again, because the average citizen has no insight into economic cause-and-effect and gladly accepts benefits today, not realizing that they will bring disaster on him and his children tomorrow. Democracy thus becomes government "of the cattle, for the cattle, by the cattle." Plato said that in a democracy any fool can get elected who calls himself the people's friend—and he despised democracy, calling it mob rule, and recom-mended instead a rule of an educated elite.[21] But the educated elite would still rule the people without their consent, and Plato's so-lution could easily end up inhibiting freedom in as many ways as does democracy in prac-tice.

It is difficult to think of a satisfactory solu-tion. People's wants are conflicting, and there is no government that can possibly reconcile them all; yet government has the coercive power to rule them. Government is needed to try and punish people for killing and assault-ing one another and to repel invaders, and for this it must have the power of the gun. Yet it has used that power to kill and assault more people than private citizens have ever done. Government is empowered to punish theft, yet it has stolen from numberless persons to en-rich its rulers and to pursue its own ends, keeping the people in poverty and subjection.

A state of no-government was described by Thomas Hobbes (1588–1679) as a "state of nature." In a state of nature each person is his own defender, and his life is in constant jeopardy from assault by others; his life, said Hobbes, is "nasty, brutish, and short." For this reason humans need government, which has the power to keep order and punish those who disturb it. Government requires vast coercive power in order to do this effectively. Yet governments have usually exacted a high price for these services—taxes, death in wars, persecution of minorities, brainwashing through a state-run educational system, and inhibition of creative efforts, especially those devoted to criticizing the government itself. Many persons have been convinced that the cure (government) is worse than the disease (state of nature).

Anarchists believe that justice, rights, happiness, and freedom could all be better preserved if there were no government at all. People would band together voluntarily for their mutual protection, and those who wished to join no group would be on their own—they would pay fees to a "protection agency" and receive from it protection against theft or bodily harm. Anarchists would also establish courts in which to try offenders

---

[21]See Plato, *The Republic,* Book 8. Many editions.

against the peace, all without the existence of a government. Government typically acts slowly, ineffectively, wastefully, like a lumbering hippopotamus. Without this impediment people would be free to make their own provisions for their protection as they saw fit. There would be no Big Brother, no stifling bureaucracy, no unresponsive government agencies.

But the groups thus banding together would have to be imbued with very similar ideals, or else civil war could easily break out. Instead of one centrally governed nation, there would be a variety of vigilante groups, each protecting their own, each reaching out to arrest nonmembers who in their opinion had committed offenses against members. And what one group would call an offense might not be recognized as such by another group; an infringement of privacy or copyright might be considered an offense by group A, but group B might consider this quite innocent; thus, a member of group B would be outraged if he were dragged into A's courts and tried for what B did not count as a crime. There are many other problems as well; yet anarchists are convinced that "government itself is the problem." They see no way to keep limited government from becoming unlimited. They believe that only the eradication of this institution and the leaving of all actions now undertaken by government in the hands of voluntary associations, to make their own decisions as to defense and pollution and countless other issues, could possibly advance general utility and, most of all, the right of individuals to conduct their lives according to their own choices, rather than be subjected to the decisions of others.[22]

---

[22]See, for example, David Friedman, *The Machinery of Freedom* (Wesport, CT: Arlington House, 1978), pp. 157–158; John T. Sanders, *The Ethical Argument against Government* (Washington, DC: University Press of America, 1980); Murray Rothbard, *For a New Liberty* (New York: Macmillan, 1973).

An alternative to the dangers of unlimited government is a *constitutional republic,* which retains government but severly limits its powers. The United States is a constitutional republic in which the Constitution, especially the Bill of Rights, is devoted mainly to setting forth *limitations* on the powers of government, so that citizens can make their own choices as long as they do not violate others' rights in doing so. Government intervenes only when people violate one another's rights; government's function is to protect those rights and not to interfere in voluntary relationships among individuals. Thus, when the First Amendment prohibits any censorship of speech or press, it does not say "unless the majority says otherwise." People have this constitutional guarantee of freedom, protecting them from the whims of a majority which—inflamed by demagogues—attempts to suppress unpopular opinions. The laws government enacts will not please everyone, but at any rate the preservation of certain "unalienable rights" is guaranteed. The same applies to the right not to incriminate oneself, the right to equal protection under the laws, the right to counsel, and numerous other rights largely contained in the Bill of Rights (the first ten amendments to the constitution) and some of the later amendments.

The right to be secure in one's home and not to be subjected to arbitrary search and seizure—and similar provisions of the Constitution—are all attempts to protect individual *privacy* against government interference. The basis of this group of rights is the conviction that the dignity and well-being of each person depends on each retaining his or her own "private space." One aspect of this privacy is the institution of private property itself, already considered; another is simply the right not to have your "space" invaded. What you say to your attorney is entirely a matter between you and her, even if you confess a murder to her; what you say to your priest is similarly privileged; your medical records are (in most states) a private matter between you and your physician, which cannot be made public.

But again it is not easy to say where lines should be drawn. If you have a communicable disease, you are a threat to others. A report must be made of it, and you might even be quarantined so that others will not contract the disease. You may be required to testify in court if you have knowledge of a crime. If you are suspected of a crime, you may be the subject of electronic surveillance (such as wire-tapping) without your knowledge (though the right to do this has been vigorously contested). A neighbor may look at you through binoculars over her fence, but may not enter your premises or publish pictures of you without your consent. There are, however, large "gray areas" in privacy law, which indeed varies from state to state. May someone follow you continuously as you walk along the sidewalk, "shadowing" you? You may feel that your privacy is being compromised, yet hasn't the other person as much right to use the sidewalk as you? When something is news, it is considered "public property"—public knowledge of events is considered more important than your wish, for instance, to keep your wife's suicide out of the newspapers; yet if someone attempts to use the newspaper's picture of this event later on a poster or brochure, that person may be prosecuted for invasion of your privacy. Exactly what the limits are to privacy is hotly disputed. In a time when crime is rampant or terrorism threatens, privacy gives way more easily than in times of security. Yet the core idea is clear; those aspects of your life which you wish no one else to know about and which threaten no one else's health or safety, are things which you are entitled to keep to yourself. There is a constant tension between the public's alleged "right to know" and the right of individuals to keep their privacy intact. Once again, the person who comes at the issue from the standpoint of rights is often in disagreement with the person who considers it solely from the standpoint of utility.

One principal aim of the American constitutional republic was the preservation of rights; utility would occur only as a consequence of the preservation of rights. Each individual has the *right to perform* peaceable acts without interference (rights to engage in actions are called "active rights") and also the right *to be protected against* violations of those rights by others (these are called "passive rights" because they do not involve what you do but what others may not do to you).

The ideal of limited government—limited by the provisions of a constitution enforced by the courts—is protection against aggression by others; (1) the armed forces, to protect you against aggression from outside the nation; (2) the police, to protect you against aggression by other people within the nation; and (3) the courts, to adjudicate disputes in a peaceful manner, so that one need not (and may not) resort to violence when disputes arise. The state is a guardian of your rights, and a referee in adjudication. Its activities (according to this view) should be limited to the protection of individual rights.

However, not everyone agrees on what one's rights are; and here lies one of the central controversies about the proper function of government. The controversy revolves around the distinction between what are called *positive* rights and *negative* rights. A negative right—including all the rights we have discussed thus far—requires of others only a duty of *noninterference,* that is, a duty of forbearance; others may not fancy your lifestyle, but as long as you are peaceful they must exhibit forbearance of your eccentricities. You have the duty to refrain from harming passersby, but you do not have the positive duty to help them if they ask for it. But a positive right is one that requires a duty of positive action from others. If you loan someone $500 for a year, at the end of the year you have a right to the $500, which means that the borrower has a duty to perform a positive act—the return to you of the $500. But aside from rights and duties agreed upon by prior *con-*

tract, the question is whether there are other positive rights, particularly positive rights which should be legislated and enforced by the state.

Chief among these is the issue of *welfare.* Does a person in need have the right to material sustenance from others? If so, these others have not only a duty of forbearance but a positive duty to give a fraction of their income to those in need. A positive right requires from others a sacrifice much greater than a negative right imposes. And it raises a host of questions. Do others have a right to your help if they have done nothing to earn it? Do others have a right to a portion of your paycheck if you are unwilling to give it, or if you believe the money is ill-spent or that the government which collects it uses most of it to administer the program rather than to help the needy? Are all the so-called needy unavoidably so, or could they get jobs rather than choose to remain on welfare? And if they could but don't, should you still be forced to share your paycheck with them? In early America the needy were usually helped privately by neighbors and townspeople, and sometimes government welfare was instituted on a local level. Today, however, hundreds of billions of dollars are collected by the federal and state governments each year for purposes of welfare, making many wage-earners so deprived themselves that they are forced to close their businesses to pay for the assistance to others, sometimes ending up on welfare themselves. And thus the "poverty industry" in Washington is spawned, collecting increasing amounts each year and yet yielding less and less in genuine help for the poor, whose numbers increase dramatically in spite of the mushrooming tax money devoted to their assistance. In view of all this, many persons insist that such public support is not a right but a privilege, justified only when freely given by others but not when forced by the coercive power of the state.

On the other hand, many others insist that welfare is indeed a right (entailing the duty of others to give); how can people pursue their goals without food and shelter? The question then becomes, how much? Should it be half your wages each year, if that is what's required to provide satisfactory care for the helpless, diseased, or aged? Should one person receive half a million dollars' worth of medical care, paid for through the taxes of others, many of whom could not afford to pay for such care for themselves? As needs grow, the amounts of money required grow even faster, and finally so much must be surrendered through taxation that many persons who could otherwise survive without help can no longer do so, thus adding them as well to an already overburdened welfare system. What if the amount required for people's needs for food and medicine exceeds the amount that is available through a constantly decreasing tax base? Such unpleasant facts have led some nations, such as Great Britain, to limit severely the amount of money spent on the sick, for the coffers would dry up if everyone's life were saved regardless of the expense; thus, those who are already sick or aged are left to die rather than be a drain on the economy—a utility-limitation on the alleged right to medical care from others.

Justice versus Rights

Another view, however, holds that welfare and other forms of aid to the troubled or needy is a moral imperative, perhaps not as a right, but in the interests of *justice.* Justice on the individual level, as we saw, is the apportionment of reward, compensation, or punishment according to *desert.* One might take the position that *all* those who are poor (below a certain level) deserve to be helped; or one might say that only some of them do (those who buy drugs with their food stamps or spend their welfare checks to buy scotch instead of feeding their children do not). One would have to review every case individually to arrive at any conclusion about individual deserts—something no welfare bureaucracy is equipped to do, and something which in any case would be almost infinitely time-consuming and permeated with graft and inefficiency. It would be difficult to believe that all the poor are *deserving* poor, especially those who have job opportunities that they regularly refuse.

What can one say about the relations of one's just deserts to one's well-being in life? Most people (it would be said) don't deserve the bad luck that they encounter. A person who throws her money away foolishly may deserve the poverty that results; but more often she has bad luck through no fault of her own—she may be crippled or diseased, or she may not be able to obtain a job that can use her skills. The more fortunate members of society should then provide for her ill luck by giving part of their income to her (via taxation). On the other hand, most of the people who do prosper cannot be said to deserve (or at least fully deserve) the prosperity they enjoy. One person is born intelligent, another is not. One person has a fine voice and makes a fortune as a singer; another has no such voice and can't make it in that profession. But having a fine voice is a kind of genetic accident, a stroke of luck, for which he can claim no credit. He may take credit for cultivating his voice, for his years of training and self-discipline, but not for having it as a gift of nature. The person with a rich father does not deserve this windfall; it's a stroke of luck, not something he has accomplished. There is no doubt that people are born unequal, in strength, in talent, in endurance, in riches, in virtually everything.

If a person is born crippled or blind, this is not an injustice, since there is no one, save possibly God, who caused the person to be born blind; but (one may add) the person born more fortunate—not diseased or blind—does not deserve his good fortune either, it's simply a stroke of luck. Thus, it is said, society should attempt to equalize what was not equal by nature. This can't be done fully, of

course—most blind people can't be given sight even through extensive surgery, and unintelligent people can't be made smart. But neither should they be left to their own resources; they should be helped—financially at least—by those who are more fortunate. It would be treating them unjustly to do less. As an empirical statement, "All men are created equal" is simply false; but society can correct this situation and achieve, at least in part, what nature has failed to do.

Perhaps then an attempt should be made in the name of justice at least to give all persons equal *opportunities*. Giving each person equal *financial* opportunities would mean taking from some and giving to others (presumably via government) until all persons are financially equal. Many persons have recommended just such condition of total equality. But if it were brought about through the coercive machinery of government, inequality would break out again at once. Some would use up the money the first week; some the first day (and be starving a few days later); others would invest it to make more; others would start an enterprise (perhaps borrowing from others) until after a year they had doubled their money. Government would then be needed to impose equality again, taking from those who had been enterprising and giving it to those who had not. And if this continued, those who worked hard would soon realize that it would be taken away from them anyway and would stop working except for themselves and their families. Then the springs of production would dry up, and soon there would be little or nothing left to distribute, and the result would indeed be equality—equality of destitution.

Even if everyone were financially equal, more important inequalities would arise. Some persons have parents who gave them attention and love and trust, so that even if they were poor, qualities of character would be instilled in the children (self-esteem, integrity, determination) which would lead them out of poverty as soon as they could fend for themselves; and children of the rich often receive little love or attention, with the result that they waste their lives and their money and become poor in a fairly short time. But how is "society" to see to it that *that* kind of opportunity—which only a home environment can provide—is equalized? Should children of uncaring parents be taken away from those parents by force? Should they be taken to institutions, where conditions might well be worse than even with bad parents? The only way to equalize this kind of opportunity—far more important than financial—is to dispose of the institution of the family and place all children in the care of the state. Many utopians from Plato on have suggested this. But again, is not the cure worse than the disease? Would being taken away from parents and growing up in a state institution not deprive children of the individual warmth and attention that even indifferent parents provide? (And would they receive equality of treatment from even the state?) Would the equality not become again an equality of nothing—an equality of upbringing in conditions of emotional indifference, lack of individual attention, and (most ominous of all) of children transformed into obedient servants of the state, to do its bidding, including betraying one's own parents if they dared speak a word of criticism against the state that had turned the children into its obedient vassals?

Some approach to equality can be realized if one doesn't mind reducing its level. You can't make stupid people smart, but you can make smart people stupid with a brain operation. You can't make ugly men handsome, but you can make handsome ones ugly by giving them scars and so on, thus making everyone about equally unattractive. Still, though none of these egalitarian ideals can be realized completely, many people have considered it an ideal of society toward which we should all aim. "Everyone should be equal, economically and in every other way possible." If this

principle should require a police state to enforce (since otherwise inequality would break out again), it would (according to egalitarians) be worth the price.

What is desired, of course, is equality at a fairly high level—not equality of poverty or equality of miserable early environment. But how is this to be achieved? A society's standard of living depends on a fairly small number of enterprising people. People who *can* be enterprising and creative in finding ways to fulfill society's needs—such as inventing labor-saving devices, making machines do the work of muscles and releasing people from drudgery, and mass-producing them, thus making them less expensive and more likely to be available to all. But people must be *motivated* to use their natural enterprise to keep working hard and producing the goods that society needs. Few persons indeed will work overtime lifelong for little or no return. But giving them a return commensurate with their achievements—which may be very great—is directly at odds with egalitarianism, which requires that all people have an equal income regardless of whether they contribute anything to society's well-being at all. Is the lazy person to receive the same income as the enterprising one who remains industrious year after year when her neighbor—who spends his day fishing—receives the same income that she does? The practical problem with egalitarianism is that it is "against human nature." But there is an argument from justice as well; don't those who work hard and use their talents well deserve more than those who don't? And isn't the heavy hand of government coercion, which could be required to enforce this equality "against nature," such a great limitation on people's freedom as not to be worth the price of forced equalization? But justice thus conceived is quite different from justice as conceived by egalitarians.

Justice would exist, according to egalitarians, only in a state of complete equality: in a society of five people the distribution would be, let us say, 5-5-5-5-5. But other champions of justice say that some deserve more than others—since deserts are unequal, rewards should also be unequal. Some people are more hard-working, they exercise their talents to better effect, and so on; and if these people are not prohibited by government from rising to the level of their ability, the distribution might be 5-7-10-15-25. Here there is an inequality but a much higher standard of living. It all depends on what model of justice you adopt. And here there is a very basic difference in people's moral convictions. Some say that equality of distribution is so important that even comparative poverty is not too high a price to pay for it. Others—perhaps a larger number—hold that the unequal distribution, because a much higher standard of living results, is more desirable; this would probably be the utilitarian position, designed to maximize happiness. It would also be the rights-position, for any interference with a person's peaceful activities would be an abridgment of a person's own right of choice. In a nation with no government controls on production except for a few such as safety regulations, the level might reach 5-10-50-100-500. Even the poorest persons in the United States are better off than the vast mass of people (except ruling elites) in many poverty-stricken nations of the world—not because the United States has more natural resources but because there is an incentive to produce and trade, which creates markets for products of all kinds; and with competition limiting the prices that can be charged, consumers are free to choose from among the products available those they find are the best buys for the money. Thus the free economy creates wealth, but also inequality, and the ideals of freedom and equality are sharply at odds with one another.

An enormously influential work, John Rawls' *A Theory of Justice* (1971), has attempted to bridge the gap between enforced egalitarianism and the freedom of individuals to be rewarded for the use of their talents.[23] Rawls attempts to create a model of a "just society," one in which perhaps not every individual, but every *group* of persons represented in the society will not suffer injustice at the hands of anyone else. (To the extent that it is groups rather than individuals under discussion, it is called *social* justice.)

Perhaps the best way to introduce Rawls' main idea is to imagine that a group of people is about to arrive at a fertile but hitherto uninhabited island, and that we are there to form a society and set up a government. What kind of society and government should this be? Different people have different needs and desires, and there will be considerable differences of opinion. Each person may want to write the laws in such a way as to favor his or her interest group; labor would want pro-labor legislation; entrepreneurs would want a laissez-faire economy; those who considered themselves ablest would want to be in power; while others would not want to entrust power-seekers with this responsibility; women would want to be sure there is no sexist legislation; minority ethnic groups would want to make sure they were neither persecuted nor exploited; and so on. How could they all come to agreement?

To solve this problem, Rawls stipulates that they all cast their vote from behind a *veil of ignorance.* Imagine that no one knows what his or her position will be in the society—whether he or she will be rich or poor, laborer or manager, farmer or tradesman, physician or accountant. Nor does anyone know whether he or she will be old or young, male or female, white or black, brilliant or stupid. Everyone will be in total ignorance of his or her own future circumstances, and even of their own present talents (which might give a clue as to their future circumstances); imagine

---

[23] John Rawls, *A Theory of Justice* (Cambridge: Harvard University Press, 1971).

all memory traces of these things to be obliterated. Why is this done? In the interests of impartiality; no one will know in advance what his or her position in society will be, so no one will be inclined to look down on any one group, or legislate against it, lest he or she turn out to be a person in that group. Obviously no one will vote for slavery, lest he turn out to be a slave. No one will vote for anti-labor legislation, lest she turn out to be a laborer. No one wants to be a victim of the legislation he voted for. The veil of ignorance will require each person to look at the entire situation from the "God's-eye" point of view rather than from the point of view of any one person or group, with special interests and special desires that do not coincide with those of other persons or groups.

Clad now in the mantle of impartiality, will there be unanimous agreement on the kind of society and the kind of government they will favor? Rawls believes the answer is yes; there are certain fundamental principles of social organization on which all persons, from behind the veil of ignorance, can agree. Thus, each individual should have the maximum freedom of decision that is compatible with the equal freedom of everyone else. This principle is not inviolable, however, for like Ross' prima facie duties each can be overridden by sufficient pressure from one or more of the others. Each interacts with the others, often requiring a compromise. Considerable freedom, for example, may be sacrificed in deference to another ideal, equality of opportunity.

Rawls is not an egalitarian; but there are limits on what people may do, even if their activities are directed at their own peaceful self-improvement. They may not initiate any activities which would cause the poorest class in a society to become yet poorer. If it makes the poorest better off, the additional money a man may earn from his invention is permissible; but if it makes them worse off, it is not permissible. It would seem that a consequence of this is that if Henry Ford's invention made

the buggy-maker worse off, the invention of the automobile would have to be prohibited. It isn't entirely clear what examples would properly fall under this heading, but generally, anything (including one's own initiative and hard work) that causes one person to be better off should not make anyone else worse off (financially)—just as a person may not use his or her property in such a way as to harm someone else. This condition would place considerable prohibitions on entrepreneurs and inventors who designed new technological and medical improvements. The consequences of actions being as complex and varied as they are, *someone* would be likely to be worse off as the result of almost any innovation. One wonders to what extent the wheels of progress would grind to a halt if this requirement were followed.

Rawls' ideal government is a fairly advanced welfare state. Everyone from behind the veil of ignorance would vote for government aid to the poor and the disabled, since they might end up being in one of those categories and would, of course, want to be helped. If this turned out to drain a very large fraction of the income of workers, it would surely reduce the creative motivations of those with marketable ideas. A basketball player who could earn $100,000 on the free market because people would voluntarily come to see him play, would end up getting perhaps less that $50,000 because of taxation to help the needy. Businesses operating on a profit margin of 10 percent would have to close up shop and discharge their employees, because the profit margin would be more than eaten up by the taxes required for contributions to welfare. Thus, while freedom of speech and press would be preserved, economic freedom (freedom of production and trade) probably would be curtailed sharply by government in Rawls' ideal society. It would not be a fully egalitarian society, but the restraints on creative activity, especially in economic enterprises, would be considerable, and the economy might well remain stagnant, with large numbers of unemployed on the dole who *would* have been employed if the stores and factories did not have to pay such high taxes in order to remain in business. At any rate, there would be numerous restrictions on "capitalist acts between consenting adults."[24]

The voters casting their ballot from behind Rawls' veil of ignorance would seem to be operating from a "least risk" attitude. They would rather not risk being poor, and be guaranteed their government benefits, than to take a leap and risk being poor but also stand a better chance of becoming truly well off. But unanimity even from behind the veil of ignorance would seem unlikely because of the diversity of human temperaments. Some people are more risk-oriented than others; to some risk is a challenge, to others a source of dread. Entrepreneurs are risk-takers; they risk their savings on a new enterprise which will pay off well if it succeeds and bankrupt them if it fails—it all depends on whether people will want to buy their product, which can't easily be predicted in advance. But might not many persons, from behind the veil of ignorance, not knowing what their place in the future society might be, vote a somewhat riskier system into being? Might they not be willing to risk *not* being helped in case they became poor (because anticipated markets didn't develop, or because entrepreneurs didn't manage them right), as long as they would have a better chance to "make it big" if they succeeded? The challenge alone, not merely the money, might be enough to induce them to vote for "no interference in entrepreneurial activities"—by themselves or by others. Is it really true that all "rational persons" from behind a veil of ignorance would vote for the least-risk system rather than a greater-risk sys-

tem, especially in view of the higher standard of living that the second would permit? It is difficult to believe that human temperaments are sufficiently alike so that *all* persons, even from behind the veil of ignorance, would favor the same system. This is especially likely if people came to believe that virtually *everyone* would be better off in a society in which people were free to produce, to buy and sell, largely without crippling bureaucratic restrictions. Here again empirical facts might well make a difference to one's moral decision.

To some extent these differences could be diminished if everyone could come to agreement on the empirical facts relevant to the issues—for example, if it were realized that an honest business person—not one who lobbies in Washington for the taxpayers' money, for such a person is merely a legalized thief— helps everyone if he succeeds. He provides himself with profits (many of which are ploughed back into the business), his customers with a new product, and employees with jobs. Thus, the opposition of many to businesspeople of all kinds (especially those who fan the flames of "business vs. labor" conflicts) would cease or diminish; they would then realize that what curtails their prosperity is government itself, by confiscating a large percentage of their income, wasting most of it, and forcing most workers to work from January to April each year for the government rather than for themselves or for those whom they would voluntarily support. But in the business community government finds a convenient scapegoat for its wasteful activities and its bloated bureaucracy; government shifts the blame, and most of the people seem to accept the government story. Agreement on the empirical data, then, might eliminate needless misunderstanding and lead to agreement where disagreement and strife existed before.

But moral judgments, as we have seen, do

---

[24]A phrase in Robert Nozick's *Anarchy, State, and Utopia* (New York: Basic Books, 1974), written partly in reply to Rawls.

not follow from empirical facts alone; armed with the same set of facts, different people will still arrive at different moral conclusions. And this "human equation" will probably never be eliminated. People have different fundamental attitudes and extremely varying temperaments. Some, as we have seen, are challenged by risk, others are in mortal fear of it. Some people are drawn to the ideal of equality of condition at all costs, others want more than anything else to be released from the ball-and-chain of enforced equality and forge ahead for themselves, even if they should fail. Some insist on rights even at the expense of utility, some espouse utility even if it sometimes violates rights, and still others are engaged in the uncomfortable task of trying to reconcile the two on all occasions. Many social planners are so dedicated to "the greatest happiness of the greatest number" that they would deny happiness to some to grant it to a majority—or would deny it to the entire present generation in order to increase it in some indefinite future. Others are convinced that freedom to choose should come first, but that once freedom is maximized, the maximization of utility will invariably follow.

It is probably too much to expect that even well-informed people will come to agreement on moral and political ideals. But it may not be too much to expect that they will differ peacefully, and be open to rational argument rather than to take arms against those with whom they disagree. A tremendous amount of disagreement can be accommodated in a society in which open and uninhibited discussion is permitted and even encouraged. And the very fact of such permission and encouragement may well persuade them to approve, or even just to tolerate, a society in which such peaceful diversity is permitted, and to be grateful that they do not reside in that vast majority of nations in the world in which it is *not* permitted.

EXERCISES

1. If someone says, "Stealing is wrong" or "It's your duty not to steal," is it possible for you to state in other words exactly what the person is saying? Can you restate it *without* using moral language (such as "good," "bad," "duty," "right," "wrong," or other ethical terms)? Or are you talking merely about what you or other people disapprove?

2. In which cases would you say that the people are *disagreeing* with one another?

a. "I think pink is a lovely color." "I think it's ugly."

b. "I think ordinary courtesy is an important moral virtue." "I think it's just a matter of etiquette."

c. "She exhibits good taste in the way she sets up her living room for guests." "I think she has awful taste—no imagination at all."

d. "The service in that restaurant is awful." "I think it's good—slow, but good."

e. "I believe abortion is always wrong." "I wouldn't go so far: I would say that *for me* it's wrong and I would never do it; but I wouldn't say that it's wrong for everyone."

f. "I can't stand rock music—Bach's music is much better." "Maybe Bach's music is better, but I still can't stand it."

3. Would you consider the following matters of morality (right or wrong behavior) or matters of taste, etiquette, or something else that doesn't involve morality? Are you harming anyone when you do, or fail to do, these things?)

a. Being prompt at attending meetings.

b. Being courteous and polite.

c. Cheating at cards.

d. Punching your time clock at work early (before you've finished working).

e. Letting garbage accumulate in your yard.

f. Killing rats in your neighborhood.

g. Killing dogs in your neighborhood.

h. Regularly checking the brakes on your car.

i. Trampling on corpses.

j. Trampling on the flag.

k. Getting even with those who have injured you.

l. Lying to those who have told lies to you.

m. Eating human flesh.

n. Engaging in homosexual behavior.

4. Would you consider it an inviolable rule under *all* circumstances

a. Never to punish those known not to be guilty?

b. Always to provide a defendant a fair trial?

c. Never to make an arrest except for "probable cause"?

d. To allow everyone who wants to to walk the streets at any hour?

e. If two people are equally qualified for a job, to always hire the one from the minority ethnic group first?

f. Never to punish your neighbor's children?

g. Never to start a fight?

5. In what ways, if any, do you think the following moral rules should be amended?

a. Always keep your promises.

b. Never kill another human being.

c. Never steal from anyone.

d. Never do evil in the hope that good may come of it.

e. Always assume the other person has good intentions unless you have contrary evidence.

6. Do the following constitute (in your opinion) restrictions on your freedom?

a. You can't travel faster than light.

b. You can't square the circle.

c. You don't have wings to fly like a bird.

d. You have two swimming pools available for your use, but one of them is too hot to suit you and the other is too cold. What you want but can't get is a pool of some temperature in between.

e. Nobody is coercing you in any way, but you can't find work and you're hungry.

f. The company is retrenching to stay afloat, and you are given the choice of accepting lower wages or being dismissed.

g. A man decides to move to the desert, where he builds a house a digs a well, which provides water. Another man later moves nearby into the same desert, builds a house and digs a well, which provides water. But the second man soon runs out of water. He comes to the first man and says, "Give or sell me some water, or I'll have to move out of the desert." The first man refuses: "I don't know when I'll run out of water myself, and

in any case it's not for sale." Has he coerced the second man? restricted his freedom? Is anyone at fault?

7. (a) A strikes B a blow on the head and knocks him against a tree, which (being already weakened by a recent storm) falls on top of B and kills him; (b) A strikes B a blow on the head and knocks him against a tree; at the same moment lightning strikes the tree and kills B. Is A the cause of B's death in the first case but not the second? Any difference in degree of blame to A? If B is injured and on the way to the hospital, and lightning strikes the ambulance, is A guilty of murder?

8. If A intending B's death poisons B's food, and B eats it and dies, A is considered the cause of B's death. But if B knows A has poisoned the food and eats it anyway, B and not A is considered the cause of B's death. Why the difference? (Is the use of the word "cause" here the same as Mill's sense, discussed in Chapter 5?)

9. Should the following acts be counted as intentional? Why? Should they count as murder or attempted murder?

a. A intends to shoot B but by mistake kills C instead.

b. Some men dynamited a prison wall to get a prisoner out; but the prisoner was at a different place at that moment; other prisoners, however, were killed by the blast.

c. The natives offered to give the pilgrims to Mecca a boat ride across the Red Sea, for a fee; but after they collected the fee they dumped the pilgrims on an abandoned island inhabited only by large land-crabs, which ate the pilgrims. The natives were convicted of murder. But they didn't intend the pilgrim's death—or did they?

d. A person jumped out of a burning building, knowing the fall would kill him. Was it suicide? (The Catholic Church doctrine is that it is not suicide, because he only intended to escape the fire, but did not intend his own death. The "Law of Double Effect.")

e. A man is walking with another along the edge of a cliff and sees a precious stone on the path before him; knowing that his companion wants to get it, he pushes him over the cliff, believing that the fall will lead to his death; but a bush breaks the fall and the man is unharmed. Is this a case of attempted murder? ("I only intended to get the jewel first.")

10. (a) A man throws a lighted cigarette from a car into some dead grass, causing a forest fire. (b) He throws it, as before, and the cigarette would have gone out except that a gentle breeze that started at that moment fanned the embers into a flame, causing a forest fire. As to causation, would you agree with those who say that the man is the cause (or principal cause) of the fire in the first case, and the breeze in the second? As to liability, should there be any difference between the two cases with regard to the man's moral responsibility for starting the fire? his legal responsibility?

11. Does a government violate the rights of citizens when it

a. Taps their telephones or uses other means of electronic surveillance without their consent?

b. Uses prisoners in medical research, promising them an earlier release if they consent?

c. Requires parents to submit to blood transfusions even though it's against their religion (Jehovah's Witnesses)? Requires the children to do so?

d. Forces a news reporter to reveal in court the source of her story?

e. Forces you to surrender part of your paycheck for undivulged purposes?

f. Publicizes your psychiatrist's personal notes about you, because he is a "public psychiatrist" employed by the city?

g. Treats a person's arrest, trial, and previous criminal record as public information?

h. Requires people to have licenses to practice medicine, law, or taxi driving?

i. Prohibits nude sunbathing except at certain specified restricted areas?

j. Requires every applicant for a job to take a test for AIDS?

k. Condemns your house and turns it into an art museum (determining the compensation you will receive)?

l. Puts your child in a foster home in order "to give it a better environment"?

12. Early in World War II the British had cracked the German code, though the Germans did not know this. Thus they learned in advance that the German air force was about to bomb Coventry. Some of the people working in the British cryptography unit had families in Coventry. But to evacuate people from Coventry would have re-

vealed to the Germans that the British had cracked their code, and so no word leaked out about the forthcoming raid. Evaluate the British conduct in this situation from the point of view of (a) long-term egoism, (b) utility, (c) justice. (Many examples of similar agonizing moral decisions are given in William Stephenson, *A Man Called Intrepid*, from which this example is taken.)[25]

13. Happiness is usually considered good or worth having *for its own sake,* not as a means toward something else: A person may say, "I want to be rich so that I can be happy," but not, "I want to be happy so that I can be rich." The question is, is *freedom* (both freedom from and freedom to) also good for its own sake, or is it only good as a *means* toward an end (such as happiness)? Argue pro or con.

14. Do the following, in your opinion, constitute injustices? Why or why not?

a. A child's parents are drunkards who care nothing about the child; the only hope for the child's well-being is the grandmother, who provides confidence, love, and understanding. But the grandmother dies.

b. A father leaves more money in his will to his handicapped child than to his other children.

c. Five men in an army platoon are selected (at random) to dig a ditch, though any of the other members of the platoon could have done it just as well.

d. A merchant charges the same price for an item to all customers, rich and poor.

e. A rich traffic violator receives a stiffer fine than a poor one.

f. All the men want to marry the attractive girl rather than the unattractive one.

g. Wealthier countries decline to share their economic output with poorer countries (through heavier taxes).

h. Three people are cast adrift on a desert island, their sole sustenance being the fish they catch; each is able to catch and eat only one fish per day. A does without fish for 2 days in order to devise a net by which he can catch more fish. His self-sacrifice pays off, and he now has a labor-saving invention. He can now either (1) hold onto his

---

[25]William Stephenson, *A Man Called Intrepid* (New York: Harcourt Brace, 1976), pp. 165–66.

savings "against a rainy day," (2) indulge himself and consume the extra fish now, (3) loan out his extra fish to B and C, and if they too are successful in building nets (for which he gave them the idea) they too will have savings, thanks to A; or (4) A can use his fish to sustain himself while building two more nets—investing his savings of consumption goods in order to increase his stock of capital goods, and then rent them to B and C for half a fish a day. Whichever of these things he does, he is not harming B or C (they are no worse off than before A's invention), but if he does (3) or (4) he inevitably benefits them, even though his *motive* may be entirely to benefit himself. But if he does (3) or (4), in many societies he would be called a "selfish capitalist exploiter," and the others would attempt to "correct his injustice" by seizing the nets he has made and using them for themselves, perhaps sharing one with him ("equal distribution of wealth"). *Was* A unjust to B and C in doing any of these four things?[26]

15. Is a person within his rights, or is he violating the rights of others, when he

a. Places solar-heating panels in his yard although the neighbors consider them an eyesore?

b. Builds a house just uphill from you, causing shade where you wanted sunlight, intercepting your favorite view from your bedroom, and possibly endangering your house because of mud slides during the rainy season?

c. Watches you in your house from the sidewalk day and night?

d. Has barbecues in his back yard of which you can't stand the smell and noise?

e. Sells the subscription list of his magazine (you are a subscriber) to other enterprises without your consent?

f. Telephones you constantly day and night although you've told him not to?

g. Consumes more natural resources than he needs, rather than leaving them for posterity?

16. Punishment. (a) Should a criminal who hasn't been caught for 30 years, and now is leading an exemplary life, be excused or have his sentence shortened or suspended? Any difference between the retributionist and the utilitarian on this? (b) If the man who killed another didn't know what he was doing (owing to stupidity), should he be punished for it?[27] (c) Should a person be punished for attempts, in the following cases? He thinks he is shooting a deer out of season, but he isn't—the season is still on. He thinks he is shooting a deer in the permitted season, but he isn't—the permitted season is over. He thinks he is shooting a bird in a tree, but it's a man.

17. "He should be kept in prison and not paroled because he continues to be dangerous to others—if let go he would kill again." "He should be kept in prison because in time he will be rehabilitated there through psychotherapy, and won't commit any more crimes." "He should be kept in, because if he's let go prematurely others will notice this and will be less likely to be deterred from violent crimes." Which of these reasons would you consider the most important and why? (All are utilitarian reasons.) What should be done if one reason applies but not the others? Which do you think should take precedence and why?

18. Should welfare be provided at taxpayers' expense for (a) those who because of ill health, physical handicap, or mental defect, cannot provide for themselves? (b) those who are able to work but can't find a job? (c) those who are able to work but refuse to do so? Why, in each case? Are your reasons those of utility, justice, or what? How much should be provided—enough to live on, as much as an average worker receives, or what?

19. "Having more liberty doesn't always mean having more happiness. A millionaire's son may become spoiled, and would have been better off with less liberty to do as he liked at an early age. Considering the high percentage of divorces, it would seem that choosing your own mate may not be the system that leads to most happiness; marriages arranged by parents may possibly have better consequences, in spite of less freedom for the partners. Sometimes people have to be coerced into doing what is best for their own happiness—if they were free they would act so as to make themselves miserable." Could you nevertheless defend a connection between freedom and happiness? Do people with more freedom have a greater *chance* to be happy?

---

[26]The example is from Irwin Schiff, *The Biggest Con* (Westport, CT: Arlington House, 1977), pp. 265–270.

[27]See Albert Tidyman, *Dummy* (Boston: Little, Brown & Co., 1974).

20. State a number of ways in which government—any government, even the most benevolent—interferes with an individual's liberties. Then state a number of ways in which government either promotes liberties or makes them possible.

21. "I enjoy doing this—therefore I should do it." If nothing interferes with this egoistic enjoyment (such as going fishing), there would appear to be no reason not to do it. According to some writers, however, when a utilitarian duty interferes with this (I could help the hungry by not going fishing), that's what I should do if it's a case of either-or (though egoists would deny this). But if something that would maximize utility (such as imprisoning an innocent scapegoat during a crime wave) conflicts with justice and rights, justice and rights should take precedence over utility. And possibly if there is a conflict between justice and rights (it would be unjust not to hire this person, who is best qualified for the job, but it's my money I'm investing and I have the right to hire my brother if I choose), then rights should triumph over justice. In other words, utility trumps egoism, justice trumps utility, and rights are the aces that trump them all. Do you agree with this? Give your reasons.

SELECTED READINGS

ARISTOTLE. *Nicomachean Ethics.* Many editions.

BRANDT, RICHARD. *Ethical Theory.* Englewood Cliffs, NJ: Prentice-Hall, 1959.

BRANDT, RICHARD. *A Theory of the Good and the Right.* Oxford: Oxford University Press, 1979.

BROAD, C. D. *Five Types of Ethical Theory.* London: Routledge & Kegan Paul, 1935.

BLANSHARD, BRAND. *Reason and Goodness.* London: Allen & Unwin, 1961.

BENTHAM, JEREMY. *Principles of Morals and Legislation.* 1789. Many editions.

CLARK, STEPHEN. *The Moral Status of Animals.* Oxford: Clarendon Press, 1977.

DEWEY, JOHN. *Human Nature and Conduct.* New York: Modern Library, 1924.

EDEL, ABRAHAM. *Ethical Judgment.* New York: Free Press, 1955.

EWING, ALFRED C. *The Definition of Good.* New York: Macmillan, 1947.

FEINBERG, JOEL. *Doing and Deserving.* Princeton, NJ: Princeton University Press, 1970.

FEINBERG, JOEL. *Social Philosophy.* Englewood Cliffs, NJ: Prentice-Hall, 1973.

FRANKENA, WILLIAM K. *Ethics.* Englewood Cliffs, NJ: Prentice-Hall, 1963.

FOOT, PHILIPPA. *Theories of Ethics.* London: Oxford University Press, 1967.

GEWIRTH, ALAN. *Reason and Morality.* Chicago: University of Chicago Press, 1978.

GLOVER, JONATHAN. *Causing Death and Saving Lives.* Baltimore: Penguin Books, 1977.

GLOVER, JONATHAN. *Responsibility.* London: Routledge & Kegan Paul, 1970.

HARE, R. M. *The Language of Morals.* Oxford: Clarendon Press, 1950.

HARE, R. M. *Freedom and Reason.* Oxford: Clarendon Press, 1963.

HARE, R. M. *Moral Thinking.* Oxford: Clarendon Press, 1981.

HARTLAND-SWANN, JOHN. *An Analysis of Morals.* London: Allen & Unwin, 1950.

HAZLITT, HENRY. *The Foundations of Morality.* Princeton, NJ: Van Nostrand, 1964.

HOSPERS, JOHN. *Human Conduct.* 2nd ed. New York: Harcourt Brace, 1982.

HOSPERS, JOHN. *Libertarianism.* San Francisco: Cobden Press, 1971.

HUME, DAVID. *A Treatise of Human Nature,* book 3. 1739.

HUME, DAVID. *An Enquiry Concerning the Principles of Morals.*

KANT, IMMANUEL. *Fundamental Principles of the Metaphysics of Morals,* 1783; *Critique of Practical Reason,* 1785.

MACKIE, J. M. *Ethics.* Baltimore: Penguin Books, 1977.

MACHAN, TIBOR. *The Great Debate.* New York: Random House, 1987.

MACINTYRE, ALASDAIR. *After Virtue.* Notre Dame: Notre Dame University Press, 1981.

MILL, JOHN STUART. *On Liberty,* 1859; *Representative Government,* 1861; *Utilitarianism,* 1863; *Principles of Political Economy,* 1865.

MOORE, G. E. *Principia Ethica.* Cambridge: Cambridge University Press, 1903.

MOORE, G. E. *Ethics.* London: Oxford University Press, 1912.

NAGEL, THOMAS. *Mortal Questions.* Cambridge: Cambridge University Press, 1979.

NOWELL-SMITH, PATRICK. *Ethics.* Baltimore: Penguin Books, 1954.

NOZICK, ROBERT. *Anarchy, State, and Utopia.* New York: Basic Books, 1974.

PAUL, ELLEN, et al., eds. *Human Rights,* 1984; *Liberty and Equality,* 1985. Oxford: Blackwell.

PERRY, RALPH BARTON. *General Theory of Value.* Cambridge: Harvard University Press, 1926.

PLATO. *Republic; Philebus; Meno; Euthyphro; Crito; Apology.* Many editions.

RASHDALL, HASTINGS. *Theory of Good and Evil.* 2 vols. London: Routledge & Kegan Paul, 1924.

RAWLS, JOHN. *A Theory of Justice.* Cambridge: Harvard University Press, 1971.

ROSS, WILLIAM D. *Foundations of Ethics.* Oxford: Clarendon Press, 1939.

ROSS, WILLIAM D. *The Right and the Good.* London: Oxford University Press, 1931.

RUSSELL, BERTRAND. *Human Society in Ethics and Politics.* London: Allen & Unwin, 1955.

REGAN, TOM. *The Case for Animal Rights.* Berkeley: University of California Press, 1984.

RESCHER, NICHOLAS. *Distributive Justice.* Indianapolis, Ind.: Bobbs-Merrill, 1966.

SANDERS, JOHN T. *The Ethical Argument against Government.* Washington, D.C.: American Universities Press, 1980.

SIDGWICK, HENRY. *The Methods of Ethics.* London: Macmillan, 1878.

STACE, WALTER T. *The Concept of Morals.* New York: Macmillan, 1937.

SMITH, ADAM. *Theory of the Moral Sentiments,* 1759. New Rochelle, NY: Arlington House, 1969.

SPENCER, HERBERT. *The Principles of Ethics.* 2 vols. 1897. Indianapolis: Liberty Press, 1979.

SMART, J. J. C., and BERNARD WILLIAMS. *Utilitarianism For and Against.* Cambridge: Cambridge University Press, 1973.

STERBA, JAMES. *The Demands of Justice.* Notre Dame, IN: University of Notre Dame Press, 1980.

STERBA, JAMES, ed. *Justice: Alternative Approaches.* Belmont, CA: Dickenson, 1979.

TAYLOR, RICHARD. *Good and Evil.* New York: Macmillan, 1970.

TAYLOR, RICHARD. *Freedom, Anarchy, and the Law.* Buffalo: Prometheus, 1973.

VON WRIGHT, G. H. *The Varieties of Goodness.* London: Routledge & Kegan Paul, 1963.

WARNOCK, G. J. *The Object of Morality.* London: Methuen, 1971.

WILLIAMS, BERNARD. *Ethics and the Limits of Philosophy.* Cambridge: Harvard University Press, 1985.

ZINK, SIDNEY. *The Concepts of Ethics.* New York: St. Martin's Press, 1962.

GLOSSARY

For terms explained in the text, see the Index.

Aesthetics. The branch of philosophy dealing with the nature and basis of judgments concerning beauty and artistic excellence. *Philosophy of art* attempts to analyze the concepts used in criticism of the arts, such as expression, symbolism, and representation, and to justify statements in which these concepts are employed.

Analogy. Resemblance, similarity. *Argument from analogy* is argument from resemblance: one typically infers that if two or more things are alike in some respects they will probably be alike also in other respects not yet examined.

Analytic statements. (1) Statements whose truth can be determined solely by analysis of the meanings of the terms they contain; or (2) statements whose negation (denial) involves a contradiction. (Example: "All fathers are male," assuming that "father" has the same meaning as "male parent.") All non-analytic statements are called *synthetic* statements. (For doubts about the analytic-synthetic distinction, see pp. 130–32.

A priori truths. Statements that are self-evidently true, or logically derivable from self-evident truths; or, truths that do not require verification or confirmation through experience. (Examples: "Tadpoles are tadpoles" is an a priori truth (also analytic), but "Tadpoles become frogs" is not, since one must observe the behavior of tadpoles to discover whether it is true. "2 + 2 = 4" is an a priori truth, but "If you pour two quarts of this liquid into a vessel containing two quarts of another liquid, there will be four quarts of mixture" is not—one must discover experimentally what happens when one does this.) Truths not knowable a priori are said to be *a posteriori* truths.

Denote. To have as an instance or class of instances. The word "dog" denotes (1) Fido, Sport, and many other individual dogs, and (2) the sub-classes of dogs, such as shepherds, Alsatians, collies, dobermans, etc. By contrast, the word "dog" *designates* ("means" in one sense of the term) that combination of properties—not easily described in detail but fairly easily recognized—by means of which a creature is identified by users of language as a dog. A term may have designation but no denotation: there are no unicorns, but the word "unicorn" means being a horse with a horn protruding from its forehead.

Empirical statement. Any statement of which observation of the world through the senses (sight, hearing, etc.) is relevant to a determination of its truth or falsity.

Entailment. Logical implication.

Epistemology. Theory of knowledge. The study of the nature and grounds (basis) of knowledge. Epistemology critically assesses claims to knowledge in all disciplines.

Ethics. The branch of philosophy dealing with moral concepts, such as good, bad, right, wrong, obligation, responsibility, justice; the analysis of such concepts and the justification of judgments (statements, claims) involving them. (Ethics and morality are not the same: ethics studies morality, as biology studies living things.)

Implication. *Material* implication: "*p* implies *q*" ("if *p*, then *q*") means that it is not the case that *p* is true and *q* false. (Example: If it's snow, it's white.) *Logical* implication (entailment): "*p* implies *q*" means that to assert *p* while denying *q* is self-contradictory. Example: If it's a square, it has four sides (since a square is defined as a four-sided figure of a certain kind, to say it's square and deny that it has four sides is self-contradictory).

Inference. To conclude something on the basis of (genuine or alleged) evidence. If I watch the rain, I *observe* that it's raining; but if I awaken and see that the entire landscape is wet, I *infer* that it has rained while I slept.

Metaphysics. The study of the nature of existence and reality, and of the kinds or types of existence. Example: If one asks "What kinds of things are there?" or "What is the fundamental furniture of the universe?" one answer might be "Substances properties, and relations." Unlike scientific statements, which also study aspects of the nature of reality, metaphysical statements are not subject to experimental confirmation or disconfirmation, but are often said to be presupposed in all the sciences, and indeed by all statements whatever.

Necessary truths. Statements that "must be true," "cannot be false," are true in all possible worlds, or whose falsity is inconceivable (these are all varying formulations). *Contingent* truths, by contrast, are true of the actual world, but need not hold true of other possible or conceivable worlds. Example: "If no dogs are cats, then no cats are dogs" is a necessary truth; but "The creature standing here before me is a dog" is contingent (contingent on the way the world is).

Philosophy. An analysis of the grounds of (basis for, reasons for believing), and the concepts expressing, a person's fundamental beliefs. (There are various overlapping definitions.)

Presupposition. A statement whose truth is assumed in what one says. If *q* could not be true unless *p* were true, *q* presupposes *p*. "Sally is away from home today" presupposes that Sally exists. (The sciences are sometimes said to presuppose metaphysics.)

Property. That which belongs to things or objects. Example: Being brown and being rectangular are properties of this table-top. The word "quality" is sometimes used synonymously with "property," but more often a quality is said to be a (real or alleged) property whose presence is sensed or felt. Example: An object has the property of redness (it emits certain photons of light), but has an experienced quality (something apparently incapable of further analysis) of redness, which persons who are not blind or color-blind can experience and those who are, cannot. Or: "The scene has a quality of strangeness or eeriness about it" (i.e., that's how it feels, without claiming that this is an actual property of the scene).

Skepticism. A method of systematic doubt concerning all claims to knowledge in a given area of study. Or: the doctrine that knowledge, as opposed to opinion, in a given area of study is impossible to attain.

Theology. The study of the reasons or grounds of belief in a divine being or beings.

An Introduction
to
Philosophical Analysis

INDEX

Items in the reading lists are not indexed.

Q

R

S